TRAINING IN
management skills

CANADIAN EDITION

TRAINING IN
management skills
CANADIAN EDITION

PHILLIP L. HUNSAKER
University of San Diego

DALE DILAMARTER
Sir Sandford Fleming College

PEARSON
Prentice
Hall

Toronto

National Library of Canada Cataloguing in Publication

Hunsaker, Phillip L.
   Training in management skills / Phillip L. Hunsaker, Dale Dilamarter. — Canadian ed.

Includes index.
ISBN 0-13-039925-6

   1. Executives—Training of. 2. Management.   I. Dilamarter, Dale, 1946- II. Title.

HD38.2.H85 2004   658.4'07124   C2002-905886-4

0-13-039925-6

Vice President, Editorial Director: Michael J. Young
Acquisitions Editor: James Bosma
Marketing Manager: Cas Shields
Developmental Editor: Rema Celio
Production Editor: Richard di Santo
Copy Editor: Judy Eaton
Production Coordinator: Andrea Falkenberg
Page Layout: Jack Steiner
Art Director: Julia Hall
Cover Design: Jennifer Federico
Cover Image: Thomas Schmidt/GettyImages

1 2 3 4 5   08 07 06 05 04

Printed and bound in Canada.

For my wife, Jo
    Phillip L. Hunsaker

For Kevin and Heather
    Dale Dilamarter

Brief Contents

Contents

Preface

Management is an applied topic. Conceptual frameworks can provide business school graduates with needed information and ideas to understand management situations, but to become effective managers they need practice in behaving as a manager and they need to receive feedback on their performance. *Training in Management Skills* fills this need.

Management is about understanding people, getting things done, and making organizations work. You will learn that the job of a manager is an exciting position that involves a variety of tasks performed in an action-packed environment. It's one where you can make a significant difference in people's lives—those of employees, customers, and co-workers. As a manager, you will become responsible for motivating others and creating a positive work environment. You will provide guidance, counsel employees, and evaluate their performance. You will hire, praise, promote, and dismiss employees. Meetings, interruptions, dealing with crises, making decisions, and solving conflicts are all part of the job.

The most significant driver of organizational success today is improving performance to achieve quality results and sustaining competitive advantage. High-performing organizations realize that how they manage people has a direct impact on results, and "how" results are achieved is as important as "what" is achieved.

Researchers have clearly identified the competencies or basic knowledge, skills, and behaviours that managers need to achieve results. *Training in Management Skills* covers the most important of these and puts you in the role of manager to experience the typical situations faced by real managers.

This text is the first Canadian edition of Phillip Hunsaker's highly successful book *Training in Management Skills*. The stimulus for creating a comprehensive management skills textbook came from Stephen Robbins and Phillip Hunsaker's *Training in Interpersonal Skills*, which deals solely with interpersonal skills. Inquiries were continually received from management professors and others who wished to provide practical training in the full range of competencies considered essential for managerial success. *Training in Management Skills* was a natural evolution to solve this problem by combining essential management concepts with training exercises for each of the critical areas. As a result, the text was developed to provide a complete management training package.

The first Canadian edition builds on the strengths of the U.S. edition. Changes include a new organizational structure based on management competency clusters, expanded coverage of concepts and approaches, and a Canadian context that has been provided for the application of management skills.

MANAGEMENT COMPETENCIES

The text organizes the key knowledge, skills, and behaviours that managers need to achieve results into four sets of competencies. They are: Self-Management Competencies, Relationship-Building Competencies, Performance Management Competencies, and Future-Building Competencies. Self-Management Competencies include the knowledge, skills, and behaviours necessary to create a realistic picture of your assets and liabilities and to act ethically, cope with stress, and manage your time. Relationship-Building Competencies help you work more effectively through others. These competencies include interpersonal communication, valuing diversity, using power wisely, managing conflict, and motivating others. Performance Management Competencies include solving problems, planning, setting goals, identifying and hiring employees, evaluating employee performance, developing employee capabilities, and building teams. Future-Building

Competencies focus on the knowledge, skills, and behaviours that allow adaptation to the constantly changing external environment.

EXPANDED COVERAGE

This first Canadian edition builds on the thoroughness of the U.S. edition by including additional concepts and approaches. These include major sections on facilitating innovation, using creative problem-solving techniques, completing an innovation audit, and developing a creative work environment. There is expanded coverage on how employers can support the work–life balance needs of employees. Chapter 8, Building a Power Base, provides a revised framework on the use of power to maximize managerial effectiveness, suggestions on how to network inside and outside the organization, and how to respond to inappropriate influence attempts. In Chapter 3, Developing Ethical Guideposts, a revised ethics checklist and process is provided. There are also new sections on the disciplining of employees, including dismissal and constructive dismissal. Considerable care has been taken to ensure a consistency of presentation and tone. This included a tighter organization of material in Chapter 4, Managing Stress and Time, Chapter 10, Innovation and Problem Solving, Chapter 11, Planning and Goal Setting, and Chapter 18, Leading Change.

CANADIAN CONTEXT

Canadian examples and research results are provided throughout the text. Examples were chosen from all regions of Canada and from a variety of workplaces, including unionized environments, where appropriate. Canadian legislation that ensures consistent treatment of all employees is reviewed, including employment standards legislation, human rights legislation, employment equity laws and pay equity legislation. With this backdrop, a Canadian perspective on the challenge of managing an increasingly diverse workforce is provided, and Canadian legislation and policy are applied to the recruitment, hiring, and performance evaluation of employees.

Message to Students

This text assists you in acquiring critical management competencies by using a proven 10-step learning model and presenting materials in an easy-to-read, straightforward style.

SKILLS LEARNING

The chapters and appendices in this text each represent key areas essential for managerial success. This ensures that you will have the necessary skills that employers are looking for. Each chapter has plenty of real-life, action-oriented exercises, role-plays, and case studies. This means that there is a lot of "learning by doing." It also means that you get to play the role of manager, which will help you to identify opportunities for growth as well as to see if a career in management will be a good fit for you.

EASY-TO-READ, STRAIGHTFORWARD LANGUAGE

Special emphasis has been placed on creating a text that has straightforward language and is easy to read. This means that you'll be able to learn the concepts faster and will be able to spend more time applying and practising your skills in a variety of new settings.

LEARNING MODEL

Each chapter of the book is organized around a learning model. This learning model contains 10 components that ask you to do the following tasks:

- Assess your basic skill level.
- Review key concepts that are relevant to applying the skill.
- Test your conceptual knowledge.
- Identify on a checklist the specific behavioural dimensions that you need to learn for each skill.
- Observe how to apply the skill through watching others in a modelling exercise.
- Practise the skill in small groups.
- Answer application questions to cement practical understanding of the concepts.
- Complete reinforcement exercises outside the classroom.
- Use a summary checklist to identify strengths as well as areas still needing improvement.
- Develop an action plan for ongoing skill improvement in your own life.

As a student, you know how important feedback is to your success. Similarly, feedback is important to an author. Please let me know what you like about the text and what you think needs improving. Your thoughts and suggestions will be welcomed. Send them directly to me at ddilamarter@canada.com.

Message to Instructors

The comprehensive coverage and practical, applied nature of *Training in Management Skills* makes it a main teaching text in business, administration, and management courses. It is particularly suitable for those courses that have a managerial scope with a strong focus on skill development. The text's learning model, based on social learning theory[1] and adapted from *Training In Interpersonal Skills* by Stephen Robbins and Phillip Hunsaker, has been widely received by college and university professors. This 10-step learning model provides an increased level of practice, which leads to greater retention of knowledge and skills. Each chapter includes a large number and variety of case studies, role-plays, action-oriented exercises, and application questions that allow students to learn, practise, and receive feedback from their peers and develop action plans for real-world applications.

The text's writing style is easy to read and understand, ensuring that your students will not get bogged down by wordiness and terminology. Its thoroughness, however, allows the text to be used for either a one- or two-semester course, depending on how much skill practice you wish to emphasize.

Training in Management Skills' brevity also allows it to serve as a supplement to general management and organizational behaviour texts that have only "back of the chapter" skill applications.

Your thoughts and suggestions on any aspect of this text are always welcome. I encourage you to send them directly to me at ddilamarter@canada.com.

Instructor Resources

INSTRUCTOR'S RESOURCE MANUAL

Each chapter of the Instructor's Resource Manual includes learning objectives, an overview, a detailed chapter outline, and teaching notes to selected chapter exercises. Additional teaching suggestions also complement the chapters. An electronic version of the manual is also included on the Instructor's Resource CD-ROM (see next page).

TEST ITEM FILE

Each chapter of the Test Item File contains multiple-choice, true/false, and essay questions. Together, the questions cover the content of each chapter in a variety of ways to test the students' knowledge of the text.

PEARSON TESTGEN

The Pearson TestGen is a special computerized version of the Test Item File that enables instructors to view and edit the existing questions, add new questions, generate tests, and print the tests in a variety of formats. Powerful search and sort functions make it easy to locate questions and arrange them in any order desired. TestGen also enables instructors to administer tests on a local area network, have the tests graded electronically, and have the results prepared in electronic or printed reports. Issued on the Instructor's Resource CD-ROM, the Pearson TestGen is compatible with both Windows and Macintosh systems.

INSTRUCTOR'S RESOURCE CD-ROM

This CD-ROM contains the electronic Instructor's Resource Manual, Pearson TestGen, and PowerPoint Electronic Transparencies. The PowerPoint transparencies, a comprehensive package of outlines and figures corresponding to the text, are designed to aid the educator and supplement in-class lectures.

SKILLS VIDEO

A Skills Video, divided into segments, focuses on a fictional video production company, Quicktakes Video. In these segments, professional actors address real business problems and the skills needed to manage them. Students receive questions throughout these segments and are asked to consider them. They then receive advice from experts in the field. The Skills Video offers a fun, hands-on way to view today's business world and learn the skills necessary to succeed within it. An instructor's Video Guide is included with the Instructor's Resource Manual.

PRENTICE HALL SELF-ASSESSMENT LIBRARY CD-ROM

This library comprises 45 self-assessments, organized by individual, group, and organizational skills. Exercises are scored automatically and analyzed. It is also available in a printed format.

Acknowledgments

This first Canadian edition of *Training in Management Skills* is the result of the effort, dedication and support of a significant number of people. Phillip Hunsaker, whose work I adapted for Canadian use, is most deserving of recognition. His skill-focused approach, talent and clarity of thought are exceptional.

At Pearson Education Canada, I wish to thank James Bosma, Acquisitions Editor; Cas Shields, Executive Marketing Manager; Rema Celio, Associate Editor; Richard di Santo, Production Editor; and Judy Eaton, Copy Editor. They are an outstanding team whose goal is to produce the finest learning materials available.

At Sir Sandford Fleming College, colleagues and students are a rich source of feedback and ideas.

Most of all, however, I wish to thank my family for their love, support and inspiration.

Dale Dilamarter
Sir Sandford Fleming College

Part 1
Introduction

Managers oversee the activities of others in order to accomplish organizational objectives. All of us recognize that a manager's job involves providing directions, but have you ever wondered what else a manager's job entails?

Part 1 of your text outlines the interpersonal, informational and decisional roles played by managers and describes how managerial work is performed. You will learn that the job of a manager is an exciting position that involves a variety of tasks performed in an action-oriented, fast-paced environment. It is a position where you can make a significant difference to an organization, its customers and its employees.

To perform well requires a common set of skills. These skills have been clearly identified by researchers who have studied how managers actually perform their roles. These are the management skills necessary for a successful career in business and management. Your text divides these skills into four competency clusters: Self-Management Competencies, Relationship-Building Competencies, Performance Management Competencies and Future-Building Competencies. In Chapter 1, Management Skills and Managerial Effectiveness, you will learn the specific skills that will be covered in each cluster.

The premise of this book, however, is that it is not good enough just to know what skills a manager needs but, rather, to practise and use them. As a result, the text puts you in the role of manager to experience the typical situations faced by real managers. Role-plays and case studies at the end of each chapter supply action-oriented exercises where you can receive feedback from your peers and develop action plans for real-world applications.

To help you learn, practise and use these management skills, the text uses the *Training in Management Skills* (TIMS) experiential learning model. To become competent in any skill, a person needs to understand it both conceptually and behaviourally, practise it, receive feedback and use the skill often enough for it to become routine. Each skill chapter uses the 10-step TIMS model to help you develop your skills. Each step of the model is explained in Chapter 1.

In this model, the majority of responsibility rests with you for your own learning. As part of the skill development model, a number of learning situations are provided in each chapter to serve as effective self-teaching for you and others. Skills learning requires that you experience an application for yourself, see the outcomes and decide whether it works for you. Only in this way can you choose what you want to do when you are in a similar situation in the future.

CHAPTER 1

Management Skills and Managerial Effectiveness

Learning Objectives

After completing this chapter, you should be able to:

- Understand the nature of management.
- Explain why skills are critical to management success.
- Describe what skills are critical to management success.
- Identify how this book will help you develop your skills.

Concepts

A career in management presents a world of challenges and opportunities. John Mayberry is the chief executive officer (CEO) at Dofasco in Hamilton, Ontario. Anne Golden is president and CEO of The Conference Board of Canada. Mary Jean Giroux is a retirement-products supervisor at London Life Insurance Co. Terry Ewacha works as the director, wholesale of Pickseed Canada Inc. Karen Gaudino is the sales and marketing manager of Creemore Springs Brewery Ltd. Even though these people have jobs with different titles and work in organizations that do different things, they all have one thing in common—they are **managers**. They all oversee the activities of other people with the purpose of accomplishing organizational goals.[1]

You may wonder what else a manager does. Although most of you have reported to a boss at work who provided directions for what you were supposed to do, becoming a manager entails a big change and a much larger scope of responsibility. As a manager you become responsible for motivating others and creating favourable conditions for doing the work. Managers provide guidance to employees and evaluate performance. They hire, praise, promote, and dismiss employees. They sign documents, run meetings, and attend ceremonial events such as retirement parties. A new manager's success no longer is measured by how well he or she performs individually. It is tied to how well the new manager encourages and enables others to perform.

Managers make new contacts and maintain a network of relationships with individuals and groups outside of the organization. Managers make decisions. They initiate and plan change to improve an existing situation. Examples of planned change include improvement projects such as re-packaging an aging product, purchasing new equipment, or improving the flow of work. Managers also deal with sudden crises caused by unforeseen events such as conflict among employees or the loss of a key worker. They participate in negotiations and have **authority** to allocate resources such as money, people or equipment to specific tasks. Managers serve as spokespeople for their organizational units.

Managers continually seek information from a variety of sources such as reports, memos, and meetings or by just walking about. A manager analyzes this information to discover problems or opportunities, or simply to monitor a situation. Managers are accountable for the achievement of organizational performance goals.

From the tasks described above, you can see that managerial work typically involves a large variety of activities each day. McGill's Henry Mintzberg produced ground-breaking research that identified the interpersonal, informational, and decisional roles played by managers described above[2] and also researched the work pattern typical of managers.[3] Interruptions occur frequently, conversations are disjointed, and important activities are mixed with trivial ones. For example, a manager may go from a budget meeting involved with spending several million dollars to a discussion about how to fix a broken photocopy machine. In addition to varied and fragmented work content, Mintzberg also cites a hectic pace, the pressure of immediate problems or crises, and a high percentage of time spent in discussions attempting to influence others or obtain information. Whereas a manager's short-term **objectives** can be quite specific and detailed, longer-term objectives are often a loosely connected 'agenda' as the manager or organization continually learns to adapt to new developments. Often short-term decisions must be made with contradictory or incomplete information.

As we have seen, a manager's job can be varied, exciting, and challenging, with lots of room to make an impact on an organization, its customers, and its employees. The success of organizations such as Dofasco, The Conference Board of Canada, Pickseed Canada Inc., London Life Insurance Co., and Creemore Springs Brewery Ltd is largely due to the quality of their management. Through practical exercises, this text puts you in the role of manager to experience the typical situations faced by real managers. In that way, you'll be able to identify opportunities for growth as well as see if a career in management will be a good fit for you.

Management Skills

At one time, managers were valued primarily for their technical know-how. Most organizations identified outstanding people in the ranks, tapped them for promotions and just trusted them to do well as managers. Today, recognition is given to the importance of having managers with strong interpersonal and communication skills.[4] In any line of work, the ability to be an outstanding technical performer does not always translate into the ability to be a good manager.

Some skills, however, are transferable. For example, the work ethic that helps someone prosper in an entry-level job will continue to be a valuable tool in management. In addition, skills such as getting along with others are just as important for managers as they are for other employees. Consequently, many new managers adapt and prosper. Success is less likely for a star performer who always relied on a skilled but solo route through the company. The performance of new managers today is rated as much on people skills as on results.[5] Interviews by PricewaterhouseCoopers indicate that the trend reaches all the way up to CEOs, who report that there are increased demands for sensitivity to human feelings because reshaping corporate culture and employee behaviour is now equal in priority to monitoring financial information.[6]

In colleges and universities, instruction in management runs the gamut from highly theoretical research-based reviews of the literature to hands-on courses where students learn about management by experiencing it in student-created and -run organizations. Skill building through experiential learning techniques such as interactive case discussions, role-plays, structured exercises, and work simulations has become an accepted added dimension to many college and university courses in management.[7]

The premise of this book is that it's not enough only to *know about* managing organizations and people. You also need to be prepared to *do it*! Today's business organizations expect college and university graduates to possess skills and use **behaviours** that go beyond content knowledge and that enable them to effectively solve the problems inherent in a diverse and rapidly changing global environment.[8]

THE IMPORTANCE OF MANAGEMENT SKILLS

Would you want to submit yourself to an appendectomy if your surgeon had read everything available on the appendix and its removal but had never actually removed one before? You'd also be apprehensive if your surgeon had years of experience operating but had never studied the sciences of physiology and anatomy. Just as competent surgeons need both a sound understanding of how the body works and surgical skills finely honed through practice and experience, competent managers need a sound understanding of the role of management and the opportunity to hone their behavioural skills through practice and experience.

Increasing amounts of evidence indicate that training programs focusing on **management skills** such as leading change, cultural awareness, communication, and self-awareness produce improvements in managerial performance.[9] This research has convinced business and public-sector organizations to cumulatively spend millions of dollars each year on development programs to improve their managers' skills. While it is true that nothing in the research suggests that skills training can magically transform every incompetent manager into a highly effective leader, the evidence strongly demonstrates that these skills can be learned.[10] Although people differ in their baseline abilities, the research shows that skills training can help most people to improve their managerial effectiveness.

KEY MANAGEMENT COMPETENCIES

If skills training can result in more effective managers, then what are the skills that need to be practised and fine-tuned? What are the success factors or competencies—including knowledge, skills, and behaviours—required for excellent performance?[11] Although particular jobs, industries, and organizations will influence the nature of these competencies, there is general agreement that an effective manager will demonstrate a common set of key competencies.[12] The most commonly identified competencies are shown in Exhibit 1-1.

Exhibit 1-1 Most Commonly Identified Management Competencies

1. Planning, goal and priority setting
2. Developing employees
3. Managing conflict
4. Interpersonal communication
5. Building a base of power
6. Motivating and influencing others
7. Managing time and stress
8. Self-awareness and self-development
9. Building teams
10. Problem solving
11. Monitoring performance
12. Managing decisions

This text—*Training in Management Skills*—has organized the knowledge or concepts needed by managers and the commonly recognized skills and behaviours into four clusters: Self-Management Competencies, Relationship-Building Competencies, Performance Management Competencies, and Future-Building Competencies.

Part 2 of the text, Self-Management Competencies, includes self-understanding and personal development, the application of ethics to managerial decisions, and coping with stress and managing time. Part 3, Relationship-Building Competencies, includes demonstrating interpersonal communication, valuing diversity, managing conflict, and developing power to influence and motivate others. Part 4, Performance Management Competencies, includes encouraging innovation, demonstrating effective problem solving, planning and goal setting, identifying and hiring employees, evaluating performance, developing employees, and building teams. Part 5, Future-Building Competencies, includes diagnosing and modifying organizational culture and leading change.

To perform effectively, managers also need **technical skills**, which provide them with the ability to apply specialized knowledge or expertise. For top-level managers, these abilities tend to be related to knowledge of the industry and a general understanding of the organization's processes and products. For middle and front-line managers, they are related to the specialized knowledge required in the areas with which they work, such as finance, human resources, manufacturing, computer systems, law, and marketing.

The Learning of Skills

"I hear and I forget. I see and I remember. I do and I understand." This famous quote, attributed to Confucius, is frequently used to support the value of learning through experience. The saying has some truth to it, but contemporary research on learning suggests that a more accurate rephrasing would be: "I understand best when I hear, see, and do!"

THE EXPERIENTIAL LEARNING MODEL

Countless studies show that people learn faster and retain more information if they have to exert some kind of active effort. To become competent at any skill, a person needs to understand it both conceptually and behaviourally, have opportunities to practise it, get feedback on how well he or she is performing the skill, and use the skill often enough that it becomes integrated into his or her behavioural repertoire.[13] One model that encompasses most of these learning dimensions is presented in Exhibit 1-2.

Exhibit 1-2 The Experiential Learning Model

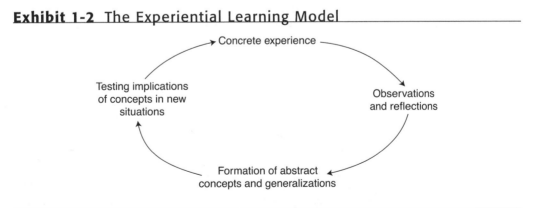

Source: D.A. Kolb, I.M. Rubin, and J.M. McIntyre, *Organizational Psychology: Readings on Human Behavior in Organizations,* 4th ed. (Upper Saddle River, NJ: Prentice Hall, 1984) 128. Reprinted with permission.

This **experiential learning** model emphasizes that the development of behavioural skills comes from observation and practice.[14] According to the model, comprehensive learning encompasses four elements: active participation in a new experience *(concrete experience)*; examination of that experience *(reflective observation)*; integration of conclusions based on the new experience into workable theories *(abstract conceptualization)*; and application of the theories to new situations *(active experimentation)*.[15] The learning of skills is maximized, according to this model, when individuals get the opportunity to combine watching, thinking, and doing.[16]

TIMS Learning Model

Using the experiential learning model and well-known learning principles, the following 10-step **training in management skills (TIMS)** learning model was created for acquiring managerial skills.[17]

1. Do self-assessment
2. Learn skill concepts
3. Check concept learning: Quiz
4. Identify behaviours that make up skill: Checklist
5. Model the skill in a demonstration exercise
6. Practise the skill in group exercises
7. Assess skill competency level in summary checklist
8. Answer questions to assist in the application of the skill
9. Do exercises to reinforce the application of the skill
10. Complete action plan for continued skill development

To help individuals appreciate the need for improvement, they need first to assess their baseline skill competency. Each skill chapter in this book begins with a self-assessment questionnaire, followed by a scoring key and an interpretation to facilitate "self-discovery."[18] The majority of the self-assessment quizzes are highly valid measurement devices that are intended to give readers insight into how much they already know about the skill in question. Second, a person needs to learn the basic concepts underlying the skill. This learning is achieved by reviewing the published materials available on the skill. The third step is providing feedback to ensure that the basic concepts are understood, which in this model is accomplished by a short quiz.

The fourth step is the identification of specific behaviours that the individual desires to learn to master the skill. This behavioural checklist, derived from the skill concepts, clarifies what specific behaviours the individual needs to acquire. It is limited to approximately seven behaviours because the research has established that people have difficulty working with more than about seven pieces of information.[19] The behavioural checklist is also used by others to evaluate how well the individual has learned the behaviours in question. The importance of this behavioural checklist cannot be overstated. It contains the only criteria by which actual behavioural performance will be judged. By keeping evaluation focused only on the behaviours identified in the checklist, we reduce the likelihood that appraisals will veer off to include personality variables, personal styles, or similar extraneous factors.

The fifth step is a modeling exercise that allows the learner to observe others exhibiting the desired skill behaviours. In the sixth step, students form small groups and practise their newly acquired skills in a series of exercises where they must apply the targeted skill behaviours. Individuals not actively involved in a group exercise learn and contribute through observation and evaluation. The seventh step, completing a summary checklist, requires learners to identify behaviours in which they still have weaknesses. The eighth step involves application questions that provide opportunities to check understanding of how skill behaviours relate to managing others. In the ninth step, reinforcement exercises further facilitate the transfer of classroom learning to real-life situations. Finally, in the tenth step, the action plan provides a framework to implement activities designed to enhance strengths or to overcome weaknesses.

Some Guidelines for Effective Skill Performance[20]

It is important to keep in mind that whenever we apply our behavioural skills with someone else we are always in some way attempting to motivate some specific behaviour in him or her. You will learn more about how to motivate others in a later chapter, but for now, just think of people's basic motivation as an effort to improve, or at least maintain, their quality of life. Because people always have freedom of choice about how they are going to respond to us, successful skill application consists of being able to inspire people to want to cooperate with us. When applying behavioural skills, we want something positive to happen for us, but so does the other person. Knowing how to create positive encounters where both parties gain something is crucial to obtaining cooperation and lasting outcomes.[21]

Another thing to keep in mind is that we tend to mirror the emotions and behaviours that we are getting from another person. Have you ever noticed, for example, that if you are talking with someone and you get angry, he or she will quite frequently get angry too? If you smile at someone, he or she will tend to smile also. When we put out something negative, we invariably get a negative reaction mirrored back to us; on the other hand, when we put out something positive, we invariably get something positive mirrored back. The skill guideline derived from this "mirroring phenomenon" is that *doing things in a positive way* is usually far more effective than doing them in a negative way. Managers who are most effective in applying people skills are usually perceived as a consistently positive force in relationships with others, in the context of getting work done.

Although the following general guidelines will vary in different skill applications such as goal setting, delegation, conflict resolution, and so on, they will help you to be positive and create win/win outcomes in the situations you face. These guidelines are described as follows:

1. *Know where you stand*   When you anticipate an encounter with someone else, know ahead of time what you would like the outcome of your skill application to be. Unless you know where you want things to go, you won't know how to conduct yourself so as to get there.

2. *Listen*   Often the key to the resolution of a situation is offered by the employee, but the manager is so intent on forcing a preconceived solution that he or she fails to hear it. Managers can learn much from their employees, but people must feel that they are being heard to keep the communication lines open. Listening indicates to employees that their opinions are important to a manager, which increases contributions and builds mutual respect. This important skill will be discussed in greater detail in Chapter 5, Interpersonal Communication.

3. *Use questions to respect freedom of choice*   The point here is that asking instead of telling will usually get better reactions from the person whom you are trying to influence. People almost always respond negatively to any attempt to invade their freedom of choice. If you are delegating, for example, and you just tell an employee to be responsible for achieving a task, quite often he or she will resent the downloading and try to avoid the responsibility or shove it back. If you present alternatives and their consequences to employees and then ask them if they will accept responsibility, however, you show respect by letting them make the decision.

4. *Be affirmative* As mentioned earlier, effective skill application involves being a consistently positive force. For example, you can correct mistakes by employees in a way that puts them down and makes them feel inferior, or you can motivate them to improve by giving implicit positive messages such as, "I can see that you want to do well and I think that I can help you learn to do better."

5. *Be honest and up-front* Successful skill application is evident when employees alter their behaviour as you suggest. They will be more willing to change if they trust and respect you because they believe that you are honest and forthright. Even if employees are willing to go along with your suggestions, they may not be able to if they are not clear about what is really required and why it is important.

6. *Be assertive* Assertiveness is being able to take a stand while treating another with care and respect. Whatever the skill you are applying, you should indicate the acceptable level of performance you expect from other people so they will know what to strive for. You should then consistently hold them to the standard. In the long run they will respect you more for it, and they will know the praise they receive for success is sincere and deserved.

A FINAL NOTE ABOUT SKILLS LEARNING

The overriding characteristic of effective skill application in any area is acting positively, so that both the manager and the employee win. But, consistent with earlier advice on freedom of choice, it is unrealistic to make this statement and expect others to begin acting this way immediately. You have to experience it for yourself, see the outcome, and decide whether it works for you. As you progress through the specific skill applications, you will experience and observe both successful and unsuccessful behaviours. You will see what works and what does not work, and then you can choose what you want to do when you are in a similar situation in the future. A number of different types of learning situations are provided so that your experiences in dealing with them will serve as effective self-teaching for yourself and others. The majority of responsibility, therefore, rests with you for your own learning. Past students who seem to get the most out of this type of learning are the ones that really want to improve their managerial skills and are willing to help others do the same.

Summary and Organization of the Text

This text has been developed to help colleges and universities teach students the managerial skills necessary for successful careers in business and management. Part 1 of the text outlines what is generally agreed to be the more important of these managerial competencies. It also describes how people learn. This forms the basis for the design of this managerial skills book—*Training in Management Skills*. You'll find that, for the most part, the chapters follow the 10-step skill development model.

In the belief that before you can understand others, you need to know and manage yourself, Part 2 of the text focuses on Self-Management Competencies. Chapter 2, Self-Awareness: Understanding and Developing Yourself, provides a battery of self-assessment tests. After you have completed and scored the tests, you'll have a realistic evaluation of your own assets and liabilities, which include insights into your emotional intelligence, values, needs, and interpersonal style in dealing with others. The remaining chapters in Part 2 cover the skills necessary to act ethically, cope with stress, and manage your time.

Part 3 of the text deals with Relationship-Building Competencies to help you work effectively through others. This skill cluster includes chapters on interpersonal communication, valuing diversity, managing conflict, building a power base, and motivating others. Part 4 covers the skills necessary to manage performance in support of organizational goals. These Performance Management Competencies include chapters on innovation and problem solving, planning and goal setting, designing work, identifying and hiring employees, evaluating performance, developing employees, and building teams. Part 5, Future-Building Competencies, is based on the need to adapt to the constantly changing external environment. This section focuses on diagnosing and modifying an organization's culture as well as leading and managing change.

Concept Quiz

Complete the following true–false quiz by circling the correct answers. Answers are at the end of the quiz. After marking your answers, remember to go back and check your understanding of any answers you missed.

True or False   1. Managers oversee the activities of other people with the purpose of accomplishing organizational goals.

True or False   2. The ability to be an outstanding technical performer always translates into the ability to be a good manager.

True or False   3. The performance of new managers today is rated as much on people skills as on results.

True or False   4. To manage others well you must know yourself.

True or False   5. The overriding characteristic of effective skill application is acting positively.

True or False   6. Listening is critically important to creating a positive attitude in others.

True or False   7. Telling, instead of asking, contributes to the development of mutual respect.

True or False   8. Being assertive and saying no to poor performance is an important key to success as a manager.

True or False   9. Learning skills is best accomplished by combining the activities of watching, thinking, and doing.

True or False   10. The majority of responsibility for successfully acquiring effective skills rests with the learner.

Answers   (1) True; (2) False; (3) True; (4) True; (5) True; (6) True; (7) False; (8) True; (9) True; (10) True

Modelling Exercise

Getting to Know About the Class and Each Other

One of the more unnerving aspects of beginning a new semester is gaining an understanding of what is expected in each class.[22] Most of us feel anxious about course requirements, getting to know new classmates, and how to carve out our roles in the class. By now you have read the course syllabus and the introductory material in this chapter. They have provided some necessary information about how the instructor wants the class to function. It is also important to give your instructor some indication of what you want or expect from the class. Specifically, some data can be useful for providing insights into why you are taking this class. To collect this data, you will need to answer some questions.

DIRECTIONS   Take out a piece of paper and place your name at the top, then write answers to the following questions:

1. What do I want from this course?
2. Why is this class important to me?
3. How does this course fit into my career plans?
4. How do I want the instructor to "run" the class?
5. What is my greatest challenge in taking this class?

When you have finished answering these questions, pair up with another class member (preferably someone you do not already know) and exchange papers. Get to know one another (using the information on these sheets as a starting point). Prepare an introduction of your partner, and share your partner's responses to the five questions with the class and your instructor.

TIME   Allow 5 minutes to answer the questions individually, 10 minutes to form pairs and share information, and 2 minutes per student for introductions.

Part 2
Self-Management Competencies

This section of your text presents concepts and practical exercises to strengthen your self-knowledge, explore your values, and use them to develop an ethical approach to management. It also provides a variety of methods to help you manage your stress levels and time. "Know thyself" has been the cornerstone of advice to managers for centuries. To manage others well, you must know yourself and manage yourself.

Chapter 2, Self-Awareness: Understanding and Developing Yourself   To know yourself better requires an assessment of your strengths and weaknesses. It also requires new knowledge about what you do, how you do it, and the consequences of your actions. Sometimes these insights can be acquired by self-observation of the consequences of your actions, but usually they are provided by others who share feedback about their reactions to your behaviour. Another way to learn about yourself is by taking self-assessment inventories that reveal certain attitudes, values, and knowledge bases. In Chapter 2, you will take a set of self-assessment inventories to establish a baseline of your important values, attitudes, motives, and styles as they apply to effective management.

Self-knowledge isn't enough for skill development. You also have to want to improve. First you have to be open to the possibility that you are not perfect and that you can become better. Next you must be open to acquiring knowledge about yourself, which the majority of the time means listening nondefensively to feedback from others. Finally, you must be willing to risk and be assertive enough to try out new behaviours, which may not work perfectly the first time, and keep practising them until you become skilled in their application. To improve your skill level requires a high degree of commitment and effort.

Chapter 3, Developing Ethical Guideposts   Today's public has high standards for the behaviours of companies. Also, the behaviour of managers is under greater scrutiny than ever before. Because the public has more access to information, misdeeds can easily become widely known, damaging an organization's reputation and a manager's career. This chapter focuses on factors affecting managerial ethics, how organizations can encourage ethical behaviour, and what you as an individual can do.

Chapter 4, Managing Stress and Time   Reports of high stress levels and job burnout among managers have risen as the work climate has become more chaotic and ambiguous.[1] Downsizing, reengineering, cost reductions, reduced job security, pressures to learn new skills, and heightened workloads create a workplace that is increasingly stressful.[2]

When managers experience high stress levels, their performance is impeded as they become more dogmatic, less tolerant of ambiguity, less able to generate creative thoughts, and more prone to see events in a short-term, crisis mentality.[3] Considering that incompetent management is the largest cause of workplace stress for employees,[4] it is imperative that managers cope effectively with stress not only for their own well-being but also for the survival of their employees and the entire organization.

One good way to reduce stress is to manage one's time effectively. Management guru Peter Drucker has said that time is a manager's scarcest resource. Of course we all have exactly the same amount of time, so time management really refers to managing yourself in such a way as to get the most from your time.

The lesson in Part 2 is that one of the keys to effective management is self-management. We can manage ourselves better by becoming more aware of our preferences, attitudes, and values, developing and using a set of ethical guidelines, and managing our own stress levels and our time.

CHAPTER 2

Self-Awareness: Understanding and Developing Yourself

Success in the knowledge economy comes to those who know themselves—
their strengths, their values, and how they best perform.
—Peter Drucker

Learning Objectives

After completing this chapter, you should be able to:

- Better understand yourself as a manager.
- Motivate yourself and others to increase self-awareness.
- Self-direct your career in management.

Concepts

Recruits rise at dawn at the leadership boot camp run by the Center for Creative Leadership at Colorado Springs. After a continental breakfast, they are subjected to a *60 Minutes*-style interview in front of television cameras, and snooped on by note-taking psychologists peering through one-way windows. But the toughest ordeal takes place in dead silence around a seminar table. That's when they see the results of questionnaires filled out by colleagues back home rating their character and job skills. "At least 15–20 percent will learn dismaying things, and everyone will feel a twinge," says David Campbell, who runs the five-day, $7,400 course for top executives. It is part of the "360-degree feedback," in which a manager's strengths and weaknesses are evaluated in lengthy questionnaires by bosses, employees, and peers.[1]

Why Increase Your Self-Awareness?

The biggest payoff for attendees of the Center for Creative Leadership's boot camp is the self-knowledge they gain from peers attending the training and colleagues back home. Feedback from peers tends to correlate with the results from the surveys of back-home colleagues. This dual feedback causes an extensive self-examination and creates the motivation to change to be more effective managers.[2]

Unfortunately, many of us have a tendency to avoid exposure to this type of self-awareness. Opening ourselves up to honest self-appraisal may result in seeing things we do not want to see. But the more you know about your unique personal characteristics, the more insight you will have concerning your basic behavioural tendencies and inclinations for dealing with others. According to Peter Drucker, "Success in the knowledge economy comes to those who know themselves—their strengths, their values, and how they best perform."[3] The more you know about yourself, the better you will be able to understand how you are perceived by others and why they respond to you the way they do. Then you can choose to decrease ineffective behaviours and try out new ones to enhance your managerial effectiveness.

This chapter's contents are designed to help you gain insights into your aptitude for managing other people: your attitudes about motivating people, level of emotional intelligence, and styles of making decisions and working with others. You will also gain insights into the consequences of your predispositions for a successful managerial career. In addition, because self-assessment is the primary step in skill development,[4] you will learn how to assess your behavioural strengths and weaknesses both individually and with the help of others. Finally, you will learn how to self-direct your managerial career.

How to Increase Your Self-Awareness

We all want to protect, maintain, and enhance our self-concepts and the images others have of us. But we also have fears, inadequacies, self-doubts, and insecurities that we do not want to reveal to others. Many of these we may not even want to admit to ourselves. So the first step in increasing our self-awareness is taking some risks by emphasizing our need to know a little more than our fear of knowing. None of us is perfect and knowledge about our strengths and weaknesses can help us gain insights into what areas we want to change and improve.

The good news is that most of us are less defensive about deficits in skills, which can be improved through practice, than about deficits in personality, which are usually thought of as relatively permanent.[5] If we can reduce our fear of knowing about skills deficits enough to satisfy our need to grow and improve them, what are some of the ways that we can gain insights about our behaviours? Two general ways allow us to do self-assessments: individual data gathering and obtaining feedback from others.

INDIVIDUAL DATA GATHERING

This section will focus on things you can do yourself to gather and analyze information that will enhance your self-awareness. One thing you can do to gather data for self-assessment is learn from your experiences. Another is to take and interpret self-assessment questionnaires.

LEARNING FROM EXPERIENCE A number of self-evaluation techniques will facilitate data collection and self-analysis. We will describe three in this section: (1) experience–goal matching, (2) keeping a journal, and (3) finding solitude to reflect. Exhibit 2-1 summarizes a number of additional techniques often used to collect and organize personal information and gain greater self-awareness.

Experience–goal matching Peter Drucker suggests that one way to learn about your strengths is by analyzing your experiences in goal achievement. It works this way: Whenever you make a key decision or take a key action, write down what you expect

Exhibit 2-1 Individual Control Self-Assessment Techniques

■ **Self-written interviews, life story, autobiographical story**   This technique requires an individual to write an autobiography that describes his or her life. It is a written narrative of personal history. Specific content statements would describe life events, education, hobbies, major changes that have occurred in the past, consequences of the described events, and the individual's feelings about these events. Also included is a description of turning points in one's life and the pros and cons of past career decisions.

■ **Written daydreams**   The individual first develops a fantasy or vision about the future or a currently preferred surrounding. Individuals then record what they have visualized for future analysis.

■ **Written future obituaries or retirement speeches**   Individuals write personal obituaries or retirement speeches that might be given at the time of their death or retirement. The individual describes what he or she will be remembered for and the comments made by coworkers and acquaintances.

■ **Ranking of significant work values**   The individual lists what he or she believes are important or relevant values and then ranks them in terms of appropriateness or desirability. Listed values may relate to the following general categories: money, financial security, material gain; helping people, social contribution; power over self, self-improvement; security, stability, predictability; mental challenge and mental stimulation.

■ **Assets and liabilities balance sheet**   The individual makes two lists. The first list articulates assets or strengths, the second articulates liabilities or weaknesses. When using this technique, it is desirable to have individuals describe specific situations and behaviours to help ensure accurate and complete assessment of personal assets and liabilities.

■ **Lifestyle representation**   Individuals describe their current lifestyle in either written or pictorial form. When using this technique, individuals are encouraged to be as behaviourally specific as possible.

Source: L.W. Mealiea and G.P. Latham, *Skills for Managerial Success* (Chicago: Irwin, 1996) 34.

---

will happen. Nine or 12 months later, compare the actual results with your expectations. If you practise this method consistently for several years, Drucker believes that it will show you what your strengths and weaknesses are. It will also indicate what you are doing, or failing to do, that deprives you of the full benefits of your strengths.[6]

Several useful implications for action typically follow from experience–goal matching analysis. First, you will know what you are good at so you can concentrate on your strengths to do what you do best to produce important results. Second, you will know where you need to work on improving your strengths and what skills you need to acquire. Third, you will discover areas of "disabling ignorance" where you need to acquire additional knowledge to fully realize your strengths. Fourth, you will discover your bad habits—the things you do or fail to do that inhibit your effectiveness and performance. For example, you may find that you are a great planner but are lax at implementation. Or, your bad habit may be failing to practise good manners and common courtesies that are the "lubricating oil" of an organization. Finally, you will be confronted with areas in which you have no talent or interest whatsoever. Drucker suggests that you should not waste any effort on improving areas of low competence because it takes far more energy and work to improve from incompetence to mediocrity than it takes to improve an area of strength from first-rate to excellent performance.[7]

Keeping a journal   Another way to learn from experiences is by keeping a journal. Journals are similar to diaries, but they are not just accounts of a day's events. A journal should include entries that address critical aspects of your managerial experience. Journal entries might include comments about insightful or interesting quotes, anecdotes, newspaper articles, or even humorous cartoons about management. They might also include reflections on personal events, such as interactions with bosses, coaches, teachers, students, employees, players, teammates, roommates, and so on. Such entries can emphasize a good (or bad) way somebody handled something, a problem in the making, the differences between people in their reactions to situations, or people in the news, a book, or a film. Managers should also use their journals to "think on paper" about management readings from textbooks or formal management programs or to describe examples from their own experience of a concept presented in a reading.[8]

At least two good reasons support keeping a journal. First, the very process of writing increases the likelihood that you will be able to look at an event from a different perspective or learn something from it. Putting an experience into words can be a step toward taking a more objective look at it. Second, you can (and should) reread earlier entries. Earlier entries provide an interesting and valuable autobiography of your evolving thinking about management and about particular events in your life.

Finding solitude to reflect   The third way to learn from experience is to seek out solitude to reflect on your experiences and learn from them. Solitude means being out of human contact, being alone, and being so for lengthy periods of time. Silence is an essential part of solitude. Silence means to escape from sounds and noises, other than the ones of nature. Solitude is especially important for managers with heavy demands on their attention and social skills who tend not to have much time alone.

What you do during time alone—walking, meditating, or just relaxing—really does not matter as long as you are achieving solitude. The amount of solitude you need for rejuvenation and reflection will vary with the demands of your environment. The benefits of solitude are many, including a chance to contemplate who you are, what your relationships are to other people, and what your goals will be. Solitude also fosters creativity because it gives you a chance to speculate without the censorship and evaluation that comes with putting forth new ideas in public.[9]

So how do you engage in solitude? What do you do in solitude or silence? Well as far as things to "get done," nothing at all. As long as you are doing "things to get done," you have not broken human contact. So do not go into solitude and silence with a list of things to accomplish. Just be there. Enjoy it. See what happens.[10]

SELF-ASSESSMENT INVENTORIES   A second method of individual data gathering is taking and interpreting self-assessment questionnaires. They have the advantage of being private and under the control of the individual using them. These same advantages are disadvantages because self-assessments are only subject to individual perspectives, which can at times be biased or defensive. Consequently, the results of self-assessments should always be checked out by soliciting feedback from relevant others to verify their validity from multiple perspectives.

Each of the following chapters in this book starts off with a self-assessment inventory to establish your baseline ability in the skills that are the focus of that specific chapter. Each chapter concludes with feedback from peers and self-evaluation to assess your level of skill development after reading the concepts and completing the exercises in that skill chapter. The self-assessment inventories presented in this section were chosen because they provide feedback on general skills that influence your overall managerial style and application of the specific skills presented in the other chapters of this book.

The four self-assessment questionnaires that follow provide feedback on characteristics found to be associated with managerial success and offer important insights to you.[11] You may want to check out other characteristics as well to get a more complete understanding of yourself. Other sources of self-assessment instruments are campus counselling centres, professional counsellors, and career search organizations.

The following four self-assessment questionnaires (SAQs) will provide you with information regarding your aptitude for management, your degree of emotional intelligence, your cognitive style for processing information and making decisions, and your assumptions about what motivates people at work. Take the time now to complete these SAQs. When you are finished, read the directions for scoring the questionnaires and the discussions of what the results say about you. You will have the opportunity to compare your scores to those of other students and discuss what you can do to improve your scores in the closing exercise of this chapter.

SAQ 1: Is Management for You?[12]

Although many want to manage because of the excitement, status, power, or rewards, managing is not something that comes automatically; it requires specific skills and competencies as well as a desire to manage.

DIRECTIONS The following 20 questions are designed to provide insight into your aptitude for management. Rate each question according to the following scale:

ML=Most like me SU=Somewhat unlike me	SL=Somewhat like me MU=Most unlike me	NS=Not sure
1. I can get others to do what I want them to do.		ML SL NS SU MU
2. I frequently evaluate my job performance.		ML SL NS SU MU
3. I prefer not to get involved in office politics.		ML SL NS SU MU
4. I like the freedom that open-ended goals provide me.		ML SL NS SU MU
5. I work best when things are orderly and calm.		ML SL NS SU MU
6. I enjoy making oral presentations to groups of people.		ML SL NS SU MU
7. I am confident in my abilities to accomplish difficult tasks.		ML SL NS SU MU
8. I do not like to write.		ML SL NS SU MU
9. I like solving difficult puzzles.		ML SL NS SU MU
10. I am an organized person.		ML SL NS SU MU
11. I have difficulty telling others they made a mistake.		ML SL NS SU MU
12. I like to work set hours each day.		ML SL NS SU MU
13. I view paperwork as a trivial task.		ML SL NS SU MU
14. I like to help others learn new things.		ML SL NS SU MU
15. I prefer to work alone.		ML SL NS SU MU
16. I believe it is whom you know, not what you know, that counts.		ML SL NS SU MU
17. I enjoy doing several things at once.		ML SL NS SU MU
18. I am good at managing money.		ML SL NS SU MU
19. I would rather back down from an argument than let it get out of hand.		ML SL NS SU MU
20. I am computer-literate.		ML SL NS SU MU

SCORING   For statements 1, 2, 4, 6, 7, 9, 10, 11, 13, 14, 16, 17, 18, and 20, give yourself 5 points for every ML; 4 points for SL; 3 points for NS; 2 points for SU; and 1 point for MU. For statements 3, 5, 8, 12, 15, and 19, reverse the scoring. That is, give yourself 1 point for each ML, 2 points for SL, and so on. Total your score.

INTERPRETATION   In this assessment, a total of 100 points is possible. A score ranging between 80 and 100 demonstrates that you may possess many of the skills and competencies that successful managers need. It also may indicate that you have a high desire to manage others. A score between 40 and 79 indicates that you may have some of the skills and competencies to manage successfully, but you need some fine-tuning. Learning new management skills and experiencing "managing" techniques may serve you well. A score below 40 indicates that your management skills are dormant or that you have a low desire to manage others. Someone in this category who wants to manage should pay particular attention to the management skills, competencies, and techniques in which he or she feels weakest.

SAQ 2: What's Your Emotional Intelligence at Work?[13]

DIRECTIONS   For each of the following items, rate how well you are able to display the ability described. Before responding, try to think of actual situations in which you have had the opportunity to use the ability.

Very Slight Ability		Moderate Ability	Very Much Ability	
1	2	3	4	5

_____	1. Conscious of the emotions within yourself.
_____	2. Relax when under pressure in situations.
_____	3. "Gear up" at will for a task.
_____	4. Know the impact that your behaviour has on others.
_____	5. Initiate successful resolution of conflict with others.
_____	6. Calm yourself quickly when angry.
_____	7. Know when you are becoming angry.
_____	8. Regroup quickly after a setback.
_____	9. Recognize when others are distressed.
_____	10. Build consensus with others.
_____	11. Know what senses you are currently using.
_____	12. Use internal "talk" to change your emotional state.
_____	13. Produce motivation when doing uninteresting work.
_____	14. Help others manage their emotions.
_____	15. Make others feel good.
_____	16. Identify when you experience mood shifts.
_____	17. Stay calm when you are the target of anger from others.
_____	18. Stop or change an ineffective habit.
_____	19. Show empathy to others.
_____	20. Provide advice and emotional support to others as needed.
_____	21. Know when you become defensive.

Very Slight Ability		Moderate Ability		Very Much Ability
1	2	3	4	5

_____ 22. Know when you are thinking negatively and head it off.
_____ 23. Follow your words with actions.
_____ 24. Engage in intimate conversations with others.
_____ 25. Accurately reflect people's feelings back to them.

SCORING Sum your responses to the 25 questions to obtain your overall emotional intelligence score. Your score for *self-awareness* is the total of questions 1, 6, 11, 16, and 21. Your score for *managing emotions* is the total of questions 2, 7, 12, 17, and 22. Your score for *motivating yourself* is the sum of questions 3, 8, 13, 18, and 23. Your score for *empathy* is the sum of questions 4, 9, 14, 19, and 24. Your score for *social skill* is the sum of questions 5, 10, 15, 20, and 25.

INTERPRETATION This questionnaire provides an indication of your emotional intelligence. If you received a total score of 100 or more, you have high emotional intelligence. A score from 50 to 100 means you have a good platform of emotional intelligence from which to develop your managerial capability. A score below 50 indicates that you realize that you are probably below average in emotional intelligence. For each of the five components of emotional intelligence—self-awareness, managing emotions, motivating one's self, empathy, and social skill—a score above 20 is considered high, while a score below 10 would be considered low.

Managers who are attuned to their own feelings and the feelings of others can use their understanding to enhance the performance of themselves and others in their organizations. The five basic components of emotional intelligence most important for managers are discussed here.[14] Review the following discussion of the five components of emotional intelligence and think about what you might do to develop those areas in which your score was low.

■ **Self-awareness** This component provides the basis for all the other components of emotional intelligence. Self-awareness means being aware of what you are feeling, being conscious of the emotions within yourself. People who are in touch with their emotions are better able to guide their own lives. Managers need to be in touch with their emotions in order to interact effectively and appreciate emotions in others. Managers with high levels of self-awareness learn to trust their "gut feelings" and realize that these feelings can provide useful information about difficult decisions. Answers are not always clear about who is at fault when problems arise, or when to let an employee go, reorganize a business, or revise job responsibilities. In these situations, managers have to rely on their own feelings and intuition.

■ **Managing emotions** The second key component of emotional intelligence is managing emotions. Operationally it means the manager is able to balance his or her own moods so that worry, anxiety, fear, or anger do not get in the way of what needs to be done. Managers who can manage their emotions perform better because they are able to think clearly. Managing emotions does not mean suppressing or denying them but understanding them and using that understanding to deal with situations productively.[15] Managers should first recognize a mood or feeling, think about what it means and how it affects them, and then choose how to act.

■ **Motivating oneself** This ability to be hopeful and optimistic despite obstacles, setbacks, or even outright failure is crucial for pursuing long-term goals in life or in business. A classic example of self-motivation occurred when the MetLife insurance company hired a special group of job applicants who tested high on optimism but failed the normal sales aptitude test. Compared to salespeople who passed the regular aptitude test but scored high on pessimism, the "optimistic" group made 21 per cent more sales in their first year and 57 per cent more in the second.[16]

- **Empathy**   The fourth component is empathy, which means being able to put yourself in someone else's shoes—to recognize what others are feeling without them needing to tell you. Most of the time people don't tell us what they feel in words but rather in tone of voice, body language, and facial expression. Empathy is built from self-awareness; being attuned to one's own emotions makes it easier to read and understand the feelings of others.

- **Social skill**   The ability to connect to others, build positive relationships, respond to the emotions of others, and influence others is the final component of emotional intelligence. Managers need social skills to understand interpersonal relationships, handle disagreements, resolve conflicts, and pull people together for a common purpose.

SAQ 3: Cognitive Style Self-Assessment[17]

Cognitive style refers to the general way you approach and attempt to solve problems. You have both similarities with and differences from other people. The differences measured here are not better or worse, merely different. Complete and score the inventory below to find out your cognitive style. Then read the interpretation to learn what it means.

COGNITIVE STYLE SELF-ASSESSMENT   This is a set of questions designed to indicate your cognitive style. The answer you choose to any question is neither "right" nor "wrong." It simply helps to point out where your cognitive preferences lie.

Below you will find a number of paired statements and words. Please give every one a score so that each pair will add up to 5. For example:

"In describing my work, I would say it is:"
a. Challenging and exciting   4
b. Routine and dull   +__1__
                                                                            = 5

Clearly, work can sometimes be challenging and sometimes dull. In the above example we have weighted four parts challenging and one part dull. The score could, in your case, be 3 + 2 or 5 + 0 or another combination.

Please choose your scores, one against another, from the following scale:

Minimum ———————————————————————————————— Maximum

0	1	2	3	4	5

1. Are you influenced more by:
   a. Values   _____
   b. Logic   + _____
                                                                      =   5

2. When you have to meet strangers, do you find it:
   a. Something that takes a good deal of effort   _____
   b. Pleasant, or at least easy   + _____
                                                                      =   5

3. Does following a plan:
    a. Appeal to you
    b. Constrain you   _____
                                                       + _____
                                                       =   5

4. Do you get along better with people who are:
    a. Creative and speculative
    b. Realistic and "down to earth"   _____
                                                       + _____
                                                       =   5

5. Are you naturally:
    a. Somewhat quiet and reticent around others
    b. Talkative and easy to approach   _____
                                                       + _____
                                                       =   5

6. Is it harder for you to adjust to:
    a. Standard procedures
    b. Frequent changes   _____
                                                       + _____
                                                       =   5

7. Is it better to be:
    a. A person of compassion
    b. A person who is always fair   _____
                                                       + _____
                                                       =   5

8. At a party, do you usually:
    a. Try to meet many new people
    b. Stick with the people you know   _____
                                                       + _____
                                                       =   5

9. When you learn something new, do you:
    a. Try to do it like everyone else does
    b. Try to devise a way of your own   _____
                                                       + _____
                                                       =   5

10. Are you at your best:
    a. When following a carefully worked out plan
    b. When dealing with the unexpected   _____
                                                       + _____
                                                       =   5

11. Do you get more annoyed at:
    a. Fancy theories
    b. People who don't like theories   _____
                                                       + _____
                                                       =   5

12. Is it better to be regarded by others as a person with a:
    a. Visionary outlook
    b. Practical outlook   _____
                                                       + _____
                                                       =   5

13. Are you more often:
    a. Soft-hearted
    b. Hard-headed   _____
                                                       + _____
                                                       =   5

14. When you buy a gift, are you:
    a. Spontaneous and impulsive
    b. Deliberate and careful   _____
                                                       + _____
                                                       =   5

15. Do you find talking to people you don't know:
    a. Usually easy
    b. Often taxing

    + _____
    = ____ 5

16. Do you think it is a worse mistake to:
    a. Show too much emotion
    b. Try to be too rational

    + _____
    = ____ 5

17. Do you prefer people who have:
    a. Vivid imaginations
    b. Good common sense

    + _____
    = ____ 5

18. Do you usually:
    a. Organize and plan things in advance
    b. Allow things to just happen and then adapt

    + _____
    = ____ 5

19. Do people get to know you:
    a. Quickly
    b. Slowly

    + _____
    = ____ 5

20. At work, would you rather:
    a. Encounter an unscheduled problem that must be solved right away
    b. Try to schedule your work so you won't be up against the clock

    + _____
    = ____ 5

21. When you are with people you don't know, do you usually:
    a. Start conversations on your own
    b. Wait to be introduced by others

    + _____
    = ____ 5

Please allocate scores on the same basis to the following choice of words and phrases so as to indicate your preferences.

22. a. Personal
    b. Objective

    + _____
    = ____ 5

23. a. Timely
    b. Casual

    + _____
    = ____ 5

24. a. Reason
    b. Feeling

    + _____
    = ____ 5

25. a. Make
    b. Design

    + _____
    = ____ 5

26. a. Easy
    b. Hard

    + _____
    = ____ 5

27. a. Unjudgmental
    b. Judgmental

    + _____
    = ____ 5

28. a. Composed
    b. Lively

$+$ _____
$=$ 5

29. a. Facts
    b. Theories

$+$ _____
$=$ 5

30. a. Imaginative
    b. Practical

$+$ _____
$=$ 5

SCORING SCHEME Look back at the scores you allocated to each of the questions. Those scores should now be added up as shown below.

Dimension E Question	Score Given		*Dimension I* Question	Score Given
2b	_____		2a	_____
5b	_____		5a	_____
8a	_____		8b	_____
15a	_____		15b	_____
19a	_____		19b	_____
21a	_____		21b	_____
28b	_____		28a	_____
Total:	_____		Total:	_____

Dimension S Question	Score Given		*Dimension N* Question	Score Given
4b	_____		4a	_____
9a	_____		9b	_____
11a	_____		11b	_____
12b	_____		12a	_____
17b	_____		17a	_____
25a	_____		25b	_____
29a	_____		25b	_____
30b	_____		30a	_____
Total:	_____		Total:	_____

Dimension T Question	Score Given		*Dimension F* Question	Score Given
1b	_____		1a	_____
7b	_____		7a	_____
13b	_____		13a	_____
16a	_____		16b	_____
22b	_____		22a	_____
24a	_____		24b	_____
26b	_____		26a	_____
27b	_____		27a	_____
Total:	_____		Total:	_____

Dimension J Question	Score Given	Dimension P Question	Score Given
3a	_____	3b	_____
6b	_____	6a	_____
10a	_____	10b	_____
14b	_____	14a	_____
18a	_____	18b	_____
20b	_____	20a	_____
23a	_____	23b	_____
Total:	_____	Total:	_____

Now transfer each of the total scores to the columns below. Thus, your total score under Dimension E should be placed next to the E, the total score under Dimension I should be placed next to the I, and so on.

	Total			Total
E	_____		I	_____
S	_____		N	_____
T	_____		F	_____
J	_____		P	_____

Your Score Is:
Write in the letter with the most points for each of the four combinations below.

I or E _____   S or N _____   T or F _____   J or P _____

Interpretation: Cognitive Style Self-Assessment[18]

Jung's personality typology was applied in the Myers–Briggs Type Indicator, which is the basis of the Cognitive Style Self-Assessment inventory you just completed. Jung observed that people's behaviour, rather than being unique, fit into patterns, and that many of the seemingly random differences in human behaviour are actually orderly and consistent, being explained by differences in psychological attitudes and functions.

THEORY OF PERSONALITY

These differences were termed *preferences*, because people actually prefer one type of functioning over another.[19] Two of these preferences concern the person's attitude toward the world. Jung believed that people tend to approach the world through either extroversion (focus on the outer world) or introversion (focus on their inner world).

The **introvert** is interested in exploring and analyzing his or her own inner world. An introvert is introspective and preoccupied with personal thoughts and reflections.[20] What is happening inside the introvert's head is much more interesting than what is outside. Therefore, the introvert seems to be in continuous retreat from the outer world, holding aloof from external happenings and feeling lonely and lost in large gatherings. This type may often appear awkward and inhibited because their best qualities are shared with only a few close people. Mistrust and self-will characterize the introvert; however, this apprehensiveness of the objective world is not due to fear but because the outer world seems negative, demanding, and overpowering. The introvert's best work is done by self-initiative without interference from others and not influenced by majority views or public opinion. In work situations, introverted managers tend to "like quiet for concentration, be careful with details, like to think a lot before they act, and work contentedly alone."[21]

The **extrovert,** on the other hand, is characterized by an interest in the outer world, by responsiveness to and a willing and ready acceptance of external events, by desire to influence and be influenced by events, a need to join in, the actual enjoyment of all kinds of noise and bustle, by a constant attention to environment, the cultivation of friends and acquaintances (none too carefully selected), and, finally, by the great importance associated with the image one projects and therefore a strong tendency to make a show of oneself. At work, extroverted managers "like variety and action, tend to be faster", "dislike complicated procedures", are often impatient with long, slow jobs, are interested in the results of their job, often act quickly (sometimes without thinking), and usually "communicate well."[22]

No one is a "pure" type, and neither extroversion nor introversion is "better" than the other. We are all in a state of balance between extroversion (E) and introversion (I), but we use one type more naturally and more frequently.

PSYCHOLOGICAL FUNCTIONS

Jung described four psychological functions that exist along two continua: the perception dimension, with sensing at one end and the intuition at the other; and the judgment dimension, with thinking at one end and feeling at the other. According to Jung, one of these four functions will tend to dominate the personality of the individual. For example, a person may be a sensation-thinking, an intuition-thinking, a sensation-feeling, or an intuition-feeling type. No one is a "pure" type, but we all strive to achieve a state of balance.

PERCEIVING   The *perception dimension* of sensation versus intuition relates to the ways in which a person becomes aware of ideas, facts, and occurrences. When using *sensing*, perception occurs literally through the use of the five senses.[23] As a result, this type is very much present-oriented, interested in practical matters, and prefers things to be orderly, precise, and unambiguous. They typically work steadily, like established routine, seldom make errors of fact, and rarely trust their inspirations.[24]

Perceiving by *intuition,* alternatively, cannot be traced back to a conscious sensory experience but, rather, it is a subconscious process, with ideas or hunches coming "out of the blue," yielding the hidden possibilities of a situation. The intuitive is future-oriented,[25] always looking ahead and inspiring others with innovations. By the time everyone else catches up, the intuitive is off on another idea. In fact, the intuitive finds it difficult to tolerate performance of routine tasks; as soon as one is mastered, another is started. Intuitives also "like solving new problems, work in bursts of energy, frequently jump to conclusions, are impatient with complicated situations, dislike taking time for precision, and follow their inspirations, good or bad."[26]

JUDGING   Jung also described two ways of making judgments based on one's perceptions; namely, by thinking or by feeling. *Thinking* is a logical and analytical process, searching for the impersonal, true versus false, correct versus incorrect. Principles are more important to the thinker than are people,[27] and the thinker often has a difficult time adapting to situations that cannot be understood intellectually.[28] Other characteristics of this type can be described in the following way: They "are relatively unemotional and uninterested in people's feelings, may hurt people's feelings without knowing it, like analysis and putting things into logical order, can get along without harmony, need to be treated fairly, are able to reprimand people or fire them when necessary, and may seem hard-hearted."[29]

Alternatively, *feeling* is a personal, subjective process, seeking a good versus bad or like versus dislike judgment. Whereas thinking occurs using objective criteria, feeling occurs on the basis of personal values and, in this sense, is different from emotion since feeling judgments are mental evaluations and not emotional reactions. The feeling type lives according to such subjective judgments based on a value system that is either related to society's values, as in the case of the extrovert, or personal values, as in the case of the introvert.

DOMINANT PROCESS

The remaining preference determines which function is the principal or dominant one (i.e., whether perceiving or judging is the primary mode). For instance, when a person follows explanations open-mindedly, then *perception* (P) is being used; if, on the other hand, one's mind is rather quickly made up as to agreement or disagreement, then *judgment* (J) is preferred.

A fundamental difference in these two preferences is manifested in terms of which process is turned off or ignored. In order for judging to take place, perception must stop; all the facts are in, so a decision can be made. On the other hand, in order for perception to continue, judgments are put off for the time being as there is not enough data, and new developments may occur.

Basically, the preference shows the difference between the perceptive types who live their lives as opposed to the judging types who run theirs. Each type is useful, but works better if the person can switch to the other mode when necessary. A pure perceptive type is like a ship with all sail and no rudder, while a pure judging type is all form and no content.[30]

The perception–judgment (P–J) preference determines the principal function. For instance, an ST who prefers perceiving would have sensation, that is, the perceiving function, as his or her principal function. The principal function of an NF who prefers judging would be feeling, the judging function.

However, in the case of the introvert, the dominant process is turned inward and the auxiliary or secondary function is shown to the world. Hence, the best side is kept for self or very close friends. The inventory you just completed measures the principal function that is used on the outside world; in the case of the introvert, it is actually the auxiliary function.

PERCEPTION–JUDGMENT COMBINATIONS

The four functional types are a means to comprehend the world. Sensation tells us something exists, thinking tells us what that something is, feeling enables us to make value judgments on this object, and intuition gives us the ability to see the inherent possibilities.[31]

In each person one of the perception dimensions and one of the judgment dimensions are favoured, so that we all prefer one of the following: (1) sensation with thinking, (2) intuition with thinking, (3) sensation with feeling, or (4) intuition with feeling. Jung's personality typology is summarized in Exhibit 2-2.

SENSATION WITH THINKING (ST)   This type is usually practical, impersonal, and down-to-earth, being interested in facts, data, and statistics and wanting everything to be orderly, precise, and unambiguous. The STs tend to value efficiency, production, and clear lines of authority. In problem solving, the ST analyzes the facts through step-by-step logic, focusing on short-term problems and using standard procedures to find solutions.[32]

Exhibit 2-2 Jung's Personality Typology (The Four Preferences) as Operationalized by Myers and Briggs

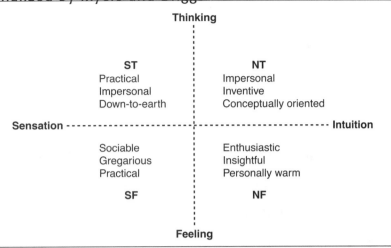

Thinking

ST
Practical
Impersonal
Down-to-earth

NT
Impersonal
Inventive
Conceptually oriented

Sensation - **Intuition**

Sociable
Gregarious
Practical

Enthusiastic
Insightful
Personally warm

SF

NF

Feeling

INTUITION WITH THINKING (NT)   NTs are inventive and concept-oriented and are likely to see the possibilities in a situation through impersonal analysis, though sometimes their conceptualizations confuse the other types. Flowcharts, graphs, and diagrams are tools that NTs feel comfortable with. These people are innovators of new ideas, frequently spark enthusiasm in others, and when solving problems, will often rely on hunches that they attempt to analyze later.

SENSATION WITH FEELING (SF)   Individuals who are SFs tend to be practical, yet also sociable and gregarious. Like the STs, they are interested in facts, but SFs are more interested in facts about people, and they, too, dislike ambiguity. SFs would strive to create an open, trusting environment where people care for one another and communicate well.[33] Although concerned for people, SFs have little inclination for global reflections on problems but, rather, look at small aspects of problems and try to solve these.[34]

INTUITION WITH FEELING (NF)   Creativity, imagination, and personal warmth are valued by the NF, who is enthusiastic and insightful, generally seeing possibilities in and for people. Their goals are proud and general, often encompassing world problems. Their ideal organization is a decentralized one that has no strict hierarchy, few rules, policies, and procedures, and encourages flexibility and open communication.[35] It is very important to NFs to be committed to organizational goals. They may seem to be "dreamers" when solving problems, because theirs is, at times, an idealistic view of the world and its difficulties; but they are persistent and committed.[36]

Exhibit 2-3 provides a summary of your overall profile as a basis for self-understanding. It also provides a look at the profiles of senior and middle managers to help you assess your similarity with successful managers.

Exhibit 2-3   Overall Profile Comparisons as a Basis for Self-Understanding

Each person has a personal way of working and living that is influenced considerably by a number of important factors. These, of course, are not by any means the only factors. However, they are very influential in the way a person organizes his or her work. We can summarize these preferences in the following way:

E=Extrovert Preference Prefers to live in contact with others and things	or	**I=Introvert Preference** Prefers to be more self-contained and work things out personally
S=Sensing Preference Puts emphasis on fact, details, and concrete knowledge	or	**N=Intuition Preference** Puts emphasis on possibilities, imagination, creativity, and seeing things as a whole
T=Thinking Preference Puts emphasis on analysis using logic and rationality	or	**F=Feeling Preference** Puts emphasis on human values, establishing personal friendships; decisions mainly on beliefs and dislikes
J=Judging Preference Puts emphasis on order through obtaining as much data as possible	or	**P=Perceiving Preference** Puts emphasis on gathering information and reaching decisions and resolving issues

As indicated in the above comparisons, the initial letter of each preference provides a shorthand reference to the factor for understanding and discussion except for intuition, which is coded N so that it does not conflict with I for introvert. These letters are used below to describe the combinations of preference alternatives and present the data on managerial style types.

There are 16 combinations from the alternatives outlined. These can be seen from the following model, which builds upon the shorthand letters that have been adopted for each factor.

Combinations of Preference Alternatives

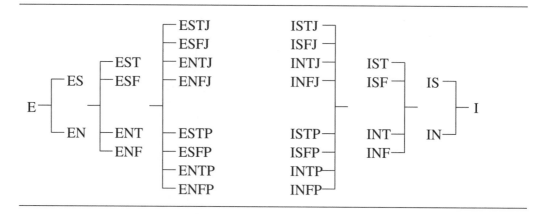

The individual descriptions, while valuable for self understanding, are insufficient for predicting managerial effectiveness. It is the combination of the various preferences that gives us a better indication of how a person will manage.

Source: Adapted from C. Margerison and R. Lewis, "Mapping Managerial Style, " *International Journal of Manpower*, Special Issue 2, no. 1 (1981): 2–20.

SAQ 4: Assumptions About Others Questionnaire[37]

This instrument is designed to help you better understand the assumptions you make about people and human nature. For each of the 10 pairs of statements, assign a weight from 0 to 10 to each statement to show the relative strength of your belief in the statements in each pair. The points assigned for each pair must total 10 in each case. Be as honest with yourself as you can and resist the natural tendency to respond as you would "like to think things are." This instrument is not a "test." It has no right or wrong answers, but rather is designed to be a stimulus for personal reflection and discussion.

1. It is only human nature for people to do as little work as they can get away with. _____ (a)

   When people avoid work, it is usually because their work has been deprived of its meaning. _____ (b)

   10

2. If employees have access to any information they want, they tend to have better attitudes and behave more responsibly. _____ (c)

   If employees have access to more information than they need to do their immediate tasks, they will usually misuse it. _____ (d)

   10

3. One problem in asking for the ideas of employees is that their perspective is too limited for their suggestions to be of much practical value. _____ (e)

   Asking employees for their ideas broadens their perspective and results in the development of useful suggestions. _____ (f)

   10

4. If people do not use much imagination and ingenuity on the job, it is probably because relatively few people have much of either. _____ (g)

   Most people are imaginative and creative but may not show it because of limitations imposed by supervision and the job. _____ (h)

   10

5. People tend to raise their standards if they are accountable for their own behaviour and for correcting their own mistakes. _____ (i)

   People tend to lower their standards if they are not punished for their misbehaviour and mistakes. _____ (j)

   10

6. It is better to give people both good and bad news because most employees want the whole story, no matter how painful. _____ (k)

   It is better to withhold unfavourable news about business because most employees really want to hear only the good news. _____ (l)

   10

7. Because a supervisor is entitled to more respect than employees in the organization, it weakens a supervisor's prestige to admit that an employee was right and the supervisor was wrong. _____ (m)

   Because people at all levels are entitled to equal respect, a supervisor's prestige is increased when that supervisor supports this principle by admitting that an employee was right and the supervisor was wrong. _____ (n)

   10

8. If you give people enough money, they are less likely to be concerned with such intangibles as responsibility and recognition. _____ (o)

   If you give people interesting and challenging work, they are less likely to complain about such things as pay and supplemental benefits. _____ (p)

   10

9. If people are allowed to set their own goals and standards of performance, they tend to set them higher than the boss would. _____ (q)

   If people are allowed to set their own goals and standards of performance, they tend to set them lower than the boss would. _____ (r)

   10

10. The more knowledge and freedom a person has regarding a job, the more controls are needed to keep that employee in line. _____ (s)

   The more knowledge and freedom a person has regarding a job, the fewer controls are needed to ensure satisfactory job performance. _____ (t)

   10

SCORING   Record the number you assign to each of the following letters in the space provided and then total each column.

Theory X		*Theory Y*	
a	_____	b	_____
d	_____	c	_____
e	_____	f	_____
g	_____	h	_____
j	_____	i	_____
l	_____	k	_____
m	_____	n	_____
o	_____	p	_____
r	_____	q	_____
s	_____	t	_____
_____ (Total)		_____ (Total)	

Theory X Score   Theory Y Score

INTERPRETATION   McGregor proposed that a manager's view of the nature of human beings tends to fall into one of two sets.[38] In the first, which is called Theory X, managers assume:

1. Employees inherently dislike work and, whenever possible, will attempt to avoid it.
2. Because employees dislike work, they must be coerced, controlled, or threatened with punishment to achieve goals.
3. Employees will shirk responsibility and seek formal direction whenever possible.
4. Most workers place security above all other factors associated with work and will display little ambition.

In contrast to these negative views about the nature of human beings, McGregor listed four other assumptions that constituted what he called Theory Y:

1. Employees can view work as natural as rest or play.
2. People will exercise self-direction and self-control if they are committed to the objectives.
3. The average person can learn to accept, and even seek, responsibility.
4. The ability to make innovative decisions is widely dispersed throughout the population and is not necessarily the sole province of those in management positions.

Do you see people as basically lazy and irresponsible or as industrious and trustworthy? Look at your Theory X and Theory Y scores. In which box did you score highest? Now, subtract your low score from your highest. The larger this number is, the more strongly you hold to the assumptions of the higher category. Conversely, the lower the number, the more flexibility you show. That is, the closer each of your Theory X and Theory Y scores is to 50, the less intensity you have about the fixed nature of human behaviour. You regard some people as hard-working and trustworthy, but see others as irresponsible and needing direction.

If you scored high only on Theory X assumptions (above 65 points), you do not have much confidence in others—an attitude that is likely to show itself in behaviours such as unwillingness to delegate, authoritarian leadership, and excessive concern with closely monitoring and controlling the people who work for you. A similar high score on Theory Y assumptions indicates a great deal of confidence in other people and may lead, at the extreme, to insufficient managerial attention. How? Excessive delegation of authority, inadequate coordination of employees' activities, and unawareness of problems that need attention are some of the possible dysfunctional outcomes of an unrealistic confidence in one's employees.

Soliciting Feedback From Others

In order to really know ourselves, it is of paramount importance to solicit feedback from others.[39] No matter how much self-examination we engage in through reflecting in solitude about our goal achievements, journal entries about life experiences, or results of self-assessment inventories, to get a true picture of our interpersonal effectiveness we need to understand how others perceive and react to us.

Before we receive meaningful feedback from others, it is beneficial to self-disclose our assumptions, frames of reference, paradigms, and motives about the behaviours they observe. When we self-disclose we force ourselves to assess who we are and why we do things, allow others to better understand our behaviour, and facilitate trust by demonstrating a willingness to share.[40]

Next we need to actively solicit feedback from others about their reactions and the consequences of our behaviours. Then we can judge whether we are being effective or need to modify what we do to achieve our goals. The monitoring and truthful evaluation of feedback facilitates behaviour changes necessary to improve managerial behaviour.[41] It should be emphasized that to receive honest feedback, we need to actively solicit it, because others, especially employees, are often reluctant to share reactions to our behaviours, especially those that they think may be perceived in an unfavourable light.[42] Our initial self-disclosures and request for feedback to improve our behaviours for the benefit of ourselves and others is a good place to set the tone for receiving honest reactions.

A MODEL FOR SELF-DISCLOSING AND SOLICITING FEEDBACK

The Johari Window[43] (see Exhibit 2-4) is a model of the different degrees of self-disclosure and solicitation of feedback utilized when someone is interacting with another person. The

Exhibit 2-4 Johari Window

| | High — Solicit Feedback — Low | |
	Known *Self*	Not Known
High Known	Open Area	Blind Area
Self-Disclose *Others*		
Low Not Known	Hidden Area	Unknown Area

Source: J. Luft, *Group Processes,* 3d ed. (Palo Alto, CA: Mayfield Publishing Company, 1984) 11–20.

model presents four "windowpanes" of potential self-awareness resulting from the information flow between ourselves and others. A description of these four cells follows.

OPEN AREA   In this high-balanced area the manager openly self-discloses and solicits feedback from others. Consequently, others know what the manager's perceptions and intentions are, and the manager's self-awareness is high because of the feedback received from others. Managers using this style know and understand themselves because of the timely and accurate feedback they receive. They can make appropriate changes when necessary. Their open sharing increases the comfort level of others and thereby increases the likelihood that they will establish open channels of communication, which can lead to full sharing of information, mutual understanding, and mutual trust. The resulting open and positive relationship maintains a source of continued feedback for ongoing self-assessment.[44]

HIDDEN AREA   Managers with relatively large hidden areas ask a lot of questions to solicit feedback but do not self-disclose much to others. Consequently, others have a difficult time knowing how the manager feels or what he or she wants. After a while, people can become irritated at continually being asked to open up and share things without any reciprocation from the manager. They may become suspicious about how the information will be used, and may begin to shut down on the quantity and quality of information they are willing to share, thereby decreasing the chances of a manager increasing self-awareness.

Managers using this conservative-probing style have an aversion to self-disclosure, but still seek to maintain open channels of communication with others by seeking feedback. This reluctance to self-disclose may reflect a manager's own insecurity or a mistrust of others. Or the manager may be afraid that if others knew all the information that they would think less of him or her, use the information to their advantage, or be angry because it hurt their feelings. Whatever the reason, conservative-probing managers are likely to create personal facades designed to mislead others. Unfortunately, once such behaviour is recognized, others are likely to withdraw their willingness to provide meaningful and candid feedback about the situation or themselves. The result may ultimately be isolation and mistrust on the part of relevant others, which closes off opportunities for receiving information relevant to self-awareness.

BLIND AREA   The blind area encompasses certain things about a manager that are apparent to others but not to the manager. These blind spots occur either because no one has ever told the manager about them or because the manager defensively blocks them out. Managers with large blind areas frequently tell others how they feel and where they stand on issues, but they are insensitive to feedback from others. Because they don't "hear" what others say to and about them, these managers do not know how they come across and what impact their behaviour has on others. Because they limit self-awareness, blind spots make a manager less effective in interactions with others. A manager may be terrible at running meetings, for example, but may not know it because no one has given him or her any feedback.

In many cases, managers with large blind spots rate their own skills highly and become egoistically involved in the correctness and importance of their actions. These types of managers tend to dominate and seek compliance from others without seeking their feelings or perceptions. They may overuse self-disclosure and fail to balance disclosure with feedback-seeking behaviours and therefore, they are not aware of their impact on others. When relevant others believe that managers are not interested in their feelings and perceptions, they not only quit trying to provide meaningful feedback, but also are likely to feel disenfranchised and withdraw their support for the relationship.[45]

UNKNOWN AREA   Finally, in the unknown area lie repressed fears and needs or beneficial potentials that neither the manager nor employees are aware of. Managers using this last style minimize the use of both self-disclosure and feedback-seeking behaviours. They tend to be perceived as impersonal and closed in their relationships with relevant others who are unaware of how these managers feel and what information they (relevant others) might have to contribute to the situation. While such managers minimize their risks during interpersonal exchanges, they create an environment characterized by withdrawal, detachment, and a reliance on rules as the basis for control. The result of such a style is an environment characterized by closed impersonal relationships and a minimum level of interaction and creativity within the system. Others are also likely to experience frustrations because they do not know where they stand with the manager and may begin to perceive the manager's behaviour as an obstacle to their own need for achievement.

APPROPRIATE LEVELS OF SELF-DISCLOSURE AND FEEDBACK   Ideally, an open interpersonal style that balances self-disclosure and feedback would produce the maximum self-awareness for the manager because he or she would be fully understood by others, and would fully understand them in return. Decisions would be based upon complete information and involved employees would be committed to their effective implementation. Unfortunately, not all environments are mutually supportive. In competitive situations, or situations providing sufficient reasons not to trust others, open self-disclosure may not be in the manager's best interest. Consequently, an appropriate style depends on both the situation and the participants themselves. If open communication is not justified, managers may want to use some of the techniques described in later chapters of this book to resolve conflicts, develop open cultures, and build supportive teams.

SOLICITING FEEDBACK

Managers can use two general strategies for collecting feedback information. First, they can actively monitor their environment by observing the behaviour of others. In this case, managers make no attempt to interact with others directly. Information is obtained by vicariously observing how others respond to their behaviour. Second, they can be direct by specifically asking others how they feel about or would evaluate the manager's behaviour.

After the feedback has been received and accepted, the best type of reinforcement for the manager is to make appropriate changes or to maintain behaviours where feedback is positive. Where necessary, the manager may want to point out changed or maintained behaviours to the individual who provided the feedback.

FROM WHOM SHOULD FEEDBACK BE SOLICITED?

Insights from others can be obtained by soliciting feedback about your skill performance from those around you who are immediately affected. If the manager is having difficulty obtaining the feedback needed by soliciting it during daily interactions, more formal interventions such as 360 degree feedback may work.

360 DEGREE FEEDBACK   The 360 degree feedback approach utilizes feedback from supervisors, employees, and co-workers to provide multiple perspectives from the full circle of people with whom the manager interacts. Managers who use formal periodic surveys or questionnaires have a greater chance of obtaining valid feedback from all sources than do those who randomly request it,[46] although some incidents may be especially ripe for immediate learning.

What are the benefits and drawbacks of these full-circle reviews?[47] The obvious advantage is the comprehensive perspective provided by soliciting information from all the individuals with whom a manager interacts during normal activities. It also allows the manager to compare his or her own perceptions with the perceptions that others have of the manager's skills, styles, and performance. The main drawback to the process is that formal questionnaires are time-consuming and complex to administer. Collecting and compiling information from a number of sources takes more time than having only one person provide feedback.

Self-Directed Career Management

Self-assessment is an ongoing process for successful managers. In order to keep abreast of rapid change in today's work world and to determine where and how they can best contribute, managers have to know themselves, continually develop themselves, and be able to ascertain when and how to change the work they do. According to Peter Drucker, successful careers are not planned. Rather, they develop when people are prepared for opportunities because they know their strengths, their methods of work, and their values. People who have done this type of self-assessment know themselves and are ready to decide where they belong or, just as important, where they do not belong. Knowing where one belongs can transform a hard-working and competent person into an outstanding performer.[48]

Self-directed career management is a process by which individuals guide, direct, and influence the course of their careers.[49] Exploration and awareness of not only yourself but also your environment are necessary conditions to self-direct your career.[50] Individuals who are proactive and collect relevant information about personal needs, values, interests, talents, and lifestyle preferences are more likely to (a) be more satisfied and productive when searching for job opportunities, (b) develop successful career plans, and (c) be productive in their jobs and careers.[51]

Exhibit 2-5 describes a self-directed career management process.[52] The organization, of course, has a big stake in you and will usually actively support your career development, but in this one area effective self-management is the key. Most of us in today's rapidly changing workplace know how important it is to keep skills current and develop new ones that are needed or anticipated to be needed. This need will only increase in the

Exhibit 2-5 A Model for Self-Directed Career Planning

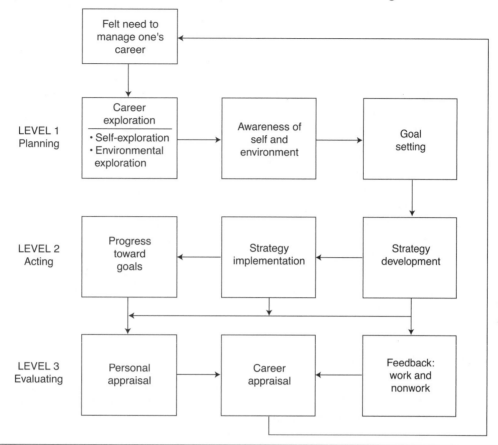

Source: L.W. Mealiea and G.P. Latham, *Skills for Managerial Success* (Chicago: Irwin, 1996) 31.

future. So self-directed career management is a continuing, lifelong process of learning and relearning.[53] And, to maximize our potential contribution and satisfaction, each of us must accept the ultimate responsibility for our own career development.

As exhibited in Level 1 of Exhibit 2-5, the first step in self-directed career management is planning. After you have assessed yourself so that you know your strengths, weaknesses, and values, you are prepared to search the environment for matching opportunities. Then you can establish realistic career goals and develop a strategy to achieve them.[54] Level 2 is the implementation stage, where you put your career plan into action, and Level 3 entails performance appraisal to make sure that you keep on track.[55]

Although the model of career management holds at all stages, individuals just beginning their careers are usually more concerned with identifying organizations that have the potential to satisfy their career goals and match their values. After settling into a job, their focus shifts to achieving initial successes, gaining credibility, learning to get along with their boss, and managing image. Managers in the middle of their careers are more likely to be concerned with career reappraisal, overcoming obsolescence due to technological advances, and becoming more of a generalist. In the later stages of their careers, managers focus more on teaching others and leaving a contribution before retirement.[56]

It has been predicted that most people starting work today can expect to change careers at least three or four times during their working lives.[57] Continual self-assessment and exploration of the environment are necessary conditions for effectively self-managing your career.[58] These activities are also necessary for all employees, however, and managers do have responsibilities to help develop employee potential also.

HELPING EMPLOYEES MANAGE THEIR CAREERS

What responsibilities do managers have for their employees' career development and what can they do to contribute? Today the key is for managers to instill in all employees the need to take responsibility for managing their own careers. Then the manager can provide support for employees to continually add to their skills, abilities, and knowledge, in order to maintain their employability within the organization. So what are some of the key forms of support that a manager can provide to help employees develop their careers?[59]

First of all, managers should inform employees about the organization's goals and future strategies so that they will know where the organization is headed and be better able to develop a personal career development plan to share in that future. Next, managers should create growth opportunities for employees to get new, interesting, and professionally challenging work experiences. Also, managers can offer financial assistance, like tuition reimbursement for college courses or skills training to help employees keep current. Finally, managers can provide time for employees to learn from these opportunities by allowing paid time off from work for off-the-job training, and managers can assure reasonable workloads so that employees are not precluded from having time to develop new skills, abilities, and knowledge.[60]

Concept Quiz

Take the following 10-question, true–false quiz concerning self-awareness and personal development. Answers are at the end of the quiz. If you miss any, go back and find out why you got them wrong. Circle the right answer.

True or False   1. You can only learn about yourself by comparing your experiences with your goals.

True or False   2. Self-awareness is the basis for all the other components of emotional intelligence.

True or False   3. Introverts are more interested in what is happening inside their heads than what is going on in the outside world.

True or False   4. Because managers work with and through other people, the more extroversion they possess, the better.

True or False   5. To get a true picture of our interpersonal effectiveness, we need to understand how others perceive and react to us.

True or False   6. In a supportive environment, high degrees of both self-disclosure and soliciting feedback would produce the maximum self-awareness for a manager.

True or False   7. After the feedback has been received, the best type of reinforcement is for the manager to make appropriate changes or to maintain behaviours where feedback is positive.

True or False   8. Because of their biases, you should not solicit feedback from those who are immediately affected by your actions.

True or False   9. Knowing where one belongs can transform a hard-working and competent person into an outstanding performer.

True or False   10. Self-directed career management is a lifelong process of learning and relearning.

Answers (1) False; (2) True; (3) True; (4) False; (5) True; (6) True; (7) True; (8) False; (9) True; (10) True

Summary Sheet

Summarize your self-assessment profile in the spaces provided on this page. Then tear out the page and turn it in to your instructor. Do not put your name on the sheet. Your instructor will aggregate your class's scores and summarize your interpersonal profiles. Then you can see how you compare to others in the class.

SAQ 1: Is Management for You? _____

SAQ 2: What's Your Emotional Intelligence at Work? _____

       Overall emotional intelligence score _____

           Self-awareness _____

           Managing emotions _____

           Motivating yourself _____

           Empathy _____

           Social skill _____

SAQ 3: Cognitive Style Self-Assessment _____

SAQ 4: Assumptions About Others _____

Theory X _____

Theory Y _____

Behavioural Checklist

The following behaviours are important for enhancing self-awareness and managing yourself. Refer to them when evaluating your own and others' skills in these areas.

Managers Skilled at Self-Awareness and Self-Management:

- Compare actual experiences with previously set goals.
  - Reflect on what went right and why.
  - Reflect on what went wrong and why.

- Keep a journal.
  - Address critical aspects of their managerial experience.
  - Reflect on personal events.

- Create time to find solitude and reflect.
  - Reflect on their experiences and learn from them during uninterrupted time.
  - Create new ideas.

- Solicit feedback from others.
  - Self-disclose so that others know their needs and intentions.
  - Use 360 degree feedback.

- Take responsibility for self-directing their careers.
  - Assess their strengths, weaknesses, and values.
  - Search the environment for matching opportunities.
  - Establish realistic career goals.
  - Develop a strategy to achieve goals.
  - Implement their career plan.
  - Ask for performance appraisals to keep on track.

Group Exercise
Self-Disclosure and Solicitation of Feedback to Know Yourself Better

Form small groups with five to seven class members you do not know well. The following activities take approximately 40 minutes to complete and should be conducted within these groups.

1. Each group member spends five minutes developing two lists: First, a list of his or her five most valuable personal strengths; second, a list of his or her five most valuable accomplishments.
2. Then each group member has three to five minutes to introduce himself or herself: Highlight your background, career goals, and most important accomplishments to date, and briefly describe what you believe are your interpersonal strengths and limitations.
3. Round robin self-disclosure and receiving feedback: One person volunteers to be the focus and shares his or her scores from the self-assessment questionnaires and feelings about their accuracy. Then, group members each give that person feedback about how closely they see assessment profile scores aligning with each person's behaviours exhibited in steps 1 and 2 of this exercise and their thoughts about the consequences.
4. After the first volunteer clarifies the feedback received, another person volunteers to be the focus, and the process continues until all group members have shared and received feedback.

Application Questions

1. How would you describe the kind of person you are to a prospective employer?
2. What is your current career plan?
3. To whom do you feel most comfortable self-disclosing about your intentions and feelings? Why? To whom do you feel least comfortable self-disclosing about your intentions and feelings? Why?
4. Who are your best resources for meaningful feedback? Why did you pick these people?
5. Do you really know yourself? What can you do to know yourself even better?
6. What are the implications of your self-assessment scores for your career planning?

Reinforcement Exercises

The following suggestions are activities you can do to reinforce the self-assessment and self-management techniques in this chapter. You may want to adapt them to the Action Plan you will develop next, or try them independently.

1. Review the section on journals earlier in this chapter. Keep a daily journal for the remainder of this semester. Record significant events and insights that will enhance your self-awareness. At the beginning of each new week, study your journal entries from the previous week to see what you can learn about yourself.
2. Share your self-assessment inventory scores with a significant other. Explain their meaning. Discuss their implications and see what you can learn from the other person's reactions and experiences with you.
3. Visit your campus counselling centre. Ask what self-assessment inventories are available.

4. Visit your campus counselling centre or placement office. Ask what career development services are provided.
5. Ask a good friend to share with you his or her perceptions of your strengths and weaknesses as a friend.
6. Practise finding solitude for 30 minutes a day for a week.

Action Plan

1. In what areas do I most need to improve my self-awareness? (See Behavioural Checklist.)
2. Why? What will be my payoff?
3. What potential obstacles stand in my way?
4. What are the specific things I will do to enhance my self-awareness? (For examples, see the Reinforcement Exercises.)
5. When will I do them?
6. How and when will I measure my success?

Skills Video

Self-Awareness

All of us have doubts, fears, and insecurities, some we can admit to, and others we cannot. Self-awareness—recognizing our own feelings and the ways they guide our behaviour—is a skill that can be sharpened with practice. It is the first step to overcoming the weaknesses we acknowledge and the weaknesses we do not.

Learning from experience is one way to enhance self-awareness. There are three techniques for learning from experience: experience-goal matching, keeping a journal, and finding solitude to reflect. Asking others for feedback about our interpersonal effectiveness is another way to increase awareness of our own feelings; it shows us how our actions affect others. As a manager, you should ask for such feedback, since employees may otherwise be reluctant to say what they think.

This video segment introduces Quicktakes Video, a small television production company started by Hal Boylston and Karen Jarvis. Quicktakes produces short films and videos for various corporate and entrepreneurial clients and is based on a real company.

We first meet Hal Boylston in a stressful moment as a problem at home follows him to the office. Then we see him confront a crisis at work that calls for a management decision. Hal fills an emergency need for a producer to do a video shoot in San Francisco by going himself, a choice that leaves his staff concerned and dissatisfied.

See whether you can spot the reasons why Hal's staff is unhappy with his decision to go on location. Decide whether you think they are justified. If Hal had another option, why do you think he did not take it?

Explain exactly how Hal's lack of self-awareness leads him to make his decision and why he chooses to ignore its possible consequences. Be alert to the behaviour of his employees too. Are there ways they could be supporting Hal more effectively?

CHAPTER 3
Developing Ethical Guideposts

Learning Objectives
After completing this chapter, you should be able to:

- Develop your own ethical parameters.
- Analyze your organization's ethics policy.
- Evaluate business situations to determine ethical courses of action.
- Create a positive ethical environment for employees.

Self-Assessment Exercise
How Important Are Ethics to You?[1]

Everyone likes to think of him- or herself as honest, moral, and ethical, especially on "big" matters. Few of us would likely cheat, steal, or lie if we perceived the stakes (or perhaps the chances of being caught) as extraordinarily high.

But how principled would you be—or *should* you be—when faced with routine business situations involving ethical choices? If your self-interest were on a collision course with your principles, how would you act?

Respond as candidly as possible to the following self-assessment situations involving potential business conflicts. Describe your level of agreement with each of the statements by circling the number in the appropriate column.

	Strongly Agree				Strongly Disagree
1. I would speak my mind if the boss asked my view of the new ad campaign, which my boss conceived and adores but which I think is dreadful.	5	4	3	2	1
2. I would never copy software without getting permission from the publisher.	5	4	3	2	1
3. If it meant making a sale that I needed for my monthly quota, I would give the customer an overly optimistic delivery date.	1	2	3	4	5

	Strongly Agree				Strongly Disagree
4. In applying for a job, I would omit a prior experience if I had been fired or had left under a cloud.	1	2	3	4	5
5. I would pad my expense account just a bit if I thought I was being shortchanged by the company in other ways.	1	2	3	4	5
6. If I saw a co-worker make false statements to a customer or a supervisor, I would tell the boss.	5	4	3	2	1
7. I would flirt with my manager if I thought it could win me a bigger raise.	1	2	3	4	5
8. I would use my office phone to make a long-distance call on personal matters if no easy alternative were available.	1	2	3	4	5
9. I would never take home paper clips, stationery, or other office supplies.	5	4	3	2	1
10. I would accept a permanent, full-time job even if I knew I could only stay for a few months.	1	2	3	4	5
11. I would never call in "sick" when I just needed some time off.	5	4	3	2	1
12. If a supplier gave me an expensive gift that I really liked, I'd return it only if keeping it would be obvious to my boss.	5	4	3	2	1
13. If I felt sexually attracted to a job candidate with lesser qualifications than the others, I wouldn't let that influence my hiring decision.	5	4	3	2	1
14. If I didn't win the promotion, I would be inclined to slack off when working for the person who did.	1	2	3	4	5
15. If my secretary weren't busy, I would ask him or her to type some personal correspondence for me.	5	4	3	2	1

SCORING AND INTERPRETATION Add the numbers you have circled to obtain your total score.

70–75	You are a strongly ethical person whom some may accuse of being too rigid.
50–69	You show average ethical awareness and thus may need to sharpen your ethical focus.
40–50	Although you show some awareness of ethical issues, your actions may not be consistently ethical.
0–40	Your ethical values appear to be below contemporary standards and could become a negative factor in your career.

Concepts

What Is Ethics? Why Is It Important?

- Your best friend asks you to download MP3s of a favourite recording artist on your company computer during lunch hours and breaks. Do you say "yes" because she is your friend even though it is a violation of the copyright? Would the company condone this activity even though it would be done on your own time?

- You are the founder and president of a small electronics company. Your whole financial future is wrapped up in the success of your firm. An engineer at a competing company makes an important scientific breakthrough that promises big profits for the rival firm at your expense. You ponder whether you should hire that engineer away in an attempt to learn the details of the discovery.[2]

- A foreign worker is seriously hurt in an accident at one of your overseas operations. Your facility there meets local standards, but the plant manager tells you the accident wouldn't have occurred in Canada because Canadian safety laws would have mandated the installation of protective equipment. Your company is under no legal requirement to install the expensive devices in foreign countries, but does it have a moral obligation?[3]

- Your assistant controller, after some not-too-subtle hints from you, is starting to look for a new job at another firm. You are relieved because you will not have to fire him; his work has been substandard for quite some time. But your relief turns to dismay when he asks you to write a strong letter of recommendation for him. Do you say "no" and run the risk that he will not leave? Or do you write the letter, knowing that you're influencing someone else to take on the problem you are finding troublesome?[4]

In the workplace, acting ethically is not just an abstraction. Especially for managers, making the right choices in ethics-laden situations, big and small, is an almost-everyday occurrence.

Ethics is commonly thought of as the rules or principles that define right and wrong conduct.[5] In this chapter, however, you are going to read many examples in which the task isn't as simple as just choosing the "correct" answer. Rather, the decision may involve the many shades of grey in between "right" and "wrong." What guideposts can you use, especially in those "grey" areas, where right and wrong are not easily defined? What processes can you follow to enhance your ethical thinking and decisions?

In this chapter, you will be encouraged to develop your own ethical decision-making process. You also will learn how managers as well as organizations can help or hinder the development of a moral climate.

WHY STUDY ETHICS?

Ethics is important for everyone, but it is particularly crucial for the manager for a number of reasons. One obvious reason is that his or her decisions set the standard for employees and help create a tone for the organization as a whole.

Second, the behaviour of managers is under increasing scrutiny. Because people have more access to information, misdeeds may become quickly and widely known. The reputation of an organization or individual, which may have taken many years to build, can be destroyed in minutes. In addition, today's public has high standards for the behaviour of managers and their companies. Customers are no longer forced to tolerate an unethical company; competition allows them to choose the company that best meets their expectations.

Behaving ethically also improves the quality of work life. If employees believe all are held to similar high standards, they likely will feel better about themselves, their colleagues, and their organization.

Further, many businesses want employees to behave ethically because such a reputation is good for business (which, in turn, can mean larger profits). Similarly, encouraging employees to act ethically can save money by reducing employee theft, downtime, and lawsuits. Because many unethical acts are also illegal, a firm that allows workers to engage in unfair practices might be prosecuted.

However, the law itself is not an adequate guide to ethics. Some unethical acts—lying under oath, for example, or embezzling—are illegal. But many legal acts are potentially unethical, and it is those situations that often require the toughest choices. For instance, charging a higher price to a naïve customer than to a savvy one is not illegal. In fact, it may be seen by some as a smart business practice. But is it *ethical*? Dismissing an employee for just cause is not illegal, but if the poor performance has been tolerated for years and the problem employee will qualify for his pension in a few more months, is firing him ethical?

How Strong Are Our Business Ethics?

Perhaps all behaviour contains a potential conflict between doing what is morally right and what is in our own self-interest. But in business—where our self-interest also constitutes our economic well-being—the dividing line between these two motives is especially blurred. Indeed, a cynic would say "business ethics" is an oxymoron, that making money and advancing one's career are so essential that observing moral niceties is a luxury few can afford.

However, interest in ethics is on the rise. Ethics education, for example, is being widely expanded in college and university curricula and in the workplace. Such attempts to codify business ethics are not new. As far back as 1750 B.C., the Babylonian ruler Hammurabi etched into an eight-foot-high stone an elaborate code of conduct, including some provisions aimed at curtailing unfair business practices.[6]

Although many companies are setting up ethics codes, ethics training, and ethics officers to help instill corporate values, many observers believe that we are currently suffering an ethics crisis. Behaviours that were once thought of as reprehensible—lying, cheating, misrepresenting, and covering up mistakes—have become, in many people's eyes, acceptable or necessary practices. Some managers have profited from illegal use of insider information. Others have covered up information about the safety of their products. Price fixing, polluting the environment, and industrial espionage are further illustrations of ethical lapses.

Pollsters often try to gauge the state of business ethics. According to a global study by Walker Information and the Hudson Institute, 62 per cent of Canadian employees believe that they work for an "ethical" company, yet only 49 per cent believe that their senior leaders have high personal integrity. This is considerably lower than the 61 per cent of employees globally who thought that their senior leaders acted with personal integrity. Canadian workers also tend not to fare well when confronted with ethical violations. While 29 per cent of Canadian employees know of or suspect ethical violations within their organization, only 38 per cent of those employees have reported the violations.[7] This could be interpreted as employees fearing censure from senior leaders who have less concern for ethical behaviour.

The Walker/Hudson study also found a strong correlation between employee commitment and the organization's ethical orientation. That is, employees are more likely to stay with an employer that is deemed to be "ethical."[8] In short, this tends to support the view that "ethical" workplaces have lower turnover rates.

There are many initiatives that attempt to increase the commitment to ethical conduct in Canadian companies. One such initiative is Ethics in Action, an award program that started in Vancouver in 1994 and has since spread to Ontario. Ethics in Action defines social responsibility as a company's obligation to consider all its stakeholders when making decisions. Stakeholders include employees, customers, suppliers, community groups, neighbourhoods, and the environment. Through awards, Ethics in Action attempts to give public recognition to companies and business leaders who have made a positive impact on communities and business practices. Business award winners have included Husky Injection Molding Systems Ltd., Print Three, Pfizer Canada Inc., and Canadian Tire.

Yet, the study and practice of ethics are not as precise as mathematics or engineering. As you will see, the variables are many and the absolutes few. Often the decision is not between good and bad or between fair and unfair alternatives as much as it is a choice among competing goods or lesser evils.

Why Ethics Questions Are Often Tougher Than They Seem

It is easy to *say* you want to do the right thing, but figuring out the proper action can be difficult because often no single "correct" answer is available. For example, if you and a friend developed a prosperous business but had serious disagreements that led to the partnership being dissolved, would you be more concerned with remaining friends or making a good deal?[9]

Most of us would agree that lying is wrong. Yet most of us also would say that at times it may be better to disguise or embellish the truth than to be totally candid. What would you do, for example, if a manager, whose support is critical to your success as a human resources officer, asked for your help to get one of his employees transferred to another division? You know the employee in question is a marginal performer. Furthermore, you know that the manager hasn't mentioned this inadequate performance in the employee's performance appraisals. Do you support the manager by not saying anything about the employee's poor, but unrecorded, performance to the heads of the other divisions? Or, do you risk your own career success and share a note about the employee's questionable performance? Put another way, is not telling the whole truth the moral equivalent of lying?

These dilemmas, and many others, have no easy answers. And opinions differ on the key questions to ask oneself when faced with an ethical dilemma. We will give you our own ethical-screening recommendations later in this chapter. Meanwhile, see Exhibit 3-1 for a simple "ethics check."

Taking the time to think through ethical quandaries and debating them with trusted associates is often wise because many situations are more complex than they may seem at first. For example, is it ethical for a salesperson to offer an expensive gift to a purchasing agent as an inducement to buy? Instinctively, you might say "no." But what if the gift comes out of the salesperson's commission? In other words, the salesperson, trying

---

Exhibit 3-1 How Will You Feel?

In their book, *The Power of Ethical Management,* Norman Vincent Peale and Ken Blanchard suggest the following ethics check:

- Is it legal? Will I be violating either civil law or company policy?
- Is it balanced? Is it fair to all concerned in the short term as well as the long term? Does it promote win-win relationships?
- How will it make me feel about myself? Will it make me proud? Would I feel good if my decision were published in the newspaper? Would I feel good if my family knew about it?

Source: K. Blanchard and N.V. Peale, *The Power of Ethical Management* (New York: William Morrow, 1988) 27.

to get ahead, is willing to make a personal investment in her clients. Does that make it any different?

Similarly, is it ethical for an employee to "blow the whistle" by complaining to authorities about an improper company practice? Sure, you might say. But what if the whistleblower does so without first consulting company officials or exhausting in-house remedies? Or, what if he is going public with his revelation because there is a financial reward? Or because he will be on the television news? Or because he mistakenly believes the company mistreated him? Would your view of the whistleblower's ethics change if you knew more about his motivation and what procedures he followed?

Organizations and individuals can do a number of things to encourage ethical behaviour. Next, we will look at what influences a person's choices and ways to improve the ethical climate.

Factors Affecting Managerial Ethics

Whether a manager acts ethically or unethically depends on several factors, including: his or her personal values; the organization's culture and structure; the issue that is being called into question; and the national culture in which the manager operates.[10]

THE INDIVIDUAL'S VALUES

People who lack a strong moral sense are much less likely to do the wrong things if they are constrained by rules, policies, job descriptions, or strong cultural norms that discourage such behaviours. Conversely, moral people can be corrupted by an organizational structure and culture that permits or encourages unethical practices. How strong is your personal moral sense?

For example, if someone in your class were selling a copy of the final exam, would you have the strength not to buy it? Would you have that resolve even if you suspected the faculty knew a copy was floating around but had done little to discourage cheating? Would a decision not to buy the exam be easier to reach if you knew that automatic expulsion was the outcome if you were caught?

THE ORGANIZATION'S CULTURE

Unwittingly perhaps, organizations often reward unethical behaviour. In fact, they may develop "counternorms" that are contrary to prevailing ethical standards. For example, although government regulations may require disclosure of certain information such as the level of hazardous chemical emissions, some organizations send out the tacit message to their employees that being secretive and deceitful is not only acceptable, but also desirable. In those organizations, employees who are too open and honest may even be punished.[11]

In addition, some managerial values can undermine integrity. Although the vast majority of managers appear to recognize that "good ethics is good business," some managers have developed ways of thinking that can encourage unethical decisions. Such thinking patterns include the following:

1. *Bottom-line mentality* People who think like this believe that financial success is the only criterion for decision making. Any ethical concerns are ignored or given a lesser priority.

2. *Exploitive mentality* This perspective sacrifices concern for others in favour of benefits to oneself. Such managers "use" people to achieve their goals.

3. *"Appearances" mentality* This reasoning suggests that anything is right if the public can be made to see it as right. Appearances are valued more than reality and, thus,

management is less concerned with doing the right thing than with what looks good.[12]

THE ORGANIZATION'S STRUCTURE

Some structures provide for strong guidance while other companies are organized in ways that create ambiguity for managers. Lax supervision is one example, or no clear code of conduct may be in place. Or perhaps a code does exist but it's often winked at. Structures also differ in the amount of time, competition, cost, and other pressures put on employees. In short, the more pressure and the less guidance, the more likely it is that managers will compromise their ethical standards.

A good structure, on the other hand, is one that constantly reminds managers about what is ethical and uniformly disciplines those who use bad judgment. Formal rules and regulations as well as clear job descriptions and written codes of ethics help reduce ambiguity.

The performance appraisal system also may weaken or reinforce ethical standards. If the appraisals focus exclusively on outcomes and ignore what means are used to reach the ends, then employees feel increased pressure to do "whatever is necessary" to reach the goals.

THE INTENSITY OF THE ISSUE

We tend to give more thought to ethical questions when the stakes are higher—when potential for harm is great, or if a lot of money or the chance of a big career gain is involved. A manager who would think nothing of taking home a few office supplies, for example, would be highly concerned about embezzlement of company funds. The distinction is made because actual pilfering of money, in addition to being prosecutable, is an act with greater consequences for both the individual and the firm.

However, deciding what is a major and what is a minor ethical issue can be a slippery slope. For example, almost everyone would consider taking a monetary bribe as unethical; it also may well be illegal. But what if the "bribe" is not monetary? What if you are a purchasing officer and several vendors are pitching similar products to you: Vendor A makes an attractive price offer; Vendor B makes a comparable offer but also invites you, a known hockey fanatic, to a big game that you otherwise would not be able to attend because of a scarcity of tickets? If you go and you choose Vendor B as your supplier, have you been "bribed" even though the prices are comparable and the company incurs no loss?

THE NATIONAL CULTURE

Some of the most difficult global business decisions involve ethical considerations because the basis of what is "right" and "wrong" is culturally determined. How rigid can you be in applying only your country's ethical and legal templates while operating in foreign lands?

For instance, using child labour in Canada is neither legal nor ethically acceptable, but in many foreign countries, the practice is routine. Which cultural norm should prevail in the foreign branches of Canadian companies?

Similarly, the issue of bribery is one of the toughest to resolve in the international context. It regularly occurs in business overseas even though most Canadians would condemn it as unethical. In 1997, the United States passed the Foreign Corrupt Practices Act, which prohibits U.S. companies from paying bribes to foreign government officials. Canada, however, does not have a similar law. Can or should Canadian firms resist joining in this universally illegal act if their competitors are doing it in response to local custom?

Consider this scenario, based on an actual situation.[13] You are marketing director for a construction firm in the Middle East. Your company bids on a substantial and much-needed project, but the cousin of the government minister who will award the contract contacts you. He suggests that in exchange for a $20,000 fee to the government minister, your chances of getting the contract will greatly improve. If you do not pay, you are sure the award will be to your competitor, which routinely makes these kinds of payments and routinely wins the contracts, too.

Your company has no code of conduct yet, although it has formed a committee to consider one. The government of your country encourages its companies to act ethically. The pertinent paragraph is somewhat vague but implies that this kind of payment would probably be in violation of the guidelines. Your boss, and those above your boss, do not want to become involved. What do you do?

How Can Organizations Encourage Ethical Behaviour?

Ethics, as we have seen, is an organizational issue, a personal issue, or a cultural issue. Management, however, can take a number of actions that, in aggregate, may help to reduce unethical practices.[14]

MAKE BETTER PERSONNEL SELECTIONS

An organization's employee-selection process—interviews, tests, and background checks—should be used to eliminate ethically undesirable applicants. The selection process should be seen as an opportunity to learn not only about the candidate's job skills but also his or her personal values.[15] Who is hired, promoted, and rewarded (or punished) sends a strong signal to employees about valued ethical standards in the organization. In Chapter 13, Identifying and Hiring Employees, we will elaborate on how to identify and hire employees.

DEVELOP A CODE OF ETHICS

Codes of ethics are an increasingly popular tool for reducing ethical ambiguity. Nearly 90 per cent of *Fortune* 1000 firms now have a formal code of ethics stating the organization's ethical rules.[16] One study of 83 corporate codes found that the content of the codes fall in three general areas: (1) be a dependable organizational citizen, (2) do not do anything unlawful or improper that will harm the organization, and (3) be good to customers.[17] Exhibit 3-2 lists the variables in each of those three clusters in order of their frequency of mention. Nortel Networks' code of business conduct is an example of a formal code. This comprehensive document outlines principles and practices to be followed by all employees and applies to Nortel's transactions throughout the world.[18]

Obviously, no code can cover every possible situation. Ideally the codes should be specific enough to show employees the spirit in which they are supposed to act but loose enough to allow freedom of judgment in unique situations.

Probably as important as the content of the code is how seriously it is taken by top management. In isolation, the code is not likely to be much more than window dressing. However, if the codes are communicated often and well, if higher-ups vigorously endorse them, and if employees who violate the codes are treated firmly and publicly, a code can provide a strong foundation for an ethics program.[19]

LEAD BY EXAMPLE

Top management sets the cultural tone through words and action. In fact, research continues to show that the behaviour of management is *the strongest single influence* on an

Exhibit 3-2 Variables Found in 83 Corporate Codes of Business Ethics

Cluster 1: Be a Dependable Organizational Citizen

1. Comply with safety, health, and security regulations.
2. Demonstrate courtesy, respect, honesty, and fairness.
3. Illegal drugs and alcohol at work are prohibited.
4. Manage personal finances well.
5. Exhibit good attendance and punctuality.
6. Follow directives of supervisors.
7. Do not use abusive language.
8. Dress in business attire.
9. Firearms at work are prohibited.

Cluster 2: Do Not Do Anything Unlawful or Improper That Will Harm the Organization

1. Conduct business in compliance with all laws.
2. Payments for unlawful purposes are prohibited.
3. Bribes are prohibited.
4. Avoid outside activities that impair duties.
5. Maintain confidentiality of records.
6. Comply with all antitrust and trade regulations.
7. Comply with all accounting rules and controls.
8. Do not use company property for personal benefit.
9. Employees are personally accountable for company funds.
10. Do not propagate false or misleading information.
11. Make decisions without regard for personal gain.

Cluster 3: Be Good to Customers

1. Convey true claims in product advertisements.
2. Perform assigned duties to the best of your ability.
3. Provide products and services of the highest quality.

Source: F.R. David, *An Empirical Study of Codes of Business Ethics: A Strategic Perspective*, Paper presented at the 48th Annual Academy of Management Conference, Anaheim, CA (August 1988).

individual's ethical or unethical behaviour.[20] Because employees use their higher-ups' behaviour as a **benchmark** for what is expected, how those in management act is probably more important than what they say.

SET REALISTIC JOB GOALS

Employees should have tangible, realistic goals. If goals are ambiguous or make unrealistic demands, they can encourage employees to take an "anything goes" attitude, but clear, realistic goals help reduce ambiguity and motivate rather than punish. Goal-setting skills will be elaborated on in Chapter 11, Planning and Goal Setting.

PROVIDE ETHICS TRAINING

Though debate continues over the value of ethics seminars, workshops, and similar programs, ethics training, at its best, can provide a number of benefits. It reinforces the organization's standards. It reminds employees that top managers put a priority on ethics. It clarifies what practices are or are not permissible. And, when managers discuss such common concerns, they may be reassured that they aren't alone in facing ethical dilemmas. Such reassurance can strengthen their resolve when they need to take an ethically correct, but unpopular, stance.[21]

USE COMPREHENSIVE PERFORMANCE EVALUATIONS

If performance evaluations focus only on economic outcomes, employees will infer that the ends justify the means. Thus, if an organization wants managers to uphold high ethical standards, it should include this dimension in the evaluation process. For instance, a manager's annual review might include a point-by-point evaluation of his or her decisions on an ethical scale as well as by more traditional economic criteria. Skills for effective performance evaluation are explained in Chapter 14, Evaluating Performance.

DO INDEPENDENT AUDITS

Having an outsider evaluate decisions and practices in terms of the organization's code of ethics can increase the likelihood of an unethical practice being detected. Such audits could be done on a regular basis and at random and be conducted by auditors responsible to the company's board of directors, which would hear the findings directly. Such autonomy not only gives the auditors clout but also lessens the opportunity for retaliation by those being audited.

CREATE ETHICS OFFICERS

More than 500 companies have created ethics officers, up from 200 just a few years ago.[22] These ombudspersons hear from employees, anonymously or by name, with a view toward counselling them on matters of fairness and working to improve the firm's ethical climate. Thus, such ethics officers can act as both a sounding board and a possible advocate for the "right" alternative.[23]

Again, this trend appears to be a welcome one, but it is not a panacea. For instance, critics contend that the ethics officer job is too often reserved for long-time company loyalists who are unlikely to challenge higher executives and/or who wield little real power. The ethics officers themselves often complain that they can recommend but have little clout with which to create real change.[24]

What You As An Individual Can Do

The organization can do much to foster ethical behaviour. But in the final analysis it is the individual manager who must make the decisions, and quite often individuals make poor choices on ethical issues. See Exhibit 3-3 for some of the reasons. Thus, it is important that you develop your own **ethical guideposts** and decision-making processes to apply for yourself. We offer some guidelines, then a step-by-step template for individual decision making.

SKILL GUIDELINES FOR DEVELOPING AND APPLYING ETHICAL GUIDEPOSTS

1. *Know and understand your organization's policy on ethics* Company policies on ethics, if they exist, describe what the organization perceives as ethical behaviour and what it expects you to do. Knowing and understanding this policy will clarify what is permissible and what discretion you have.
2. *Anticipate potential ethical conflict* Managers should be alert to situations that may promote unethical behaviour. Under unusual circumstances, even an otherwise eth-

Exhibit 3-3 Why Do Individuals Make Poor Choices on Ethical Issues?

1. The individual and/or the organization is immature.
2. Economic self-interest is overwhelming.
3. Special circumstances outweigh ethical concerns.
4. People are uneducated in ethical decision making.
5. Possible rewards outweigh possible punishments for unethical behaviour.
6. The prevailing attitude is "All's fair in love, war, and business."
7. There is powerful organizational pressure to commit unethical acts.

Source: O.C. Ferrell and G. Gardiner, *In Pursuit of Ethics: Tough Choices in the World of Work* (Springfield, IL: Smith Collins Co., 1991) 9–13

ical employee may be tempted to act out of character. The manager needs to anticipate those unusual situations and be proactive.

For example, a manager may know that an important client has a reputation for cutting corners. He or she also may know that this quarter's sales goals are high, putting added pressure on the salespeople. If so, the manager could seek to blunt any temptation by meeting with the customer to tactfully restate the company's ethical credo. Further, the manager probably will want to give the sales staff helpful advice on how to rebuff questionable overtures and meet goals through ethical means.

3. *Think before you act* Ask yourself, "Why am I doing what I'm about to do? What led up to the problem? What is my true intention in taking this action? Is my reason valid? Or are there ulterior motives behind it—such as proving myself to my peers or manager? Will my action injure someone?"

Also ask yourself: "Would I disclose to my boss or family what I am about to do?" Remember, it is *your* behaviour and *your* actions. You need to make sure that you are not doing something that will jeopardize your reputation or your organization.

4. *Ask yourself what-if questions* As you ponder your decision, you should also be asking what-if questions. For example: "What if I make the wrong decision? What will happen to me? To my job?" "What if my actions were described, in detail, on a local TV news show or in the newspaper? Would that public notice bother or embarrass me or those around me?" "What if I get caught doing something unethical? Am I prepared to deal with the consequences?"

5. *Seek opinions from others* Asking for advice from other managers is often wise. Maybe they have been in a similar situation and can give you the benefit of their experience. Or maybe they can just listen and act as a sounding board for you.

6. *Do not allow yourself to become isolated* Managers can easily become isolated from what is occurring in the office, but it is the manager's responsibility to be aware of all activities. You can combat isolation by promoting an open-door policy and continually looking for ways to improve ethical behaviour.

7. *Do what you truly believe is right* You have a conscience, and you are responsible for your behaviour. Whatever you do, if you truly believe it is the right action to take, then what others will say is immaterial. You need to be true to your own internal ethical standards. Ask yourself: "Can I live with what I have done?"

ETHICAL SCREEENING

Ethical screening refers to running a contemplated decision through an ethics test. This screening makes the most sense when, as is often the case, the contemplated action is in that grey area between clearly right and clearly wrong.

The following process contains nothing magical.[25] Other authors will offer other litmus tests. What is important is that you are familiar with the basic steps you should take when faced with an ethical dilemma.

Step 1. Gather the facts   You should find out the answers to pertinent questions: Does the situation present any legal questions? What are the precedents for this kind of decision? What do our company rules and regulations say?

Step 2. Define the ethical issues   It may be helpful to talk the situation over with someone to clarify these issues. Such issues might include conflicts of interest, dealing with confidential information, proper use of company resources, or more intangible questions concerning kindness, respect, or fairness.

Step 3. Identify the affected parties   Major corporate decisions, such as shutting down a plant, can affect thousands of people. Even a much more modest action—hiring or not hiring an individual with a disability, for example—can involve many more people than you might initially think.

Step 4. Identify the consequences   Try to predict the consequences for each party. Concentrate on those outcomes with the highest probability of occurring and especially those with negative outcomes. Both the short- and long-term results should be considered. Closing down the plant, for example, might create short-term harm but in the long term the firm may be financially healthier.

Do not neglect the symbolic consequences, either. Every action sends a message, good or bad. If you hire the disabled worker, that act may send a message that is larger and more meaningful than all your words about equal opportunity. It is not just what you say, it is what you do that your employees will pick up on.

Step 5. Consider your character and integrity   It is fair to ask yourself the following questions.

- What would my family, friends, co-workers, and manager think of my actions?
- How would I feel if my decision were publicly disclosed in the newspaper or via e-mail?
- Does this decision or action agree with my religious teachings and beliefs (or with my personal principles and sense of responsibility)?
- Would I want everyone to make the same decision and take the same action if faced with these same circumstances?
- How would I feel if I were on the other side of this decision?

Step 6. Think creatively about alternatives   More alternatives can often be identified than just the choice between doing or not doing something. Try to be imaginative when considering options. For example, what could you do if a grateful client sends you an expensive fruit basket that you cannot ethically accept? To keep it would be wrong. But if you returned it, you might appear ungrateful and make the client feel foolish; you could even cause the fruit to spoil.

So, another possibility might be giving the gift to a homeless shelter, then penning the client a thank-you note mentioning that you passed the fruit along to the more needy. You would not have violated your policy or set a bad example for your staff. Meanwhile, you also would have graciously informed the client about your policy and probably discouraged future gift giving.

Step 7. Check your intuition   Quite apart from the rational decision-making process, you should also ask yourself: "How does this feel in my gut? Will I be proud of myself?"

Step 8. Prepare to defend your action   Will you be able to explain adequately to others what you are about to do? Will they also likely feel it is ethical or moral?

Concept Quiz

Complete the following true–false quiz by circling the correct answer. Answers are at the end of the quiz. After marking your answers, remember to go back and check your understanding of any answers you missed.

True or False	1.	An explicitly written code of conduct is an increasingly common tool for reducing ethical ambiguity.
True or False	2.	Management's words and actions have little to do with how employees behave.
True or False	3.	Tasks that are unrealistic and highly stressful may cause an employee to resort to unethical measures.
True or False	4.	Managers should take into consideration employees' values only after they are hired and can be observed in a work environment.
True or False	5.	An ethically sound corporate culture can lead to long-term success for the company.
True or False	6.	A manager's ethics are especially important because management sets the standard for employees.
True or False	7.	Some unethical acts are legal.
True or False	8.	An organization's culture and structure influence how ethically its employees act.
True or False	9.	Business operations in foreign lands often present difficult ethical choices because of differences in cultural norms.
True or False	10.	Because an individual facing an ethical dilemma needs to rely on his or her reasoning skills and moral compass, rarely can anything be gained by discussing the circumstances with others.

Answers (1) True; (2) False; (3) True; (4) False; (5) True; (6) True; (7) True; (8) True; (9) True; (10) False

Behavioural Checklist

The following behaviours are important to ethical management. Use them when evaluating your ethical management skills and those of others.

The Ethical Manager:

- Disseminates the organization's policy on ethics.
- Hires and promotes individuals with high ethical standards.
- Leads by ethical example.
- Sets job goals that are realistic.
- Provides ethics training.
- Anticipates potential ethical conflicts.
- Avoids isolation and seeks opinions from others.
- Applies the ethical-screening process to ethical dilemmas.

Modelling Exercise
Competing Ethical Criteria[26]

DIRECTIONS The entire class should read the following situation. Then two class members volunteer to act out the roles of John Higgins, director of research, and Jasmine Singh, who heads his design team. The role-players read their assigned role only and prepare to explain their position at the forthcoming meeting. Do NOT read the other person's role. The remainder of the class reads both roles and reviews the Observer's Rating Sheet. Upon completion of the dialogue, class members rate Higgins's application of ethical management skills.

Observers should also note what points Higgins and Singh make and be prepared to suggest additional arguments and alternatives.

TIME 20 minutes.

ACTORS John Higgins, director of research for Softec, a software developer; Jasmine Singh, leader of design team charged with developing a critical component for a new software application.

SITUATION John Higgins appointed Jasmine Singh about three months ago to head the design team for a new software application. The success of the new application is crucial to the firm's profitability. The new component has a tight development deadline of 18 months. In fact, the CEO issued a statement indicating that the company's financial future may hinge on the timely development of this new application.

The CEO's statement also applauded the promotion of Jasmine Singh to a key role. She is an Indo-Asian female, and the first woman in company history to lead such a unit. The company has traditionally lagged in the hiring and promotion of minorities.

Now, more than halfway through the project, certain members of the all-male team have been complaining about Singh. The project is on schedule, and no one has faulted Singh's technical knowledge. But general criticisms ("She does not know how to lead men" and "She does not understand teamwork") have been made and discussed publicly. The grousing has started to snowball, and recently the pace of work has slowed. Higgins suspects some team members are quietly sabotaging the project.

HIGGINS'S ROLE You respect and admire Singh as an employee as well as a human being. You are sure she has a lot to offer the company as she grows professionally. You do not want to crush her hopes—or stymie her potential—by reneging on this big chance you gave her.

On the other hand, neither you nor the firm can risk having this software project fail for whatever reason, so you are considering removing her as team leader. You and Singh have always had a good working relationship until now, but you fear that if you take her off the project, she will become embittered and perhaps even file a gender-discrimination complaint with the Human Rights Commission. Furthermore, you feel sure some will see her removal as symbolic of the traditional shortchanging of minorities by the firm.

You feel torn between your responsibility to the company and to a valued employee. You want to explain to Singh the ethical quandary you find yourself in and how the economic considerations are at war with the moral ones. Your goal is to try to understand the other person's view and to try perhaps to reach an ethical solution that is satisfactory to both parties and the company. You have asked Singh to meet with you to discuss "a critical question" relating to her work role.

SINGH'S ROLE   The men on the design team have been difficult, almost mutinous, but you think they would be that way with any woman or minority group member in charge. You are qualified for this job. You have earned it. You want it. You are prepared to endure insults and whatever other hurdles are placed in your way; those challenges are the price pioneers must pay. You owe it not only to yourself but also to other women and minorities to persevere and not let Higgins cave under pressure from the men who are upset because their "white males only" club has been disrupted.

If this question is one of ethics, it is a clear issue of fairness and equity, one that can only be resolved by allowing you to complete the job assigned to you.

Observer's Rating Sheet

Upon completion of the dialogue, class members, using the following scale, rate Higgins's application of ethical management skills. Write concrete examples in the space for comments below each criteria skill to use in explaining your feedback.

1 Unsatisfactory	2 Weak	3 Adequate	4 Good	5 Outstanding

_____ Disseminated the organization's policy on ethics

_____ Hired and promoted individuals with high ethical standards

_____ Led by ethical example

_____ Set job goals that are realistic

_____ Provided ethics training

_____ Anticipated potential ethical conflicts

_____ Avoided isolation and sought opinions from others

_____ Applied the ethical-screening process to ethical dilemmas

Group Exercises

In the three exercises that follow you will be asked to practise ethical management skills, sharpen your ethical sensitivity, and stretch and expand your moral reasoning and ethical judgment capability.

Group Exercise 1: The Selkirk Group Role-Play

DIRECTIONS Upon completion of the dialogue, class members rate Carrie's application of ethical guideposts. Also note other options the role-players may have missed.

TIME 20 minutes.

ACTORS Carrie Makson, vice-president of The Selkirk Group; Pat Jergen, corporate account manager.

SITUATION Pat Jergen, a 20-year advertising veteran, is reputed to be the best account manager at The Selkirk Group, a mid-sized advertising agency in Winnipeg. Carrie Makson, the company's vice-president, has come across an opportunity to get an enormous new corporate account with Agri-Gate Chemical, a large agricultural chemical company. This account, if landed and handled properly, could mean an entirely new scope and size of business for the advertising agency. Over the past five years, however, Agri-Gate has been widely accused of dumping hazardous waste and polluting the environment.

CARRIE MAKSON'S ROLE You have been a vice-president at The Selkirk Group for 10 years and a friend and admirer of Pat Jergen for almost as long. You have recently felt pressure from the board of directors to increase your corporate business, and the Agri-Gate account would more than remedy the problem. In addition, you feel your present job has put you on a plateau. Thus, you desperately want this new account not only for the agency's sake but also for the good of your career and Pat's.

You want Pat to handle the Agri-Gate effort personally, but you know that he is likely to have major reservations about taking the new account because of Agri-Gate's environmental record. You know that Pat feels strongly about the environment; in fact, you once bailed him out of jail after he was arrested in a pro-environment demonstration. Pat almost got fired because his arrest was filmed by a local television station. You intervened with the CEO and saved Pat's job, arguing that what he did on his own time was not the company's concern. You still believe that, but you wonder: Where do we draw the line? Can an employee legitimately refuse to take an important assignment because of his or her beliefs?

If the Agri-Gate account is not landed because of Pat's personal feelings, the boss will not be so easily placated as he was when Pat was arrested. Meanwhile, you don't quite know how Pat will react. He may be outraged that you would even consider assigning the Agri-Gate account to him. Whatever his feelings, you need Pat to complete and manage the deal. But you don't want to order him to do so because he might quit, which would leave you and the company in a pickle. Pat could easily move to another advertising agency, and you are concerned that he might because the environmental issue is so important to him. In any event, the time has come to talk to him.

PAT JERGEN'S ROLE You rose quickly at The Selkirk Group, from copywriter to corporate account manager. You know the advertising business inside out and have many contacts in the industry. Other agencies have courted you but you believe in loyalty and you like your job and The Selkirk Group. You love the people there and are friendly with

Carrie Makson, who helped smooth the waters some time ago when you were arrested in an environmental protest. Carrie knows the depth of your commitment to the environment, knows how you ride a bicycle to work, recycle everything, and stay active in environmental politics.

You feel strongly that people need to make sacrifices for their beliefs. Not to do so is hypocrisy. In your mind, the environment must come first. Believing that, you know that you sometimes need to take a stand or no one else will.

You've heard some rumours about Agri-Gate Chemical being wooed by The Selkirk Group. You hope that doesn't happen, or if it does, that you aren't involved. That would surely put your principles to the test. But, meanwhile, Carrie has asked to see you. Could it be about that?

Observer's Rating Sheet

Use the following scale to rate each role-player on what arguments he/she comes up with. Also write specific examples in the space for comments to use in explaining your feedback.

1 Unsatisfactory	2 Weak	3 Adequate	4 Good	5 Outstanding

_____ Disseminated the organization's policy on ethics

_____ Hired and promoted individuals with high ethical standards

_____ Led by ethical example

_____ Set job goals that are realistic

_____ Provided ethics training

_____ Anticipated potential ethical conflicts

_____ Avoided isolation and sought opinions from others

_____ Applied the ethical-screening process to ethical dilemmas

Additional points:

Group Exercise 2: Minicases[27]

DIRECTIONS Form groups of four to six people and select a leader. Discuss each of the following minicases and arrive at a consensus on the best ethical courses of action.

Limit yourself to the options presented. Note that some cases have more than one satisfactory solution, and others may have no good solution. So it's important to decide on the *one best solution* of those offered.

Allot no more than five minutes per case before moving on to the next one. The group leader should be prepared to present and defend the group's decision to the class.

TIME 40 minutes.

MINICASE 1 You work for a Southern Ontario auto parts manufacturer that has apparently made a successful bid for a big project. Final approval has become bogged down in the bureaucracy of the car manufacturer, though it is likely the funds will be allocated; the question is when. You feel you need to get started in order to meet the tight deadline. You start negotiating with a supplier. You decide to tell the supplier:

a) "Approval is imminent. It is an important deal that will benefit us both in the long run. So, like us, you need to shoulder your share of the startup costs between now and when the contract is okayed. So let's get going on preliminary work without a contract."
b) "The program is a 'go.' I'll spare you the details."
c) "Start work now and we will cover your costs when we get the contract."
d) "The program is almost certain to be approved. Let's quickly put together an interim contract to cover us on the first, tentative phase of the work."

MINICASE 2 Office supplies are disappearing from the stockroom almost as soon as they're brought in. You're told unofficially that two employees, who are well paid and should know better, are taking them for their children's school. Should you:

a) Lock up the supplies and issue them only as needed and signed for?
b) Tell the two suspected pilferers that supplies are for office use only?
c) Install video cameras to monitor the stockroom to get proof?
d) Send a reminder to all employees that supplies are for office use only and that disregard for this rule could result in disciplinary action?

MINICASE 3 Your operation is being relocated. The human resources regulations governing moving expenses, kilometrage reimbursement, and storage of personal goods are so complex that you fear they may dissuade your "team" from making the move. Relocating without your experienced staff would be difficult for you. Do you:

a) Tell the staff the regulations are so complex that you can't go into them now but assure them that everything will work out all right in the end?
b) Not mention the regulations but instead stress the excitement of the move and the importance of the team remaining intact?
c) Present them with a highly simplified version of the regulations and encourage them to come along?
d) Give them a complete copy of the regulations and promise to work with them to get the answers they need?

MINICASE 4 You make the low bid on an electronics system for the Canadian Armed Forces. However, because of staffing problems, you believe it will take you several months longer than it would your competitor to build the system. When the Armed Forces asks for further details on the schedule before deciding to whom to award the contract, do you:

a) Say your schedule will be "essentially the same" as what you believe your competitor's would be?
b) Predict you will complete the job as quickly as your competitor, then tell your engineers they must do it faster than they say it can be done?
c) Sidestep the time issue and instead stress the quality of your firm's work?
d) Admit that your people say you won't meet the competitor's schedule even though you suspect this revelation may cause you to lose points on the evaluation?

MINICASE 5 A friend of yours wants to transfer to your division. He is a loyal and hardworking, if not exceptionally talented, employee. You have a job opening, and one other candidate, whom you do not know, has applied. Do you:

a) Select the friend in whom you have confidence?
b) Select the other person, whom you are told is qualified?
c) Request a qualifications comparison from human resources?
d) Ask human resources to extend the search for additional candidates and establish a hiring committee to make the choice?

MINICASE 6 Your newest employee is a niece of a company vice-president. Her performance is poor, and she doesn't get along with her co-workers. Do you:

a) Call her in and discuss her inadequacies?
b) Ask human resources to counsel her and put her on a performance improvement plan?
c) Go see her uncle?
d) Because she is new, do nothing for now in the hope she will improve?

MINICASE 7 You discover that an employee hired four months ago—and who appears to be competent—falsified his employment application by claiming to have completed post-secondary education when he did not. Do you:

a) Do nothing because you are happy with his work and post-secondary education is not a job prerequisite?
b) Recommend he be fired for lying?
c) Point out the discrepancy to him and tell him that he is on probation?
d) Refer the matter to human resources?

MINICASE 8 A current supplier offers you a chance to be a paid consultant on matters not pertaining to your company's business. He assures that you would work only on weekends and that the arrangement could remain confidential if you so choose. Should you:

a) Accept the job?
b) Turn down the position?
c) Accept the job if the legal department poses no objection?
d) Report the offer to your supervisor?

Group Exercise 3: Anticipating Unethical Situations

DIRECTIONS Break into groups of four to five students and study the following situation. Your goal is to come up with as many relevant questions and options as possible for the meeting between Anna and Jessica. Then compare results with the other groups.

TIME 20 minutes.

SITUATION Jessica has filled an entry-level sales position at Myers Equipment for about 18 months. Her performance has been exceptional. Anna, the inside sales manager and Jessica's supervisor, knows that Jessica is ambitious, a hard worker, and a widowed mother of three who is devoted to her children and gives all her off-hours attention to her family. Anna knows that Jessica not only needs more money but also deserves a promotion.

However, the only job opening on the horizon is in outside sales in another unit, which Anna does not supervise. If Anna talked to the outside sales manager about Jessica's work, Jessica would probably get the job. That would be just. It would also make Jessica happy and help her to better provide for her family.

That outside sales slot normally is filled by a more experienced salesperson, although Anna thinks Jessica would grow into the job. However, Anna has other concerns. For one, the new job would put Jessica in with a group of other experienced and extremely competitive salespeople. Anna believes that the unit is productive but not well supervised, and she has heard rumours that some outside salespeople use dubious methods to meet their goals. There reportedly have been complaints from customers to the company about the outside sales crew, but nothing has been done because the outside sales force is highly regarded by upper management due to its sales volume. Anna feels that Jessica, who is young and somewhat naïve, would find her peers there to be poor role models with questionable ethics. In turn, Jessica's ethics might be affected.

Anna also fears Jessica would feel under intense pressure because of the highly competitive nature of outside sales. Sales goals there are high, and so is the peer pressure as well as management pressure to do whatever it takes to meet those goals.

Jessica has been ethical in all her actions so far. But Anna is worried that in any major conflicts in the new job, Jessica may be tempted to act unethically because of what she observes in her colleagues, the pressure to produce, and the needs of her family.

Jessica, for her part, does not yet know about the opening in outside sales. She knows only that she deserves a break and desperately needs more money. When Anna asks Jessica to her office to talk about this promotion possibility, Jessica hopes that her big chance has come at last.

QUESTIONS FOR DISCUSSION

1. What questions should Anna ask of Jessica?
2. What questions should Jessica ask of Anna?
3. What safeguards could Anna insist on as a way of protecting Jessica from acting unethically?
4. What could Jessica ask for to reduce the likelihood that time and competitive pressures would be too intense?
5. Does Anna have any options besides promoting Jessica to outside sales or not doing so?
6. In what ways could others help?

Application Questions

1. Describe an ethical situation you've faced recently. How did you handle it? Would you handle it any differently now? How? Why?
2. What questions will you ask yourself when you next encounter an ethical dilemma?
3. Think about managers for whom you have worked. Which did you think were highly ethical and which were not? What makes you say this? Did they act differently in similar situations? Why or why not?

Reinforcement Exercises

The following are suggested activities for reinforcing the application of ethical guideposts described in this chapter. You may want to adapt them to the Action Plan you will develop next, or try them independently.

1. Check the newspapers and business periodicals for news of a controversial business decision—closing a plant, for example, or disciplining an employee for some infraction. List the various alternatives that might have been available and the ethical guideposts that apply.
2. When your class or school has a speaker or guest lecturer from the business community, ask him/her to describe the kinds of ethical dilemmas faced in his/her business and how they are resolved.
3. When you interview with a corporate recruiter, ask if the firm has a code of ethics and/or ethics training and, if appropriate, to see a copy of the code or a training syllabus.
4. Ask your friends and/or relatives what kinds of ethical situations they run into in their jobs and how they handle them.
5. Search the Internet for company websites of interest to you. See whether you can find a published code of ethics for the company. What does that tell you?

Summary Checklist

Take a few minutes to reflect on your performance in the preceding exercises. Assess how your analysis compared to other students (and if you were a presenter, how others rated your skill). Make a check (√) next to those behaviours on which you may need improvement. Ethical managers:

_____ Anticipate potential ethical conflicts.

    1. Ask what-if questions.

    2. Be alert to situations that promote unethical behaviour.

    3. Be alert to unusual circumstances that may tempt otherwise ethical employees.

_____ Consider all points of view.

    1. Identify all affected parties.

    2. Consider actual and symbolic consequences to everyone concerned.

_____ Devise creative alternatives.

    1. Always look for more than one choice.

    2. Consider all possibilities before deciding what to do.

_____ Can defend the morality of their decisions.

    1. Be able to explain the rationale for actions to others.

    2. Will others feel those actions are ethical?

_____ Think before acting.

    1. Ask, "Why am I doing what I'm about to do?"

    2. Consider all the consequences.

    3. Would you disclose to your boss or family what you are about to do?

_____ Have a good inner sense of right and wrong.

    1. Develop your own personal code of ethics.

    2. Know your organization's policy on ethics.

    3. Do what you truly believe is right.

_____ Lead by example.

    1. Management's behaviour is the strongest influence on employee behaviour.

    2. Actions speak louder than words.

_____ Seek opinions from others before deciding.

    1. Avoid becoming isolated.

    2. Others in similar situations may have sound advice.

    3. Others can act as a sounding board.

Action Plan

1. Which ethical behaviours do I most want to improve? (For examples, see Summary Checklist.)
2. Why? What will be my payoff?
3. What potential obstacles stand in my way?
4. What are the specific things I will do to improve? (For examples, see the Reinforcement Exercises.)
5. When will I do them?
6. How and when will I measure my success?

CHAPTER 4

Managing Stress and Time

Learning Objectives

After completing this chapter, you should be able to:

- Perceive symptoms of stress.
- Identify causes of stress.
- Reduce causes of stress.
- Develop resiliency to stress.
- Reduce stress symptoms.
- Focus activities to achieve priority goals.
- Help employees manage their stress.

Self-Assessment Exercise

For each of the following questions, select the answer that best describes your behaviour when you are experiencing stress.

When I feel anxious and stressful:	Usually	Sometimes	Seldom
1. I try to determine the sources.	_____	_____	_____
2. I do not want to bother my friends by talking about it.	_____	_____	_____
3. I check my priorities and organize my activities.	_____	_____	_____
4. I refrain from seeking help so I will not appear weak.	_____	_____	_____
5. I try to relax or meditate to gain composure.	_____	_____	_____
6. I have a couple of drinks to feel better.	_____	_____	_____
7. I exercise to work it off.	_____	_____	_____
8. I drink plenty of coffee to keep my energy level up.	_____	_____	_____
9. I confront the stressor directly.	_____	_____	_____
10. I take time for recreation in order to relax.	_____	_____	_____

SCORING AND INTERPRETATION   For questions 1, 3, 5, 7, 9, and 10, give yourself 3 points for "Usually," 2 points for "Sometimes," and 1 point for "Seldom." For questions 2, 4, 6, and 8, give yourself 3 points for "Seldom," 2 points for "Sometimes," and 1 point for "Usually." Sum up your total points.

27 or higher	You're good at managing stress.
22–26	You have some room for improvement.
Below 22	You need to find a more effective way to manage your stress.

Concepts

Carla could not get her mind off work. During weekend hikes with her husband, this marketing professional tried to concentrate on the beautiful landscape. Instead, her mind drifted back to the office and how much work was piled in her "in" box. "I reached a stage where I was thinking about work 24 hours a day," she said. "I couldn't sleep. I would go into work feeling like a zombie." She became short-tempered and irritable. Some days, thinking about work made her so stressed that she had difficulty breathing. She didn't realize it at the time, but she was suffering from burnout.

In today's fast-paced society, burnout runs rampant as people increasingly cram more into their already-packed schedules. And with laptop computers, pagers, e-mail, voice mail, and cell phones and the time zone demands of a global economy, workers are tethered to their jobs more than ever. Certainly, some people feel energized by the crisis, surprise, and excitement that are inherent in many jobs. To them, long hours and tons of work are a way of life. For others, they spell burnout—a state of fatigue and frustration brought about by devotion to a cause, way of life, or relationship that fails to produce the expected reward.[1]

Many of you may feel like Carla in the preceding vignette, and wish you had read this chapter about stress management skills earlier. As you well know, you don't need to wait until you are a manager to feel overwhelmed with the amount of stress in your life. The list of stress-causing elements for students never seems to end: monster reading assignments, difficult homework problems, simultaneous exams, papers, multiple group projects, boring subjects, balancing school with work, relentless parents, fickle friends, difficult roommates, unreliable automobiles, not enough money. Any of these sound familiar?

The list of stressors is even greater for those of you who are already managers. Today's work environment is increasingly characterized by heavier workloads, longer hours, fewer resources, more ambiguities, and less job security. Recent reports show that 55 per cent of Canadians have high levels of stress, 33 per cent report high levels of burnout, and 36 per cent report high levels of stress at work.[2]

What Is Stress?

Think of how you would react to seeing an automobile speeding straight at you as you were crossing an intersection. How do you feel when you are faced with nonphysical stressors such as giving a speech, making a deadline, or resolving a disagreement? **Stress** is the body's psychological, emotional, and physiological response to any demand that is perceived as threatening to a person's well-being. These changes prepare a person to cope with threatening environmental conditions called *stressors* either by confronting them (fight) or by avoiding them (flight).[3] This is called the *stress response*. Stress is created by a multitude of overlapping factors that threaten the achievement of our goals at work, in relationships, in school, and in life in general. Although stress can be separated into "work" and "non-work" components, it is the *combined* result that affects individuals. Stress stimulates and challenges us to perform at higher levels; however, too much stress for too long a time has negative effects on both our work quality and personal life. It wasn't until 1956 when Canadian doctor Hans Selye published his ground-breaking book, *The Stress of Life,* that we learned that stress can play a very significant role in the development of many types of disease.[4] The reality is that stress will not go away, but it can be managed to lessen its negative consequences.

Why Is Stress Management Important?

Work stress is an equal opportunity dilemma. It affects men and women from all cultures and job situations. Stress affects employees ranging from executives to secretaries, and from student interns to retiring veterans. A majority of Canadian employees are reporting increases in stress-related illnesses.[5] Managers also believe that stress is a significant and growing problem in the workplace.[6]

ORGANIZATIONAL COSTS

According to a report developed for Health Canada by Dr. Martin Shain of the Centre for Addiction and Mental Health in Toronto, the economic consequences of excessive workplace stress include high absenteeism, high medical and drug claim costs, less efficiency, loss of courteousness with customers, and a loss of creativity.[7]

In another Health Canada report, produced by Linda Duxbury of Carleton University and Chris Higgins of the University of Western Ontario, a close relationship was found between work–life conflict and burnout. Employees with high work–life conflict also reported less organizational commitment, which increases turnover.[8] At Sun Life of Canada in Toronto, stress-related claims make up 30 per cent of total disability claims according to Doug Smeall, assistant vice-president of group life, health and disability.[9]

Another harmful employee response to stress is the use of alcohol and other drugs, leading to more accidents, costly errors, and decreases in task performance levels. Compared to their nonuser co-workers, employees who use drugs and alcohol are far less productive, miss ten or more times as many workdays, and are three times as likely to injure themselves or someone else.[10]

Frustration and stress can also result in aggression and sabotage. If employees blame the organization for the stress-induced symptoms, they may adopt aggressive behaviours in an effort to "get even." This aggression can take the forms of verbal or physical abuse, intentional slowdowns, and acts of sabotage such as making intentional mistakes, damaging products, and starting negative rumours. Left unchecked, such reactions to stress can cause irreparable harm to an organization.[11] An all-too-frequent example is a fired employee returning to the former workplace and killing the former boss and several co-workers. Another is a sales representative insulting the president of a key account during a business dinner because he or she has overindulged in alcohol or didn't understand important cultural differences.

In summary, the organizational costs of stress are higher operating costs, lower productivity, lower quality of service, and less profit.

INDIVIDUAL COSTS

Workers experiencing high job stress typically have increased job dissatisfaction, reduced productivity, and more illnesses than those with low stress.[12] People with inadequate stress coping skills often become ineffective and may exhibit physical symptoms such as headaches, elevated blood pressure, fatigue, and depression.[13]

HEALTH IMPAIRMENT   Chronic stress is often accompanied by increased cholesterol levels and elevated blood pressure, two conditions that precipitate a number of serious health impairments.[14] Medical experts attribute between 50 and 75 per cent of all illness to stress-related sources. Perhaps the most significant stress-related illness in industrialized countries is coronary heart disease, which kills about 25 per cent of male workers. In fact, a significant correlation between job dissatisfaction and heart disease has been discovered among workers from more than 40 different occupations.[15]

Chronic high stress contributes to a variety of other physical ailments, including fatigue, arthritis, and allergies. Its potential to cause depression and anxiety is widely recognized. While attempting to cope with the ailments and discomforts brought on by stress, some individuals compound their problems by turning to alcohol or drugs.

JOB BURNOUT   When prolonged exposure to stress uses up available adaptive energy, exhaustion can take the forms of depression, mental breakdown, or what is termed *burnout*.[16] **Job burnout** is a feeling of exhaustion that develops when an individual simultaneously experiences too much pressure and too few sources of satisfaction.[17] Business owners, managers, professionals, and technical personnel have especially high probabilities of suffering from burnout.[18] When we confront continual role ambiguity, performance pressures, interpersonal conflicts, or economic problems while trying to fulfill personal and organizational expectations, the most likely effects are fatigue, frustration, helplessness, and exhaustion.[19]

PERFORMANCE DECLINE   The relationship between stress and performance resembles an inverted U-curve, as shown in Exhibit 4-1. Stress is like a violin string: the optimal degree of tension is essential to obtaining the proper performance. A string that is too tight or too loose will not produce the desired effect. Insufficient stress leads to boredom, apathy, and decreased motivation. Increasing stress enhances performance by increasing arousal and concentration. Group leaders and members, for example, become more

Exhibit 4-1 Inverted-U Relationship Between Stress and Job Performance

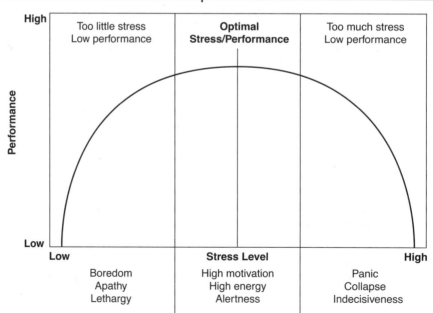

receptive to problem-solving information provided by others when the group is under increased stress.[20] After an optimal level of stress is attained, however, further increases in stress for long periods of time overload our ability to cope, create anxiety, and deplete energy. As a result, our ability to perform effectively decreases.[21]

Although managers can't eliminate all stressors that negatively affect employees, they can do things to modify stressors and help employees manage stress more productively. But, before they help their employees, managers need to develop better stress coping skills themselves. Managers who are overwhelmed by personal stress often underperform themselves and are consequently unable to help others. So it's important for managers to be competent in the skills of personal stress management. Then they can model and teach these important skills to employees.

What Skills Are Needed to Cope with Stress?

Individual and organizational stress management consists of three general skills. First is to *become aware* of negative stress symptoms. Second is to *determine the sources*. Third is to *do something constructive* to cope with the stress. The last step includes developing your resiliency to stress, dealing directly with the stressor, and alleviating the immediate stress that you are experiencing.

The stress management process illustrated in Exhibit 4-2 demonstrates that potential stressors can originate from personal, organizational, job, or environmental sources. The arrows indicate the direction of influence of the factors in Exhibit 4-2. Personal awareness of experiencing stress comes from recognizing symptoms like those listed in Exhibit 4-3. If nothing is done to cope with the stress or symptoms constructively, negative physical, emotional, and behavioural consequences occur. However, constructive stress management techniques can be applied either to prevent potential factors from causing stress in the first place or, after stress is experienced, to prevent its negative consequences.

Exhibit 4-2   Model of the Stress Management Process

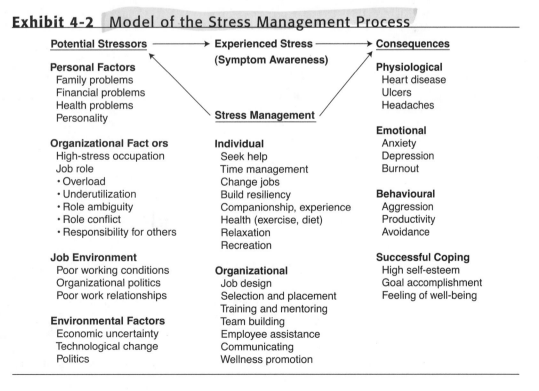

Potential Stressors	Experienced Stress (Symptom Awareness)	Consequences
Personal Factors		**Physiological**
Family problems		Heart disease
Financial problems		Ulcers
Health problems	**Stress Management**	Headaches
Personality		
		Emotional
Organizational Fact ors	**Individual**	Anxiety
High-stress occupation	Seek help	Depression
Job role	Time management	Burnout
• Overload	Change jobs	
• Underutilization	Build resiliency	**Behavioural**
• Role ambiguity	Companionship, experience	Aggression
• Role conflict	Health (exercise, diet)	Productivity
• Responsibility for others	Relaxation	Avoidance
	Recreation	
Job Environment		**Successful Coping**
Poor working conditions	**Organizational**	High self-esteem
Organizational politics	Job design	Goal accomplishment
Poor work relationships	Selection and placement	Feeling of well-being
	Training and mentoring	
Environmental Factors	Team building	
Economic uncertainty	Employee assistance	
Technological change	Communicating	
Politics	Wellness promotion	

How Can Awareness of Stress Symptoms Be Enhanced?

If you can learn to recognize the signs of stress sooner, you can take some form of action quickly. If not, the problem becomes more difficult to solve later on.[22]

Individuals experiencing unhealthy levels of stress often exhibit *physical symptoms* such as headaches, elevated blood pressure, and fatigue.[23] If they are unable to escape from their stressors, people may resort to common *psychological substitutes* such as negativism, boredom, dissatisfaction, irritability, anger, feelings of persecution, criticism, apathy, hopelessness, depression, withdrawal, forgetfulness, procrastination, or inability to make decisions.[24]

Intermittent checking of your own stress symptoms may aid self-diagnosis and provide insights into the nature of personal stress. Warning signs include constant fatigue, recurring headaches, bad breath, inability to sleep, moodiness, compulsive eating, and chronic worrying. Complete the questionnaire in Exhibit 4-3 to check your own stress symptoms.

Managers should be on the lookout for similar symptoms in their employees. Any continuing negative change in employees' work behaviour may also be a warning signal. For example, when employees who are usually reliable, industrious, and friendly start missing numerous work days, coming in late, exhibiting irritable and noncooperative behaviours, appearing absent-minded, making unusual errors, or decreasing their performance, they are likely to be experiencing too much stress.

What Are the Major Stressors?

Many factors contribute to the stress experienced by employees. The organizational environment can certainly provide many stressors, but so can a number of personal and environmental factors. Let's take a look at each of these.

MAJOR ORGANIZATIONAL STRESSORS

Although things like time pressures and work overload have been cited as sources of stress for years, others of particular concern for managers today include the nature of occupations, job roles, and interpersonal relationships.[25]

HIGH-STRESS OCCUPATIONS   Certain occupations cause more stress than others. They allow incumbents little control over their jobs, impose relentless time pressures, carry weighty responsibilities, or have threatening or unpleasant physical conditions, such as extreme heat, cold, noise, crowding, or lack of privacy.[26] Occupations such as manager, secretary, and air traffic controller possess these high-stress characteristics, while jobs such as stock handler, actuary, and artisan do not.[27]

JOB ROLE   Whatever the occupation, certain negative characteristics of a person's role at work can increase the likelihood of experiencing stress. You may have already experienced the number one job role stressor: work **overload**. Overload occurs when people are expected to accomplish more than their ability or time permits.[28] Students often encounter overload at the end of each semester. On the other hand, **underutilization** of time or abilities causes stress for skilled workers who often feel anxiety about wasting their lives doing unimportant things.[29]

Stress also occurs when people are expected to work without a clear understanding of their job definition, performance expectations, preferred methods of meeting those expectations, or consequences of their behaviours. This type of **role ambiguity** often occurs in class projects or research assignments. If it is a group project, **role conflicts** can also occur when duties or responsibilities conflict with one another. If you are put in

Exhibit 4-3   Checklist of Stress Symptoms

Check the box that most closely describes how often you have experienced each symptom during the past month.

	Never	Rarely	Sometimes	Often	Always
Constant fatigue	[ ]	[ ]	[ ]	[ ]	[ ]
Low energy level	[ ]	[ ]	[ ]	[ ]	[ ]
Recurring headaches	[ ]	[ ]	[ ]	[ ]	[ ]
Gastrointestinal disorders	[ ]	[ ]	[ ]	[ ]	[ ]
Bad breath	[ ]	[ ]	[ ]	[ ]	[ ]
Sweaty hands or feet	[ ]	[ ]	[ ]	[ ]	[ ]
Dizziness	[ ]	[ ]	[ ]	[ ]	[ ]
High blood pressure	[ ]	[ ]	[ ]	[ ]	[ ]
Pounding heart	[ ]	[ ]	[ ]	[ ]	[ ]
Constant inner tension	[ ]	[ ]	[ ]	[ ]	[ ]
Inability to sleep	[ ]	[ ]	[ ]	[ ]	[ ]
Temper outbursts	[ ]	[ ]	[ ]	[ ]	[ ]
Hyperventilation	[ ]	[ ]	[ ]	[ ]	[ ]
Moodiness	[ ]	[ ]	[ ]	[ ]	[ ]
Irritability	[ ]	[ ]	[ ]	[ ]	[ ]
Inability to concentrate	[ ]	[ ]	[ ]	[ ]	[ ]
Increased aggression	[ ]	[ ]	[ ]	[ ]	[ ]
Compulsive eating	[ ]	[ ]	[ ]	[ ]	[ ]
Chronic worrying	[ ]	[ ]	[ ]	[ ]	[ ]
Anxiety	[ ]	[ ]	[ ]	[ ]	[ ]
Inability to relax	[ ]	[ ]	[ ]	[ ]	[ ]
Feeling inadequate	[ ]	[ ]	[ ]	[ ]	[ ]
Increase in defensiveness	[ ]	[ ]	[ ]	[ ]	[ ]
Dependence on tranquillizers	[ ]	[ ]	[ ]	[ ]	[ ]
Excessive use of alcohol	[ ]	[ ]	[ ]	[ ]	[ ]
Excessive smoking	[ ]	[ ]	[ ]	[ ]	[ ]
Totals	__ × 0	__ × 1	__ × 2	__ × 3	__ × 4
	0 + [ ] + [ ] + [ ] + [ ] = ___				

SCORING AND INTERPRETATION   Tally the number of responses you checked in each column. Next multiply the column totals by the factor indicated. Finally, add the products to get your stress symptoms score. Check your total score against the following scale to determine how well you are reacting to the stress you are currently experiencing.

Score	Stress State
Below 10	Relaxed
11–15	Alert
16–20	Tense
21–25	Stressed
Over 26	Panicked

a supervisory position with responsibility for the group's task performance, you may experience even more stress.

INTERPERSONAL RELATIONSHIPS   Poor work relationships with co-workers is another frequent source of stress. Working for a boss you do not like is the most stressful relationship aspect of a job for the majority of workers.[30] Of course, disciplining and giving poor performance reviews are stressful for managers. Racial or gender discrimination and sexual harassment are other examples of stressful situations. It can also be stressful to be assigned to a team where members do not get along. Finally, when people compete for power and play politics, stress levels rise.

MAJOR PERSONAL STRESSORS

Of the 168 hours each week, most people only spend about 40 hours at work. The challenges individuals face during their nonwork hours also create stress that spills over into the work environment. The primary sources of nonwork stress are home, financial, and health problems, and personality.

HOME PROBLEMS   Problems at home can be a major stressor in North America.[31] A growing stressor is the dilemma of two-career families that must balance the conflicting demands of childcare, career moves, time conflicts, priorities, and expectations. Other common home stressors are relationship difficulties, discipline troubles with children, conflicts with relatives, and caring for elderly parents.

FINANCIAL PROBLEMS   Regardless of income level, many people are poor money managers or have wants that exceed their earning capacity. All too frequently individuals overextend their financial resources, which causes stress, which distracts from work effectiveness.

HEALTH PROBLEMS   Diseases, injuries, or psychological problems, either your own or those affecting family members and close friends, exact a toll in anxiety and stress. Stress caused by poor health creates a circular dilemma because stress itself is a major cause of health problems.

One of the contributors to stress-related health problems occurs when a person experiences too much change in too short a period of time.[32] To determine whether the rate of change in your life has the potential to contribute to stress-related illness, complete the Life Change Unit Scale in Exhibit 4-4.

Stress occurs each time a person experiences a change, and those changes add up in a cumulative fashion. Too much change eventually overloads the endocrine system, thereby depleting the stress-coping resources and suppressing the immune system. This reaction makes the body more susceptible to certain types of disease.

PERSONALITY   People with what is called the Type A personality have a chronic sense of time urgency and excessive competitive drive to achieve more and more in less and less time. To determine whether you are a Type A personality take the self-assessment inventory in Exhibit 4-5.

Exhibit 4-4 Life Change Unit Scale

Fill in the mean values for the life events you have experienced in the past 12 months, then total your personal points.

Rank	Life Event	Mean Value	Personal Points
1.	Death of spouse	100	0
2.	Divorce	73	0
3.	Separation from mate	65	65
4.	Detention in jail or other institution	63	0
5.	Death of close family member	63	0
6.	Major personal injury or illness	53	0
7.	Marriage	50	50
8.	Fired at work	47	0
9.	Reconciliation with mate	45	0
10.	Retirement from work	45	0
11.	Major change in health of family member	44	0
12.	Pregnancy	40	0
13.	Sex difficulties	39	0
14.	Gain new family member (birth, roommate)	39	0
15.	Business readjustment (bankruptcy, reorganization)	39	0
16.	Major change in financial state (better or worse)	38	38
17.	Death of a close friend	37	0
18.	Change to different line of work	36	36
19.	Major change in number of arguments with spouse (or significant other)	35	0
20.	Mortgage or loan for major purchase (home, business, etc.)	31	0
21.	Foreclosure of mortgage or loan	30	0
22.	Major change in responsibilities at work (e.g., promotion, demotion, transfer)	29	0
23.	Son or daughter leaving home	29	0
24.	Trouble with in-laws	29	0
25.	Outstanding personal achievement	28	28
26.	Wife/husband begins or stops work	26	0
27.	Begin or end formal education	26	0
28.	Major change in living conditions	25	25
29.	Revision of personal habits (e.g., eating, schedule)	24	0
30.	Trouble with boss	23	0
31.	Major change in work hours or conditions	20	20
32.	Change in residence	20	0
33.	Change in schools	20	0
34.	Major change in recreation (type, amount)	19	0
35.	Major change in church activities (more, less)	19	19
36.	Major change in social activities	18	0
37.	Mortgage or loan for moderate purchase (e.g., car, TV, appliance, etc.)	17	0

(continued)

Exhibit 4-4   (continued)

Rank	Life Event	Mean Value	Personal Points
38.	Major change in sleeping habits	16	_0_
39.	Major change in number of family get-togethers	15	_15_
40.	Major change in eating habits	15	_0_
41.	Vacation	13	_0_
42.	Christmas	12	_0_
43.	Minor violations of the law (e.g., traffic ticket)	11	_0_
TOTAL POINTS			_____

INTERPRETATION   People with a score totaling less than 150 generally have good health the following year. Those with scores between 150 and 200 have a 37 per cent chance of developing health problems, while those with scores between 200 and 300 have a 51 per cent chance. People scoring more than 300 have an 80 per cent chance of having a major illness.

Source: This scale was first published as "The Social Readjustment Rating Scale" by T. H. Holmes and R.H. Rahe, *Journal of Psychosomatic Research* 11 (1967): 213–8.

Exhibit 4-5   Type A Personality Self-Assessment

Circle the number on the scale that best characterizes your behaviour for each trait.

1. Casual about appointments	1	2	3	4	5	6	7	8	Never late
2. Not competitive	1	2	3	4	5	6	7	8	Very competitive
3. Never feel rushed	1	2	3	4	5	6	7	8	Always feel rushed
4. Take things one at a time	1	2	3	4	5	6	7	8	Try to do many things at once
5. Slow doing things	1	2	3	4	5	6	7	8	Fast (e.g., eating, walking)
6. Express feelings	1	2	3	4	5	6	7	8	"Sit on" feelings
7. Many interests	1	2	3	4	5	6	7	8	Few interests outside work

SCORING   Total your score on the seven characteristics. Now multiply the total by 3. A total of 120 or more indicates that you are a hard-core Type A. Scores below 90 indicate that you are a hard-core Type B. The following gives you more specifics:

Points	Personality Type
120 or more	A+
106–119	A
100–105	A–
90–99	B+
Less than 90	B

Source: Adapted from R.W. Bortner, "Short Rating Scale as a Potential Measure of Pattern A Behavior," *Journal of Chronic Diseases* (June 1969): 87–91. Used with permission.

Type A people were originally thought to be more likely to experience stress on or off the job and have a much higher chance of having a heart attack as a result.[33] More recent research has found that it is only the hostility and anger characteristics of the Type A personality that are contributors to coronary heart disease.[34]

So, if you are a workaholic but still get along well with others, you probably are not unduly susceptible to heart disease because of this aspect of your personality. People who are quick to anger, have a persistently hostile outlook, and a cynical mistrust of others are at risk.

MAJOR ENVIRONMENTAL STRESSORS

Most of what goes on outside of our personal and work environments is beyond our control. Because economic and technological factors do affect our well-being, however, they can be sources of worry and concern.

ECONOMIC UNCERTAINTY   An abundance of economic uncertainty in society today has the potential to cause anxiety. Employees have recognized that "jobs aren't for life" and organizations are not necessarily going to "look after them." As jobs have become more temporary, employees worry about constantly managing their career as well as performing on the job. The constant possibility of downsizing can generate fear of being terminated and forced to find other means of income. Stock market declines affect where our pension funds are invested and increase fears of insecurity in old age.

TECHNOLOGICAL CHANGE   Most of us experience constant pressure just trying to keep up with continual upgrades for personal computers and Internet enhancements. More serious stress can be created by automation, computerized systems, and robotics, which displace workers and force them to relearn skills for different occupations.

What Constructive Things Can Be Done to Manage Stress?

In this section, we will examine strategies that you can use to cope with excessive stress as well as identify what can be done to manage stress risk in the workplace.

INDIVIDUAL COPING STRATEGIES

The ultimate responsibility for stress management rests with you as an individual. A number of proven methods can help you to either cope with stress or directly modify stressors or both. In this section, we will discuss time management and how to develop stress resiliency. Some of these skills take time to develop while others such as seeking help or social support can often decrease anxiety immediately.

MANAGING TIME   Losing control of our time can generate serious anxiety, frustration, and even panic for most of us. Time management strategies entail deciding what goal is to be accomplished and by what deadline. All tasks necessary to accomplish the goals need to be listed and prioritized. Estimates of how long it will take to accomplish the tasks need to be computed. Activities can then be planned, starting with the most important task first. Finally, the prioritized tasks are implemented until the goal is accomplished.[35] Let's take a closer look at each of the seven components of this vital skill and some of the techniques that facilitate them.

1. *Determine your values*   **Values** are enduring beliefs about what is worthwhile. They determine which behaviours and objectives are desirable to you and which are not. Clarifying what is important to you helps you to decide what kind of person you want to be and what things you want to accomplish.

2. *Determine your goals and objectives*   You can't be sure whether you are spending your time wisely unless you know what tasks contribute to your **long-term goals**.

Once you know the kind of person you want to be and the values that will guide your behaviour, you can determine your long-term goals in important areas such as career, family, religion, recreation, and relationships. That is, you can determine what you have to do to achieve the goals that will contribute to your satisfaction in life.

Next, determine what **intermediate goals** you need to achieve to accomplish your long-term goals. An example of an intermediate goal is, "In the next four years I will graduate from Business Administration with a specialization in International Trade."

Now you can look at **short-term goals** for a year, a semester, a month, a week, and finally, a day. As you probably have already surmised, if we reverse the order, each short-term goal should be compatible and contribute to the next longer-term goal. Otherwise you are not getting the best use of your time. If what you are doing right now does not contribute to your goals for today, why are you doing it?

3. *Prioritize your objectives*   Some short-term goals are more important than others in contributing to your intermediate and long-term goals. Therefore, the next step is to prioritize your objectives in each time frame from most to least important. The most stress-resilient individuals maintain a balance of life activities.[36] At any given time, however, you will find that certain goals are clearly more important than others. During exam time, for example, developing friendships may be less important than learning certain subject matter.

Once you know what you want to accomplish, you are ready to determine what you have to do to achieve your goals. Now you can organize and schedule your time and resources to achieve your goals. The next step is determining what tasks are required to achieve your objectives, how to do them, and when to do them.

4. *List activities*   You need to identify the specific actions necessary to achieve your goals. Record these activities on a sheet of paper, an index card, or a computer-generated schedule. This record should be made for each time frame—long, intermediate, and short term.

5. *Prioritize activities*   This step involves imposing a second set of priorities. Here, you need to emphasize both importance and urgency. If the activity is not important, consider eliminating or postponing it. If it is not urgent, it can usually wait. Completing this step helps you identify activities you *must* do, activities you *should* do, those you will do *when you can,* and those you can *eliminate or postpone*. See Exhibit 4-6 for examples of urgent and important activities.

One approach to prioritizing is the **ABC system**. To apply it, give tasks an A, B, or C value depending upon their urgency and importance. *A tasks* are urgent and important. They can yield extraordinary results or disastrous consequences if they are not attended to immediately. *B tasks* are those that should be done as soon as possible. They have important consequences but are not pressing emergencies. *C tasks* can be put off indefinitely without creating dire consequences. They should only be attended to if you have extra time.

Exhibit 4-6   Urgent and Important Activities

	Not Important	Important
Urgent	Co-workers desire to know who will attend a luncheon tomorrow C - task	Preparation for key client presentation tomorrow A - task
Not Urgent	Review junk mail for ideas C - task to delegate	Plan next year's objectives B - task

6. *Schedule activities*   After prioritizing your activities, the next step is to plan *when* you will do each of them. Time spent scheduling when you will do things can save you hours of anxiety, confusion, and making up for things you forgot to do. It can also provide you with a feeling of being in control of yourself and how you are spending your time. You need to schedule both immediate and future activities.

Next, determine what you will be doing over the longer term, for example, the next month or next week. A number of planning aids such as "Week at a Glance" or "Month at a Glance" calendars or electronic organizers are available to help you. Remember to schedule your activities well in advance. For a week, do it Friday or Sunday before the action actually begins. Do not block activities in so tightly that you have no flexibility for unexpected emergencies. Some people are most productive in the mornings, others at midday or in the evening. Once you know your productivity cycle, you should schedule your larger and most important activities when you are able to give them the most effort.

Finally, develop a *daily plan* for what you will do and when you will do it. Each morning (or the night before) identify what you want to accomplish during the day. This to-do list should identify five to seven things you want to do during the day. It will allow you to spend time actually doing tasks versus trying to remember them.

Complete the most important urgent activity first, then tackle other important tasks. Follow with those you should do, and so forth. Be realistic about what you can really accomplish in your schedule. Given the nature of your activities, you may be unable to complete everything. The key, however, is to concentrate on the A tasks, or must-do items, making sure they do get done. Fifteen minutes here or a half-hour there add up in getting a must-do done. Do not make the mistake of working on C tasks, or "when you can" activities, just because they are easier to accomplish. You will be spending time on activities that really won't add to your effectiveness.

This to-do list will help you avoid the *reaction mentality* of putting out fires for other people when they approach you about help with their problems. Now you are in control of your time because you know what you need to do when. Of course you have to be able to say "no" when you have something more important and urgent to accomplish. To get the most out of your *to-do list,* check your planning calendar and focus on high-priority tasks you have scheduled for the current day. Then list all activities you want to accomplish, prioritize them, and plan your day.

7. *Follow your schedule* To help you stick with your plan, tips to eliminate time wasters, minimize disruptions and avoid procrastinating are described next

Constantly ask yourself: What is the most effective use of my time right now? To do this apply the 80/20 Rule (sometimes referred to as the Pareto Principle), which states that 80 per cent of our activities are trivial and only provide 20 per cent of the results that we desire, while 20 per cent of what we do is really vital and contributes to 80 per cent of our desired results.

To apply this principle, first determine which activities give you the most payoff—the vital 20 per cent—versus the trivial 80 per cent, which really are time wasters. Then expand the time allocated to the high payoff activities. Next, constantly check to make sure that what you are doing is the most effective use of your time at the moment.

Disruptions are time wasters that can steal your time before you know it.[37] These include interruptions such as phone calls and unscheduled visitors. During your most productive time, you need to insulate yourself from the time wasters. Go somewhere, if possible, where you won't be disturbed. Have calls screened, or let them roll over to the answering machine. Close your door to keep interruptions to a minimum. Obviously, the degree of insulating yourself will depend on your job, your organization's policies, your boss, and your employees. However, you must attempt to protect your productive time at all costs. But if you are disturbed, take it in stride, deal with the issue, then return to your task as soon as you can.

None of us consciously wants to procrastinate, but all of us do it at one time or another, some more than others. The first thing to do is to figure out why you do it. Be honest with yourself about what you are doing, why, what it costs you, and what benefits you derive from it. Unpleasant or overwhelming tasks and unclear goals or ambiguous task sequencing are enough to make most of us want to postpone doing things. On the other hand, a number of psychological reasons—like fear of failure, fear of change, tendency to overcommit, and addiction to cramming—can contribute to the tendency to procrastinate.

Next do something about it. Suggestions for overcoming procrastination for each of the external and internal reasons are provided in Exhibit 4-7.

DEVELOPING RESILIENCY   The same stressors do not cause the same reactions in all people. Some people seem to fall apart at the slightest problem, while others apparently thrive when confronted with a stressor. Those who don't experience stress in a negative way and cope better with stressors have *resiliency*. Three significant factors that moderate reactions to stressors include differences in personality hardiness, social support, and good health.

1. *Personality hardiness*   Hardiness is a combined personality characteristic of people who believe that they are in control of their lives, have the ability to respond to and transform potentially negative situations, and actively seek out novelty and challenge. Hardy people welcome change and have a high tolerance for ambiguity. Consequently, "hardy" individuals experience far lower than average rates of illness in high-stress environments.[38]

Two of the most important characteristics of hardy individuals include high self-esteem and an internal locus of control. First we will explain how these factors affect stress, then we will share some ideas for developing them to make you more resilient to stress.

High self-esteem causes people to feel good about themselves and have high confidence in their abilities to cope effectively. Consequently, people with high self-esteem experience less stress when experiencing threatening situations than do those with low self-esteem.[39] People with high self-esteem often exhibit a "self-serving bias," where they take credit for success and blame external factors for failure. Those with low self-esteem tend to do the opposite by attributing their successes to factors outside their control and taking personal blame for their failures or unpleasant experiences. This leads to greater stress because people cannot benefit from past successes to feel more confident in a recurring situation.

An acknowledged pioneer of the self-esteem movement, psychotherapist Nathaniel Branden, described six essential practices to building self-esteem.[40] The first is *living consciously,* which means keeping yourself aware of what you are doing; for example, really listening to a salesperson who is talking to you. Second is *self-acceptance:* the willingness to take responsibility for your own actions and thoughts without evaluating them. Third is *self-responsibility:* realizing that you are the author of your choices and responsible for attaining goals in your life. Fourth is *self-assertiveness:* being willing to stand up for your ideals in appropriate ways. Fifth is *living purposefully,* which is identifying the things you want out of life and the actions needed to obtain them, then applying yourself and monitoring your results to stay on track, as opposed to just drifting through life. Finally, Branden advises that you should practise *personal integrity:* living with congruence between what you profess and what you do. Examples are telling the truth, honouring commitments, exemplifying in action the values you profess, and dealing with others fairly and benevolently.

Exhibit 4-7 Methods for Dealing with Procrastination

Environmental Reasons	Potential Solutions
Unpleasant task	Do it first thing.
	Find someone else to do it.
Overwhelming tasks	Divide and conquer by breaking it into smaller pieces.
	Ride the momentum. Once you get going, keep at it.
Unclear goal	Ask for clarification.
	Clarify if your own goals.
Unclear task sequence	Ask for clarification.
	Plan how to do it yourself.
Psychological Reasons	
Fear of failure	Realize that fear is natural and can actually provide added energy.
Fear of change	Accept that change is an opportunity for growth.
Tendency to overcommit	Just say no, but explain.
Addiction to cramming	Admit that cramming is dangerous because it does not allow time to correct mistakes or attend to urgent tasks that may arise.

Source: Adapted from M. Mancini, *Time Management* (Burr Ridge, IL: Irwin/Mirror Press, 1994) 41–53.

People with an *internal locus of control* believe that they make a difference and that the course of events in their normal daily life is primarily under their own control. People with an *external locus of control*, on the other hand, believe that whatever happens is either a matter of chance or determined by forces external to them. Externals are more likely to feel helpless to deal with stressors, so they experience more stress.[41]

One way to shift your locus of control is by **reframing**, which in this case means changing your perception from being helpless to being in control of altering the situation to cope with stressors yourself. Instead of assuming that you must passively accept an overtime assignment, for example, you could reframe it as an opportunity to negotiate with your boss to delegate other tasks that you do not like to do.

After you reframe, self-esteem can be built through a **small-wins strategy**. Instead of perceiving a large, perhaps overwhelming situation, look at a smaller part of it that you can tackle immediately. As you work for small, concrete outcomes that are more likely to be attained, you have a better chance for visible success and heightened confidence.

Another way to demonstrate your internal locus of control is to get *proper training* to perform more effectively on the job. You will then have a higher probability of experiencing small wins, which in turn can increase self-esteem and confidence. The more *experience* you get, the more confidence you will have dealing with recurring situations that originally were threatening because of their novelty.[42] New hires who have never given a sales presentation before, know little about the product, and doubt their ability to make presentations in an articulate manner, may feel much more pressure on a sales call than more experienced salespeople who already know the client and product well.

2. *Social support*   Positive relationships with colleagues, family members, and friends can significantly lessen the impact of stress.[43] Social support provides comfort and assistance that can buffer people from negative stressors.[44] Consequently, it is important

to spend time nurturing and building relationships with supportive others. The natural place to start is with people who already support you at work, home, or social groups. Other ways to build additional social support range from professional help to joining interest groups. Most companies also have Employee Assistance Programs for counselling and other assistance. In addition, simply sharing your dilemmas with an understanding co-worker can release anxiety.

3. *Health maintenance*   Appropriate exercise, diet, and rest are three keys to maintaining a healthy mind and body to cope with stressors. Regular physical exercise improves self-esteem as well as physical capacity to cope with stressors. Exercisers experience lower degrees of anxiety, depression, and hostility than nonexercisers.[45] A balanced diet can help you maintain optimal weight and avoid anxiety from too much sugar or caffeine. Finally, getting enough sleep can help you keep an alert mind for rationally coping with stressors.

   If all you do is work, you're bound to experience stress, no matter how much you love your job. Everyone needs hobbies and recreational interests that have no purpose beyond the relaxation and pleasure they bring.

   Temporary relaxation techniques such as concentrating on relaxing all your muscles while you listen intently to your own breathing for 20 minutes, two times a day, can reduce stress.[46] This exercise decreases muscle tension, which in turn decreases heart rate, breathing rate, and blood pressure.[47] Long-term payoffs include increases in coping effectiveness, work performance, and sociability, as well as decreases in blood pressure, anxiety, depression, and hostility.[48] You can sample this relaxation technique in the exercise at the end of this chapter.

ORGANIZATIONAL COPING STRATEGIES

Organizations have plenty of incentive to decrease stress at work. In addition to ethical and humanitarian reasons, work-related stress costs organizations millions of dollars each year through sickness, accidents, turnover, and absenteeism. Workplaces where employees experience high pressure—too much to do with constant imposed deadlines, and too little influence over the day-to-day organization of their work—are particularly stressful. So too are imbalances between employee effort to achieve organizational goals and rewards such as acknowledgment, compensation, or career advancement.[49] Particularly effective are management practices that address low employee control and low rewards. Early intervention by an employer through early assessment, decision making, and referral also significantly reduce loss due to workplace stress. These management practices include more open communication and employee participation in decision making, person–job fit training, job redesign, and Employee Assistance Programs and wellness initiatives.

1. *Open communication and employee participation in decision making*   One way of addressing the low control, low reward aspect of stressful workplaces is increasing employee participation in decision making. This means getting employees more involved in the organization and design of their own day-to-day work such as shift/time scheduling and how to introduce new technology. Developing a culture that respects, appreciates, and listens to employees is critical to a healthy workplace. For example, stress levels run high when rumours or newspaper articles hint of an impending layoff but employees are not given clues as to who may be affected or when the event will occur. Because trust is based on communication clarity,[50] we are not suggesting that managers share every conceivable potential problem. Sharing to this extent could create unfounded anxieties unnecessarily and reduce a manager's credibility. However, when employees are kept informed about what is actually going on, trust increases, ambiguity decreases, and so does the general level of anxiety.

2. *Person–job fit*   Selection and placement procedures can prevent role overload by ensuring that employee education level, abilities, and experience match the requirements of the job.[51] Personality factors can also be assessed to ensure a good person–job fit. Putting introverted people in sales positions or extroverted people in isolated research jobs can cause stress because of mismatches in job demands and personality preferences.

3. *Training*   When employees have been trained properly, it increases their sense of control in their work, thereby eliminating a major source of stress. Training should include role clarification that specifies job duties in order to reduce the likelihood of role ambiguity and conflict. When jobs require group interaction, their design should include team building. Team spirit and a supportive climate can prevent many common stressors from occurring.

4. *Job redesign*   Careful job analysis can reveal role ambiguity, overload, underutilization, and conflict. Further analysis may also reveal working conditions with high noise levels, poor air quality, and poorly designed equipment and workstations. Then jobs and working conditions can be redesigned to eliminate these problems and reduce the distress they cause.[52] You might find through job analysis, for example, that the tedium of performing one simple operation repeatedly on an automobile assembly line—such as installing weather stripping for doors—can be eliminated by having work teams rotate tasks (e.g., attaching antennas, installing floor mats, etc.) every hour throughout the work shift.

5. *Employee assistance programs and wellness initiatives*   By providing and encouraging the use of free counselling, in-house or by referral, an organization acknowledges the existence of stress-related problems among personnel and demonstrates its support of those who suffer from them. Although businesses generally recognize the importance of a healthy workplace, some have been slower to develop programs. For example, of the greater than 450 businesses responding to Health Canada's National Wellness Survey in 2000, 83 per cent cited stress as the major health risk in their organization; 64 per cent of the companies offered some wellness initiatives, and 17.5 per cent offered comprehensive programs.[53]

Because nonwork-related stress often carries over into the job, assistance can also be offered for health, financial, and home problems. Wellness programs focus on employees' total physical and mental condition.[54] Organizations offer a variety of opportunities including physical exams, counselling, and workshops on how to quit smoking, control alcohol use, lose weight, eat better, reduce stress, and develop a regular exercise program, often in the organization's own gym. One successful initiative is BC Hydro's Employee Lifestyle Program. A 1996 cost/benefit study showed a $1.2 million reduction in annual sick leave costs and almost a $1.0 million gain in productivity and substantial employee retention gains. Employee participation rates have risen annually to a high of 80 per cent of all BC Hydro employees in 2000.[55]

Concept Quiz

Complete the following true–false quiz by circling the correct answer. Answers are at the end of the quiz. After marking your answers, remember to go back and check your understanding of any answers you missed.

True or False   1. The first step in stress management is determination of the sources.

True or False   2. Work overload, when people are expected to accomplish more than their ability or time permits, is the number one job role stressor.

True or False   3. Personality characteristics are stress moderators.

True or False	4. Prioritizing activities should precede prioritizing your objectives.
True or False	5. Reframing and adopting a small-wins strategy can give you a sense of control over stressful situations.
True or False	6. The stress response prepares a person to cope with threatening environmental conditions.
True or False	7. One thing that helps productivity is that people leave the stress from personal sources at home.
True or False	8. Management issues such as the balance between employee control/job demand and effort and reward are known to increase stress significantly.
True or False	9. Positive relationships lessen the impact of stress.
True or False	10. Keeping employees uninformed about what is going on or is about to happen decreases stress levels.

Answers   (1) False; (2) True; (3) True; (4) False; (5) True; (6) True; (7) False; (8) True; (9) True; (10) False

Behavioural Checklist

The following skills are important to effective stress and time management. Use them when evaluating your skills and those of others.

The Effective Stress and Time Manager

- Is aware of stress symptoms.
- Identifies stressors.
- Reduces causes of stress.
- Develops stress resiliency.
- Reduces stress symptoms.
- Focuses activities to achieve priority goals.
- Helps employees manage stress.

Modelling Exercise
The Stress of Success Role-Play

DIRECTIONS   After the class reads the situation, pick two role-players. The role-players then read their own role, *but not the other role,* and prepare for the role-play. The class reads both roles, and reviews the observer's rating form to prepare for providing meaningful feedback at the end of the role-play.

ACTORS   Terry Peterson, account executive at Creative Ad Services, Inc., a marketing communications firm; Cory Smith, the firm's president.

SITUATION   Terry Peterson handles more accounts than any other representative and is acknowledged as one of the best account managers at Creative Ad Services. This reputation is quite an honour in the Toronto business environment, which tends to glorify people who live on a few hours of sleep, always doing, doing, doing. Many people in the company have health problems but continue to work at outrageous levels.

The firm's president, Cory Smith, has just received two of the most lucrative accounts the firm has ever had. Of course Cory wants to assign the new accounts to the best performers, and Terry is one of them. The accounts are important to the firm, especially in light of the poor financial results so far this year. The manager overseeing the accounts will be well rewarded financially if everything goes smoothly and will perhaps be given a promotion. The accounts will require a lot of extra attention and effort.

TERRY PETERSON'S ROLE   You are one of the top producers at Creative Ad Services, handling 15 accounts and a minimum of 30 crisis calls from clients every day. While you enjoy success, having a prestigious client list, and a healthy income, you are concerned about your increasing stress level. You also feel that at 32, it is time to develop a serious relationship and think about having a family. Unfortunately, the only thing anyone at the company cares about is "produce, produce, produce, and work, work, work."

Your stressful situation is beginning to have adverse effects on your health. You're gaining a lot of weight and you spend your entire weekend working with little sleep. Although your doctor said that you need a break, you know that people in your company who take pit stops are soon derailed from the fast track.

Yesterday, your boss, Cory Smith, asked you to consider taking on two new accounts that are vital to the company. The financial rewards and promotion opportunities are attractive, but you are already on overload with your current accounts. You agree with your doctor's recommendation to take a break and get away for a while before you have a breakdown.

You are asking yourself, "What kind of life do I want, and what do I need to do to get it?" when you hear your boss knock on your door. How do you want to handle the situation?

CORY SMITH'S ROLE   It has not been a great year for Creative Ad Services. The company is facing a loss after two breakeven years. You have had to cut back on personnel and you know that all account managers are under a tremendous amount of pressure, but Creative Ad Services compensates them accordingly.

These conditions motivated you to put on a major push to acquire some new clients. After an incredible number of hours, meetings, and negotiations, you landed two spectacular new accounts that could save your firm. These accounts are crucial to the firm's future and you want special attention and extra effort given to them.

You do not want anything to go wrong with these new accounts so you asked your best account manager, Terry Peterson, to look them over yesterday. You are a little apprehensive about the situation because Terry really seems to be stressed out lately and does not look well. Terry has consistently been your highest performer and your father always told you that "if you want something done right, and on time, give it to a busy person."

You decide to go over to Terry's office to see whether the new assignments are acceptable. You know what you want, and whom you want to do it.

Observer's Rating Sheet

On completion of the exercise, class members rate each role-player's application of stress management skills. Use the following scale to rate each role-player between 1 and 5. Write concrete examples in the space under each factor for comments to use in explaining your feedback.

1 Unsatisfactory	2 Weak	3 Adequate	4 Good	5 Outstanding
Stress Management Behaviours				**Rating** **Terry**
Points out stress symptoms				_____
Identifies stressors				_____
Modifies stressors				_____
Develops resiliency				_____
Reduces stress symptoms				_____
Focuses on priority goals				_____
Helps employees (protects self against superiors)				_____
				Rating **Cory**
Points out stress symptoms				_____
Identifies stressors				_____
Modifies stressors				_____
Develops resiliency				_____
Reduces stress symptoms				_____
Focuses on priority goals				_____
Helps employees (protects self against superiors)				_____

Group Exercises

Three different types of group exercises are presented here. First is a case for you to practise your awareness, analysis, and action planning skills. Second is a role-play to practise your skills. Finally, you will learn the relaxation response technique to apply whenever you need to reduce your stress level.

Group Exercise 1: Case Analysis: A Hectic Day at Stirling & Besterfield Chartered Accountants[56]

Andrew Burkholder awoke to the ring of the telephone next to his bed. It was after midnight. Andrew thought instantly of his aging parents in Kelowna and reached for the receiver with a feeling of dread. Instead it was the sergeant at police headquarters downtown, making what was to him a routine call.

"Mr. Burkholder. The back door down here at Stirling & Besterfield is unlocked. You're gonna have to come down and check the place out with our officer and lock up the building."

Andrew was both relieved and agitated. "So what else can go wrong at work?" he asked himself as he grappled in the dark for jeans and a sweatshirt.

Andrew was a senior partner in Stirling & Besterfield, a small chartered accounting firm that had come into its own in the 10 years since Andrew had started to work there. At that time it had only two accountants: Seung Chow, managing partner, and himself. It now has 18.

As Andrew drove toward town, he began to recall the events of the preceding day at work. It had been one of those days that were becoming increasingly common. Such days left him exhausted—so much so that at home he had begun to argue with his wife and to scold his three children for minor things that had once left him unruffled.

Yesterday the turmoil had started early in the morning when the chairperson of the board of directors burst into his office and created a disturbance because she had not yet received last month's statistical data. She had to review it prior to that afternoon's board of directors' meeting. Andrew had intended to get the statistical information together, but in what little spare time he could find between customers he had made out the monthly report for the Bank of Montreal instead. That deadline could not be ignored.

After the board chair departed, Andrew went to tell Chow that he needed another clerical person to help relieve his workload. Chow asserted that the firm was currently overstaffed and that more efficient use of the personnel on board would solve the problem. Andrew agreed with him that the present number of personnel should be adequate, but their efficiency was poor. Chow took this comment as a direct criticism of his niece and two cousins that he had hired, and a heated argument developed. Eventually their tempers cooled, and Andrew returned to his office and resumed his work.

About two o'clock in the afternoon, Andrew stepped out of his office and spotted two clients waiting at the counter. Not one clerical staff member was in evidence. His quick investigation disclosed three staff members downstairs having coffee. Another had gone out for cigarettes, and the fifth was in the supply room stocking up on desk supplies. Andrew called Chow out of his office and quickly pointed out the situation. Chow snapped, "You take care of it!" Then he ducked back into his office and slammed the door. Andrew herded the staff out of the lunchroom with a sharp reprimand and then went to see Anita Farelli, who was supposed to supervise them.

Anita was in her mid-twenties and had worked for Stirling & Besterfield for nearly five years. At first she had shown marginal interest in her work, but after she got married and her husband went back to school, her interest picked up; now she was progressing quite rapidly.

Andrew asked Anita for an explanation of the staff situation. Anita advised him that she had no real control over the staff. She told Andrew that she had asked Chow for help but got none, and that on occasions when she had attempted to discipline certain staff members, Chow had reprimanded her for doing so. By this time Andrew was very frustrated, but he managed to keep himself under control.

Just before five o'clock, Andrew's secretary (a Chow cousin) brought him the typed letters that he had dictated earlier that day. As Andrew prepared to sign them, he noted that two contained so many errors that he needed to stay late and retype them himself.

Now, as the steeple clock in the centre of town struck once, Andrew Burkholder drove into the parking lot pondering why the back door was unlocked. Hadn't Chow been the last person to leave? "But Seung always checks both doors before he leaves the building...could I myself have forgotten?"

QUESTIONS FOR DISCUSSION

1. What symptoms of stress is Andrew exhibiting in this case?
2. What are the sources of Andrew's stress? For which is he responsible?
3. What could Andrew do to improve his management of stress in this situation?
4. How could Andrew apply time management techniques?

Group Exercise 2: Role-Play: Time Management at D.C. Howe Inc.

DIRECTIONS   After the class reads the situation, pick three role-players. The role-players then read their own role, *but not the other roles,* and prepare for the role-play. The class reads all roles, and reviews the observer's rating form to prepare for providing meaningful feedback at the end of the role-play.

ACTORS   Pat Pool, director of sales; Chris Criley, sales representative; Lorin Lipper, Chris's assistant.

SITUATION   D.C. Howe Inc. is a high-velocity investment company with heavy quotas and deadlines to meet on a daily basis. Pat Pool is a 20-year veteran with the company and has worked up to the position of director of sales. Pat has been successful in this industry and has high expectations for all people in the company. It is well known that Pat doesn't have a problem bombarding people with heavy workloads. Chris Criley is a recent graduate who was hired last year as a sales representative. Chris was characterized by most people as an extremely nice person who always gives maximum effort, and would do anything required for a respected person. Lorin Lipper has been with the company for 10 years and is the assistant for five sales representatives, including the company's newest hire, Chris Criley.

At the moment, Pat is starting to leave Chris's office after dropping off a second set of portfolios Pat just delegated to Chris to analyze for tomorrow. Lorin is just entering the office with a list of urgent messages that arrived for Chris earlier this morning. As Chris asks Pat about the necessity of completing the portfolios by tomorrow, an impromptu meeting begins between the three of them.

PAT POOL'S ROLE   You feel that you have earned your stripes the hard way and you want your employees—including Chris Criley, the newest employee—to work hard for the money you pay. You also feel that you shouldn't have to do a lot of the busywork because of your seniority, so you delegate most of it to Chris, the new kid on the block. As a matter of fact, you want to see how much work Chris will do for you, even if it means taking advantage of your seniority. Chris has the utmost respect for you and wants to excel within this company.

At 8:00 A.M. this morning you realize that you have five large portfolios to analyze today, but you also have to clean up some work from yesterday, a golf game at 10:00 A.M., and a corporate lunch at the club following the game. After the usual martinis, you would just as soon knock off after lunch and beat the traffic home, because the restaurant is closer to your home than the office.

In order to carry out your plans, you decide to delegate the portfolios to Chris. Because you know that Chris already has a heavy workload, and that the analysis will be quite involved, you do not want to give them all to Chris at the same time. You decide to drop the work off in parts so that this huge downloading won't be so obvious. You are aware that the analyses will take a significant amount of time but you're going to tell Chris that you need them first thing tomorrow morning.

CHRIS CRILEY'S ROLE   This morning you woke up late, took a quick shower, grabbed a cup of coffee, and ran out the door. Halfway to work you realized you forgot your briefcase, which contained some important notes for a meeting with your lawyer today and it was necessary that you return home and get it. Traffic was bumper to bumper, which made you a little late for work. At the moment you are going through an ugly divorce and custody battle and you have a difficult time staying focused because of all the things on your plate.

Your job is important to you because money is tight and you are using your savings for your mortgage and lawyer fees. You have been working as a sales rep for D.C. Howe since graduating a year ago. You are really looking forward to the early promotion to associate, which Pat mentioned to you a couple of months ago because of your record production figures. You feel that Pat is somewhat demanding at times, but you want to make a positive impression because Pat is the one who determines who gets what in the company. At times Pat gives you more work than you can handle, but you don't have much of a choice. You make the best of the situation and complete your work no matter how unhappy you may be. Today you have a long list of important personal things you need to do, so you are hoping for a light day at work so you can knock off a little early. Your *to-do list* includes the following "A" priority tasks:

1. Meetings with three regular clients for one-hour financial planning sessions starting at 9:00 A.M.
2. Determine whom to cold-call from a list of 30 potential clients to inform about a new IPO [initial public offering of a new stock], because, in order to keep up to Pat's expectations, you need to replace two clients who passed away last month.
3. Pick up your daughter from school and drop her off at ballet class at 4:00 P.M.
4. Meet with lawyer at 5:00 P.M. to discuss tomorrow's court appearance.

You have a great assistant who has been with the company for 10 years. Lorin is aware of your personal dilemmas and has been almost like a mother helping you learn the ropes at D.C. Howe and lending an ear when you need to unload about problems on the home front. She is at your disposal if you need her, but you know that she also reports to four other busy reps, and you do not want to take advantage of her generosity or interfere with her other responsibilities.

Your goal for today is to accomplish all that you can at work before your personal agenda takes over. You think that you will have just enough time to get everything done as long as Pat does not surprise you with more work.

Lorin Lipper's Role   You are assistant to five sales reps, including the nice, bright, new hire, Chris Criley. You have been with D.C. Howe for 10 years and know all there is to know about it. You also know about Chris's pending divorce and legal dilemmas. Chris is a nice young man who is always polite and considerate to you. You have gone out of your way when you could to help Chris learn the ropes at D.C. Howe and lend an ear when Chris needed to unload about problems on the home front. You are more than willing to help Chris out if you can, but you do not want to embarrass anyone, so you will only do so if you are asked.

You've noticed that Chris has been running behind for the past few days with all the legal hassles, his daughter's summer visitation with him, and the loss of two major clients. You've actually had to cover a couple of times when Chris had to be out of the office to deal with personal crises. You are aware that Pat asks more than necessary from Chris, and you would like to confront Pat about these unrealistic expectations. Even though you know that confronting Pat would be inappropriate, you also know that Chris will never say anything, even if the stress is substantial. You are actually concerned about Chris's health and mental well-being if the current situation continues much longer.

Before Chris arrived late for work this morning, you received four messages you need to pass on:

1. Chris's daughter is sick and needs to be picked up at school.
2. Chris's lawyer needs to meet at 4:00 P.M. instead of 5:00 P.M. today.
3. Chris's father has been admitted to the hospital for tests and observation due to chest pains last night, but is currently experiencing no problems.
4. The president's assistant has requested that Chris make a presentation at the board of directors meeting tomorrow about trends in the Asian financial markets. The scheduled speaker canceled and in order to show appreciation for his hard work over the past year, the president thought Chris should be asked to substitute.

Observer's Rating Sheet

On completion of the exercise, observers rate the person role-playing Chris Criley on application of time management skills using the following rating scale. Write in concrete examples in the space below each skill component for comments to use in explaining your feedback.

1=Unsatisfactory   2=Weak   3=Adequate   4=Good   5=Outstanding
Rating　　*Skill Component*

_____　　Determines priorities and sticks with high ones.

_____　　Plans and organizes tasks to achieve daily and longer-term goals.

_____　　Schedules activities according to top priorities.

_____　　Delegates.

_____　　Avoids interruptions.

_____　　Says no to unimportant tasks.

_____　　Schedules most important activities during peak productivity cycle.

Group Exercise 3: Relaxation Response

PURPOSE   To learn the relaxation-response technique to reduce stress.

TIME   15 minutes for the exercise; 5 minutes for debriefing.

INSTRUCTIONS   The instructor will slowly read the following guidelines to class members while they relax with their eyes closed.

1. Select a comfortable sitting or reclining position.
2. Close your eyes.
3. Direct your attention to your own breathing process. Think about nothing but your breath as it flows *in* and *out* of your body.
4. Continue to focus on your breathing while you follow the next steps for tensing and relaxing your body.
5. Tense your toes and feet (curl the toes, turn feet in and out). Hold and study the tension. Relax.
6. Now tense your lower legs, knees, and thighs. Hold the tension, study the tension, then relax your legs.
7. Now tense your buttocks. Hold and study the tension. Relax.
8. Tense your fingers and hands. Hold and study the tension. Relax.
9. Tense your lower arms, elbows, and upper arms. Hold and study the tension. Relax.
10. Tense your abdomen. Hold and study the tension. Relax.
11. Now tense your chest. Hold and study the tension. Relax. Take a deep breath and exhale slowly.
12. Tense your lower back. Hold and study the tension. Relax.
13. Now tense your shoulders. Hold and study the tension. Relax.
14. Now tense your neck. Hold and study the tension. Relax.
15. Finally, check and relax every part of your body. Concentrate on your breathing and the relaxed feeling for a couple of minutes.
16. (Wait a couple of minutes.) When you are ready, open your eyes and check how you feel.

DEBRIEFING   Participants now share how they feel, their general reactions to the exercise, which parts of the exercise were most difficult, and how they can practise relaxation on their own. Participants may also share other relaxation techniques they have experienced, such as visualization or meditation.

Application Questions

1. What are your most common stress symptoms? How do these symptoms affect your performance in school, your relations with friends, and your happiness?
2. What are your major stressors? If you are not currently experiencing stress symptoms, how do you account for this state of affairs?
3. How do you and other students you know cope with end-of-the-semester stressors such as term papers and final examinations? What are the short-term and long-term consequences of these various methods?
4. How do you react to the stress of giving a speech? Check out how five of your friends feel about public speaking. Why is it considered stressful? Why do some people perceive it as more stressful than do others?
5. What are your major time wasters? What can you do to overcome them?

Reinforcement Exercises

The following suggestions are activities you can do to reinforce the stress management techniques in this chapter. You may want to adapt them to the Action Plan you will develop next, or try them independently.

1. Interview a practising manager to determine the most stressful parts of his or her job and how he or she manages the resulting stress.
2. Attend a stress management seminar. Many are available free of charge through colleges and universities, hospitals, and community education programs.
3. Make a to-do list for tomorrow. List eight things you would like to do tomorrow. Now decide which things are A tasks (really must be done to achieve important goals), which are B tasks (can probably be put off without dire consequences if you don't get to them), and which are C tasks (would be nice to do but really do not have to be done at all). Now try it out by starting with your top A and sticking with it until completed.

Summary Checklist

Take a few minutes to reflect on your performance and look over others' ratings of your skill. Now assess yourself on each of the key learning behaviours. Make a check (√) next to those behaviours on which you need improvement.

_____ I am aware of stress symptoms
     1. Physical problems (e.g., fatigue, headaches, dizziness)
     2. Psychological problems (e.g., inability to sleep, compulsive eating)
     3. Emotional problems (e.g., moodiness, irritability, aggression)

_____ I identify stressors.
     1. Personal
     2. Work-related
     3. Environmental

_____ I develop resiliency to stressors.
     1. Work on increasing self-esteem.
     2. Maintain social support.
     3. Maintain my health through diet, exercise, and sleep.

_____ I reduce my stress symptoms by:
     1. Seeking help.
     2. Managing my time productively.
     3. Managing my job stress.
     4. Exercising regularly.
     5. Relaxing.

_____ I directly eliminate stressors by:
     1. Changing jobs or tasks.
     2. Avoiding stressful people.
     3. Planning ahead.

_____ I focus on priority goals.

    1. Determine my values.

    2. Determine my life goals and priorities.

    3. Practise good time management.

_____ I help employees cope with stress.

    1. Watching for stress symptoms.

    2. Make them aware of employee assistance programs.

    3. Appropriate selection and placement.

    4. Provide proper training.

    5. Wellness promotion.

Action Plan

Diagnosing Stress and Managing It Effectively

1. Describe a stressful situation(s) you are experiencing at home, work, or school.
2. What symptoms of stress do you experience?
3. What causes the stress (what are the stressors)?
4. What are the consequences of the stress?
5. What can you do to eliminate or reduce the stressor?
6. What can you do to better cope with the stress you are experiencing?
7. When will you do the things listed in questions 5 and 6?
8. What will be your payoff?
9. What potential obstacles stand in your way?
10. How and when will you measure your success?

Skills Video

Managing Stress

Few of us are able to compartmentalize every aspect of our lives. In addition to the sources of stress we find in the workplace (such as deadlines, quotas, workloads, relationships, changes, and poorly defined job roles), we all bring our own individual stressors such as financial, home, and health problems. When work and home pressures collide, for example, there is often an increase in stress in both areas.

The first step to developing coping skills is to recognize what factors or situations create stress for us. Once we have done that, there are a number of effective strategies for coping with stress. Changing the situation, for instance, includes relying on such stress relievers as better planning, time management, to-do lists, schedules, and prioritizing. An extreme but sometimes necessary response to stress is to change jobs or even careers. Changing ourselves to handle stress better can include making such efforts as increasing self-esteem, developing an inner locus of control, working toward smaller and more manageable goals, keeping healthy through diet and exercise, and enjoying recreation and relaxation regularly.

You may recognize in Susan's day some familiar sources of stress. Susan's son calls her at work with a school problem that seems to have no solution and leaves her feeling guilty. Ray is worried about Susan's use of recording equipment on a shoot and their conversation does not go well. In her chance meeting with Andrew, Susan begins to acknowledge some of the sources of stress she feels and admits that it is not all about Ray.

Try to pinpoint what it is about Ray's approach to Susan that adds stress to their interaction. Does she contribute to the strain on their relationship? What other factors are working on Susan as her day draws to a close? Does she have control over any of these?

QUESTIONS

1. How could Susan have avoided the stressful conversation with her son?
2. Specifically how is Ray a source of stress for Susan? Is he responsible in any way for their difficulties communicating? How could Susan improve her interpersonal relationship with Ray?
3. How can Susan relieve some of the stress she feels? Do you think Andrew's suggestion that she take a vacation will help? Why or why not?

Part 3
Relationship-Building Competencies

Managers need to have relationship-building skills in order to behave competently across a broad range of organizational situations. Regardless of whether managers are solving problems, working with teams, or creating change, they need to be able to communicate effectively, cope with diversity, manage conflicts, build a power base, and motivate others.

Chapter 5, Interpersonal Communication   You can have the greatest vision, plans, and work designs, but if you cannot effectively communicate what is required, you will not succeed as a manager. Communication is the glue that holds an organization together and allows a manager to coordinate all the activities of many different people to accomplish organizational objectives. A successful manager is skilled in both formal and informal communications.

Managers are frequently required to address various groups of employees, customers, and other managers, as well as write various memos and reports. Oral and written presentation skills are the subjects of Appendix A and B, respectively.

Chapter 6, Valuing Diversity   The values, needs, interests, and expectations of workers have never been homogeneous, but the increased diversity in Canada's workforce requires managers to be sensitive to differences constantly. Managers need to understand that it is difficult for some employees to put in overtime hours without substantial notice, to work weekends, to be gone overnight on business, or to accept a transfer to a new location. Similarly, physical barriers such as narrow doorways or stairs can be troublesome for some employees. Managers cannot assume that all employees share a common understanding of language. In addition, managers have to be sure that employees are sensitive to co-workers who are different. That means being observant of expressions of sexism, racism, agism, and more subconscious biases within the work group.

Chapter 7, Managing Conflict   Every relationship, including those in organizations, experiences conflicts where incompatible differences emerge. It's true that conflict has the potential to destroy relationships and organizations. On the other hand, the lack of conflict can make an organization static, apathetic, and nonresponsive to the need for change and innovation. Managers need skills to maintain an optimum level of conflict and guide employees in productive problem-solving efforts to learn and profit from it.

Chapter 8, Building a Power Base   To accomplish organizational goals, you need to have a power base that allows you to influence others to do what you need done. Effective managers learn to acquire personal power and develop relationships with employees that allow them to be influential and function as leaders.

Chapter 9, Motivating Others   You can't do it all yourself. In fact, the manager's job is to get things done through the efforts of others. Therefore, effective managers are skilled at determining what their employees want and don't want from work and showing them how to get it by working hard to achieve organizational objectives.

5

Interpersonal Communication

Learning Objectives

After completing this chapter, you should be able to:

- Identify and avoid the barriers to effective communication.
- Send clear, understandable messages.
- Listen actively to others.
- Utilize nonverbal signals.
- Solicit meaningful feedback.
- Adapt to style, gender, and cultural diversity.
- Give appropriate feedback.

Self-Assessment Exercise

What Is Your Communication Style?

Think of how you usually communicate with others in everyday situations. For each of the following 18 *pairs* of statements, distribute three points between the two alternatives depending upon which is most characteristic of your style. The point range is 0–3: 0 = Never; 1 = Rarely; 2 = Sometimes; 3 = Always. *The numbers you assign to each pair of statements should add up to 3.*

1A	_____	I am open to getting to know people personally and establishing relationships with them.
1B	_____	I am not open to getting to know people personally and establishing relationships with them.
2A	_____	I react slowly and deliberately.
2B	_____	I react quickly and spontaneously.
3A	_____	I am open to other people's use of my time.
3B	_____	I am not open to other people's use of my time.
4A	_____	I introduce myself at social gatherings.
4B	_____	I wait for others to introduce themselves to me at social gatherings.

5A	_____	I focus my conversations on the interests of the parties involved, even if it means that the conversations stray from the business or subject at hand.
5B	_____	I focus my conversations on the tasks, issues, business, or subject at hand.
6A	_____	I am not assertive, and I can be patient with a slow pace.
6B	_____	I am assertive, and at times I can be impatient with a slow pace.
7A	_____	I make decisions based on facts or evidence.
7B	_____	I make decisions based on feelings, experiences, or relationships.
8A	_____	I contribute frequently to group conversations.
8B	_____	I contribute infrequently to group conversations.
9A	_____	I prefer to work with and through others, providing support when possible.
9B	_____	I prefer to work independently or dictate the conditions in terms of how others are involved.
10A	_____	I ask questions or speak more tentatively and indirectly.
10B	_____	I make emphatic statements or directly express opinions.
11A	_____	I focus primarily on the idea, concept, or results.
11B	_____	I focus primarily on the person, interaction, and feelings.
12A	_____	I use gestures, facial expressions, and voice intonation to emphasize points.
12B	_____	I do not use gestures, facial expressions, and voice intonation to emphasize points.
13A	_____	I accept others' points of view (ideas, feelings, and concerns).
13B	_____	I do not accept others' point of view (ideas, feelings, and concerns).
14A	_____	I respond to risk and change in a cautious or predictable manner.
14B	_____	I respond to risk and change in a dynamic or unpredictable manner.
15A	_____	I prefer to keep my personal feelings and thoughts to myself, sharing only when I wish to do so.
15B	_____	I find it natural and easy to share and discuss my feelings with others.
16A	_____	I seek out new or different experiences and situations.
16B	_____	I choose known or similar situations and relationships.
17A	_____	I am responsive to others' agendas, interests, and concerns.
17B	_____	I am directed toward my own agendas, interests, and concerns.
18A	_____	I respond to conflict slowly and indirectly.
18B	_____	I respond to conflict quickly and directly.

Source: Adapted from T. Alessandra and M.J. O'Connor, *Behavioral Profiles: Self-Assessment* (San Diego: Pfeiffer & Company, 1994). Permission granted from the author.

SCORING AND INTERPRETATION People develop habitual ways of communicating with others based on behaviours that were reinforced when growing up. Your communication style can be understood by looking at how open or self-contained you are, and how direct or indirect you are.

To determine your degrees of openness and directness, transfer your scores from the questionnaire to the table below. Then, total each column to get your O, S, D, and I scores.

Communication Style Scoring Sheet

O	S	D	I
1A _____	1B _____	2B _____	2A _____
3B _____	3A _____	4A _____	4B _____
5A _____	5B _____	6B _____	6A _____
7B _____	7A _____	8A _____	8B _____
9A _____	9B _____	10B _____	10A _____
11B _____	11A _____	12A _____	12B _____
13A _____	13B _____	14B _____	14A _____
15B _____	15A _____	16A _____	16B _____
17A _____	17B _____	18B _____	18A _____
O Total _____	S Total _____	D Total _____	I Total _____

Compare the O and S scores. Which is higher? Write the higher score in the following blank and circle the corresponding letter: _____   O   S

Compare the D and I scores. Which is higher? Write the higher score in the following blank and circle the corresponding letter: _____   D   I

Are you more **Open** [higher O score] or **Self-Contained** [higher S score] when you communicate? When an Open person communicates, he or she is more relationship-oriented, supportive of others' needs, and shares feelings readily. A Self-Contained person is more task-oriented and not prone to sharing feelings.

Are you more **Direct** [higher D score] or **Indirect** [higher I score] when you communicate with others? Direct people are more extroverted and may express their thoughts and feelings quite forcefully. Indirect people may hold back and appear more introverted. Direct communicators range from highly assertive to aggressive, while indirect communicators go the other way from moderately assertive to passive.

We all use a number of communication style variations, but the one used most easily and skillfully is called our predominate style. Four different predominate communication styles can be discerned by how direct and open a person is. If your scores are highest on open and direct, you have a *Socializer Style*. If your scores are highest on self-contained and direct, you have a *Director Style*. If your scores are highest on indirect and self-contained, you have a *Thinker Style*. If your scores are highest on indirect and open, you have a *Relater Style*.

Your communication style affects all other aspects of communication discussed in this chapter: what specific communication barriers you face, how you send messages, how you listen to others, how you use nonverbal signals and how you react to diversity of communication styles. We will talk more about the ramifications of your communication style later in this chapter.

Concepts

Read about the following events that all occurred the same day at a large hotel in Vancouver to learn how miscommunication can cause myriad problems in daily business operations.[1] Think about what common communication problems were operating in these situations and what the probable consequences were.

EPISODE 1 The manager of convention sales, Kim Wong, was reviewing last quarter's sales report in preparation for a performance review with each of her three employees. Concerned particularly about Jan Decker's performance, Kim called Jan into her office.

"Jan, I just saw your last quarter's sales numbers. I thought we had agreed upon a goal of six major conventions [1,000 or more room nights] for the quarter. The data state that you booked only four conventions. What happened?"

"I don't understand the problem," Jan responded. "Six was our goal, a target. It was something we were trying to reach."

Clearly upset, Kim was trying to control her frustration. "Jan, six was our goal all right, but it wasn't some 'pie-in-the-sky' number. It was the minimum number of bookings we were counting on. You're responsible for getting us the big conventions. Ted and Dawn handle the smaller ones, but you know we rely on the big conventions to keep our occupancy rates up. I told Dave [the hotel's general manager and Kim's immediate boss] we'd book at least six big conventions in the second quarter. Now I've got to explain why we missed our goal!"

EPISODE 2 A memo had gone out a number of months previously from the hotel's director of human resources to all managers. The topic of the memo was a change in the hotel's leave-without-pay policy. The director of human resources just received a complaint from a buyer in the food and beverage department. The employee's request for a two-week leave without pay to handle personal and financial problems related to the death of his mother had been denied by his manager. He felt his request was reasonable and should have been approved. Interestingly, the memo in question specifically stated that leaves of up to three weeks because of a death in the family were to be uniformly approved. When the human resources director called the beverage manager to follow up on the employee complaint, she was told by the manager, "I never knew there was a change in the policy on leaves without pay."

EPISODE 3 The following conversation took place between two accounts payable clerks in the accounting department. "Did you hear the latest? The general manager's daughter is marrying some guy from Hamilton who's serving a five-year sentence for stealing."

"You're kidding!"

"No, I'm not kidding! I heard it this morning from Chuck in purchasing. Can you imagine the heartache the family must feel?"

This rumour had some basis in fact but was far from accurate. The previous week, the general manager had announced the engagement of his daughter to a Hamilton businessman who had just been awarded a five-year computer services contract with Dofasco, a major steel manufacturer.

Why Is Communication Important?

In extreme cases, the effectiveness of **communication** can make the difference between life and death. Examples of miscommunication occur all too frequently on the operating table, in aircraft emergencies, and in fatal industrial accidents. In addition, daily communication breakdowns contribute to numerous organizational problems ranging from minor irritations and conflicts to low productivity and quality due to employee injuries and deaths (particularly in industries where workers operate heavy machinery or handle hazardous materials).[2]

The events described in the opening hotel vignette demonstrate three common communication problems. First, words mean different things to different people. In the first situation, for Kim Wong a goal meant a minimum level of attainment, while to Jan Decker it meant a maximum target that one tried to reach. Second, the initiation of a message provides no assurance that it has been received or correctly understood. Third, communications often become distorted as they are transmitted from person to person. As the marriage rumour illustrates, "facts" in messages can lose much of their accuracy as they are transmitted and translated.

These episodes illustrate the potential for communication problems and how easily they can plague managers. The importance of effective communication for managers can't be overemphasized because almost everything a manager does involves communicating.[3] For example, managers can't make an informed decision without getting all the relevant information. Once a decision is made it must be communicated to those charged with implementing it. The best idea, the most creative suggestion, or the finest plan will not make any difference unless effectively communicated.

Managers work with their employees, peers, immediate supervisors, people in other departments, customers, and others to get their own department's objectives accomplished. Interactions with these various individuals all require communication of some type. We are not suggesting that good communication skills alone make a successful manager. However, ineffective communication skills can lead to a continuous stream of problems for the manager.

What Is the Interpersonal Communication Process?

Communication begins when one person sends a message to another with the intent of evoking a response. Often, for a variety of reasons, however, the response that occurs is not what the sender desired. *Effective* communication occurs when the sender transmits ideas and feelings completely and accurately, and the receiver interprets the message exactly as the sender intended. Communication is *efficient* when it uses less time and fewer resources. Communicating with each employee individually, for example, is less efficient than addressing all employees as a group. Effectiveness, however, means the accurate conveyance of information, which is more important than the speed of transmission. Explaining a new operating procedure to each staff member individually, for example, might be less efficient than calling a meeting where everyone can hear about it together, but if staff members have unique sets of problems, they may require individual coaching. It may be more effective to meet with each one individually. What a manager wants to achieve is effective communication in the most efficient way.

Exhibit 5-1 depicts the interpersonal communication process.[4] The main components of this model are the sender, the receiver, the message, and the channel. The communication process includes the sequential steps of encoding, transmitting, and decoding.

STEPS OF THE COMMUNICATION PROCESS

First, the message is **encoded** into a format that will get the idea across. Then it is **transmitted** through various channels *orally* (e.g., speeches, meetings, phone calls, or informal discussions), *nonverbally* (e.g., touch, facial expression, and tone of voice), *in writing* (e.g., letters, memoranda, reports, and manuals), or *electronically* (e.g., e-mail, voice mail, facsimiles).

No matter how effectively a message is encoded and transmitted, communication will

Exhibit 5-1 The Communication Process Model

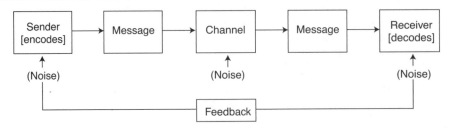

not be effective if the receivers fail to perceive and understand the sender's message. **Decoding** is the receiver function of perceiving the communication and interpreting its meaning. It is often more than half the equation.

Noise is anything that interferes, at any stage, with the communication process. The success of the communication process depends to a large degree on overcoming various sources of noise. **Feedback** is the manager's primary tool for determining how clearly a message was understood and what effect it had on the receiver.

Basic Interpersonal Communication Skills

Most communication problems can be avoided by applying six essential skills for effectively sending and receiving interpersonal messages. They include avoiding barriers to communication, sending understandable messages, actively listening, utilizing nonverbal signals appropriately, giving and soliciting meaningful feedback, and adapting appropriately to diversity of communication styles. After reading about the main barriers to communication, you will be presented with some methods to overcome them. You will have an opportunity to practise these techniques in later exercises.

What Are the Barriers to Communication?

Barriers to communication, such as semantics, mistrust, or different frames of reference, are often responsible for confusion and misunderstanding. Misinterpretation occurs when the receiver understands the message differently from the way in which the sender intended. A deadly example of misinterpretation occurred in 1990 when a Colombian Avianca pilot told controllers that the plane was "running low on fuel," as it approached New York's Kennedy Airport.[5] Because the controllers heard this phrase all the time, they took no special action. Unfortunately, this time the pilot intended a different meaning. Consequently, the jet ran out of fuel and crashed 26 kilometres from the airport, killing 73 people. Had the pilots used the phrase "fuel emergency," the controllers would have been obliged to clear the Avianca flight to land immediately. The next section describes some of the primary sources of misunderstanding and then provides techniques to overcome these barriers.

FRAMES OF REFERENCE

As illustrated in the Avianca incident, a person's frame of reference often leads two people to perceive the same communication differently. Even if two individuals hear the actual words accurately, they may assign different meanings to them, depending on the combination of their past experience and current expectations.

SEMANTICS

Semantics pertains to the meaning and use of words. A common example of semantic noise is evident when people from different cultures try to communicate. In another airline tragedy, Chinese pilots flying a U.S.-built airliner crashed in a fog in 1993 in Urumqu, China, killing 12 people. The cockpit recording of the pilots' last words as they tried to figure out the meaning of the message on the jet's ground proximity warning system were, "What does 'pull up' mean?"[6]

Many professional and social groups adopt a specialized technical language called jargon that simplifies communication within the in-group. But sophisticated technical or financial terms can intimidate and confuse outsiders, especially when members of a specialized group use them to project a professional mystique. The military and aerospace companies are examples of organizations that actually produce telephone book-sized dictionaries to define all of their acronyms.

VALUE JUDGMENTS

Value judgments are a source of noise when a receiver evaluates the worth of a sender's message before the sender has finished transmitting it. Often such value judgments are based on the receiver's previous experience either with the sender or with similar types of communications. A manager may tune out when an employee begins to describe a scheduling problem because "workers are always complaining about something." In businesses where union leaders are perceived as political exploiters, managers will rarely hear their messages without making some inference as to the speaker's intent. When listeners form value judgments, speakers are usually aware of them because nonverbal signals, like frowns or smiles, give them away. Subsequently, the senders become guarded and defensive, which often inhibits transmission of their real concerns.

SELECTIVE LISTENING

Value judgments, needs, and expectations cause us to hear what we want to hear. When a message conflicts with what a receiver believes or expects, **selective listening** may cause the receiver to block out the information or distort it to match preconceived notions. Feedback to an employee about poor performance, for example, may not be "heard" because it doesn't fit the employee's self-concept or expectations.

FILTERING

Filtering is selective listening in reverse; in fact, we might call it "selective sending." When senders convey only certain parts of the relevant information to receivers, they are said to be filtering their message. Filtering often occurs in upward communication when staff members suppress negative information and relay only the data that will be perceived by managers as positive. Filtering is common when people are being evaluated for promotions, salary increases, or performance appraisals.

DISTRUST

A lack of trust on the part of either communicator is likely to evoke one or more of the barriers we've just examined. Senders may filter out important information if they distrust receivers, and receivers may form value judgments, make inferences, and listen only selectively to distrusted senders.

How Do You Send Clear, Understandable Messages?

Many times these barriers to effective communication can be neutralized or avoided altogether if communicators are simply aware of them and guard against their negative effects. Applying effective sending and receiving behaviours can also eliminate barriers. First let's examine behaviours that help send messages more effectively.[7]

USE MULTIPLE CHANNELS

Using more than one channel or mode of transmission can increase the impact of a message. For example, matching facial and body gestures to a message and diagramming it on a piece of paper uses three channels. This kind of multiple-mode communication ensures that the receiver has the opportunity to receive the message through more than one sense.

BE COMPLETE AND SPECIFIC

The sender can make the message complete and specific by providing sufficient background information and details. Once the receiver understands the sender's frame of reference, he or she is more likely to interpret the message accurately. By referring to concrete deadlines and examples, like 4:00 P.M. on Friday instead of "as soon as possible," a sender can decrease the probability of misinterpretation.

CLAIM YOUR OWN MESSAGE

To claim a message as your own, use personal pronouns such as "I" and "mine." These labels indicate to the receiver that you take responsibility for the ideas and feelings expressed in the message. General statements like "everyone feels this way" leave room for doubt (someone might not feel that way, which could damage your credibility). But an "I message" such as "I feel strongly about this" is an unambiguous personal opinion. It is probably more effective to say "I think improvement is necessary," rather than, "Don't you think you can do better?" which could put the receiver on the defensive.

BE CONGRUENT

Make sure your messages are congruent with your actions. Being incongruent by saying one thing and doing another confuses receivers. If, for example, managers tell employees that they are "always available" to help them but then appear condescending and preoccupied when people come to them with problems, they are communicating something quite different from the verbal message.

SIMPLIFY YOUR LANGUAGE

Complex rhetoric and technical jargon confuse individuals who do not use such language themselves. You should also refrain from using "lingo" (i.e., the company's own words and phrases for people, situations, events, and things). For example, describing your company as a "leading provider of e-business information solutions" does not clearly describe your company's products or services and their benefits.

MAINTAIN CREDIBILITY

Sender credibility is reflected in the receiver's belief that the sender is trustworthy (i.e., what he or she says is accurate). Things you can do to maintain credibility include only trying to influence others when you have sufficient *expertise* on the topic, being *reliable* by providing all relevant information accurately, and being *supportive* of others' concerns. For example, managers who squelch dissent, over-estimate accomplishments, or make false claims soon lose credibility and, consequently, their communication effectiveness.

OBTAIN FEEDBACK

Effective communication means both top-down and bottom-up communication. All too often managers concentrate on communicating messages to employees without providing a mechanism for staff to respond and give feedback.[8] Without feedback, you have no immediate way to know whether your message has been understood as you intended. When you ask for feedback, on the other hand, the receiver's response will indicate the degree of understanding. You can then modify the original message if necessary. Some rules for giving and receiving feedback effectively are summarized in Exhibit 5-2.

How Do You Receive and Understand Messages Accurately?

The final step to ascertain whether you understand another's message accurately is to provide feedback by sharing your understanding of what has been communicated and to ask for feedback to confirm your interpretation. This and other skills necessary for understanding messages accurately are contained in the technique of active listening.

Listening is an intellectual and emotional process in which a receiver processes physical, emotional, and intellectual messages from a sender in search of meaning. Listening to others is our most important means of gaining the information we need to understand people and assess situations. Poor listeners miss important messages and emerging problems. Disinterest makes listening effectively difficult. To listen well, you have to *care* about the

Exhibit 5-2 Guides for Giving and Receiving Feedback

Criteria for Giving Feedback

1. Make sure your comments are intended to help the recipient.
2. Speak directly and with feeling.
3. Describe what the person is doing and the effect the person is having.
4. Don't be threatening or judgmental.
5. Be specific, not general (use clear and recent examples).
6. Give feedback when the recipient is open to accepting it.
7. Check to ensure the validity of your statements.
8. Include only things the receiver can do something about.
9. Don't overwhelm the person with more than can be handled.

Criteria for Receiving Feedback

1. Don't be defensive.
2. Seek specific examples.
3. Be sure you understand (summarize).
4. Share your feelings about the comments.
5. Ask for definitions.
6. Check out underlying assumptions.
7. Be sensitive to the sender's nonverbal messages.
8. Ask questions to clarify.

Source: Summarized from P.L. Hunsaker and A.J. Alessandra, *The Art of Managing People* (New York: Simon & Shuster, 1986) 209–13.

speaker and the message. Then you need to put energy into the process.[9] This process is called active listening.

Active listening means refraining from evaluating other people's words, trying to see things from their point of view, and demonstrating that you are truly trying to understand.[10] Active listeners search for the intent and feeling of the message and indicate their understanding both verbally and nonverbally. Active listeners do not interrupt. They look for verbal and visual cues that the other person would like to say something more.

The three main skills in active listening are sensing, attending, and reflecting. **Sensing** is the ability to recognize the silent messages that the speaker is sending through nonverbal clues such as vocal intonation, body language, and facial expression. **Attending** refers to the verbal, vocal, and visual messages that an active listener sends to the speaker to indicate full attention. These cues include direct eye contact, open posture, affirmative head nods, and appropriate facial and verbal expressions.

When **reflecting**, the active listener summarizes or paraphrases to test understanding and gives feedback on the content and feeling of the sender's message. All of these actions encourage the speaker to elaborate, make the speaker feel understood, and can improve the speaker's own understanding of the problem or concern. Reflecting also includes asking questions to obtain additional information, motivate additional communication, and explore the sender's feelings.

How Can You Utilize Nonverbal Cues?

As much as 93 per cent of the meaning that is transmitted in face-to-face communication can come from nonverbal channels.[11] Nonverbal communications are more reliable than verbal communications when they contradict each other. Nonverbal communications function as a lie detector to aid a watchful listener in interpreting another's words. Most people choose to believe the vocal meaning instead of the nonverbal one when contradictions are present.

People also judge books and other people by their covers. Managers who look and act like executives, for example, communicate an *image* that makes them more successful than those who do not.[12] Furthermore, by "reading" a person's *facial expressions*, we can detect unexpressed feelings[13] of anger, fear, sadness, disgust, surprise, and happiness.[14] *Eye contact* can communicate things such as honesty, interest, openness, and confidence.[15] *Posture* provides clues about the attitude of the bearer,[16] and *gestures* can signify entire meanings all by themselves.

To the sender of a message, a receiver's visual nonverbal cues serve as feedback. For example, disagreement can be indicated in a side-to-side headshake, while a smile and nod will signal agreement. Caution in reading nonverbal movements is always advisable, however, especially when communicating with people from different cultures where the same gesture can mean entirely different things. The North American "V" for "victory" or "peace," for example, means "up yours!" in England when the palm faces inward.[17]

Visual, tactile, and vocal aspects of communication, plus the use of time and space, make up the nonverbal dimensions.[18] The components, consequences, and examples of each of these are illustrated in Exhibit 5-3.

How Can You Adapt to Diversity of Communication Styles?

Effective communication is a challenge even when the workforce is culturally homogeneous, but when participants possess a variety of languages and cultural backgrounds, it becomes even more difficult. First, we'll examine how to cope with differences in communication styles. Then we'll look at cultural and gender differences.

Exhibit 5-3 Means of Nonverbal Communication[19]

	Components	**Examples**	**Meanings Communicated**
Visual	Image Facial expressions Eye movements Posture Gestures	Clothing; hygiene Frown; smile; sneer Looking away; staring Leaning in; slumped Handshake; wave	Values; competence Unexpressed feelings Intentions; state of mind Attitude Intentions, feelings
Tactile	Touch	Pat on the back Gentle touch on an arm	Approval Support and concern
Vocal	How things are said	Loudness, pitch, rate, vocal intonations, rhythm, pitch, clarity	Different meanings (e.g., sarcasm, disapproval, agreement, surprise)
Spatial[20]	Body closeness Furniture arrangement	0–1 metre Large pieces far apart	Feelings of intimacy Formal and serious

DIFFERENCES IN COMMUNICATION STYLES

Have you ever wondered why it seems so difficult to talk with some people, and so easy to talk with others? Can you remember immediately liking or disliking people the first time you met them? The chances are that your reactions were caused by differences in communication styles.

One frequently occurring communication barrier is the tendency to favour one, usually one's own, communication style, often at the cost of being insensitive to other styles. Ideally managers should be conscious of their own stylistic preferences and dislikes, be able to detect such preferences and dislikes quickly in other people, and be able to adjust their own styles to match those of other people. If managers attempt to achieve this ideal, a surprising number of payoffs result, both in personal insights and in interpersonal skills.[21]

Review your scores on the "*What Is Your Communication Style*" self-assessment exercise at the beginning of this chapter. Although you probably have a number of style variations you can utilize, the predominate style you use most easily and skillfully was indicated at the end of the communication style scoring sheet. Let's review the four dominant communication styles and then explore how managers can practise "style flexing" to get on the same wavelength as their conversational partners.

THE SOCIALIZER STYLE Socializers communicate in an open and direct manner. The animated and lively Socializers speak quickly and are less concerned than other styles about facts and details. They can be emotional and relatively comfortable sharing their own feelings and hearing about the feelings of others. To communicate productively with Socializers, take time to empathize and understand their feelings.

THE DIRECTOR STYLE Directors keep feelings self-contained but are direct about what results are expected. Their communications are oriented toward immediate productivity so Directors can be impatient or strong willed. They prefer to shape situations to achieve their goals. Directors like expressing and reacting to tough emotions, but may be uncomfortable either receiving or expressing tender feelings. You can maintain productive communications with a Director if you are precise, efficient, and well organized. You should keep communications businesslike.

THE THINKER STYLE   Thinkers also keep feelings self-contained but are indirect about concerns for task accomplishment. Thinkers sometimes appear aloof and critical mainly because of their search for solid, tangible, and factual evidence. Thinkers tend to avoid being confrontational and think before they speak.

Thinkers suppress their feelings because they may be uncomfortable with emotion. To get on the same communication wavelength with Thinkers, try to be systematic, organized, and prepared. Take time to explain the alternatives and the advantages and disadvantages of your point of view.

THE RELATER STYLE   Relaters are indirect about what is desired but open about feelings. Relaters tend to be supportive and accepting when they talk with others. They want to know how other people feel about a decision before they commit themselves. Because they dislike interpersonal conflict, Relaters often tell others what they think others want to hear rather than what is really on their minds.

Relaters like expressing and receiving tender feelings of warmth and support, but abhor tough emotions like anger or hostility. To communicate effectively with Relaters, support their feelings and show personal interest in them. Move along in an informal manner and show that you are "actively listening."

CULTURAL DIFFERENCES

Differences in backgrounds create differences in meanings attached to particular words and behaviours, regardless of whether communicators are of different sexes, or are from different countries or different subcultures in the same country. Even if two communicators are speaking the same language, the same words and phrases may mean different things to people from different cultures. For example, the phrase "that would be very hard to do" to a Canadian means that some adjustments or extra contributions may be necessary, but the deal is still possible. To a Japanese person, the phrase clearly means, "No, it won't be possible." For a nonverbal example, many Canadians think that maintaining eye contact is important and those who don't are dishonest or rude. Japanese people, on the other hand, lower their eyes as a gesture of respect when speaking with a superior.[22]

GENDER DIFFERENCES

Gender can create subculture communication barriers within the same country. For example, men frequently complain that women talk a lot about their problems, and women criticize men for not listening. What men are doing is asserting their independence and desire for control by providing solutions, which women do not necessarily want in their quest for support, understanding, and connection.[23]

Because of these differences, most people interact differently with same-sex than with different-sex communicators. Male managers' communication behaviours are often characterized by task orientation, dominance, challenges to others, and attempts to control the conversation. For example, males talk more and interrupt more often than do females. Females are usually more informative, receptive to ideas, focused on interpersonal relations, and concerned for others. They are more reactive and show more emotional support.[24]

Women are more precise in their pronunciation than men, who, for example, tend to shorten the ends of words (e.g., using "in" instead of "ing").[25] Men and women also differ in word choice. Women tend to select more intense adverbs, such as "awfully friendly," whereas men use words that are more descriptive and defining.

Women more often use qualifying terms, which are phrases that soften or qualify the intent of our communication. They make language less absolute and less powerful. Examples include "maybe," "you know what I mean," "it's only my opinion," and so on.[26]

Women also frequently use tag questions, which are qualifying words at the end of a sentence that ask the other for confirmation of the statement presented. When using these tags, they automatically defer to others: "It's time for a break now, right?" "We did a great job, didn't we?" By adding the tag question, the speaker gives the impression of being unsure and surrenders decision-making power.[27]

Women learn to listen with empathy and to be responsive and sensitive to others' emotions. Men, on the other hand, are encouraged to be rational and strong, and to deny feelings in order to maintain rationality and control. Women's stronger empathy is thought to be valuable in maintaining collaborative, growth-enhancing relationships.

How Can You Facilitate Communication With Diversity?

Even with the best of intentions, the unknowing manager can get into deep trouble when communicating with people with different gender or cultural backgrounds. Some specific guidelines can help facilitate communications when diversity is present.[28]

1. *Assume differences until similarity is proven* Effective cross-cultural communicators know that they don't know how people with different backgrounds perceive a situation or interpret certain forms of communication. They avoid stereotypes and do not assume that a person from another culture interprets a word or behaviour the same way that they do.

2. *Emphasize description rather than interpretation or evaluation* Effective cross-cultural communicators are patient and delay judgment until they have observed and interpreted the situation from the perspectives of all cultures involved.

3. *Empathize* When trying to understand the words, motives, and actions of a person from another culture, try to interpret them from the perspective of that culture rather than your own. When you view behaviours from your own perspective, you can completely misinterpret the other's actions if he or she has different values, experiences, and objectives.

4. *Treat your interpretations as guesses until you can confirm them* Check with others from that culture to make sure that your evaluation of a behaviour is accurate if you are in doubt. To communicate effectively in sensitive situations or in handling cultural misunderstanding or conflict, consider using an intermediary with a background in both cultures.[29]

Concept Quiz

Complete the following true–false quiz by circling the correct answers. Answers are at the end of the quiz. After marking your answers, remember to go back and check your understanding of any answers you missed.

True or False   1. Efficient communication is almost always better than effective communication.

True or False   2. Communication takes more time than any other managerial activity.

True or False	3. People develop habitual ways of communicating with others based on behaviours that were reinforced when growing up.
True or False	4. Feedback is the receiver function of perceiving communication and interpreting its meaning.
True or False	5. An army colonel should avoid using technical military jargon when addressing the general public.
True or False	6. Sally is filtering when she tells her supervisors only about sales successes but not about setbacks.
True or False	7. Active listening involves sensing, attending, and reflecting.
True or False	8. You should not ask questions in order to avoid confusing a sender.
True or False	9. In Canada, direct eye contact is usually a sign of honesty, interest, openness, and confidence.
True or False	10. Interpret the meaning of a foreign speaker's statements from your own point of view.

Answers (1) False; (2) True; (3) True; (4) False; (5) True; (6) True; (7) True; (8) False; (9) True; (10) False

Behavioural Checklist

The following skills are important to effective communication. Use them when evaluating your communication skills and those of others.

The Effective Communicator:

- Avoids barriers to communication.
- Sends clear, understandable messages.
- Actively listens to others.
- Utilizes nonverbal signals.
- Gives appropriate feedback.
- Adapts to the diversity of other communicators.
- Solicits meaningful feedback.

Modelling Exercise
Controversial Issue Debate

PURPOSE To practise all the interpersonal communication skills in a highly charged situation and receive feedback on your effectiveness.

DIRECTIONS Two class members volunteer to participate in a debate in front of the class. The debaters can choose any contemporary issue on which they disagree. Or they can role-play their differences by debater A selecting one position on the issue and debater B taking the counterposition. Some examples: business ethics, value of unions, stiffer course policies for late assignments, gun control, and money as a motivator. The debate is to proceed, with only one catch. Before each debater speaks, he or she must first summarize, in his or her own words and without notes, what the other has said. If the summary isn't what the first debater meant, it must be corrected and restated until it is. Then the second debater says his or her piece, and the first debater restates the second debater's position satisfactorily before responding.

OBSERVER'S ROLE In addition to rating both debaters' interpersonal communication skills on the rating sheet, the observers should remind each debater to paraphrase the other's statements until acknowledged as correct, before stating his or her own points.

TIME 15 minutes.

Observer's Rating Sheet

On completion of the exercise, class members rate each debater's application of inter-personal communication skills. Use the following scale to rate each role-player between 1 and 5. Write concrete examples in the space below each criterion to use in explaining your feedback.

1 Unsatisfactory	2 Weak	3 Adequate	4 Good	5 Outstanding
Communication Behaviours			**Debater A Rating**	**Debater B Rating**
Avoids communication barriers			_____	_____
Sends understandable messages			_____	_____
Actively listens (attends, paraphrases, questions)			_____	_____
Utilizes nonverbal signals well			_____	_____
Gives effective feedback			_____	_____
Adapts to diversity (style, gender, culture)			_____	_____
Solicits meaningful feedback			_____	_____

Group Exercises

Three different types of group exercises follow. First is a business case to apply your conceptual understanding of effective communication. Second is an active listening exercise applied to solving personal problems where you have an opportunity to practise your behavioural skills. Third is an experiential exercise to practise your nonverbal communication skills.

Group Exercise 1: A Case of Deadly Communication Problems[30]

DIRECTIONS Individually read the following case and answer the questions at the end. Then form groups of five or six and discuss your answers, or discuss your answers in the class as a whole.

DEADLY COMMUNICATION PROBLEMS At 7:40 P.M. on January 25, 1990, Avianca Flight 52 was cruising at 37,000 feet above the southern New Jersey coast. The aircraft had enough fuel to last nearly two hours—a healthy cushion considering the plane was less than half an hour from touchdown at New York's Kennedy Airport. At this point a series of delays began. First, at 8:00, the air traffic controllers at Kennedy told the pilots on Flight 52 that they would have to circle in a holding pattern because of heavy traffic. At 8:45, the Avianca copilot advised Kennedy that they were "running low on fuel." The controller at Kennedy acknowledged the message, but the plane was not cleared to land until 9:24. In the interim, the Avianca crew relayed no information to Kennedy that an emergency was imminent, yet the cockpit crew spoke worriedly among themselves about their dwindling fuel supply.

Flight 52's first attempt to land at 9:24 was aborted. The plane had come in too low and poor visibility made a safe landing uncertain. When the Kennedy controllers gave Flight 52's pilot new instructions for a second attempt, the crew again mentioned that they were running low on fuel, but the pilot told the controllers that the newly assigned flight path was okay. At 9:32, two of Flight 52's engines lost power. A minute later; the other two cut off. The plane, out of fuel, crashed on Long Island at 9:34. All 73 people on board were killed.

When investigators reviewed the cockpit tapes and talked with the controllers involved, they learned that a communication breakdown caused this tragedy. A closer look at the events of that evening help to explain why a simple message was neither clearly transmitted nor adequately received. First, the pilots kept saying they were "running low on fuel." Traffic controllers told investigators that it is fairly common for pilots to use this phrase. In times of delay, controllers assume that everyone has a fuel problem. However, had the pilots uttered the words "fuel emergency," the controllers would have been obliged to direct the jet ahead of all others and clear it to land as soon as possible. As one controller put it, if a pilot "declares an emergency, all rules go out the window and we get the guy to the airport as quickly as possible." Unfortunately, the pilots of Flight 52 never used the word "emergency," so the people at Kennedy never understood the true nature of the pilots' problem.

Second, the vocal tone of the pilots on Flight 52 didn't convey the severity or urgency of the fuel problem to the air traffic controllers. These controllers are trained to pick up subtle tones in a pilot's voice in such situations. Although the crew of Flight 52 expressed considerable concern among themselves about the fuel problem, their voice tones in communicating to Kennedy were cool and professional. Finally, the culture and traditions of pilots and airport authorities may have made the pilot of Flight 52 reluctant to declare an emergency. A pilot's expertise and pride can be at stake in such a situation. Declaration of a formal emergency requires the pilot to complete a wealth of paperwork. Moreover, if a pilot has been found to be negligent in calculating how much fuel was needed for a flight, the Federal Aviation Administration can suspend his or her licence. These negative consequences strongly discourage pilots from calling an emergency.

QUESTIONS FOR DISCUSSION

1. Analyze the communications between pilots on Flight 52 and the air traffic controllers at Kennedy Airport using the process model in this chapter.
2. Could active listening skills have prevented this crash? Cite examples.
3. Avianca is a Colombian airline. A large number of planes that fly into major world airports are international carriers. How is it possible for world air traffic controllers to be effective when they and many pilots do not share the same native language?

Group Exercise 2: Listening to Understand Problems

PURPOSE   To practise the skills of active listening when trying to be compassionate and understand another's problem.

DIRECTIONS   Form groups of three individuals. Each person will play the role of listener, speaker, and observer. Decide who will play each role for the first round.

1. If you are the *speaker*, choose an unresolved interpersonal problem such as an un-cooperative co-worker. Explain it and your feeling about it to the listener. Continue to share and expand until you feel certain the listener completely understands both the problem and your feelings about it. (Take no more than 10 minutes.)
2. The *listener* should use as many of the active listening skills as possible to understand (not solve) the speaker's problem (e.g., attending, paraphrasing, questioning, and so on). Your goal is to have the speaker say, "Yes, you understand my problem and how I feel about it perfectly."
3. The *observer* should remain totally silent during the exercise and take notes on the listener's effective and ineffective listening behaviours.
4. At the conclusion of the exercise, first the observer and then the speaker should give the listener feedback on points they felt indicated effective or ineffective listening skills. (Take no more than 5 minutes for this feedback.)
5. Steps 1 through 4 should be repeated two more times so that each person in the group has a chance to play each role once.

DEBRIEFING   As a class, develop a list of effective listening "do's and don'ts."

TIME   15 to 20 minutes per session. 10 minutes for debriefing.

Observer's Rating Sheet

On completion of the exercise, rate each actor's application of interpersonal communication skills. Use the following scale to rate each role-player between 1 and 5. Write concrete examples in the spaces between behaviours to use when explaining your feedback.

1 Unsatisfactory	2 Weak	3 Adequate	4 Good	5 Outstanding

Communication Behaviours	Sender Rating	Listener Rating
Avoids communication barriers	_____	_____
Sends understandable messages	_____	_____
Actively listens (attends, paraphrases, questions)	_____	_____
Utilizes nonverbal signals	_____	_____
Gives effective feedback	_____	_____
Adapts to diversity (styles, gender, culture)	_____	_____
Solicits meaningful feedback	_____	_____

Group Exercise 3: Getting to Know You: Connecting by Rubber Bands

PURPOSE To practise nonverbal communication skills to send messages about yourself and learn about another person.

PREPARATION Requires a room with space to move about freely.

DIRECTIONS Class members stand up and move all furniture out of the way if possible to allow open space in the classroom in which to move about. The instructor then reads the instructions for the following nonverbal activities for students. At the end of the exercise, first dyads and then the entire class debriefs the experience.

ACTIVITY 1 All members of the class stand up and silently mill around greeting each other nonverbally. After you have greeted everyone (about 2 minutes), nonverbally choose a partner for Activity 2. Remember, at no times are participants allowed to speak to each other.

ACTIVITY 2 Stand about two feet apart facing your partner. Put your hands out in front of you, almost touching the hands of your partner. Pretend that your hands are connected by rubber bands and that you are facing your partner in a mirror. Nonverbally move your hands around in creative ways while they are "connected" to your partner's. (3 minutes)

ACTIVITY 3 Stay in your hand-mirroring position. Now pretend that your feet are also connected by rubber bands, about two inches away from your partner's feet. Again, nonverbally, move both your hands and feet around. Be creative: See if you can move around the room, encounter other dyads, etc. (3 minutes)

ACTIVITY 4 With your partner, nonverbally choose another dyad. Sit down together and share what you learned about your partner from participating in Activities 1, 2, and 3 to the other dyad. Rotate sharing until all are finished (10 minutes).

DEBRIEFING At the end of the exercise, first dyads and then the entire class debriefs the experience. The purpose of the debriefing is to analyze what you learned about yourself and your partner during the nonverbal exercise. The following questions will help get you started. (10 minutes)

1. What were the main mechanisms you and your partner used for communicating nonverbally in this exercise?
2. How did you feel about interacting in this close interpersonal space with your partner? Why? Would it have been different with another partner?
3. What were the primary ways you influenced each other nonverbally?
   For example, who invited the other to be his or her partner and how did it happen nonverbally? How did you nonverbally decide to choose another dyad?
4. What else did you learn about yourself, your partner, or others in the nonverbal exercise? For example, how comfortable were you during the nonverbal milling? Why? How did other dyads respect your personal space and how did you feel about it?

TIME 25 minutes for the exercise; 10 minutes for debriefing.

Application Questions

1. What does your professor do in class or your manager do at work to ensure sending clear messages? What could he or she do to improve the clarity of the messages?
2. What do the students in your class or employees at work do in terms of active listening to improve the communication process? How could they improve?
3. Describe some common nonverbal gestures that are widely known in Canada but would be misunderstood in other parts of the world.
4. Describe how you feel when a person whom you just met is standing in your intimate zone. What do you do about it? What are your options?

Reinforcement Exercises

The following suggestions are activities you can do to reinforce the interpersonal communication techniques in this chapter. You may want to adapt them to the Action Plan you will develop next, or try them independently.

1. Watch a talk show on television and observe how the host and guests are communicating. Is the host actively listening to the guest's problems? Are the guests actively listening? Is anyone attempting to clarify the messages using the clarity-enhancing techniques outlined in the chapter?
2. The next time a friend shares a problem with you, apply your active listening skills. Attend, ask open-ended questions, and paraphrase without trying to provide a solution or talk about one of your own experiences. When you think you really understand how your friend perceives and feels about the problem, paraphrase your understanding and ask whether you have a complete understanding. When you receive an affirmative response, go ahead and share your own reactions or advice, but not before. Afterwards think about what you learned about your interpersonal communication skills from this exercise.

Summary Checklist

Take a few minutes to reflect on your performance and look over others' ratings of your skill. Assess yourself on each of the key learning behaviours. Make a check (√) next to those behaviours on which you need improvement.

_____ Identify and avoid communication barriers.

1. Different frames of reference.
2. Not recognizing semantic differences.
3. Value judgments.
4. Selective listening.
5. Inappropriate filtering.
6. Distrust.

_____ Send clear, understandable messages.

1. Use multiple channels.
2. Be complete and specific.
3. Claim messages as your own.
4. Be congruent.
5. Simplify language.

_____Develop credibility.
> 1. Demonstrate expertise.
> 2. Be reliable.
> 3. Be supportive of others.

_____ Actively listen.
> 1. Paraphrase to test your understanding.
> 2. Use nonverbal signals.
> 3. Ask clarifying questions.

_____ Be aware of the nonverbal signals of others.
> 1. Be conscious of visual components like eye movements, gestures, and facial expressions in yourself and others.
> 2. Listen for vocal intonations.
> 3. Observe spatial arrangements.

_____ Give appropriate feedback.
> 1. Specifically describe actions.
> 2. Avoid being judgmental or threatening.
> 3. Include only things the receiver can do something about.

_____ Adapt to style, gender, and cultural diversity.
> 1. Assume differences.
> 2. Empathize.
> 3. Treat interpretations as guesses.

_____ Solicit meaningful feedback.
> 1. Seek examples.
> 2. Avoid being defensive.
> 3. Ask for definitions.
> 4. Check out assumptions.
> 5. Ask clarifying questions.

Action Plan

1. Which interpersonal communication behaviour do I most want to improve? (See Summary Checklist.)
2. Why? What will be my payoff?
3. What potential obstacles stand in my way?
4. What are the specific things I will do to improve? (For examples, see the Reinforcement Exercises.)
5. When will I do them?
6. How and when will I measure my success?

CHAPTER 6

Valuing Diversity

Learning Objectives

After completing this chapter, you should be able to:

- Encourage and support diversity to meet organizational needs.
- Be creative and flexible in dealing with difficulties faced by diverse employees.
- Be accountable by recruiting broadly and selecting employees fairly.
- Assist diverse employees through training and orientation.
- Break down barriers standing in the way of appreciating diversity.

Self-Assessment Exercise

Complete the following self-assessment exercise to determine your instincts and knowledge about workplace diversity. Respond as candidly as possible to the statements. Describe your level of agreement with each statement by circling the number in the appropriate column according to the following scale.

Strongly Agree 1	Agree 2	No Opinion 3	Disagree 4	Strongly Disagree 5
1. Only a minority of Fortune 500 firms say they are implementing initiatives to manage diversity.		1 2 3 4 5		
2. Prejudice and stereotyping are so ingrained in our cultural makeup that an individual can do little about them.		1 2 3 4 5		
3. Homogeneous groups are more likely to come up with more ideas than diverse groups.		1 2 3 4 5		
4. Mental speed slows down and performance of many complex tasks decreases steadily as people age.		1 2 3 4 5		
5. Employees, no matter what their culture, will work hard if they're shown that it's in their own self-interest.		1 2 3 4 5		
6. Having a diverse workforce brings many advantages but few problems.		1 2 3 4 5		
7. Firms should seek diversity principally to get the government off their backs.		1 2 3 4 5		

Strongly Agree 1	Agree 2	No Opinion 3	Disagree 4	Strongly Disagree 5

8. Because of the growing importance of world trade, firms are finding it increasingly necessary to teach foreigners about Canada's culture. 1 2 3 4 5

9. If minority employees adapt to the dominant organizational culture, then diversity is assured. 1 2 3 4 5

10. Diversity is largely in the hands of the individual manager, not the organization's top leaders. 1 2 3 4 5

SCORING Add the numbers you have circled to obtain your total score.

INTERPRETATION

40–50	You have excellent instincts about the role of diversity in the workplace.
30–39	You show average or better awareness of diversity issues.
20–29	You have some sense of diversity's place, but you need to increase your knowledge.
0–19	You definitely need to bolster your knowledge and scrutinize your instincts before getting involved in diversity issues.

Concepts

- Miyako, a person of Japanese origin, performed well as part of a team that assembled semiconductors. She was quick, attentive to detail, and got along well with group members, but when rewarded with a supervisory job, she seemed almost to change personalities. She became withdrawn and reluctant to take responsibility. You wonder: *What did I do wrong?*

- Charles was the firm's premier drill-press operator for 20 years. He knew his job and did it masterfully, coming and going on a schedule he largely devised and asking for nothing more than a paycheque and a yearly raise. Mildred, an equally skilled drill-press operator, replaced him, but she complained of "isolation," "lack of feedback," and "not feeling like an integral part of the operation." You want women and minorities to get ahead, but you find yourself asking: *Why can't they be like the old-timers?*

- You appointed two teams to come up with ways to sell more bread products. The first team—consisting of exceptionally able supervisors and favourite rank-and-filers— came up with warmed-over versions of old ideas, such as trying to break into the school market, special holiday breads, and a line of "natural," whole-grain products. The other group, however, comprising more recent hires who had complained generally about lack of input, blew you away when it suggested *pav* and *poyee* (a type of brown bread) as well as other types of traditional breads from the regions of India. This group targeted the growing Indian population that was not really served in your area. You scratched your head and pondered: *Do my best people have a blind spot? How can I give more responsibility to the newcomers without alienating my most trusted associates?*

Understanding and managing people who are similar to us is challenging—but understanding and managing those *who are dissimilar from us and from each other* can be even tougher. As the workplace becomes more diverse and as business becomes more global, managers can no longer assume that all employees want the same thing, will act in the same manner, and can be managed the same way. Instead, managers must understand how cultural diversity affects the expectations and behaviour of everyone in the organization.

What Is Diversity?

Diversity is not a synonym for equal employment opportunity, nor is it another word for affirmative action, though either or both of those may aid diversity. Instead, diversity refers to the vast array of physical and cultural differences that constitute the spectrum of human differences.

Achieving workforce diversity means hiring and including people with different human qualities, such as age, ethnicity, gender, and race, from various cultural groups. It is important to remember that diversity includes everyone, not just racial or ethnic minorities.[1]

Six core dimensions of diversity form the inside wheel of Exhibit 6-1. The inherent differences of age, ethnic heritage, gender, mental/physical abilities, race, and sexual orientation have impact throughout a person's life. These fixed dimensions shape individuals' self-image and perspective of the world.

The outside wheel in Exhibit 6-1 represents secondary dimensions that can be acquired or changed throughout one's lifetime. They have less impact than the core dimensions but still influence how people think of themselves and how others perceive them. Secondary dimensions such as work style, communication style, and educational or skill level are particularly relevant in the organizational setting. The challenge for managers is to recognize that each person can bring value and strengths to the workplace based on his or her own unique combination of diversity characteristics.[2]

Exhibit 6-1 The Diversity Wheel

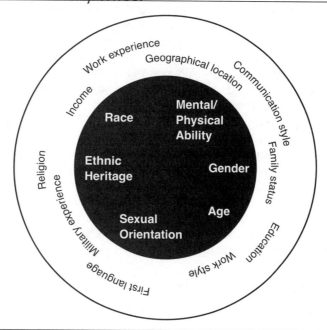

Source: M. Loden, *Implementing Diversity* (Homewood, IL: Irwin, 1996) 14. Used with permission. © Irwin Co. Reprinted by permission of the McGraw-Hill Companies.

The challenge of managing this increasingly diverse workforce is to provide an inclusive workplace where differences are recognized and valued—and where, as a result, productivity is fostered. That's easier said than done. And diversity, if it's not managed well, can cause distrust, communication problems, and even resistance to authority.

Old Versus New

Less than 25 years ago, North American organizations were peopled by a clear majority of male Euro-Americans. Since then, the percentages of males and of employees with European origins have shrunk and will continue to shrink.

The historical approach to managing diversity was to expect minorities to adapt so they blended into the organization's dominant culture. But now few minority employees feel as though they have to "play it safe" by hiding their differences. Although many managers haven't had much pressure to adapt to diversity in the past, they certainly are challenged to do so today. If managers fail to accept and promote diversity as a valuable corporate asset, they may pay the price of decreased work effort and low performance.[3]

The globalization of business also is bringing a cross-cultural mandate. With more businesses selling and/or manufacturing more products and services abroad, managers increasingly see the need to relate to their foreign customers, including the need to have managers and salespeople who can understand overseas customers.

Workers who believe their differences are not merely tolerated but valued by their employer are likely to be more loyal, productive, and committed. Further, a firm with a reputation for providing opportunities will have a competitive advantage in the labour market and will be sought out by the most qualified employees. FedEx, for instance, not only makes it a point to show in its television ads the diversity of its workforce, but it prescreens each of its television ads on an in-house cable television system and solicits feedback from its 90 000 employees.[4]

What's more, just as women and minorities may prefer to work for an employer who values diversity, so may they prefer to patronize such organizations. Minorities now control billions of consumer dollars, and a multicultural workforce can provide a company with greater knowledge of the preference of shoppers.

Because people with different backgrounds often come with different perspectives, work-team diversity promotes creativity and innovation.[5] Effectively managed, such teams come up with more options and create more solutions than do homogeneous groups. Remember the third example at the beginning of this chapter about the new, more diverse group that came up with more creative ideas to sell more bread products to the expanding Indian population.

A diverse workforce also enhances organizational flexibility. Successfully managing diversity requires a corporate culture that tolerates many different styles and approaches. Such a culture tends to enable organizations to become more free-ranging in other areas such as manufacturing or marketing.

So the goal of diversity is not diversity for its own sake. Rather, it's to bring in new points of view and ideas. For example, a culturally diverse group that designs a marketing campaign for a new product likely can help develop better plans for reaching different cultural market segments.

Canadian Legal Requirements[6]

A brief overview of Canadian legislation and its intent is presented here.

EQUALITY

Employment (labour) standards legislation is present in the federal jurisdiction and every province and territory. These laws establish minimum employee entitlements and set a limit on the maximum number of hours employees are permitted to work each day or week. In most jurisdictions, they also require equality in the pay received by men and women performing similar work.

EQUAL OPPORTUNITY

Equal opportunity legislation makes it illegal to discriminate, even unintentionally, against various groups. Reactive in nature, since it is complaints-driven, the focus of such legislation is on the types of acts in which employers should *not* engage. Legislation in this category includes:

1. *The Charter of Rights and Freedoms*—federal legislation that is the cornerstone of equal opportunity.

2. *Human rights legislation*, which is present in every Canadian province and territory. It prohibits discrimination in all areas, terms, and conditions of employment on the basis of such characteristics as race, colour, national or ethnic origin, and sex.

EQUITY

Equity legislation is aimed at hastening the pace of change for certain groups that, historically, have been disadvantaged in employment. Such laws fall into two categories:

1. *Employment equity laws*, which require employers to be proactive in hiring and promoting qualified individuals from four designated groups: women, visible minorities, Aboriginal people, and persons with disabilities.

2. *Pay equity legislation*, which is one component of employment equity but much narrower in focus. It is aimed at reducing the differences in pay between male-dominated and female-dominated job classes caused by the undervaluing of work traditionally performed by women.

Specific applications of the legislation may be found in other chapters. For example, Chapter 13, Identifying and Hiring Employees, deals with the implications of the legislation for recruitment and selection. Next, issues beyond legal compliance are discussed.

How Organizations Can Promote Diversity

There are issues that organizations face beyond complying with the legal requirements of diversity. Overall, three challenges exist for organizations and their managers: a fairness and justice challenge, a decision-making and performance challenge, and a flexibility challenge. Let us explore the nature of these challenges in greater depth. Then we will look at how managers can meet those challenges.

FAIRNESS AND JUSTICE

How can you allocate jobs, promotions, and rewards in a way that honours diversity without making anyone feel cheated? This challenge is difficult because seniority plays a large role in promotions and rewards—and many minorities may be recent hires. On the other hand, rectifying this imbalance by actively recruiting and promoting women and minorities reduces the job prospects for the remainder of the workforce. That practice, in turn, could adversely affect performance and morale.

DECISION MAKING AND PERFORMANCE

Many organizations have found that tapping into diversity reveals new ways of viewing traditional problems. The tapping-in process, however, is not automatic. Research has shown that many supervisors do not know how to manage and lead diverse work groups. Further, supervisors are often unsure how to communicate with employees with different cultural backgrounds and sometimes even different languages.[7]

FLEXIBILITY

Being sensitive to the needs of different kinds of employees is the first step to flexibility. The second step is developing flexible employment approaches. Such approaches can include benefit packages customized to fit needs of different groups, such as single workers with no children, same-sex partners in long-term committed relationships, and workers caring for aged parents. Flexibility may entail flextime and other scheduling options, such as job sharing, that give workers input into the length and scheduling of their work weeks. Further, it could mean designing jobs and buildings to be sensitive to the special needs of disabled workers (and customers), establishing informal networks among minority employees to provide social support, and creating programs to encourage feedback to employees about their personal styles of dealing with minorities.

Diversity's Importance to Managers

If the percentage of women and minority workers is increasing and the skills and talents of such workers aren't being fully utilized, the organization will suffer a clear loss of potential productivity. Thus, managing a diverse workforce has quickly become a core competency for effective managers. The overall challenge is to harness the wealth of differences, but that is a sensitive, potentially volatile, and sometimes uncomfortable task.

Simply sending employees to diversity training does not guarantee that diversity will be valued. In fact, one study of 785 human resources professionals revealed that both the adoption and success of diversity training was strongly related to top management's support for the program.[8] Also affecting the success of diversity training was whether attendance was mandatory for all managers, whether a long-term evaluation of results was conducted, and whether managers were rewarded for increasing diversity.

What Can the Individual Manager Do?

Diversity issues for managers are many. They include issues such as coping with employees' unfamiliarity with English; learning which rewards are valued by different ethnic groups; developing career development programs that fit the skills, needs, and values of different individuals and groups; and rewarding others for effectively recruiting, hiring, and training a diverse workforce. However, some positive steps are available to managers at every level to improve their handling of diversity issues.

FULLY ACCEPT DIVERSITY

Yes, it is true that diversity management probably won't be effective unless top management, by word and action, endorses it, but it's also true that acceptance of the principle of multiculturalism starts with the individual.

Managers should look into their hearts and minds to root out prejudice, even if it's latent. They must accept the value of diversity for its own sake—not just because diversity will increase employee creativity, make workers more contented, and maybe even cut costs, and not just because to do so will accredit the manager as a "team player." Valuing diversity is important because it is the right thing to do. Equally important, managers must reflect this acceptance in what they say and do.

Managers who truly want to promote diversity must shape organizational culture to allow diversity to flourish. As you will learn more about in Chapter 17, Diagnosing and Modifying Organizational Culture, the behaviour of managers is a key determinant of organizational culture. A manager who is committed to the advantages that diversity can bring to the organization and the world at large cannot just go through the motions, but needs to truly believe as well as act.

RECRUIT BROADLY

Managers need to cast their nets widely to get a diverse applicant pool. It's easier to rely on current employee referrals as a source of job applicants. But that tends to produce candidates who are similar to the present staff, as will be explained in greater detail in Chapter 13, Identifying and Hiring Employees. Some nontraditional sources are women's job networks, over-fifty clubs, urban job banks, training centres for the disabled, ethnic newspapers, and gay-rights organizations.

SELECT FAIRLY

Once a manager has a diverse group of applicants, he or she must ensure that the selection process doesn't discriminate. As you will see in Chapter 13, Identifying and Hiring Employees, assessments used for selection are often culturally biased. As a result, people from different cultures, minorities, or even those who are functionally illiterate may not understand the meaning of test questions, causing them to be rejected as candidates for jobs they actually could perform well.

One way to make assessments valid for diverse employees is to use job-specific tests. For example, a firm that is hiring word-processing people may give applicants a timed test to measure their typing speed and accuracy. Such tests would measure the specific skills, not subjective personal characteristics.

PROVIDE ORIENTATION AND TRAINING

Making the transition from an outsider to an insider is difficult for everyone but may be especially challenging for women and minorities. Thus, many organizations have programs to create opportunities for diverse groups and train them to succeed. They may have support groups within the organization to give emotional support and/or career guidance. Others may encourage mentoring in which a trusted coach or advisor is teamed up with minority employees, teaching them the cultural values of the organization, and coaching them on how to make the most of their chances for advancement. Many firms now require their managers to serve as mentors.

Because diversity means two-way understanding, many organizations provide special workshops to raise diversity awareness among current employees as well as offering programs for new employees.

STRIVE TO BE FLEXIBLE

With dual-career households now so common, work/family programs seek to give employees flexibility in balancing their home and work demands. Some of the most common forms of these include flextime, the compressed work week, job sharing, and telecommuting, all of which are discussed in detail in Chapter 12, Designing Work. Another resource is *The Manager's Work–Family Toolkit,* published by the Ottawa-based

Vanier Institute of the Family. It is an excellent guide to assist organizations' move toward more work/family policies and programs.[9]

SEEK TO MOTIVATE INDIVIDUALLY

Motivating is one of a manager's key tasks, and motivating a diverse workforce requires special efforts because not everyone has the same needs and goals. For instance, studies tell us that men generally place more importance on having autonomy in their jobs than women do.[10] On the other hand, women are more likely to value the opportunity to learn, good interpersonal relations, and convenient work hours. Thus, managers need to recognize that what motivates a single mother with two young children and who is working full-time to support her family may be different from the needs of a young, single, part-time employee, or an older employee who's only working to supplement his or her retirement income.

Most of our knowledge of motivation is based on studies by North American researchers on North American workers. Consequently, the underlying belief that most people work to help promote their own well-being and get ahead may be at odds with people in more collectivist countries, such as Venezuela, Singapore, Japan, and Mexico, where the link to the organization is the individual's loyalty to the organization or to society rather than to his or her self-interest.[11] Thus, employees in or from collectivist cultures may be more receptive to team-based job design, group goals, and group performance evaluations. Reliance on the fear of being fired in such cultures is also likely to be less effective because of the belief that the fired person will be taken care of by extended family, friends, or community.

One study, for example, showed that Japanese-owned *maquiladoras* (foreign-owned businesses in Mexican border towns) were better able to motivate and retain employees than the U.S.-owned *maquiladoras*.[12] Researchers credited the Japanese success to the similarity between the Japanese and Mexican cultures. U.S. firms expected their Mexican workers to take individual initiative and get the job done at all costs. The Japanese culture, however, with its emphasis on teamwork and avoiding uncertainty, was a better fit with the Mexican workers, who were easier to train in the structured Japanese ways.

As differences in the employee pool continue, managers will need to study socialization much more closely. Studying the ethnic background and national cultures of workers will be necessary.

REINFORCE EMPLOYEE DIFFERENCES

Managers should encourage individuals to value and promote diverse views, creating traditions and ceremonies that celebrate diversity.

In these ways and others, a manager may accentuate the positives of diversity. However, it's misleading to claim that having employees from different backgrounds only provides benefits.

Diversity also can create a lack of cohesiveness. Because of the lack of similarity in language, culture, and/or experience, diverse groups are often less tightly knit than homogenous groups. Mistrust, miscommunication, stress, and attitudinal differences reduce cohesiveness, which in turn can lessen productivity.

Perhaps the most common negative effect is communication problems, including misunderstanding, inaccuracies, inefficiencies, and slowness. Group members may assume they interpret things similarly when actually they do not, or they may disagree because of their different frames of reference.[13] Managers need to accept the likelihood of these side effects while working hard to keep them at a minimum.

Concept Quiz

Complete the following true–false quiz by circling the correct answers. Answers are at the end of the quiz. After marking your answers, remember to go back and check your understanding of any answers you missed.

True or False	1.	If an organization complies with government legislation, then it's doing all it needs to do on diversity.
True or False	2.	Six core dimensions of diversity are age, ethnic heritage, gender, mental/physical abilities, race, and sexual orientation.
True or False	3.	The percentages of males and of employees with European origins in the workplace are growing and will continue to grow.
True or False	4.	To manage diversity, expect people who are different to hide their differences or adapt to the dominant culture.
True or False	5.	Workers whose differences are not merely tolerated but valued are likely to become more loyal and productive employees.
True or False	6.	A diverse workforce enhances an organization's flexibility.
True or False	7.	Human rights legislation has eliminated prejudice from the workplace.
True or False	8.	The success of a diversity training program depends strongly on the degree of support from top management.
True or False	9.	One way to make tests more valid for diverse employees is to make them job-specific rather than general aptitude or knowledge tests.
True or False	10.	Most of our knowledge of motivation is based on studies by North American researchers on North American workers, and thus may not be valid for those from other cultures.

Answers (1) False; (2) True; (3) False; (4) False; (5) True; (6) True; (7) False; (8) True; (9) True; (10) True

Behavioural Checklist

The following behaviours are important to managing a diverse workforce. Use them when evaluating your skills and those of others.

Effective Managers of Diversity:

- Encourage and support diversity.
- Respond to diversity difficulties with creativity and flexibility.
- Recruit broadly and select fairly.
- Provide diverse employees with orientation and training.
- Sensitize mainstream employees to diversity issues.
- Motivate people based on their unique individual needs.
- Reinforce the value of employee differences.

Modelling Exercise
A Problematic Promotion

DIRECTIONS The entire class should read the descriptions of the four actors and the following situation. Then four students should be selected to play the roles of Sam, Charlotte,

Harry, and Edgar. Role-players should then read their assigned roles. They should not read the other roles. The rest of the class should read all four roles and review the Observer's Rating Sheet in preparation for observing and critiquing them.

TIME 30 minutes.

ACTORS Sam, an experienced, able technician, who has been with Acme Medical Products for three years—a manager at his previous place of employment, he's one of the few minority group persons working for this company in a technical position; Edgar, a well-regarded technician, who has been with the company for 10 years and aspires to management; Charlotte, the division vice-president, who is committed to seeing more women and minorities progress at the firm; Harry, the department head, who must choose between Sam and Edgar.

SITUATION Sam was hired three years ago at the behest of Charlotte, who thinks, with some justification, that Acme's record of hiring and promoting minorities is poor. In fact, the company was the object of a Canadian Human Rights Commission action several years ago, though the action was settled by the higher-ups before it garnered too much publicity. Due to a reorganization, a new manager's spot has been created. The question is: Who should get it? Charlotte and Harry have a meeting set to discuss the candidates, who at this point have been narrowed to Sam and Edgar. After the meeting, Charlotte and Harry will jointly interview the two contenders, then discuss the results between themselves and try to pick the new manager.

SAM'S ROLE You left your previous employer, where you were a manager, in hopes that you could achieve a similar position with Acme, a larger, more prestigious, and better-paying firm. You were not promised a managerial spot, but certainly you made your aims known in the job interviews and those who hired you didn't discourage you from thinking you had a good shot. It has been three years now, and you had hoped you would have been promoted before now. This new spot ought to have your name on it. If it does not, you will be forced to conclude that you made a mistake in joining Acme. You will probably leave if that is the case, though you are not sure whether you should make that threat at today's interview.

CHARLOTTE'S ROLE Being a company officer, you know a lot about Acme. You know that the company historically has not done much to attract and reward minorities, but the Canadian Human Rights Commission complaint a few years back did put fear into the top ranks of the firm. Maybe they are not pursuing minorities for the right reason, but at least they are pursuing them. For example, improving the numbers and positions of minorities is a key element of your assigned management objectives. So, if Sam and others like him get ahead, you will get more money. That is good, but that is not your primary motivation. You genuinely want to see a multiethnic, multicultural workforce because, well, the world is multiethnic and multicultural. You feel the firm must approximate the makeup of its customers if it is going to sell to them effectively. What is more, it is the right thing to do. Sam is a good man, respected by nearly everyone. You are unlikely to get a better minority candidate. You have always tried to empower Harry and let him make decisions in his department. In this case, however, he may not understand the "big picture" the way you do, and you may have to overrule him.

EDGAR'S ROLE You have been with the company for 10 years. You are the senior technician in this department, and you are long overdue for a promotion. This manager's slot rightfully ought to be yours. Sam is a good man, but he is a johnny-come-lately compared to you. You have worked hard for a decade, enduring sometimes cruel and capricious bosses. You gave up your vacation plans one year to meet a pressing deadline. You have taken special courses to improve your skills. You have made a point of getting along with everyone. You cannot think of a single enemy in the department, remarkable in a company known for the intensity of its infighting.

If the executives turn you down, you'll have no choice but to go elsewhere—and you think a lot of the other technicians will follow you out the door. In today's interview you hope to show Charlotte and Harry how promoting you is a no-risk move that not only is the right thing to do but will help morale throughout the department.

HARRY'S ROLE You feel caught in the middle. You support diversity, but you do have an investment in making this department the best it can be. Sam is probably every bit the technician that Edgar is, but Edgar has paid his dues; Sam has not. You suspect Charlotte favours Sam because of some things she has said. But if she forces the issue and orders you to promote Sam, you feel sure there will be a rank-and-file rebellion. She does not realize how tenuous morale is. Edgar is highly competent and well liked, and he has earned his stripes. How can anyone beat those credentials?

Observer's Rating Sheet

During the dialogue, observers should note closely how Charlotte and Harry discuss the issues. What points do they make and what questions do they pose? Be prepared to suggest additional queries and draw conclusions about what arguments the pair makes. Notice what questions they ask of the two candidates and how the candidates respond.

Using the following scale, rate Charlotte's and Harry's application of techniques discussed in this chapter. Also write in comments that will help explain your feedback.

1 Unsatisfactory	2 Weak	3 Adequate	4 Good	5 Outstanding

Overall, how well did Charlotte:

	Rating	Comments
■ Encourage and support diversity	_____	
■ Creatively respond to diversity difficulties	_____	
■ Orient and train diverse employees	_____	
■ Reinforce the value of employee differences	_____	
■ Sensitize employees to diversity issues	_____	
■ Motivate people based on unique needs	_____	

Overall, how well did Harry:

	Rating	Comments
■ Encourage and support diversity	_____	
■ Creatively respond to diversity difficulties	_____	
■ Orient and train diverse employees	_____	
■ Reinforce the value of employee differences	_____	
■ Sensitize employees to diversity issues	_____	
■ Motivate people based on unique needs	_____	

DEBRIEFING At the completion of the exercise provide the role-players with feedback from your observations. Then discuss the following questions as a class:

1. What appeared to be the motivations of each of the four players based on the behaviours you observed?
2. How did those motivations reveal themselves in the discussions?
3. What was not discussed?
4. Whom would you pick for manager? Why?
5. What are the possible repercussions of your decision? How would you deal with them?

Group Exercises

In the following three exercises you will be asked to show an understanding of diversity issues. The first exercise involves looking at how prejudices are formed, the second concerns being flexible about employees' needs, and the third entails choosing a work team.

Group Exercise 1: Choosing Music[14]

STEP 1 Imagine that you are travelling in a rental car in a city you have never visited before. You face an hour-long drive on an uncrowded highway before you reach your destination. You decide that you would like to listen to the car radio while making the trip.

The rental car has four radio-selection buttons, each with a preset station. Each button plays a different type of music. Button A plays country music, B plays rock, C plays classical, and D plays jazz.

To which type would you choose to listen for the duration of the trip? (Assume you want to relax and stick with one station. You don't want to bother with switching around among stations.)

STEP 2 Form four groups, depending on the type of music chosen. In each group, debate the following questions and appoint a spokesperson from within the group to report your answers to the class.

QUESTIONS

1. What are your feelings about each of the other three sorts of music?
2. What words would you use to describe people who like to listen to each of the other three forms of music? Specify for each type.
3. Have you listened to enough of the other three types of music to form a valid conclusion about the kinds of people they attract? Why or why not?

STEP 3 Have each spokesperson report the responses of his/her group to the questions in Step 2.

STEP 4 Reconvene as a class and discuss the following questions.

1. What was the purpose of this exercise?
2. What did you notice about the words used to describe the other groups?
3. Upon what sorts of data do you think these images were based?
4. What terms do we normally use to describe such generalized perceptions of other groups?
5. What could be some of the consequences of these perceptions?
6. What parallels are there to other kinds of group differences, such as race, gender, culture, ethnicity, nationality, age, and so on?

7. If an organization was interested in helping employees to value music lovers in the other three genres, what might it do?

Group Exercise 2: Motivation in Action[15]

Consider the following descriptions of three employees working in the same organization. Then individually write down your answers to the questions that follow.

MARVIN He is 55 years old, a college graduate, and a vice-president of the firm. His parents came to Canada from Poland. His two children are married, and Marvin is a grandfather. He lives in a condo with his wife, who does volunteer work and is active in their church. Marvin is healthy and likes to play golf and handball.

KRISHAN She is 30 years old, and traces her roots to India. She is a clerical worker and a single parent with two children under the age of 10. She completed high school after moving to Canada, and she has begun to attend evening classes at a local community college. She is a practising Hindu. Although her health is excellent, one of her children has a severe learning disability.

YURI A recent immigrant from one of the former Soviet republics, he is 42 and speaks halting, heavily accented English. He earned an engineering degree overseas but, being unlicensed in Canada, he is employed as a parts clerk. He is unmarried and has no children but sends much of his paycheque to relatives back in Eastern Europe. A few others from his country also work at your firm or in your city.

Based on this information, answer the following questions:

1. What do you expect the goals and priorities of each of those employees to be?

Marvin: _____

_____

Krishan: _____

_____

Yuri: _____

_____

2. Indicate which employee(s) you think would be motivated by the following additional benefits:

a. on-site daycare _____

b. fitness centre _____

c. tuition reimbursement _____

d. executive bonus plan _____

e. rigorous affirmative-action plan _____

f. enhanced retirement benefits _____

g. supervisory training _____

h. financial aid for special education _____

i. corporate country club membership _____

j. having a mentor _____

k. being a mentor _____

l. English classes _____

m. more time off _____

n. flextime _____

o. job sharing _____

3. Form groups of five to six members and share your answers. Discuss your differences and their implications for managing diversity.

4. Groups share with the entire class what they learned from their discussions.

Group Exercise 3: How Homogeneous Should a Diverse Group Be?

INSTRUCTIONS Split into groups of three or four members. Read the situation. Pick two class members to come to the front of the class and read the following conversation between Fred and Sally as if they were actually having the discussion. Then answer the questions in your groups. Finally, compare answers among the groups and discuss their implications for diversity.

SITUATION You are the CEO, and you think the firm's diversity practices need to be reviewed. It has been a long time since they were looked at, so you assign Fred and Sally, two senior supervisors, to decide how to overhaul the firm's practices. Fred and Sally think the task would be best handled by a team. When they meet to decide the composition of the team, the following discussion takes place.

Fred   Well, the big boss wants this review done, so I guess we need to form a committee. That shouldn't be hard. Then it's the committee's problem, not ours.

Sally   True, but it's important that we get the right people on the panel. Otherwise, we're just wasting everyone's time. Whom do you think should be on it?

Fred   How 'bout Schultz over in Accounting. He's a good guy, and he did a good job when we put him on the committee to oversee the vending machines in the cafeteria.

Sally   Yeah, but this is more important and more difficult than that. What does Schultz know about diversity?

Fred   What does anybody know about diversity? It's just a numbers game anyway. I say: Schultz is one.

Sally   Okay, but we're going to need a lot of minorities, right?

Fred   Why? They know about being black or Asian or whatever, but do they know any more about diversity in general than, say, you or me?

Sally   Well, maybe not individually, but in aggregate they're going to be more sensitive to diversity issues. You wouldn't set up a panel to study women's issues and have it be all men, would you?

Fred	I suppose not, though (laughing) I bet that would produce some interesting ideas. But, seriously, let's put Tom Warner on this diversity committee, too.
Sally	Another old white guy?
Fred	Old and white but also experienced, capable, and loyal. Wouldn't you agree?
Sally	Of course. But what's our purpose? To get some fresh eyes looking at this program, not just to ratify the status quo. We need people like Consuelo Martinez, Le Ly Thuc, and Samuel Cooper, that black man in the machine shop.
Fred	They barely have five years' seniority between them. They have no clout and only modest leadership ability. Who's going to chair this thing, anyway? You cannot pick some newcomer like Consuelo Martinez or Samuel Cooper and have them head a committee that has heavyweights on it like Warner or Schultz.
Sally	(Sharply) Well, we don't need alleged heavyweights like Warner and Schultz, either. They may be experienced but they would be way out of their element on a committee like this. In fact, I think the panel should be composed entirely of women and minorities. Seniority doesn't have anything to do with it. What we need are fresh ideas, not someone with a zillion years of experience who wouldn't know innovation if it smacked them in the nose.
Fred	No way! You and I are going to be held responsible for creating this group and, by extension, for its product. I don't want to be associated with this effort if it's going to be staffed solely by employees who lack any institutional memory and any real respect from the rank and file. I say pick five veterans whom we know will do a good job. Whether they're white, black, or green, who cares? We need competence, not a formula.
Sally	Absolutely not. We need minorities because that's what diversity is all about. Let's pick a full team from among the best and the brightest of our people of colour. They are the ones affected by diversity policies. And they are the ones most sensitive to diversity issues. Any committee with white males will totally lack credibility.
Fred	You're impossible, Sally. And we're at an impasse. We're going to need to kick this back up to the CEO.

QUESTIONS FOR DISCUSSION

1. Who is correct: Fred? Sally? Both? Neither?
2. If Fred is right and the most highly qualified persons are nonminorities, should they be included?
3. Should white males comprise the entire committee? Is it proper to have a diversity committee without minority members?
4. If Sally is correct and the committee is staffed by minorities only, is that a diverse committee? Is it proper to have a diversity committee without white males?
5. What do you as CEO decide?

Application Questions

1. Does your organization (employer or school) show signs of bias against certain groups of people? What is your first "gut" response to that question? Why do you feel this way?
2. How might a manager's role for promoting diversity change as the organization changes by becoming more diverse?
3. How can more diversity contribute to greater creativity and better problem solving?

4. What diversity programs have you observed at school or work? Were they effective? Why or why not?

5. What steps could be taken to change these practices? Do you think your organization would be willing to do so?

Reinforcement Exercise

The following are suggested activities for enhancing your awareness and reinforcing the techniques described in this chapter for valuing diversity. You may want to adapt them to the Action Plan you will develop next, or try them independently.

1. Ask your minority friends what kinds of biases they perceive in school or in the workplace. Do you agree with their assessments? Even if you think they are wrong or exaggerate the problem, try to imagine yourself in their role.

2. Think of places where you have worked. Were minorities expected to adapt to that culture? Did the employer make any concessions to diversity? If so, what were those efforts? Were the minority employees content? If not, could their discontent have been reduced by more sensitivity by management?

3. Use the following checklist to gather the information indicated.[16] Use your existing knowledge of the organization or ask someone who might know. (If you do ask others, explain to them that it is for a class project.)

   Does your organization...

   _____ Have signs and manuals in English only, although several employees are more comfortable in other languages?

   _____ Ignore important holidays celebrated by people of certain cultures, such as Yom Kippur, Cinco de Mayo, or Chinese New Year?

   _____ Limit social events to married people?

   _____ Restrict training opportunities available to women and minorities?

   _____ Emphasize male-oriented sporting events, such as football?

   _____ Limit its recruitment efforts to colleges and universities with predominantly white students?

   _____ Hire predominantly females for secretarial and clerical positions?

   _____ Discourage styles of dress that express varied cultural and ethnic backgrounds?

4. What items in the preceding checklist, if any, did you find that may represent bias?

5. What steps could be taken to change the practices you cite in question 4? Do you think your organization would be willing to do so?

Summary Checklist

Take a few minutes to reflect on your performance in the preceding exercises. Assess yourself as to how your analysis compared to other students (and if you were an actor in the role-play, how others rated your skill). Make a check (√) next to those behaviours you may need to improve.

_____ Encourage and support diversity.

   1. Examine your own prejudices.

   2. Promote diversity for its own sake.

_____ Recruit broadly.

   1. Seek applicants from nontraditional sources.

   2. Build relationships with minority organizations.

_____ Select fairly.
  1. Use performance-related tests.
  2. Focus on specific skills, not personal characteristics.

_____ Provide diverse employees with orientation and training.
  1. Encourage support groups.
  2. Consider mentoring.
  3. Meet regularly with minority groups or representatives.

_____ Sensitize mainstream employees to diversity issues.
  1. Offer diversity awareness training.
  2. Reward those who promote diversity.

_____ Respond to diversity difficulties with creativity and flexibility.
  1. Be open to alternative work schedules.
  2. Establish work/family programs.

_____ Motivate people based on their unique individual needs.
  1. Learn about ethnic backgrounds and national cultures.
  2. Talk to workers about their goals.
  3. Consider differences when making assignments.

_____ Reinforce the value of employee differences.
  1. Encourage employees to value and promote diverse views.
  2. Create traditions and ceremonies that honour diversity.

Action Plan

1. How can I improve my sensitivity to diversity issues?
2. What will be the payoff for doing so?
3. What potential obstacles stand in my way?
4. What are the specific things I will do to improve my sensitivity?
5. When will I do them?
6. How will I measure my improvement?

CHAPTER 7
Managing Conflict

Learning Objectives

After completing this chapter, you should be able to:

- Assess sources of a conflict.
- Modify your conflict management style appropriately.
- Empathize with others in conflicts.
- Deal with emotions.
- Negotiate conflict resolution.
- Stimulate appropriate conflict.
- Implement procedures to manage conflict.

Self-Assessment Exercise

Indicate how often you do the following when you differ with someone by inserting the appropriate number after the statements. Answer as you actually do behave, not as you would like to behave.

5 Usually	4 Quite a bit	3 Sometimes	2 Occasionally	1 Seldom

When I differ with someone:	Points
Set A:	
1. I explore our differences, not backing down, but not imposing my view either.	_____
2. I disagree openly, then invite more discussion about our differences.	_____
3. I look for a mutually satisfactory solution.	_____
4. Rather than let the other person make a decision without my input, I make sure I am heard and also that I hear the other out.	_____
Sum the points for questions 1 through 4 to get your **Set A score** =	_____

5 Usually	4 Quite a bit	3 Sometimes	2 Occasionally	1 Seldom

When I differ with someone: Points

Set B:
5. I agree to a middle ground rather than look for a completely satisfying solution. _____
6. I admit I am half wrong rather than explore our differences. _____
7. I have a reputation for meeting a person halfway. _____
8. I expect to get out about half of what I really want to say. _____

Sum the points for questions 5 through 8 to get your **Set B score** = _____

Set C:
9. I give in totally rather than try to change another's opinion. _____
10. I put aside any controversial aspects of an issue. _____
11. I agree early on, rather than argue about a point. _____
12. I give in as soon as the other party gets emotional about an issue. _____

Sum the points for questions 9 through 12 to get your **Set C score** = _____

Set D:
13. I try to win the other person over. _____
14. I work to come out victorious, no matter what. _____
15. I never back away from a good argument. _____
16. I would rather win than end up compromising. _____

Sum the points for questions 13 through 16 to get your **Set D score** = _____

Set E:
17. I prefer to avoid the other person until the problem is solved. _____
18. I would rather we both lose than risk an emotional confrontation. _____
19. I feel that most differences are not worth worrying about. _____
20. I try to postpone discussing the issue until I can think it through thoroughly. _____

Sum the points for questions 17 through 20 to get your **Set E score** = _____

SCORING AND INTERPRETATION

■ Total your choices for each set of statements, grouped as follows:

Set A (items 1–4): _____
Set B (items 5–8): _____
Set C (items 9–12): _____
Set D (items 13–16): _____
Set E (items 17–20): _____

- Sets A, B, C, D, and E represent the following different conflict resolution strategies:

A = Collaborating	I win, you win.
B = Compromising	Both win some, lose some.
C = Accommodating	I lose, you win.
D = Competing/Forcing	I win, you lose.
E = Avoiding	I lose, you lose.

- Treat each set separately to determine your relative frequency of use.

- A score of 17 or above on any set is high. When you differ with someone you do these things more often than most people.

- Scores of 8 to 16 are moderate. When you differ with someone you behave in these ways the same as most people.

- Scores of 7 or less are considered low. When you differ with someone you behave in these ways less often than most people.

Everyone has a preferred conflict-handling style. High scores in a set indicate the strategies you rely upon or use most often. Scores do not indicate proficiency at using a strategy. The key thing to consider when analyzing your style is whether it is appropriate for the conflict situations you usually encounter with respect to the outcomes you desire. The five styles and their appropriated uses will be explained in the section "*Know the Basic Styles of Handling Conflicts.*"

Source: Adapted from T.J. Von der Embse, *Supervision: Managerial Skills for a New Era* (New York: Macmillian Publishing Co., 1987); and K.W. Thomas and R.H. Kilmann, *Management-of-Differences Exercise* (1971).

Concepts

It is difficult, if not impossible, to think of a relationship of any type that does not encounter disagreements at one time or another. Unless relationships are able to withstand the stress involved in their inevitable conflicts, and manage them productively, they are not likely to endure.[1] Because of inherent characteristics such as scarce resources, interdependence, different goals, and the need for coordination, conflict is a natural phenomenon in organizational life. Consequently, it is not surprising that some organization researchers have concluded that "no skill is more important for organizational effectiveness than the constructive management and resolution of conflict."[2] This chapter provides concepts for understanding and skills for managing conflict productively in both personal and organizational situations.

What Is Conflict?

Conflict is a disagreement between two or more parties (individuals, groups, departments, organizations, countries, etc.) who perceive that they have incompatible concerns. Conflicts exist whenever an action by one party is perceived as preventing or interfering with the goals, needs, or actions of another party. Conflicts can arise due to a variety of organizational experiences, such as incompatible goals, differences in the interpretation of facts, negative feelings, differences of values and philosophies, or disputes over shared resources.[3]

Conflict is natural to organizations and can never be completely eliminated. If not managed properly, however, conflict can be dysfunctional and lead to undesirable consequences such as hostility, lack of cooperation, violence, destroyed relationships, and even company failure. But, when managed effectively, conflict has many beneficial properties. It stimulates creativity, innovation, and change, and can even result in better relationships. If organizations were completely devoid of conflict, they would become apathetic, stagnant, and unresponsive to change. Given this reality, comprehensive conflict management should encompass both conflict stimulation and conflict-resolution techniques.[4] Typically when managers talk about conflict problems they are referring to conflict's dysfunctional effects and they are seeking ways to eliminate them.

What Are the Main Sources of Conflict?

Conflicts do not just magically appear out of thin air. They have causes. Research indicates that while conflicts have varying causes, they can generally be separated into three categories: communication problems, structural design, and personal differences.[5]

COMMUNICATION PROBLEMS

Disagreements frequently arise from semantic difficulties, misunderstandings, poor listening, and noise in the communication channels. People are often quick to assume that most conflicts are caused by lack of communication. In reality, plenty of communication is usually going on during a conflict. The mistake many people make is equating good communication with having others agree with their views; they assume that if others do not accept their position, a communication problem must be at fault.[6] After a closer analysis, what might look like an interpersonal conflict based on poor communication is quite often determined to be a disagreement caused by things such as different role requirements, incompatible goals, or different value systems.

STRUCTURAL DESIGN

When performing the organizing function, management divides up tasks, groups common tasks into departments, sets up a hierarchy of authority to coordinate departments, and establishes rules and regulations to facilitate standardized practices between departments. Exhibit 7-1 illustrates a functional organization chart. This structural differentiation

Exhibit 7-1 Functional Organization Chart

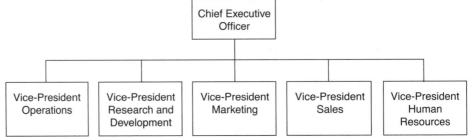

Strengths:
- Lower headquarters–subsidiary conflicts
- Increases international orientation of all managers
- Facilitates coordination within function
- Effective when market demands are similar

Weaknesses:
- Often creates problems in cross-functional coordination
- Slower response to specific market changes
- Ineffective when international market demands differ

Source: Adapted from J.S. Blac and L.W. Porter, *Management* (Upper Saddle River, NJ, Prentice Hall, 1999) 271.

creates interdependence between units and the need to coordinate activities. Unfortunately, integration efforts frequently result in conflict when various units disagree over goal priorities, decision alternatives, performance criteria, and resource allocations. The "goodies" that people want—budgets, promotions, pay increases, additions to staff, office space, influence over decisions, and the like—are scarce resources that must be divvied up. The creation of horizontal units (departments) and vertical levels (the management hierarchy) brings about efficiencies through specialization and coordination, but at the same time produces the potential for structural conflicts.

PERSONAL DIFFERENCES

Conflicts can evolve out of individual idiosyncrasies and personal value systems. The chemistry between some people makes it hard for them to work together. Factors such as cultural background, education, experience, and training mold each individual into a unique personality with a particular set of values and different behavioural styles. The result is people who may be perceived by others as abrasive, untrustworthy, or strange by individuals with different backgrounds. The conflicts created by these types of personal differences are exacerbated when people from different countries or subcultures interact with each other. Stereotypes and prejudice are often the culprits, but ignorance and misunderstanding also create confusing conflicts.

What Are the Key Conflict Management Skills?

If conflict is dysfunctional, what skills and knowledge does a manager need to manage it successfully? Although many of the skills discussed earlier in this book can help—for example, listening, valuing diversity, managing stress, and self-awareness—you need to be able to do a number of specific things to deal effectively with conflicts. The following skills are discussed in the order that they are usually applied in a conflict situation. First, you need to assess the nature of the conflict: what created it, who is involved, what the consequences are, and so on. Second, you need to decide which conflicts to take on and which to avoid. Third, you need to understand the different conflict-handling styles, including your own preferred style. Fourth, it helps to determine the other party's preferred conflict style and empathize with that position. Fifth, you are now ready to determine your objectives, assess your options, and decide on a game plan to achieve the preferred one. Sixth, it is often necessary to deal effectively with the emotional aspects of conflict before a rational solution can be worked out. Seventh, at times you will determine that it is appropriate to negotiate a satisfactory outcome, or eighth, even stimulate conflict to provide optimal long-term results for all involved.

ASSESS THE NATURE OF THE CONFLICT

The best approach to resolving a conflict can quite often be determined by understanding its causes. Consequently, the first, and perhaps most important, thing you need to do is to identify the source of the conflict (e.g., cultural differences, communication problems, structural differences, personal style incompatibilities, and so on).

Next examine the long-term and short-term consequences of the conflict. Is the conflict dysfunctional and hindering the achievement of personal and organizational goals? Is there hostility, decreased communication, negative stereotypes, lack of cooperation? Are any functional consequences of value, which you may want to maintain, such as increased problem awareness, clarification of priorities, personal or organizational learning, or improvements in operating practices? Sometimes you may want to let the conflict just play out. Other times, immediate intervention will be required.

JUDICIOUSLY SELECT THE CONFLICTS YOU TRY TO MANAGE

Not every conflict justifies your attention. Some might not be worth the effort; others might be unmanageable. Although avoidance might appear to be a "cop-out," it can sometimes be the most appropriate response. You can improve your overall managerial effectiveness, and your conflict management skills in particular, by avoiding trivial conflicts. Choose your battles judiciously, saving your efforts for the ones that have serious consequences. Regardless of our desires, reality tells us that some conflicts are unmanageable.[7] When antagonisms are deeply rooted, when one or both parties wish to prolong a conflict, or when emotions run so high that constructive interaction is impossible, your efforts to manage the conflict are unlikely to meet with much success. Do not be lured into the naïve belief that a good manager can resolve every conflict effectively. Some are not worth the effort. Some are outside your realm of influence. Still others may be functional and, as such, are best left alone.

KNOW THE BASIC STYLES OF HANDLING CONFLICTS

Even though most of us have the ability to vary our conflict response according to the situation, each of us has a preferred style for handling conflicts.[8] The Self-Assessment Exercise at the beginning of this chapter can help you identify the conflict-handling style you use the most. You might be able to change your preferred style to suit the context in which a certain conflict exists; however, your basic style indicates how you are *most likely* to behave in most conflict situations.

Managers can draw upon five basic conflict-resolution approaches when attempting to resolve dysfunctional conflicts: avoidance, accommodation, forcing, compromise, and collaboration.[9] The five basic conflict-handling style options are presented graphically in Exhibit 7-2. Each has particular strengths and weaknesses, and no one option is ideal for every situation. You should consider each one a tool in your conflict management toolbox. Even though you might be better at using some tools than others, the skilled manager understands the potential of each tool and knows when each is most effective.

Exhibit 7-2 Conflict-Handling Styles

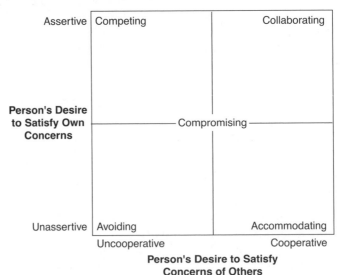

Not every conflict requires an assertive action. Sometimes **avoidance**—withdrawing from or postponing the conflict—is the best solution. When is avoidance a desirable strategy? It is most appropriate when the conflict is trivial, when emotions are running high and time is needed for the conflicting parties to cool down, or when the potential disruption from a more assertive action outweighs the benefits of resolution.

The goal of **accommodation** is to maintain harmonious relationships by placing another's needs and concerns above your own. You might, for example, yield to another person's position on an issue because it is much more important to him or her. This option is most viable when the issue under dispute is not that important to you or when you want to "build up credits" for later issues.

When **forcing**, you attempt to satisfy your own needs at the expense of the other party. In organizations, a manager using his or her formal authority to resolve a dispute most often illustrates this style. Forcing works well when you need a quick resolution on important issues where unpopular actions must be taken, and when commitment by others to your solution isn't crucial.

A **compromise** requires each party to give up something of value. Typically management and labour, in negotiating a new labour contract, take this approach. Compromise can be an optimum strategy when conflicting parties are about equal in power, when it is desirable to achieve a temporary solution to a complex issue, or when time pressures demand an expedient solution.

Finally, **collaboration** is the ultimate win–win solution. All parties to the conflict seek to satisfy their interests. It is typically characterized by open and honest discussion among the parties, active listening to understand differences, and careful deliberation over a full range of alternatives to find a solution that is advantageous to all. When is collaboration the best conflict option? When time pressures are minimal, when all parties seriously want a win–win solution, and when the issue is too important to be compromised.

EMPATHIZE WITH THE OTHER CONFLICT PARTIES

If you choose to manage a conflict situation, it is important that you take the time to get to know the players. Who is involved in the conflict? What interests does each party represent? What are each player's values, personality, feelings, and resources? Your chances of success in managing a conflict will be greatly enhanced if you can view the conflict situation through the eyes of the conflicting parties.

Empathizing is more difficult for most of us when the other conflict parties are from another country and culture. As international trade increases, so does the frequency of business negotiations among people from different countries and cultures regarding joint ventures, acquisitions, mergers, licensing, distribution agreements, and sales of products and services. To manage such negotiations successfully, businesspeople need to know how to influence and communicate with members of cultures other than their own.[10]

Do North Americans negotiate with the same expectations and approaches as Arabs? Are Japanese negotiation styles similar to Russian styles? Do Brazilian negotiators possess the same characteristics as those from China? The answer to all of these questions is no. A growing literature exists documenting that people from different countries negotiate in widely different ways.[11] Exhibit 7-3 illustrates how negotiation styles of people from three different countries differ.

When preparing for negotiations with people from different cultures it is especially important to imagine what the situation looks like through their eyes. This ability may require some research on your part if you are not familiar with the country's culture. The fact of international negotiations is that no formula guarantees success.

Exhibit 7-3 National Styles of Persuasion

	North Americans	**Arabs**	**Russians**
Primary negotiating style and process conflict	Factual: Appeals made to logic	Affective: Appeals made to emotions	Axiomatic: Appeals made to ideals
Counterparts' arguments countered with	Objective facts	Subjective feelings	Asserted ideals
Making concessions	Small concessions made early to establish a relationship	Concessions made throughout as a part of the bargaining process	Few if any concessions made
Response to counterparts' concessions	Usually reciprocate counterparts' concessions	Almost always reciprocate counterparts' concessions	Counterparts' concessions viewed as weakness and almost never reciprocated
Relationship	Short term	Long term	No continuing relationship
Authority	Broad	Broad	Limited
Initial position	Moderate	Extreme	Extreme
Deadline	Very important	Casual	Ignored

Source: E.S. Glenn, D. Witmeyer, and K.A. Stevenson, "Cultural Styles of Persuasion," *International Journal of Intercultural Relations* 1, no. 3 (Fall 1977). Reprinted with permission from Elsevier Science.

You should address specific questions about the people of the other culture such as the following:

- What is important to them?
- Who has power?
- What is at stake?
- What is their time frame?
- Where do they draw their personal and organizational bottom line?[12]

DEAL WITH THE EMOTIONAL ASPECTS OF CONFLICT

When feelings such as anger, fear, or resentment are strong, it is usually better to deal with the emotional aspects of conflict first before trying to settle substantive issues. Why? When we are highly emotional, our ability to think through all the consequences of our actions is not optimal. The following three steps are designed to help alleviate negative emotions for both parties, which better prepares them to deal with the substantive issues in a more constructive manner.

1. *Treat the other person with respect* During emotional disagreements, words of disrespect are often spoken carelessly, but they can block communication and create wounds that may never fully heal. We all have initiated or endured disrespectful

statements like "That's the dumbest idea I've heard in years," or "You're such an idiot," or much worse. Nonverbal behaviours—such as the way you look at the other, not listening, or sarcasm in your voice—can also convey disrespect.

After such an outburst, you often apologize and explain that you were just mad and did not really mean what you said. But the other person has heard and reacted to what you said, and may think that it took a burst of anger for you to speak the truth and that your apology is just a feeble attempt to backpedal out of the situation. Consequently, the receiving party is on the defensive and less likely to trust what you say next.

To avoid slipping into a disrespectful conversation, you need to check your own emotions. It helps to get the end in mind, which usually means understanding how the other sees the situation, getting what you need, and maintaining the relationship. It frequently requires an act of willpower, but it is worth it to keep the situation rational and respectful.

2. *Listen and restate to the other's satisfaction* The goal here is to understand the other person's point of view and feelings, and to make that person feel understood. Your job is to understand, not necessarily to agree. When you indicate that you understand the other's feelings, it is amazing how quickly the feelings subside. This acknowledgment opens the way for you to share your point of view with a much higher probability of being understood.

3. *Briefly state your views, needs, and feelings* After demonstrating respect for the other person and conveying your understanding of his or her feelings and point of view, it is your turn to share your position. During a conflict you will usually communicate better if you keep your message short and to the point, avoid loaded words that might upset the other party, do not exaggerate or leave things out, and disclose your feelings about the issue and what has transpired.

DETERMINE TOUR OBJECTIVES

You should look next at your goals. The best solution is closely intertwined with your definition of "best." Three goals seemed to dominate our discussion of strategies: (1) the importance of the conflict issue, (2) concern over maintaining long-term interpersonal relations, and (3) the speed with which you need to resolve the conflict. All other things held constant, if the issue is critical to the organization's or relationship's success, collaboration is preferred. If sustaining supportive relationships is most important to you, the best strategies, in order of preference, are accommodation, collaboration, compromise, and avoidance. If it is crucial to resolve the conflict as quickly as possible, forcing, accommodation, and compromise, in that order, are preferred.

IMPLEMENT THE OPTIMAL LONG-TERM STRATEGY FOR ALL INVOLVED

Start by looking at your preferred conflict-handling style (see the Self-Assessment Exercise), and gaining an awareness of the styles with which you feel most comfortable. Next consider the source of the conflict. What works best depends, to a large degree, on the cause of the conflict.[13] Communication-based conflicts revolve around misinformation and misunderstandings. Such conflicts lend themselves to collaboration. In contrast, conflicts based on personal differences arise out of disparities between the parties' values and personalities. Such conflicts are most susceptible to avoidance because these differences are often deeply entrenched. When managers have to resolve conflicts rooted in personal differences, they frequently rely on forcing—not so much because it placates the parties, but because it works! The third category, structural conflicts, seems to be amenable to most

Exhibit 7-4 When to Use the Different Conflict Management Styles

Conflict Management Style	When to Use	When Not to Use
Collaborating	When issues are complex and require input and information from others When commitment is needed When dealing with strategic issues When long-term solutions are needed	When time is critical When others are not interested or do not have the skills When conflict occurs because of different value systems
Accommodating	When the issues are unimportant to you When your knowledge is limited When there is long-term give and take When you have no power	When others are unethical or wrong When you are certain you are correct
Competing	When time is critical When issues are trivial When any solution is unpopular When others lack expertise When issues are important to you	When issues are complex and require input and information from others When working with powerful competent others When long-term solutions and commitment are needed
Avoiding	When issues are trivial When conflict is too high and parties need to cool off	When a long-term solution is needed When you are responsible for resolving the conflict
Compromising	When goals are clearly incompatible When parties have equal power When a quick solution is needed When conflict is rooted in different value systems	When an imbalance in power is present When the problem is complex When long-term solutions are needed

Source: Based on M.A. Rahim, "A Measure of Styles of Handling Interpersonal Conflict," *Academy of Management Journal* (June 1983): 368–76; M.A. Rahim, *Managing Conflict in Organizations,* 2d ed. (Westport, CT: Praeger, 1992).

of the conflict strategies depending on other variables in the situation. Exhibit 7-4 illustrates when you should and should not use each conflict management strategy.

This process of blending your personal style, your goals, and the source of the conflict should result in identifying the strategy or set of strategies most likely to be effective for you in any specific conflict situation. Keep in mind, however, that most conflict situations involve interdependent parties that need each other over the long term to achieve joint objectives. Overall, over the long run, interdependent relationships can only endure when collaborative solutions are reached and both parties feel that they have achieved what they need. Otherwise, one party may win a battle but lose the war when the losing party, whom the winner needs, leaves for a more beneficial relationship. So, in the long run, either both sides win, or both parties lose.

You can do a few things to facilitate win/win outcomes.[14] First, do your homework so that you are prepared, know the facts, and understand the other's situation. Second, do not underestimate the others' knowledge about the situation or the importance of their commitment to their position. Third, always share the credit for solutions, even if it means just letting the other person save face and win something. After all, the real goal in interdependent relationships is more than just getting your own way; it is making sure that both parties feel that they win and are on the same side.

OPTION OF LAST RESORT[15]

When interdependent parties try for collaborative solutions and fail, they can sometimes agree to disagree, and still cooperate in their joint endeavours. Often, putting aside disagreements is necessary in value conflicts where each party is strongly committed, but agreement is not necessary to continue the relationship. If agreement is required, a positive relationship can still be maintained by agreeing to no deal: if the two parties cannot find a collaborative solution, they agree not to continue their relationship, because it is not right for both of them, and they part as friends, open to future collaborative possibilities.

Before moving to this option of last resort, however, the parties should attempt to negotiate a solution that will allow both to achieve satisfactory, although not optimal, outcomes. A subset of skills can contribute to successful negotiating, which we will discuss next.

NEGOTIATION

Negotiation is a process in which two or more parties exchange goods or services and attempt to agree upon the exchange rate for them.[16] For our purposes, we will also use the term interchangeably with **bargaining**.

We know that lawyers and car salespeople spend a lot of time negotiating. Actually, managers do also. They have to negotiate salaries for incoming employees, cut deals with other managers and supervisors, bargain over budgets, work out differences with associates, and resolve conflicts with employees. First two broad bargaining strategies will be discussed, then specific negotiation tactics will be summarized.

Bargaining Strategies

The two general approaches to negotiation are distributive bargaining and integrative bargaining. It is important to know the distinction between the two and when each is appropriate. A graphic comparison of the two is shown in Exhibit 7-5.

Exhibit 7-5 Distributive Versus Integrative Bargaining

Bargaining Characteristic	Distributive Bargaining	Integrative Bargaining
Available resources	Fixed amount of resources to be divided	Variable amount of resources to be divided
Primary motivations	I win, you lose	I win, you win
Primary interests	Opposed to each other	Convergent or congruent with each other
Focus of relationships	Short term	Long term

Source: Based on R.J. Lewicki and J.A. Litterer, *Negotiation* (Homewood, IL: Irwin, 1985) 280.

DISTRIBUTIVE BARGAINING

You see a used car advertised for sale in the newspaper. It appears to be just what you have been looking for. You go out to see the car. It is great and you want it. The owner tells you the asking price, which is more than you want to pay. The two of you then negotiate over the price. The negotiating process you are engaging in is called **distributive bargaining**. Its most identifying feature is that it operates under zero-sum conditions. That is, any gain I make is at your expense, and vice versa. Referring to the used-car example, every dollar you can get the seller to cut from the car's price is a dollar you save. Conversely, every dollar more he or she can get from you comes at your expense. Thus the essence of distributive bargaining is negotiating over who gets what share of a fixed pie.

One of the most widely cited examples of distributive bargaining is labour–management wage negotiations. Typically, labour's representatives come to the bargaining table determined to get as much money as possible out of management. Because every cent more that labour negotiates increases management's costs by the same amount, each party bargains aggressively and treats the other as an opponent who must be defeated. Exhibit 7-6 depicts the distributive bargaining strategy. Parties A and B represent the two negotiators. Each has a target point that defines what he or she would like to achieve. Each also has a resistance point, which marks the lowest outcome that is acceptable—the point below which he or she would break off negotiations rather than accept a less favourable settlement. The area between their resistance points is the settlement range. As long as their aspiration ranges overlap somewhat, a settlement area exists where each one's aspirations can be met.

When engaged in distributive bargaining, your tactics should focus on trying to get your opponent to agree to your specific target point or to get as close to it as possible. Examples of such tactics are: persuading your opponent of the impossibility of getting to his or her target point and the advisability of accepting a settlement near yours; arguing that your target is fair, while your opponent's is not; and attempting to get your opponent to feel emotionally generous toward you and thus accept an outcome close to your target point.

INTEGRATIVE BARGAINING

Assume a sales representative for a women's sportswear manufacturer has just closed a $15,000 order from a small clothing retailer. The sales rep calls in the order to her firm's credit department. She is told that the firm cannot approve credit to this customer because

Exhibit 7-6 Staking Out the Bargaining Zone

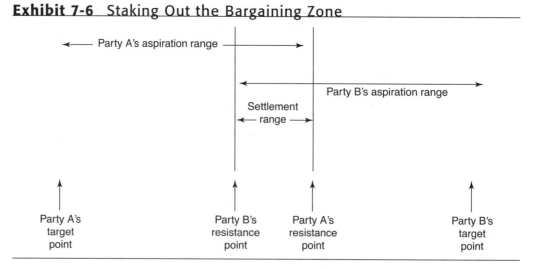

of a past slow-pay record. The next day, the sales rep and the firm's credit supervisor meet to discuss the problem. The sales rep does not want to lose the business; neither does the credit supervisor, but he also doesn't want to get stuck with an uncollectible debt. The two openly review their options. After considerable discussion, they agree on a solution that meets both their needs: The credit supervisor will approve the sale, but the clothing store's owner will provide a bank guarantee that will assure payment if the bill is not paid within 60 days.

The sales–credit negotiation is an example of **integrative bargaining**. In contrast to distributive bargaining, integrative problem solving operates under the assumption that at least one settlement exists that can create a win–win solution.

In general, integrative bargaining is preferable to distributive bargaining. Why? Because the former builds long-term relationships and facilitates working together in the future. It bonds negotiators and allows each to leave the bargaining table feeling that he or she has achieved a victory. Distributive bargaining, on the other hand, leaves one party a loser. It tends to build animosities and deepen divisions between people who have to work together on an ongoing basis.

Why, then, do we not see more integrative bargaining in organizations? The answer lies in the conditions necessary for this type of negotiation to succeed. These conditions include openness with information and frankness between parties, sensitivity on the part of each party to the other's needs, the ability to trust one another, and a willingness by both parties to maintain flexibility. Because many organizational cultures and interpersonal relationships are not characterized by openness, trust, and flexibility, it is not surprising that negotiations often take on a win-at-any-cost dynamic.

Guidelines for Effective Negotiating

The essence of effective negotiation can be summarized in the following 10 guidelines. Careful attention to them can increase your odds of successful negotiation outcomes.

1. *Consider the other party's situation* Acquire as much information as you can about your opponent's interests and goals. What are his or her real needs versus wants? What constituencies must he or she appease? What is his or her strategy? Jerry Anderson, president of the Minneapolis-based architectural-glass fabricator, Apogee Enterprises, is consistently successful at reaching consensus in negotiations between architects, engineers, and building contractors. He attributes a large amount of his success to forethought. "Always try to figure out where the other guy is coming from," he says. "If you think enough about it, you can usually come up with a reading."[17] This information will help you understand your opponent's behaviour, predict his or her responses to your offers, and frame solutions in terms of his or her interests. Additionally, when you can anticipate your opponent's position, you are better equipped to counter his or her arguments with the facts and figures that support your position.

2. *Have a concrete strategy* Treat negotiation like a chess match. Expert chess players have a strategy. They know ahead of time how they will respond to any given situation. How strong is your situation and how important is the issue? Are you willing to split differences to achieve an early solution? If the issue is important to you, is your position strong enough to let you play hardball and show little or no willingness to compromise? These questions should be addressed before you begin bargaining.

3. *Begin with a positive overture* Establish rapport and mutual interests before starting the negotiation. Then begin bargaining with a positive overture, perhaps a small concession. Studies show that concessions tend to be reciprocated and lead to agreements. Reciprocating your opponent's concessions can further develop a positive climate.

4. *Address problems, not personalities* Concentrate on the negotiation issues, not on the personal characteristics of your opponent. When negotiations get tough, avoid the tendency to attack your opponent. If other people feel threatened, they concentrate on defending their self-esteem, as opposed to solving the problem. It is your opponent's ideas or position that you disagree with, not him or her as a person. Separate the people from the problem, and avoid personalizing differences.

5. *Maintain a rational, goal-oriented frame of mind* Use the previous guideline in reverse if your opponent attacks or gets emotional with you. Do not get hooked by emotional outbursts. Let the other person blow off steam without taking it personally while you try to understand the problem or strategy behind the aggression.

6. *Insist on using objective criteria* Make your negotiated decisions based on principles and results, not emotions or pressure.[18] Agree upon objective criteria that can help both parties to assess the reasonableness of an alternative. Let's say you are negotiating the monthly rent for an apartment close to campus. An objective criterion might be the average rent paid for similar student apartments as reported by your school's Student Housing Department. Or, you are negotiating the price of a used car at a dealership. In this case, a bank loan officer can tell you the "book value" of cars that are of the same year, make, model, and condition as the one you are looking at. If the other party's underlying rationale does not meet these criteria, avoid emotional pleas, or stubbornness.

7. *Pay little attention to initial offers* Treat an initial offer as merely a point of departure. Everyone has to have an initial position. These initial offers tend to be extreme and idealistic. Treat them as such. Focus on the other person's interests and your own goals and principles, while you generate other possibilities.

8. *Emphasize win–win solutions* Inexperienced negotiators often assume that their gain must come at the expense of the other party. As noted with integrative bargaining, zero-sum results need not be the case. Often, win–win solutions can be found. But assuming a zero-sum game means missed opportunities for trade-offs that could benefit both sides. So if conditions are supportive, look for an integrative solution. Create additional alternatives, especially low-cost concessions you can make that have high value to the other party. Frame options in terms of your opponent's interests and look for solutions that can allow your opponent, as well as yourself, to declare a victory.

9. *Create an open and trusting climate* Skilled negotiators are good listeners, ask questions, focus their arguments directly, are not defensive, and have learned to avoid words and phrases that can irritate an opponent. In other words, they are adept at creating the open and trusting climate necessary for reaching an integrative settlement.

10. *Be open to accepting third-party assistance* When stalemates are reached, consider using a neutral third party. Mediators can help parties come to an agreement, but they do not impose a settlement. Arbitrators hear both sides of the dispute and then impose a solution. Conciliators are more informal and act as a communication conduit, passing information between the parties, interpreting messages, and clarifying misunderstandings.

What About Conflict Stimulation?

What about the other side of conflict management—situations that require managers to *stimulate* conflict? Few of us personally enjoy being in conflict situations, so the idea of purposely creating them seems to be the antithesis of good management. Yet the evidence demonstrates that in certain situations, an increase in conflict is constructive.[19] Following are some suggestions that managers might want to use to stimulate conflict.[20] Some, such as changing the organization's culture (discussed in Chapter 17) and restructuring the organization (discussed in Chapter 12), are more effective if you are a higher-level manager with position authority. The others—using communication strategies, bringing in outsiders, and appointing a devil's advocate—can be applied at any managerial level.

1. *Communicate that conflict has a legitimate place in the organization* The initial step in stimulating functional conflict is for managers to convey to employees the message, supported by actions, that conflict is encouraged in the organization. This atmosphere entails changing the organizational culture so that individuals who beneficially challenge the status quo, suggest innovative ideas, offer divergent opinions, and demonstrate original thinking are rewarded visibly with promotions, salary increases, and other positive reinforcers.

2. *Send ambiguous messages about potentially threatening developments* Disclosing news that a plant might close, a department could be eliminated, or that a layoff is likely will reduce apathy, stimulate new ideas, and force reevaluation. The goal is to create healthy conflict in the spirit of joint problem solving to produce renewed interest and creative solutions.

3. *Bring in outsiders* A widely used method for shaking up a stagnant unit or organization is to bring in—either by hiring from outside or by internal transfer—individuals whose backgrounds, values, attitudes, or managerial styles differ from those of present members. Many large organizations have used this technique over the last decade in filling vacancies on their boards of directors. Women, minority group members, consumer activists, and others whose backgrounds and interests differ significantly from those of the rest of the board have been purposely selected to add a fresh perspective.

4. *Restructure the organization* Centralizing decisions, realigning work groups, increasing formalization, and increasing interdependencies between units are all structural devices that disrupt the status quo and act to increase conflict levels.

5. *Appoint a devil's advocate* A devil's advocate is a person who purposely presents arguments that run counter to those proposed by the majority or against current practices. He or she plays the role of the critic, even to the point of arguing against positions with which he or she actually agrees in order to stimulate discussion. A devil's advocate acts as a check against groupthink and practices that are left in place with no better justification than "that's the way we've always done it." When thoughtfully listened to, the advocate can improve the quality of group decision making.

In contrast, others in the group often view devil's advocates as time wasters, and their appointment is almost certain to delay any decision process. Another thing to consider is rotating the person playing the devil's advocate role so that he or she does not become stereotyped as a "yes, but" type of person.

How Do You Manage Conflict Between Groups and Departments?

Groups that are able to cooperate with other groups are usually more productive than those that are not.[21] But the potential areas of conflict are many. Conflict erupted at Apple Computer in the early 1980s, for example, even though groups were in independent divisions. The newly created Macintosh division was assigned the task of developing a creative breakthrough product as quickly as possible and was receiving a disproportionate share of the company's publicity and resources. At least the Apple II division, which was bringing in most of the company's profits, viewed it that way. This situation led to jealousy, resentment, and name calling between the two divisions.

Because it can have destructive organizational consequences, it is important to detect, reduce, and act to prevent the recurrence of dysfunctional intergroup conflict. On the other hand, even dysfunctional conflict is useful in that it signals needed changes.

Also, functional intergroup conflict that serves to improve the quality of decision making and stimulate creative breakthroughs should be judiciously managed to achieve the most beneficial results for the organization.[22] Consequently, the critical issue is not how to eliminate intergroup conflict but how to manage it productively to obtain positive change and avoid negative consequences. Persistent dysfunctional intergroup conflict, however, needs to be confronted.[23]

As with interpersonal conflict, attempts to manage intergroup conflict can result in win–lose (competing and accommodating), lose–lose (avoiding), win–win (collaborating), or compromise (bargaining) outcomes. Win–lose outcomes are brought about by all-or-nothing competitive strategies that encourage one group to win at the expense of the other. Because organizations consist of ongoing relationships, zero-sum strategies create destructive political environments. Instead of solving problems, avoiding strategies leave problems to fester and erupt later. At best they allow temporary productivity until the groups can address the conflict more effectively. Compromise strategies allow both groups to gain a little but neither to obtain all that its members desire. Because win–win strategies allow both groups to obtain their goals through creative integration of their concerns, the best practice is to try win–win strategies first. If they do not work, a compromise strategy can provide some benefits to both groups. Organizations with effective intergroup coordination strategies can often manage conflict effectively without it becoming destructive at all. Techniques that can prevent[24] and reduce[25] intergroup conflict are presented next.

SUPERORDINATE GOALS

One of the most effective ways to reduce intergroup conflict is to determine an overriding goal that requires the cooperative effort of the conflicting groups. Such a goal must be unattainable by either group alone and of sufficient importance to supersede all their other goals. One fairly common **superordinate goal** is survival of the organization. Overall survival usually requires the elimination of suboptimal strategies on the part of conflicting groups. In the airline industry, for example, several unions have agreed to forgo pay increases and have even accepted temporary pay reductions when the survival of an airline was threatened.

This strategy eliminates win–lose situations as groups shift efforts toward cooperation and pull together to maximize organizational effectiveness. Setting up an appraisal system that rewards total organizational effectiveness rather than individual group accomplishments also supports these efforts by promoting cooperation rather than competition between groups.

A derivative strategy to restore alliances and increase cooperation is focusing on a common enemy. At the international level, bickering nations unite against a common adversary in times of war or natural catastrophe. Players on athletic teams that normally compete in a particular league join together to produce an all-star team and challenge another league. Like all these factions, warring groups will suppress their conflicts and join together to help their organization compete successfully against another. Sometimes, however, they must be reminded that the opposition is out there.

INCREASED COMMUNICATION

In cases where groups are not competing for scarce resources or trying to achieve inherently conflicting goals, devising means to increase communication can do much to correct misunderstandings, reduce negative stereotypes, and develop more positive feelings among group members. Requiring groups to meet together to solve common problems can reduce stereotypical images and faulty perceptions, and contribute to mutual understanding.

NCR Corp. (formerly National Cash Register Company) began tearing down the walls between its engineering and manufacturing groups by putting people from design, purchasing, manufacturing, and field support in adjacent cubicles to allow them to communicate with one another throughout the design and manufacturing process. This process reduced assembly time from 30 minutes to five and permitted assembly without special tools. The free flow of information across groups enabled NCR to get better products to market much faster.[26]

PROBLEM SOLVING

Problem solving is a more structured means of bringing together conflicting groups for a face-to-face confrontation. The purpose of a problem solving meeting is to identify and solve conflicts through a mutual airing of differences, complaints, and negative feelings. An effort is made to work through differences and bring about a greater understanding of the opposing group's attitudes, perceptions, and position. The problem solving approach requires considerable time and commitment but it can be effective when conflicts stem from misunderstandings or different perceptions. Specific problem solving strategies and techniques can be found in Chapter 10, Innovation and Problem Solving.

NEGOTIATING

As previously described, negotiating is a form of problem solving in which two groups with conflicting interests alter their positions in order to reach a mutually agreeable resolution. One of the most publicized forms of negotiating is when unions bargain for better wages, working conditions, benefits, and job security, while management bargains for lower labour costs and increased efficiency. Many informal forms of intergroup bargaining go on constantly, like when one department agrees to stay in an old office space in exchange for new computer equipment.

When choosing representatives, groups should be aware that personality, experience, training, and chosen strategy make a difference in how well a negotiator negotiates.[27] The guidelines for successful negotiating described for interpersonal negotiating also apply in an intergroup situation.

EXPANSION OF RESOURCES

When the major cause of intergroup conflict is limited resources, the likely outcome is a win–lose situation in which one group succeeds at the expense of another. If at all possible, the organization should eliminate this source of conflict by expanding its resource base. Additional investments may pay off handsomely in terms of increased productivity.

CHANGES IN ORGANIZATIONAL STRUCTURE

When the reasons for intergroup conflict are scarce resources, status differences, or power imbalances, changes in organizational structure may be the answer.[28] Structural changes can include: rotating group members on a semipermanent basis, creating liaison or coordinator positions, and eliminating special-interest groups that exist within the organization. Marshall Industries, for example, rotates new employees through a variety of assignments in different groups to ease the competitive effects of single-group identification, enhance understanding of interaction in the whole system, and provide total organization identification. Marshall Industries regroups people from different departments with different specialties into overlapping, cross-trained teams. This approach decreases identity with one particular department and increases understanding of the requirements and needs of other groups.[29] In other situations, conflicting groups can be relocated, task responsibilities can be redefined, and hierarchies can be decentralized. Sometimes two conflicting groups can be merged into one. If the conflict clearly centres on the personal animosities of two or more strong individuals, the key instigators can be removed.

Restructuring has produced increased quality, productivity, and cooperation for companies such as Corning Glass Works, Ford Motor Company, and Hewlett–Packard, which are shifting their focus from how individual departments function to how different departments work together. Companies such as the Royal Bank of Canada are creating network groups of department managers with appropriate business skills, personal motivations, resource control, and positions to shape and implement organizational strategy. The free flow of information to all network group members who need it and the emphasis on horizontal collaboration and leadership have clarified joint business goals and helped meet deadlines.[30]

SMOOTHING

Smoothing is a means of providing conflicting groups with some incentive to repress their conflict and avoid its open expression. The smoothing process plays down the differences between the groups and accentuates their similarities and common interests. The rationale is that eventually the groups will realize they are not as alienated from one another as they initially believed. Because this approach circumvents full confrontation of the sources of conflict, they will probably resurface in the future and possibly cause a more serious disturbance. Smoothing is at best a temporary solution.

AVOIDANCE

Some groups may be able to ignore dysfunctional situations temporarily by looking the other way or disregarding the threatening actions of others in the hope that the situation will resolve itself. But most conflicts do not fade; usually, they worsen with time. Although avoidance is ineffective in the long run, certain controlled conditions can be established to lessen the short-term consequences of conflict. Sometimes conflicting groups can be physically separated; sometimes the amount of interaction between them can be limited. Procrastination, disregard for the demands of others, and attempts at peaceful coexistence are all variations of the avoidance process.

Concept Quiz

Complete the following true–false quiz by circling the correct answer. Answers are at the end of the quiz. After marking your answers, remember to go back and check your understanding of any answers you missed.

True or False	1.	Conflicts cannot be ignored because they always hinder organizational effectiveness.
True or False	2.	Most people have the ability to vary their conflict response according to the situation.
True or False	3.	Every conflict does not justify a manager's attention.
True or False	4.	Some conflicts are unmanageable.
True or False	5.	Most conflicts are caused by lack of communication.
True or False	6.	You should suppress emotions and deal with conflict logically.
True or False	7.	Accommodation requires each party to give up something of value.
True or False	8.	Forcing is effective for resolving important issues where unpopular actions need implementing.
True or False	9.	Collaboration is an effective strategy for arriving at an expedient solution under time pressures.

True or False 10. Effective negotiators make sure they get public credit for a win and spread the word that the other party lost.

Answers (1) False; (2) True; (3) True; (4) True; (5) False; (6) False; (7) False; (8) True; (9) False; (10) False

Behavioural Checklist

Look for these behaviours when evaluating your own and others' conflict management skills.

For Effective Conflict Resoution:

- Assess the nature of the conflict.
- Be judicious in selecting conflicts in which to engage.
- Determine your own conflict management style.
- Know your options.
- Evaluate and empathize with the other conflict party.
- Deal with the emotional components of the conflict.
- Determine your objective.
- Stimulate conflict when appropriate.
- Implement the optimal long-range strategy for all involved.

Modelling Exercise

INSTRUCTIONS Two people volunteer to be role-players. One person is to play Lee, the supervisor. Another plays B.J., a conservative, senior cost accountant. The class uses the Observer's Rating Sheet to evaluate the skills of Lee and to prepare notes for feedback after the role-play. Everyone reads the situation, but the role-players read only their own role. The observers read both roles and review the Observer's Rating Sheet located at the end of this exercise.

ACTORS Lee Lattoni; B.J. O'Malley

SITUATION Lee Lattoni supervises an eight-member cost accounting department in a large metals fabricating plant in Calgary, Alberta. Lee was promoted about six months ago to this supervisory position after only a year as an accountant. It was no secret that Lee got the promotion predominantly because of education. Lee has an MBA, whereas no one else in the department has a university degree.

LEE LATTONI'S ROLE Your transition to supervisor has gone smoothly; you have encountered little in the way of problems until now. Business has been prospering at the plant for some time, and it has become apparent that you need an additional cost accountant in the department to handle the increased workload. In fact, it has been on your mind for over a month. Department members have been complaining about the heavy workload. Overtime has become commonplace and is adversely affecting your department's efficiency statistics. You do not think you will have any trouble supporting your request for a new, full-time position with your boss.

The search for a new employee should be relatively hassle-free. The reason is that you have already spotted someone you think can fill the slot nicely. The person you have in mind is currently working in the production control department of the plant.

Unofficially, you have talked with the production control supervisor and the plant's personnel director about moving Regi Simpson, a young clerk in production, into your department. Regi has been with the company for eight months, has shown above average potential, and is only six units shy of a bachelor's degree (with a major in accounting), which Regi has been earning in part-time studies. You are aware that the department currently is made up of older male employees who have worked their way up through the ranks based on experience and longevity. None of them has a university degree, and the attitude of most members is that advanced education is just a frivolous waste of time. They are a macho, raucous group who tell a lot of chauvinistic jokes, but always get the job done well. You are aware that Regi may have a problem gaining acceptance in this group but Regi is certainly a qualified candidate and deserving of the promotion.

You met with Regi earlier in the week and discussed the possibility that cost accounting will have a vacancy. Regi was interested in the position. After further discussion over lunch—all unofficially—you said that although you could not make any promises, you were prepared to recommend Regi for the job. However, you emphasized that it would be a week to 10 days before a final decision and an official announcement were made.

You are in your office when B.J. O'Malley comes in. B.J. works for you as a cost accountant and has been at the plant for 26 years. You like B.J. but consider B.J. closed-minded and the most extreme of the chauvinistic old timers. If Regi were to join the department, you would expect B.J. to be the least receptive. Why? B.J. was raised by a conservative working class family and you have heard B.J. speak disparagingly about university students.

B.J. O'MALLEY'S ROLE   You are a cost accountant in the plant, working for Lee. You are 58 years old, were raised in a conservative working class family, and have been working at the Calgary plant since it opened 26 years ago. You have heard rumours that Lee is planning to bring Regi Simpson, a young inexperienced employee, into the department. You understand the need to hire another cost accountant, because the workload has become too heavy and the department's overtime budget is out of hand. The current department is made up of older employees who have worked their way up through the ranks based on experience and longevity. None of them has a university degree and the attitude of most members is that advanced education is just a frivolous waste of time. They are a macho, raucous group who have a lot of fun and tell a lot of chauvinistic jokes, take breaks throwing darts at each month's Playboy centrefold, but always get the job done well. You are concerned that Regi will cause problems for your group and you believe there must be equally qualified and experienced locals around who could do the job better.

You believe that Lee should be sensitive to your feelings. You are not prejudiced; you just want to maintain the camaraderie and efficiency of your department. You want Lee to talk with all department members before making an appointment. You view the department as a close-knit, homogeneous group and you do not want to add a newcomer who will have trouble fitting in. In the back of your mind, you know that if all the department members get to vote on who joins the department, a young, inexperienced university student who will probably need constant handholding is unlikely to be hired. However, you also know that if you do not speak up, no one else will. You are quite upset and have decided to go to Lee's office and let Lee know that you have no intention of working with an uppity, know-it-all university student who probably does not know the first thing about cost accounting.

TIME   Not to exceed 15 minutes.

Observer's Rating Sheet

Evaluate Lee Lattoni's conflict management skills on the following scale. Write concrete examples in the space for comments below each behaviour to use in explaining your feedback.

1 Unsatisfactory	2 Weak	3 Adequate	4 Good	5 Outstanding

_____ Assesses the nature of the conflict.

_____ Judicious in selecting conflicts in which to engage.

_____ Determines own conflict management style.

_____ Knows options.

_____ Empathizes with other.

_____ Deals with the emotions.

_____ Determines the objective.

_____ Negotiates effectively.

_____ Stimulates conflict when appropriate.

Group Exercises

The following three exercises are designed to give you a chance to practise your conflict management skills in small groups and receive feedback from others about your strengths and weaknesses. The first exercise consists of a set of short conflict cases for you to analyze and select the best approach for managing. Next is a role-play where you can practise negotiating for a used car. Last is an exercise that challenges you to resolve a values-based conflict among several group members.

Group Exercise 1: Deciding How to Manage Conflicts[31]

DIRECTIONS Form groups of three to five members. Each group member is to begin by independently ranking the five alternative courses of action in each of the following four incidents. You are to rank the responses from the most desirable or appropriate way of dealing with the conflict situation to the least desirable. Rank the most desirable course of action "1," the next most desirable "2," and so on, with the least desirable or least appropriate action as "5." Enter your rank for each item in the space next to each choice. Next, identify the conflict style being used with each of the possible courses of action (competing, accommodation, avoidance, compromise, or collaboration).

DISCUSSION After each person has completed the steps for all four incidents, group members are to compare their answers for each situation. Begin with Incident 1. When completed do the same for the remaining incidents. For each incident, (1) defend why you answered as you did; (2) if you do not all agree, discuss why not; (3) reach a group consensus with some of you changing your answers as a result of the discussion; and (4) prepare to present your group's consensus answer and rationale for each incident to the rest of the class. Confine the analysis and discussion of each incident to 10 minutes or less.

INCIDENT 1 Pete is lead operator of a production molding machine. Recently, he has noticed that one of the men from another machine has been coming over to his machine and talking to one of his men (not on break time). The efficiency of Pete's operator seems to be falling off and causing some rejects because of his inattention. Pete thinks he detects some resentment among the rest of the crew. If you were Pete, what would you do?

  a) Talk to your worker and tell him to limit his conversations during on-the-job time.
  b) Ask the foreman to tell the lead operator of the other machine to keep his operators in line.
  c) Confront both men the next time you see them together (as well as the other lead operator, if necessary), find out what they are up to, and tell them what you expect of your operators.
  d) Say nothing now; it would be silly to make a big deal out of something so insignificant.
  e) Try to put the rest of the crew at ease; it is important that they all work well together.

INCIDENT 2 Sally is the senior quality control (QC) inspector and has been appointed group leader of the QC people on her crew. On separate occasions, two of her people have come to her with different suggestions for reporting test results to the machine operators. Paul wants to send the test results to the supervisor and then to the machine operator, because the supervisor is the person ultimately responsible for production output. Jim thinks the results should go directly to the lead operator on the machine in question, because the operator is the one who must take corrective action as soon as possible. Both ideas seem good, and Sally can find no ironclad procedures in the department on how to route the reports. If you were Sally, you would:

a) Decide who is right and ask the other person to go along with the decision (perhaps establish it as a written procedure).
b) Wait and see; the best solution will become apparent.
c) Tell both Paul and Jim not to get uptight about their disagreement; it is not that important.
d) Get Paul and Jim together and examine both of their ideas closely.
e) Send the report to the supervisor, with a copy to the lead operator (even though it might mean a little more work for QC).

INCIDENT 3 Ralph is a module leader; his module consists of four complex and expensive machines and five crew members. The work is exacting, and inattention or improper procedures could cause a costly mistake or serious injury. Ralph suspects that one of his crew is taking drugs on the job, or at least is showing up for work under the influence of drugs. Ralph feels he has some strong indications, but he knows he does not have a "case." If you were Ralph, you would:

a) Confront the man outright, tell him what you suspect and why, and that you are concerned for him and for the safety of the rest of the crew.
b) Ask that the suspected offender keep his habit off the job; what he does on the job is part of your business.
c) Not confront the individual right now; it might either "turn him off" or drive him underground.
d) Give the man the "facts of life"; tell him it is illegal and unsafe to use drugs, and that if he gets caught, you will do everything you can to see that he is fired.
e) Keep a close eye on the man to see that he is not endangering others.

INCIDENT 4 Gene is supervisor of a production crew. From time to time in the past, the product development section tapped the production crews for operators to augment their own operator personnel to run test products on special machines. This use of personnel put little strain on the production crews because the demands were small, temporary, and infrequent. Lately, however, the demand seems almost constant for four production operators. The rest of the production crew must fill in for these missing people, usually by working harder and taking shorter breaks. If you were Gene, you would:

a) Let it go for now; the "crisis" will probably be over soon.
b) Try to smooth things over with your own crew and with the development supervisor; we all have jobs to do and cannot afford a conflict.
c) Let development have two of the four operators they requested.
d) Go to the development supervisor or his or her supervisor and talk about how these demands for additional operators could best be met without placing production in a bind.
e) Go to the supervisor of production (Gene's boss) and get him or her to "call off" the development people.

TIME Not to exceed 10 minutes per incident.

Group Exercise 2: Used Car Role-Play[32]

DIRECTIONS One volunteer assumes the role of the buyer and another assumes the role of the seller. Role-players read only their own role and prepare for the role-play.

Other class members read both roles and review the Observer's Rating Sheet. After the role-play discussion, observers will provide feedback to the people playing the Buyer and Seller, using the Observer's Rating Sheet as a guide.

ACTORS Buyer and Seller.

SITUATION You are about to negotiate the purchase/sale of an automobile. Before advertising it in the local newspaper, the seller took the car to the local Volkswagen dealer for an independent assessment. The dealer's write-up stated:

- 1998 VW Jetta GL; standard shift.
- Midnight black with black upholstery, tinted glass.
- AM/FM, cassette. 49 000 kilometres.
- Steel-belted radial tires expected to last 100 000 kilometres.
- 15 kilometres per litre.
- No rust; dent on passenger door barely noticeable.
- Mechanically perfect except exhaust system, which may or may not last another 16 000 kilometres (costs $300 to replace).
- "Blue book" retail value, $15 000; wholesale, $13 200.
- Car has spent its entire life in the local area.

BUYER'S ROLE Your car was stolen and wrecked two weeks ago. You do a lot of travelling in your job, so you need a car that is economical and easy to drive. The Jetta that was advertised looks like a good deal, and you would like to buy it right away if possible. The insurance company gave you $12 000 for your old car. You have only $2100 in savings that you had intended to spend on a vacation trip—a chance you really do not want to pass up.

Your credit has been stretched for some time, so that if you borrow money, it will have to be at an 18 per cent interest rate. Furthermore, you need to buy a replacement car quickly, because you have been renting a car for business purposes, and it is costing you a great deal. The Jetta is the best deal you have seen, and the car is fun to drive. As an alternative, you can immediately buy a used 1997 Ford Escort for $11 400 (the wholesale value); it gets 12 kilometres per litre and will depreciate much faster than the Jetta.

The seller of the Jetta is a complete stranger to you. Before beginning this negotiation, set the following targets for yourself:

1. The price you would like to pay for the car
2. The price you will initially offer the seller
3. The highest price you will pay for the car

SELLER'S ROLE You have bought a used Mercedes from a dealer. The down payment is $14 100 on the car, with steep monthly payments. You are stretched on credit, so if you cannot make the down payment, you will have to borrow at 18 per cent. You are going to pick up the Mercedes in two hours, so you want to sell your old car, the Jetta, before you go.

You advertised the Jetta, which is in particularly good condition, in the newspaper and have had several calls. Your only really good prospect right now is the person with whom you are about to bargain—a stranger. You do not *have* to sell it to this person, but if you do not sell the car right away, you will have to pay high interest charges until you do sell it.

The Mercedes dealer will only give you $13 200 for the Jetta, because he will have to resell it to a Volkswagen dealer. The local VW dealer is not anxious to buy the car from you because he just received a shipment of new cars; in any case, he probably would not give you more than $13 200 either.

Before beginning this negotiation, set the following targets for yourself:

1. The price you would like to receive for the car
2. The price you will initially request
3. The lowest price you will accept for the car

TIME Not to exceed 15 minutes.

Observer's Rating Sheet

Evaluate the parties' conflict management and negotiation skills on the following scale. Write concrete examples in the space for comments below each behaviour to use in explaining your feedback.

1 Unsatisfactory	2 Weak	3 Adequate	4 Good	5 Outstanding
			Buyer	**Seller**
■ Determines objectives.			_____	_____
■ Plans a concrete strategy before negotiating.			_____	_____
■ Knows options.			_____	_____
■ Begins with a positive overture.			_____	_____
■ Maintains a rational, goal-oriented frame of mind.			_____	_____
■ Empathizes with other party's position.			_____	_____
■ Addresses problems, not personalities.			_____	_____
■ Does not take initial offers too seriously.			_____	_____
■ Insists on objective criteria.			_____	_____

Group Exercise 3: The Alligator River Conflict[33]

OBJECTIVES To demonstrate how different perceptions, values, and attitudes lead to conflicts. To learn about your own conflict management style and practise conflict resolution skills.

TIME 50 minutes (5 minutes for set-up, 30 minutes for the exercise, and 15 minutes for debriefing).

PROCEDURE
1. Read The Alligator River Story, which follows.
2. After reading the story, individually rank the five characters in the story beginning with the one whom you consider as the most offensive and ending with the one whom you consider the least objectionable. Briefly note your reasons.

THE ALLIGATOR RIVER STORY

There once lived a woman named **Abigail** who was in love with a man named **Gregory**. Gregory lived on the shore of a river. Abigail lived on the opposite shore of the same river. The river that separated the two lovers was teeming with hungry alligators. Abigail wanted to cross the river to be with Gregory. Unfortunately, the bridge had been washed out by a heavy flood the previous week. So she went to ask **Sinbad**, a river boat captain, to take her across. He said he would be glad to if she would consent to go to bed with him prior to the voyage. She promptly refused and went to a friend named **Ivan** to explain her plight. Ivan did not want to get involved at all in the situation. Abigail felt her only alternative was to accept Sinbad's terms. Sinbad fulfilled his promise to Abigail and delivered her into the arms of Gregory. When Abigail told Gregory about her amorous escapade in order to cross the river, Gregory cast her aside with disdain. Heartsick and rejected, Abigail turned to **Slug** with her tale of woe. Slug, feeling compassion for Abigail, sought out Gregory and beat him brutally. Abigail was overjoyed at the sight of Gregory getting his due. As the sun set on the horizon, people heard Abigail laughing at Gregory.

3. Now form *groups* of five or six members. Compare rankings and share reasons for them.
4. Reach a group consensus decision on a final set of rankings, that is, talk it through until all are satisfied your agreed-upon ranking is the best you can do in your group. Do not just add up ranks or take a quick vote, talk through and explain all positions until all agree on a common set of rankings.
5. Using the Observer's Rating Sheet, give each group member feedback on the conflict management skills he or she exhibited during the group ranking.

	Individual Ranking Form	
Rank	Character	Reasons
First (Worst)		
Second		
Third		
Fourth		
Fifth		

Rank	Group Consensus Ranking	
	Name	Reasons
First (Worst)		
Second		
Third		
Fourth		
Fifth		

Observer's Rating Sheet

Evaluate conflict management and negotiation skills demonstrated by each group member on the following scale. Write concrete examples in the space for comments below each behaviour to use in explaining feedback. Rate and provide feedback to one group member at a time, until all have received feedback.

Names of Group Members

1 Unsatisfactory	2 Weak	3 Adequate	4 Good	5 Outstanding

- Assesses the nature of the conflict. _____ _____ _____ _____ _____

- Judicious in selecting conflicts to engage in. _____ _____ _____ _____ _____

- Determines own conflict management style. _____ _____ _____ _____ _____

- Knows options. _____ _____ _____ _____ _____

- Empathizes with other party's position. _____ _____ _____ _____ _____

- Deals with the emotions. _____ _____ _____ _____ _____

- Determines the objective. _____ _____ _____ _____ _____

- Does not take initial offers too seriously. _____ _____ _____ _____ _____

- Insists on objective criteria. _____ _____ _____ _____ _____

Application Questions

1. Most people dislike conflict because it is dysfunctional. Do you agree or disagree? Why?
2. Is conflict inevitable in organizations? Why?
3. When is conflict likely to hinder an organization? When can it help?
4. What are the key steps in diagnosing a conflict situation?
5. What type of outcomes would you desire when resolving a conflict with a significant other? How about with a used-car dealer?

Reinforcement Exercises

1. Describe in detail three recent interpersonal conflicts you have experienced. How did your basic conflict-handling style influence your actions? To what degree do you believe your conflict style is flexible? The next time you find yourself in a conflict situation: (a) be sure to recall your basic conflict style; (b) consider its appropriateness to this specific situation; and (c) if inappropriate, practise exhibiting more appropriate conflict resolution behaviour.
2. Think of a recent conflict you had with a colleague, friend, or relative. What was the source of the conflict? What goals did you seek? How did you handle the conflict? Was it resolved consistently with your goals? What other ways of handling this conflict might have been more effective?
3. Take the role of a third-party consultant for an individual or a group involved in a conflict. Advise the party/parties as to their options. Note how your advice works.

Summary Checklist

On the basis of your experiences and observations, assess yourself on each of the following conflict skill behaviours. Make a check (√) next to those behaviours on which you think you need improvement.

_____ Assessing the nature of the conflict.

_____ Being judicious in selecting conflicts in which to engage.
1. Some conflicts might not be worth the effort.
2. Others might be unmanageable.
3. Save your efforts for conflicts that have serious consequences.

_____ Determining my own conflict management style.
1. Competing.
2. Accommodating.
3. Avoiding.
4. Collaborating.
5. Compromising.

_____ Knowing my options.
1. Knowing when it is appropriate to use each of the five conflict management styles.
2. Agreeing to no deal.

_____ Empathizing with the positions of others.
1. Get to know the players.
2. What interests does each party represent?
3. What are each player's values, personality, feelings, and resources?
4. View the conflict situation through the eyes of the conflicting parties.

_____ Dealing with emotions.
1. Treat the other person with respect.
2. Listen and restate to the other's satisfaction.
3. Briefly state your views, needs, and feelings.

_____ Negotiating.
1. Consider the other party's situation.
2. Have a concrete strategy.
3. Begin with a positive overtone.
4. Address problems, not personalities.
5. Maintain a rational, goal-oriented frame of mind.
6. Insist on using objective criteria.
7. Pay little attention to initial offers.
8. Emphasize win–win solutions.
9. Create an open and trusting climate.
10. Be open to accepting third-party assistance.

_____ Stimulating conflict when appropriate.
1. Communicate that conflict has a legitimate place in the organization.
2. Send ambiguous messages about potentially threatening developments.
3. Bring in outsiders with different backgrounds, values, and attitudes.
4. Restructure the organization to disrupt the status quo.
5. Appoint a "devil's advocate."

Action Plan

1. Which behaviour do I most want to improve? (For examples, see Summary Checklist.)
2. Why? What will be my payoff?
3. What potential obstacles stand in my way?
4. What are the specific things I will do to improve?
   (For examples, see the Reinforcement Exercises.)
5. When will I do them?
6. How and when will I measure my success?

Skills Video

Managing Conflict

Conflicts are not negative; they are a natural feature of every organization and can never be completely eliminated. However, they can be managed to avoid hostility, lack of cooperation, and failure to meet goals. When channelled properly, conflicts can lead to creativity, innovative problem solving, and positive change.

Recall the five basic conflict resolution approaches available to managers: avoidance, accommodation, forcing, compromise, and collaboration. Each has its specific function, but in all cases, treating all parties with respect and using listening skills will go a long way towards achieving positive results.

There are two main conflicts taking place at Quicktakes in this segment. Janet and Tom have a disagreement about the quality of Tom's current project, which quickly escalates into an impasse over when Tom will fix the problems, if at all. Eddie and Andrew discuss how much money Andrew spends in his London office. The two have different ideas about what level of expense is appropriate for the amount of income Andrew generates.

Each of these conflicts moves up the line to Hal Boylston's office. Eddie lets Hal know the result of his conversation with Andrew, and Janet brings her dissatisfaction with Tom to Hal for resolution. Look for the roots of these conflicts, and the reason one escalates and the other does not. Do you agree with Eddie that his conflict with Andrew has been resolved? What do you think will happen to resolve the situation between Janet and Tom?

QUESTIONS

1. What conflict resolution strategy did Janet choose? Do you think she made the right choice? What other options did she have?
2. What could Tom do differently to bring the conflict to a more positive resolution?
3. What strategies do Eddie and Andrew use in their discussion? Does anyone win, and if so, who?
4. What strategy does Hal use in the conflict between Eddie and Andrew? Why?
5. How does Hal manage the conflict between Janet and Tom? Do you think his strategy is successful? What else does he need to do to resolve the problem to the company's benefit?

CHAPTER 8

Building a Power Base

Learning Objectives

After completing this chapter, you should be able to:

- Perform an assessment of your power base.
- Enhance your position and personal power.
- Use power to achieve organizational and personal goals.
- Counteract inappropriate influence attempts.

Self-Assessment Exercise[1]

DIRECTIONS Answer true or false to indicate your beliefs about the following statements.

	True	False
1. Managers need power to do their jobs.	_____	_____
2. Power is misused when it is used for personal gain at another's expense.	_____	_____
3. Courtesy is one of the most effective tools for getting things done.	_____	_____
4. Power allows individuals, groups and organizations to accomplish worthwhile goals.	_____	_____
5. Special skills and expertise are sources of power.	_____	_____
6. A person who has power can usually protect his or her interests from the manoeuvring of others.	_____	_____
7. It is necessary and effective to constructively criticize employees for their mistakes.	_____	_____
8. Withholding my viewpoint and relevant facts to get along with someone with different prejudices would be a sell-out of my integrity.	_____	_____

	True	False
9. Being cordial to people, even if I don't like them, is as important as being good at my job.	_____	_____
10. I should not have to curry favour to get people to cooperate with me or to do the job they are paid to do.	_____	_____

SCORING Award yourself one point for each answer that matches the following key:

1. True	4. True	7. True	10. False
2. True	5. True	8. False	
3. True	6. True	9. True	

INTERPRETATION Interpret your score according to the following directions. Keep in mind that this self-perception instrument has a wide variety of possible interpretations. The following descriptions are intended only to help you take a closer look at your own attitudes and potential behaviour in organizational situations.

If you scored 0 to 3, your view of organizational power and influence may be naïve. People are likely to take advantage of you.

If you scored 8 to 10, you are extremely power oriented. You may actually be abrasive in your use of power and probably tolerate little pressure from others without fighting back. You may even turn an ordinary problem into an unnecessary confrontation for the pleasure of winning the point.

If you scored 4 to 7, you tend to be cooperative or moderately competitive in your use of power, depending on how you read the situation. You do not mind confrontations, but usually will not provoke them.

Concepts

Power is a reality of organizational life, yet most people have mixed feelings about it. Power allows an organization, group, or individual to accomplish worthwhile goals. On the other hand, power is viewed negatively when it is misused or abused. Power can be manipulative and coercive when it is used for personal gain at another's expense. For example, it can be used to reward or punish others unfairly, to take credit for an accomplishment when it is not deserved, or to escape blame or punishment when it is deserved. Power, in itself, is neither good nor bad. Rather, it is the *use* of power that is "good" or "bad." Learning how power is acquired and used wisely will help you manage others and your own career more effectively.

What Is Power?

Power is the capacity or potential to influence the behaviour of others.[2] Influence, however, entails securing the consent or agreement of others. Power and influence work hand in hand. Probably the most important aspect of power is that it is a function of *dependence*.[3] The more person A's well-being is dependent on person B, the more power person B has in the relationship. Dependence, in turn, is based on the alternatives that A is aware of and the importance that A places on the alternative(s) that B controls. If, for example, your boss has the authority to fire you, you desperately need your job to pay your bills, and you don't think it would be possible to find a comparable job, your boss is likely to have considerable power and influence over you.

Further, when you alone control a resource that others want, you have power because others are dependent on you to provide it to them so they can meet their needs. As the importance and scarcity of the resource you control increases and the availability of substitutes decreases, the more dependence others have on you, and the more power you possess. At Intel, a technological company, engineers are clearly a powerful group because the company is extremely dependent on their knowledge to maintain its products' technical advantages and quality. At Procter & Gamble, however, marketing is the key to success, making marketers a powerful occupational group.

A second aspect of power is that it need not be exercised, but only recognized, to be effective. Just knowing that your boss has the right to fire you for poor performance will affect your behaviour. That is, you are likely to comply with the manager's legitimate requests.

Why Is Power Important?

Managers need power to do their jobs. Power is a means to facilitate goal attainment, solve problems, create strategy, evaluate performance, motivate others, and manage teams. Also, employees rate powerful yet cooperative managers as competent, effective, and supportive.[4]

In the real world of organizations, however, the "good guys" do not always win. At times, in order to get things done or to protect your interests against the manoeuvring of others, you will have to play "hard ball." To play hard ball effectively, you need to have power.

How Can Power Be Acquired?

Power originates from both an individual's *personal characteristics* and *position* within an organization.[5]

POSITION POWER

Position power is associated with the holder of a position or role within an organization. In formal organizations, managerial positions come with *legitimate power* or authority, which provides the right to give directions and expect those directions to be carried out. Employees accept the position authority of a manager regarding legitimate activities as a part of the psychological contract of a job description. Managers need to realize, however, that position power is relative; giving commands is risky, especially if the manager's performance depends on the creative action or expertise of employees.[6] Furthermore, if legitimate authority alone is consistently used to influence behaviour, others will likely seek to gain counterbalancing power. Even the mere possession of formal authority isolates the manager from those employees who inherently resist influence, or are simply uncomfortable with authority figures.[7] Nevertheless, formal authority is often necessary to resolve complex differences of opinion, as when a higher-level manager dictates a solution to how differences are to be resolved between two or more battling departments.

People in managerial positions also have the discretion to allocate rewards (*reward power*). Managers can give out desirable work assignments, appoint people to interesting or important projects, provide favourable performance reviews, and recommend salary increases. Managers can also enact punishments (*coercive power*), such as dishing out undesirable work shifts and assignments, putting people onto boring or low-profile projects, writing unfavourable appraisals, recommending undesirable transfers or even demotions, and limiting merit raises. Coercion tends to lead to resentment, conflict, and lower employee morale, and should be avoided.

PERSONAL POWER

You don't have to be a manager with formal authority to have power; you can derive power from personal characteristics. There are several bases of personal power. You can influence others if you possess needed expertise, have personal charisma, have access to important information, or are able to develop positive, respectful relationships.

EXPERTISE   In today's knowledge-intensive world, *expertise power* has become an increasingly powerful source of influence. As jobs become more specialized and complex, organizations have become dependent on experts with special skills to achieve goals. Expertise is credibility gained from experience on the job or education. Software analysts, tax accountants, environmental engineers, and marketers are examples of individuals in organizations who influence others as a result of their expertise power.

CHARISMA   Charisma exists when others identify with and are attracted to someone they admire.[8] If others seek your acceptance because they like and admire you, you have what is known as **referent power**. If others wish to model themselves after your behaviours, you have considerable influence over what they do.

ASSOCIATION POWER   We have all heard the saying, "It's not what you know, but whom you know." In most organizations, success usually results from a combination of both. However, some people who possess no position or personal power themselves are able to influence others because they have close respectful associations with other people who do have position and/or personal power. Staff members with no formal organizational authority who develop close advisory relationships with high-ranking managers have *association power*.

INFORMATION POWER   When others need information to which only you have access, you have *information power* because others are dependent on you for what they need to know. People in accounting, information systems, marketing, and purchasing often have access to information others seek, which gives them considerable influence. Control over the distribution of critically needed information enables people to define reality for others, which can influence how they perceive situations and how they behave. One example would be people in marketing research who generate information on how consumers respond to new or existing products or services. Another example is receptionists and secretaries who have access to information needed by others, sometimes even their bosses.

NETWORKING   Networking is a special form of information power. It is the process of establishing, maintaining, and utilizing a broad network of contacts who are willing to share information and knowledge and to make their influence available to you.[9] Networking is building a web of relationships for mutual benefit, and it occurs both inside and outside the organization. Think of it as building a community of friends. Some tips on how to build your network include:

- *Make the effort*   Networking takes time and is hard work. Make the first move by smiling, introducing yourself, and asking people about themselves and their business. Alternatively, actively listen to conversations and find information that could be used as a lead-in to "small talk." Find common interests that you can discuss.
- *Network everywhere*   Many people think of traditional professional gatherings, industry associations, conferences, or shared interest groups as the only place to network; however, the opportunities are endless. Expand the notion to include social gatherings, charities, local clubs, recreational events, or wherever people gather.

- *Networking is a two-way process*   Be prepared to give and get information, resources, advice, or referrals, but first take the time to set out realistic and specific objectives. View these relationships as a means to exceed what you could accomplish on your own initiative. This may mean attempting to cultivate contacts with a broad range of people in strategic positions or serving on community committees whose membership includes influential people. For example, knowing that your objective is to establish professional contacts, or to learn more about consumer issues, or to seek out experts in your field will help you to achieve your goals. At the same time, develop long-lasting relationships by being a generous resource for your contacts. Think of what you can offer them and deliver more than you promise. In every encounter, ask: What can I learn? What can I contribute?

- *Swap business cards*   Exchanging business cards will serve to remind you of the contacts you've made. At the end of the conversation, ask for a business card and offer yours. Maintain a professional image by carrying your cards in an attractive case. This will avoid the embarrassment of dog-eared or wrinkled cards.

- *Organize and follow up*   Some people find it convenient to record important details in a small notebook *after* a conversation. Be sure to set up a system to organize and keep your contact list up-to-date. Exchange ideas and expertise on a regular basis to keep up-to-date on trends, patterns, or changes. Use appropriate opportunities to keep in regular contact.

IMAGE MANAGEMENT

Managing one's image is also an attempt to increase personal power. It is the process of shaping the image you project during interactions with others in order to favourably influence how others see and evaluate you.[10] Image management is utilized by individuals at all organizational levels as they interact with senior managers, peers, and employees as well as with suppliers, customers, and other people outside the organization. Organization members are especially likely to use **impression management** tactics such as publicizing successes, doing favours, or "dressing for success" to affect the perception of their bosses, on whom they are dependent for evaluations, raises, and promotions.[11]

Some individuals, however, attempt to use deception to influence another's perceptions. Deception includes lying, which is concealing or distorting truthful information, and behaviours that do not reflect true feelings or beliefs. Because honesty and trust are so important for productive long-term relationships, deception can be a serious flaw that can undermine your power. The biggest cost of lying is that you may lose the trust of other people who depend on you and on whom you depend.[12]

Given these considerations, a definition of positive impression management might be an attempt to convey as positive an impression as possible without lying about one's capabilities, achievements, and experiences.

Assess Your Power

Before you consider how to use the power you possess, you need to perform a comprehensive evaluation of your specific situation. The following three-step process is recommended.

1. *Assess the organizational culture*   Begin by assessing your organization's culture to ascertain which behaviours are deemed desirable and undesirable. One of the fastest and most effective means for tapping the power aspects of an organization's culture is to learn as much as you can about the organization's performance appraisal system and the criteria used for determining salary increases, promotions, and other rewards.

Then turn your attention to the reward system. Determine who gets the raises and promotions, and who does not. These reward-allocation decisions can tell you which behaviours are highly valued in your organization and which behaviours are not.

2. *Assess the power of others* People are either powerful or they are not, right? Wrong! Power is differential. On some issues, a certain person may be powerful. Yet that same person may be relatively powerless on other issues. Consequently, you need to determine which individuals or groups will be most powerful in different situations.

First, determine who has formal authority to affect the issues you are concerned about. Then consider which individuals, coalitions, and departments may have vested interests in the decision's outcome. This determination helps to identify the stakeholders and their interests. Next, specifically assess the power of each stakeholder or group of stakeholders. This assessment includes not only position power or formal authority, but also personal power and the scarce resources each controls, such as key information or expert knowledge.

Also assess your boss's power status in the organization and his or her position on issues of concern to you. The support of a powerful boss can obviously benefit you. On the other hand, weak support of your boss is likely to be of little help and no support will be harmful to your cause.

3. *Assess your own power* Determine where you stand relative to others who hold power. Examine the source of your personal power. Does your position in the organization provide power through the authority to reassign people, approve time off, hand out salary increases, initiate suspensions, or fire employees? Are you fortunate enough to have charisma, that magnetic personality that draws others to you? Are others dependent on you for expertise or specialized information? Do you have positive relationships with others who support you and your position on the issue?

Also examine the dynamics between yourself and other stakeholders. Determine the degree to which the other stakeholders support or resist you. Identify: where your allies are; where resistance is likely to be; the intensity of support or resistance; and the amount of personal, positional, and coalitional power you and your supporters can exert to counter the resistance of opponents.

Using Power to Maximize Your Managerial Effectiveness

How do you turn your conceptual understanding of power into effective influence strategies? In this section you will learn how to translate your power bases into specific actions to obtain the outcomes you desire. You will also learn specific strategies appropriate for different kinds of situations.[13] There are three categories of influence strategy: persuasion (based on reason, needs, or personal values), exchange, and retribution and intimidation.

PERSUASION STRATEGIES (I'D LIKE YOU TO DO THIS BECAUSE...)

1. *Reasoning* Reasoning is the use of facts and data to make a logical or rational presentation of ideas. In part, you are the expert. This strategy attempts to show people that it is in their best interest to comply and is most likely to be effective in a culture characterized by trust, openness, and logic, and where the vested interests of other parties in your request are low.

2. *Consultation* This involves gaining cooperation by involving an individual or group in the decision-making process. In many cases, the other party will identify with the issue, blunt his or her criticism, and most likely accept the decision.

3. *Personal appeal* This is an attempt to gain cooperation by appealing to someone's loyalty or sense of friendship.
4. *Ingratiation* This involves gaining cooperation by putting people into a good mood. Examples include friendliness, flattery, creating goodwill, and being supportive prior to making a request. It is more effective for obtaining favours than for selling ideas. Being friendly works best when you are already well liked and have a productive interpersonal relationship with the target of influence.

EXCHANGE (IF YOU DO THIS, YOU RECEIVE...)

1. *Bargaining* This involves the exchange of benefits or favours to negotiate outcomes acceptable to both parties. Bargaining is essential where two conflicting parties are interdependent and must rely on each other for goal accomplishment. Bargaining is easier to apply where the organizational culture promotes give-and-take cooperation.
2. *Coalition building* Coalitions exist when a number of other people in the organization have similar interests and support the same outcome. Forming coalitions and using them effectively is complex and requires planning and coordination. They are most effective where final decisions rely more on the quantity than on the quality of support. Consequently, managing coalitions is worth the energy when important outcomes are at stake in situations such as a committee meeting where the decision will be made by majority rule.

RETRIBUTION AND INTIMIDATION (DO THIS OR ELSE!)

1. *Legitimating* This is an attempt to gain cooperation by referring to one's formal authority. This strategy can work if the request is seen as legitimate. It may also be appropriate in bureaucratic-structured organizations that have cultures with great respect for authority. It is only appropriate in less structured organizations where managers have power because they are either liked or feared.
2. *Pressure* Examples of this approach are demanding compliance with requests, issuing reminders, ordering individuals to do what you need done, and pointing out that rules require compliance. This strategy is most effective when the balance of power is clearly in your favour, for example, when because of your position you have considerable ability to reward and punish others, and their power over you is low. The drawback to this method is that the target is likely to feel resentful and look for later opportunities to retaliate.
3. *Sanctions* This is the use of organizationally derived rewards and punishments to obtain desired outcomes. Examples include preventing or promising a salary increase, threatening to give an unsatisfactory performance appraisal, and withholding a promotion. This strategy is similar to pressure, except the influence here depends solely on your position. Obviously, it is not an approach for influencing senior managers; and even when used with employees, it may be perceived as manipulative or illegitimate.

Ways to Respond to Inappropriate Influence Attempts

Managers tend to be most effective when they assume others are reasonable and well intentioned. Unfortunately, this is not always the case. Therefore, it is important to be able to protect ourselves from those who abuse us or seek personal gain at our expense. Examples include overbearing bosses or individuals who are manipulative or use high-pressure tactics.

Often inappropriate influence tactics occur in organizational climates that have ambiguous goals, significant organizational change, and/or scarce resources. In these situations, open communication and transparent processes, clarifying goals and expectations, and handling yourself in a manner that is beyond reproach will tend to limit manoeuvring.

Because power is a function of dependence, the long-term strategy should be to gain more power in order to reduce or eliminate a dependency on another person or group. In the short run, however, you may have to attempt to position yourself so that you and the other individual are dependent upon one another, or are *interdependent*. Then over time, shift the discussion to common goals and how each of you can assist the other in meeting those goals. If unsuccessful, confront the individual. Be sure to describe the offending behaviour accurately, express how it makes you feel, and make specific suggestions for change. If necessary, specify the actions you are prepared to take if the behaviour persists. If still unsuccessful, take the issue to a higher authority such as your boss or a senior manager.

For individuals who use deceit or manipulative tactics, confront them as stated above. Outright deceit is probably not that common. Ingrained moral or ethical codes prevent most people from deliberately lying, especially if the chances of being found out are high.[14] Refuse to bargain with those who use high-pressure tactics and suggest fairer approaches to negotiate. For individuals who insist on offering gifts or favours, consider the person's motive, the appropriateness of the offer, and the potential consequences. If it's not appropriate, simply decline the offer.

Consider the Cost–Benefit Equation

Before you attempt to influence someone, be sure to weigh all the potential costs of using your power against its potential benefits. Some forms of power are accepted more readily than others, and in many instances, the costs of applying influence exceed the benefits derived. While the benefits of power are quite obvious, the costs are often overlooked. It has been noted, "Power is effective when held in balance. As soon as power is *used*, it gets out of balance and the person *against whom* the power is used automatically resorts to some activities designed to correct the power imbalance."[15]

Ask yourself: Is this the most effective and efficient way to achieve my short-term goals? What are the potential consequences of using this strategy? For example, will it minimize resentment or avoid other negative reactions? Such analysis usually suggests a preference for strategies emphasizing reason, friendliness, and rewards to obtain compliance, and an avoidance of coercive approaches.[16] Remember, whenever you use the "do this or else" approach, you run the risk that your bluff will be called or that future negative reactions will be worse than your immediate gains. In other words, in cost–benefit terms, the results may not be desirable; you may win the battle but lose the war.

Concept Quiz

Complete the following true–false quiz by circling the correct answer. Answers are at the end of the quiz. After marking your answers, remember to go back and check your understanding of any answers you missed.

True or False   1. Most people try to conceal their influence attempts because the application of power is unethical.

True or False   2. The degree of power one person holds over another is primarily a function of dependency in the relationship.

True or False   3. It is what you know, not whom you know, that determines your power in an organization.

True or False   4. Position power is also called authority or legitimate power.

True or False   5. A manager does not have to be concerned about acquiring power in larger organizations because with enough resources the "good guys" always win.

True or False	6. You cannot have power in a large organization unless you have a position that has formal authority.
True or False	7. Expertise and the right to give rewards are forms of personal power.
True or False	8. Networking is a two-way process that expands one's access to information.
True or False	9. Coalitions are individuals or groups that have similar interests and support the same outcome.
True or False	10. "Winning the battle but losing the war" is an important consideration when deciding on specific power tactics.

Answers (1) False; (2) True; (3) False; (4) True; (5) False; (6) False; (7) False; (8) True; (9) True; (10) True

Behavioural Checklist

The following skills are important when building a power base. Use them when evaluating your power-building skills and those of others.

The Effective Power Builder:

- Identifies where the power is in the organization.
- Applies formal authority sparingly.
- Strives to develop personal power bases.
- Frames desires in terms of organizational benefits.
- Considers the cost–benefit equation before selecting an influence strategy or power tactic.
- Responds to inappropriate influence attempts.

Modelling Exercise
Role-Play: Power and the Truck Trading Problem[17]

All class members should read the following situation.

SITUATION A large electric appliance company has six repair technicians. It is necessary for them to drive to various locations in the city to complete their work. Each repair technician drives a small truck and takes pride in keeping it looking good. The technicians have a possessive feeling about their trucks and like to keep them in good running order. Naturally, they would prefer to have new trucks because it gives them a feeling of pride.

A new truck has just been allocated to the crew. The new truck is a Chevrolet. The supervisor has just called a meeting to determine who will get the new truck.

Here are some facts about the trucks and the repair technicians in the crew who report to Sean Marshall, the supervisor of appliance repairs. Most technicians do all of their driving in the city, but Jo and Charlie cover the jobs in the suburbs.

Jo:	17 years with the company, has a 2-year-old Ford truck
Bo:	11 years with the company, has a 5-year-old Dodge truck
Jean:	22 years with the company, has a 3-year-old Ford truck
Charlie:	5 years with the company, has a 3-year-old Ford truck
Fran:	3 years with the company, has a 5-year-old Chevrolet truck

DIRECTIONS After the class reads the previous situation, pick one role-player to be the supervisor and five more role-players to be crew members. The role-players read the reminders for role-playing and their own role, but not the other roles, and prepare for the role-play.

The remainder of the class will be observers and provide feedback on the power dynamics in the role-play. They should be divided into five equal groups, each of which is assigned to observe one of the specific role-players. Observers should NOT read any of the roles. The observers' job is to see whether they can determine which power bases and political tactics the various role-players are applying. They also provide specific feedback to their assigned role-player on his or her effectiveness in applying power in the exercise. Observers should review the Observer's Rating Sheet to prepare for providing meaningful feedback at the end of the exercise.

SEAN MARSHALL'S ROLE You are the supervisor of a crew of repair technicians, each of whom drives a small service truck to and from the various jobs. Every so often you get a new truck to exchange for an old one, and you have to decide which of your crew will receive the new truck. Even though you always try to be fair, the decision often generates hard feelings because each crew member feels entitled to the new truck. No matter what you decide, most of the crew is unsatisfied. You now have to face the issue again because a new Chevrolet truck has just been allocated to you for distribution.

Most of the crew drive in the city and make fairly short trips. The exceptions are Jo and Charlie, who cover the suburbs. In order to solve the problem this time you have decided to allow the crew to decide who gets the new truck. You will tell them about the new truck and will frame the problem in terms of what they think would be the fairest way to assign the truck. You will avoid taking a position yourself because you want to do what the crew thinks is fair.

If the crew is unable to reach a consensus, you can always exercise your supervisor's authority to make the final decision. You know that it is your responsibility as supervisor to guide and direct the meeting.

JO'S ROLE You have to do more driving than most of the other technicians because you work in the suburbs. You have a fairly old truck and feel that your large amount of driving makes you the best candidate for a reliable new truck. You were an automobile mechanic prior to becoming an appliance technician and you know that several trucks have problems that can be easily fixed to make them perfectly satisfactory for their current drivers. If any of these drivers argues for the new truck, you will explain how to make easy repairs rather than discarding them. You plan to use your expertise assertively in favour of winning the new truck for yourself.

JEAN'S ROLE When a new Chevrolet truck becomes available, you think you should get it because you have the most seniority and do not like your present truck. Your personal car is a Chevrolet, and you prefer the Chevy truck you drove before you were allocated the current Ford. You have known Sean Marshall's boss since you both hired on as technicians more than 20 years ago. If your seniority does not work to get you the new truck, maybe a tactful bit of name dropping will do the job.

FRAN'S ROLE You have the least desirable truck in the company. It is five years old, and before you got it, it was in a bad wreck. It never has driven well and feels unsafe, but you have put up with it for three long years and feel the next one should be yours. You have an admirable accident record. In fact, the only accident you ever had occurred when you sprung the door of Charlie's truck when he opened it as you backed out of the garage. You hope the new truck is a Ford because you prefer them to other brands. You are well liked by the rest of the crew because of your charismatic personality. You plan to use friendliness, flattery, and humility to really sweet talk the crew during the meeting in hopes of securing the new truck for yourself.

CHARLIE'S ROLE The heater in your present truck is inadequate. The door lets in too much cold air, and you attribute your frequent colds to this problem. You want a warm truck because you have a good deal of driving to do. As long as it has good tires, brakes, and is comfortable you don't care about its make. Although Fran never admitted it, you know that it was Fran who backed into the door of your truck, and it has never been repaired to fit right. You also know that Dodge trucks have better maintenance records than other makes, and that an allocation is currently pending for another new truck next month. You plan to use this information to bargain for the new truck for yourself.

BO'S ROLE You feel you deserve a new truck. Your present truck is old, and because the senior person has a fairly new truck, you should get the next one. You have taken excellent care of your present Dodge and have kept it looking like new. A person deserves to be rewarded for treating a company truck like a personal vehicle. You plan to use this logic to reason with the others that those who conscientiously maintain their vehicles should get their just desserts.

Observer's Rating Sheet

On completion of the exercise, rate how well the role-players applied the power-building skills using the following rating scale. Write concrete examples in the space below each skill component to use when explaining your feedback. Also note examples of behaviours that demonstrate applications of power tactics and influence strategies and indicate how effective they were.

1 Unsatisfactory	2 Weak	3 Adequate	4 Good	5 Outstanding

Name of Person Observed _____

■ Identified where the power is in the organization. _____

■ Applied formal authority sparingly. _____

■ Worked to develop personal power bases. _____

■ Framed desires in terms of organizational benefits. _____

■ Considered the cost–benefit equation before selecting tactics. _____

■ Responded to inappropriate influence attempts. _____

Group Exercises

Three different types of group exercises are presented here. First is a case for you to practise your awareness, analysis, and action-planning skills. Second is an exercise for you to apply and get feedback about your personal power strategies. Third is an opportunity to solicit the help of others to analyze and plan how to better build your power base.

Group Exercise 1: Case Analysis of The Bill and Mary Show[18]

INSTRUCTIONS The following case can be discussed in small groups or by the class as a whole. It should take about 15 minutes to read and think about the questions, then another 20 to 30 minutes to discuss the case.

CASE Mary Cunningham was a hot topic at Bendix Corporation long before September 1980, when Bill Agee stood before more than 600 employees and denied that her rapid advancement had anything to do with "a personal relationship that we have." Cunningham joined the company right after obtaining her MBA from Harvard in June of the previous year. She was hired as executive assistant to the CEO, Bill Agee, after a three-hour interview in New York at the Waldorf–Astoria. "A meeting of kindred spirits," she said. Exactly one year later, Agee gave her a promotion to vice-president for corporate and public affairs. Three months after that came another promotion to vice-president for strategic planning. Agee tried to confront the uproar that immediately followed by announcing to employees that his new vice-president and he were "very, very good friends" but not romantically involved. The comment backfired, creating a national media furor so intense and so focused on Cunningham's youth, blonde hair, and shapely figure that in the fall of 1980 the Bendix board of directors forced her resignation.

Inside Bendix, gossip about the relationship between Cunningham and Agee escalated after her June promotion, and all sorts of additional events kept the noise level up. A television camera focusing on former President Gerald Ford at the Republican National Convention happened to find Agee and Cunningham sitting next to him. Some Bendix people suggested that Agee was less accessible than he had once been, and Cunningham's growing influence with him did not help to allay suspicions. She had called herself his "alter ego" and "most trusted confidante"; he said she was his "best friend."

Top corporate executives in the United States had been accused of almost everything imaginable except having romances with one another. But, what was one to think? Here were two attractive people working together, travelling together, even staying in the same two-bedroom suite at the Waldorf Towers. They had to be having an affair—that would explain Cunningham's sprint up the ranks. On the other hand, was Cunningham, as Gail Sheehy portrayed her in a four-part newspaper series, a brilliant, idealistic corporate missionary destroyed by jealous cynics? Barbara Seaners interviewed Cunningham, and feminist leaders like Gloria Steinem rallied to her defence, asking whether her treatment meant that young, talented, attractive, ambitious, and personable female executives were permitted only slow climbs upward, lest they invite gossip.

Insisting that their relationship had been platonic until after she left Bendix, Agee and Cunningham married in June 1982. By then, Agee had converted to Catholicism and divorced his wife of 25 years. Cunningham's six-year marriage to Howard Gray, an executive with American Express, was annulled. The same year, after resurfacing as a vice-president at Seagram's, Cunningham acted as Agee's unpaid adviser during Bendix's attempted takeover of the Martin Marietta Corporation. Their ambitious plan collapsed, however, when Bendix was swallowed by the Allied Corporation in a merger that cost hundreds of Bendix employees their jobs. The fiasco was blamed, in part, on the chair's young wife, the strategic planner.

In 1988, Bill Agee was named CEO of the Morrison Knudsen Corporation in Boise, Idaho. Six years later, in 1994, Morrison Knudsen posted losses of $310 million and lurched toward bankruptcy. In February 1995, Bill Agee was ousted as MK stock fell from $30 a share to $5; employees and retirees alike watched their futures evaporate. In February, too, Mary Agee resigned as executive director of the nonprofit Morrison Knudsen Foundation, a position critics say she used to benefit the Nurturing Network, a nonprofit women's organization that she founded in 1983.

The Boise community did not regret the Agees' demise. It was not only the shareholders' losses and the hundreds of MK workers Bill Agee fired, but the fact that the Agees rubbed Boise the wrong way almost from the start—so much so that after being excluded from the town's private clubs and most prestigious boards, the couple and their two children abruptly relocated in 1992, to a $3.4 million estate in Pebble Beach, California. From that Pacific Coast setting 965 kilometres away from their offices, Mary Agee managed her charity and Bill Agee ran Morrison Knudsen by phone, fax, FedEx, and from a $17 million corporate Falcon jet that peeved MKers dubbed "Mary's taxi."

Now, with more than a dozen lawsuits filed by shareholders charging that Bill Agee and the Morrison Knudsen board wasted assets and managed the company recklessly, Mary Agee's role was under legal as well as public scrutiny regarding the use of MK assets to benefit the Nurturing Network. The lawyers also eyed the close relationship linking MK and its foundation with the Nurturing Network—a complex web of friendships, business interests, and moral commitments. In 1992, half the MK board members had wives on the Nurturing Network board, and Bill Agee served on both boards. "Once so many of the directors and their wives had joined with the Agees in...a moral crusade," the *New York Times* pointedly asked, "how likely was it that they would challenge Mr. Agee in the boardroom?"

QUESTIONS FOR DISCUSSION

1. What are the major power issues in this case?
2. What were Mary Cunningham's original power bases when she first joined Bendix? What other sources of power did she acquire? How?
3. What bases of power did Bill Agee have? Did he acquire any more?
4. How did the effectiveness of Bill Agee's power bases change? Why? What were the consequences?
5. What could Bill and Mary have done differently to avoid the negative outcomes?

Observer's Rating Sheet

When you finish reading the case, rate how well both Bill Agee and Mary Cunningham applied power-building skills, using the following rating scale. Write concrete examples in the space below for each skill component to use when discussing your ratings.

1 Unsatisfactory	2 Weak	3 Adequate	4 Good	5 Outstanding

Bill   Mary

- Identified where the power is in the organization. _____ _____

- Applied formal authority sparingly. _____ _____

- Worked to develop personal power bases. _____ _____

- Framed desires in terms of organizational benefits. _____ _____

- Considered the cost–benefit equation before selecting tactics. _____ _____

- Responded to inappropriate influence attempts. _____ _____

Group Exercise 2: Role-Play: Power Plays Within Universal Care, Inc.

This role-playing exercise enables class members, working in groups of 7 to 10, to experience influence behaviours when confronted with obvious differences in power. You will assume the position of a vice-president who has a place on the board of directors. Because a variety of crises have been plaguing the firm, the CEO just resigned and you and other company vice-presidents must now elect a replacement from among your peers. When told by your instructor, your group will assemble as a board of directors to nominate, discuss, and eventually elect the new CEO using the bylaws of Universal Care, Inc. Following the board meeting and election, you will then discuss what you learned.

PURPOSE The exercise serves three purposes: (1) to create complex and realistic roles from sketchy data; (2) to confront issues and negotiate decisions when actors have explicit power differences; and (3) to stimulate introspection about your personal reactions to having more or less power than other group members and the behaviours you use to deal with power discrepancies.

TIME 45 to 60 minutes.

MATERIALS One index card per student (5″ × 7″ suggested) and one felt-tip marker per group.

BACKGROUND ON UNIVERSAL CARE, INC. Universal Care, Inc. (UCI), was founded 15 years ago by a physicist, a biologist, a chemist, and an engineer. The company has grown erratically into what is now a $5 billion multidivisional firm. UCI branched beyond its entrepreneurial beginnings in molecular research into diverse lines of business, all related to health care. The firm currently has products in pharmaceuticals, genetic engineering, medical instrumentation, residential nursing, and prosthetics (including a mechanical heart).

During the past year, UCI has increasingly come under a variety of pressures, even attacks. Several lawsuits against the firm for alleged product malfunctions that resulted in injury or death were won by the plaintiffs. Fortunately, no class action suits have yet been settled against the company, although two are pending—one involving a heart implant valve alleged to be associated with three patient deaths. Other biotech firms alleging infringement of patents on DNA-related products have filed three suits. Several of these incidents have made the front pages of major daily newspapers, each raising questions about the propriety of the firm's products and/or operations.

Management is faced with the likelihood of a significant fourth-quarter loss that is expected to result in negative earnings for the year (which ends in two months). The expected loss is due to a combination of: legal judgments against UCI; reserves set aside for possible future legal losses; intensified competitive action in several product segments, causing loss of market share; and the difficulty in assimilating seven recent acquisitions (especially in the residential nursing segment). Additionally, a number of key employees in research and management have recently defected, leaving human resource gaps in some key areas. (A few of these former employees left after blowing the whistle on questionable company practices.)

Under these intense pressures, the CEO today announced a personal decision to resign and take early retirement, effective in two weeks. Because of the rapid growth of the firm in the past few years, no serious effort had been given to developing a successor. Now, however, the company faces a pressing need for a new CEO, and the corporate bylaws are explicit on the process. According to the wishes of the founders (who withdrew from active management within two years of UCI's going public six years ago), the bylaws state that a new CEO must be elected from the ranks of incumbent managers who sit on the board of directors.

You are a vice-president of UCI and a member of the board of directors. You are quite concerned by the sudden resignation of the CEO and the need to elect a replacement quickly. A special board meeting has been scheduled solely for the purpose of electing a new CEO. You have a little time to prepare for that meeting and to communicate selectively with some of your peers on the board.

ROLE-PLAY PREPARATION

1. Students form "companies" of 7 to 10 members. Sit in a circle or around tables, if possible, facing one another within a company.
2. Students read "Background on Universal Care, Inc."
3. While students are reading, the instructor distributes to each group a number of 5"x 7" index cards equal to the number of team members, and one marker each.
4. After reading the background note, each person within a company selects a vice-presidency, such as finance, operations, the medical instruments division, etc.
5. One person per team marks the index cards with numbers, beginning with 200 and working up in 100 unit denominations until all cards are used (equal to the number of team members). Numbers should be written so that when folded into a tent shape, a number will appear on both sides. Now, that person shuffles and deals the cards face down, one to a person.
6. The number on the card each person receives represents the number of shares of stock that he or she owns or controls by proxy. Once the directors (vice-presidents) move into the election phase of the board meeting, shares of stock become important in electing a new CEO. Students write the title (vice-presidency) they are assuming and display their card in front of them for others to see.

PHASE 1: E-MAIL COMMUNICATIONS Because of Universal's problems, all VPs are out in the field putting out fires. Although they cannot communicate face to face with one another, they keep in touch by e-mail. You initiate e-mails by writing notes (on paper) and pass them to others with whom you want to communicate. As an "interested executive and board member," the instructor is concerned about the forthcoming board meeting for the specific purpose of selecting a new CEO (who must be one of the VPs).

As VPs you can communicate to whomever you want about whatever you want, but most likely you will discuss the pending election, candidates, qualifications, and so on. If you want several people to receive the same message, provide a routing by listing names. Use this phase as an opportunity to get into your role. You have about 5 minutes for this e-mail phase.

PHASE 2: FACE TO FACE AT COMPANY HEADQUARTERS When the instructor calls time on the e-mail phase, everyone stands up. All VPs are now back at company headquarters, waiting for the board meeting to begin. You may now caucus with whomever you choose. Join up with the person or persons you want to meet with and then back away from the table for your conversations. This time is not for a meeting of the whole—you'll get that opportunity soon enough.

PHASE 3: BOARD MEETING When instructed to by the facilitator, take a seat for the board meeting. The facilitator will pick a VP and introduce him or her: "The outgoing chair and CEO has asked that [person] with _____ shares of stock chair this meeting. The

CEO has also provided a written reminder that the bylaws are specific on how to elect a new CEO. Discussions and nominations are in order, as are questions to the candidates and perhaps a formal statement from candidates. Once the group is ready to vote, follow these guidelines. Voting must be public by voice, beginning with the person who controls the greatest number of shares, working to the smallest in descending order. When it is your time to vote, you can split votes (shares) among the candidates, or can abstain; however, if you abstain, you cannot re-enter voting for that round of voting. If an impasse (no clear winner) occurs, then on the next round of voting anyone who previously abstained can now vote. To elect a new CEO requires a vote of two-thirds of all outstanding shares. You may begin your board meetings." When finished, report your results to the instructor.

DEBRIEFING Discuss the following questions in your groups to bring out reactions to power differences and to methods of exerting influence or political behaviour.

1. For those with low power (200–400 shares), what was your initial reaction once you realized the significance of the number you were dealt? What did this suggest to you about the possible strategy you might follow to be heard and perhaps be influential? How about high-power people?
2. Who received the most e-mail messages? Why? What is the significance of this phase?
3. What did people with low power do during the e-mail phase to increase their base of power? How about the high-power players?
4. Describe the nature of coalitions formed within your company and the extent to which they remained together or either broke up or consolidated.
5. What other influence behaviours did you either observe or engage in? Why were influence behaviours more or less effective?
6. Of those of you with high power, did anyone choose not to seek the CEO position, and if so, why?
7. What were your overall reactions to having to confront the reality of working with people where formal power was hierarchically differentiated? Did high-power or low-power people feel more comfortable with this situation, and why?

Group Exercise 3: Personal Power Strategies for Allocating Resources

In preparation for this exercise, students should review the bases of power and influence tactics described in the text. They should also be advised in advance to bring $1 to class on the day of the exercise and to be prepared to risk it if they wish to participate.

PURPOSE To increase awareness of power bases and strategies participants actually use, and to provide feedback on how their political effectiveness can be enhanced.

TIME Total time is 45 minutes: 30 minutes for the exercise; 15 minutes for feedback and debriefing.

INSTRUCTIONS The class is divided into groups of six to eight participants. Each group member must contribute $1 to a pot. It is possible that a participant will lose his or her $1. On the other hand, it is possible that he or she will receive more than originally contributed or even the whole pot. The money distribution will be made at the end of the exercise according to the following procedure:

Each group's task is to decide how to divide the money in the pot any way they want between two-thirds of its members, i.e., two people in a group of six will not get their money back. It is not legitimate to use any sort of chance procedure like drawing straws, or to avoid the exercise like agreeing to return each person's money after the exercise regardless of what happens. The final decision is to be determined by group consensus, i.e., all must agree to the final allocation. Do not make a hasty decision. Wait until all have argued their viewpoints and are ready to decide.

The objective for each individual participant is to get as much money as possible for him or herself. The 30-minute time limit in which the group must make its consensus decision is critical. The time limit is important, because if a group cannot decide how to allocate the money in 30 minutes, the instructor gets the entire pot!

REFLECTION   Immediately following the end of the exercise, each participant should write down the answers to the following questions:

1. What were your feelings during this exercise?
2. What power bases did you draw upon?
3. What influence strategies did you utilize?
4. How successful were you in achieving your goals? Why?
5. What did you learn about yourself with respect to how you feel and deal with power and influence?

DEBRIEFING   One at a time, *each participant* should: (1) discuss answers to the preceding questions with others in the group; (2) receive feedback regarding the effectiveness of his or her personal power tactics; and (3) solicit suggestions about how they could be improved. After each individual has received feedback, the *total group* discusses: (1) why the winners (those who received the most money) were more successful than the losers (who lost their money); (2) how the outcome might be different under different circumstances; and (3) what they learned about using power in conflict situations.

Application Questions

1. Can you be an effective manager and avoid power and influence?
2. You have just joined a large organization as a first-line supervisor. Using your power-building skills, what can you do to increase the probability of succeeding on this job?
3. How are you currently involved in power and influence on your job, in your classes, and with those with whom you live?
4. How do you currently practise impression management? Give examples.

Reinforcement Exercises

The following suggestions are activities you can do to reinforce the power-building techniques in this chapter. You may want to adapt them to the Action Plan you will develop next, or try them independently.

1. Review six recent issues of *Canadian Business*, *Business Week*, or *Fortune* magazine. Look for articles on reorganizations, promotions, and departures from upper management. Do these articles suggest that power and influence factors were involved in the management changes? Explain.
2. Interview three managers from three different organizations. Ask them to describe the roles that they perceive power and influence to play in decision making in their organization. Ask for examples that they have participated in or been affected by.

Summary Checklist

Take a few minutes to reflect on your performance and look over others' ratings of your power-building skills. Now assess yourself on each of the key learning behaviours. Make a check (√) next to those behaviours on which you need improvement.

_____ Identify where power is in the organization.

1. Assess the organizational culture for desirable behaviours, the performance-appraisal system, and the criteria used for determining salary increases, promotions, and other rewards.

2. Assess your own power by examining your personal power (expertise, charisma, information, and associations) and your position power (formal authority).

3. Assess the power of others by determining who has formal authority, and finding out who controls scarce resources.

_____ Apply formal authority sparingly.

1. Use discretion to allocate rewards and enact punishments.

2. Be on the lookout for resistance to formal authority.

_____ Develop personal power bases.

1. Acquire needed expertise.

2. Develop personal charisma.

3. Gain access to important information.

4. Build positive relationships with powerful associates.

5. Develop and expand your network inside and outside the organization.

_____ Frame desires in terms of organizational benefits.

1. Avoid actions that appear to blatantly further your own interests at the expense of the organization's.

2. Emphasize the benefits that will accrue to the organization.

_____ Consider the cost–benefit equation before selecting an influence strategy.

1. Weigh all potential costs of a strategy against potential benefits.

2. Consider all potential consequences, such as minimizing resentment and avoiding other negative reactions.

_____ Respond to inappropriate influence attempts.

1. Clarify goals and expectations.

2. Insist on open communication and transparent processes.

3. Accurately describe the offending behaviour, express how it makes you feel, and make specific suggestions for change.

4. Suggest fair approaches to negotiation.

Action Plan

Think of a situation in which you want to increase your power. Develop a plan to do so, applying what you have learned in this chapter.

1. Why do I want to increase my power? What will be my payoff?
2. Where is the power in the organization?
3. How can I increase my power and decrease my dependency on others?
4. What are the specific things I will do to increase my personal power?
5. When will I do them?
6. How and when will I measure my success?

CHAPTER 9
Motivating Others

Learning Objectives

After completing this chapter, you should be able to:

- Determine motivational factors to keep employees on the job.
- Identify the factors that motivate people to perform.
- Diagnose sources of performance problems.
- Apply appropriate methods to motivate employees to perform better.

Self-Assessment Exercise

How Do I Motivate Others?

For each statement, enter the number from the rating scale that best describes what you do when another person needs to be motivated:

All of the time 1	Most of the time 2	About half the time 3	Less than half of the time 4	Never 5

_____	1. I assume that performance problems are caused by lack of motivation.
_____	2. I always establish a clear standard of expected performance.
_____	3. I always offer to provide training and information, without offering to do tasks myself.
_____	4. I am honest and straightforward in providing feedback on performance and assessing advancement opportunities.
_____	5. I use a variety of rewards to reinforce exceptional performances.
_____	6. When discipline is required, I give specific suggestions for improvement.
_____	7. I design task assignments to make them interesting and challenging.
_____	8. I strive to provide the rewards that each person values.
_____	9. I make sure that people feel fairly and equitably treated.
_____	10. I make sure that people get timely feedback from those affected by task performance.

All of the time 1	Most of the time 2	About half the time 3	Less than half of the time 4	Never 5

_____ 11. I carefully diagnose the causes of poor performance before taking any action.

_____ 12. I always help people establish performance goals that are challenging, specific, and time bound.

_____ 13. Only as a last resort do I attempt to reassign or release a poorly performing individual.

_____ 14. Whenever possible I make sure valued rewards are linked to high performance.

_____ 15. I consistently intervene when performance is below expectations and below capabilities.

_____ 16. I try to combine or rotate assignments so that people can use a variety of skills.

_____ 17. I try to arrange for an individual to work with others in a team, for the mutual support of all.

_____ 18. I make sure that people use realistic standards for measuring fairness.

_____ 19. I provide immediate compliments and other forms of recognition for meaningful accomplishments.

_____ 20. I always determine whether a person has the necessary resources and support to succeed in a task.

SCORING AND INTERPRETATION[1]   Add up your point ratings for the 20 questions to obtain your total score for how you motivate others. You can determine how well you motivate others by comparing your scores to three standards:

1. The maximum possible score of 120 points.
2. The scores of your classmates.
3. A norm group of 500 business school students. In comparison to the norm group, if you scored:

101 or above	you are in the top quartile.
94–100	you are in the second quartile.
85–93	you are in the third quartile.
84 or below	you are in the bottom quartile.

Concepts

People make at least two decisions about motivation every day when they come to work. One is whether to stay in the organization or look for another source of work. The other is how much effort to put into performance on the job. Consequently, managers need to be concerned about two corresponding aspects of motivation: motivating workers to stay on the job and motivating them to perform at their best.

Motivation consists of a conscious decision to direct effort in an activity to achieve a goal that will satisfy a predominate need. This definition of motivation contains three elements: (1) some need or goal that triggers action; (2) a selection process that directs the choice of action; and (3) the intensity of effort that is applied to the chosen action. In essence, motivation governs behaviour selection, direction, and level of effort.[2]

This chapter provides specific methods for motivating employees to stay on the job and to perform at their best. First, what motivates workers to stay in an organization will be discussed. Then the discussion will shift to the determinants of job performance, followed by what we know about the needs that motivate people to perform. Finally, methods you can apply to motivate employees will be described.

What Motivates Workers to Stay on the Job?

In a recent survey of nearly 1300 U.S. managers and employees, Kepner-Tregoe, a New Jersey human resources consulting firm, found that nearly two-thirds said their companies have suffered increased worker turnover since 1996. They said the loss of high-performing employees has "dulled their companies' competitive edge and led to a decline in quality and in customer service."[3] These consequences are serious, and because it is the high-performing employees who usually leave for more desirable surroundings and rewards, it is important to determine what causes them to leave.

In a survey of 500 000 employees at more than 300 U.S. firms, the Hay Group, a large human resources consulting firm, discovered that among 50 factors affecting employee staying power, pay ranked the lowest. If pay is not the motivator, what is? In its study, the Hay Group found that giving employees the opportunity to learn new skills ranked highest. Coaching and feedback from managers was another top factor. The employees perceived a problem here because top performers receive less of both, because managers think the "stars" do not need their help. Yet ironically they value feedback the most, which points to the third major factor causing employee retention problems: a "bad boss." Even if organizations have all other programs right, if managers do not treat their direct reports equitably and with respect, then none of the other factors matters.[4]

One of the greatest mistakes managers make in implementing a reward system that will retain and motivate employees is assuming that they know precisely what employees want in return for doing their jobs. Two of the main reasons for these mistakes is that managers assume that all workers want the same outcomes, which are the same ones that the managers think workers prefer. Several studies have indicated a low correlation between workers' actual priorities for work rewards and the priorities attributed the same rewards by their bosses.[5] In general, managers most often believe that what workers want most from their jobs are things such as good wages, job security, promotions, and good working conditions. The workers themselves, however, usually rank aspects such as challenging work, recognition for good work, participation in decisions that affect them, and sympathetic understanding of personal problems higher than job security and good wages.[6]

If managers do not provide workers with opportunities to obtain the rewards they desire in the organization, the workers will go somewhere else where they can get what they want. It is important to be aware that their immediate managers, for the most part, can easily provide the things employees want most. Consequently, a manager should always take advantage of opportunities to provide more challenging work, recognition for good work, participation in decisions that affect employees, and sympathetic understanding of personal problems. These efforts are free, and they pay great motivational dividends.

What Motivates People to Perform Well on the Job?

The desire to perform well isn't always enough to ensure good performance. It is also necessary to have the ability to perform. The determinants of task performance can be summarized in the model in Exhibit 9-1.[7]

Exhibit 9-1 Determinants of Task Performance

Performance = Ability × Motivation
Ability = Aptitude × Training × Resources
Motivation = Desire × Commitment

Performance is the product of a person's ability multiplied by his or her motivation. Ability is the product of aptitude multiplied by training and resources. Motivation is the product of desire and commitment. All elements in these equations are necessary for high performance. For example, a worker could have 100 per cent motivation, but if he or she only has 10 per cent of the required ability, performance will not be satisfactory, no matter how hard the worker tries.

Given these multiple determinants of task performance, the first question a manager should ask when below-par performance is observed is whether it is caused by lack of ability or lack of motivation. If the manager determines that the problem is lack of ability, rather than motivation, no amount of pressure or encouragement will help. What the employee needs is training, additional resources, or a redesign of the job. Chapter 15, Developing Employees, discusses skills for enhancing ability. In this chapter, the focus is on increasing motivation by enhancing desire and commitment.

Motivation was earlier defined as a conscious decision to direct effort in an activity to achieve a goal that will satisfy a predominate need. Therefore, it is needs that drive, or motivate, behaviour to satisfy the tension they create. An unsatisfied need creates tension, which sets off a drive to satisfy that need. In order to motivate employees, a good place to start is to determine what types of needs exist and what is required to satisfy them.

BASIC NEEDS

Perhaps the best known theory of motivation is Abraham **Maslow's hierarchy of needs**.[8] Maslow proposed that every individual has a five-level hierarchy of needs that he or she attempts to satisfy, beginning with physical well-being and progressing successively through safety, belonging, esteem, and self-actualization (see Exhibit 9-2). According to Maslow, once a lower-level need has been largely satisfied, its impact on behaviour diminishes. The individual then is freed up to progress to the next higher-level need, and it becomes a major determinant of behaviour. Each of these needs is described, followed by an example.

PHYSIOLOGICAL NEEDS Physiological needs refer to our physical survival. These basic needs include the needs for food, water, and shelter. They can be satisfied at work by receiving enough pay to purchase the basics for survival such as groceries, water, clothing, and housing.

SAFETY NEEDS When physiological needs are reasonably satisfied, the safety needs become aroused. For example, if you are having an asthma attack and cannot breathe, all you care about is getting a breath of fresh air. Once your attack has subsided, however, you become concerned with safety, security, and protection from another life-threatening event. At that point you might be motivated to find a prescription inhaler or other drug that you could keep on hand to feel more secure in case you have another asthma attack. Safety needs can be satisfied at work by receiving job security, medical benefits, and safe working conditions.

SOCIAL NEEDS Once you feel reasonably secure and have had enough to eat and drink, social needs begin to drive your behaviour. They are the needs people have for affiliation,

Exhibit 9-2 Maslow's Hierarchy of Needs

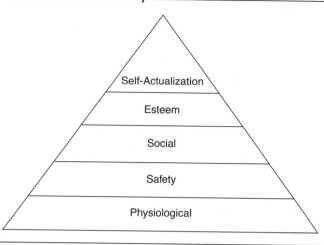

Source: A.H. Maslow. "A Theory of Human Motivation," *Psychological Review* 50 (1943): 370–96.

for giving and receiving affection, and for friendship. Social needs can be satisfied at work by having good relationships with co-workers and participating in company social functions.

ESTEEM NEEDS Two types of esteem needs motivate us after we have fairly well satisfied our physiological, safety, and social needs. One type is those needs that relate to one's *self-esteem*, including needs for self-confidence, independence, achievement, competence, and knowledge. The second type of esteem needs concern esteem from others. They include things that affect your reputation, such as needs for recognition, status, appreciation, and respect. Esteem needs can be satisfied at work by being recognized for accomplishments and receiving promotions.

SELF-ACTUALIZATION NEEDS These highest-level needs only begin to really affect our behaviour after all lower-level needs have been reasonably satisfied. They are the needs for fulfillment by becoming the person we feel we have the potential to become. Self-actualization motivates us to continue self-development and learning. Self-actualization needs can be satisfied at work by receiving tuition reimbursement for continuing education, attending training sessions, and having opportunities to exercise your creativity in endeavours that fully utilize your skills and abilities.

So how does the need hierarchy work in a real situation? Imagine that Theresa, a technical writer and single parent, has been earning a good salary and benefits that enable her to provide for her family's physical well-being—ample food, comfortable housing and clothing, good medical care. Then her company announces it is downsizing (reducing the number of employees), and she fears being laid off (which triggers a safety need). She is unlikely to be overly concerned about the higher-order need of belonging to a group or her own self-esteem need to perform creative and technically accurate work. Rather, she is likely to be motivated to do whatever she believes will enable her to keep her job and/or to begin looking discreetly for other employment. Once the layoffs have been announced and Theresa realizes she is not on the list, she breathes a sigh of relief, and focuses back on her work with a higher-order need energizing her behaviour.

As the preceding example demonstrates, current circumstances automatically determine which level of inherent basic needs will be aroused and acted on. Another category of needs, however, is learned or socially acquired. Depending on your personal experience, you may have one or two strong socially learned needs. These needs are learned through repeated positive reinforcement in previous experiences, and they motivate our behaviour whenever we perceive an opportunity to satisfy them.

LEARNED NEEDS

David McClelland and his colleagues have studied three learned motives that he believes are especially important for motivating people at work.[9] They are the needs for achievement, power, and affiliation. These higher-level needs are associated with Maslow's social, esteem, and self-actualization categories. But, since most of the employees that a manager supervises have their basic physiological and safety needs satisfied by the organization, the higher, learned motives are the ones that hold the most potential for motivating others. Because individuals have learned to value these acquired needs differently, the manager's job is to determine which ones specific individuals are most concerned about, and then provide opportunities for them to satisfy these needs in the organization.

THE ACHIEVEMENT MOTIVE Because achievement is highly valued in most Western societies, most of us like to think of ourselves as being achievement oriented. However, people's **achievement motives** vary in intensity, as do all motives. People who really have a high need to achieve are self-motivated; they seek tasks that will provide them with a sense of accomplishment. For example, they may choose an opportunity to confront a challenging but doable task rather than attend the company's Friday afternoon pizza social.

The achievement motive can be measured by what people say, do, or write. Several behavioural characteristics distinguish the achievement-motivated person.[10]

1. Achievers prefer a moderate level of difficulty or challenge. Just as they avoid tasks that are too easy, they also shy away from those that are extremely difficult. Being realistic, they know their limitations. The most desired task is one that requires a high level of exertion but carries a reasonable probability of success.
2. High achievers also like to feel that they are in reasonable control of an outcome. If the element of chance or luck is a primary factor in success, or if others over whom they have little influence are involved, they experience a reduced incentive to try.
3. Achievement-motivated people also like to receive frequent and specific feedback about how well they are doing. This preference does not mean they need constant praise from their supervisors. Ideally the task itself should provide enough feedback so they can evaluate themselves; self-approval is a strong motivator for an achiever.

THE POWER MOTIVE As you learned in Chapter 8, Building a Power Base, power is the capability to influence others to behave as you want. People who have a high need for power, or **power motive**, find satisfaction from being in charge and influencing others. Although it is important to have high achievers in an organization, it is also necessary to have some take-charge types for whom power is the dominant motive. These people are willing to specify organizational goals and influence others to achieve them. It is difficult to be a successful manager without a need for power, especially in large organizations. Managers must learn to take satisfaction in acquiring and exercising the means for influencing others.

Managers with strong power needs can be classified into two types, depending upon how they exhibit their needs.[11] Managers with high personal power needs exemplify the stereotypical self-serving, exploitative, dominating boss. Such a need for power reflects the aim of personal gain through manipulation and control of others without exhibiting self-control and inhibition. A personal-power boss may coerce and even threaten employees in a forceful attempt to get them to carry out commands. Such a manager then takes credit for their successes. Contrary to what is presented in soap operas, these managers usually don't make it to the top of an organization because people they stepped on earlier find ways to sabotage their careers.[12]

Managers with high institutional power needs, on the other hand, temper their influence over others with inhibition and self-control. They are altruistic and believe power should be used more for the good of the organization than for personal advantage. Satisfaction is obtained more from the process of influencing others to carry out their work in pursuit of organizational goals than from their own personal success. Research indicates that higher-level managers in large organizations are more likely to be successful if they possess a high need for power that is institutionalized combined with low affiliation needs.[13]

THE AFFILIATION MOTIVE People with a high need for affiliation, or **affiliation motive**, find satisfaction in the quality of their social and interpersonal relationships. Affiliators avoid isolation (whereas achievers often welcome it), because interaction with others is so important for them. Such people easily develop wide circles of friends both in and out of the workplace. They are prone to show concern for the feelings of others and to be sympathetic to opposing views. Given the opportunity, they often try to help others work through problems.

People who are high affiliators most often make weak bosses. One study found that only 20 per cent of the "above-average" sales departments in a research sample were supervised by managers whose affiliation needs were more dominant than their power needs. Of the "below-average" departments in their sample, 90 per cent were run by affiliation-motivated managers. By contrast, power-motivated managers ran 80 per cent of the best and only 10 per cent of the worst departments. The researchers concluded that because of their need to be liked, affiliation-motivated managers made "wishy-washy decisions." They bent company rules to make particular individuals happy, and in the process they were seen as unfair.[14]

DIAGNOSING AND USING LEARNED MOTIVES TO MOTIVATE OTHERS Correctly recognizing motive patterns helps a manager motivate employees by selecting assignments that energize them. For example, the achiever is excited by his assignment to a challenging project. The power-motivated person enjoys representing her group in a negotiating session. Be cautious in making attributions about another's motives, however. The better you know another person, the better you will be able to identify the motivation patterns underlying his or her behaviour.

How Do People Decide How to Behave to Satisfy Their Needs on the Job?

Need-based theories of motivation are useful to managers because they provide a general answer to the question of what needs or motives drive human behaviour. They are often referred to as the *content* theories of motivation. If you are going to motivate people to behave in ways that will accomplish organizational objectives as well as satisfy their own needs, however, you should understand how and why workers select specific behaviours to satisfy these needs. *Process* theories of motivation explain how and why workers select behaviours and how they determine whether their choices were successful. Because people are creatures of perception, thought, and a certain degree of rationality, they are capable of making informed choices about where and how to channel energy. In making choices, the human tendency is to embrace the most advantageous option or at least avoid functioning at a disadvantage. With this tendency in mind, the process considerations for understanding how people decide what to do to satisfy their needs include goals, expectations, reinforcements, and perceptions of equity.

HOW DO GOALS ENHANCE MOTIVATION?

A **goal** is the desired outcome of an action. This section will summarize what we know about using goals to motivate others to strive for organizational objectives. Later, Chapter 11, Planning and Goal Setting, will review the characteristics of effective goals, how to set goals, how to obtain commitment to goals, and how to apply goal setting through the management by objectives process.

PARTICIPATION IN GOAL SETTING Goals become motivational when an individual desires them and strives to achieve them. It is critical, therefore, that goals are understood and accepted by those striving to achieve them. Employees are more likely to "buy into" goals if they have a part in determining what they will be and how they will be accomplished.[15] Ironically, however, while participation often produces greater commitment to goals and perceptions of self-control and fairness,[16] participation does not necessarily lead to higher performance than manager-assigned goals. One workable combination is for managers to assign goals, hold people responsible for results, grant people the autonomy to plan their actions and exercise control over how they do their work, and then measure results. People who have the capability to do the task and are committed to achieving it generally will perform well regardless of their degree of participation in setting the goal itself.[17]

CHARACTERISTICS OF EFFECTIVE GOALS To activate energetic, task-focused behaviour, a person needs clear, specific, and challenging goals. Especially when delegating tasks, managers should describe clearly what is wanted and provide specific feedback as to the appropriateness of work being done.[18]

Even though goal achievement is internally rewarding, motivation is usually increased when people believe that increased efforts will produce desired results that will lead to fair rewards they value. To get the best from their people, managers should clarify the links between effort–performance and fair rewards. This premise underlies the motivational process theories based on expectancy and equity that we will discuss next.

HOW DO EXPECTANCIES ABOUT EFFORT, PERFORMANCE, AND REWARDS AFFECT WORK MOTIVATION?

Motivation based on expectancy theory focuses on a person's beliefs about the relationships among effort, performance, and rewards for doing a job. The basics of expectancy theory for managers can be converted into a series of three questions that people often ask themselves about their work situation.[19]

1. *Does how hard I try affect my performance?* To be motivated, you must have a positive answer to this question. You must believe that your personal efforts have the potential to make a positive performance difference. You must also have the capacity for internal attribution, or a willingness to take personal credit or blame for your performance. Positive task motivation begins when you see a link between personal effort and task performance.
2. *Are personal consequences linked to my performance?* To be motivated, you must believe that task performance results will enable you to obtain personal consequences or payoffs. Increased motivation is possible when you perceive a positive personal consequence arising from satisfactory task performance.

3. *Do I value the consequences that occur?* Motivation will depend on how much you value a particular expected personal outcome or payoff. If you really do not care about the potential payoff, it provides little if any incentive value. Suppose you want recognition, but your boss simply gives you another assignment and sends you off on another trip to the boondocks. You thus discount the value of possible payoffs, and your expectation of being rewarded in a meaningful way diminishes. A person must value the payoff if the expectancy loop is to be positive and motivational.

Motivation is enhanced when a person answers yes to all three of the preceding questions. Conversely, when one or more answers are negative, motivation potential diminishes.[20]

It is important for managers to realize that not all people value the available outcomes or rewards in the same way. One of the first things managers who want to motivate by expectancies must weigh is whether employees place a greater value on extrinsic or intrinsic rewards.

HOW DOES THE NATURE OF REWARDS AFFECT MOTIVATION?

Two basic sources provide **rewards** or payoffs. Many people depend on and highly value **extrinsic rewards**—rewards that are externally bestowed, such as praise from a supervisor, a promotion or pay raise, or the grade received on a term paper. Others place a high value on **intrinsic rewards**—their own personal feelings about how well they performed the task or simply the satisfaction they derived from doing it. Managers need to realize the distinction between the two and how their employees view them. For example, in work conditions where employees seek extrinsic rewards but believe their degree of effort is not clearly visible to supervisors, "social loafing" or low effort is likely to occur. However, where intrinsic involvement in the task is high, social loafing will be low even when effort is not visible to the manager.[21]

Although most people look for some mix of intrinsic and extrinsic rewards, people clearly differ as to which is the more compelling motivational force.[22] If a manager always praises an achievement-motivated professional who excels largely for the feelings of intrinsic satisfaction, this person will probably begin to view the manager as shallow or phony. The professional may think, "I know I did a superb job on this project. Why does my manager keep stating the obvious and acting so condescending?"

Even within extrinsic rewards, people look for different types of rewards. Praise may be perfectly acceptable to the person motivated by relatedness needs or affiliation, but may do nothing for the person expecting a more tangible payoff. Typical extrinsic rewards are favourable assignments, trips to desirable destinations, tuition reimbursement for courses in which a good grade is earned, pay raises, bonuses, and promotions.

HOW DO PERCEPTIONS OF EQUITY AFFECT MOTIVATION TO WORK?

Along the path to expectancy motivation, things can go wrong. One of the most disruptive situations is when the payoffs or personal outcomes are perceived to be inequitable or unfair. Managers need to be aware of inequity perceptions and reduce gaps where possible.

Perceptions of equity moderate motivation. If expectancy motivation is to work, people must perceive an underlying fairness among effort–performance–reward relationships. **Equity theory** suggests that motivation is moderated by the perceived fairness or discrepancy between personal contributions and rewards relative to others. Two basic dimensions define the equity process.[23]

RATIO OF PERSONAL OUTCOMES TO INPUTS People often think in terms of the ratio of their personal outcomes to work inputs. That is, their perceptions of equity depend on how they answer the question: What is the payoff to me (in terms of status, benefits, recognition, money, promotion, and job assignments) relative to my inputs of effort exerted, skills, job knowledge, and actual task performance?

EXTERNAL COMPARISONS People also compare their own outcomes/input ratio to those they perceive for other people doing comparable work. These comparisons may be made on three levels.

1. *Comparisons to specific other individuals* For example, Bev might conclude, "I guess Kerri really has been outperforming me." Bev would expect Kerri to be getting more in the way of rewards and recognition.
2. *Comparisons to another reference group* Workers might think, "Our department is getting much better treatment than the shipping department." This comparison recognizes differences in payoffs and concludes that "our group" is getting a better deal.
3. *Comparisons to general occupational classifications* At times people compare themselves to people in similar positions in other organizations. A physical therapist at a private clinic might observe, "According to the national salary survey data, my pay is at only the 20th percentile, way below what someone with my experience should be earning." Another common comparison is across gender within the same occupation, where women often experience discrepancies and earn 20 per cent to 40 per cent less pay than men.

ADJUSTING FOR EQUITY GAPS You might think that equity concerns would be activated only when a person believed he or she was being taken advantage of, or was undercompensated relative to others. Not necessarily. Although it may be the more common experience, people sometimes conclude that they are overcompensated. This conclusion might have been the case in the second comparison previously listed if the workers thought, "Our group is receiving better treatment but performing no better than the group in shipping."

The equity concept affects motivation whenever a person perceives a meaningful difference in personal or group outcomes and then adjusts behaviour or perceptions to reduce the gap.[24] In a research experiment, those who survived a job layoff and thought their co-workers' dismissals were random worked harder than when they believed those caught in the layoff had produced less.[25] Similarly, if Bernice believes she is inequitably overcompensated, she might intensify her efforts to produce more to be worthy of the superior benefits she receives, or she may simply change her frame of reference to reduce the perceived equity gap, say, by comparing her pay with national rather than company data. Conversely, when people perceive that they are undercompensated relative to the frame of reference, they will likely reduce or redirect their efforts in an attempt to beat the system so they end up with a fair deal. These adverse consequences are more pronounced with extrinsic inequities (especially monetary rewards) than intrinsic inequities.[26]

Methods of Motivating Employees

ENHANCE COMMITMENT TO GOALS
We know that organizational goals become motivational only when individuals also desire them and strive to achieve them. We also know that to motivate energetic, task-focused behaviour, people need clear, specific, and challenging goals. Therefore, it is important to make sure that goals are understood and accepted by those striving to achieve

them. One way to get this understanding and "buy in" is to ensure that employees participate in setting goals and how they will be accomplished. Then managers should make sure to provide specific feedback as work toward goals is being completed.

Another way to apply goal setting to enhance motivation is to apply the more formal management by objectives (MBO) process described in Chapter 11, Planning and Goal Setting.

STRENGTHEN EFFORT–PERFORMANCE–REWARD EXPECTANCIES

A manager can benefit from applying expectancy theory. First, the theory is most applicable to those jobs in which an individual has discretion as to how and when work is performed. For example, it would have somewhat greater applicability for airline reservation agents (who can either be thorough and helpful or abrupt and indifferent) than for operators on a machine-paced assembly line. But it likely has even greater relevance for professionals such as accountants, market researchers, stockbrokers, and systems analysts.

To get the best from their people, managers should emphasize anticipated reward value, whether extrinsic or intrinsic.[27] The manager's job is to strengthen effort–performance–reward expectancies. For employees who have difficulty attributing outcomes to their performance, managers must make sure they realize performance–reward connections and then provide performance feedback.

CLARIFY PERFORMANCE–REWARD LINKAGES Not all employees know about or understand how extrinsic organizational rewards link to performance. The managerial challenge is to clarify rewards available to employees and relate them to personal and team performance.[28] Even though many organizations provide little performance-based pay differentiation among people of the same salary grade, a manager can bestow other extrinsic rewards. For example, a manager can allocate more favourable job assignments to those who meet or surpass performance expectations. The key is to make obvious in advance the payoffs people can expect for certain levels of performance, then follow up on satisfactory performance with feedback and appropriate rewards.[29]

PROVIDE PERFORMANCE FEEDBACK Managers need to provide feedback both to demonstrate that they know what others are doing and to acknowledge improved performance or a job well done. Especially for employees who seem unsure of themselves or tend to attribute success externally, a manager should point out ways in which the employee is improving.[30] Praising specific accomplishments or improvements helps bolster employee esteem and promote internal attribution. It helps forge the link between focused effort, performance improvement, and the personal outcome of recognition from powerful others and personal feelings of pride.

PROVIDE SALIENT REWARDS

We learned from expectancy theory that it does little good to try to motivate someone to put forth extra effort in performance if they do not desire the reward you offer as a consequence. The important question for a manager to ask is, "Do employees feel that the rewards they can obtain for high performance are worth the effort?" We know that all employees do not value the same rewards equally, and that managers are not the best judges of what employees prefer. Therefore, perhaps the best way to make sure that employees are offered salient rewards is to ask the employees themselves what they prefer. Of course, we also know a wide diversity of answers will result.

One method for adapting to the diversity in preference for work rewards is to offer cafeteria-style benefits.[31] This increasingly popular practice is to let people select from among a portfolio or menu of benefits. One way to implement such a plan is to allocate performance-based credits that employees can cash in on a variety of benefits including bonuses, increased insurance or health benefits, extended vacations, or tuition reimbursements for education.

For example, Arthur has a wife who stays at home with their three children. He may be quite concerned that he has comprehensive family medical coverage with minimum deductibles. Felicia, on the other hand, is single and in her early twenties. She might prefer increased vacation allowances and educational reimbursement benefits in exchange for a higher deductible in her medical insurance plan. Such flexibility in selecting benefits, while not necessarily related to employee output, helps promote a positive answer to the expectancy question: Do I value the rewards available to me?

REINFORCE THE RIGHT BEHAVIOUR

Quite often what managers say they want, what they reward, and what they get from employees are not the same.[32] If innovation is espoused, but doing things by the book is what is rewarded, it does not take a psychologist to figure out what the manager actually values. Another example of rewarding A while hoping for B is a business that says it wants to take care of its customers, then rewards managers for cutting costs in ways that negatively impact customers. The lesson is that often, without thinking, managers reinforce the wrong behaviour. Such errors in judgment suggest that the selective use of rewards should be a key tactic in managers' efforts to motivate employees. One approach that can help avoid such errors is to apply reinforcement theory through behaviour modification.

Behaviour modification is a technique of changing behaviour through the use of contingent rewards or punishments. Behaviours that lead to positive consequences (rewards) tend to be repeated, whereas behaviours that lead to negative consequences (punishments), or are not reinforced, tend not to be repeated. Consequently, if behaviours are not reinforced, or are punished, they will be extinguished. Also, by providing valued rewards at the right times, a person is more likely to change his or her behaviour in a desired direction.[33] Several types of reinforcement and their consequences are described next.

Positive reinforcement occurs when a reward, such as praise or a bonus, is given after a desired behaviour occurs. It can include actions such as calling or writing a note to congratulate an employee for completing a project on time and under budget.

To eliminate an undesired behaviour, **punishment** can be applied. For example, a manager could punish a late employee as a reprimand in hopes that the behaviour would not be repeated. Punishment usually is effective in stopping a specific undesired behaviour, but it does not reinforce desired behaviours and often causes negative feelings with associated detrimental consequences. It is usually better to try and decrease the frequency of the undesired behaviour by withholding any reward when it occurs.

This process of **extinction** can be especially useful when someone is inadvertently being rewarded for doing the wrong thing, as in the preceding examples of rewarding A while hoping for B. Therefore in the case of the managers who say they want employees to do whatever is necessary to take care of their customers, but then reward people for cutting costs in ways that negatively impact customers, those rewards for any activities, including cost cutting, that negatively impact customers need to be stopped. Now employees no longer have any incentive for cutting costs in ways that negatively impact customers, so this behaviour will probably be extinguished over time. The employees still have no incentive to take the desired actions, so to get exactly what you want in terms of changed behaviour, in this case of customer service, positive reinforcement is preferred.

Even highly valued rewards, however, lose their motivating potential unless they are given at the correct times. It is the timing of reinforcements that lets employees know which behaviours are being encouraged. As we saw in the cases of rewarding A while hoping for B, giving rewards at the wrong times can inadvertently increase an undesirable behaviour. For example, if an employee comes into a manager's office and complains that a fully warranted raise is long overdue, and the manager grants the raise as a result, the employee may learn to complain more rather than work harder. In addition, not giving a reward when a desired behaviour occurs may extinguish it. For example, a customer service representative who has a superb performance record will likely lose motivation if he or she receives the same yearly pay raise as those whose performance is mediocre.

REWARD IN A TIMELY MANNER

We know that to motivate a behaviour change, we need to reward desirable behaviours. Unfortunately, most organizations have established reward systems that postpone rewards for months, for example, until annual performance reviews are scheduled. These delays dilute the motivational potential of rewards because it is difficult to tie them to specific performance. As you will learn in Chapter 14, Evaluating Performance, annual performance reviews can be valuable opportunities to provide feedback on past performance and set new goals, which may cause employees to leave with a new set of commitments. However, like New Year's resolutions, this high soon wears off because the employee has little to look forward to until next year. To motivate employees to perform at their best throughout the year, more frequent reinforcement is required.

So, how frequently should positive behaviours be rewarded? The schedule you utilize to reward positive behaviours can make a big difference. Is it better to reward employees every time they do well, or only periodically?

The fastest way to establish a desirable behaviour is through **continuous reinforcement**: reinforce the desired behaviour continuously each and every time it occurs. The drawback is that the desired behaviour also diminishes quickly once you stop reinforcing it. Say, for example, that you consistently praise an employee for arriving at work on time. What will happen if you must be away from work for an extended training program? The employee may slip back into being late because without the reinforcement of the expected rewards behaviour is extinguished.

An alternative is **intermittent reinforcement**, where the reward is not provided every time it is warranted, but on a random basis that is frequent enough to hook the person to continuing the desired behaviour. Although it may take longer to get someone to change his or her behaviour, intermittent reinforcement is the most powerful way to get sustained changes in behaviour. With this schedule people will continue producing the desired behaviour for a long time even without reinforcement, because they are always expecting to "hit the jackpot" on the next try. Have you ever experienced the addictive nature of playing a slot machine, which only pays off infrequently and intermittently?

ADMINISTER REWARDS EQUITABLY

Once appropriate rewards have been determined for each employee, linkages have been clarified to performance, and the best reinforcement schedule determined, managers still need to consider how workers feel about the equity of the distribution. Motivation is moderated by the perceived fairness or discrepancy between personal contributions and rewards relative to others.

The important question is, "Do employees feel that work-related benefits are distributed fairly?" If they don't, and especially if they believe that they are on the short end of the distribution, people will make their own adjustments to compensate. Remember the earlier example of the customer service representative who performed better than colleagues did but received the same pay increase each year as everyone else? The likely result was that the representative stopped performing as well because performance was not being rewarded equitably. If any of the motivation enhancement skills are going to work, people must perceive an underlying fairness among effort–performance–reward relationships.

An important thing to remember about fairness is that it concerns perceptions about equity that may or may not be valid. Nevertheless, whether they are accurate or distorted, they are accurate in the mind of the beholder. Consequently, managers need to monitor employees' perceptions of equity closely by gathering data and asking clarifying questions. It is possible that this monitoring may uncover false assumptions about how the organization values various behaviours, or faulty comparisons regarding the performance of others. If misperceptions are discovered, they can be clarified, which may reinstate employees' acceptance of the fairness in the reward system. On the other hand, such monitoring may uncover overlooked inequities that management needs to correct.

TIE PAY TO PERFORMANCE

It seems intuitively obvious that if you want to motivate people to perform you will tie their level of pay to the quantity and/or quality of work that they produce. Uniform systems of pay may seem equitable, but from a motivational perspective, such nonperformance payments do not necessarily encourage stellar performance.

Performance-based compensation schemes are consistent with the expectancy theory of motivation. Employees compare rewards received for performance with what they expect to receive. They also compare what they receive with what others receive (the equity factor). In the following paragraphs, some methods of administering performance-based compensation are explained.

PIECEWORK OR STANDARD-HOUR SYSTEMS The classic performance-based reward system is based on piecework, or payment for the amount produced consistent with specified quality standards. Piecework systems do motivate workers when a person can directly affect his or her rate of output, and the output (quality and quantity) can easily be measured or verified. Some programmers' pay depends on how many lines of code they write; magazine writers are often paid by the number of words in their articles.

A pay-for-performance variation is to use a **standard-hour plan**. Such plans specify the normal time required to complete a task, coupled with a standard rate of pay. For example, the standard for a technician to complete a job may be 45 minutes at a rate of $40. A more skillful technician may be able to complete more jobs per day, receiving pay for each at the standard rate.

Two difficult issues plague any piece- or standard-rate plan.[34] One is evaluating work methods to arrive at an equitable standard and rate. Because managers like to periodically adjust one or both compensation factors, the issue of equity can be controversial. The second concern is the quality–quantity tradeoff. Without appropriate quality controls, quality may be sacrificed to reach quantity targets. As previously noted, behaviour tends to focus on what is measured.

MERIT PAY Rather than tie pay only to output, an alternative is to provide a base salary or hourly wage and then an incentive or bonus based on output. Where the base plus merit, or merit pay, incentive system is used, the performance-based portion depends on some measurable level of output over which the employee has control. Output could be measured by volume, defect rate (or quality), or cost savings. Sales representatives often earn a base salary plus commissions based on the level of sales above a set base figure.

BONUS AND PROFIT-SHARING PLANS Many compensation plans are based on the overall performance of the enterprise rather than the individual's contribution. Profit sharing has become common in many firms including Domino's Pizza, where everyone owns stock and profits are distributed back to members.[35] In merit-based pay plans, a pool of money is divided among eligible employees based on some performance evaluation or rating system. The objective of profit-sharing plans such as bonuses and stock options is to link everyone's fate to overall organization performance, reinforcing corporate cultures that emphasize group results over individual performance.

For Wal-Mart, corporate profit growth is a primary goal, and the profit-sharing plan is keyed to it.[36] Every employee who works at least 1000 hours per year is eligible for profit sharing. The firm contributes a percentage of every eligible employee's wages or salary (an average of 6 per cent over the last 10 years) into a fund, from which the employee can withdraw cash when leaving the company. This plan helps employees commit to long-term corporate and personal financial growth.

GAINSHARING PLANS Gainsharing is an umbrella for approaches to encourage employees at all levels to be responsible for improving organizational efficiency. Gainsharing plans link financial rewards for all employees to improvements in performance of the entire business unit.[37]

While the number of companies in Canada reporting performance-based pay has increased, especially in the last decade, it is far from being the norm. In unionized work environments, however, performance-based pay is more the exception than the rule. There are three major issues that continue to be stumbling blocks. First, labour unions believe that the introduction of performance-based pay should only be negotiated as part of the collective bargaining process. Second, there is concern that production standards could be set abnormally high. Third, there is a concern that performance-based pay could cause an increase in the pace of work, leading to health and safety problems.[38]

EMPOWER EMPLOYEES TO ACHIEVE

Empowerment describes conditions that enable people to feel competent and in control and energized to take the initiative, and to persist at meaningful tasks.[39] Empowerment aspires to bring about positive self-perceptions (self-concept, self-esteem, and self-efficacy) and task-directed behaviours. A manager can empower employees by giving them the authority, tools, and information they need to do their jobs with greater autonomy. As a result, employees' feelings of self-efficacy are enhanced and they are enabled to use their potential more fully, which satisfies their higher-level needs for achievement, recognition, and self-actualization.

As a management practice, empowerment also means managers open communications, delegate power, share information, and cut away at the debilitating tangles of corporate bureaucracy. The manager who deliberately works to empower his or her employees gives them licence to pursue their visions, to champion projects, and to improve practices consistent with organizational missions and goals. The manager who shares responsibilities with employees and treats them as partners is likely to get the best from them.[40]

Empowered people usually intensify their task focus and are energized to become more committed to a cause or goal. They experience self-efficacy, which stimulates motivation by enabling people to see themselves as competent and capable of high performance.[41]

Empowerment also is manifested in active problem-solving behaviours that concentrate energy on a goal. The empowered person is more flexible in behaviour, tries alternative paths when one is blocked, and eagerly initiates new tasks or adds complexity to current ones.[42] Behaviour becomes self-motivated when the individual seeks to carve out greater personal autonomy in undertaking tasks without the manager's help.

Empowerment success stories abound. At BPCO, a manufacturing plant producing building products in Pont-Rouge, Quebec, a participatory management approach was introduced. Policies were developed jointly by management and labour and workers now have direct input into the decision-making process. Although change was slow, more and greater responsibilities were given to workers including the replacement of supervisors with unionized team leaders. As a result, people now try to find solutions to their problems together.[43] At Kruger, a manufacturer of newsprint in Bromptonville, Quebec, empowerment takes the form of union–management problem-solving groups and performance improvement groups. Results include lower absenteeism, fewer accidents, and a higher quality of paper produced.[44]

REDESIGN JOBS

Chapter 12, Designing Work, describes how well-designed jobs lead to high motivation, high-quality performance, high satisfaction, and low absenteeism and turnover. For these outcomes to occur, managers need to ensure that workers experience challenging work, believe they are doing something meaningful because their work is important to other people, feel personally responsible for how the work turns out, and receive feedback on how well they perform their jobs.[45] If these conditions exist, employees can experience high-level motivators such as increased responsibility, achievement, recognition, growth, and learning. Additional benefits of jobs rating high in motivational design are decreased boredom and lower absenteeism.

MAKE AVAILABLE OPPORTUNITIES TO LEARN

Making available opportunities to learn is motivational because it enables employees to grow and develop, which provides a route to fulfilling their potential. As employees learn new skills, they become competent to complete more complex tasks. This competency satisfies their needs for achievement, enhances their sense of self-efficacy, and helps them progress towards self-actualization. Honeywell Limited's Scarborough, Ontario, factory, which makes heating and cooling valves, has provided an outstanding example of learning motivation in action. Honeywell developed a Learning for Life program to improve productivity and quality. The company introduced computer-based manufacturing and realized that they could only be successful if skill levels, knowledge, and decision making of employees were also addressed. Through this program, factory throughput increased by 180 per cent and the quality of its product by 92 per cent.[46] Another outstanding example is Alcan Aluminum Limited in Kemano, B.C., which launched its Personal Education Program following extensive consultations with its labour partner, the Canadian Auto Workers. This program is designed to enhance employees' reading, writing, numeracy, and computer skills to enable them to adapt to a plant reorganization and modernization.[47]

Some companies, recognizing the payoff for the organization that has multiskilled, committed employees, have added incentives to continue learning by basing salaries on the number and quality of skills employees possess.[48] This pay basis provides satisfaction for basic needs and esteem needs. When increased education and skills lead to promotions to higher positions in the company, learning also satisfies needs for growth and self-actualization.

Managers can provide some forms of learning personally through helping, mentoring, and coaching employees. More will be provided on these opportunities in Chapter 15, Developing Employees. A large variety of companywide programs can also be set up to provide incentives to learn, including on-the-job training, in-house seminars, tuition reimbursement for courses and degree programs, and sponsorship for attending continuing education certification programs, workshops, conferences, or correspondence courses.

Concept Quiz

Complete the following true–false quiz by circling the correct answer. Answers are at the end of the quiz. After marking your answers, remember to go back and check your understanding of any answers you missed.

True or False   1. Motivation consists of a conscious decision to direct effort in an activity to achieve a goal that will satisfy a predominate need.

True or False   2. All workers want the same outcomes, so managers can effectively motivate people by providing rewards that managers think workers prefer.

True or False   3. People will always do their best on a job if they have the necessary training, skills, and abilities.

True or False   4. Because most employees have their basic physiological and safety needs satisfied, the higher, learned needs are the ones that hold the most potential for motivation.

True or False   5. It is not good to promote people with high institutional power needs to management positions because they become self-serving, exploitative, and dominating bosses.

True or False   6. Employees are more likely to "buy into" goals if they have a part in determining what they will be and how they will be accomplished.

True or False   7. The most important question in expectancy theory is: does how hard I try really affect my performance?

True or False   8. Most people prefer intrinsic rather than extrinsic rewards.

True or False   9. Motivation is moderated by the perceived fairness or discrepancy between personal contributions and rewards relative to others.

True or False   10. Even highly valued rewards lose their motivating potential unless they are given at the correct times.

Answers (1) True; (2) False; (3) False; (4) True; (5) False; (6) True; (7) False; (8) False; (9) True; (10) True

Behavioural Checklist

The following skills are important to motivating others. Use them when evaluating your own motivation skills and those of others.

The Effective Motivator:

- Enhances commitment to goals through clarification and participation.
- Strengthens effort–performance–reward expectancies.
- Provides salient rewards.
- Utilizes positive reinforcement.
- Rewards in a timely manner.
- Administers rewards equitably.
- Ties pay to performance.
- Empowers employees to achieve.
- Redesigns jobs to motivate employees.
- Makes available opportunities to learn.

Modelling Exercise
Reshaping Unacceptable Behaviours[49]

One of the most challenging aspects of management is transforming inappropriate behaviours into appropriate behaviours. Managers commonly take insufficient action to transform negative actions into positive ones. Some of these insufficient responses include: assuming that ignoring an employee's shortcomings will make them go away; praising positive aspects of an individual's performance in hopes that the praise will encourage him or her to rechannel unproductive energies; discussing problems in vague, general terms in a group meeting, in hopes that the unproductive person will take the "hint" and change; and getting upset with an individual and demanding that he or she shape up.

DIRECTIONS One volunteer assumes the role of the manager, Andre Tate, and another assumes the role of a staff member, Shaheen Matombo. Role-players read only their own role, and prepare for the role-play. Other class members read both roles and review the Observer's Rating Sheet. After the role-play discussion, observers will provide feedback to the person playing the manager, Andre Tate, on his or her performance, using the Observer's Rating Sheet as a guide. Then, the class discusses other options to resolve this problem.

ANDRE TATE'S ROLE Shaheen has been a member of your staff for only three months. You don't know much about her other than that she is a single parent who has recently entered the workforce after a difficult divorce. She is often 10 to 20 minutes late for work in the morning. You are the manager of a hectic customer relations office for a utility company. The phones start ringing promptly at 8:00. When she is late for work, you have to answer her phone, which interrupts your work schedule. This morning, you are particularly annoyed. She is 25 minutes late, and the phones are ringing like crazy. Because you have been forced to answer them, it will be difficult for you to complete an important assignment by the noon deadline. You are getting more upset by the minute.

While you are in the middle of a particularly unpleasant phone conversation with an irate customer, you look out your window and see Shaheen bounding up the steps to the building. You think to yourself, "This is ridiculous, I've got to put a stop to her tardiness. Maybe I should just threaten to fire her unless she shapes up." Upon further reflection, you realize this action would be impractical, especially during this period of retrenchment after the rate hike was turned down. Given the rumours about a possible hiring freeze, you know it may be difficult to refill any vacancies.

Also, Shaheen is actually a pretty good worker when she is there. She is conscientious and has a real knack with cranky callers. Unfortunately, it has taken her much longer than expected to learn the computer program for retrieving information on customer accounts. She frequently has to put callers on hold while she asks for help. These interruptions have tended to increase an already-tense relationship with the rest of the office staff. She has had some difficulty fitting in socially; the others are much younger and have worked together for several years. Shaheen is the first new hire in a long time, so the others are not used to breaking someone in. Three of your staff have complained to you about Shaheen's constant interruptions. They feel their productivity is going down as a result. Besides, she seems to expect them to drop whatever they are doing every time she has a question. They had expected their workload to be lighter when a new person was hired, but now they are having second thoughts. (In the past, you have had enough time to train new hires, but your boss has had you tied up on a major project for almost a year.)

Shaheen enters the office obviously flustered and disheveled. She has "I'm sorry" written all over her face. You motion for her to pick up the blinking phone line and then scribble a note on a tablet while you complete your call: "See me in my office at 12:00 sharp!" It is time you got to the bottom of Shaheen's disruptive influence on an otherwise smooth-flowing operation.

SHAHEEN MATOMBO'S ROLE   Boy, what a morning! Your babysitter's father died during the night, and she called you from the airport at 6:30 A.M. saying she would be out of town for three or four days. You tried three usually available backups before you finally found someone who could take Keen, your three-year-old. Then Shayla, your seventh-grader, went through five outfits before she was satisfied that she had just the right look for her first yearbook picture. It is a miracle that Buddy, your oldest, was able to pull himself out of bed after getting only five hours of sleep. On top of football and drama, he has now joined the chess team, and they had their first tournament last night. Why did it have to fall on the night before his final in physics? This morning you wished you had his knack for juggling so many activities. By the time you got the kids delivered, you were already 10 minutes behind schedule. Then an incredible accident on the expressway slowed traffic to a crawl.

As you finally pull off the downtown exit ramp, you notice you are almost 20 minutes late for work. "My kingdom for a cell phone!" you groan. "Although by now I probably couldn't get an open line into the office, anyway." As you desperately scan the side streets for a parking space, you begin to panic. "How am I going to explain this to Andre? He will be furious. I'm sure he is upset about my chronic lateness. On top of that, he is obviously disappointed with my lack of computer skills, and I am sure the others complain to him about having to train a newcomer." You are sure that one of the reasons you got the job was that you had completed a computer class at the local college. Unfortunately, the carryover to the incredibly complex computer program you use at work had been minimal. (It seems to defy every convention of logic.)

"What am I going to tell him about my being late for work so often?" Unfortunately, you have no easy answer. "Maybe it will get better as the kids and I get used to this new routine. It's just very difficult to get the kids to the bus stop and the sitter, commute 20 minutes, and arrive precisely at 8:00. I wonder if he would allow me to come in at 8:30 and only take a half-hour lunch. Staying late wouldn't work because they close down the computers at 5:00, unless I could do some paperwork for half an hour."

Then what about the problems with the computer and the other staff members? "Sooner or later he's going to get on my case about those things. Is it my fault I don't think like a computer? Some people might be able to sit down and figure this program out in a couple of hours, but not me. So is that my fault or should someone be giving me more training? I wish the others weren't so cliquish and unwilling to help me out. I wonder why that's the case. It is as if they are afraid I will become as good as they are if they share their experience with me. I wish Andre had more time to help me learn the ropes, but he always seems to be in meetings."

"Well, I'm probably going to catch it this morning. I've never been this late. Maybe I'll be back home full-time sooner than I expected."

Observer's Rating Sheet

On completion of the exercise, evaluate Andre's motivation skills. Rate the motivation skills between 1 and 5 using the following scale. Write in concrete examples in the space for comments below each criteria skill to use in explaining your feedback.

1 Unsatisfactory	2 Weak	3 Adequate	4 Good	5 Outstanding

_____ Enhanced commitment to goals through clarification and participation.

_____ Strengthened effor--performance--reward expectancies.

_____ Provided salient rewards.

_____ Utilized positive reinforcement.

_____ Rewarded in a timely manner.

_____ Administered rewards equitably.

_____ Tied pay to performance.

_____ Empowered employees to achieve.

_____ Made available opportunities to learn.

Group Exercises

Three different types of group exercises are presented here. First is a short case for you to practise diagnosing motivational problems. Second is an interview role-play to determine what motivates a team member. Third is a team problem-solving exercise for improving motivation.

Group Exercise 1: Case Study: Ralph Henry's Motivational Crisis

Ralph Henry had worked as a production chemist at Systems Diagnostics Corporation (SDC) for seven years. The last four of those years were with the MED group, during which he received two promotions to become the group's senior chemist. Conscientious and thorough in his work, Ralph was a stickler for detail in the lab yet always willing to help others. Co-workers liked Ralph's pleasant, friendly manner and his lively conversations about sports and running (his major avocations). However, beyond the immediate group, Ralph was rather private. He interacted with few people outside the MED group and rarely attended social functions and company parties.

Ralph had always enjoyed his career as a chemist. He was particularly pleased with the laboratory environment, which allowed him to work freely and independently, pursuing whatever challenge or idea that came along. It was no big surprise, then, when Ken Chang asked Ralph to become supervisor of the MED group and take over a role Chang had held for three years.

THE REORGANIZATION Systems Diagnostics Corporation makes diagnostic reagent kits and pharmaceutical instrumentation for hospitals, clinical laboratories, and some government agencies. The firm was having difficulties containing costs and had recently announced the third consecutive decline in quarterly profits. Although sales were steady, with the latest announcement of profit erosion, senior management also announced a reorganization to consolidate product lines. As a result of the reorganization, Ken Chang was promoted to production manager of a newly created division, leaving vacant his former position as supervisor of the MED group. While a supervisor, Ken spent much of his time outside the group and, in doing so, granted considerable autonomy to his chemists.

When offered the supervisor's position, Ralph initially balked. He explained to Ken his reluctance to leave the lab bench and his feelings of uneasiness about supervising a group of longtime peers. All of his education was in pure science; he had no management training or experience. Ken promised that Ralph could participate in management training seminars and expressed his confidence that Ralph would quickly master the art of management.

THE PROMOTION After a week of contemplation, Ralph accepted. When his appointment was announced, members of the MED group were delighted and hosted a congratulatory luncheon for Ralph.

Six months into the supervisory job, Ralph's attitude was as conscientious and upbeat as ever. Much of his time was spent thoroughly checking each group member's work. Unlike Ken in the role of supervisor, Ralph required that all product tests be documented in detail and often requested that routine lab testings be repeated to confirm accuracy. Rather than delegate difficult problems to group members, Ralph took on most of these complex lab tasks himself and often worked late into the evening.

THE CRISIS In mid-December a major crisis required Ralph's immediate attention. The deadline on a large Canadian Forces contract assigned to the MED group was moved from mid-February to mid-January. Management wanted very much to make good on this contract because the Canadian Forces was a potential major customer. However, because of technical difficulties and because SDC had a tradition of shutting down during the holidays, Ralph did not believe MED would meet the deadline. To respond to the pressure, Ralph called a meeting of all group members, something he rarely did. He spelled out the situation:

"As you are all aware, we are having a big technical problem with the Canadian Forces contract. To compound our troubles, I just got word from management that the deadline has been moved up one month to mid-January. This change really puts us in a jam because the plant is scheduled to shut down for 10 days over the holidays.

"Personally, I know the project is more important than my holiday plans, so I'm cancelling them. What I'd like to know is who will be willing to work with me, say, a few of the 10 days. Of course you will get overtime pay. How many of you will be willing to work with me?"

The group was silent. Not one of the 10 members raised a hand or spoke up.

QUESTIONS FOR DISCUSSION

1. What motivates Ralph Henry? How do these forces impact on his behaviour as a chemist? As a supervisor?
2. What likely motivates the other chemists in the MED group? How well does Ralph understand these motivational forces and adjust his supervisory behaviour to bring out their best? Compare the motivational impact on the chemists of Ken Chang's approach to supervision with that of Ralph Henry.
3. Why the "no hands" response to Ralph's request for help? What does it indicate about Ralph's development as a supervisor? Given no volunteers, what does Ralph do now?

Group Exercise 2: Role-Play: Uncovering Rewards that Employees Value[50]

PURPOSE   To provide an opportunity to practise determining the motivational factors that keep employees on the job and motivate them to perform.

DIRECTIONS   The class divides into pairs of students. In each pair, one student plays the role of a team leader who is developing a plan to highly motivate the team member being interviewed. The other student plays the role of the team member being interviewed. The twist to this role-play is that the team member reflects on his or her actual motivators (rewards that he or she would like to attain).

The team leader might ask several questions while conducting an interview for approximately 3 minutes. In addition, when the team member reveals an important piece of information, the team leader will dig for more details. Suggested interview questions are as follows:

1. Why are you working on this team?
2. What can the company do to make you really happy?
3. What would be a fair reward for performing up to your capacity? On a scale of 1 to 10, how badly do you want this reward?
4. What would be an outstanding reward for you for performing up to your capacity?
5. What would be a fantasy reward for you for performing up to your capacity? On a scale of 1 to 10, how badly do you want this reward?
6. What do you hope to get out of this job?

DEBRIEFING A brief class discussion might follow the completion of the interviews. A key issue to address in the discussion is the extent to which each interview appeared helpful in motivating the team member. For example, were the interviews an effective method of uncovering the value that team members attached to specific rewards?

Group Exercise 3: Improving Motivation at Lightning Rod Steel

PURPOSE This team-based exercise is designed to (1) analyze the motivational implications of data generated by a group of engineers working for Lightning Rod Steel (LRS), (2) develop and present to the class a theory-supported action plan for improving motivation of the engineers, and (3) use the same criteria developed by the engineers to assess motivational factors affecting you in a work situation.

TIME 35 to 45 minutes.

DIRECTIONS Perform the following five tasks:

1. Assemble the class into teams of five to seven students each.
2. As a team, read the background material, including Exhibit 9-3. (about 3 to 4 minutes)
3. Have each team first analyze the Lightning Rod situation to determine the presumed lack of motivation among engineers. Then, use one established theory of motivation as the basis for developing an action plan of recommendations to "improve the motivation" of the steel company engineers. What specific actions should the managers take? Make sure your plan is feasible and reasonable for the managers to accept. (10 to 15 minutes)
4. Have each team member score the 19 motivational factors listed by the engineers in Exhibit 9-3. Determine how much each factor contributes to your motivation in an ideal work situation. Assign points from 0 to 5, where 5 means "extremely desirable" and 0 indicates "unimportant." Record your points in the "Your Ideal Scores" section of the exhibit. Then think of any factors important to you that are missing from the list. Compare your responses to those of the engineers and your team members. Plan to comment to the class on why your team scores were similar to or different from the engineers' scores. (10 minutes)
5. Present your recommendations and observations to the class. Debrief the activity to look for insights into how motivational expectations and motives differ among your peers. (15 minutes)

BACKGROUND OF LIGHTNING ROD STEEL (LRS)

Lightning Rod produces a number of rolled, bar, and tubular steel products from a single mill fueled by two electric hearth furnaces that melt recycled scrap metal. Kent Olsen, the director of manufacturing services, and his two engineering managers are concerned that, given a recession-induced soft market for steel and the constant need to cut costs by improving efficiencies, "we aren't getting 100 per cent from our engineering staff." Engineers number about three dozen and are of two types. Design engineers work on special projects for plant modernization. Industrial engineers update work standards, work method improvements, compensation incentives, and similar projects.

Olsen approaches your consulting group with a couple of questions: "One of the issues we have been unable to resolve among ourselves is how to determine the productivity of engineering professionals, and then how to improve it. Second, why aren't more of our

Exhibit 9-3 What LRS Engineers Expect at Work

Note: Scores reflect the group mean, with 5 points maximum.

Engineers' Scores

Work Factors	Your Ideal Conditions	Actual Experience	Ideal Scores
1. Open and honest communication	4.8	2.2	_____
2. A sense of fairness and justice	4.3	2.0	_____
3. Seeing the results of my work	4.3	2.7	_____
4. The opportunity to get my job done	4.2	2.5	_____
5. Feedback about how I am doing	4.0	2.0	_____
6. Interesting work assignments	4.0	2.2	_____
7. Opportunity for advancement	4.0	0.5	_____
8. Being compensated for performance	4.0	1.5	_____
9. Upward and/or lateral job mobility	4.0	0.8	_____
10. Recognition for work accomplishments	3.8	1.8	_____
11. A say in things that affect me	3.8	1.8	_____
12. A sense of involvement in the company	3.7	2.0	_____
13. Being informed of policies/job openings	3.5	0.7	_____
14. Working for a winning/successful team	3.2	1.7	_____
15. Even work distribution (no peaks/valleys)	3.0	2.0	_____
16. Equitable access to benefits	3.0	2.8	_____
17. A variety of tasks (job rotation)	2.8	1.8	_____
18. Security of not working myself out of job	2.5	1.5	_____
19. Good physical working environment	2.0	1.3	_____

engineers being pirated away by our seven operating general managers for higher paying managerial jobs?" He hands you a page (Exhibit 9-3) developed by the engineers during a recent training session. The data were developed in response to the question, "Brainstorm a list of what you would like to experience more often or have more of in your work situation, then evaluate ideal and actual conditions on a 0-to-5-point scale." Olsen continues, "Maybe this gives you some clues as to what we could do better to motivate engineers."

Application Questions

1. Think of a coach, teacher, or supervisor who really motivated you to enhance your performance in a specific task. What did this person do that motivated you so?

2. What are the predominate needs that you want to satisfy in task situations? Are you more concerned about compensation, status, achieving something worthwhile, being in charge of others, socializing with members of a team, learning something new?

3. Have you ever had a mentor at work or school? What was it about this person that was valuable to you? If you have not had a mentor, what characteristics would you like to have in one?

4. What motivates you to stay on a job or in an educational program versus looking for another better alternative?

5. As long as you are receiving the job benefits you agreed to when you started a job, does it matter to you that others are receiving better or worse deals? Why or why not?

Reinforcement Exercises

1. Interview several professors about what motivates them in their jobs. Compare the answers and determine whether professors are intrinsically or extrinsically motivated, what needs they seek to satisfy on the job, and how they decide where to invest their efforts. Repeat these interviews with people in different occupations and see if you can determine any differences.

2. Practise behavioural modification. Choose a friend, a small child, or a pet. Decide on a behaviour that you want to modify. Provide rewards after the desired behaviour occurs to positively reinforce its reoccurrence. Punish with a negative reaction on your part, or do not reinforce, undesired behaviours so that they will be extinguished. After a week of reinforcement, how successful were you in modifying the behaviour? Share your experiences with your class or a group of classmates. What were the common lessons you learned?

3. Interview a human resources director in any type of organization (company, school, hospital, etc.) about the compensation packages available for hourly employees, skilled workers, and managers. What did you learn about how the organization uses pay to motivate employees? Did you find differences in the compensation for different types of employees? If so, on what motivational assumptions do you think these differences were based?

4. Talk to five or six of your friends about their career plans and why they are choosing particular careers. What can you determine from your conversations about what motivates different people to choose different careers?

Summary Checklist

Take a few minutes to reflect on your performance and look over others' ratings of your motivation skills. Now assess yourself on each of the key learning behaviours. Make a check (√) next to those behaviours on which you need improvement.

_____ Enhancing commitment to goals.
　　1. Encourage participation.
　　2. Clarify.
　　3. Make specific goals.
　　4. Ensure that goals are challenging.

_____ Strengthening effort–performance–reward expectancies.
　　1. Emphasize anticipated reward value.
　　2. Clarify performance–reward linkages.
　　3. Provide performance feedback.

_____ Providing salient rewards.
　　1. Do not assume that all people want the same thing.
　　2. Do not assume that you know what people want for rewards.
　　3. Ask the employees themselves what rewards they prefer.
　　4. Offer cafeteria-style benefits.

_____ Utilizing positive reinforcement.
　　1. Beware of rewarding A while hoping for B—you get what you actually reward.
　　2. Provide rewards after desired behaviours occur to positively reinforce their reoccurrence.
　　3. Punish, or do not reinforce, undesired behaviours so that they will be extinguished.

_____ Rewarding in a timely manner.

    1. To get the fastest change in behaviour, reinforce the desired behaviour continuously each and every time it occurs.

    2. Use intermittent reinforcement where the reward is provided on a random basis to get sustained changes in behaviour.

_____ Administering rewards equitably.

    1. Determine whether employees feel that work-related benefits are distributed fairly.

    2. Clarify misperceptions.

    3. Correct inequities.

_____ Tying pay to performance.

    1. Use piecework to pay for the amount produced when workers can directly affect their rate and quality of output.

    2. Use merit pay where a salary plus merit incentive system is based on some measurable level of output over which the employee has control.

    3. Use profit sharing, bonuses, and stock options to link everyone's fate to over-all organization performance and reinforce corporate cultures emphasizing group results over individual performance.

    4. Use gainsharing to link financial rewards for all employees to improvements in performance of the entire business.

_____ Empowering employees to achieve.

    1. Give employees the authority, tools, and information they need to do their jobs with greater autonomy.

    2. Open communications, delegate power, share information, and cut away debilitating corporate bureaucracy.

    3. Give employees license to pursue their visions, to champion projects, and to improve practices consistent with organizational mission and goals.

    4. Share responsibilities with employees and treat them as partners.

_____ Making available opportunities to learn.

    1. Help, mentor, and coach employees yourself.

    2. Provide opportunities for on-the-job training, in-house seminars, and tuition reimbursement for courses, degree programs, and sponsorship for workshops and conferences.

Action Plan

1. Which motivation behaviour do I most want to improve? (For example, see Summary Checklist.)
2. Why? What will be my payoff?
3. What potential obstacles stand in my way?
4. What are the specific things I will do to improve? (For examples, see the Reinforcement Exercises.)
5. When will I do them?
6. How and when will I measure my success?

Part 4
Performance Management Competencies

Organizations exist to achieve some purpose; therefore, someone has to define that purpose and the means for its achievement. A manager is that someone. Performance management competencies include defining an organization's goals, establishing an overall strategy for achieving those goals, and developing a comprehensive hierarchy of plans to integrate and coordinate activities.

Managers have to divide work into manageable components and coordinate results to achieve objectives. Organizing includes determining what tasks are to be done, who is to do them, how the tasks are to be grouped, who reports to whom, and where decisions are to be made. To manage performance effectively, managers need skills in designing work, identifying and hiring employees, evaluating performance, developing employees, and creating work teams.

Even if the best structural arrangements have been determined and the best people have been hired, trained, and motivated, plenty of things can still go amiss. To ensure that things are going as they should, a manager must monitor performance. Actual performance must be compared with the previously set goals. If there are any significant deviations, it is the manager's responsibility to get the process back on track.

Chapter 10, Innovation and Problem Solving   Almost everything a manager does involves making decisions to solve problems. Before acting, effective managers identify critical problems, assimilate the appropriate data, make sense of the information, and decide on the best course of action to take to resolve the problem.

Chapter 11, Planning and Goal Setting   One element of planning that permeates just about every manager's job—from CEOs to project managers to first-line supervisors—is setting objectives. Objectives, or goals, refer to desired outcomes for individuals, groups, or entire organizations. Setting goals keeps employees properly focused on the work to be done and helps organizational members keep their attention on what is most important.

Creating strategy is the process of identifying and pursuing an organization's mission by aligning the organization's internal capacities with the external environmental demands. This alignment is accomplished by developing a long-range plan that will realize the stated organizational goals.

In order to anticipate and interpret changes in their environments, managers in both small and large organizations need to scan their environments continually for information relevant to their present or future situations. Information needs to be obtained from all possible sources about all institutions outside the organization that might affect the organization's performance. Although every specific organization is different, its environment usually includes suppliers, customers, competitors, unions, government regulatory agencies, and public pressure groups.

Chapter 12, Designing Work　The design of a person's job has significant motivational impact on behaviour and goal achievement. As a manager you want to design jobs that maximize your employees' performance. Designing work is the process of incorporating tasks and responsibilities that utilize your employees' important talents into jobs that are meaningful, productive, and satisfying.

Chapter 13, Identifying and Hiring Employees　If the people working for you lack skills, experience, or motivation, their work performance is sure to reflect it. Managers need to know how to identify and attract qualified applicants to do the work they have designed; then they have to select the most capable recruits, hire them, and match them to the jobs where they can best perform.

Chapter 14, Evaluating Performance　Performance evaluation is the process of monitoring activities to ensure that they are being accomplished as planned and correcting any significant deviations. Managers can't really know whether their employees are performing properly until they've compared the actual performance with the desired standard.

Chapter 15, Developing Employees　Today's manager is increasingly more like a coach than a boss. Managers create a climate in which their players can excel. They define the overall objectives, set expectations, define the boundaries of each player's role, ensure that players are properly trained and have the resources they need to perform their roles, attempt to enlarge each player's capabilities, offer inspiration and motivation, and evaluate results. As coaches, contemporary managers help employees develop as they guide, listen to, encourage, and motivate them.

Consistent with the coaching role, today's managers are increasingly giving up authority and empowering their employees. Letting employees make independent, job-related decisions and letting them learn from their mistakes is a form of development. Managers also need the skills to act as mentors and counsellors when appropriate.

Chapter 16, Creating Teams　Because work in organizations is increasingly organized around teams, employees have had to become team players. This means developing the kinds of skills necessary to contribute to high-performance teams. These skills include problem solving, group decision making, active listening, feedback, conflict resolution, and other interpersonal skills.

Being a team player is especially challenging for people who have grown up in cultures that encourage and reward individual achievement. They typically find it difficult to think like a team player and sublimate their personal ambitions for the good of the team. Consequently, teams benefit when managers model cooperative team behaviours and instill them in their employees.

CHAPTER 10

Innovation and Problem Solving

Learning Objectives

After completing this chapter, you should be able to:

- Stimulate creativity and innovation in yourself and others.
- Apply the six steps of the problem-solving process.
- Utilize the strengths and avoid the weaknesses of groups in solving problems.

Self-Assessment Exercise

How Creative Are You?

DIRECTIONS Place a check mark by the 10 words in the following list that best characterize you.

____ energetic	____ persuasive	____ observant	____ fashionable	____ self-confident
____ persevering	____ original	____ cautious	____ habit-bound	____ resourceful
____ egotistical	____ independent	____ stern	____ predictable	____ formal
____ informal	____ dedicated	____ factual	____ open-minded	____ forward-looking
____ tactful	____ inhibited	____ enthusiastic	____ innovative	____ poised
____ acquisitive	____ practical	____ alert	____ curious	____ organized
____ unemotional	____ dynamic	____ polished	____ courageous	____ clear-thinking
____ helpful	____ efficient	____ perceptive	____ quick	____ self-demanding
____ good-natured	____ thorough	____ impulsive	____ determined	____ understanding
____ realistic	____ modest	____ involved	____ flexible	____ absentminded
____ sociable	____ well-liked	____ restless	____ retiring	

SCORING For each of the following adjectives that you checked, give yourself 2 points:

energetic	resourceful	original	enthusiastic	dynamic
flexible	observant	independent	perceptive	innovative
persevering	dedicated	courageous	curious	self-demanding
involved				

For each of the following adjectives that you checked, give yourself 1 point:

thorough	determined	restless	informal
alert	open-minded	forward-looking	self-confident

The rest of the adjectives receive no points.

ADD UP YOUR TOTAL NUMBER OF POINTS:

INTERPRETATION

16–20	Very creative
11–15	Above average
6–10	Average
0–5	Below average

Other research concludes that innovators have a common mindset or way of looking at the world rather than a common set of personal traits. Innovators tend to challenge industry norms, love to constantly experience new things, and develop a deep sense of the frustrations and unspoken needs of customers.[1]

Source: Copyright © 1981 Adapted from E. Raudsepp, *How Creative Are You?* (New York: Putnam, 1981) 22–4.

Concepts

Dofasco is Canada's second-largest steel maker, producing over four million tons of steel annually with approximately 7300 employees at its Hamilton, Ontario, facility. Dofasco's cost per ton of steel produced is one of the lowest in North America, and, since 1996, the company has consistently ranked as one of North America's most profitable steel makers.[2] For three consecutive years (1999–2001), Dofasco has been named to the Dow Jones Sustainability World Index as one of the world's most sustainable companies.[3] The sustainability ranking is based on the company's financial, social, and environmental record. The picture, however, wasn't always this bright.

In the early 1990s, Dofasco faced increasing global competition, depressed prices, aging technology, and a workforce in need of skills training. In 1992, Dofasco lost $2.96 per share.[4]

How was Dofasco able to turn its performance around? John Mayberry, president and CEO, attributes the change to a new company mission with a goal to look at steel from a customer point of view, introduce new innovative technology, and develop a new corporate culture based on performance and innovation.[5] The most far-reaching change was the creation of a working environment that rewarded and fostered innovation. Problem-solving teams were introduced, problems were analyzed, and employees were sent around the world to learn best practices and set goals and plans for improvement.

The Importance of Effective Problem Solving

High-performance organizations have always relied on innovation to stay in the forefront of their industries and, today, they face ever increasing challenges from a rapidly changing economic, social, technological, competitive, and international environment. Their future depends on the ability to question old ways of thinking, and this chapter provides an organized approach for doing so.

Managerial success depends on making the right decision at the right time.[6] However, **decision making** is just one component of the innovation and problem-solving process. Unless a problem has been defined and its root causes identified, managers are unlikely to be able to make an appropriate decision about how to solve it. Effective managers, like Dofasco CEO John Mayberry, know how to gather and evaluate information that clarifies a problem. They know the value of generating more than one action alternative and weighing all the implications of a plan before deciding to implement it. They acknowledge the importance of following through and evaluating to make sure that changes are effective. In this chapter, you will learn how managers can encourage innovation. You will also learn how to apply the problem-solving process to generate creative solutions to problems. Then you will have opportunities to apply and improve your problem-solving skills in the exercises that follow.

Encouraging Innovation

Innovation is defined as the entire process by which ideas are generated, developed, and transformed into value. Rather than involving accidental discovery, innovation is a manageable process. It is a process filled with inspiration and intuition and, at the same time, is systematic, disciplined, and detailed. Innovation can result in a new product or service such as a digital camera, or it can result in a new process that improves workflow, decreases paperwork, or reduces the cost of making steel. Ultimately, an organization's "capacity for perpetual innovation" is its means of sustaining competitive advantage.[7]

Innovation is so important to both business and a healthy economy that the federal government has made it a priority initiative for Canada.[8]

CHARACTERISTICS OF MANAGERS WHO ENCOURAGE CREATIVITY[9]

Managers play a significant role in innovation by crafting meaningful challenges and fostering a creative environment for their employees. They allow their people freedom, expect some errors, and are willing to learn from inevitable failures. Managers who are afraid of mistakes, on the other hand, restrict the freedom of their employees to experiment and be creative.

Productive managers of creativity can live with half-developed ideas. They do not insist that an idea be 100 per cent proven before supporting its development. They are willing to listen to employees and encourage them to press on with "half-baked" proposals that hold promise. The goal, however, is not to let employees go off in all directions but, rather, to concentrate efforts in selected areas that can produce sustained competitive advantage.[10]

Creative managers have a feel for the times when the company rulebook needs to be ignored and will stretch normal policies for the greater long-term good. Managers who permit no deviation from standard operating procedures will make predictable progress and avoid mistakes, but will not realize breakthroughs that calculated risk taking can promote.

Productive managers are good listeners. They listen to their staff, try to pull out good ideas, and build on suggestions. They do not try to impose new policies or procedures on people without listening to the other side first.

Creative managers do not dwell on mistakes. They are more future oriented than past oriented. They do not hold the mistakes of others against them. They are willing to begin with the world as it is today, and work for a better future by learning from their mistakes.

When good ideas are presented, productive managers are willing to decide on the spot to try them without waiting for further studies. They are courageous enough to trust their intuition and commit resources to implementing promising ideas.

Finally, productive managers are enthusiastic and invigorating. They encourage and energize others. They enjoy using the resources and power of their position to push projects forward and make improvements.

A CREATIVE WORKING ENVIRONMENT

Organizations like Dofasco promote creativity and innovation by having high expectations of results while providing a stimulating environment that encourages "play" and freedom to explore ideas. Everyone in the organization is expected to be creative in his or her job and supportive of the innovation process. In other words, these organizations instill a performance and innovation culture that is clearly focused on the customer and the future.[11]

At Dofasco, innovative technologies and a state-of-the-art facility have allowed the company to reinvent its product line. Dofasco linked its strategic innovation orientation with employee performance by having staff search the world for ideas. One result of this effort was the introduction of hydroform tubing in automotive applications. Dofasco is the only North American steel producer to use this method of production, which involves less welding and results in a finished product that is lighter and stronger.[12]

Another example of how a creative climate can pay off is the Minnesota Mining & Manufacturing Company (3M) in Minneapolis, where employees are encouraged to devote about 15 per cent of their work time to non-job-related creative thinking. Doing "Skunkworks duty," as it is known at 3M, has resulted in such creative products as Post-It notes, three-dimensional magnetic recording tape, and disposable medical masks. 3M figures that nearly 70 per cent of its annual sales comes from creative ideas that originated with the workforce.[13] Another way that 3M develops breakthrough products is by staying in touch with customers. For example, 3M's "Lead User" process attempts to locate and research individuals and organizations whose needs are ahead of market trends and create solutions to address their needs. The rationale for this is that it will be only a matter of time before lead users' needs become everyone's needs.[14]

At W. L. Gore & Associates, developers of Teflon and Gore-Tex, employees are urged to take risks. The feeling is that if they are not making mistakes, they are doing something wrong. This philosophy has propelled W. L. Gore from a glorified mom-and-pop operation to a company with 37 plants worldwide that turns out everything from electronics to dental products.

FACILITATING INNOVATION

To facilitate innovation, a manager needs to recognize that innovation leaders are found throughout an organization[15] and that there are various roles in the innovation process. These roles are the idea champion, the sponsor, the orchestrator, and the rule breaker.[16] The idea champion comes up with an innovative solution to a market need. The sponsor encourages the champion and helps by providing resources such as facilities, money, or time to work on the idea. The orchestrator arranges or obtains political support for the idea, and the rule breaker ensures success by overcoming organizational barriers to bring the application to market. Four sets of competencies are required for innovation. These are: creating, executing, managing, and commercializing.[17] Few individuals excel in all four, so a manager needs to bring together various people who, in total, have these complementary competencies.

The lesson here is that innovation is the entire process by which ideas are generated, developed, and transformed into value. For this to be successful, a manager needs to recognize those who are idea champions, bring the various people and competencies together, and support all the roles in the innovation process. In an innovation culture, everyone has a responsibility to support the process. To support the process, the Conference Board of Canada has developed a set of questions or audit (see Exhibit 10-1) to help organizations and their managers facilitate innovation.[18]

What Are the Steps in the Problem-Solving Process?

Now that we know how to develop the conditions necessary for innovation, let's look at the steps needed to create ideas—the problem-solving process.

A problem exists when the actual situation is not what is needed or desired. Many people tend to think of problems as "bad"—something unwanted or unforeseen. But it's also useful to think of problems in a positive light. For example, an unfulfilled market need represents a business opportunity and is a "good" problem. In a general sense, then, problem solving is a six-step process of eliminating the gap or difference between actual and desired outcomes. The first step is to recognize and acknowledge that a problem exists. Next, the problem needs to be defined and analyzed. This is followed by generating a variety of alternative solutions. Selecting the best solution from among feasible alternatives comes next. The solution is implemented and, finally, the solution is evaluated.

1. AWARENESS OF THE PROBLEM

A major responsibility for all managers and employees is to maintain a constant lookout for actual or potential problems—both "good" and "bad." Managers fulfill this responsibility by keeping channels of communication open and examining deviations from present plans as well as from past experience.[19] Four situations usually alert managers to possible problems: (1) a deviation from past experience, (2) a deviation from a set plan, (3) when other people communicate problems to the manager, and (4) when competitors outperform the overall organization.[20] New market opportunities are best discovered by talking to existing or potential customers about the product or service.

CLARIFY OBJECTIVES Before setting out to assess the current or actual situation, clarify the objectives. A business objective that has been set and agreed to previously, such as reducing production defects by 3 per cent, represents the desired outcome. It is a documented statement of what you intend to accomplish and it provides the standard against which to compare the current situation.

ASSESS THE CURRENT SITUATION First, determine whether the current situation is meeting the objectives or goal. Do the actual conditions match the desired ones? If not, what is the difference between actual and desired? If the matching process reveals a difference, determine how large the gap is and then attempt to determine why it exists.

2. DEFINE AND ANALYZE THE PROBLEM

Serious mistakes can be made if managers act before they know exactly why a problem exists or before they have identified the source(s) of a problem. The way a problem is actually defined has a major impact on what alternatives are considered, what decision is reached, and how the action plan is implemented.

For example, problems can be categorized as either routine or nonroutine. Routine problems are those that are anticipated or arise on a regular basis and can be solved by implementing the company policies, procedures, or guidelines that have been effective in the past. An example is the reordering of supplies as soon as inventory on hand falls below a certain quantity. Nonroutine situations, on the other hand, are unique and not

Exhibit 10-1 The "Simple Innovation Audit"

- **The Vision Test:** What is our global vision? What will we be global best at? (and do we really know what we're best at?) On what should we focus?

- **The Benchmarking Test:** How will we know we're global best? What technology, foresight, and competitive intelligence are needed? Do we know what we don't know?

- **The "Awareness" Test:** Why should we invest in innovation? How will innovation help our organization to flourish? Will our organization flourish without innovation?

- **The Smarter-Not-Harder Test:** Have we considered smart solutions before costly ones? Have we explored creative solutions in addition to resource-intensive ones? Are we prepared to "kill" ideas or terminate projects?

- **The Groundwork Test:** Do we have the right "stuff" to innovate: the right people and business processes, the right structure and reward systems? What groundwork must be laid to ensure that our global-best ideas, products, and processes will be successful?

- **The Sustainability Test:** Can we sustain our capacity to innovate—economically, culturally, environmentally? Are we investing in the next quarter and the next generation?

- **The Perverse Policy Test:** Does a new policy (or practice, product, process) inhibit innovation in any way? Do any corporate policies or practices inhibit innovation?

Source: The Conference Board of Canada, The Road to Global Best Leadership, Innovation and Corporate Culture, Innovation Challenge Paper #1, May 2002 p. 5.

usually anticipated by managers. As a result, they require greater definition, analysis, and a solution that is tailored to fit the specific dilemma. Because more than one way can usually be found to solve nonroutine situations, it is critical to consider all possible solutions and arrive at several alternatives from which to choose a solution.

To identify a nonroutine problem accurately, it must be understood from all points of view. Take the time to gather all relevant information and investigate all plausible alternatives before settling on the most probable cause(s). The idea is to determine the root cause(s) of the problem. Encourage all stakeholders to participate in problem definition and analysis. If problem solving is perceived as a joint learning experience, all parties will be much more likely to contribute needed information.

Beware of mistaking symptoms for the source of the problem. For example, you receive medication from your doctor to control a skin rash, which is only a symptom that something is wrong. The medication clears the rash, but the actual cause of the problem is not identified until you or the physician look for clues. When you discover that the onset of the rash coincided with the arrival of a new plant in your living room, you have identified the problem: an allergy to that plant.

One technique for facilitating a thorough problem analysis is the **cause-and-effect diagram**.[21] A cause-and-effect diagram, or fishbone chart, is constructed to represent the relationship between an effect and all possible causes influencing it. As illustrated in Exhibit 10-2, the effect or problem is stated on the right side of the chart and the major influences or causes are listed on the left. Although a problem may have various sources, the major causes can usually be summarized under the four M categories of manpower,

Exhibit 10-2 Cause-and-Effect Diagram (Fishbone Analysis)

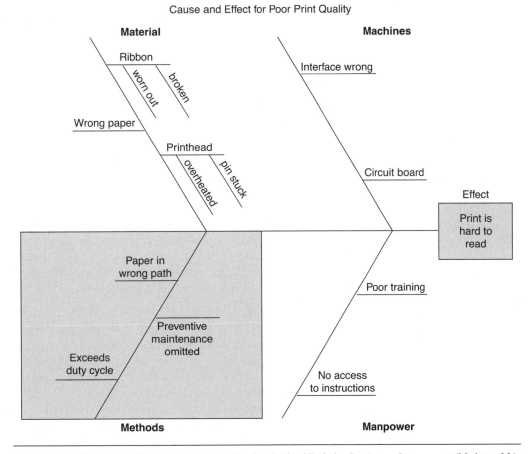

Cause and Effect for Poor Print Quality

Source: M. Brassard, *The Memory Jogger: A Pocket Guide of Tools for Continuous Improvement* (Methuen, MA: GOAL/QPC, 1988) 26.

methods, machines, and material. Data can then be gathered and shared to determine the relative frequencies and magnitudes of contribution of the different potential causes.

SET PRIORITIES If more than one problem has been identified and defined, the next step is to set priorities regarding which problem will be worked on first and which ones will be put aside temporarily or indefinitely. Priorities can be established by answering the following three questions. How urgent is the problem? That is, what will happen if nothing is done immediately? How serious is it? That is, how much will a solution impact desired objectives? Is the problem getting better or worse? That is, what's the problem's potential for growth? The problem that is the most serious, urgent, and becoming worse should be dealt with first, even if the solutions seem more difficult.

PROBLEM STATEMENT Before generating potential solutions, it's useful to develop a problem statement. Problem statements begin with the words, "In what ways can..." or "How might..." or "How to..." Examples of problem statements are: In what ways can productivity be improved? How might sales be increased? How do we reduce toxic emissions? By stating the problem in this way, it opens your mind to the range of possibilities for solving it.

3. GENERATE ALTERNATIVE SOLUTIONS

After successfully defining the problem, strive to find the best possible solution. The first step is to generate as many solutions as possible. Overcoming mental blocks and the application of a few good techniques will help.

COMMON CAUSES OF MENTAL BLOCKS   Mental blocks can inhibit your ability to generate solutions. Some common causes of mental blocks are:

- Defining the problem too narrowly
- Defining the problem too vaguely
- Assuming there is only one right answer
- Becoming preoccupied with the first solution that comes to mind
- Wanting to solve the problem too quickly

Attempt to avoid these blocks. Be alert for similarities and differences as well as distinguishing features in situations. Keep open and receptive to your ideas and the ideas of others by looking at the problem from different perspectives. Be aware of your biases, dislikes, and weaknesses as well as your strengths. Keep an active mind. The key to generating ideas and potential solutions is perseverance. Essentially, generating ideas is an art and becomes an acquired skill with time and experience.

CHECKLISTS   One way to generate alternative solutions is to ask a directed set of questions. The stimulus comes from forcing yourself to answer questions that you would not normally pose. The most basic set of questions is the familiar who, what, where, when, how, and why. This powerful checklist, often recommended to journalists, is simple enough to start the thinking process but not over-complicate it. For example, the questions can be used as a checklist in the early data-gathering stages or to help you build on existing ideas. The answers to these questions will usually be facts rather than actions. So, it is useful to use the answers in conjunction with your problem statement. For example, "Who does X?" may be "Donna." To use this question in a problem-solving context, you might have to add: If Donna does X, *in what ways can* or *how might* we make it easier for her or lighter for her and so on. This second-stage questioning makes the facts come alive and adds to the creative process.

A second checklist of questions is the mnemonic SCAMPER.[22] S = Substitute? C = Combine? A = Adapt? M = Modify? or Magnify? P = Put to other uses? E = Eliminate? or Minify? R = Reverse? or Rearrange?

To use SCAMPER, identify the problem you want to think about. Establish the facts by asking who, what, where, when, how, and why. Then, ask SCAMPER questions to generate a variety of ideas. Let's carry on with the earlier example, In what ways can we make it easier for Donna? You can start looking for ideas by asking: What can be *substituted* for X? What can be *combined* with X to make it easier? What can be *adapted* for X? How can I *modify* X? What can I *magnify* or add to X? What *other uses* can I find for X? What can be *eliminated* from X? What is the *reverse* of X? What *rearrangement* of X might be better?

MINDMAPPING[23]   Another technique that can help you organize your thoughts and content is mindmapping. This whole-brain, visually interesting version of outlining helps you pull together all your ideas, memories, associations, and connections quickly. Mindmapping allows information to flow more freely from mind to page, streaming off naturally into organized branches. The technique takes advantage of the mind's tendency to work in short, intense mind bursts by allowing you to dump your ideas and thoughts onto paper in just a few minutes. Mindmapping is like a personal brainstorming session.

It gives you a chance to make new connections with the information and organize it into its primary pieces or branches and the appropriate subtopics and details.

Mindmapping is extremely easy to use. The basic process includes the following steps:

- **Focus** Print the central idea in a circle or box in the centre of the page.
- **Free association** Allow your ideas to flow freely without judgment.
- **Connect ideas** Print key ideas or thoughts on lines connected to the centre focus.
- **Branches** First branches are key ideas; related ideas are connected as subbranches.
- **Key words** Print key words only: mindmapping is a form of brain shorthand and needs only a few key words to capture an idea.
- **Symbols/images** Use any symbols or images that make sense to you.
- **Colour** Use colour to stimulate your thought processes and to help you organize the material.

Mindmapping allows you to get information down on paper the way your mind handles it rather than in a rigid outline form. Each mindmap is a unique product of the person who produces it. Exhibit 10-3 illustrates a mindmap.

BRAINSTORMING Brainstorming is a demonstrated approach for achieving high participation and increasing the number of action alternatives.[24] To engage in brainstorming sessions, people meet in small groups and feed off one another's ideas, which provide stimuli for more creative solutions. With brainstorming, the focus is on quantity: participants generate as many ideas as they can, no matter how far-fetched. Rules for effective brainstorming allow no criticism or evaluation of ideas as they are generated, allow only one idea at a time from each person, and encourage people to build on each other's ideas.

Brainstorming groups are encouraged to be freewheeling and radical. Through the use of a nonevaluative environment that is intentionally fun, brainstorming ensures involvement, enthusiasm, and a large number of solution alternatives.

Brainstorming generally works well in a participative, team-oriented climate where people are comfortable with each other and are committed to pulling together toward a common goal. In some situations it may not be effective, however. For example, a hostile or political climate might inhibit the free flow of ideas. In restrictive interpersonal climates, more structured techniques such as the nominal group or Delphi technique may be more effective.

Exhibit 10-3 Mindmapping Example

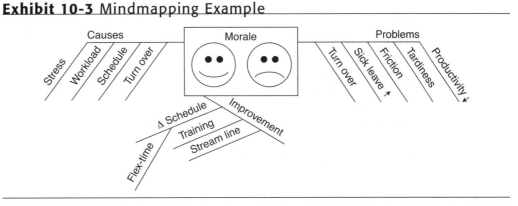

Source: T. Allesandra and P. Hunsaker, *Communicating at Work* (New York: Simon & Schuster, 1993) 225.

NOMINAL GROUP TECHNIQUE In the **nominal group technique**, participants meet together in a highly structured format that governs the decision-making process.[25] First, participants independently write down their ideas about the problem. Second, each presents one idea to the group in a round-robin fashion without discussion. These ideas are summarized and written on a flip chart or blackboard so all can see them. After a group discussion to clarify and evaluate the ideas, an independent ranking of the proposals takes place. These rankings are pooled to determine the proposal with the highest aggregate ranking, which is the group's decision.

The nominal group technique offers the advantages of multiple idea generation, balanced participation, and participant satisfaction. It is time-consuming and does require participants to meet together at a common location. In any group decision-making situation, the advantages and disadvantages of a proposed technique should be weighed with respect to the nature of the participants and the specific decision being made.

DELPHI TECHNIQUE In the **Delphi technique**, participants do not meet together but interact through a series of written judgments and suggestions.[26] After each participant has been presented with the problem, he or she writes down comments and possible solutions and sends them to a central location for recording and reproduction. Each participant then receives a copy of all other comments and solutions to use as a springboard for additional ideas or comments. These are also returned to the central location for compilation and reproduction, after which an independent vote on solution priority is taken.

The Delphi technique allows for the pooling of a variety of ideas, viewpoints, feedback, and criticism at minimal expense, because participants do not have to congregate at a common meeting place. It does, however, take an extended period of time and really offers no control over the decision-making process. Depending on the nature of the decision group, participants' lack of face-to-face interaction can be either an asset or a liability.

4. DECIDE THE COURSE OF ACTION

After goals have been clarified, information gathered, situations assessed, and problems identified, the next step is to develop a particular course of action that will either restore formerly acceptable conditions or improve the situation in a significant way.

ESTABLISH DECISION-MAKING CRITERIA Decision-making **criteria** are statements of objectives that need to be met for a problem to be solved. Effective criteria should be specific, measurable, attainable, complementary, ethical, and acceptable to those who will implement the decision.

Specific, Measurable, and Attainable "I need to reduce scrap material waste by 10 per cent, avoid a reduction in product quality, and increase production by 5 per cent," is an example of a concise decision-making criterion statement. Decision-making criteria should be specific: "I will increase productivity by 5 per cent," not just "I want to increase productivity." Second, they should be measurable: Saying you want to increase employee morale is not as good a criterion statement as saying that you will increase employee morale as indicated by a 4 per cent reduction in absenteeism over the next three months. Third, to gain commitment to meeting criteria, there should be sufficient time, resources, and expertise available to make them attainable.

Complementary The criteria must also complement one another. The achievement of one should not reduce the likelihood of achieving another. For example, you would not improve the quality and detail of your written reports at the expense of spending the necessary time with those who must interact with you.

Ethical Decision criteria should conform to what is considered morally right by society. Criteria should be legal, fair, and observant of human rights. Organizations need to establish a commonly agreed upon set of ethical standards to guide decisions when individuals are confronted with conflicting obligations, cost–benefit tradeoffs, and competing value choices.

Acceptable Even the best technical decision will not be workable if it is unacceptable to the parties involved. You may be convinced, for example, that the best solution for meeting a production deadline without increasing costs is to have the department work weekends for the next month without additional compensation. However, this action plan may not be viable if it is not acceptable to those on whom its implementation depends. Negative reactions to changes can create more problems than are solved. Sensitivity to emotional factors, personal values, family issues, and individual objectives is vital in choosing a successful action plan.

EVALUATE BENEFITS AND RISKS OF ALTERNATIVES It is important to look at all the long-run consequences of the alternatives being considered. This step is sometimes overlooked because of our tendency to avoid spending extra time and energy and our fear of discovering negative consequences in preferred solutions. Important criteria to consider in evaluating action alternatives are each alternative's probability of success and the associated degree of risk that negative consequences will occur. If the chance of failure is high and the related costs for an alternative are great, the benefits of it may not justify its use. Risk can be personal as well as economic—just ask the person whose reputation is on the line or who is soon to undergo a performance review.

The degree of risk can range from none to potentially catastrophic. **Certainty** exists when the exact results of implementing a problem solution are known in advance, like when you put your money in a savings account for one year. **Known risk** is present when the probability that a given alternative will produce specific outcomes can be predicted. For example, an executive may know that by taking a commercial airline flight tonight, he or she has a 99.5 per cent probability of arriving on time for a business meeting in Winnipeg tomorrow morning. **Uncertainty** exists when decision makers are unable to assign any probabilities to the consequences associated with an alternative. **Turbulence** occurs when the environment is rapidly changing and decision makers are not clear about relevant variables, available solution options, or potential consequences of decisions. In times of recession, economic reforms, or military conflict, turbulence usually prevails.[27]

DECIDE ON A PLAN As alternatives are evaluated according to these criteria, many will be clearly unsatisfactory and can be eliminated. Sometimes the evaluation will reveal that one alternative is decidedly superior to all others. At other times none of the proposed action plans will be acceptable, signalling a need to develop additional alternatives. Most often, however, several alternatives will appear feasible, and the best one must be selected. Exhibit 10-4 illustrates a decision-making grid that summarizes the preceding criteria for evaluating alternatives. Such a grid can help to visualize which alternative offers the maximum benefits with minimal risks and costs. The decision-making goal is to select the

Exhibit 10-4 Decision-Making Grid

Alternatives	Criteria					
	Benefits	**Probability of Success**	**Costs**	**Risks**	**Associated Consequences**	**Timing**
Alternative A						
Alternative B						
Alternative C						

best solution alternative for solving the entire problem while minimizing additional negative consequences for anyone else in the organization.

Perfect Rationality In a world of perfect rationality, all problems can be clearly defined, all information and alternatives are known, the consequences of implementing each alternative are certain, and the decision maker is a completely rational being who is concerned only about economic gain. These conditions allow for an optimal solution to every problem and provide the basics for ideal management decision making. The real world, however, is made up of real people with real problems, and it rarely conforms to these ideal conditions.

Bounded Rationality Usually real-world limitations prevent obtaining and processing all relevant information that might optimize decision making. Consequently, most managers exhibit bounded rationality when they reach satisfactory rather than "perfect" decisions. Bounded rationality is necessary in the face of constraints on time, money, and intellectual resources.[28] Even though the goal of the decision model presented here is to optimize decision outcomes, **satisficing**—choosing the first satisfactory alternative that meets minimal requirements—probably describes the majority of daily managerial decision making.

5. IMPLEMENT THE SOLUTION

Decision and action plans are of little value unless they are implemented effectively, and how the action plan is to be accomplished connects the decision with reality. Implementation includes assigning tasks and responsibilities, and establishing an implementation schedule.

ASSIGN TASKS AND RESPONSIBILITIES It is important to clarify both verbally and in writing what each person involved will do to make the new action plan work. To avoid misunderstandings, it is essential to specify who is to do what, by when, and how.

ESTABLISH AN IMPLEMENTATION SCHEDULE To be implemented effectively, all necessary tasks need a specified time schedule for completion. One way to approach scheduling is to start at an end point (the date by which the objective should be completed) and work backward. Action implementation steps can be listed in priority order and assigned reasonable time periods for completion, starting with the last step before the objective is accomplished.

A **Gantt chart** is a graphic planning and control method that breaks a project down into separate tasks and estimates the time needed for their completion. The chart has a space for planned starting and completion dates and actual dates filled in as implementation occurs. A sample Gantt chart appears in Exhibit 10-5.

Gantt charts help to make certain that all implementation tasks are considered in relation to each other and appropriate people are assigned to each task. They provide checkpoints for all tasks to ensure that they are finished on time. Gantt charts are developed by defining goals and setting completion dates, then bracketing time blocks based on the time required and completion date of each task.

Once an action plan is implemented, managers often move on to another task. It is of key importance, however, to follow through to be sure that the solution is working effectively and that no additional problems have been created. Following through entails the development and maintenance of positive attitudes in everyone involved in the implementation process. Several guidelines help establish the positive climate necessary for the implementation steps.

Exhibit 10-5 Gantt Chart

Activity Description (Responsibility)	Dec 2002 7 14 21 28	Jan 2003 4 11 18 25	Feb 2003 1 8 15 22	Mar 2003 1 8 15 22 29	Apr 2003 5 12 19 26	May 2003 3 10 17 24
Process planning, routing, and scheduling (Chuck Teplitz: Project Manager)						
Materials procurement (David Burt: Procurement)						
Parts fabrication (Don Helmich: Manufacturing)						
Part No.1						
2						
3						
4						
5						
6						
7						
8						
9						
10						
11						
12						
Subassemblies (Pam Schwerin: Assembly) A						
B						
C						
D						
E						
Subassemblies (Pam Schwerin: Assembly)						

☐ Planned starting and completion dates
█ Work completed

Source: L.W. Rue and L.L. Byars, *Management Skills and Applications,* 9th ed. (Homewood, IL: Richard D. Irwin, 2000) 174. Adapted from E.S. Buffa, *Modern Production Management,* 4th ed. (New York: John Wiley & Sons, Inc., 1973) 576.

- Visualize yourself in the position of those doing the implementing so that you understand their feelings and perspectives.
- Establish sincere respect and concern.
- Make sure necessary resources are available.

With this kind of positive climate, several sequential steps in the follow-through process are necessary for implementation. They include establishing the criteria for measuring success, monitoring the results obtained, and taking corrective action when necessary.

ESTABLISH CRITERIA FOR MEASURING SUCCESS Unless circumstances change, the criteria for measuring problem-solving success are the time, quality, and quantity goals already developed in the action-planning stage. These criteria serve as benchmarks for measuring and comparing the planned versus actual results.

6. EVALUATE THE SOLUTION

The data on the results can be compared with the established criteria. If the new performance meets the criteria, no further action is necessary other than continued monitoring. If the new results do not measure up, the next step is to determine why. Then, take corrective action by applying the problem-solving process again. Be sure to investigate whether the real problem was examined, rather than symptoms, and challenge your data and assumptions. For any new corrective action plan, new measures and schedules need to be determined and new data need to be gathered and tested against the criteria.

When Is Participation Appropriate for Decision Making?

Who should be involved in the problem-solving process? Just the manager? A committee? A coalition of key individuals? The entire department? All stakeholders to be affected by the decision?

DEGREES OF DECISION PARTICIPATION

Evidence indicates that participation can enhance morale, satisfaction, and productivity, but in emergencies or when others do not have sufficient information, an autocratic decision may be more appropriate.[29] Degrees of decision participation can be grouped into the following three broad levels.[30]

- **Autocratic** The manager solves the problem alone using information personally available or solicited from employees. Employees are not involved in analyzing the problem or generating solutions.

- **Consultative** The manager shares the problem with employees either individually or as a group and solicits their ideas and suggestions. The manager then makes an independent decision, which may or may not reflect employees' inputs.

- **Group** The manager shares the problem with employees or stakeholders as a group. Together they generate and evaluate alternatives and attempt to reach a consensus agreement on a solution, which the manager accepts and implements.

Victor Vroom and Phillip Yetton have published a diagnostic framework for matching the amount of participation in decision making with situational requirements.[31] Their five possible decision-making processes, described in Exhibit 10-6, vary in the degrees of participation they allow.

CRITERIA FOR PARTICIPATION

When deciding how much participation to use when making a decision, several factors need to be considered. Three of the most important are the quality requirements, the degree necessary for employees or stakeholders to accept the decision, and the time required to make the decision.

QUALITY REQUIREMENTS Whether a decision is best made by an individual or a group depends on the nature and importance of the problem. Important decisions that have large impacts on organizational goal achievement need to be the highest quality possible. In complex situations, it is unlikely that any one individual will have all the necessary information to make a top-quality decision. Therefore, the decision maker should at least consult with others who are either closer to the problem or more "expert" in dealing with it. One person with appropriate knowledge and experience, on the other hand, can decide what to do to solve simple routine problems.

Exhibit 10-6 Types of Participation in Decisions

Key: A = Autocratic, C = Consultant, G = Group: I and II denote variations of a process.

AI You solve the problem or make the decision yourself, using information available at the time.

AII You obtain the necessary information from your employee(s), then decide on the solution to the problem yourself. You may or may not tell your employees what the problem is in getting the information from them. The role played by your employees in making the decision is clearly one of providing the necessary information to you, rather than generating or evaluating alternative solutions.

CI You share the problem with relevant employees individually, getting their ideas and suggestions without bringing them together as a group. Then you make the decision that may or may not reflect your employees' influence.

CII You share the problem with your employees as a group, collectively obtaining their ideas and suggestions. Then you make the decision that may or may not reflect your employees' influence.

GII You share the problem with your employees as a group. Together you generate and evaluate alternatives and attempt to reach agreement (consensus) on a solution. Your role is much like that of chairperson. You do not try to influence the group to adopt "your" solution, and you are willing to accept and implement any solution that has the support of the entire group.

Source: Adapted from V.H. Vroom and A.G. Jago, *The New Leadership* (Upper Saddle River, NJ: Prentice Hall, 1988) 35.

ACCEPTANCE REQUIREMENTS The effectiveness of the action plan decided upon is a combination of its quality and the effort put into implementing it. A top-quality decision, if not implemented appropriately, will not be effective. A lower-quality decision that receives enthusiastic support from all involved may be more effective than a higher-quality alternative that implementers do not buy into.

Those stakeholders affected by a decision are usually more highly motivated to implement the action plan if they have had an opportunity to influence it. Being involved usually increases participants' understanding and generates a feeling of commitment to make "our" decision work, whereas an arbitrary, autocratic decision that is handed down often results in passive acceptance or even active resistance to implementation.

TIME REQUIREMENTS Allocating problem solving and decision making to a group requires a greater investment of time in meetings, which is unavailable for usual tasks. But the level of acceptance and probability of efficient execution is greater for participative decisions than autocratic methods. Also, a higher-quality decision may result from the inclusion of a variety of perspectives and approaches. It is important to determine whether additional time investment produces significantly higher degrees of quality, acceptance, and commitment.

CHOOSING THE APPROPRIATE DEGREE OF PARTICIPATION

The specific needs for quality, acceptance, and time provide the impetus for choosing among the five degrees of participation in any given decision situation. The answers to seven questions about decision quality and acceptance can indicate the most appropriate degree of participation in any given decision situation.[32] Exhibit 10-7 illustrates the appropriate sequence of these three questions regarding quality and four questions regarding acceptance in a decision-tree format.

Exhibit 10-7 Decision Tree for Deciding the Optimum Participation in Decision Making

A	B	C	D	E	F	G
Would any of the quality requirements make one solution likely to be more rational than another?	Do I have sufficient information to make a high-quality decision?	Is the problem structured?	Is acceptance of decision by subordinates critical to implementation?	If you were to make the decision by yourself, is it reasonably certain that it would be accepted by your subordinates?	Do subordinates share the organizational goals to be obtained in solving this problem?	Is conflict among subordinates likely in preferred solution?

1-AI
2-AI
3-GII
4-AI
5-AI
6-GII
7-CII
8-CI
9-AII
10-AII
11-CII
12-GII
13-CII
14-CII

Source: Adapted from V.H. Vroom and A.G. Jago, *The New Leadership* (Upper Saddle River, NJ: Prentice Hall, 1988) 62.

It is possible that more than one style may be appropriate for a problem situation. In that case, the optimal style indicated by this model is the more autocratic one because it will require the least amount of time to implement. Therefore, the decision tree is most useful in situations where time is a critical factor. In situations where it is important to increase things such as morale, employee development, or group cohesiveness, it may be more appropriate to choose a more time-consuming decision style that emphasizes team development.

ADVANTAGES AND DISADVANTAGES OF GROUP DECISION MAKING

As we have just discussed, groups usually take more time than individuals to make decisions, but groups are often more creative and group involvement is essential for gaining acceptance of decisions that members must implement. Although groups are often able to produce more and better solutions to problems than are individuals[33] and more commitment to higher-quality decisions,[34] extensive research has demonstrated that groups have both strengths and weaknesses in reaching decisions.[35] These aspects are summarized in Exhibit 10-8.

ADVANTAGES OF MAKING DECISIONS IN GROUPS When a number of people meet in a group to solve a problem, one advantage is that they usually have greater amounts of knowledge available than one individual working alone. They have more diverse viewpoints, which lead to more options and creative solutions. More people also means more approaches to solving the problem, which can eliminate constantly trying to approach a problem in a way that will not work. By participating in the discussion and problem-solving process, group members have a better understanding of the decision and why it was made. Being a part of the decision process contributes to an increased probability of acceptance and implementation of the decision because of the group ownership of "our decision" versus one by some authority figure.

DISADVANTAGES OF MAKING DECISIONS IN GROUPS Although groups have the potential for making more creative and effective decisions, the increased number of individuals involved and group dynamics often create barriers.

More Time Investment Group decisions are usually more time-consuming than individual ones because of the interaction required. Individuals in groups need to get to know each other, build rapport, satisfy social needs, and clarify communications. Groups also spend time organizing, resolving conflicts, and developing operating procedures. In addition, the time group members spend solving problems is time away from other work responsibilities.

Individual Agendas Individual group members may have competing goals or prior commitments that lead to disagreements about alternative solutions and destructive conflict. Groups may also be subject to domination by a few strong individuals who may not have the best ideas. At times an individual who personally stands to lose may block even the best group decision.

Shared Responsibility Ambiguous responsibility regarding who is actually accountable for the final decision and implementation of a group decision can be an issue. At times this shared responsibility can lead to more risky decisions than are appropriate because individuals feel less personally responsible for negative consequences because the group made the decision.

Pressure to Conform One of the main disadvantages of making decisions in groups is the potential social pressure to conform to premature decisions before all the information

Exhibit 10-8 Advantages and Disadvantages of Group Problem Solving

Advantages Groups Have Over Individuals	Disadvantages Groups Have Compared to Individuals
■ **More knowledge and information** A group of people meeting together to solve a problem has more breadth and, quite often, more depth of experience and knowledge than any one individual. This is especially true if members come from diverse backgrounds.	■ **Competing goals** Group members often have prior commitments to other reference groups or have personal agendas that conflict. These differences can lead to disagreement about alternative solutions and destructive conflict.
■ **Diversity of viewpoints** A number of people with different experiences can generate more options and creative alternatives. They also bring a greater number of approaches to solving the problem.	■ **Time consuming** People have to plan and coordinate group meetings and then wait for everyone to arrive. The processes of being understood, resolving interpersonal conflicts, and irrelevant side conversations also detract from group problem-solving efficiency.
■ **Increased understanding** By participating in the problem-solving process, group members have a better understanding of the decision and why it was made.	■ **Social pressure to conform** Especially in highly cohesive groups, members often conform to majority opinions that are not optimal in order to gain liking and acceptance.
■ **Increased acceptance** Group members are also more likely to accept a decision they understand. Also, a participative decision, in North American democratic-type societies, is often perceived as more legitimate than an autocratic decision by a single manager, which might be considered arbitrary.	■ **Domination by a few** High status, power, or just an assertive personality can cause certain members to dominate group discussions and influence decisions that they prefer. If the dominating people do not have the best ideas and those who do are kept silent, the quality of the group decision will suffer.
■ **Better implementation** Participation in a decision creates a feeling of ownership of "our decision" versus one by some authority figure. People want to show that they are right and consequently will work hard to implement it themselves as well as encouraging others to do the same.	■ **Ambiguous responsibility** Since no one individual is held responsible for a group's decision, there is often uncertainty about who is accountable for implementing decisions and who gets the credit or blame for outcomes. Often this can lead to decisions that are more risky than appropriate for the organization, because no one in particular will be held accountable if the decision fails.

Source: Adapted from N.R.F. Maier, "Assets and Liabilities in Group Problem Solving," *Psychological Review* 74 (July 1967): 239–49.

Exhibit 10-9 Symptoms of Groupthink

- **Illusions of group invulnerability** Members of the group feel they are invincible, resulting in risk taking.
- **Collective rationalization** Refusal to consider contradictory data or to thoroughly consider unpleasant alternatives.
- **Illusion of group morality** Members of the group feel it is "right" and morally correct.
- **Stereotypes of competitors** Shared negative opinions; treating other groups as weak, evil, or stupid.
- **Pressure to conform** Direct pressure to conform is applied to a member who suggests other alternatives or that the group may be wrong.
- **Self-censorship** Members do not share personal concerns if contrary to overall group opinion.
- **Illusions of unanimity** Erroneously believing that all are in agreement and accepting consensus prematurely.
- **Mind guarding** Members of the group protect the group from hearing disturbing ideas or viewpoints from outsiders.

Source: I.L. Janis, *Groupthink: Psychological Studies of Policy Decision and Fiascoes,* 2d ed. (Boston: Houghton Mifflin Company, 1982). © Houghton Mifflin Company. Adapted with permission.

has been processed thoroughly. In highly cohesive groups this pressure to conform can lead to the **groupthink** phenomenon.[36] Groupthink exists when members' desire to agree is so great that it tends to override the concern for realistic appraisal of alternative courses of action.[37] Exhibit 10-9 highlights symptoms to look for to determine whether groupthink exists.

THE MANAGER'S ROLE IN MAKING GROUP DECISION MAKING EFFECTIVE
Whether a group will be effective or ineffective depends primarily on the skills of its members and its leader. For example, lower-status group members usually defer to those with higher status, even though they may be the ones with the best ideas.[38] Group leaders need to ensure that all participants feel free to contribute by not trying to persuade others in the problem-solving group to adopt the leader's own preference. The leader's role is to establish a cooperative environment in which all opinions are heard and evaluated before a solution is reached.[39] If the leader is not aware of the dynamics of group process or is not effective in the role of facilitator, a cohesive group may fall into the pattern of groupthink.

Groupthink can be avoided if a leader remains neutral, encourages criticism, asks for new ideas, and brings in outside consultants to present alternative views. The following strategies can also be used to avoid groupthink.[40] Assign a critical evaluator role to each member of the group and emphasize the need to air doubts. Another strategy is for the leader to remain impartial and refrain from stating preferences. A third option is to encourage members to discuss their deliberations with people outside the group and relay these opinions to the group. Outside experts can even be invited to meetings for the express purpose of challenging prevailing views. A devil's advocate can be assigned to raise deliberate opposition to the proposals being considered. Finally, after a tentative decision has been reached, a second-chance meeting can be called, in which members air every possible doubt.

Concept Quiz

Decide whether the following 10 statements are true or false, and circle the right answer. Answers are at the end of the quiz. After marking your answers, remember to go back and check your understanding of any answers you missed.

True or False	1. A problem exists whenever the actual situation is not what is desired.
True or False	2. It is more important to analyze a problem thoroughly than to generate many solutions.
True or False	3. Brainstorming, Nominal Group Technique, and the Delphi Method are all techniques used to decide a course of action.
True or False	4. Gantt charts indicate which problems should be solved first.
True or False	5. Acceptance and implementation of action plans are enhanced by involving all affected stakeholders in generation and analysis of alternatives.
True or False	6. The last step in problem solving is deciding on the best solution to the problem.
True or False	7. Autocratic decisions may result in passive acceptance or even active resistance to implementation.
True or False	8. Groupthink facilitates realistic appraisals of alternative courses of action.
True or False	9. Shared responsibility is a strength for identifying who is actually accountable for the implementation of a group decision.
True or False	10. Brainstorming promotes a higher quantity of far-fetched ideas.

Answers (1) True; (2) True; (3) False; (4) False; (5) True; (6) False; (7) True; (8) False; (9) False; (10) True

Behavioural Checklist

The following skills are important to problem solving. Use them when evaluating your own problem-solving skills and those of others.

The Effective Problem Solver:

- Encourages innovation by creating a learning environment, absorbing risks, encouraging others, and committing resources.
- Identifies problems by establishing trust, clarifying objectives, and assessing the situation.
- Analyzes problems by separating symptoms from sources and determining all causes.
- Decides on an action plan by establishing criteria, developing alternatives, and choosing the best one.
- Implements the action plan by assigning responsibilities and establishing a schedule.
- Follows through by measuring performance and taking corrective actions.
- Decides who should participate in decision making based on quality, acceptance, and time.
- Avoids the problems in group decision making by remaining neutral, encouraging critical evaluation, asking for new ideas, and allowing second-chance decision meetings.
- Applies techniques to promote group problem solving.

Modelling Exercise[41]

INSTRUCTIONS One person volunteers to play Jan, the manager of human resources for Beacon Lights. Another person volunteers to play the role of Sean, Jan's administrative assistant. Everyone, including the person playing Sean, should read Jan's role, but Jan is not to read Sean's role. Class members not playing one of the roles should also review the Observer's Rating Sheet, which they will use to rate Jan's performance in solving the problem and providing feedback at the end of the exercise.

JAN'S ROLE You have been manager of human resources for Beacon Lights for 10 years. Just when you thought you had your job "down pat," the sky fell in. A strong labour union has been trying to organize your plant, a job applicant recently filed a claim against your company for discriminatory hiring practices, the president and vice-president of sales were forced to resign last month because of the company's poor performance, and on top of all that, your long-time administrative assistant just died of a heart attack.

A month ago you hired Sean to replace your administrative assistant. Sean has two years of experience, so you could save some salary money, and you think that Sean should have no difficulty picking up the pieces. Sean asked for some temporary help recently, but you really cannot afford it right now and said you would keep Sean informed about the more urgent items you wanted to concentrate on first. Your former administrative assistant had no problems getting the job done and you do not expect that Sean will either.

You have been asked to give a talk at a national convention on a new productivity program your company has pioneered, and you are looking forward to getting away from the office for a few days to catch your breath. You gave your talk to your new administrative assistant, Sean, a couple of days ago so there would have been plenty of time to get it typed and reproduced.

This morning you have come into the office to proofread and rehearse your talk prior to catching a plane this evening and you are shocked to find a note saying your administrative assistant called in sick this morning. You rush over to Sean's desk and frantically begin searching for your paper. You find it mixed in with some material for the quarterly report that should have been sent in two weeks ago, a stack of overdue correspondence, and two days' worth of unopened mail.

As you dial Sean's home phone number, you realize that you are perspiring heavily and your face is flushed. This foul-up is the worst one you can remember in years.

SEAN'S ROLE You hear the phone ring and it is all you can do to get out of bed and limp into the kitchen to answer it. You really feel rotten. On the way home last night, you slipped on your kid's skateboard in the driveway and sprained your knee. You can hardly move today and the pain is excruciating. You are also a bit hesitant to answer the phone because you figure it is probably your boss, Jan, calling to chew you out for getting behind in your work. You know you deserve some blame, but it was not all your fault. Since you began working for Jan a month ago, you have asked several times for a thorough job description. You feel you do not really understand Jan's priorities or your specific job responsibilities. You are replacing an administrative assistant who died suddenly after working for Jan for 10 years. You were hired to pick up the pieces, but you have found working with Jan extremely frustrating. Jan has been too busy to train you properly and she assumes you know as much about the job as your predecessor. This assumption is particularly a problem because you have not worked as an administrative assistant for three years, and you feel a bit "rusty."

Jan's talk is a good example of the difficulties you have experienced. Jan gave you the talk a couple of days ago and said it was urgent—but that was on top of a quarterly report that was already overdue and a backlog of correspondence, filing, and so on. You never filled out a report like this before, and every time you asked Jan a question you were told that you would have to discuss it with her later as Jan ran off to a meeting. When you asked if it would be possible to get some additional help to catch up on the overdue work, Jan said the company could not afford it because of poor sales. This response irked you because you knew you were being paid far less than your predecessor. You knew Jan faced some urgent deadlines so you had planned to return to the office last night to type Jan's speech and try to complete the report, but two hours in the emergency room at the hospital put an end to that plan. You tried calling Jan to explain the problem, only to find out Jan has an unlisted number.

You sit down and prop up your leg, and wince with pain as you pick up the phone.

TIME Not to exceed 15 minutes.

Observer's Rating Sheet

On completion of the exercise, evaluate Jan's problem-solving skills. Rate the problem-solving skills between 1 and 5 using the following scale. Write concrete examples in the space for comments below each criteria skill to use in explaining your feedback.

1 Unsatisfactory	2 Weak	3 Adequate	4 Good	5 Outstanding

_____ Identified problems by establishing trust, clarifying objectives, and assessing the situation.

_____ Analyzed the problem by separating symptoms from sources and determining all causes.

_____ Decided on an action plan by establishing criteria, developing alternatives, and choosing the best one.

_____ Implemented the action plan by assigning responsibilities and establishing a schedule.

_____ Followed through by measuring performance and taking corrective actions.

_____ Decided who should participate in decision making based on quality, acceptance, and time.

_____ Avoided the problems in group decision making by remaining neutral, encouraging critical evaluation, asking for new ideas, and allowing second-chance decision meetings.

_____ Encouraged innovation by creating a learning environment, absorbing risks, encouraging others, and committing resources.

_____ Applied techniques to promote group problem solving.

Group Exercises

Three different types of group exercises are presented here. First is a short case for you to practise your conceptual problem-solving skills. Second is an opportunity to apply the decision tree to determine the appropriate degree of participation in several different problem situations according to the criteria of quality, acceptance, and time restraints. Third is an exercise demonstrating the advantages of group versus individual problem solving.

Group Exercise 1: Dealing with Academic Dishonesty Case Discussion[42]

PURPOSE To apply the creative problem-solving process to a current situation familiar to participants.

DIRECTIONS All steps in this exercise can be conducted by the instructor with the entire class, or autonomous groups can apply the process themselves.

STEP 1 Read the following description of academic dishonesty.

STEP 2 Form groups of five or six members and discuss the case questions in your groups.

STEP 3 Groups share their solutions with the entire class.

STEP 4 Groups analyze their application of the problem-solving process using the Observer's Rating Sheet.

TIME 55 to 85 minutes. Allocate 30 minutes for group problem solving, 30 minutes for class discussions, and 25 minutes for groups to analyze their problem-solving process. If time is limited, eliminate the 30-minute class discussion, leaving 55 minutes for group problem solving and debriefing.

THE PROBLEM OF ACADEMIC DISHONESTY

Someday it will happen to every professor. A student will turn in such an excellent, well-written paper that its authenticity is in serious doubt. Or, during a test, the professor looks up and sees one student copying from another or from crib notes lying on the floor. Studies show that about 40 per cent of students cheat in a given term, and it is not only the lazy student looking for a shortcut. In fact, overachievers are more likely to cheat than underachievers when a professor springs a test on them and they feel they are losing control of their ability to prepare for class. For example, a student who is taking a full course load, working part-time, and still trying to have a social life may not feel adequately prepared for a test and feel pressured to cheat. The question for professors is what to do about it.

QUESTIONS FOR DISCUSSION

1. What types of student cheating behaviour have you observed?
   a) How did you detect the cheating?
   b) Whose responsibility was it to control the cheating?
   c) Was the cheating dealt with? If so, how? If not, why not?
2. Apply the problem-solving process to develop an action plan to prevent the problem of academic cheating. Be prepared to present your plan to the class.

Group Exercise 2: Choosing a Decision Style[43]

OBJECTIVE To learn how to apply the Vroom and Yetton decision participation model.

PREPARATION Review the earlier section in this chapter titled "When Is Participation Appropriate for Decision Making?" Make sure you understand the five decision participation styles (Exhibit 10-5) and the decision participation tree (Exhibit 10-6). (10 minutes)

STEP 1: INDIVIDUAL CASE ANALYSES Individually read each of the three hypothetical cases that follow. Decide which of the five decision participation styles from Exhibit 10-6 you would use in each situation. Record your decisions. (10–15 minutes)

CASE A You are manufacturing manager in the northeastern division of a large electronics plant. Upper management is always searching for ways to increase efficiency.

Recently management installed new machines and introduced a simplified work system, but to everyone's surprise (including your own) the expected increase in productivity has not been realized. In fact, production has begun to drop, quality has fallen, and the number of employee resignations has risen.

You do not believe anything is wrong with the machines. You have requested reports from other companies that are using them, and their responses confirm this opinion. You have also called in representatives from the firm that built the machines. These technicians have examined the machines thoroughly and report that they are operating at peak efficiency.

You suspect that some elements of the new work system may be responsible for the decreased output and quality, but this view is not shared by your five immediate direct reports—the four first-line supervisors who head your four production sections and your supply manager. They have attributed the drop in production to various factors: poor operators, insufficient training, lack of adequate financial incentives, and poor worker morale. Clearly, it is an issue surrounded by considerable depth of individual feeling. A high potential for discord exists among your five key employees, and this development may be just the tip of the iceberg.

This morning you received a phone call from your division manager, who had just reviewed your production figures for the last six months and was clearly concerned. The division manager has indicated that the problem is yours to solve in any way that you think best but has requested that you report within a week what steps you plan to take.

Certainly you share your manager's concern and you know that, despite their differing views, your employees share it as well. Your problem is to decide what steps must be taken by whom in the effort to reverse the decline.

CASE B You are the general supervisor in charge of a large work gang that is laying an oil pipeline. It is now necessary to estimate your expected rate of progress in order to schedule material deliveries to the next field site.

You know the nature of the terrain you will be travelling and have the historical data you need to compute the mean and variance in the rate of speed over that type of terrain. Given these two variables, it is a simple matter to calculate the earliest and the latest times at which materials and support facilities will be needed at the next site. It is important that your estimate be reasonably accurate. Underestimates result in idle workers, and overestimates result in securing materials for a period of time before they are to be used.

Up to this point, progress has been good. Your five group supervisors and other members of the gang stand to receive substantial bonuses if the project is completed ahead of schedule.

CASE C You are supervising the work of 12 engineers. All 12 have similar levels of formal training and work experience, a condition that enables you to use them interchangeably on most projects. Yesterday your manager informed you that a request had come in from an overseas affiliate for four engineers to go abroad on extended loan for a period of six to eight months. For a number of reasons, he argued (and you agreed) that this request should be met from your group.

All your engineers are capable of handling this assignment and, from the standpoint of present and future projects, no particular reason dictates why any one should be retained over any other. The major problem is that most members of the organization consider the location of the overseas assignment undesirable.

STEP 2: GROUP DISCUSSION After individuals have recorded their opinions of the most appropriate decision participation style in each of these cases, proceed with the following steps:

1. Divide the class into groups of five to six people.
2. Each person shares with others in the group why he or she chose a particular decision style for each of the three cases. Focus on determining all the reasons why people chose different decision styles. One person should write down the styles chosen for each case and note briefly the associated reasons. The group should not try to reach a consensus; you merely want to discover how many different approaches were taken and why. (20 minutes)
3. Using the decision-making tree in Exhibit 10-6, individually answer the questions at the top and work through the decision tree until you reach the recommended decision style for each of the three cases. (10 minutes)
4. Repeat step 4 as a group. Now establish consensus as to the appropriate decision style prescribed by this model. (10 minutes)
5. Check your answers with the authors' recommendations, which your instructor will provide. Discuss any variations and reread the chapter explanation if misunderstandings persist. Speculate as to why differences occurred. The recorder should note the outcome of this group discussion. (10 minutes)

STEP 3: CLASS DISCUSSION Reconvene as a class. The recorders report group outcomes, including discrepancies between the original (individual) analyses and the decision tree's solutions. Note any sharp disparities among the groups' responses, and try to determine why they occurred.

Participate in a class discussion based on the following questions:

1. To what extent do you agree with the model? What are its strengths and weaknesses in application?
2. Do you have a preferred decision style (AI, AII, CI, CII, GII)? Why or why not? Will knowledge of this model make any difference in your decision-style flexibility?
3. How closely does your decision behaviour match that prescribed by the model? What evidence do you have that you are concerned more with time (efficiency) or with participation in choosing a decision style? (15 minutes)

TIME Count on approximately 75 minutes for the entire exercise. If the total class discussion is left out, the exercise takes about 55 to 60 minutes.

Group Exercise 3: Winter Survival Exercise[44]

PURPOSE This exercise is designed to demonstrate the potential advantages of participative group decision making compared to individual decision making.

TIME 80 minutes for the complete exercise. If less time is available, skip step 7 and shorten step 6 by the time needed. For example, leaving out step 7 saves 20 minutes, and if 5 minutes are taken off of step 6, the exercise can be completed in 55 minutes.

DIRECTIONS All of the class reads the Winter Survival Situation. (5 minutes)

STEP 1 *Individually rank* the 12 items shown in the following Winter Survival Tally chart according to their importance to your survival in the Winter Survival Situation. In the "Individual Ranking" column, indicate the most important item with 1, going through to 12 for the least important. Keep in mind the reasons why each item is or is not important. (5 minutes)

STEP 2 Form groups of five or six members. Reach a *group consensus* of the best rank-order for the 12 items and record it in the second column of the Winter Survival Tally chart. Remember that a consensus means that everyone agrees it is the best ranking the group can agree on, it is not simply an average of the individual rankings. (30 minutes)

STEP 3 Enter the *expert's ranking*, which will be provided by the instructor, in the third column.

STEP 4 Compute the absolute difference (i.e., ignore minus signs) between the *individual ranking* and the *expert's ranking* for each item and record this information in column four. Put the sum of the absolute differences for each item at the bottom of column four.

STEP 5 Compute the absolute difference for each item between the *team's ranking* and the *expert's ranking*. Sum these absolute scores at the bottom of column five. (5 minutes for steps 3 through 5)

STEP 6 Compare the differences between your absolute difference score and your group's absolute difference score. Based on these results, discuss the merits of individual versus team decision making. (20 minutes)

STEP 7 Share your group's absolute difference scores and conclusions with the class. The class discusses common conclusions about the merits of individual versus team decision making. (20 minutes)

The Winter Survival Situation

You have just crash-landed somewhere in the woods of Southern Manitoba or Northern Minnesota. It is 11:32 A.M. on a day in mid-January. The small plane in which you were travelling crashed on a small lake. The pilot and co-pilot were killed. Shortly after the crash, the plane sank completely into the lake with the pilot and co-pilot's bodies inside. Everyone else on the flight escaped to land without getting wet and without serious injury.

The crash came suddenly before the pilot had time to radio for help or inform anyone of your position. Because your pilot was trying to avoid a storm, you know the plane was considerably off course. The pilot announced shortly before the crash that you were 72 kilometres northwest of a small town that is the nearest known habitation.

You are in a wilderness area made up of thick woods broken by many lakes and rivers. The snow depth varies from above the ankles in windswept areas to more than knee-deep where it has drifted. The last weather report indicated that the temperature would reach –15°C in the daytime and –26°C at night. Plenty of dead wood and twigs can be found in the area around the lake. You and the other surviving passengers are dressed in winter clothing appropriate for city wear—suits, pantsuits, street shoes, and overcoats. While escaping from the plane, your group salvaged the 12 items listed in column one on the Winter Survival Tally chart. You may assume that the number of persons in the group is the same as the number in your group, and that you have agreed to stay together.

	Step	1 Your Individual Ranking	2 Group Consensus Ranking	3 Survival Expert's Ranking	4 Difference Between 1 and 3 Values	5 Difference Between 2 and 3 Values
Winter Survival Tally Chart						
Items						
Ball of steel wool						
Newspapers (one per person)						
Compass						
Hand axe						
Cigarette lighter (without fluid)						
Loaded .45-calibre pistol						
Sectional air map made of plastic						
Twenty-by-twenty-foot piece of heavy-duty canvas						
Extra shirt and pants for each survivor						
Can of shortening						
Quart of 100-proof whiskey						
Family-size chocolate bar (one per person)						
Totals						

Application Questions

1. Explain why it is so important to establish an atmosphere of trust in situations of group problem solving. Can you cite situations in which you have not trusted others with whom you were involved in solving a problem? Compare them with situations in which you have felt trust. Have you ever felt that others in a group distrusted you? Why?

2. What four purposes are served by clarifying objectives early in the problem solving process? Whose objectives should be considered?

3. Explain this statement: "No problem solution can be better than the quality of diagnosis on which it is built."

4. With regard to selecting an action plan, indicate whether you agree or disagree with each of the following statements and why: (a) Experience is the best teacher; (b) Intuition is a helpful force; (c) Advice from others is always beneficial; and (d) Experiment with several alternatives.

5. What difficulties might you anticipate when using the problem-solving process? Why? What additional difficulties might arise because of personal attributes? Which of these have you experienced? Explain. What were the consequences? How can these difficulties be avoided?
6. Explain under what circumstances you would want to use participation to solve a problem. When would you rather solve the problem individually?
7. How can a manager encourage problem solving by department members?

Reinforcement Exercises

1. Interview several managers about how they make decisions. Compare the answers you receive to the steps in the problem-solving model. Also, check the degree of participation that these managers used against those recommended by the participation decision tree.
2. Ask some other people to help you solve a problem that you are concerned with. Get their ideas by applying the problem-solving model and techniques for enhancing creativity, such as brainstorming.
3. Help a group you are involved with such as your family, roommates, church group, or sport team creatively solve a problem it is having difficulty with by applying the problem-solving skills you have acquired from this chapter.
4. Watch a movie or television show where the objective is to solve a crime. Note the problem-solving process that the actors apply and compare it to the problem-solving techniques you have learned about in this chapter. What did you learn from this comparison?

Summary Checklist

Take a few minutes to reflect on your performance and look over others' ratings of your problem-solving skills. Now assess yourself on each of the key learning behaviours. Make a check (√) next to those behaviours on which you need improvement.

_____ Proactively identifying problems.
    1. Establish trust with people involved in the situation.
    2. Clarify objectives.
    3. Assess the current situation.
    4. Identify problems.

_____ Defining and analyzing the problem identified.
    1. Separate symptoms from sources.
    2. Determine all causes.

_____ Generating alternative solutions.
    1. Develop action alternatives.
    2. Use a variety of techniques.

_____ Deciding the course of action.
    1. Establish decision-making criteria.
    2. Evaluate alternatives.
    3. Choose the best alternative.
    4. Develop a plan of action.

_____ Implementing the solution (plan of action).

    1. Assign tasks and responsibilities.

    2. Establish an implementation schedule.

    3. Reinforce commitment.

    4. Activate the plan.

_____ Establishing criteria for success.

_____ Evaluating the solution.

    1. Determine how to measure performance.

    2. Monitor and evaluate the results.

    3. If required, take corrective action.

_____ Deciding who should participate in the decision process based on:

    1. Quality requirements.

    2. Acceptance requirements.

    3. Time availability.

_____ Avoiding group decision-making problems.

    1. Remain neutral.

    2. Encourage critical evaluation and devil's advocates.

    3. Ask for new ideas.

    4. Bring in outside experts.

    5. Allow second-chance meetings to reconsider decisions.

Action Plan

1. Which problem-solving behaviour do I most want to improve?
2. Why? What will be my payoff?
3. What potential obstacles stand in my way?
4. What are the specific things I will do to improve? (For examples, see the Reinforcement Exercises.)
5. When will I do them?
6. How and when will I measure my success?

CHAPTER 11

Planning and
Goal Setting

Learning Objectives
After completing this chapter, you should be able to:

- Perform SWOT analyses.
- Determine distinctive competencies.
- Create plans to achieve goals.
- Formulate competitive strategies.
- Create strategic and operational goals.
- Obtain employee commitment to goals.

Self-Assessment Exercise
How Well Do I Plan and Set Goals?

In this two-part assessment, the first part explores how well you plan. The second part helps you assess your goal-setting skills.

Part I: Am I a Good Planner?[1]
The following assessment is designed to help you understand your planning skills. Answer either yes or no to each of the following questions.

	Yes	No
1. My personal objectives are clearly spelled out in writing.	____	____
2. Most of my days are hectic and disorderly.	____	____
3. I seldom make any snap decisions and usually study a problem carefully before acting.	____	____
4. I keep a desk calendar or appointment book as an aid.	____	____
5. I use "action" and "deferred action" files.	____	____
6. I generally establish starting dates and deadlines for all my projects.	____	____

	Yes	No
7. I often ask others for advice.	_____	_____
8. I believe that all problems have to be solved immediately.	_____	_____

Part II: How Well Do I Set Goals?[2]

For each of the following questions, select the answer that best describes how you set goals for yourself. Respond as you have behaved or would behave, not as you think you should behave. Indicate how much you agree or disagree with each statement. When you finish, review the items that received the lowest scores.

Disagree 1	Strongly Disagree 2	Neutral 3	Strongly Agree 4	Agree 5

_____ 1. I am proactive rather than reactive.

_____ 2. I set aside enough time and resources to study and complete projects.

_____ 3. I am able to budget money to buy the things I really want without going broke.

_____ 4. I have thought through what I want to accomplish in my education.

_____ 5. I have a plan for completing my education.

_____ 6. My goals for the future are realistic.

SCORING AND INTERPRETATION

Part I: Am I a Good Planner?

According to the author of this first questionnaire, the perfect planner would have answered as follows. If you answered differently, look for reasons that the alternative is more desirable as you read the Concepts section.

(1) Yes (2) No (3) Yes (4) Yes (5) Yes (6) Yes (7) Yes (8) No

Part II: How Well Do I Set Goals?

This assessment helps you focus on basic aspects of the goal-setting processes in your personal life. Several keys help in making any goal-setting process effective, and we discuss those throughout the Concepts section that follows. Our intent with this brief assessment is to get you thinking about goal setting as it relates to your school, personal, and work settings.

In the first part of the assessment, we focus on whether your personal goal setting is *passive* or *active*. Question 1 queries your general tendency toward "action," and Questions 4 and 5 select a specific example of proaction versus reaction (i.e., having a plan for completing your education). Allocating "resources" for the completion of goals is queried in Questions 2 and 3. Question 6 focuses on a cornerstone of effective goal setting: creating goals that are attainable, yet challenging. If your score on any of these questions is "3" or less, you should pay particular attention to the corresponding material that follows.

Concepts

Most of us have goals we want to achieve. As managers, we also have organizational goals we are charged to accomplish through the efforts of those who work for us. Consequently, we should make sure employees have a clear idea of what they are trying to accomplish in their jobs. Then, we need to help employees determine how best to achieve their objectives.

Planning

Planning involves defining the organization's objectives, establishing an overall strategy for achieving those goals, and developing the means to integrate and coordinate necessary activities. Planning is concerned with both ends (what needs to be done) and means (how it is to be done). Depending on their level in the organization, managers are concerned with different types of planning.

Strategic plans apply to the entire organization. They establish the organization's overall objectives, and seek to position the organization in terms of its environment. Strategic planning is done by top-level managers to determine the long-term focus and direction of the entire organization. Wal-Mart's strategy, for example, is to build large stores in rural areas, offer an extensive selection of merchandise, provide the lowest prices, and then draw consumers from the many surrounding small towns. All other shorter-term and specific plans for lower-level managers are linked and coordinated so that they contribute to the organization's strategic plan.

Operational plans specify the details of how the overall objectives in the strategic plan are to be achieved. Operational plans are of a short-term nature, usually one year or less. They are formulated to achieve specific objectives assigned to lower-level managers regarding their contribution to the organization's strategic plan. The Wal-Mart store manager in Windsor, Ontario, for example, would be doing operational planning when making out a quarterly expense budget or weekly employee work schedules.

The planning process is essentially the same for managers at all levels of the organization. The breadth, time frames, specificity, and frequency vary, however, becoming smaller in scope as managerial level decreases. Top-level strategic planning is also unique because of the environmental scanning and analysis of overall organizational resources that are required. Because the majority of managers are at supervisory or mid-level positions, we will summarize both the strategic aspects of planning and the planning process, while the remainder of the chapter will focus on goal setting at the operational level.

HOW THE PLANNING PROCESS WORKS

The nine-step planning process is illustrated in Exhibit 11-1. The steps include identifying the overall goal, analyzing the environment for opportunities and threats, analyzing your

Exhibit 11-1 The Planning Process

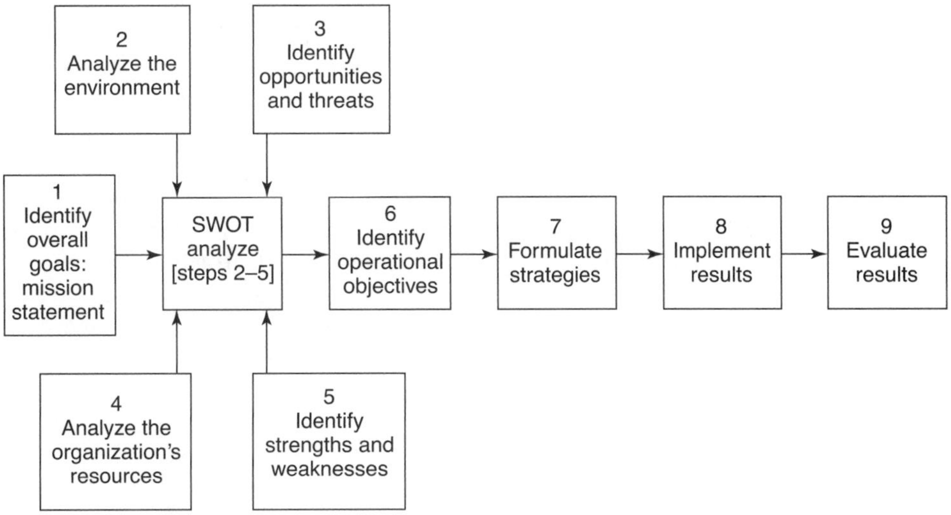

own resources for strengths and weaknesses, formulating specific objectives, deciding how to implement the plan, and determining how to evaluate results.

STEP 1: IDENTIFY OVERALL GOALS In order to create a plan, managers must first identify what the organization is trying to achieve. Goals are the foundation of all other planning activities. They refer to the desired outcomes for the entire organization, groups, and individuals. Goals provide the direction for all management decisions and form the criteria against which actual accomplishments can be measured.

Goals differ in breadth, time frame, specificity, and frequency of change just as plans do. At the highest level, every organization should have a **mission statement** that defines its purpose and answers the questions: Why do we exist? What do we do? What business are we in? Defining the organization's mission forces management to identify the scope of its products or services carefully. For example, Rubbermaid's mission statement gives direction to managers and employees alike when it states that the company seeks "to be the leading world-class creator and marketer of brand-name, primarily plastic products which are creatively responsive to global trends and capable of earning a leading market share position."[3]

The organization's mission establishes the overreaching goal or basis on which objectives and strategies are formulated, providing guidance for all managers. Every unit or department in an organization needs to have an overriding goal or mission statement of its own that indicates its major contribution to the overall organization mission. Mission statements help managers focus on their units' strengths, which give the organization a competitive advantage. Rubbermaid's management, for instance, understands that its company's strength lies in producing plastic products, marketed under their brand name, where they can be the market leader. Even if management saw opportunities in steel products, or in selling to large retailers who would sell Rubbermaid products under the retailer's house brand, Rubbermaid's mission statement would deter management from pursuing those opportunities. Although some companies can make money by following those strategies, they do not play to Rubbermaid's mission and strengths.

Once managers know the purpose for their organization, they can perform a **SWOT analysis** to examine the fit between their organization's **S**trengths and **W**eaknesses, and the environmental **O**pportunities and **T**hreats. The first step is environmental scanning to determine what is taking place in the organization's environment. Then they can begin the essence of strategic planning, the SWOT analysis to identify a niche that the organization can exploit to achieve its mission. Because an organization's environment largely defines management's options, a successful strategy will be one that aligns well with the environment.

STEP 2: ANALYZE THE ENVIRONMENT Once the mission has been identified, managers should look outside their organization to ensure that their goals align well with current and future environments.[4] This environmental scanning can be challenging for managers because of their numerous day-to-day responsibilities. Some companies have special departments with primary responsibility for helping managers keep track of environmental forces.[5] Nevertheless, because all decisions about what plans and strategies to pursue in obtaining goals need to be grounded in a thorough assessment of the external situation, all managers must constantly evaluate environmental forces as they diagnose issues and weigh decisions.

These external forces include both macro and micro factors. Macro-environment, or **PEST** factors, include **P**olitical factors such as government legislation and trade agreements, **E**conomic factors such as Bank of Canada interest rates or long-term prospects for the general economy, **S**ocial factors such as demographic trends and public opinion, and **Technology** factors that can provide cheaper means of production and faster communication. Micro-environmental factors are those that directly affect the organization. These organization-specific factors include changes in competitors (e.g., new entrants, substitute goods and services), customers, laws and regulations, and suppliers.[6]

Understanding and being aware of developments in all these factors will give a manager a solid foundation for knowing where to look and for analyzing the data retrieved about the business environment. Several behaviours can facilitate the environmental scanning process.[7]

Make Scanning a Priority To combat the problem of being too busy to keep up with the latest developments, managers should shift the priority given to environmental scanning from something they do if time permits to something that is a vital part of their job. It can be implemented by ongoing activities ranging from attending relevant seminars and college and university courses to learn the latest innovations in the field, to daily reading of trade publications and newspapers, or "surfing the Net" to stay current with political, economic, social, technical, and competitor developments.

Anticipate Change Any environmental factor can change without warning. You can adapt easier and more effectively if you have anticipated and planned for possible changes than if you are caught by surprise and have to catch up in a crisis mode. Anticipation means never taking the present environment for granted and always being proactive by continually scanning the environment for clues about potential developments. A classic example of what happens if you do not anticipate change is the reaction of the entertainment and recording industries to new copying devices and transmission technologies. While illegal copies of MP3s and movies have soared, both industries have been slow to develop strategies to capitalize on the commercial potential of the Internet.[8]

Flexible Thinking Forming strong opinions about events in the future and preparing for them to occur in the predicted manner is a risky means of dealing with the environment. The intent of environmental scanning is to keep one step ahead of changes and thus outperform the competition. Successful environmental scanning entails constantly thinking ahead and staying open to all change possibilities. The key to successful anticipation and effective adaptation is flexibility of opinions about how to best prepare for environmental changes.

Consult with Colleagues You need to get as many different takes on as many environmental factors as possible to be best informed and develop a comprehensive analysis. You can get help by consulting colleagues who are specialists from different business functions such as finance, marketing, and purchasing. Some managers even obtain data from their counterparts at competing companies when chatting at professional conventions or business club meetings.[9] Students intuitively do the same thing when they seek out others who have completed the final exam in earlier sections of an instructor's course to get guidance on what to expect and how to prepare.

Be Patient with Ambiguity The causes of environmental change are often ambiguous and a culmination of many uncertain events. When scanning the environment, expect to find a lot of ambiguous information that may not make sense at first. But keep at it and try to determine ways in which certain environmental factors affect others. As you mull over potential alternative outcomes, trust your intuition to provide needed insights and hunches that can be checked out.

STEP 3: IDENTIFY EXTERNAL OPPORTUNITIES AND THREATS After thoroughly analyzing the environment, managers can determine and evaluate opportunities that the organization can exploit and threats that the organization faces.[10] Keep in mind, however, the same environment can present opportunities to one organization and pose threats to another in the same or a similar industry because of their different resources. For example, telecommuting technologies have enabled organizations that sell computer modems, fax machines, and the like to prosper. On the other hand, organizations such as the Canada Post Corporation, whose business it is to get messages from one person to another, have been adversely affected by this environmental change.

STEP 4: ANALYZE THE ORGANIZATION'S RESOURCES Next we move from looking outside the organization to looking inside in order to evaluate the organization's internal resources. What skills and abilities do the organization's employees have? What is the organization's cash flow? Has it been successful at developing new and innovative products? How do customers perceive the image of the organization and the quality of its products or services?

Every organization is constrained to some degree by the resources and skills it has available. A small six-person computer software design firm with annual sales of less than $2 million might see a huge market for on-line services, but the company's minimal resources limit its ability to act on this opportunity. In contrast, Microsoft's management was able to create the Microsoft Network because it had the access, people skills, name recognition, and financial resources to pursue this market.

STEP 5: IDENTIFY INTERNAL STRENGTHS AND WEAKNESSES The analysis in Step 4 should lead to a clear assessment of the organization's internal resources, such as capital, worker skills, patents, and the like. It should also indicate organizational abilities such as training and development, marketing, accounting, human resources, research and development, and management information systems. An organization's **strengths** refer to the internal resources that are available or things that it does well. **Weaknesses** are activities that the organization does not do well, or resources it needs but does not possess. Strengths that represent unique skills or resources and give the organization a competitive edge are called its **distinctive competence**. For example, Black & Decker bought General Electric's small appliance division—which made coffee makers, toasters, irons, and the like—renamed it, and capitalized on Black & Decker's reputation for quality and durability to make these appliances far more profitable than they had been under the GE name.

STEP 6: IDENTIFY OPERATIONAL OBJECTIVES The results of the SWOT analysis provide a clear understanding of environmental opportunities and threats and the organization's internal strengths and weaknesses. It can then lead to the identification of a unique set of opportunities, or **niche**, where the organization has a competitive advantage. Using this information, managers can formulate more specific operational objectives that will contribute to its mission.

The purpose of setting operational objectives is to convert managerial statements of business mission and company direction into specific performance targets. Objectives create a standard against which organization progress can be measured.[11] The objectives established should include both short-range and long-range performance targets. Short-range objectives spell out the immediate improvements and outcomes management desires. Long-range objectives prompt managers to consider what to do now to position the company to perform well over the long term.

To achieve one of Wal-Mart's visions of maintaining consistent growth, founder Sam Walton gave employees their goal for the 1990s of doubling the number of stores and increasing dollar volume per square foot 60 per cent by the year 2000. It was a tangible and meaningful goal. It only took five years for Wal-Mart to increase dollar volume per square foot by 45 per cent and be two-thirds of the way toward doubling the number of stores.[12] At this rate, Wal-Mart was able to achieve the goal years earlier than projected.

STEP 7: CREATE STRATEGIES According to Michael Porter at Harvard's Business School, no firm can successfully perform at an above-average profitability level by trying to be all things to all people. Porter proposed that management must select a **competitive strategy** that will give the organization a distinct advantage by capitalizing on its strengths and the industry it is in.[13]

Porter recommends that managers can choose among three generic competitive strategies. These three strategies are: (1) **cost-leadership**, where the organization strives to be the low-cost producer in the industry, like Costco Wholesale Corporation, which operates an international chain of membership warehouses ("Costco Wholesale") that offer lower prices by eliminating frills and keeping overhead costs low; (2) **differentiation**, where an organization seeks to be unique in its industry in ways that are widely valued by buyers, such as Tim Horton Donuts, whose three attributes—Fast, Fresh and Friendly— are the core of the company's identity; and (3) **focus**, where an organization seeks uniqueness in a narrow market segment, like Vancouver-based Clearly Canadian Beverage Corporation. At times, managers develop a hybrid of these strategies. For example, Loblaw's tries to gain advantage by being competitively priced (cost and quality) and by differentiating through in-store service and ambience.

The strategies management chooses depend on the organization's strengths and competing organizations' weaknesses. Management should avoid a position in which it has to "slug it out" with everybody in the industry. Rather, the organization should work on its strength where the competition is lacking. Success depends on selecting the right strategy that fits the complete picture of the organization and the industry of which it is a part in order to gain the most favourable competitive advantage.

While strategy selection can be a deliberate, planned course of action such as positioning a company within a marketplace or attempting to outwit a competitor with a ploy, successful strategies can also be developed unintentionally. McGill's Henry Mintzberg says that a strategy is also of a pattern of activities—a consistency of behaviour. A manager who always accepts challenging assignments can be described as pursuing a high-risk strategy.[14] Mintzberg also says strategy is a perspective—an ingrained way of seeing the world— where individuals within an organization are united by common thinking and behaviour, such as "The Canadian Tire Way."[15]

In practice, strategy is more often crafted, that is, a cobbling of constantly evolving ideas that work rather than finding a perfect fit for a particular situation. Regardless of how strategy is formed, it sets the stage for the entire organization. Porter suggests that strategy and operational effectiveness must fit together in order to create a sustainable competitive advantage.[16] Through strategy, a company attempts to create a difference between itself and rival companies. Through operational effectiveness, a company attempts to perform similar activities better than rivals—such as reducing defects, serving customers, or developing better products faster. Subsequently, the manager of each unit within the organization translates both strategy and operational effectiveness goals into a set of operational plans that will give the organization a sustainable competitive advantage.

STEP 8: IMPLEMENT STRATEGIES No matter how effectively an organization has planned its strategies, it cannot succeed if the strategies are not implemented well. Front-line managers spend much of their time implementing strategies. Other chapters in this book address a number of issues related to strategy implementation. For instance, Chapter 9, Motivating Others, discussed ways to motivate people. Chapter 12, Designing Work, explores work design as a means of achieving strategic goals, and shows that many of the new organization structural designs are ways for organizations to cope with environmental and strategic changes. Chapter 15, Developing Employees, looks at how developing employees can contribute to competitive advantage. Chapter 16, Creating Teams, shows how creating teams is an important part of implementing strategy, and Chapter 18, Leading Change, offers suggestions for improving leadership effectiveness.

STEP 9: EVALUATING RESULTS The final step in the strategic management process is evaluating results. How effective have our strategies been? What adjustments, if any, are necessary?

The progress toward goals needs to be constantly evaluated and strategies must be adjusted to ensure that the desired results are being achieved. A growing number of firms use a balanced scorecard approach.[17] This measures performance from four different perspectives: the customer, business and production process improvement, innovation and growth, and finance. Progress from the customer perspective can be evaluated by measuring customer satisfaction, customer retention, and the growth in market share. Reduced error rates and reduction in cycle times can measure how business and production processes are improving. Innovation and growth progress can be measured by tracking employee retention or by the amount of time spent in employee training and development. Profit as well as return of assets can measure progress from the financial perspective. BC Hydro uses a similar approach.[18] Its Triple Bottom Line Report documents the progress made toward its business across three bottom lines—environmental, social, and economic. The message is clear: Today's managers need to be concerned with results beyond financial returns.

Environmental scanning should be an ongoing process: competitors introduce new products, technological innovations make a production process obsolete, and societal trends reduce demands for some products or services, while boosting demand for others. As a result, planning is an evolutionary process requiring the need to be alert to opportunities and threats that might demand modifying or in some cases totally abandoning the original goals and/or plans to achieve them.[19]

With clearly understood plans, managers and employees can get on with the goal-setting process so that energy can be directed toward achieving organizational objectives.

Goal Setting

One of the most basic skills in planning is goal setting. Goals are the foundation of all other planning activities. They provide the direction for management decisions as well as the criteria against which actual accomplishments can be measured. Consequently, we have devoted the following section to helping you learn how to effectively set goals for yourself and your employees.

Goal setting serves four main purposes.[20] First, it provides a clear, documented statement of what you intend to accomplish. When written, objectives are a form of acknowledgment and reminder of commitment. Second, setting objectives establishes a basis for measuring performance. Third, knowing what is expected and desired provides positive motivation to achieve goals. And fourth, knowing exactly where you're going is much more likely to get you there than trying different solutions in a haphazard way.

CHARACTERISTICS OF EFFECTIVE GOALS

Five basic characteristics can guide you in defining and setting goals. Goals should be (1) specific, (2) challenging, (3) set with a time limit for accomplishment, (4) established with the participants, and (5) designed to provide feedback to the employee. Let's elaborate on each of these points.

SPECIFIC Goals are only meaningful when they are specific enough to be verified and measured. The more specific the goals, the more explicitly performance is regulated. If the goal is vague (e.g., "do the best you can"), people interpret it in many different ways, depending on their own personal experience, ability, and ambition. In contrast, if a goal is specific (e.g., "increase sales by 20 per cent"), it helps eliminate ambiguity and reduce the leeway for idiosyncratic interpretations.[21] When confusion over the desired result is eliminated, the likelihood of it being achieved is increased.

CHALLENGING Goals should be set so as to require the employee to stretch to reach them. If they are reached too easily, they offer no challenge. If set unrealistically high, they create frustration and are likely to be abandoned. So the employee should view goals as challenging yet reachable.[22] Examples are Hewlett-Packard's 50 per cent performance improvement per year and Intel's double the number of chip components each year.[23]

Keep in mind that one person's "*challenging*" is another person's "*impossible*," and may be a third person's "*easy*." It's a question of perception. Stretch goals are more likely to be perceived as challenging rather than impossible if the person has a high degree of self-confidence, ability, and ambition, and has previously had more success in goal attainment than failure.[24] For people without these qualities, the same goal might be broken down into less challenging steps, or subgoals, which add up to the same outcome over time when all are completed.

TIME LIMITS Open-ended goals are likely to be neglected because no sense of urgency is associated with them. Whenever possible, goals should include a specific time limit for accomplishment.[25] So instead of stating, "I'm going to complete the company management training program, with a score in the upper 25 per cent of the class," a time-specific goal would state, "I'm going to complete the company management training program, with a score in the upper 25 per cent of the class, by February first of next year."

EMPLOYEE PARTICIPATION Goals can typically be set in two ways: the manager can *assign* them to the employee or they can be *participatively* determined in collaboration between the boss and employee. Most people seem willing to accept the request of managers, providing what they ask makes sense.[26] However, participation does increase a person's goal aspiration level and leads to the setting of more difficult goals.[27] Also, participation makes the whole goal-setting process more acceptable than when it is imposed from above, and accepted goals are more likely to be achieved.[28]

One method of obtaining employee participation will be described in the management by objectives section that follows. By requesting that employees obtain inputs from external and internal customers about what the employees might include as goals, management can enhance the quality and variety of goals.

FEEDBACK Feedback shows you how you are progressing in relation to your desired outcome. It lets people know whether they are on track and whether their level of effort is sufficient or needs to be increased. It can also induce them to raise their goal level after attaining a previous goal and inform them of ways in which to improve their performance. Because of these factors, higher performance is more likely if individuals are given feedback while they are striving to achieve goals.[29]

Feedback can be provided in many ways. It can be in the form of memos, charts, printouts, reports, computer displays, or personal interaction. The ideal frequency of feedback depends on how frequently it is required to keep organizational processes on target. For example, productivity and on-time delivery goals need to be tracked daily, because immediate corrective action is called for. Cost management, however, might only require monthly information to be most useful. Ideally, feedback on goal progress should be self-generated rather than provided externally.[30] Encouraging employees to solicit frequent feedback from internal and external customers on their own and to drop by the manager's office when they have questions are examples. When an employee is able to monitor his or her own progress, the feedback is less threatening and less likely to be perceived as part of a management control system.

SETTING EFFECTIVE GOALS

Every organization and every department within an organization is unique. Consequently, the goal-setting process has to be applied with a particular context in mind. At Toronto-based Maple Leaf Foods, for example, goals include being the lowest cost producer, continually creating shareholder value, customer satisfaction, the pursuit of quality, and employee development.[31] The objective of the federal government's multiculturalism program, on the other hand, is to foster a society with fair and equitable treatment of people of all origins and backgrounds who feel a sense of belonging and attachment to Canada.[32] Regardless of the context, however, seven steps need to be followed to obtain the optimum results from goal setting.[33] Let's look at these requirements and discuss how differences in circumstances can be addressed.

SPECIFY THE GENERAL OBJECTIVE AND SPECIFIC TASKS TO BE DONE Goal setting begins by defining what it is that you want your employees to accomplish. The best source for this information is job descriptions. They describe what tasks employees are expected to perform, how these tasks are to be done, and what outcomes employees are responsible for achieving.

Naturally, goals should differ depending on an employee's organizational level and type of work. The key question to ask is "What are the most important outcomes for this specific employee to accomplish?" Because outcomes for which goals are not set will usually not be pursued, goals need to be set for every important outcome. However, do not set too many goals for a given person because goal overload causes confusion about what to do and when to do it.[34]

SPECIFY HOW THE PERFORMANCE IN QUESTION WILL BE MEASURED Hundreds of outcomes can be measured. If the wrong outcomes are measured, they will undermine rather than further goal obtainment. An old management adage says it all: "What gets measured gets done." The corollary is that what isn't measured won't get done. If a professor places 30 per cent of a course grade on student participation, for example, but does not take roll or even know the students' names, attendance may be low while people prepare papers and read assignments for tests that receive concrete marks.

If you have done an effective job defining an employee's tasks in step 1, you should be in good shape to determine what specific outcomes from these tasks are to be measured. Typically, work outcomes are measured in physical units (i.e., quantity of production, number of errors), time (i.e., meeting deadlines, coming to work each day), or money (i.e., profits, sales, costs). Of course, for many jobs, developing valid individual measures of performance is difficult or even impossible. For example, upper-level management jobs are complex and often difficult to measure, so measures of overall yearly performance in terms of market share or profit margin might be used.

Similarly, when employees are part of a work team, it is often difficult to single out their individual contributions. In such cases, the available outcome measures can be combined with inputs (behaviours) that are controllable by the employee and that are assumed to lead to successful outcomes. So a senior executive might be evaluated on criteria such as "listens to employees' concerns" or "explains how changes will affect employees" in addition to "completes monthly forecast by the 25th of the preceding month."

Another difficult area to measure is "soft" outcomes such as customer satisfaction. It can be done, however. Examples are customer questionnaires rating their satisfaction with specific employees, amount of repeat business, or how often customers recommend the company to others. Measurements can be made of employee actions that are assumed to lead to desired outcomes (e.g., greeting customers, or asking if the customers need help when they enter the department). Such behaviours can even be turned into quantitative goal measurements, for example, by having mystery shoppers complete a checklist to determine how many of the required employee actions were shown.

SPECIFY THE STANDARD OR TARGET TO BE REACHED The next step requires identifying the *level* of performance expected. In step 2, it might be determined that one of the criteria by which a salesperson will be judged is number of repeat customer purchases. In this step, you need to specify a target; for example, at least 30 per cent of last month's customers will repeat purchases in the current month. If properly selected, the target will meet the requirements of being both specific and challenging for the employee.

An important question is, "How difficult should you make these standards?" The answer is, difficult but achievable. Jack Welch's goals at General Electric were described as so hard they were "loony tunes stuff," but they worked. Welch increased shareholder value by $100 billion from the time he took over GE in 1980 to the time he left in 2001.[35] How did he do it? The key is that those who are trying to reach it must perceive the standard as attainable. As a manager, for instance, you might think that Sean is capable of improving sales in his territory next quarter by 7 per cent. But if Sean believes that 5 per cent is as good as he can do, 7 per cent appears unachievable to him. In this case, it is important for the manager first to determine how Sean perceives the situation, and then build his confidence through counselling and the provision of necessary support so that 7 per cent is perceived as attainable.

SPECIFY THE TIME SPAN INVOLVED Qualitative goals, such as "install new customer service information system," are often critical. However, such goals need to be accompanied by deadlines: e.g., "complete project within six months." So, after targets are set, deadlines for each goal need to be put in place. Typically, the time span increases at upper levels of management. The goals of operative employees tend to be in the range of one day to several months; middle managers' goals are more likely to fall into the three-months-to-a-year range; and top-level managers' goals will often extend to two, three, or five years. For example, Smith Kline, Beecham has set a goal to reduce the development time for new drugs from 7.8 to 5.5 years, which would save the company hundreds of millions of dollars. Similarly, all the major automobile manufacturers are trying to reduce the time needed to develop new models; examples are BMW's hoped-for reduction from five to three years and Ford's ambitious goal of two years.[36]

Even though putting a time target on each goal is important because it reduces ambiguity, keep in mind that deadlines should not be chosen arbitrarily. The reason is that people tend to focus on whatever time span is attached to any given goal. If daily goals are assigned, the time focus will be one day. If quarterly goals are set, actions will be directed accordingly. The message here is twofold. First, to rephrase Parkinson's Law, effort toward a goal will be expended to fill the time available for its completion. Give people a month to complete a task that requires a week, and they'll typically take the full month.

A second factor is that overemphasis on short-term goals can undermine long-term performance. Short-range time targets encourage people to do *whatever is necessary* to get immediate results, even if it's at the expense of achieving long-term goals. Abundant examples can be found in companies with expatriate managers with one- or two-year assignments abroad, or fast-track managers transferred to different parts of the organization every couple of years as long as they achieve their yearly goals. These short-term successes often result at the expense of inappropriate resource depletion, or the destruction of important trust relationships with customers or suppliers. By the time the replacement manager arrives, the previous one has been promoted to another position elsewhere in the company or perhaps hired away by a headhunter.

PRIORITIZE GOALS When someone is given more than one goal, it is important to rank the goals in order of importance. The purpose of this step is to encourage the employee to take action and expend effort on each goal in order of and proportion to its importance. Priorities are applied in the rating and reward system that you will devise next.

RATE GOALS AS TO THEIR DIFFICULTY AND IMPORTANCE People like to succeed and they like to get rewarded for doing so. Consequently, if you are not careful, goal setting often encourages people to choose easy goals in order to ensure success, especially if people are rewarded only for attaining a goal. Employees with hard goals that they did not meet might have performed much better than others who had easy goals and exceeded them. Many times, those who "fail" are punished and those who succeed with easy goals are rewarded. These rating systems can cause employees to become risk averse, demoralized, and cynical.

Goal setting needs to take into account the difficulty of the goals selected and whether individuals are emphasizing the right goals. When ratings of difficulty and importance are combined with the actual level of goal achievement, you will have a more comprehensive assessment of overall goal performance. This procedure gives credit to individuals for trying difficult goals even if they don't fully achieve them. So, an employee who sets easy goals and exceeds them might receive a lower overall evaluation than one who sets hard goals and partially attains them. Similarly, an employee who reaches only low-priority goals and neglects those with high priorities could be evaluated lower than one who tries for important goals and only partially achieves them.

DETERMINE COORDINATION REQUIREMENTS Managers are responsible for making sure that objectives set for employees support overall organizational goals. Goals for every person in every area should be integrated with overall company objectives and strategy. Consequently, goal setting for any specific person or group starts with asking, "How do this unit's performance outcomes contribute to the overall organization's goals?"[37]

Actually, the objectives for any particular person or group should mesh with the objectives of all others who might be affected by them. If not, a potential for conflict arises. It is important in such cases to ensure that these goals are coordinated. Failure to coordinate interdependent goals can lead to territorial fights, abdication of responsibility, and overlapping of effort. The failure of an accounting professor to teach students what they need to know about financial analysis may lead to difficulties in the investments class, which assumes that the subject has been covered in the prerequisite class.

OBTAINING COMMITMENT TO GOALS

The mere existence of goals is no assurance that employees accept and are committed to them. Although managers can sometimes influence an employee's immediate actions, commitment to pursue a goal on your own comes from inside you. If you are not internally committed to your goals, goal setting will not work. The best way to persuade others to pursue specific goals is to appeal to their values and needs. This means that to obtain commitment from employees, managers need to explain how achieving organizational objectives can support each employee's personal goals. But what are the specific things managers can do to increase acceptance and commitment?[38]

EXPLAIN GOAL RELEVANCE TO PERSONAL NEEDS AND VALUES Although requests from the boss have built-in legitimacy because employees are being paid to do what is asked of them, internal commitment is not guaranteed. The way to build commitment is to provide the reasons and rationale for a goal, and how its achievement will ultimately benefit the employee. In other words, the results should be meaningful to employees and make a difference to them.[39] Explaining how goal achievement will guarantee organizational success, which is vital for job security, for example, or showing how the employee could gain useful skills in achieving the goal, which will help career development, will tie organizational success to personal values. The Conference Board of Canada, for example, has developed "Business Basics for the Workplace." This training program is distributed free of charge to Canadian companies and is designed to increase employees' awareness of their value to their organization.[40]

PROVIDE MANAGERIAL SUPPORT When goal setting involves routine activities, most people can determine and take the needed actions on their own. But when it entails the achievement of difficult objectives or the performance of complex tasks, management support is often essential for goal accomplishment. Managers exhibit support by encouraging initiative, expressing confidence, and helping employees reduce barriers that stand in the way of goal attainment. The latter includes making sure employees have the necessary equipment, supplies, time, training, and other resources to complete their tasks. Support can also entail providing help from other people and removing organizational roadblocks such as bureaucratic rules. Employer sponsorship is one type of support experienced by employees in Carleton University's innovative female-only Management Development Program. Because the program is hands-on and workplace-based, employers give employees access to the inner workings of their organization, pay tuition, and give time off to attend the two-days per month program.[41]

USE PARTICIPATION Employee participation in goal setting is a key to getting goals accepted. To be effective, participation must be authentic, that is, employees must perceive managers as truly seeking and utilizing their input. If a manager attempts to co-opt employees by pretending to want their participation when, in fact, specific goals, levels of performance, or target dates are already established, they will be quick to label the exercise as phony. Valuable ideas for improvement are generated when a manager encourages open communication, earns trust, and actually implements some of the ideas. If ideas are not used, employees quickly lose their motivation to participate in the future.

CONVINCE EMPLOYEES THAT GOAL ATTAINMENT IS WITHIN THEIR CAPABILITIES People must believe that they are capable of attaining or making substantial progress toward the goal before they will commit serious energy to it. Individuals differ in terms of their skills and abilities. If these differences are taken into consideration, each person's goals will realistically reflect his or her capabilities. Further, matching goal difficulty and an individual's capabilities increases the likelihood that the employee will see the goals as fair, realistic, attainable, and acceptable.

Where a person's abilities aren't adequate to meet satisfactory goals, this matching effort may signal the need for additional skill training. Benchmarks, based on what other companies have achieved, are useful in showing that a certain level of achievement is possible, as are role models within the company. Finally, helping employees develop suitable strategies for approaching the task and explicit expressions of confidence can boost their confidence.

USE REWARDS In light of the saying, "What's worth doing is worth doing for money," offering money, promotions, recognition, time off, or similar rewards to employees contingent on goal achievement is a powerful means to increase goal commitment. Recognition for goal attainment or goal progress is extremely important because everyone values being given credit and appreciation for his or her work. When the going gets tough on the road toward meeting a goal, people are prone to ask themselves, "What's in it for me?" Linking rewards to the achievement of goals helps employees to answer that question. You learned how to use rewards to motivate people in Chapter 9, Motivating Others.

GOAL SETTING APPLIED THROUGH THE MANAGEMENT BY OBJECTIVES PROCESS

Management by objectives (MBO) is one application of goal-setting. In this management system, specific performance objectives are jointly determined by employees and their supervisors, progress toward objectives is periodically reviewed, and rewards are allocated on the basis of this progress.

MBO converts overall organizational objectives into specific objectives for organizational units and individual members. Because lower-level managers jointly participate in setting their own goals, MBO works from the "bottom up" as well as from the "top down." The result is a hierarchy that links objectives at one level to those at the next level. For the individual employee, MBO provides specific personal performance objectives and thus each person has an identified specific contribution.

Four elements of effective goal setting are common to MBO programs. They are goal specificity, participative decision making, an explicit time period, and performance feedback.[42]

GOAL SPECIFICITY The objectives in MBO should be concise statements of expected accomplishments. It is not adequate, for example, merely to state a desire to cut costs, improve service, or increase quality. Such desires have to be converted into specific objectives that can be measured and evaluated. To cut departmental costs *by 7 per cent*, to improve service by ensuring that all telephone orders are processed *within 24 hours of receipt*, or to increase quality by keeping returns to *less than 1 per cent of sales* are examples of specific objectives.

PARTICIPATION The objectives in MBO are not unilaterally set by the boss and then assigned to employees. MBO replaces imposed goals with participatively determined goals. The manager and employees jointly choose the goals and agree on how they will be measured.

TIME LIMITS Each objective has a specific time period in which it is to be completed. Typically the time period is three months, six months, or a year. So managers and employees have specific objectives and stipulated time periods in which to accomplish them.

PERFORMANCE FEEDBACK The final ingredient in an MBO program is feedback on performance. MBO seeks to give continuous feedback on progress toward goals. Ideally, ongoing feedback allows individuals to monitor and correct their own actions. This feedback is supplemented by periodic managerial evaluations, when progress is reviewed. Evaluations apply at the top of the organization as well as at the bottom. The vice-president of sales, for instance, has objectives for overall sales and for each major product. The vice-president will monitor ongoing sales reports to determine progress toward the sales division's objectives. Similarly, district sales managers have objectives, as does each salesperson in the field. Feedback in terms of sales and performance data is provided to let these people know how they are doing. Formal appraisal meetings also take place at which managers and employees can review progress toward goals and further feedback can be provided.

Although the purpose of the MBO management system is to convert organizational goals into departmental goals and then into individual goals, the specifics of how companies implement MBO programs varies. Some practitioners say more flexibility is needed in fast-paced business environments and view the MBO management system as too cumbersome. Others suggest that it is more realistic to evaluate performance than to attempt to *measure* it. No matter what process is used, goal-setting is the basis for effective performance appraisal, which we will learn about in Chapter 14, Evaluating Performance.

Concept Quiz

Goal setting is a vital skill for planning, motivating, and measuring performance. It is necessary at the personal, supervisory, and organizational levels. To see how well you understand goal-setting skills, complete the following true–false quiz by circling the correct answer. Answers are at the end of the quiz. After marking your answers, remember to go back and check your understanding of any answers you missed.

True or False	1. Specific goals reduce ambiguity about what an employee is expected to do.
True or False	2. Goals should be set beyond what a person can realistically achieve to maximize motivation.
True or False	3. To avoid confusing employees, managers should never deviate from original plans.
True or False	4. Participation reduces employee commitment to goals.
True or False	5. Feedback on goal progress is best if self-generated.
True or False	6. Everything an employee does on his or her job can and should be quantified and have a goal set for it.
True or False	7. Because of their immediacy, short-term goals should take priority over long-term goals.
True or False	8. Achieving an easy goal should be evaluated more positively than coming up short on a difficult goal.
True or False	9. Competitive strategy that provides a distinct advantage should be used to achieve goals.
True or False	10. People accept goals more readily when the goals are tied to rewards they desire.

Answers (1) True; (2) False; (3) False; (4) False; (5) True; (6) False; (7) False; (8) False; (9) True; (10) True

Behavioural Checklist

Look for these specific behaviours when evaluating your planning and goal-setting skills and those of others.

The Effective Planner and Goal-Setter:

- Formulates goals that contribute to the organization's mission.
- Conducts SWOT analyses.
- Determines distinctive competencies to formulate competitive strategies.
- Establishes specific and challenging goals for each key task.
- Explains how task goals contribute to individual needs and values to gain employee commitment.
- Allows the employees to participate actively in goal setting.
- Prioritizes goals according to difficulty and importance.
- Specifies deadlines for each goal.
- Builds in feedback mechanisms to assess goal progress.
- Commits rewards based on goal attainment.

Modelling Exercise
Role-Play: Goal Setting at Extra-Life Batteries

DIRECTIONS The class should read the following information about the actors and the situation, but do NOT read the roles. Then two students volunteer to play the roles of R.J. Simpson and Pat Bell. Volunteers then read their own role (not the other person's role) and prepare for the role-play. The remainder of the class reads both roles and reviews the Observer's Rating Sheet. When the role-play begins, the observers rate R.J. Simpson's goal-setting effectiveness and note examples they can use to provide specific feedback at the end of the role-play.

TIME Not to exceed 20 minutes for the role-play; about 15 minutes for feedback.

ACTORS R.J. Simpson, vice-president marketing at Extra-Life Batteries; Pat Bell, new marketing director at Extra-Life Batteries

SITUATION R.J. Simpson made a recent offer to Pat Bell to join Extra-Life Batteries as the company's new marketing director at a salary of $75,000 a year plus a performance-based bonus. Pat has accepted. Pat will replace the previous director, who held the job for three years and had moderate success in increasing sales. Pat previously was a marketing manager at an Ottawa-based telecommunications company where she successfully led the introduction of several new high-tech products into the marketplace.

Extra-Life is a 150-employee company in the consumer battery industry. The company manufactures its own brand of rechargeable battery and has developed a superior technology that dramatically increases battery life. Extra-Life has commercialized this proprietary technology by licensing production rights to companies around the world, including some with well-known brand names. The company made money with its own brand of battery but sales were low in its licensed business, resulting in an overall loss. The company has targeted Europe because the high use of rechargeable batteries and Original Equipment Manufacturers (OEM) in an attempt to increase sales. It also seeks to increase sales by developing a strategic partner such as a battery distributor, battery marketer, or an end user like a cordless phone manufacturer.

This meeting is to set goals for the marketing department in the coming year. These goals will be used to judge Pat's performance and as a basis for allocating performance-based bonuses for the sales representatives of up to $20,000 each.

R.J. SIMPSON'S ROLE You are delighted to have hired Pat Bell, a person with such an excellent record in the high-tech sector. Although the battery industry is new to her, you are confident that the knowledge, skills, and experience she gained in marketing high-tech products will be an asset. Extra-Life is at a crucial juncture with its marketing program this year after moderate success over the past few years. If sales don't improve next year, several product lines may have to be dropped, which means production staff layoffs, loss of investor confidence, and difficulty in financing research and development for a promising new product. You want to make sure that Pat has extremely clear-cut goals and is motivated to achieve them.

PAT BELL'S ROLE You feel that you are at the right place at the right time. You were able to develop your skills in a time of growth in the telecommunications sector and were able to change jobs before the downturn. You were also fortunate to have had superior products to market as well as a team of dedicated staff. Nevertheless, you have to pat yourself on the back because you were able to capitalize on your team's skills by implementing some creative marketing strategies. You have enjoyed a significant degree of independence and freedom to do as you choose as a marketing manager. The battery industry is new to you and you have never marketed proprietary technology or an entire product line. Nevertheless, you feel that your experience of introducing high-tech products into the marketplace can help to increase Extra-Life's sales, raise the company's market profile, and boost your career. Your priorities are to get the right staff and do things your way. You especially look forward to launching Extra-Life's new product in about a year's time.

Observer's Rating Sheet

The class is to evaluate R.J. Simpson's goal-setting skills on a scale of 1 to 5 (5 being highest). Write concrete examples in the space provided after each skill component to use in explaining your feedback.

Skill Component	Rating
■ Formulates goals that contribute to the organization's mission	_____
■ Conducts SWOT analyses	_____
■ Formulates competitive strategies based on distinctive competencies	_____
■ Sets specific and challenging goals	_____
■ Relates goals to personal needs and values	_____
■ Sets deadlines for each goal	_____
■ Provides for employee participation	_____
■ Prioritizes goal difficulty and importance	_____
■ Builds in feedback mechanisms	_____
■ Commits rewards based on performance	_____

Group Exercises

The following three exercises are designed to give you a chance to practise your planning and goal-setting skills in small groups and receive feedback from others about your strengths and weaknesses. The first exercise for you to analyze is a case describing the planning and goal-setting approach of a practising manager. Next is a role-play in which you can practise participative goal setting with a surrogate direct report. Last is an exercise that gives you a chance to set goals for a relevant person in this class, your instructor.

Group Exercise 1: Case: I Can See Clearly Now[43]

"The most important thing for any organization is to have everyone focused on the same objectives and to have the objectives clearly defined." So says Kathleen Cote, chief executive officer of Computervision Corporation of Bedford, Massachusetts. Computervision Corporation [*www.cv.com*] is a leading supplier of desktop and enterprise-wide product design and development software and services. Its vision is to be the partner of choice for the most important thing its customers do—product development. The company pioneered CAD/CAM (computer-aided design/computer-aided manufacturing) hardware and software years ago. It was flying high for the subsequent 10 years as revenues and profits soared. Then, as patents expired and competitors entered the market, the once-profitable company started posting losses, which accumulated over the next three years to nearly $1.3 million. Cote headed the operating committee that developed the strategic plan for Computervision's turnaround and ultimate survival. Her work in that area led to her being named president and chief operating officer of the company. The following year she was appointed to the top management job.

Cote's management style happens to be people oriented, and she knew how she wanted to run the company. What the company had to do to become successful again and what she had to do as CEO to make that happen were crystal clear in her mind: The company had to clearly define its objectives, and she had to make sure that everyone was focused on those objectives. Cote stated, "The top three things I am working on have to be the top three things everyone is working on. We are only going to be successful together." How did she go about creating a focused environment?

The first thing Cote did was to have her senior managers identify where Computervision was winning business and where it was losing business. On the basis of that analysis, they decided to shift the company's focus to providing product development solutions through software and services and putting less of an emphasis on hardware. The top managers then established corporate objectives and communicated them down through the organization. Those objectives were then used to clearly define individual performance objectives. In addition, Cote was firmly committed to sticking to the objectives. She said, "I'm a firm believer that if you stay on course and never get off, you will have great success. There really is no surprise if you have a plan in place."

Cote isn't just focused on establishing and communicating common objectives for organizational employees. She is also strongly committed to making sure objectives are met. Managers (and all organizational employees) are held accountable for meeting their respective objectives and doing what they say they are going to do. Says Cote, "I don't like surprises. If something isn't going right, let me know what you can do about it to work through the issues and the problem." According to Cote, achieving the objectives entails showing employees how they are a part of making the plans happen and making them feel that they play an important role in helping the company meet its goals.

How has Computervision performed under Cote's leadership? The company posted a net income of $9.8 billion, a profit of $22.8 million, during her first year as chief operating officer, and a profit of $26 million in Cote's next three quarters as CEO. But,

Computervision did suffer a loss of $5.9 million in the fourth quarter of that year. That loss abruptly ended the company's string of 11 consecutive profitable quarters. But, despite the unexpected fourth-quarter loss, industry and financial analysts expect Computervision to continue its history of solid profits.

QUESTIONS FOR DISCUSSION

1. What is your reaction to Cote's philosophy that the most important thing for any organization is to have everyone focused on the same objectives and to have the objectives clearly defined? Do you agree? Why or why not? What would be the drawbacks of such a philosophy?
2. What role did strategic plans play in Computervision's turnaround? What role should they play in the company's future? What role should operational plans play?
3. One of the major criticisms of formal planning is that planning may create rigidity, particularly in a dynamic environment. How do you think Kathleen Cote would respond to that criticism?
4. How might the commitment concept affect planning at Computervision?
5. Would you call Computervision's approach to setting objectives a more traditional approach or more of an MBO approach? Explain your choice.

Group Exercise 2: Role-Play: Prioritizing Goals for a Theatrical Company

DIRECTIONS The class should read the following information about the actors and the situation, but do *NOT* read the roles. Then two students volunteer to play the roles of Taylor Williams and Pat MacDonald. Volunteers then read their own role (not the other person's role) and prepare for the role-play. The remainder of the class reads both roles and reviews the Observer's Rating Sheet. When the role-play begins, the observers rate Taylor Williams' goal-setting effectiveness and note examples they can use to provide specific feedback at the end of the role-play.

TIME Not to exceed 20 minutes for the role-play; about 15 minutes for feedback.

ACTORS Taylor Williams, director, publicity and sales; Pat MacDonald, newly hired publicist.

SITUATION Although well known for excellence, a long-established theatre company is experiencing a steady decline in ticket sales. The company presents six productions per year. Ticket sales (box office and subscriptions) make up over 80 per cent of annual revenue while donations make up less than 20 per cent. This heavy dependence on ticket sales is unusual for a professional theatre company. A higher level of financial support from patrons and corporations sustains most theatre groups.

Recently, the board of directors outlined the company's challenges as the need to (1) sustain current ticket sales while boosting corporate and patron contributions, (2) attract new audiences while retaining loyal patrons, (3) maintain performance excellence, and (4) improve the company's public image.

Both Taylor Williams and Pat MacDonald are currently in Taylor's office.

TAYLOR WILLIAMS' ROLE You are happy to have hired a new publicist because your department is understaffed and has a heavy workload. Pat MacDonald is a bright and capable addition to your staff, and desires to learn the job quickly. You are concerned that his recent business education has not provided some of the essential knowledge and skills desired for the job, but with some extra classes and training, these can be upgraded. You want to set goals for Pat's job and professional development.

PAT MACDONALD'S ROLE You are happy to have this job because Publicity and Sales is a small department. You will be involved in all aspects of the department, with tasks ranging from writing press releases, preparing fact sheets, and special event planning to liaising with the advertising agency that prepares promotional campaigns. You know that your contribution will be valued and it will be easy to see the results of your work. You feel fortunate to have been hired for this position because you have no theatre or writing experience. You did, however, excel in some of your marketing courses and are eager to learn. You are somewhat confused at the moment because the department has so many priorities and you feel the need for more direction from Taylor Williams.

Observer's Rating Sheet

The class is to evaluate Taylor Williams' goal-setting skills on a scale of 1 to 5 (5 being highest). Write concrete examples in the space provided after each skill component to use in explaining your feedback.

Skill Component	Rating
■ Formulates goals that contribute to the organization's mission.	_____
■ Conducts SWOT analyses.	_____
■ Formulates competitive strategies based on distinctive competencies.	_____
■ Sets specific and challenging goals.	_____
■ Relates goals to personal needs and values.	_____
■ Sets deadlines for each goal.	_____
■ Provides for employee participation.	_____
■ Prioritizes goal difficulty and importance.	_____
■ Builds in feedback mechanisms.	_____
■ Commits rewards based on performance.	_____

Group Exercise 3: Goal Setting for Your Instructor

PURPOSE This exercise will help you learn how to write specific, verifiable, measurable, and relevant goals as might evolve from an MBO program.

TIME Approximately 20 to 30 minutes.

INSTRUCTIONS
1. Break into groups of three to five students.
2. Spend a few minutes discussing your class instructor's job. What does he or she do? What defines good performance? What behaviours will lead to good performance?
3. Each group is to develop a list of five goals that, although not established participatively with your instructor, you believe might be developed into an MBO program at your college or university. Try to select goals that seem most critical to the effective performance of your instructor's job.
4. Each group selects a leader who will share his or her group's goals with the entire class.
5. The class then discusses the goals presented by the groups, focusing on their (a) specificity, (b) ease of measurement, (c) importance, and (d) motivational properties.
6. Continue until all groups have shared their goals and the class has discussed them. Then find out your instructor's reactions.

Application Questions

1. Does goal setting emphasize short-term results at the expense of long-term effectiveness?
2. How does goal setting deal with employees who have multiple goals, some of which are conflicting?
3. What barriers in an organization can you identify that may limit the effectiveness of a goal-setting program? How can these barriers be overcome?
4. Explain what an instructor can do to use goal setting with students in a classroom.
5. How can an organization develop and sustain a competitive advantage? How can you do the same for your career?

Reinforcement Exercises

The following suggestions are activities you can do to reinforce the planning techniques and goal-setting skills in this chapter. You may want to adapt them to your Action Plan or try them independently.

1. Visit the websites for companies that you are interested in and see what they say about their missions, objectives, and strategies; for example, go to www2.canadiantire.ca or, www. mapleleaf.com, etc. The same can be done by looking through companies' annual reports.
2. Perform a SWOT analysis on a local business you feel you know well. What, if any, competitive advantage has this organization staked out?
3. Locate and read the strategic plan for your college or university. Does it cover all the necessary steps effectively? Is it current? Does it provide a good fit with the most relevant environment to provide a competitive niche?
4. Set specific and challenging goals for yourself in this class. Do the same for your other classes. Prioritize and rate them for difficulty.

Summary Checklist

Review your performance and look over others' ratings of your planning and goal-setting skills. Now assess yourself on each of the key learning behaviours. Put a check (√) next to those behaviours on which you need improvement.

_____ Formulating goals that contribute to the organization's mission.
1. Know the overall goals of the organization.
2. Be mindful of the organization's mission statement.

_____ Conducting SWOT analyses.
1. Assess organizational strengths.
2. Assess organizational weaknesses.
3. Assess environmental opportunities.
4. Assess environmental threats.

_____ Formulating strategies based on distinctive competencies.
1. Determine the organization's unique skills and resources.
2. Determine the niche where the organization has sustainable competitive advantage.
3. Develop objectives and plans to take advantage of the niche.

_____ Establishing specific and challenging goals for each key task.
1. Identify operational objectives that provide specific performance targets.
2. Develop achievable goals that stretch capabilities.

_____ Relating task goals to personal needs and values.
1. Assess individual differences in skills, values, and needs.
2. Develop commitment to goals by adjusting to individual differences.

_____ Setting deadlines for each goal.
1. Balance required quality with time requirements.
2. Determine a specific time limit for realistic accomplishment.

_____ Having employees actively participate in setting their goals.
1. Determine coordination requirements.
2. Get ideas from all people collaborating in goal implementation.
3. Sincerely seek and utilize employees' inputs.

_____ Prioritizing goals based on difficulty and importance.
1. Determine which goals will contribute most to the organization mission.
2. Determine the difficulty and time required to achieve each goal.
3. Determine the time urgency for completion of each goal.
4. Determine which goals should be completed first and by when.

_____ Building in feedback mechanisms to assess goal progress.
1. Determine how performance will be measured quantitatively and qualitatively.
2. Specify standards and targets to be reached.
3. Set up time frames for providing feedback.

_____ Commiting rewards based on performance toward goal attainment.
1. Explain goal relevance to personal needs and values.
2. Link rewards to achievement of goals.

Action Plan

Planning Your Career

The following questions can help you formulate a strategic plan for achieving your career goals. Periodically rethinking them can also help you keep your career from drifting.

1. What is your mission statement? What business are you in? What is your product (the service or value you create for others)? Who is your market (what type of employer or client is willing to buy your service)?
2. What are your strengths and weaknesses as an employee or self-employed provider of services? What are your core skills and competencies?
3. What external opportunities and threats do you anticipate? Where could you best use your competencies following graduation? What could go wrong in managing your own career?
4. Where would you like your career to be in 5 or 10 years? What is your vision?
5. How do you plan to get there? What actions do you need to undertake now to reach your career vision?
   a. What added education/training do you need?
   b. What organizational experiences do you need?
   c. What people are critical to your progress?
6. How do you know you are still on the right course? What milestones do you have for periodically checking up on your career progress?

Skills Video

Planning

In this episode, we find out that John got the production manager job at Quicktakes. We meet up with John on his first day on the job. We join him at his first meeting at Quicktakes and are reintroduced to Hal and Karen, the owners of the company. We also meet Alexandra, the company's general manager. It seems that the purpose of this meeting is to give John an idea of how the company is organized, what its goals are, and how things are run.

What can you learn from this meeting that relates to what you have learned about planning? Before considering this question, we might want to make some assumptions about the management of the company. Given that this meeting is set up to introduce John to the company, we assume that the people invited are those that the owners believe are important in setting the direction and focus of the company, or are those most responsible for keeping it running. This may not be a correct assumption, but it is logical that John might get this idea. He will only know for sure after he has been at Quicktakes for a while.

This meeting is John's first real chance to learn about who is really running Quicktakes and about how the people interact. In this meeting he gets some idea about how Hal and Karen operate and interact on the job. It is likely that someday, maybe soon, you will be in a meeting like this and you will be in John's shoes. Think about the kinds of information you would hope to get, the expectations you might have of new employers, and the kinds of things you would hope your new employer thinks are important. With these things in mind, you might now consider how you think John feels after this meeting.

A couple of important areas are covered in this orientation meeting. First, we get some idea about the culture at Quicktakes. This comes across in the comments Hal makes to John about a dress code and the degree of formality that you observe in the meeting. You also get some hints about what Hal and Karen, and to some degree Alexandra, think Quicktakes' main product focus is. They tell John about things they think make them different from their competitors and things that they seem to think are important.

It is interesting that John asks about plans and goals more than once. This gives us an idea about what is important to John. He does not necessarily get the answer he is looking for and seems to think that there might be more to planning than what is currently considered at Quicktakes.

QUESTIONS

1. Hal and Karen talk about their ideas for the company. Do you think they are both moving in the same direction and aiming for the same target? If not, how do you think this affects the ongoing operation of the company?

2. It was explained to John that it is difficult to plan because of changes in economic conditions and areas of public interest. What areas of Quicktakes' operation might economic and market factors affect the most? Do you think that these issues make it impossible to develop a general plan and goal for the company? What areas might be important to consider anyway?

3. There was discussion of things that Quicktakes does other than video production. Why do you think they do these other things? To what degree should a small company like Quicktakes spread itself across multiple products?

CHAPTER 12
Designing Work

Learning Objectives
After completing this chapter, you should be able to:
- Diagnose job characteristics.
- Apply the Job Characteristics Model to design satisfying jobs.
- Design jobs to maximize employee preference, performance, and work–life balance.

Look closely at any organization and you will see that it is composed of thousands of tasks. These tasks, in turn, are grouped into jobs. When jobs are designed with consideration of both the organization's needs and technology and the skills, abilities, and preferences of employees, they can motivate employees to achieve their productive potentials. On the other hand, if jobs just evolve by chance, productivity and satisfaction are not as likely.[1]

Jobs, like people, come in all shapes and sizes. Also like people, jobs cause different individuals to react differently. Some employees, for instance, are bored by jobs that others would find challenging. Some people favour routine tasks, others abhor any job without challenge. Some do their best work while analyzing small details while other workers thrive only when focusing on the big picture.

A major determinant in effective job performance is appropriate **job design**.[2] Job design refers to the way tasks are combined to form complete jobs. Effective job design is important to a manager because it involves trying to shape the right jobs to conform with the right people, taking into account both the organization's goals and the employee's satisfaction. This, in turn, not only leads to more highly motivated employees but also to higher productivity, lower absenteeism, and higher employee retention. Complete the following self-assessment exercise to determine your current understanding of job design.

Self-Assessment Exercise

Respond as candidly as possible to the statements seeking to explore your instincts and knowledge about job design. Describe your level of agreement with each statement by circling the number in the appropriate column.

	Strongly Agree				Strongly Disagree
1. I do not think much can be done about the fact that all jobs are essentially boring.	1	2	3	4	5
2. If I gave workers some control over their tasks I would feel diminished as a manager.	1	2	3	4	5
3. I believe employees' feelings about their jobs are central to how they perform.	5	4	3	2	1
4. I think everyone has the same desire to improve himself or herself as I do.	1	2	3	4	5
5. I do not pay much attention to what others say or seem to think about my job, and my co-workers do not care what others think about theirs either.	1	2	3	4	5
6. Feedback helps me and others to perform better.	5	4	3	2	1
7. I would not want my employees working from home or on the road because that would encourage them to goof off or be distracted.	1	2	3	4	5
8. I believe many workers function better when they can see a project through from beginning to end rather than just being involved in one phase of the task.	5	4	3	2	1
9. Jobs that I have held that had a substantial impact on the lives of other people were the most rewarding.	5	4	3	2	1
10. I think that a manager can help employees by reminding them how interesting and important their jobs are.	5	4	3	2	1

SCORING AND INTERPRETATION Add the numbers you have circled to obtain your total score.

40–50	You have very good instincts about jobs and how employees respond to them.
30–39	You show good awareness of the principles of motivating people through job design.
20–29	You have some sense of how the structure of jobs affects workers, but you need to increase your knowledge.
0–19	You greatly need to increase your knowledge and scrutinize your impulses related to job design.

Concepts

Why Design Jobs?

In the early 1900s, cigar makers paid people to read stories to employees. During the same period, textile manufacturers allowed kittens to play on the factory floor. A century later, some modern firms permit workers to listen to music on individual headsets, play computer games, or spend time in cyberspace chat rooms. The aims of such activities, past and present, are the same: Fight boredom and improve productivity.[3] Even though no universally accepted way to improve work productivity exists, several approaches to job design have evolved over the years.

THE JOB SPECIALIZATION APPROACH

Historically, job design was concerned with making jobs smaller and more specialized. This approach, popularized by Frederick Taylor more than a century ago, involved fitting people to jobs as a way to achieve maximum efficiency. His assumptions were that employees will gradually adjust and adapt to any work situation and their attitudes are much less important than the needs of the organization. Thus, Taylor's concept of *scientific management* involved making jobs smaller, more specialized, and standardized, such as on an assembly line. Many manufacturing and production-oriented firms still are organized along those principles.

Although early results indicated that the scientific management approach did make workers more efficient and productive in the short term, research suggests that repetitive jobs also lead to dissatisfaction, poor mental health, a low sense of accomplishment, and no opportunities for personal growth.[4] Consequently, motivating employees is a real challenge. Further, the principles of scientific management are not applicable to the increasing numbers of "knowledge workers" who are required to scan the environment for new data to generate creative alternatives for jobs in areas such as advertising or investment banking. Scientific management ideas also do not fit well with the trend to empower both employees and work teams. Thus, many organizations have sought other design options.

JOB EXPANSION APPROACHES

The more recent approaches to job design entail fitting jobs to people. Such methods assume that employees often are underutilized and that they desire more challenge and responsibility. The **job enlargement** approach attempts to overcome the drawbacks of specialization by horizontally expanding a job by increasing the job scope—the number of different tasks required in a job and the frequency with which these tasks are repeated. A secretary's job could be enlarged, for example, by adding to typing duties additional tasks such as sorting and delivering mail, keeping supply cabinets full, and greeting visitors.

Job enlargement has been found to provide more job satisfaction, enhance customer service, and generate fewer errors.[5] It does overcome the lack of diversity of overspecialized jobs, but job enlargement is often not sufficient to create real meaning and challenge for most employees.

Job enrichment attempts to design more meaning and challenge into jobs by adding planning and evaluating responsibilities. It increases job depth—control over one's own work. When a job is enriched, employees are responsible for planning and completing an entire activity on their own, including the assessment and correction of their own performance. So instead of requiring salespeople in a department store to call a supervisor whenever a customer has a complaint, they might be authorized to handle as they see fit any complaints that would cost the store $100 or less.

REDESIGNING JOBS TODAY

The changing nature of work is certain to challenge managers to better define work and design jobs. The jobs that people perform should not evolve by chance or from a standardized procedure that was used in the past. Managers should design jobs deliberately and thoughtfully to reflect the organization's changing needs as well as the abilities and preferences of its employees.

In some cases, redesigning jobs may mean offering flexible work arrangements and scheduling to encourage work–life balance. In other situations, it might mean completely restructuring how the work is done, for example, by forming teams rather than having individuals do the work alone.

Increasingly, technology comes into play, allowing managers much more latitude in job design. An interesting example of large-scale work redesign occurred at Chiat/Day, a large advertising agency in California. Its headquarters has no executive suites, no permanent work cubicles, desks, filing cabinets, or other trappings of an office. Why? Because the firm has made its office into a virtual workplace where employees are free to work where they please.[6]

Half of Chiat/Day's workers telecommute either from home or on the road. The only space at headquarters that employees can call their own is the high-school style locker where each can stow personal belongings. Employees who choose to go into the office stop first in the lobby to pick up their laptop computers and portable phones. Then they pull up a desk-on-wheels, plug in their telecommunications, and go to work.

A virtual office staffed by highly mobile employees is not for every firm or every organization, but at Chiat/Day, where the mission involves freewheeling creativity and out-of-the-box thinking, the firm has moved to meet the challenge. In this chapter, we will identify the primary dimensions of jobs and describe how these dimensions can be mixed and matched by managers to maximize employee preference, performance, and work–life balance.

What Makes a Job?

We all know that a lifeguard's job is radically different from an accountant's or a stonemason's. But what is it that makes these jobs so dissimilar? A pragmatic answer to that question is provided by the **job characteristics model (JCM)**. According to researchers who developed and tested the JCM, any job can be described in terms of five core job dimensions, or characteristics.[7]

1. *Skill variety* The degree to which a job requires a variety of different activities so that the worker can employ a number of different skills and talents.
2. *Task identity* The degree to which a job requires completion of a whole and identifiable piece of work.
3. *Task significance* The degree to which a job has a substantial impact on the lives of other people.
4. *Autonomy* The degree to which a job provides substantial freedom and discretion to the worker in scheduling tasks and in determining how the work will be carried out.
5. *Feedback* The degree to which the worker gets direct and clear information about the effectiveness of his or her performance.

Exhibit 12-1 offers examples of job activities that rate high or low for each characteristic. Exhibit 12-2 presents the model.

Exhibit 12-2 shows how the first three characteristics—skill variety, task identity, and task significance—combine to create meaningful work. If a job has those three characteristics, we can predict that the employee will see his or her job as being important, valuable, and worthwhile. The fourth characteristic, autonomy, gives workers a sense of responsibility for the results. The fifth characteristic, feedback, gives the employee information on how effectively he or she is performing.[8]

Today, advances in job enrichment involve the strengthening of some or all of the five core dimensions—skill identity, task identity, task significance, autonomy, and feedback. The most effective job enrichment increases all five core dimensions, but a person's need for growth will determine how effective a job enrichment program will be. *Growth-need strength* is the degree to which individuals want personal and psychological development. Though almost all people respond positively to job enrichment, those with high growth-need strength particularly welcome it.[9]

Exhibit 12-1 Examples of High and Low Job Characteristics

	High	**Low**
Skill Variety	An auto-repair shop operator who does electrical repairs, rebuilds engines, does body work, and handles customer complaints	A body shop worker who spray paints 8 hours a day
Task Identity	A cabinetmaker who designs a piece of furniture, selects the wood, builds the object, and finishes it to perfection	A worker in a furniture factory who operates a lathe solely to make table legs
Task Significance	Nursing the sick in a hospital intensive care unit	Sweeping hospital floors
Autonomy	A police detective who schedules his or her own work for the day, makes contacts without supervision, and decides on the most effective techniques for solving a case	A police dispatcher who must handle calls as they come in according to a routine, highly specific procedure
Feedback	An electronics factory worker who assembles a modem and then tests it to see whether it operates properly	An electronics factory worker who assembles a modem and then routes it to a quality control inspector who tests it and makes adjustments, if necessary

Source: Adapted from G. Johns, *Organizational Behavior: Understanding and Managing Life at Work,* 4th ed. (New York: Harper/Collins, 1996) 204.

Exhibit 12-2 The Job Characteristics Model

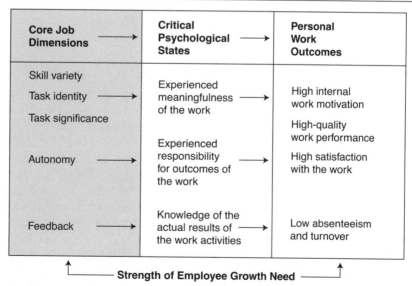

Source: J.R. Hackman, "Work Design," in J.R. Hackman and J.L. Suttle, eds., *Improving Life at Work* (Glenview, IL: Scott Foresman, 1977) 129.

Well-designed jobs lead to high motivation, high-quality performance, high satisfaction, and low absenteeism and turnover. These outcomes occur when workers experience three critical psychological states: (1) they believe they're doing something meaningful because their work is important to other people; (2) they feel personally responsible for how the work turns out; and (3) they learn how well they perform their jobs.[10]

When a job is well designed according to these core dimensions, people usually experience feelings of general satisfaction, internal work motivation, growth satisfaction, and work effectiveness. These intrinsic rewards—that is, rewards the person derives directly from performing the job—are essential to motivation. In one study of manufacturing plants, it was found that employees initiated more patent applications, made more novel and useful suggestions, and were rated by their managers as more creative when their jobs were challenging and their managers did not control their activities closely.[11]

Many jobs today are being designed to increase motivation by offering more intrinsic rewards. For example, Opel, a German subsidiary of General Motors, operates one of the most productive plants in Europe. Opel considers employee motivation a key to its excellence and has built into its operation the characteristics of motivating tasks. As a result, employees have full responsibility over large segments of the production. In addition, workers make decisions about work procedures and can try innovative approaches to assembly, work flow, and materials. Any employee can stop the production line whenever deemed necessary. Workers seek advice and help from one another and give frank feedback to each other. Thus, tapping employee ingenuity, listening to ideas, and allowing workers some freedom and control over their work has resulted in substantial increases in productivity.[12]

At the Abitibi-Price paper plant in Alma, in the Lac St-Jean region of Quebec, workers and management turned around a business that was threatened with closure by re-designing jobs and the workplace. Union and management, who were previously adversaries, cooperated to jointly develop strategies and performance indicators related to production costs, customer satisfaction, equipment performance, environmental protection, and employee development. To implement these strategies, joint labour–management work committees were established to reduce the negative impact of technological changes on jobs and develop programs in areas such as training, quality assurance, and health and safety. Using this cooperative approach, grievances became virtually non-existent as productivity increased, accident frequency decreased dramatically, and paper quality and client satisfaction skyrocketed.[13]

LOOKING AT THE SAME JOB DIFFERENTLY

Different people work and perform differently. Too many people work in ways that are not their ways, and that almost guarantee nonperformance. According to management expert Peter Drucker, how a person performs is a given and can only be slightly modified. So, because it is unlikely that how a person performs can be completely changed, it is important to try to match people to jobs that they are good at, so they can achieve results by working in ways that they best perform.[14] Let us look at a couple of examples.

Cheri works at a fast-food restaurant—and hates it. "All day, every day, I ask people what kind of burger they want and if they also want French fries and a soda. It's not like our menu is complicated, or something. This is a job a trained monkey could do—and *should*."

Bonnie, meanwhile, has the same role and thinks it's great. "Sure, the menu is pretty limited, but the people aren't. They come in all sizes, shapes, ages, and colours and I find them endlessly fascinating. Plus, it gives me a good feeling to know I'm doing something worthwhile by serving hungry people."

Bonnie and Cheri look at exactly the same job differently. The fact that people respond to their jobs as they perceive them rather than responding objectively to the job itself greatly complicates the job design process. The central element of the **social information processing (SIP) model** says that what others tell us about our jobs is important.

The SIP model contends that employees form attitudes and behaviour in response to the social cues provided by others, such as co-workers, supervisors, family members, or customers/clients.[15] Although the objective characteristics of their jobs were the same for Cheri and Bonnie in the preceding example, each may have picked up on different signals from those with whom they had contact.

Take John, who was highly motivated when he took a job selling classified ads by phone for a small newspaper. However, before his first month was over, he felt deflated and unhappy. Why? His colleagues consistently bad-mouthed their jobs and the firm, put up derisive signs ("How can I fly with the eagles when I'm surrounded by turkeys?" and "Even a bad day on vacation is better than a good day at work!"). They also complained that the managers didn't trust them and never listened to their opinions. The objective characteristics of John's job hadn't changed, but he had reconstructed his perceived reality on the basis of messages received from his peers.

What do individual perceptions mean for the manager? In short, they mean that a manager should pay at least as much attention to the employees' perception of their jobs as to the actual characteristics of the work. The manager should listen to what employees say about their jobs and periodically ask for their opinions. You can also remind employees about the importance of the work and encourage them to apply their autonomy to making their jobs more interesting. New hires or newly transferred workers are usually more receptive to such social cues than those with greater seniority who may have fallen into a routine, which is all the more reason, however, to continually give all employees performance feedback and ask them for suggestions for improvement.

Designing Jobs for Maximum Performance

How can you design or enrich jobs to maximize your employees' performance? Using the JCM as a guide, the logical way to design jobs is by improving the five core dimensions: skill identity, task identity, task significance, autonomy, and feedback. Applying the SIP model, shape employees' perceptions by speaking positively about their work.

How can you actually enrich a job? The following suggestions, derived from the JCM, specify the types of changes in jobs that are mostly likely to lead to improvements in each of the five core dimensions.[16]

1. **Combine tasks** Put existing fragmented tasks together to form a new, larger module of work and increase skill variety and task identity.

For instance, instead of having an assembly-line worker install just the coils on a toaster and have other assemblers add the other parts, a toaster might be assembled from start to finish by one operator.

2. **Create natural work units** Design tasks to form an identifiable and meaningful whole to increase employee "ownership" of the work and encourage workers to view their jobs as important.

Take, for example, 10 typists in a pool who handle a random assignment of letters, reports, and other tasks. As a result, the typists do not identify with the work or with the person or department for whom it is performed. To create a natural work unit, the manager might assign continuing responsibility for a specific department's work to one or more typists. Or, one or more typists could handle the letters, another such group handle the reports, the budget, whatever. As a result, typists to whom work is assigned naturally rather than randomly have a much greater chance of performing the whole job to completion and identifying with it.

3. **Establish client relationships** The client is the user of the product or the service that the employee works on. Building direct relationships between the worker and the client increases skill variety, autonomy, and feedback.

A cook who never sees the diners might be encouraged to circulate among the clientele to get direct praise or criticism. Or, the mechanic who actually repaired a transmission might meet the automobile owner and explain the procedure.

4. **Expand jobs vertically** Give employees responsibilities formerly reserved for management to increase autonomy.

Ways to expand jobs vertically at a packaging plant might include giving workers greater authority in setting schedules. The employees might also decide on work methods, check on quality, and advise or help to train less-experienced workers.

5. **Open feedback channels** Feedback not only tells employees how well they are performing but also whether their performance is improving, deteriorating, or remaining constant. Ideally, employees should receive feedback directly as they do their jobs, rather than just occasionally.[17]

For instance, people who are responsible for the work do quality control in many organizations. Placing quality control close to the workers can dramatically increase the quantity and the quality of data that are available to them.

Working with Teams

In the modern workplace, people increasingly are working in groups and teams. For example, a group of workers might be responsible for assembling an entire automobile or an electric appliance. Can much be done about the design of group-based work? Due to the relatively recent nature of teams, we know more about the individually based job design than we do about design at the group level.[18] But researchers offer some suggestions.[19]

First, the JCM principles seem as valid for group endeavours as they are at the individual level. So managers should expect a group to perform at a high level when: (1) the group task requires members to use a variety of relatively high-level skills; (2) the group task is a whole and meaningful piece of work with a visible outcome; (3) the outcomes of the group's work on the task have significant consequences for other people; (4) the task provides group members with autonomy in deciding how they do the work; and (5) work on the task generates regular, trustworthy feedback about how well the group is performing.

Second, group composition is critical to the success of the work group. Managers should try to ensure that: (1) individual members have the necessary expertise to do the work; (2) the group is large enough to get the job done; (3) members possess interpersonal as well as task skills; and (4) membership is moderately diverse in terms of talents and perspectives. You will learn more about working with teams in Chapter 16, Creating Teams.

Designing Jobs for Work–Life Balance

Today, many employees are looking to balance their work and home life. Dramatic increases in the number of women in the labour force, the need to care for aging family, increases in the number of single-parent families, and ongoing restructuring of the labour force have all led to growing conflicts between the demands of employment and the demands of family. Roughly half of Canadian employees are experiencing conflict between their work and personal lives.[20]

One of the ways that companies can respond is to design jobs with flexible work arrangements. For example, the time of day set aside for work or the location at which it must be performed can be changed. Most people work an 8-hour day, 5 days a week, at a more or less fixed location. These are full-time employees who start and leave at fixed times. But an increasingly popular way to design work to match the employee is to use scheduling options that benefit the worker without sacrificing organizational aims. Such variation includes flextime, compressed work weeks, job sharing, and telecommuting.

Flextime is short for "flexible hours" and provides employees another option to reduce work–life conflicts. It allows workers some discretion over when they arrive at and leave work. Employees still must work a specified number of hours per week, but they are free to vary the hours within certain limits. For example, the required core hours during which all employees must be at their jobs might be the six hours between 9 A.M. and 3 P.M., but workers would be free to add the additional two hours in the morning by coming in at 7 A.M., or in the evening by staying until 5 P.M. Another variation of flexible hours is the compressed work week, where employees work fewer but longer days, such as four 10-hour days each week.

Flextime has become an extremely popular option. The many potential benefits include improved motivation and morale, reduced absenteeism because employees can better balance work and family responsibilities, and the ability of the organization to recruit higher-quality and more diverse employees.[21] Merck Frosst Canada & Co., Canada's largest pharmaceutical company, and RBC Financial Group, Canada's largest financial institution, have developed flexible work arrangements including flextime.[22] Despite its benefits, however, only one in four Canadian employees reports a flextime schedule.[23]

On the other hand, flextime cannot be used for every job. It works well with tasks in which an employee's interaction with people outside his or her department is limited. It is not viable when key people must be available during standard working hours, when work flow requires tight scheduling, or when specialists are called upon to maintain coverage of all functions in a unit.[24]

Job sharing is a special sort of part-time work that allows two or more people to split a traditional 40-hour-a-week job. One person might perform the same job, say, from 8 A.M. to noon and another from 1 P.M. to 5 P.M. Or, the two could alternate full days. Job sharing, while growing, is less widespread than flextime. According to Statistics Canada, approximately 10 per cent of the workforce follows a compressed work week.[25] Alcan, in Jonquiere, Quebec, and the *Toronto Star* are examples of companies with job sharing.[26]

Job sharing allows the organization to draw upon the talents of more than one individual for a given job. It also creates the opportunity to acquire skilled workers—for instance, retirees and parents of young children—who might not otherwise be available on a full-time basis. The major drawback from management's perspective is the difficulty of finding compatible pairs who can successfully coordinate the intricacies of one job.[27]

Telecommuting or telework refers to employees who do their work at home or on the road using a computer linked to the office. Executives have practised forms of telecommuting for years, and now thousands of employees telecommute by doing such tasks as taking orders over the phone, filling out reports and other forms, and processing or analyzing data. At the Canadian Imperial Bank of Commerce (CIBC), employees can work away from their office or branch for all or part of the work week. An employee can work at home or at other CIBC office locations that may be closer to home.[28] Not all employees embrace telecommuting. Some feel they miss out on important meetings and informal interactions that spark new policies and ideas. Similarly, some business transactions require face-to-face communication. Activities that entail the development of trust and an understanding of context such as negotiation, deal-making, or design need personal interaction to be successful.[29]

Even among those for whom telecommuting is a possibility, other issues must be addressed: Are employees who work from home disadvantaged in office politics and in competition for salary increases and promotions or seen as less committed to the organization? Do distractions in the home—children, neighbours, and the proximity of the television and the refrigerator—significantly reduce productivity? Will those workers for whom telecommuting is not viable feel jealousy toward those who can telecommute? In short, telecommuting is a novel, emerging issue. It is unclear yet whether telecommuting will have a long-term future in the workplace.

Job design is an ongoing, dynamic process. For employees, what we do on the job plays a major role not only in our economic standing but also in our social, health, and psychological status. For employers, employee satisfaction, customer satisfaction, and corporate performance are linked. Job design attempts to identify the most important needs of both the employee and the organization, and then try to remove any obstacles that thwart those needs.

A recent employer survey indicates that roughly half of Canadian organizations leave the implementation of flexible work arrangements to the discretion of managers.[30] Clearly, managers can play a significant role in work design by creating choices that support the organization's mission and supporting employees in decisions that meet their needs.

Concept Quiz

Complete the following true–false quiz by circling the correct answer. The answers are at the end of the quiz. After marking your answers, remember to go back and check your understanding of any answers you missed.

True or False 1. *Scientific management* refers to the idea that jobs should be made to fit people.

True or False 2. Technology is increasingly an important element of modern job design.

True or False 3. All workers want personal and psychological development to roughly the same degree.

True or False 4. Task identity is the degree to which a job requires completion of a whole and identifiable piece of work.

True or False 5. Employees form attitudes and behaviour in response to social cues provided by others.

True or False 6. The Job Characteristics Model (JCM) is more valid for individuals than for group endeavours.

True or False 7. Flextime works best for employees whose interaction with people outside their department is limited.

True or False 8. Job sharing allows two or more people to split a traditional 40-hour-a-week job.

True or False 9. Building direct relationships between the worker and the client increases skill, variety, autonomy, and feedback.

True or False 10. Jobs that possess autonomy give workers a sense of responsibility for the results.

Answers (1) False; (2) True; (3) False; (4) True; (5) True; (6) False; (7) True; (8) True; (9) True; (10) True

Behavioural Checklist

The following behaviours are important for diagnosing job characteristics and designing jobs to maximize employee performance.

Effective Job Designers:

- Study the characteristics of each job.
- Take into account each employee's desire to improve himself or herself.
- Note what signals or social cues workers are receiving from others about their jobs.
- Seek to enrich jobs using the five core dimensions of skill variety, task identity, task significance, autonomy, and feedback.
- Try to improve employees' perception of their jobs.
- Consider work–life balance options.

Modelling Exercise

The Job Design Process

DIRECTIONS The entire class should read the following situation. Then three students should be assigned to play the roles of Charles, Jenny, and Rhonda. The rest of the class should observe and critique them.

Role-players should read and prepare for their assigned role but should not read the others' roles. After reading the situation, observers should read all three roles and review the Observer's Rating Sheet.

TIME 30 minutes.

ACTORS Rhonda, manager of the Acme Bakery; Charles, a tourism and hospitality student working his first summer at Acme Jenny, a business administration student in her second summer at Acme

SITUATION Rhonda is manager of a busy bakery where Charles and Jenny, both college students, are working for the summer. The bakery specializes in dinner rolls and bread, most of which are sold just prior to the weekend. Most of Charles's and Jenny's work is dictated by production schedules but some time is discretionary, and Rhonda usually assigns them whatever task is a priority at that moment.

Neither Charles nor Jenny is highly skilled, but Jenny is more experienced at bakery work. Both began the summer with energy and enthusiasm. However, Charles has since lost his edge and has complained at length about the tedium of the work. His performance has fallen off, too. Jenny, on the other hand, remains ebullient and a good worker, which is why she was rehired.

The least-desirable job for an inexperienced worker is stacking trays of dinner rolls on racks as the bakers fill up the pans with dough. The employee must be quick and pay attention all the time, otherwise the bakers will be tossing the dough into already-filled pans, and the whole operation will need to come to a stop, costing money and aggravation. On the other hand, packing bread for shipment is hardly creative but is not quite so fast-paced, and a worker can take a break if he or she needs to.

Here are the tasks and schedules:

CHARLES

Schedule: Works 2:30 P.M. to 11:30 P.M. Wednesday through Sunday (with one hour for dinner break).

Tasks:

Wednesday: 3 hours stacking trays of rolls on racks; 4 hours cleaning bread pans before dough is put in them; 1 hour sweeping the floor and stowing newly arrived supplies.

Thursday: 5 hours stacking trays of rolls on racks; 3 hours cleaning bread pans.

Friday: 6 hours stacking rolls on racks; 2 hours cleaning bread pans; 1 hour sweeping.

Saturday: 1 hour stacking rolls on racks; 3 hours cleaning bread pans; 2 hours sweeping; 2 hours as directed.

Sunday: 1 hour stacking rolls on racks; 4 hours cleaning bread pans; 3 hours as directed.

JENNY

Schedule: Works 1 P.M. to 10 P.M. Saturday through Wednesday (with one hour for dinner break).

Tasks:

Saturday: 4 hours packing bread; 3 hours stacking roll trays on racks; 1 hour helping Rhonda with mail and clerical tasks.

Sunday: 4 hours packing bread; 2 hours stacking rolls on racks; 2 hours helping Rhonda on mail and clerical tasks.

Monday: 4 hours packing bread; 4 hours stacking rolls on racks.

Tuesday: 4 hours packing bread; 4 hours stacking rolls on racks.

Wednesday: 2 hours stacking rolls on racks; 1 hour cleaning bread pans; 3 hours packing bread; 2 hours as directed.

RHONDA'S ROLE Making the students happy with their work is not your highest priority. Still, it would be nice if everyone liked his or her job and performed it well. You are especially fond of Jenny. She and Charles are equals in terms of pay and status (such as it is), but you try to give her a break by assigning her mostly to the bread-packing job, which is slightly less tedious than stacking trays of rolls. You also use her as a clerical assistant whenever possible. Charles has been disappointing in that he complains a lot and his performance has fallen off after a good early start. If he quits, you're going to be in a pickle because finding someone in mid-summer to replace him won't be easy.

JENNY'S ROLE You like your job, which is why you came back for a second year. The work is not glamorous, but it is a nice change of pace from studying and, now that you have some experience, Rhonda has given you a slightly better schedule and an array of tasks. You especially enjoy helping with the mail and clerical tasks. You think you deserve the breaks she has given you because you worked so hard last summer, often stacking trays of rolls for what seemed like days at a time.

CHARLES'S ROLE You knew this job would mean hard work, but you hoped for a more equitable division of tasks. It is not Jenny's fault, but it does trouble you that she seems to get the better schedule and assignments. Stacking trays of rolls is an especially deadening job, but one on which you cannot let your attention drift for a second. Compared to it, sweeping the floor is a pleasure. You do not know whether you can gut it out the whole summer. There has got to be a better way to make some tuition money than this!

MODELLING EXERCISE OBSERVATIONS

During the dialogue, observers should note how Rhonda treats Charles and Jenny, what questions she asks, how flexible she seems, and how the two workers respond. Be prepared to suggest additional questions or alternatives and to draw conclusions about Rhonda's commitment to making a good-faith effort to redesign the jobs.

Observer's Rating Sheet

Using the following scale, rate Rhonda's application of techniques discussed in this chapter. Also write comments in the spaces below each of the behavioural criteria that will help explain your feedback.

1 Unsatisfactory	2 Weak	3 Adequate	4 Good	5 Outstanding

_____ Found out what was wrong with the present situation.

_____ Explored employees' motivation.

_____ Examined each worker's growth-need strength.

_____ Considered the role of social cues.

_____ Analyzed what would work for the firm as well as for employees.

_____ Showed creativity in developing alternatives.

_____ Involved employees in the search for solutions.

_____ Looked at schedule options as well as changes in assignment of tasks.

Group Exercises

In the three exercises that follow you will be asked to practise the elements of good job design. The first exercise is designed to encourage you to brainstorm about how you would redesign a job. The second exercise gives you a detailed work situation to analyze, and the third exercise allows you to "overhear" and critique a conversation between two managers who are planning a job redesign.

Group Exercise 1: Brainstorming Job Redesign[31]

STEP 1: IDENTIFY A TARGET JOB   Class members volunteer to share the description of a job they now hold or have held. The student selected should explain the job thoroughly so that everyone becomes familiar with it. If several students volunteer, the class and/or the instructor can select a job that seems the most interesting. (10 minutes)

To help identify a job that will be a good candidate for job redesign, make sure it meets the following criteria.

1. *A specific problem or exploitable opportunity is identified*. Unless a specific organizational problem can be identified, the diagnosis should stop there.
2. *The problem or opportunity involves employee motivation, satisfaction, or work effectiveness*. If the issues are irrelevant to these matters, work redesign is unlikely to help.
3. *The redesign is likely to help resolve the problems*. Many factors affect poor performance, motivation, and satisfaction. Is the design of the work one of the reasons?
4. *Specific aspects of the job can be pinpointed as being most troublesome*. What deserves special attention?
5. *The employees are ready for change*. Check the level of employee knowledge and skill, growth-need strength, and overall satisfaction. If one or more of these factors is low, the decision might be to proceed with work redesign cautiously, if at all.
6. *The organization is hospitable to change*. If work design is called for, the organization must be ready to embrace it.

STEP 2   The class interviews the person who holds (or held, or knows) the target job so that everyone understands the job activities. Before proceeding, make sure the group is in agreement on the activities performed by the person holding the job. Check to see whether anyone has questions about the job. Ask the following questions to gain further information about the job. (15 minutes)[32]

CONTROL AND INFLUENCE:

Do you have influence over the pace of your work?
Do you have a say in your work assignments and goals?
Is there an opportunity for you to comment on your performance appraisal?

INFORMATION AND UNCERTAINTY:

Do you have access to all the information you need at work?
Is there adequate planning for changes that affect you at work?
Do you receive complete information for your work assignments?

CONFLICT AT WORK:

Does the organization apply policies clearly and consistently?
Are job descriptions and task assignments clear and unambiguous?
Are policies and procedures in place for resolution of conflicts?

JOB SCOPE AND TASK DESIGN:

> Do your work activities and assignments provide adequate variety?
> Do you receive timely, constructive feedback on your work?
> Is your work important to the overall mission of the enterprise?
> Do you work on more than one small piece of a big project?

STEP 3 Form groups of three to seven students. With the information from above, brainstorm as many possible changes in the job as you can think of. (20 minutes)

RULES FOR BRAINSTORMING
1. Write down all ideas that are produced.
2. Praise one another's ideas, help each develop ideas, and add to others' ideas whenever possible.
3. Do *not* evaluate or criticize anyone's ideas. The creative process is a fragile one. Ideas—not criticism—are needed at this point.

After you've finished brainstorming, then you can be critical. Go over your brainstormed list and delete proposed changes that (a) will not affect core job characteristics, (b) are technologically impossible or obviously not cost effective, or (c) are too abstract and general.

Then pick a spokesperson to report your recommended changes to the rest of the class.

STEP 4 Each group's representative reads off that group's list of recommendations. (10 minutes)

STEP 5: JOB INCUMBENT'S REACTIONS Ask the person who holds (or held, or knows) the job to comment on the job redesign ideas. How realistic are they? What impact would they have? Have they ever been tried there? Would they likely improve motivation, satisfaction, or performance? (5 minutes)

Group Exercise 2: Redesigning Assembly-Line Jobs[33]

TIME 80 minutes.

INSTRUCTIONS Meet in groups of five to seven people. Take 10 minutes to read each part of the Hovey and Beard Co. case as directed. Take another 10 minutes to come to a group decision on the questions at the end of each part.

PART I THE HOVEY AND BEARD CO. CASE
The Hovey and Beard Co. manufactures wooden toys of various animals. One part of the manufacturing involves spraying paint on the partially assembled toys. This operation was staffed entirely by women.

The toys are cut, sanded, and partially assembled in the wood room. Then they are dipped in shellac and, finally, painted. The toys are predominantly two-coloured, though a few are painted with more than two colours. Each additional colour requires an extra trip through the paint room.

For a number of years, production of these toys had been entirely by hand. However, to meet tremendously increased demand, the painting operation recently has been re-engineered so that the eight operators (all women) who are painting sit in a line by an endless chain of hooks. These hooks are in continuous motion, past the line of operators and into a large oven. A woman sits at her own painting booth designed to carry away fumes and to backstop excess paint. The operator takes a toy from the tray in front of her, positions it in a jig inside the painting cube, sprays on the color according to a pattern, then releases the toy and hangs it on the hook passing by. The pace at which the hooks move had been calculated by the engineers so that the women, when fully trained, should be able to hang a painted toy on each hook before it passes her reach.

The operators working in the paint room are on a group bonus plan. Because the operation was new to them, they are receiving a learning bonus that decreases by regular amounts each month. The learning bonus is scheduled to vanish in six months, by which time it was expected that they would be on their own—that is, be able to meet the standard and to earn a group bonus when they exceed that standard.

DISCUSS What do you expect will happen over the next few months? Will production go up, down, or stay the same?

All the groups meet briefly as a full class. Make a tally of how many groups think production will go up, how many think it will go down, and how many think it will stay the same.

Now read Part II of the case.

PART II

By the second month of the training period, trouble had developed. The employees learned more slowly than had been anticipated, and it began to look as though their production would stabilize far below what was planned. Many of the hooks were going by empty. The women complained that they were going by too fast, and that the time-study engineer had set the rates wrong. A few women quit and had to be replaced with new operators, which further aggravated the learning problem. The team spirit that the management had expected to develop automatically through the group bonus was not in evidence except as an expression of what the engineers called "resistance." One woman whom the group regarded as its leader (and the management regarded as the ringleader) was outspoken in making various complaints of the group to the supervisor: The job was messy, the hooks moved too fast, the incentive pay was not being correctly calculated, and it was too hot working so close to the drying oven.

DISCUSS If you were a consultant, what would you recommend?

Now read Part III.

PART III

A consultant who was brought into this picture worked entirely with and through the supervisor. After many conversations with the consultant, the supervisor felt that the first step should be to get the employees together for a general discussion of the working conditions. The supervisor took this step with some hesitation, but he took it on his own volition.

All eight operators attended the first meeting, held immediately after the shift was over at 4 P.M. They voiced the same complaints again. The hooks went by too fast, the job was too dirty, the room was hot and poorly ventilated. For some reason, it was this last item that they complained of most. The supervisor promised to discuss the problem of ventilation and temperature with the engineers, and he scheduled a second meeting to report back to the employees. In the next few days the supervisor had several talks with the engineers. They and the plant manager felt that the complaint was trumped up and that the expense of any effective corrective measure would be prohibitively high.

The supervisor came to the second meeting with some apprehensions. The operators, however, did not seem to be much put out, perhaps because they had a proposal of their own to make. They felt that if several large fans were set up so as to circulate the air around their feet, they would be much more comfortable. After some discussion, the supervisor agreed that the idea might be tried. The supervisor and the consultant discussed the question of the fans with the plant manager, and three large propeller-type fans were purchased.

The fans were brought in. The women were jubilant. For several days the fans were moved about in various positions until they were placed to the satisfaction of the group. The operators seemed completely satisfied with the results, and the relations between them and the supervisor improved visibly.

The supervisor, after this encouraging episode, decided that further meetings might also be profitable. He asked the operators if they would like to meet and discuss other aspects of the work situation. They were eager to do so. The meeting was held, and the discussion quickly centered on the speed of the hooks. The operators maintained that the time-study engineer had set the hooks at an unreasonably fast speed and that the operators would never be able to reach the goal of filling enough of them to make a bonus.

The turning point of the discussion came when the group's leader frankly explained that the point was not that they could not work fast enough to keep up with the hooks, but that they could not work at that pace all day long. The supervisor explored the point. The employees were unanimous in their opinion that they could keep up with the belt for short periods if they wanted to, but they didn't want to because if they showed they could do this for short periods they would be expected to do it all day long. The meeting ended with an unprecedented request: "Let us adjust the speeds of the belt faster or slower depending on how we feel." The supervisor agreed to discuss this request with the plant manager and the engineers.

The reaction of the engineers to the suggestion was negative. However, after several meetings the engineers conceded that some latitude could be given within which variation in the speed of the hook would not affect the finished product. After considerable argument with the engineers, it was agreed to try out the operators' ideas.

With misgiving, the supervisor had a control with a dial marked "low, medium, fast" installed at the booth of the group leader; she could now adjust the speed of the belt anywhere between the lower and upper limits that the engineers had set.

DISCUSS What do you think the results of this action will be? Will production go up, down, or stay the same? Will satisfaction go up, down, or stay the same?

Now read Part IV.

PART IV

The operators were delighted, and spent many lunch hours deciding how the speed of the belt should be varied from hour to hour throughout the day. Within a week the pattern had settled down to one in which the first half hour of the shift was run on what the operators called a medium speed (a dial setting slightly above the point marked "medium"). The next two and one-half hours were run at high speed; the half hour before lunch and the half hour after lunch were run at low speed. The rest of the afternoon was run at high speed with the exception of the last 45 minutes of the shift, which was run at medium.

In view of the operators' reports of satisfaction and ease in their work, it is interesting to note that the constant speed at which the engineers had originally set the belt was slightly below medium on the dial of the control that had been given the women. The average speed at which the women were running the belt was on the high side of the dial. Few, if any, empty hooks entered the oven, and inspection showed no increase of rejects from the paint room.

Production increased, and within three weeks (some two months before the scheduled ending of the learning bonus), the operators were operating at 30 to 50 per cent above the level that had been expected under the original arrangement. Naturally their earnings were correspondingly higher than anticipated. They were collecting their base pay, a considerable piece-rate bonus, and the learning bonus that, it will be remembered, had been set to decrease with time and not as a function of current productivity. The operators were earning more now than many skilled workers in other parts of the plant.

DISCUSS What do you think will be the final reaction of plant management? If you were part of Hovey and Beard's top management team, what would you recommend?

Group Exercise 3: Getting Ready to Redesign Work

DIRECTIONS Split into three groups. Each group should read the situation and the dialogue that follows it, then try to answer the questions. Reconvene as a class and compare answers.

SITUATION The vice-president of human resources and organizational development at a large manufacturing firm has received numerous complaints from employees in the human resources department that their work is undervalued and that they do not feel "a part of the company." The vice-president calls Leo and Clare, the two managers in the HR department, to his office. He tells them to find out what is going on and report what changes, if any, can and should be made. His tone is less than friendly.

Leo and Clare have the following conversation:

Leo: What is this problem about our employees feeling unwanted and unloved? Don't they know how good they have it compared to those who work in other parts of this outfit? If they operated a lathe or a router for a few days, they would wish they were back on the clerical side, don't you agree?

Clare: Of course. But our boss wants us to improve things. The question is how do we start?

Leo: Well, how do we know that what we do will have any effect?

Clare: Work can always be better—it just can't be made perfect. So we have got to sort out the chronic whiners from those with legitimate gripes. I suggest we interview everybody, then compare notes. Maybe we can get a consensus about the kinds of problems we face.

Leo: That is a lot of work.

Clare: I don't see any way around it if we are going to improve things.

Leo: Okay, but then what?

Clare: I don't know.

A week later, Leo and Clare meet again after having talked to all the employees in the department. They were bombarded with complaints. The HR workers feel the manufacturing employees are given special treatment while the clerical workers are expected to do unrewarding jobs without the possibility of bonuses, scheduling options (the manufacturing employees can choose to work a 10-hour day, four days a week), or getting any significant feedback on their work.

Leo: So what do you think now?

Clare: I think we have a lot of work to do. I definitely do not want to take any more heat from the VP about this. I say: Give them what they want. Where should we start?

Leo: Well, if we think this scheduling complaint is valid, we could draw up some alternatives and present them to top management.

Clare: I don't care if it is valid. I just want to stop the flak. Why don't you handle that? I will find out how the bonus system works on the manufacturing side and then we can see whether we can adapt it for the white-collar rank-and-file.

Leo: What about the feedback question?

Clare: What about it, Leo. Who can change that?

QUESTIONS FOR DISCUSSION

1. Should Leo and Clare have known about this situation before being called in by the vice-president? Why or why not?
2. Did they go about their investigation in the right way? Why or why not?
3. What important factors did Clare not include in her rush to get the job done?
4. What is the answer to Leo's question about who can improve the feedback? Why?

Application Questions

The following checklist can be used to get an idea of how flexible work arrangements and work–life balance measures are being developed, implemented, and communicated within an organization. Use the checklist to evaluate your own college, university, or an organization for which you would like to work. The more statements that can be checked "yes," the better positioned that organization is to meet the work–life balance needs of its employees.[34]

ATTITUDES AND CULTURE:

_____ Managers encourage employees to stay home with children or elderly parents in the event of a medical emergency or when their usual care arrangements are unavailable.

_____ Managers are conscious of the need to help employees manage their workloads in a way that enables them to participate fully in their personal lives.

_____ Managers are flexible around hours of work in order to assist employees in balancing their work and home activities.

_____ Managers in our organization are supportive of work–life balance — demonstrated by "walking the talk" or by encouraging employees to take advantage of work–life balance policies.

_____ One of the criteria for promotion or hiring into management positions is solid understanding of the importance of, and commitment to, work–life balance initiatives.

_____ Our organization has developed measurements to hold individuals and managers accountable for creating supportive work environments.

PROGRAMS:

_____ Our organization has conducted surveys and/or focus groups with employees to learn about their work–life balance needs and desires.

_____ Our organization has a formal work–life balance policy or program in place.

_____ Our organization offers or plans to offer one or more of the following programs:

- Dependant care initiatives (e.g., emergency child or elder care, referral or information services, workplace childcare).

- Stress management (e.g., employee assistance program or wellness/health promotion activities).
- Flexible work arrangements (e.g., compressed work week, flextime, or telework).
- Reduction in working time (e.g., job sharing, gradual retirement, or voluntary part-time).
- Vacation and other social benefits (e.g., flexible benefits, leave for personal reasons, maternity, paternity, and/or parental leave, sick leave, or vacation flexibility).

_____ Our organization has a process in place to monitor progress and usage of work–life balance programs.

_____ Work–life programs are linked to recruitment and retention strategies, business development goals, and organizational development initiatives.

_____ Our organization participates in external work–life councils, committees, or consortiums to benchmark progress and learn from others' experience.

COMMUNICATION:

_____ Employees are aware of their options when it comes to work–life programs or initiatives in our organization.

_____ Employees are provided with regular opportunities to express views about work, life, and family balance.

_____ Managers have received appropriate training and possess the proper tools and skills that are necessary to implement organizational work–life balance policies.

_____ Our organization regularly reminds managers that work–life balance is important.

_____ Our organization publicizes work–life balance programs at all levels of the organization across all work locations.

Source: "Work–Life Balance in Canadian Workplaces": http://labour-travail.hrdc-drhc.gc.ca/worklife/welcome-en.cfm, Checklist for Employers, Human Resources Development Canada. Reproduced with the permission of the Minister of Public Works and Government Services Canada, 2003.

Reinforcement Exercises

The following are suggested activities for reinforcing the job design techniques described in this chapter. You may want to adapt them to the Action Plan you will develop next, or try them independently.

1. Examine the motivating potential in your job or a job you have held. For each of the following questions, circle the number of the most accurate description of the job. Be as objective as you can in describing the job by answering these questions.[35]

A. How much autonomy is present in this job? That is, to what extent does the job permit a person to decide on his or her own how to go about doing the work?

1	2	3	4	5	6	7
Very little. The job gives a person almost no say about how and when the work is done.			Moderate. Many things are standardized and not under control of the jobholder, but he or she can make some decisions about the work.			Very much. The job gives the employee complete responsibility for deciding how and when the work is done.

B. To what extent does the job involve doing an identifiable piece of work? That is, is the job a complete piece of work with an obvious beginning and end? Or is it a small part of an overall piece of work, which is finished by other people or by machines?

1	2	3	4	5	6	7

The job is only a tiny part in the overall piece of work. The results of this person's effort cannot be seen in the final product or service.

The job is a moderate-sized chunk of the overall piece of work. The person's contribution can be seen in the final outcome.

The job involves doing the whole piece of work from start to finish. The person's activities can be easily seen in the final product or service.

C. How much variety is present in the job? That is, to what extent does the job require a person to do many different things at work, using a variety of his or her skills and talents?

1	2	3	4	5	6	7

Very little. The job requires the person to do the same routine things over and over again.

Moderate variety.

Very much. The job requires the person to do many different things, using a number of different skills and talents.

D. In general, how significant or important is the job? That is, are the results of the person's work likely to affect the lives or well-being of other people significantly?

1	2	3	4	5	6	7

Not significant. The outcome of the work is not likely to affect anyone in any important way.

Moderately significant.

Highly significant. The outcome of the work can affect others in important ways.

E. To what extent does doing the job itself provide the person with information about his or her work performance? That is, does the actual work itself provide clues about how well the person is doing—aside from any feedback co-workers or supervisors may provide?

1	2	3	4	5	6	7

Very little. The job itself is set up so a person could work forever without finding out how well he or she was doing.

Moderately. Sometimes doing the job provides feedback to the person, sometimes it does not.

Very much. The job is set up so that the person gets almost constant feedback as he or she works about how well he or she is doing.

SCORING AND INTERPRETATION To score the questionnaire, place your responses to Questions C, B, D, A, and E, respectively, in the blank spaces in the following equation:

Motivating   C   B   D   A   E

$$\text{Potential} = \dfrac{[\quad] + [\quad] + [\quad]}{3} \times [\quad] \times [\quad] = \underline{\quad}$$

Score (MPS) _____

200–343   means the job is high in motivating potential

120–199   means the job is moderate in motivating potential

0–119   means the job is low in motivating potential

2. Thinking of that same job, what could be done to make it more motivating?

	Yes	No	Maybe
A. Could the skill variety be increased?	_____	_____	_____
B. Could the task identity be improved?	_____	_____	_____
C. Could the task significance be enhanced?	_____	_____	_____
D. Could more autonomy be granted?	_____	_____	_____
E. Could more feedback be given?	_____	_____	_____

Summary Checklist

Take a few minutes to reflect on your performance in the preceding exercises. Assess yourself as to how your analysis compared to other students (and if you were a presenter, how others rated your skill). Make a check (√) next to those behaviours on which you may need improvement.

_____ Understanding the present situation.

1. Know your employees' strengths and weaknesses.
2. Perform an analysis of each affected job.
3. Evaluate how the job stacks up on the five-element JCM model.
4. Know what work–life balance options exist

_____ Showing creativity in coming up with alternatives.

1. How can jobs be combined?
2. Can natural work units be established?
3. Is it possible to have the worker interact with the client?
4. Should jobs be expanded vertically to give rank-and-file employees more autonomy, control, and authority in their jobs?
5. Can feedback channels be opened?
6. Are telecommuting, job sharing, and flextime or other work–life balance options possible?

_____ Involving employees in the search for solutions.

1. Elicit comments about what is wrong.
2. Encourage realistic suggestions.

_____ Making sure your recommendations work for the organization as well as the employees.

  1. Is performance enhanced?

  2. Is the job enrichment likely to cause problems with unaffected groups of employees?

  3. Will customer satisfaction be enhanced?

Action Plan

1. What are specific things I can do to improve when designing jobs? (See Summary Checklist.)
2. What will be the benefits of these improvements?
3. What potential obstacles stand in my way?
4. When will I start these improvements?
5. How and when will I measure my success?

CHAPTER 13
Identifying and Hiring Employees

Learning Objectives

After completing this chapter, you should be able to:

- Plan human resources needs.
- Find applicants for specific jobs.
- Use selection devices that are valid and reliable.
- Competently interview job candidates.
- Comply with federal, provincial, or territorial human rights legislation.

Hiring is one of the manager's most important—and often among the most difficult—tasks. Every decision to hire someone is a prediction of that candidate's ability to do the job and get along with his or her co-workers. "All we can do is bet on the people whom we pick," says Jack Welch, the much-admired former CEO of General Electric. "So my job is picking the right people."[1]

As Welch suggests, this prediction carries with it enormous stakes. The happiness of the employee, the morale of the workforce, the reputation of the manager, and even the functioning of the entire organization may rest on the performance of that candidate. Yet many supervisors come unprepared to this challenge. The skills that a person acquires prior to becoming a manager are no guarantee that he or she will be good at hiring.

Self-Assessment Exercise

In the following self-assessment, respond as candidly as possible to the statements seeking to gauge your instinct and knowledge about hiring and promotion. Act as if you were a hiring manager and describe your level of agreement with each of the statements by circling the number in the appropriate column.

	Strongly Agree				Strongly Disagree
1. I want to hire people like me because they are known quantities.	1	2	3	4	5

	Strongly Agree				Strongly Disagree
2. I think speed is of the essence when trying to fill openings.	1	2	3	4	5
3. I can use tests to eliminate most of the guesswork from the hiring process.	1	2	3	4	5
4. I believe the best job candidates are almost always found close to home.	1	2	3	4	5
5. I can tell most of what I need to know about a person by studying his or her résumé.	1	2	3	4	5
6. When I interview someone for a job, I want the session to be informal and unstructured so I can find out what he or she is really like.	1	2	3	4	5
7. Any organization I work for is likely to have a human resources department that will relieve me of most hiring responsibility.	1	2	3	4	5
8. I need to be careful in my interviewing that I do not violate federal, provincial, or territorial human rights legislation.	5	4	3	2	1
9. To lure the best applicants I may have to resort to nontraditional recruitment methods.	5	4	3	2	1
10. I believe hiring from within is almost always a sound idea.	1	2	3	4	5

SCORING AND INTERPRETATION Add the numbers you have circled to obtain your total score.

40–50	You have some of the knowledge and many of the instincts to serve you well as a hiring supervisor.
30–39	You show average awareness of the nuances of hiring and promotion.
20–29	Although you seem aware of some of the implications of hiring decisions, you need to increase your knowledge.
0–19	You definitely need to bolster your knowledge and scrutinize your impulses before you make any hiring or promotion decisions.

Concepts
Why Do I Need to Know About Hiring?

After three years as a salesperson, you have just been promoted to assistant sales manager for your insurance firm's district office. *Terrific!* You have proven to be what you always knew you were: An outstanding salesperson with enormous potential for advancement.

Before you can bask in the glow of this triumph, the sales manager gives you your next assignment: Choose someone to replace you as salesperson. "It has got to be someone who is at least as good as you," he says. "Someone who is extremely capable, hard-working, easy to get along with, and who will serve this company well for many years. You know how short-staffed we are. So this has to be a good hire, or we are all sunk."

He adds, "I hate hiring and am not very good at it. So here is your chance to show what you can do. Do this well and you could make a real mark for yourself. Botch it and well...," he leaves the sentence unfinished but you get the idea.

You are honoured—and scared out of your wits. You have never hired anyone before. And now the future of the district office seems to rest in your hands. But where do you go to find good people? What about government legislation that influences hiring and recruitment? Should you just err on the safe side and interview your friends? Or do you need to interview at all? Why has no one taught you this stuff before? As a salesperson, you learned how to make a good first impression—strong handshake, eye contact, proper appearance, "good" personality—and you learned your firm's products and how to close a deal. But is that going to be enough to allow you to choose the right person?

Many firms boast that "Our staff is our most important asset." Fewer, though, follow through by choosing those staff members in a thoughtful way. Too often contemplation is sacrificed for speed, and what should be careful selection from among several highly qualified applicants becomes a choice among predictable candidates selected in a narrow, biased manner. Too often the result is, at best, the wrong person for the job and, at worst, a weak link that can turn into a morale problem, a blemish on the supervisor, or even a nasty lawsuit. Yet, hiring and promotion, if done well, can be a boon to the organization and even yield a sustainable competitive advantage.[2]

Employee selection involves choosing the right person for the job. It is vital to any organization for the following reasons:[3]

- Success depends in large measure on attracting and retaining competent people. For any organization, people really are its biggest asset.

- A manager's performance will always hinge on how employees perform.

- Hiring is costly. Studies show the average cost of turnover, whether righting a hiring mistake or replacing a long-time employee, is about two and one-half times the salary of the departing worker. The costs are even higher when it is an executive who is leaving.

- Yet, annual turnover rates in the retail, services, and health-care sectors are 37 per cent, 21 per cent, and 19 per cent, respectively, according to Saratoga Institute Canada, a Vancouver-based management consulting firm that tracks attrition data.[4]

- Lawsuits over discriminatory staffing policies cost companies millions of dollars.

Thus, in large measure a supervisor's success—and by extension, the organization's success—depends on his or her employees.

In this chapter we will cover the first half of the manager's job as it pertains to staffing: human resources planning, recruitment, and selection of new employees. Elsewhere in this book, we will discuss training (Chapter 15, Developing Employees), performance appraisals (Chapter 14, Evaluating Performance), and motivating employees (Chapter 9, Motivating Others).

The Human Resources Function

Organizations cannot afford to have more workers than they need, yet neither can they afford to do without the needed number of employees. Therefore, the staffing function begins with planning personnel requirements, then increasing or decreasing the number of employees.

In large organizations such as Stelco Inc. or BCE, Inc., many staffing activities—grouped under the title **human resources management (HRM)**—are conducted by personnel specialists, not the supervisor. However, not all managers work in organizations with a formal human resources department. The small business manager, for example, usually does his or her own hiring without benefit of an HR specialist.

Even in a multi-million dollar firm with a formal HR department, the manager is still likely to be involved in recruiting applicants, reviewing applications, and choosing among candidates, as well as coordinating employee training and providing career advice. So HRM is of great importance to every manager.

When performing the staffing functions, a manager usually works to some extent with the HR department, if one is available. The manager can benefit from HR's skills in screening and interviewing candidates and from its familiarity with laws regarding hiring practices. Nevertheless, managers usually interview and make the final decisions themselves. For the purpose of explaining these skills, this chapter will assume the manager is solely involved and will have final say on who is selected and how.

PLANNING

Human resources planning is the process by which managers ensure that they have the right number and right kinds of people in the right places at the right times. How many people will an organization need in the future? The answer is determined by the organization's objectives, strategies, and sales forecasts. After assessing current capabilities and future needs, managers should be able to estimate shortages—both in number and type of workers—and to highlight those areas in which the organization will be overstaffed. A program can then be developed to match these estimates with forecasts of future labour supply.

Managers typically begin this process by doing a *human resources inventory,* which is based on forms completed by employees. Such an inventory may include name, education, training, prior employment, languages spoken, special capability, and specialized skills of each employee. It allows managers to assess available talent and skills.

Another part of the current assessment is the *job analysis,* which defines jobs and what is necessary to perform those jobs. The analysis explains, for instance, the duties of a Secretary II and what knowledge, skills, abilities, and behaviours are needed to perform those duties. This analysis helps determine employee compensation and training needs, and is a prerequisite for evaluating employee performance as well as recruiting and selecting employees. The job analyst gets this information by observing the employee performing the job, interviewing the employee, asking the employee to fill out a job questionnaire, having the employee keep a log of what he or she actually does, or some combination of these methods.

The two parts of a job analysis are a **job description** and **job specifications.** The job description tells what a jobholder does, how it is done, and why it is done. Job specifications, on the other hand, focus on the person, not the job, and give the minimal acceptable qualifications or competencies that an employee must have to perform the job successfully.

The job description can be used to describe the job to potential candidates as well as for training workers and appraising their job performance. The job specifications help determine whether candidates are qualified. In other words, these job specifications are the criteria used to evaluate the ability of a candidate to perform the job.

Exhibit 13-1 shows what kinds of information job descriptions and job specifications include.

One thing not listed in the job specifications is the personal traits needed to "fit in" with the department. Yet, not getting along with peers is the most common reason employees are unhappy on the job.[5] For this area, the interview, which we'll discuss in the section about selection devices, can be especially helpful.

Exhibit 13-1 Contents of Job Descriptions and Job Specifications

The job description tells the basic tasks and responsibilities of a job. It answers the question: "What does this job entail?" Such a description commonly includes the following:

- Job title (Clerk, bookkeeper, technician, etc.)
- Supervision (Who does the employee report to? Who, if anyone, reports to the employee?)
- Location (Where is the job performed? Shop, office, etc.)
- Tasks, duties, activities (What does the employee actually do on the job?)
- Performance standards (What is the level of acceptable performance, e.g., the sale of $100,000 worth of goods annually?)
- Working conditions (Hazards, heat, noise, etc.)
- Tools, equipment, materials, etc. (Drill presses, forklifts, computers, etc.)

Job specifications identify the qualifications or competencies needed to perform a job satisfactorily. It answers the question: "What kind of person is needed?" The traits identified may include the following:

- Skills and ability (Key 60 words per minute)
- Credentials (College degree, teacher certification)
- Training (Trained to operate heavy-duty bulldozer)
- Experience (Held same or similar job for at least 12 months)
- Personal qualities (Good judgment, initiative, collaborative, ambition)
- Physical effort (Able to lift 23 kilogram bags)
- Sensory demands (Specific level of sight, hearing, smell)

Source: Adapted from R.N. Lussier, *Supervision: A Skill-Building Approach* (Burr Ridge, IL: Irwin, 1994) 285.

Once managers know their current HR status—whether they are understaffed or overstaffed—they can begin to do something about it. If they are short of staff, they can begin the recruitment process, which means locating, identifying, and attracting applicants. A carefully planned recruitment process is critical to selecting the most qualified candidate and also ensures that every candidate is dealt with professionally and in a non-discriminatory manner.

Recruiting Qualified Applicants

Where can a manager recruit potential job candidates? Exhibit 13-2 shows the major sources of potential candidates as well as the advantages and disadvantages of each source.

Many managers prefer to fill jobs from within, if possible. It is usually simpler to fill the higher-level job being vacated, and employee morale and motivation is enhanced when good people are given greater responsibility, status, and income. But the person promoted must also be replaced, which can result in substantial shifts. One organization experienced 545 job movements to fill 195 initial openings.[6] In addition, those not promoted may be dissatisfied, especially if their new boss is a former peer. Of course, training costs tend to increase as well.

Exhibit 13-2 Major Sources of Potential Job Candidates

Source	Advantages	Disadvantages
Internal search	Low cost; builds employee morale; candidates are familiar with the organization	Limited supply; may not increase the diversity and mix of employees; creates additional openings and possible dissatisfaction among unsuccessful candidates
Advertisements	Wide distribution; can be targeted to specific groups	Generates many unqualified candidates
Employee referrals	Knowledge about the organization provided by current employee; may generate strong candidates because a good candidate reflects on the current employee	May not increase diversity and mix of employees
Public employment agencies	Free or inexpensive	Candidates tend to be unskilled or minimally trained
Private employment agencies	Wide contacts; careful screening; guarantees often given	High cost
School placement	Large, centralized body of candidates	Limited to entry-level positions
Temporary-help services	Fills temporary needs	Expensive; candidates may lack understanding of organization's goals and activities
Independent contractors	Fills temporary needs, but usually for more specific, longer-term projects	Little commitment to organization beyond current project

How recruitment is done depends on the labour market, the type of opening, and the size of organization. It is generally easier to recruit in a large labour market, such as Vancouver or Toronto, because of the greater supply of workers. In such markets, recruitment tends to be directed locally to newspapers, commercial employment agencies, colleges and universities, listing vacancies with Canada Employment offices, or referrals by current employees.

The greater the skill required in the job or the higher the position in the organization's hierarchy, the more the recruitment is likely to expand to become a regional, or even a national, search. Similarly, the larger the organization, the easier it usually is to recruit applicants. Large organizations such as Montreal-based Bombardier Inc. naturally have a large pool of internal candidates. Typically, large organizations also attract many external applicants because of the prestige inherent in working for the larger company and the perception of greater opportunity for job promotions.

Do certain recruiting sources produce superior candidates? In short, no. It was long believed that employee referrals produced the best candidates because the referring employees knew the job and the person being recommended and had a personal stake in suggesting only the most well-qualified applicants. But the most recent research indicates that employee referrals are no more productive or stable than recruits obtained from other sources.[7]

RECRUITING TRENDS

In recent years, three recruiting trends have surfaced. First, organizations are showing more creativity by using alternative sources to increase the diversity of applicants.[8] For example, in the five major banks (the Bank of Nova Scotia, the Bank of Montreal, the Royal Bank, the Canadian Imperial Bank of Commerce, and TD Canada Trust), the representation of visible minorities exceeds that of the Canadian labour force. To increase access to job information, some banks hold regular "job fairs" and send job posters to outreach groups and local community associations.[9]

Another development is increased reliance on temporary-help firms as a source of new employees. This way a firm gets a chance to assess a potential permanent employee with minimal commitment. Thus, some organizations use temporary positions as the ultimate "job performance test" before hiring an individual permanently.[10]

Yet another trend is the use of the Internet for recruitment. Particularly when seeking candidates with technical or computer-related skills, posting a vacancy on the Internet can provide wide access to potential candidates.[11]

Selecting the Best Candidate

Once a list of candidates is obtained from whatever source, the task is to choose among them. It becomes an exercise in prediction. Subsequent performance will show whether the prediction was correct, that is, the person hired performs the job successfully.

Unfortunately, hiring a person who performs poorly is not easily righted. This error brings obvious burdens, including the cost of training, added costs or loss of profits due to the employee's incompetence, and the cost of severance as well as the expense of further recruiting and selection.

Overlooking a candidate who would have performed successfully can also create a problem. It can open the organization to charges of discrimination, especially if applicants from minority groups were disproportionately rejected.

Selection committees, consisting of diverse members, can reduce these errors by assessing candidates' qualifications, as well as providing new insights and cancelling out misperceptions.

So, one aim of any selection process should be to reduce the likelihood of making errors while increasing the probability of making correct decisions. The second aim is to ensure that the selection process is conducted in a fair, consistent, equitable, and transparent manner.

SELECTION DEVICES

Managers can use a number of selection devices to reduce errors. They include the candidate's résumé and application form, tests, interviews, background investigations, and, where a bona fide occupational requirement exists, a physical exam.

Any such device must demonstrate **validity.** That is, a proven relationship must be shown between the device and some relevant criterion. For instance, managers should not use a test score as a selection device unless clear evidence indicates that, once on the job, persons with high scores on this test outperform those with low scores.

A selection device must also show **reliability.** It must measure the same thing consistently. If a test is reliable, an individual's score should remain fairly consistent over time, not fluctuate randomly.

Let's look at some of the more common selection devices. They include the application form, written tests, performance simulation tests, background investigations, a physical exam, and the interview.

THE APPLICATION FORM At one end of the spectrum, a simple application may require only name, address, and phone number. At the other end, a comprehensive personal resumé details the candidate's activities, skills, and accomplishments. Even though some of this data (for example, college or university grades) may be valid for predicting performance for some jobs, typically few of the items on an application form are valid predictors.[12]

Some experts believe that as many as 30 per cent of all résumés contain false information.[13] Such a statistic may be incentive to do some checking. Most of the time double-checking will yield little important new data, but the possibility is always there. A survey published in 2001 by the Conseil Quebecois du Commerce de Detail (CQCD), in cooperation with Samson, Belair, Deloitte & Touch, found that Quebec retailers lost approximately $835,000 a day from shoplifting, whereas theft by employees created losses of over $491,000 a day. The study strongly recommends reference, credit, and education checks for new hires.[14] Professional firms can be hired to do background checks, including previous job and credit histories. Just having a candidate consent to this verification process can be a security measure in itself.

WRITTEN TESTS Tests may measure intelligence, aptitude, ability, and interest. Such tests have been used for years, though their popularity tends to run in cycles. After a period in the 1960s and 1970s when written tests were often characterized as discriminatory and nonvalid, their popularity seems to be growing. The cost and time required to validate such tests has decreased, and their use has increased as managers have become more aware of how testing can decrease the likelihood of poor hiring decisions.[15]

Research shows that tests of intellectual ability, spatial and mechanical ability, perceptual accuracy, and motor ability are moderately valid predictors for many semiskilled and unskilled operative jobs in industrial firms. Intelligence tests also are reasonably good predictors of success for supervisory positions. However, an enduring criticism of written tests is that intelligence, for example, is not necessarily a good indicator of general performance.[16]

PERFORMANCE SIMULATION TESTS Composed of actual job behaviours, these tests more easily meet the requirement of job relatedness. For example, can a candidate for a technical writing job actually write a technical manual? The best known performance-simulation tests are work sampling and assessment centres.

Work sampling involves giving applicants a miniature model of a job and having them perform the tasks. Such tests have almost always produced validity scores superior to those of written aptitude, personality, or intelligence tests.[17]

Assessment centres can measure a candidate's managerial potential. Executives, supervisors, or trained psychologists evaluate candidates as they go through two to four days of exercises simulating real problems they would face on the job. Such activities might include interviews, in-basket problem-solving exercises, group discussions, and business-decision games. Though expensive to administer, such centres have consistently demonstrated results that predict later job performance in managerial positions.[18]

An alternative format is the micro assessment—a set of paper-based or computer-based questions and exercises that take up to three hours to complete. The questions and exercises simulate the range of activities required to perform a specific job successfully.

The assessment can be completed on-site or submitted electronically by internal, local, national, or international applicants.

BACKGROUND INVESTIGATIONS The two types of background investigations are (1) verification of application data and (2) reference checks. More than one-third of job applicants have been found to exaggerate or misrepresent dates of employment, job titles, past salaries, or reasons for leaving an earlier position.[19] Some organizations, in weighing the liability that potential employees may create, seek as much in-depth background information as possible.[20]

Reference checks in which the employer contacts persons suggested by the applicant are often used. But debate continues about how much valid information is learned in this way. For one thing, an applicant normally would only furnish the names of people expected to speak highly of him or her. Second, past employers are increasingly reluctant to give candid evaluations for fear of legal repercussions.[21]

PHYSICAL EXAM In Canada, pre-employment physical examinations are only permitted where employers have demonstrated that specific physical requirements are necessary in order to perform the job. An example of a job-related physical ability test is the Physical Abilities Requirement Evaluation (PARE) required to become a regular member of the Royal Canadian Mounted Police. Firefighting is another example of a job that requires specific physical requirements. Pre-employment drug and alcohol testing is illegal because it cannot be established as a bona fide occupational requirement.[22]

Because the validity of a selection device varies from job to job, you should use only those devices that predict for a given job. Exhibit 13-3 shows the quality of selection devices for different sorts of jobs. You will notice that written tests are reasonably effective for routine jobs, but work samples are even better. For managerial selection, the assessment centre is strongly recommended. The interview works best for less-routine jobs, particularly middle- and upper-level positions. Verification of application data is valuable for all jobs, while reference checks and physical exams rarely provide valuable information.

THE INTERVIEW Along with the application form, the interview is an almost universal selection device. Not many of us have ever been hired for a job without one or more interviews. It is also the only selection device that is two-way, that is, the applicant learns facts about whether to accept the job, just as the manager learns whether to offer it.

Exhibit 13-3 Quality of Selection Devices as Predictors

Note: Validity is measured on a scale from 5 (highest) to 1 (lowest.) A dash means the device is not applicable.

Device	Senior Management	Middle/Lower Management	Complex Nonmanagerial	Routine Operative
Application form	2	2	2	2
Written tests	1	1	2	3
Work samples	—	—	4	4
Assessment centre	5	5	—	—
Interviews	4	3	2	2
Verification of application data	3	3	3	3
Reference checks	1	1	1	1
Physical exam	1	1	1	2

Unfortunately, though, many interviews are poorly conducted and may result in distorted findings.[23] This finding does not mean that interviews cannot be valid and reliable devices, but, rather, that untrained interviewers tend to make common mistakes.

The unstructured interview—short, casual, and composed of random questions—has been proven to be an ineffective selection device.[24] The information gathered in such interviews is often biased and unrelated to future job performance.

Specific interviewing problems can include the following:[25]

- Interviewers often hold a stereotype of what represents a "good" applicant and tend to favour applicants like themselves. (A *similarity error* occurs when the interviewer has a bias in favor of a candidate who looks or acts like the interviewer.)

- A candidate's overall potential may be judged on the basis of a single characteristic, such as where the candidate went to college or university or how he or she dresses. (This bias is known as the *halo error*.)

- The order in which applicants are interviewed often influences evaluation, as does the order in which information is elicited. (A common judgment error is the *contrast error* in which the interviewer rates the candidate on a comparison to the preceding interviewee.)

- Interviewers tend to decide about a person early in the interview and then spend the rest of the time seeking information to support that decision.

- Negative information tends to be given unduly high weight.

- Conclusions may be skewed depending on how much prior knowledge the interviewer has about the applicant.

- Interviewers forget much of the content of an interview within minutes after it is over.

Having interviewers ask a standardized set of questions, use a uniform method of recording information, and standardize the rating of the applicant's qualifications enhances the validity of the interview as a selection device. Interviews are most valid in determining an applicant's intelligence, degree of motivation, and interpersonal skills.[26] Although an interview may not determine how well someone will perform, it may indicate how he or she will fit in with other members of the work group.

Interviewing Techniques

Because the interview is so essential no matter what the job, the technique of interviewing deserves amplification. Not only is the interview widely used, but it also tends to have a disproportionate influence on selection. The candidate who performs poorly in the interview is likely to be cut from the pool of applicants regardless of experience, test scores, letters or recommendations, or other signs of suitability. Conversely, the candidate who performs well in the interview may be hired even though he or she isn't the best candidate.[27]

What can managers do to make interviews more valid and reliable? Exhibit 13-4 gives some specific suggestions.

Questions make the interview, allowing you to get the information you need to make a decision. The kinds of questions you might use include the following:[28]

Closed-ended These require a limited response, often "yes" or "no," and are most appropriate in dealing with fixed aspects of the job. For example:

- "Have you used the software package *Simply Accounting*?"
- "Do you prefer the night shift or the day shift?"

Exhibit 13-4 Suggestions for Interviewing

1. Structure a fixed set of questions for all applicants; match the questions to the selection criteria and make sure all criteria are covered.
2. Have detailed information about the job for which applicants are interviewing.
3. Minimize any prior knowledge of applicants' background, experience, interests, test scores, and other characteristics.
4. Ask questions that require applicants to give detailed accounts of actual job behaviours.
5. Use a standardized evaluation form.
6. Take notes during the interview.
7. Avoid short interviews that encourage premature decision making.

Source: Based on D.A. DeCenzo and S.P. Robbins, *Human Resources Management*, 4th ed. (New York: Wiley, 1994) 208–9.

Open-ended These require an unlimited response and are appropriate for determining abilities and motivation. For instance:

- "What is it about this job that interests you?"
- "What were your major achievements in your last job?"

Probing These questions require a clarification and are used to improve understanding. Unplanned, these queries are used in a semi-structured or unstructured interview. For instance:

- "What do you mean by 'It was tough'?"
- "Can you give me an example of how you cut costs?"

Behavioural These require the candidate to describe what he or she would do in a given situation. The answers may help assess capabilities. For instance:

- "What would you do and say if the customer swore at you?"
- "How would you respond if the machine made a screeching sound?"

In short, good interviewing is an art. To do it well you need to know what to do and how to do it. Once you know the skills needed, it is a matter of practice. Here, then, are some steps to keep in mind as you seek to sharpen your interviewing skills.

Skill Guidelines for Interviewing Canadiates[29]

1. Review job description and job specifications This review helps remind you of the criteria on which you want to assess the candidate. Reviewing the job requirements also helps to reduce interview bias.

2. Prepare a structured set of questions for all applicants Structured questions will ensure a common base from which to compare all candidates' answers. It will also prevent you from forgetting some key query.

Emphasize questions that cannot be answered with a mere "yes" or "no." Inquiries beginning with a *how* or *why* tend to evoke extended answers. Avoid leading questions that tip off the desired response (e.g., "Would you say you're ethical?") or that force the applicant to choose among your options (e.g., "Are you an extrovert or an introvert?").

Because the best predictor of future behaviour is past behaviour, good questions may include queries that focus on previous experience relevant to the current opening.

(Examples: "What have you done in your previous job that demonstrates your creativity?" or "What goals did you have in the last job that you accomplished? And which ones didn't you accomplish and why?")

3. Review the candidate's application/résumé before meeting him or her The application is a critical piece in creating a complete picture of the candidate. You may also identify areas you wish to explore in the interview, for example, areas not defined in the résumé/application but that are essential for the job.

4. Open the interview by putting the applicant at ease Interviews are naturally stressful, and only rarely is the interviewee not at least a bit nervous. If you want genuine insights into what this person is really like, you need to put the applicant at ease.

Introduce yourself. Be friendly, and begin with some small talk about, say, the traffic or the weather to give the candidate time to adjust. It is also helpful to briefly preview the topics to be discussed, so the candidate knows the purpose and range of the interview. Explain if you will be taking notes, and encourage him or her to ask questions.

5. Ask your questions and listen carefully to the answers Ask all the questions on your list, but also pose follow-up questions that flow from the answers given. Focus on the responses as they relate to information about the job.

Ask situational questions. Avoid the traditional "What are your strengths and weaknesses?" query, which is likely to produce a rehearsed answer. Instead ask candidates to describe a time when they had to carry out an unpopular decision or perhaps a situation in which they felt their ethics were challenged, and ask them how they handled it.

If you feel the candidate's response is superficial or inadequate, seek elaboration in a nonhostile way. "Tell me more about that issue," you might say, or "Could you amplify on that one point a bit more?"

6. Give the candidate a chance to ask questions Questions from the candidate not only help the candidate learn more, but also may give the interviewer insight into the candidate's understanding and areas of concern.

7. Close the interview by explaining what happens next Applicants typically are anxious about the status of the hiring decision. Be candid about others being interviewed and the steps remaining in the hiring process. Tell the applicant when you expect to make a decision and how you plan to notify him or her about your decision.

8. Write your evaluation of the applicant while the interview is still fresh in your mind Do not wait until the end of the day or the end of the week to put your assessment on paper. The sooner you record your observations, the more likely you are to remember the details.

Human Rights Legislation in Canada

Human rights law is based on the principle that employment decisions should be made on the applicant's ability to do the job and those factors related to job specifications, qualifications, and performance. *The Canadian Human Rights Act* applies to the federal government and to federally regulated industries such as banking, railways, airlines, and telecommunications. Provincial or territorial human rights acts or codes, however, cover the vast majority of businesses. All of these laws are very similar across Canada. Each jurisdiction has a list of grounds or characteristics of discrimination that are against the law. These lists are somewhat different, but there is a common group that appears in most laws. This group includes age, sex, race, ethnic origin, colour, religion, sexual orientation, marital or family status, mental or physical disability, and dependence on alcohol or drugs.

Most jurisdictions in Canada, including the federal government, use the same basic system for handling complaints. The process starts with a human rights commission investigating the complaint and attempting to settle it. If unsuccessful, the complaint is sent to a tribunal or board of inquiry that can award remedies such as compensation for valid complaints. Tribunal and board decisions can be appealed to the courts.

The Employment Equity Act (revised 1996) is designed to put human rights legislation into practice. It provides equal employment opportunity within the federal government, federally regulated industries, and, through the federal contractors program, those enterprises with over 100 employees who do business with the Government of Canada. Under employment equity legislation, the numbers of women, visible minorities, persons with disabilities, and Aboriginal peoples in the workforce are to reflect their composition in Canadian society. This is to be accomplished through accelerated entry and promotion of qualified candidates, targeted recruitment, elimination of employment barriers, and reasonable accommodation such as adjusting work schedules, upgrading facilities, and redesigning job duties. The Canadian Human Rights Commission enforces this law. Although the provinces and territories do not have employment equity legislation, human rights legislation may provide for special employment programs to overcome discrimination. Similarly, labour-management or collective agreements may also provide special antidiscrimination initiatives.

Human rights legislation also requires valid testing and limits what questions can be asked on an application or during an interview. Two rules guide decisions about whether a question is discriminatory: (1) every question should be job related and (2) every general question should be asked of all candidates. Exhibit 13-5 identifies questions or topics that are likely to be viewed as permissible or discriminatory. Be sure to become knowledgeable with the federal, provincial, or territorial laws that apply to your situation.

Exhibit 13-5 Which Interview Questions Comply with Canadian Human Rights Legislation?

No...	Yes...
What is your age?	Are you of legal working age?
What is your marital status?	
Are you planning to start a family soon?	
Do you have children?	Are there any restrictions on your ability to travel, as required?
How's your health?	
How many days did you miss on your last job because of illness or injury?	We expect employees to work from 8:00 A.M. to 4:00 P.M. Can you meet these attendance requirements?
Do you suffer from night blindness?	The position you applied for requires driving a vehicle at night. Can you drive at night?
Have you ever been arrested?	This job requires that you work with cash. Have you ever been convicted of any finance-related crime for which you have not received a pardon?
Are you a Canadian citizen?	Are you legally entitled to work in Canada?

It is important to keep detailed and accurate records of the entire recruitment and selection process. This includes a written record of procedures and steps taken to meet human rights requirements or any other requirements under a collective agreement, if one exists. This documentation will not only make future recruitment and selection processes easier but also offers protection against complaints that hiring practices were unfair.

Job Offer, Orientation, and Training

Once the best candidate is selected, a job offer is made. Offers are often in writing and contain the terms and conditions of employment. The offer is either accepted or rejected. If it is rejected, an offer may be made to the next most-qualified applicant. If the process has yielded no other qualified candidates, the selection procedure must start anew.

After the candidate has accepted the offer, those not hired should still be kept in mind for any possible future openings. It is common courtesy to notify them that someone else has been selected, and a rejection, if made diplomatically, will retain their goodwill.

The first day on a new job is confusing for anyone. Thus, new employees should be given a proper orientation that introduces the new employees to their job responsibilities, their co-workers, and the organization's policies. A job description should be given to the new hire and explained in detail.

Tell the new employee the firm's objectives, policies, and rules. Explain your performance expectations and encourage the new hire to ask questions. Give a tour of the facilities and a look at the firm's product or service. Done properly by the supervisor, orientation should speed the building of a positive working relationship with the new employee.

A supervisor also is responsible for training and developing employees. Not only must new workers be trained in the new job, but current employees must be retrained and their skills updated to meet rapidly changing environments and job requirements. These responsibilities will be discussed further in Chapter 15, Developing Employees.

Concept Quiz

Complete the following true–false quiz by circling the correct answer. Answers are at the end of the quiz. After marking your answers, remember to go back and check your understanding of any answers you missed.

True or False   1. Early in the interview you should provide the applicant with as much detail as possible about the job being interviewed for.

True or False   2. No cost is associated with making a poor hire except the expense involved in going through the recruitment and selection process again.

True or False   3. A good interviewer avoids asking questions that can be answered with a simple "yes" or "no."

True or False   4. The use of assessment centres as a selection device is particularly helpful for hiring assembly-line workers.

True or False   5. Interviewing is commonly used as part of the selection process no matter what the level of job.

True or False   6. In large organizations, many staffing activities are conducted by a personnel specialist rather than the supervisor.

True or False   7. A job specification contains the minimal acceptable qualifications an employee must have to perform the job successfully.

True or False   8. Help-wanted advertisements typically produce the best candidates.

True or False   9. Interviews yield the most valid information and the least bias if they are informal and unstructured.

True or False   10. In general, the larger the organization, the easier it is to recruit job applicants.

Answers (1) True; (2) False; (3) True; (4) False; (5) True; (6) True; (7) True; (8) False; (9) False; (10) True

Behavioural Checklist

The following behaviours are important to recruitment and selection of new employees. Use them when evaluating your hiring skills and those of others.

Effective Hiring Managers:

- Use appropriate recruiting sources to find applicants.
- Employ valid and reliable selection devices when choosing among candidates.
- Act with certain knowledge of laws and government regulations.
- Reduce biases by interviewing candidates in a consistent and structured way.

Modelling Exercise
The Selection Process[30]

DIRECTIONS The entire class should read the following situation. Then, working together, the class develops a job description and job specifications for the position described. When in doubt about the details, class members should use their imagination. The objective is for the class to agree that these two lists are reasonable and complete. The instructor records the job description and job specifications on the chalkboard or overhead projector. Then the class discusses what recruitment sources Sam, the manager, should use. It lists them in descending order, and the instructor records the recommendations.

When the job description, job specifications, and list of recruitment avenues are complete, the class develops a set of interview questions. In addition to the questions, the class also should consider other ways to determine whether a candidate would be appropriate (e.g., observing some aspects of the candidates' behaviour during the interview). It should also take into consideration the goal of more closely matching the age and ethnicity of the employees to that of the clientele.

Next, four class members volunteer to act out the roles of Sam and the three candidates. Each candidate explains his or her background and why he or she would be right for the job. (Actors should feel free to add details to their descriptions.) Sam should interview each candidate for no more than five minutes.

TIME 30 minutes.

ACTORS Sam, the owner/manager of Sammy's Restaurant; Candidate #1: an eager college student without experience; Candidate #2: a woman who appears to be about 60 years old, with eight years of experience in the 1960s; Candidate #3: a man with four years of experience as a server in five different restaurants; Candidate #4: a middle-aged woman from a minority group with little job experience.

SITUATION Sam owns and manages Sammy's, a family-style restaurant that needs to hire a server. Although the pace is quick, and the pay is minimal, because the restaurant is part of a small chain an ambitious employee who performs well can advance within the organization.

SAM'S ROLE You recognize that as a result of hiring inexperienced people, the restaurant has suffered a high attrition rate, so you would like to get a more seasoned server. However, you're also aware that the salary and benefits are not competitive with other industries.

The restaurant is in an older neighborhood populated by many senior citizens and minority group members (Asian and Indo-Asian). Your current servers are young and white. You think that hiring an older, minority server, provided he or she was capable, would be a good idea.

MODELLING EXERCISE OBSERVATIONS

During the dialogue, observers should note closely how Sam treats each candidate, what questions he asks, and how the candidates respond both verbally and nonverbally. Be prepared to suggest additional questions and to draw conclusions both about Sam's interviewing technique as well as who seems to be the best-qualified applicant.

Observer's Rating Sheet

Using the following scale, rate Sam's application of techniques discussed in this chapter. Also write in comments in the spaces below each technique that will help explain your feedback.

1 Unsatisfactory	2 Weak	3 Adequate	4 Good	5 Outstanding

_____ Put the candidates at ease.

_____ Interviewed objectively.

_____ Covered the important points.

_____ Used open-ended questions.

_____ Asked the same questions of each candidate.

_____ Gave candidates a chance to ask questions.

_____ Complied with human rights or employment equity legislation.

Finally, the class discusses:

1. **The candidates** How did they appear? What could each have done differently?
2. **Selecting a candidate** By a show of hands, the class votes for which candidate it would recommend hiring. Why? List the pros and cons of each candidate.
3. **Interviewing technique**
   - How did the manager's style of questioning help or hurt the information-gathering process?
   - Did the candidates reveal anything about their acceptability in nonverbal ways?
   - How did the interviewing experience feel to the candidates? To Sam?

Group Exercises

In the three exercises that follow you will be asked to practise good hiring skills.

Group Exercise 1: Choosing a Payroll Manager[31]

SITUATION The chief financial officer in a large organization asks her two young assistants to help recruit and select a new payroll manager. She requests that the pair choose three semifinalists and then set up a second set of interviews for her. The assignment was given to Jack and Sue, who had the following conversation:

Jack: The controller wants us to come up with payroll manager candidates. Any ideas?

Sue: That's a really tough job. The payroll department handles a large volume of work.

Jack: Yeah, we have more turnover in that department than in any other department in the company.

Sue: It is not our fault people leave. Some excellent people have been in that department. It is just that the working conditions are difficult.

Jack: True. Well...let's develop the job description and specifications for this payroll manager position.

Sue: Okay. The person should have a degree in accounting, that's for sure.

Jack: This person gets to work in a nicely heated and air-conditioned office.

Sue: He or she should have really excellent accounting skills.

Jack: The candidate will have to maintain all the payroll records and pay all employees on time.

Sue: You just reminded me how many times the payroll department had to work overtime to get the cheques out on time. Remember when the cheques came out late on several occasions, and everybody got really mad?

Jack: Give me another idea we can use.

Sue: The person must be computer literate.

Jack: The person will supervise 10 people and report to the controller.

Sue: The payroll department is at corporate headquarters.

Jack: Sound decision-making skills are needed.

Sue: Well, I guess that does it.

Jack: Yeah, but we need to decide on a recruiting method.

Sue: The usual, I guess: Advertise in the paper.

Jack: Any other possibility? Headhunter maybe?

Sue: Okay, headhunter and classified ad. But what selection methods do you think would work best for this position?

Jack: An interview, probably. Because it is a supervisory position, we'll separately interview the candidates. You ask your questions and I'll ask mine. That way we'll probably cover all the bases. Then we'll compare notes and give the chief financial officer a list of semifinalists, whom she can then interview.

Sue: Anything else we need to think about?

Jack: Lunch, I'm hungry.

DIRECTIONS Divide into groups of four or five students each. Respond to the following exercise, then compare your answers to those of the other groups.

TIME 30 minutes.

1. Write out the job description based on information provided by Jack and Sue.
   Job description:
2. Write out the job specifications based on information provided by Jack and Sue.
   Job specifications:
3. What information was lacking in each case?
   a) Job description also requires:
   b) Job specifications also require:
4. Assuming no internal candidates are available, should other recruiting sources be used? Why or why not? If other means should be used, which ones and why?
5. Jack and Sue's primary mistakes were:
6. Are Jack and Sue on the right track to doing an effective job of recruiting and selecting? Why or why not?

Group Exercise 2: Questions for New Hires[32]

SITUATION 1 Procter & Gamble is looking for new graduates for a sales management training program. Each hiree will spend 18 to 24 months as a sales representative calling on retail grocers. After this training period, successful candidates can expect to be promoted to a sales supervisory position.

SITUATION 2 The Assembly of First Nations has an opening for a project manager to work in the Social Development unit. The primary duties are to coordinate a variety of projects and to liaise/communicate effectively with First Nations communities, the public, and the federal and provincial governments.

DIRECTIONS Choose either Situation 1 or Situation 2. Break into groups of three. Take up to 10 minutes to compose five challenging job interview questions that you think would be relevant in the hiring of these individuals. Then exchange your five questions with another group.

Each group should allocate one of the following roles to its three members: *interviewer, applicant,* and *observer.* The person playing the applicant should rough out a brief résumé of his or her background and experience, then give it to the interviewer.

Role-play a job interview for an additional 10 minutes. The interviewer should include, but not be limited to, the questions provided by the other group.

Observer's Rating Sheet

After the interview, evaluate the interviewer's behaviours by rating the following skills. Write comments in the spaces below each behaviour to use in explaining your feedback.

	Yes	No	Sometimes
Prepared questions well.	_____	_____	_____
Asked open-ended questions.	_____	_____	_____
Followed up with probing questions.	_____	_____	_____
Avoided illegal questions.	_____	_____	_____
Took diversity into account.	_____	_____	_____

Group Exercise 3: Sharpening Questions and Answers[33]

DIRECTIONS Break into five groups and discuss the following questions. One member of each group will present the group's best question for each alternative to the entire class.

For the following five closed-ended questions and the answers they might elicit, how would you rephrase these questions to make them open-ended? What would be appropriate answers to the revised questions?

1. *Q:* Do you work well under pressure?
   A: Pressure doesn't bother me.
2. *Q:* Do you think you will like the job if it is offered to you?
   A: I just like working.
3. *Q:* Do you require a lot of supervision?
   A: I do not need anyone telling me what to do.
4. *Q:* Do you get along well with people?
   A: Everyone likes me.
5. *Q:* Do you want to tell me anything else about yourself?
   A: No.

Application Questions

1. What types of questions have you been asked during an actual job interview? Open-ended? Closed-ended? Probing? Hypothetical? Other? Give an example of each.
2. Which of those questions were the toughest? Could you do a better job of answering them now? Why? What would your new answers be?
3. What recruiting source was used to hire you for one or more jobs?
4. What selection methods were used for a job you were offered? If a test was used, what type of test was it?
5. Were you, or was anyone you know, asked illegal discriminatory questions during an interview or on an application? If so, specify the area or areas (age, gender, race, etc.).

Reinforcement Exercises

The following are suggested activities for reinforcing the identifying and hiring techniques described in this chapter. You may want to adapt them to the Action Plan you will develop next, or try them independently.

1. Write a job analysis for a job you hold or have held. Write a job description and job specifications.
2. List the recruitment devices most applicable to any job you are likely to apply for in the future.
3. List what you think would be the best selection devices for your likely job.

Summary Checklist

Take a few minutes to reflect on your performance in the previous exercises. Assess yourself as to how your analysis compared to other students (and if you were a presenter, how others rated your skill). Make a check (√) next to those behaviours on which you may need improvement.

_____ Planning to fill human resource needs.
    1. Conduct human resources inventories.
    2. Complet job analyses.
      a. Write job descriptions.
      b. Write job specifications.

_____ Recruiting qualified applicants.
    1. Know the sources of potential job candidates.
    2. Use alternative sources to increase diversity of applicants.
    3. Use the Internet to access potential candidates.

_____ Employing valid and reliable selection methods for choosing the best candidates.
    1. Application forms.
    2. Written tests.
    3. Performance simulation tests.
    4. Background investigations.
    5. Physical exams.
    6. Interviews.

_____ Acting within laws and government regulations.
    1. Be familiar with federal, provincial or territorial human rights legislation prohibiting discrimination.
    2. Be aware of federal employment equity legislation and where it applies.
    3. Have knowledge of antidiscrimination regulations requiring valid testing.
    4. Have knowledge of antidiscrimination rules prohibiting discriminatory questions.

_____ Performing skilled interviews.
    1. Prepare a fixed set of questions for all applicants.
    2. Put the applicant at ease.
    3. Ask open-ended questions.
    4. Avoid illegal, discriminatory questions.
    5. Follow up with probing questions.
    6. Listen carefully to answers.
    7. Give candidate a chance to answer questions.
    8. Close the interview by explaining what happens next.

Action Plan

1. Which hiring skills do I most want to improve?
2. Why? What will be my payoff?
3. What potential obstacles stand in my way?
4. What are the specific things I will do to improve? (For examples, see Reinforcement Exercises.)
5. When will I do them?
6. How and when will I measure my success?

Skills Video

Interviewing Job Candidates

Structured interviews, with their prepared situational, willingness, and job knowledge questions, are designed to assist interviewers in reaching objective conclusions about candidates. All three types of questions are hypothetical job-oriented questions with predetermined answers that are consistently asked of all applicants. When applicants' answers are compared, the result is usually an unbiased basis for comparing their job skills, willingness and motivation to work, and quality of judgment and decision-making skills.

You may already have interview experience, on either side of the desk. Have you ever interviewed for a job and been nervous and anxious to make a good impression? You may have worried about saying too much or too little, or you may have felt unprepared for the questions you were asked.

Although you might at first identify with Quicktakes' new job applicant, Mary Byrns, you should also try to see the situation in the video from Hal's point of view. He is looking for a new producer, and in a small company such as Quicktakes, it is difficult to invest a lot of time in training new employees who have little or no experience. Hal needs someone who can get off to a quick start and maintain a high degree of self-motivation. Try to evaluate Mary's potential as a self-starter based on her behaviour in the interview.

Evaluate Hal's interviewing skills. Since there is no human resources department at Quicktakes, Hal, like managers at many small-to-medium-sized firms, has the responsibility both for screening job candidates and for making the final hiring decision. How well does he put Mary at ease? How does he react to her volunteering information about herself? Does he make any interviewing errors?

QUESTIONS
1. Did Hal conduct a structured interview? Explain your answer.
2. Hal has rated Mary a "strong candidate for the job." How do you think he arrived at this conclusion? Do you agree with his assessment? Why or why not?
3. What other facts about Mary's background and experience do you think Hal should have before he makes a decision about whether to hire her? (Assume that her résumé provides a brief job history and basic personal data.) How should Hal go about finding this information?
4. What should Mary know about Quicktakes before she decides whether to accept any offer that Hal may make? How can she find this out?
5. How could Hal have better prepared himself for the interview? How could Mary?

CHAPTER **14**
Evaluating Performance

Learning Objectives
After completing this chapter, you should be able to:

- Conduct performance evaluation interviews.
- Create evaluation criteria and performance indicators from stated goals.
- Apply the most effective methods to measure performance.
- Avoid rating errors.
- Provide meaningful feedback for development.
- Use fairness in discipline.

Self-Assessment Exercise

For each of the following questions, select the answer that best describes how you would prefer to conduct a performance evaluation.

		Usually	Sometimes	Seldom
1.	Compare performance results to original objectives.	_____	_____	_____
2.	Make sure the person knows what others do not like about his or her personality.	_____	_____	_____
3.	Focus on employee's behaviour, not the employee's characteristics.	_____	_____	_____
4.	Ask the recipient to summarize what I have said to ensure that my feedback is clearly understood.	_____	_____	_____
5.	Focus my comments on generalities rather than specific job-related behaviours.	_____	_____	_____
6.	Use objectives previously set with the employee as a basis for measuring performance.	_____	_____	_____

	Usually	Sometimes	Seldom
7. Be sure to use only evaluation criteria applicable to any management situation.	_____	_____	_____
8. Use multiple sources of information for measuring actual performance.	_____	_____	_____
9. Sometimes revise the standard of measurement rather than correct the employee.	_____	_____	_____
10. Conduct the performance feedback interview whenever a convenient opportunity arises, rather than scheduling it in advance.	_____	_____	_____

SCORING For Questions 1, 2, 4, 6, 8, and 9, give yourself 3 points for "Usually," 2 points for "Sometimes," and 1 point for "Seldom." For Questions 3, 5, 7, and 10, give yourself 3 points for "Seldom," 2 points for "Sometimes," and 1 point for "Usually."

INTERPRETATION Sum up your total points. A score of 27 or higher means you have a good understanding of the performance evaluation process. A score of 22 to 26 suggests you have some room for improvement. A score below 22 indicates that you should concentrate on improving this skill.

Concepts

The following individual quotes were reportedly taken from actual employee performance evaluations in a large corporation.[1]

- "Since my last report, this employee has reached rock bottom...and has started to dig."
- "This employee is really not so much of a 'has-been,' but more of a definite 'won't-be'."
- "This young lady has delusions of adequacy."
- "He sets low personal standards and then consistently fails to achieve them."
- "This employee is depriving a village somewhere of an idiot."
- "This employee should go far...and the sooner he starts, the better."

The preceding quotes will not help an employee's performance or career. They are not things managers want to hear about their employees either, because in today's competitive environment highly qualified employees are the primary source of sustained competitive advantage for most organizations.[2] In fact, these types of comments about employees' performance won't help anyone. Employees, too, are frustrated with performance appraisals. They report that reviews are inconsistent, discourage collaboration, and can be too subjective, especially when a supervisor wields all of the power.[3] Performance appraisals are also questioned because they bring together two conflicting purposes—learning and evaluation.[4] For example, it is difficult for employees to be honest about mistakes and learn from them when they are being evaluated. All of these concerns are an indication of the degree of frustration that can occur if the performance evaluation process is not carried out effectively.

So, why is performance evaluation so critical? **Performance appraisal** is the process of periodically measuring employees' progress toward agreed-upon objectives, providing constructive feedback, reinforcing successes with rewards, and taking corrective action if goals are not being achieved. Performance review is one of the primary tools for helping managers meet organizational goals and compete effectively internationally. Appraisals are important to obtain the best performance from employees, to help develop objectives for training programs, and to obtain employee feedback. They are important to employees because they often serve as the basis for promotions, terminations, training opportunities, and pay adjustments. When conducted effectively, performance appraisals can increase productivity and morale and decrease absenteeism and turnover. But when handled poorly, they can have the opposite effects.[5] This chapter is designed to help you develop the skills to manage the performance evaluation process effectively.

As you learned in Chapter 11, Planning and Goal Setting, setting goals is a prerequisite to performance evaluation. The goal-setting process provides a documented statement of what you intend an employee to accomplish, a form of acknowledgment, and a reminder of commitment. Setting objectives also establishes a basis for measuring performance and provides positive motivation to achieve goals.[6] In this chapter you will learn about how to measure progress toward goals and provide feedback to enhance employee performance and goal achievement.

The Evaluation Process

Evaluation is the process of monitoring activities to ensure that employees are accomplishing planned goals, rewarding performance, or correcting any significant deviations. Managers can't really know whether their employees are performing properly until they have evaluated what activities are being undertaken and have compared the actual performance with desired standards. It helps to think of the **evaluation process** as consisting of three separate and distinct steps: (1) measuring actual performance, (2) comparing actual performance against a standard, and (3) taking managerial action to reward performance or correct deviations or inadequate standards. If performance is positive, the employee's behaviour can be rewarded with praise, pay increases, or promotions. If performance is below standard, managers can seek to correct it or, depending on the nature of the deviation, discipline the employee.

FOCUS ON OBJECTIVES

If the manager has utilized goal setting as described in Chapter 11, Planning and Goal Setting, the standards of performance already exist and have been agreed upon by both the manager and employee. These standards are the specific, tangible, and verifiable objectives against which progress can be measured.

WHAT PERFORMANCE SHOULD BE MEASURED?

An evaluation system should be concerned only with an employee's actual performance. It should be based on those aspects of behaviour that are observable and are important to perform the job.

To determine actual performance, managers need to acquire information about it. This process is known as *measuring*, a key step in the evaluation process. Two important questions here are how to measure and what to measure.

The most frequently used sources of comprehensive and objective information for measuring actual performance are personal observation, statistical reports, oral reports, written reports, and computer-accessed databases. The effective manager tends to use multiple sources, recognizing that different sources provide different types of information. Personal observations obtained by talking with an employee, for instance, can be a rich source of detailed performance data.

What we measure is also critical to the evaluation process. Selecting the wrong criteria can have serious dysfunctional consequences. Besides, what we measure determines, to a great extent, those areas in which people in the organization will attempt to excel.[7]

Some evaluation criteria are applicable to any management situation. For instance, because all managers, by definition, influence the activities of others, criteria such as employee attendance or turnover rates can be measured. Keeping costs within budget is a common measure for monetary costs. Any comprehensive evaluation system, however, needs to recognize the diversity of activities among managers. A production manager in a manufacturing plant might use measures of the quantity of units produced per day, number of units produced per labour-hour, or percentage of units rejected by customers because of inferior quality. The manager of an administrative department in a government agency might use number of orders processed per hour or average time required to process service calls. Marketing executives often use such criteria as percentage of market captured, average dollar value per sale, or number of customer visits per salesperson.

The behaviours or characteristics measured by a performance appraisal should be related to the job and to succeeding on the job. For example, if the appraisal measures "grooming," then good grooming should be important for success in the job. Because of this requirement, a supervisor and others responsible for the content of performance appraisals should make sure that what they measure is relevant to a particular job.

In Canada, human rights law is based on the principle that employment decisions should be made on a person's ability to do the job and those factors related to job specifications, qualifications, and performance. Therefore, just as hiring should be based on a candidate's ability to perform the essential tasks of a particular job, performance evaluations should be based on the employee's success in carrying out those tasks. The ratings in a performance appraisal should not be discriminatory; they should not be based on an employee's race, sex, age, marital or family status, or any other prohibited grounds but on an employee's ability to meet standards of performance. Managers are bound to conduct evaluations in good faith, acting in a fair, consistent, and objective manner. As such, employees should know in advance what those standards are and have an opportunity to comment on the assessment.

It is especially important that managers make certain that their performance appraisals do not result in adverse effects on minorities, women, or older employees. Suggestions to make performance appraisal systems fair, consistent, and objective include: (1) deriving the content of the appraisal system from job analyses; (2) emphasizing work behaviours rather than personal traits; (3) ensuring that the results of the appraisals are communicated to employees; (4) ensuring that employees are allowed to give feedback during the appraisal interview; (5) training managers to conduct proper evaluations; (6) ensuring that appraisals are written, documented, and retained; and (7) ensuring that personnel decisions are consistent with the performance appraisals.[8]

PERFORMANCE APPRAISAL CRITERIA The three most popular sets of criteria used in appraising performance are individual task outcomes, behaviours, and traits.[9] **Individual task outcomes** measure ends, rather than means. A salesperson, for example, might be assessed on overall sales volume, dollar increase in sales, or number of new accounts established. When specific outcomes are difficult to attribute directly to one employee's actions, **behaviours** that contribute to these goals might be all you can measure. If the employee being appraised is part of a team, for example, the team's task outcome can be measured, but the contribution of each individual on the team may be difficult to identify. In this case, example behaviours you could measure would be things such as attendance, number of contact calls made per week, or number of deadlines achieved. Individual **traits** or characteristics such as "good attitude," "highly motivated," and "dependable" are weaker criteria than other task outcomes or behaviour because they are more difficult to correlate with goal achievement. Therefore, caution should be exercised if they are used.

MEASURING PERFORMANCE: RATING METHODS FOR COMPARING PERFORMANCE TO STANDARDS

The comparison step determines the degree of variation between actual performance and the standard. Because some variation in performance can be expected in all activities, it is critical to determine the acceptable range of variation. Deviations in excess of this range merit corrective action. In the comparison stage, managers should be particularly concerned with the size and direction of the variation. But, how should these comparisons be made and documented? Six methods are described next.[10]

CHECKLISTS On a checklist appraisal the manager simply answers yes or no to a series of questions about an employee's performance. Examples of checklist questions are provided in Exhibit 14-1. Items on the list can then be scored or reviewed to determine a rating for the employee's evaluation. Although checklists are easy to complete, they require a great deal of thought and analysis to be sure that meaningful questions are included for each job. They usually do not provide ways to adjust the answers for special circumstances that may affect performance.[11] To make up for this weakness, checklists are sometimes combined with essays.

WRITTEN ESSAYS The written essay requires no complex forms or extensive training to complete. Based on remembered observations, the appraiser writes a narrative describing an employee's past performance, strengths, weaknesses, potential, and suggestions for improvement—but the results often reflect the ability of the writer. The quality of the performance review may be determined as much by the evaluator's memory, perception, and writing skill as by the employee's actual level of performance. Essay appraisals are often used to supplement checklist questionnaire appraisals to allow for a description and explanation of ratings.

CRITICAL INCIDENTS With this method, the manager writes down anecdotes that describe what the employee did that was especially effective or ineffective. A list of critical incidents provides a set of examples to show the employee specific behaviours that are desirable and those that call for improvement. The key here is that only specific behaviours, not personality traits, are cited. A drawback is that the definition of a critical

Exhibit 14-1 Example Checklist Appraisal Questions

	Yes	No
1. Does the employee willingly cooperate with others in completing work assignments?	_____	_____
2. Does the employee have adequate job knowledge to perform duties in a satisfactory manner?	_____	_____
3. In terms of quality, is the employee's work acceptable?	_____	_____
4. Does the employee meet deadlines for the completion of work assignments?	_____	_____
5. Does the employee's record indicate unexcused absences?	_____	_____
6. Does the employee follow safety rules and regulations?	_____	_____

Source: S.E. Catt and D.S. Miller, *Supervision: Working with People*, 2nd ed. (Homewood, IL: Richard D. Irwin, 1991) 374. © Irwin Co. Reprinted by permission of the McGraw-Hill Companies.

incident is unclear and may be interpreted differently by different managers. Also, managers need to keep a log of incidents, which is a lot of work, for incidents that may occur at inconvenient times.

GRAPHIC RATING SCALES In this commonly used method, a set of performance factors, such as quantity and quality of work, depth of knowledge, cooperation, loyalty, attendance, honesty, and initiative, are listed. The manager then goes down the list and rates each on incremental scales. The scales typically specify five levels, so a factor such as *job knowledge* might be rated from 1 ("poorly informed about work duties") to 5 ("has complete mastery of all phases of the job").

Though they don't provide the depth of information that essays or critical incidents do, graphic rating scales are easy to use and less time-consuming to develop and administer. They also allow for quantitative analysis and comparison. On the other hand, the ratings are subjective so that what one manager deems "excellent" may be only "average" to another. Some of these problems can be overcome by providing descriptions of excellent or poor behaviours in each area. An example of a graphic rating scale is provided in Exhibit 14-2.

BEHAVIOURALLY ANCHORED RATING SCALES This approach combines major elements from the critical incident and graphic rating scale approaches. The manager rates employees on items along a continuum, but the points are examples of actual behaviour on the given job. Examples of job-related behaviour and performance dimensions are found by asking participants to give specific illustrations of effective and ineffective behaviour regarding each performance dimension. These behavioural examples are then translated into a set of performance dimensions, each dimension having varying levels of performance. The results of this process are behavioural descriptions, such as "anticipates, plans, executes, solves immediate problems," "carries out orders," and "handles emergency situations." An example of a behaviourally anchored rating scale is illustrated in Exhibit 14-3.

MULTIPERSON COMPARISONS With this method, a specific individual's performance is evaluated against the performance of one or more others. It is a relative rather than an absolute measuring device. The three most popular comparisons are group order ranking, individual ranking, and paired comparisons.

The **group order ranking** requires the manager to place employees into a particular classification, such as top one-fifth or second one-fifth. When managers use this method to appraise employees, they deal with all their employees. Therefore, a forced distribution will be created that does not consider the degree of difference between employees in each category. For example, if a manager has 20 employees, only 4 can be in the top fifth and, of course, 4 must also be relegated to the bottom fifth.

The **individual ranking** approach rank-orders employees from best to worst. If the manager is required to appraise 30 employees, this approach assumes that the difference between the first and second employee is the same as that between the twenty-first and twenty-second. Even though some of the employees may be closely grouped, this approach allows for no ties. The result is a clear ordering of employees, from the highest performer down to the lowest, but no indication of the degree of difference is provided.

The **paired comparison** approach compares each employee with every other employee and rates each as either the superior or the weaker member of the pair. After all paired comparisons are made, each employee is assigned a summary ranking based on the number of superior scores he or she achieved. This approach ensures that each employee is compared against every other, but it can obviously become unwieldy when many employees are being compared.

Exhibit 14-2 Sample Graphic Rating Scale

Name_____ Dept._____ Date_____

	Outstanding	Good	Satisfactory	Fair	Unsatisfactory
Quantity of work Volume of acceptable work under normal conditions Comments:	[ ]	[ ]	[ ]	[ ]	[ ]
Quality of work Thoroughness, neatness, and accuracy of work Comments:	[ ]	[ ]	[ ]	[ ]	[ ]
Knowledge of job Clear understanding of the facts or factors pertinent to the job Comments:	[ ]	[ ]	[ ]	[ ]	[ ]
Personal qualities Personality, appearance, sociability, leadership, integrity Comments:	[ ]	[ ]	[ ]	[ ]	[ ]
Cooperation Ability and willingness to work with associates, supervisors, and staff toward common goals Comments:	[ ]	[ ]	[ ]	[ ]	[ ]
Dependability Conscientious, thorough, accurate, reliable with respect to attendance, lunch periods, reliefs, etc. Comments:	[ ]	[ ]	[ ]	[ ]	[ ]
Initiative Earnestness in seeking increased responsibilities, self-starting, unafraid to proceed alone Comments:	[ ]	[ ]	[ ]	[ ]	[ ]

Source: J.M. Ivancevich, *Human Resource Management: Foundations of Personnel,* 7th ed. (New York: Irwin/McGraw-Hill, 1998) 272. © Irwin Co. Reprinted by permission of the McGraw-Hill Companies.

Exhibit 14-3 Sample Behaviourally Anchored Rating Scale (BARS)

Engineer's Name: _____

9 _____	This engineer applies a full range of technical skills and can be expected to perform all assignments in an excellent manner.
8 _____	
7 _____	This engineer is able to apply in most situations a good range of technical skills and can be expected to perform most assignments well.
6 _____	
5 _____	This engineer is able to apply some technical skills and can be expected to adequately complete most assignments.
4 _____	
3 _____	This engineer has difficulty applying technical skills and can be expected to bring in most projects late.
2 _____	
1 _____	This engineer is confused about using technical skills and can be expected to disrupt the completion of work because of this deficiency.

Source: J.M. Ivancevich, *Human Resource Management: Foundations of Personnel*, 7th ed. (New York: Irwin/McGraw-Hill, 1998) 277. © Irwin Co. Reprinted by permission of the McGraw-Hill Companies.

360 DEGREE FEEDBACK The 360 degree feedback evaluation consists of a process whereby employees compare their own assessment of competencies with the way they are seen and experienced by other significant persons such as their manager, peers, staff, direct reports, and so on. Employees receive a gap analysis between how they see themselves and how others perceive them. This type of feedback can be helpful as it can give a sense of an individual's impact on others in such areas as cooperation with workers outside their department or attitude towards customers and suppliers.

The purpose of 360 degree feedback is to provide an employee with a good all-around perspective and is most useful when used for developmental purposes rather than for compensation or promotion decisions. To be useful, survey respondents need to be fully aware of the scope of the individual's work responsibilities. In addition, high levels of organizational trust are necessary, as are the skills to give and accept feedback. When the measured competencies are relevant to the organization's business and strategic directions and when feedback is accepted, employees are more likely to begin the hard process of changing behaviours.

THINGS TO WATCH OUT FOR WHEN RATING PERFORMANCE

Several common potential errors can occur when rating performance and they can invalidate the accuracy of an appraisal. They include rushing, bias, leniency, central tendency, recency emphasis, focusing on activities, and the halo effect. **Bias** occurs when managers develop feelings about employees based on work-related interactions that may have little to do with their performance. These feelings can be negative, positive, or neutral, and they may be related to personality, race, religion, or other nonwork-related factors. Feelings should be separated from objective assessments when rating work performance.

Managers with positive feelings (bias) towards certain employees tend to be lenient when rating their performance. **Leniency** is the grouping of ratings at the positive end of the performance scale instead of spreading them throughout the scale. Consequently, employees are rated higher than actual performance warrants.[12]

When managers have neutral feelings about employees, they exhibit a **central tendency** when rating their performance. Central tendency occurs when performance appraisal statistics indicate that most employees are evaluated as doing average or above-average work, even though in actuality a distribution is present because all employees do not perform the same all the time on specific tasks.[13]

The **recency emphasis** occurs when performance evaluations are based on most recent work performed. It sometimes occurs because of the difficulty in remembering things that happened six months to a year ago versus work performed one or two months before evaluation. It also can occur when a manager is **rushing** the evaluation process because of a heavy workload or lack of sufficient time. Rushing also can make managers susceptible to **focusing on activities**, which occurs when employees are rated on how busy they appear versus how well they perform in achieving results.

The next rating error occurs when managers allow a single prominent characteristic of an employee to influence their judgment on all other items in the performance appraisal. This problem often results in the employee receiving approximately the same rating on every item.[14] It can go either way, however. The **halo effect** often occurs when a manager has positive feelings about an employee, causing him or her to rate the employee positively on all criteria because of outstanding performance in one specific area that has impressed the manager.[15] On the other hand, if the manager feels negatively about an employee, the **horns effect** may occur. In this case, a manager rates an employee low on all criteria based on unfavourable performance on only one.[16]

Bias, leniency, central tendency, recency, and activity errors make it difficult to separate superior from marginal performance. These errors also make it difficult to compare ratings from different managers. For example, it is possible for a good performer who is evaluated by a manager with a negative bias, or who is committing central tendency errors to receive a lower rating than a poor performer who is rated by a manager with a positive bias or one who is committing leniency errors.[17]

Rushing, recency emphasis, personal biases, and halo or horns effects can also cause errors in performance appraisals. Rushed managers with biases tend to look for employee behaviours that conform to their halo or horns first impressions of employees, and they do not take the time to seriously consider contradictory evidence.

TAKING MANAGERIAL ACTION

Managers can choose among three courses of action in this final step of the evaluation process: (1) they can do nothing; (2) they can correct the actual performance; or (3) they can revise the standard. Doing nothing is not really a feasible alternative if performance is not acceptable, so let's look more closely at the latter two options.

CORRECT ACTUAL PERFORMANCE If the source of variation from anticipated results is deficient performance, managers will want to take corrective action. Examples of such corrective action include a change in work methods, reorganization of work groups, or providing employees with training. First you will want to determine how and why performance has deviated. This analysis will take more time, but it will increase the chances that you can permanently correct significant variances between standard and actual performance, rather than just provide a band-aid for a problem that will reemerge later.

REVISE THE STANDARD Sometimes the variance is a result of an unrealistic standard—that is, the goal may be too high or too low. In such cases it is the standard that needs corrective attention, not the performance. A more troublesome problem is the revising of a performance standard downward. If an employee falls significantly short of reaching the target, the natural response is to shift the blame for the variance to the standard.

Students, for example, who make a low grade on a test may claim the test was too difficult. Rather than explore the idea that they are not familiar enough with the concepts and application, students argue that the standards are unreasonable. Similarly, salespeople who fail to meet their monthly quota may attribute the failure to an unrealistic quota. It may be true that standards are too high, resulting in a significant variance and acting to demotivate those employees being assessed against it. Keep in mind, however, that if employees or managers do not meet the standard, the first thing they are likely to attack is the standard itself. If you believe the standard is realistic, hold your ground. Explain your position, reaffirm to the employee that you expect future performance to improve, and then take the necessary corrective action to turn that expectation into reality.

Performance Evaluation as a Means of Providing Constructive Feedback

Many managers are reluctant to give performance feedback. In fact, unless pressured by organizational policies and controls, a large number of managers are likely to ignore this responsibility.[18] At least three reasons can be cited for this avoidance behaviour.[19] First, managers are often uncomfortable discussing performance weaknesses with employees. Given that almost every employee could stand to improve in some areas, managers fear a confrontation when presenting negative feedback. Second, many employees tend to become defensive when their weaknesses are pointed out. Instead of accepting the feedback as constructive and a basis for improving performance, some employees challenge the evaluation by criticizing the manager or redirecting blame to someone else. Finally, employees may tend to have an inflated assessment of their own performance. So even when managers are providing "good news," employees are likely to perceive it as "not good enough!"

In spite of managers' reluctance to give performance feedback, their employees still need it, so the solution is to train managers in how to conduct constructive feedback sessions. An effective review—one in which the employee perceives the appraisal to be fair, the manager to be sincere, and the climate to be constructive—can result in the employee's leaving the interview with a positive attitude, with knowledge about the performance areas in which he or she needs to improve, and motivated to correct the deficiencies.[20] These things are more likely to happen if the performance review is designed more as a coaching activity than a judgmental process.

THE VALUE OF FEEDBACK IN A PERFORMANCE EVALUATION

An important reason to be skilled at giving feedback in a performance interview is because it can increase employee performance in a number of ways.[21]

First, feedback can induce a person who previously had no goals to set some. And, as was demonstrated previously, goals act as motivators to higher performance. Second, where goals exist, feedback tells people how well they are progressing toward those goals. To the degree that the feedback is favourable, it acts as a positive reinforcer. Third, if the feedback indicates inadequate performance, this knowledge may result in increased effort. Further, the content of the feedback can suggest ways—other than exerting more effort—to improve performance. Fourth, feedback often induces people to raise their goal sights after attaining a previous goal. Fifth, providing feedback to employees conveys that others care how they are doing. So feedback is an indirect form of recognition that can motivate people to higher levels of performance.[22]

POSITIVE VERSUS NEGATIVE FEEDBACK

Just as managers treat positive and negative feedback differently, so, too, do recipients. Positive feedback is more readily and accurately perceived than negative feedback. Further, while positive feedback is almost always accepted, the negative variety often meets resistance.[23] Why? The logical answer seems to be that people want to hear good news and block out the bad. Positive feedback fits what most people wish to hear and already believe about themselves. As a result, you may need to adjust your style accordingly.

Does this tendency mean you should avoid giving negative feedback? No! What it means is that you need to be aware of potential resistance and learn to use negative feedback in situations where it is most likely to be accepted.[24] What are those situations? Research indicates that negative feedback is most likely to be accepted when it comes from a credible source or if it is objective in form. Subjective impressions carry weight only when they come from a person with high status and credibility.[25] Negative feedback that is supported by hard data or specific examples has a better chance of being accepted than do subjective evaluations.

THE PERFORMANCE EVALUATION FEEDBACK PROCESS

As a coaching activity, the performance appraisal identifies areas where employee growth and development are needed.[26] The feedback interview is the last step in the performance evaluation process. It follows the establishment of performance standards, the gathering of performance data, and actually rating performance. During the performance interview the ratings are shared with the employee in an effort to clarify any personnel decisions that have been made based upon them, and to help the employee learn and develop. Following are some guidelines for conducting a successful performance evaluation interview.

The performance evaluation interview can be broken down into four stages.[27] It begins with *preparation*, followed by the *opening*, a period of *questioning and discussion*, and a *conclusion*. During the last three stages of the performance review interview, a problem-solving approach is recommended. This is where the manager acts as a partner and works jointly with the employee to create a development plan. To use this format, you need to practise your communication skills, especially effective listening, during these stages of the performance review interview.

PREPARATION **Schedule the interview in advance and be prepared.** Simply calling an employee in and giving feedback that is not well organized serves little purpose for you or your employee. For a performance review interview to be effective, you should plan ahead.[28] Review the employee's job description. Go over your rating sheet. Identify the issues you wish to address and have specific examples to reinforce what you are saying. Have you carefully considered the employee's strengths as well as weaknesses? Can you substantiate, with specific examples, all points of praise and criticism? Given your past experiences with the employee, what problems, if any, do you anticipate popping up in the review? How do you plan to react to these problems? Once you have worked out these kinds of issues, you should schedule a specific time and place for the review and give the employee ample advance notice. Make sure that what you do is done in private and can be completed without interruptions. You may need to close your office door, have your phone calls held, and so on.

OPENING **Put the employee at ease.** The performance review can be a traumatic experience for the best of employees. People don't like to hear their work criticized. Add the fact that people tend to overrate themselves and you have the ingredients for tension and confrontation. Because the employee is apt to be nervous, be supportive and understanding.

Be sure that the employee understands the purpose of the interview. Employees are often concerned about whether the results of the evaluation interview will be used for personnel decisions or to promote their growth and development.[29] In the problem-solving approach, the interview provides recognition for things the employee is doing well and an opportunity to discuss any job-related problems. Any uncertainty the employee may have about what will transpire during the review and the resulting consequences should be clarified at the start.[30]

QUESTIONING AND DISCUSSION **Keep it goal-oriented.** Feedback should not be given primarily to "dump" or "unload" pent-up feelings on the recipient.[31] If you have to say something negative, make sure it is directed toward the *recipient's* goals. Keep in mind who your feedback is designed to help. If it is you, just to get something off your chest, for example, it is probably a good idea just to keep these statements to yourself. This kind of "feedback" undermines your credibility and lessens the credibility and influence of future feedback.

Make it well-timed. Feedback is most meaningful to a recipient if the interval between his or her behaviour and the receipt of feedback about that behaviour is short. To illustrate, a sales associate who makes a mistake during a sales presentation is more likely to respond to a manager's suggestions for improvement right after the mistake, immediately following the presentation, or a few days later, rather than to feedback provided by the manager several months later. If you have to spend time re-creating a situation and refreshing someone's memory of it, the feedback you are providing is likely to be ineffective.[32] Moreover, if you are particularly concerned with changing behaviour, delays providing feedback on the undesirable actions lessen the likelihood that the feedback will be effective in bringing about the desired change.[33] Of course, making feedback prompt merely for the sake of promptness can backfire if you have insufficient information, if you are angry, or if you are otherwise emotionally upset. In such instances, *well-timed* may mean "somewhat delayed."

Minimize threats. Create a helpful and constructive climate.[34] Try to maximize encouragement and support, while minimizing threats.[35] Little value comes from reminding a person of some shortcoming over which he or she has no control. Negative feedback should be directed toward work-related behaviour that the employee can do something about.[36] For example, to criticize an employee who is late because he forgot to set his alarm is valid. To criticize the same employee for being late when the subway he takes to work every day had a power failure, trapping him underground for half an hour, is not valid. He could do nothing to correct what happened. Additionally, when the manager gives negative feedback concerning something that is controllable, it may be a good idea to indicate specifically what can be done to improve the situation. This tactic takes some of the sting out of the criticism and offers guidance to recipients who understand the problem but do not know how to resolve it.

Obtain employee participation. The more employees talk, the more satisfied they will be with the review.[37] So, let employees do the majority of the talking. Get the employee's perceptions of what you are saying, especially if you are addressing a problem. Of course, you are not looking for excuses. But you need to be empathetic to the employee. Get his or her side. Maybe something has contributed to the issue. Letting employees speak involves them in the review, and just might add information you were unaware of.

Encourage the employee to engage in self-evaluation. If the climate is supportive, employees may openly acknowledge performance problems you have identified, thus eliminating your need to raise them. They may even offer viable solutions to these problems.

Criticize performance but not the person. Feedback, particularly the negative kind, should be descriptive rather than judgmental.[38] If something needs to be criticized, direct the criticism at specific job-related behaviours that negatively affect the employee's performance.[39] It is the person's performance that is unsatisfactory, not the individual person. No matter how upset you are, keep the feedback job-related and never criticize someone personally because of an inappropriate action. Telling people they are "stupid," "incompetent," or the like is almost always counterproductive. It provokes such an emotional reaction that the performance deviation itself is apt to be overlooked. Remember that you are criticizing a job-related behaviour, not the person. You may be tempted to tell someone he or she is "rude and insensitive" (which may well be true); however, such a comment is hardly impersonal. Better to say something like "You interrupted me three times with questions that were not urgent when you knew I was talking long distance to a customer in Scotland."

Focus on specific behaviours. Feedback should be specific rather than general.[40] General statements are vague and provide little useful information, especially if you are attempting to "correct" a problem. Document your employee's performance ratings with specific examples.[41] Avoid statements such as "You have a bad attitude" or "I'm really impressed with the good job you did." They are vague, and while they provide information, they don't tell the recipient enough to correct the "bad attitude" or on *what basis* you concluded that a "good job" had been done. You can generate more positive results from saying something like, "Jack, you called yesterday to say that you would have to miss the project proposal meeting because you did not have time to read the preliminary report, and today you are leaving work three hours early for your daughter's soccer game. I am concerned about your commitment and involvement to completing the new project proposal on time. Is there anything we need to discuss about it?"

Statements that focus on specific behaviours tell the recipient *why* you are being critical or complimentary. These supporting statements add credibility to your ratings and help employees to better understand what you mean by "good" and "bad." Tell your employee how you came to your "conclusion" on his or her performance. Hard data help your employees to identify with specific behaviours.

When criticizing, soften the tone but not the message. If criticism is necessary, do not water down the message, do not dance around the issue, and certainly do not avoid discussing a problem in the hope that it will just go away. State your criticism thoughtfully and show concern for the employee's feelings, but do not soften the message. Criticism is criticism, even if it is constructive. When you try to sell it as something else, you are liable to create ambiguity and misunderstanding.

Do not exaggerate. Don't make extreme statements in order to make a point. If an employee has been late for four out of five recent meetings, do not say "You are *always* late to meetings." Avoid absolutes such as *always* or *never*. Such terms encourage defensiveness and undermine your credibility. An employee only has to introduce one exception to your "always" or "never" statement to destroy the entire statement's validity.

Give positive as well as negative feedback. Avoid turning the performance review into a totally negative feedback session.[42] Also, identify the things that were done correctly and reinforce them. State what was done well and why it deserves recognition.

Tailor the feedback to fit the person. Take into consideration the person to whom the feedback is directed. You should consider the recipient's past performance and your estimate of his or her future potential in designing the frequency, amount, and content of performance feedback.[43] For high performers with potential for growth, feedback should be frequent enough to prod them into taking corrective action, but not so frequent that it is experienced as controlling and saps their initiative. For adequate performers who have settled into their jobs and have limited potential for advancement, little feedback is needed because they have displayed reliable and steady behaviour in the past, know their tasks, and realize what needs to be done. For poor performers—that is, people who will need to be removed from their jobs if their performance doesn't improve—feedback should be frequent and specific, and the connection between acting on the feedback and negative sanctions such as written warnings, suspension or termination should be made explicit.

CONCLUSION **Ensure understanding.** To be effective your feedback should be concise and complete enough so that the recipient clearly and fully understands it.[44] Consistent with our discussion of listening techniques in Chapter 5, Interpersonal Communication, you should have the recipient rephrase the content of your feedback to see whether it fully captures the meaning you intended. As the review nears its conclusion, encourage the employee to summarize the discussion that has taken place.[45] This process gives the employee an opportunity to put the entire review into perspective. It will also tell you whether you have succeeded in clearly communicating your evaluation.

Detail a future plan of action. In areas of performance inadequacies, the final part of the review should be devoted to helping the employee draft a detailed, step-by-step plan to improve the situation.[46] This plan includes what has to be done, when, and how you will monitor the activities. Offer whatever assistance you can to help the employee. Your role should be supportive: "What can I do to provide assistance?" Do you need to make yourself more available to answer questions? Do you need to give the employee more freedom or responsibility? Would securing funds to send the employee to professional meetings or training programs help?[47] It must be made clear that it is the employee, not you, who has to make the corrections. On the other hand, do not forget that good performance should be reinforced, and that new performance goals need to be set even for exceptional employees. Some additional guidelines for improving performance appraisal interviews are provided in Exhibit 14-4.

Exhibit 14-4 Guidelines for Improving Performance Appraisal Interviews

The following guidelines can provide a framework for improving employee performance review feedback evaluations.

- Review evaluations written by other experienced supervisors to see what works and what doesn't.
- Keep notes throughout the evaluation period. Do not rely on recall at the end of the time.
- Seek input from other observers when appropriate.
- Base written evaluations on multiple, firsthand observations.
- Know what you are looking for. Evaluate the right things. Concentrate exclusively on factors directly related to job performance.
- Don't include rumours, allegations, or guesswork as part of your written evaluations.
- Be complete. Include the good, the bad, and the ugly.
- Do not be afraid to criticize. Do not forget to praise.
- Focus on improvement. Use the evaluation to set goals for better performance.
- Never use an evaluation as a threat or as punishment.
- Supplement periodic written evaluations with frequent verbal feedback. Negative written evaluation should not come as a surprise.
- Do not put anything in writing that you would not say to the employee in person.
- Do not beat around the bush or sugarcoat needed criticism. Say what has to be said and move on.
- If checklists are part of the evaluation, be sure written comments are consistent with the items checked.
- Be as specific as possible. Use examples. Generalities don't help much in targeting action or improvement plans.
- Relate evaluations to previous reviews. Are things better? Worse? The same?
- Allow plenty of time to prepare evaluations properly. Do not work under pressure.

Exhibit 14-4 continued

- Avoid completing an evaluation when you are angry or frustrated.
- Choose words carefully. The goal is clarity.
- Let the evaluation "cool" overnight before distributing it.
- Be willing to change an evaluation if new information becomes available.

Source: R.D. Ramsey, "How to Write Better Employee Evaluations," *Supervision* (June 1998): 5ff. Reprinted by permission. © National Research Bureau, P.O. Box 1, Burlington, IA 52601–0001.

Evaluating Team Performance

Performance evaluation concepts have been almost exclusively developed with only individual employees in mind. This fact reflects the historical belief that individuals are the core building blocks around which organizations are built. As more organizations use teams, there is a need to evaluate team performance effectively. Information on team performance will be covered in Chapter 16, Creating Teams.

Disciplining Employees[48]

Unfortunately, there are incidents such as theft, destruction of company property, and alcohol or drug use that require a manager to discipline an employee. In these difficult times, what's the process to follow? A fair and just disciplinary process has three main parts: policies and regulations, a system of progressive penalties, and an appeal process. A company that follows this process will satisfy the Canadian courts, which have repeatedly insisted upon the fair treatment of an employee during disciplinary action or termination.[49]

Company policies and regulations should be widely distributed and known to employees. Examples of policies and regulations are: *the use of alcohol or drugs during working hours or reporting to work under the influence of drugs or alcohol are strictly prohibited;* or *the selling of unauthorized goods or gambling are not permitted on company premises;* or *employees are expected to meet established standards of quality.* The purpose of these policies and regulations is to identify what is and what is not acceptable behaviour. A company will have met this criterion if employees have been given these regulations in writing, at an orientation session, or in an employee handbook.

A system of progressive penalties should be in place. Penalties can progress from verbal warnings to written warnings to suspension to termination. The severity of the penalty should be in proportion to the type of offence and the number of times it has occurred. For example, a first offence of unexcused lateness would usually receive a verbal warning, and a fourth offence, termination. More severe offences such as drug use on the job, however, may result in immediate termination if specified in the company regulations.

Lastly, an appeal process should be available. This allows an employee to question the fairness of the process and the disciplinary action taken.

GUIDELINES FOR DISCIPLINING EMPLOYEES

A manager plays a significant role in all disciplinary actions. Here are some guidelines to ensure that the process is fair and the actions taken can be defended.

BURDEN OF PROOF A person is always considered innocent until proven guilty and, therefore, the burden of proof is on the employer. Get the facts. Don't base any disciplinary decisions on hearsay or general impressions. Be sure that the evidence collected is substantial and supports the charge of wrongdoing.

DUE PROCESS Follow the established progressive discipline procedures. Adequately warn the employee of the disciplinary consequences of the misconduct. Do not deny an employee an opportunity to tell his or her side of the story. All employees have the right to legal counsel and all unionized employees have the right to bring a union representative to a disciplinary meeting. Keep careful records of evaluations, memos that outline necessary improvements, or warnings.

PENALTY Be sure that the action taken is without discrimination, and is consistent with similar situations appropriate to the alleged misconduct and the past work history of the employee.

DISCIPLINARY MEETING To ensure the dignity of the employee, conduct the meeting in private unless the employee has requested legal counsel. Provide a clear explanation of the problem behaviour.

DISCIPLINE WITHOUT PUNISHMENT

Formal punishment often creates bad feelings that can linger for a long time, reducing employee cooperation. To avoid this shortcoming, some employers suggest a non-punitive approach. This means getting an employee to accept the rules and reducing the disciplinary action. The process usually involves a verbal reminder of the reason for the rule and the fact that he or she has a responsibility to meet performance standards. A written record of the incident should be kept in the manager's file. If a second incident occurs, a written reminder should be sent to the employee with a copy placed in the employee's HR file. In addition, hold a private meeting with the employee expressing the need to act responsibly. If a third incident occurs, meet with the employee to investigate the possibility that the person is ill-suited for the job. Give the employee a paid one-day leave. Tell the employee to consider whether or not the job is right for him or her and whether or not the employee wants to abide by the company's rules. When the employee returns, ask for his or her decision. If the answer is positive, work out a plan to assist the employee to change his or her behaviour.

Non-punitive discipline is consistent with the current trend to increase employees' control of their job and working conditions. Although appropriate for less severe violations of the company rules, some behaviours such as criminal acts or fighting require the formal approach previously outlined.

Dismissal[50]

Dismissal is the involuntary termination of a person's employment. Dismissal should only occur when sufficient or just cause exists and after all reasonable attempts have been made to restore the effectiveness of the employee. It is the most drastic disciplinary step and, because of the serious implications, a manager should involve specialists from human resources or obtain legal advice prior to acting. While good employer–employee relations are always the goal, it is especially important that an employer be honest, reasonable, and respectful at the time of dismissal.

GROUNDS FOR DISMISSAL

Dismissal for just cause is based on four principles: unsatisfactory performance; misconduct; lack of qualifications; and changed requirements of or elimination of the job. Unsatisfactory performance is a persistent failure to meet established job standards and can include excessive absenteeism and chronic lateness. Misconduct is deliberate violation of company rules and can include disobedience of the boss's authority, theft, or drug or alcohol use at work. Lack of qualifications is an inability to do the job although the employee is diligent in attempting to carry out his or her duties. Because the employee is trying to do the job, every effort should be made to re-assign the person. Changed requirements of the job is the inability to do the job because the nature of the job has changed. For example, the introduction of advanced technology can change the job or even eliminate it. Again, in this case, every effort should be made to find for the employee another job of equal level within the company.

THE EMPLOYMENT CONTRACT

The employer–employee relationship in Canada is governed by an employment contract, which may be in writing or based on mutual understanding. If the contract is for a specific length of time, the employee cannot be dismissed without just cause. However, employees are often hired under an implied contract where employment is for an indefinite amount of time. In this case, an employee may only be terminated after either party gives *reasonable notice*.[51]

Canadian employers can only terminate an employee's contract *without* reasonable notice when just cause exists. If just cause does not exist, termination without notice is considered wrongful dismissal, leaving the door open for a company to be sued. Reasonable notice may be defined in an employment contract or, in the case of implied contracts, reasonable notice is often interpreted as three to four weeks for every year of service. Usually an employee stops work and is given a lump sum of money equal to his or her pay for the period of notice. If the employee does not consider the amount to be acceptable, the company can be sued for wrongful dismissal. The court will review the situation and make a final decision on the amount of notice to be provided. The courts will take into account factors such as the employee's age, salary, length of service, and level of job. Notice periods are usually less than two years.[52] If a company is deemed to have acted "in bad faith," such as being untruthful, misleading, or unduly insensitive, the courts may order additional compensation. The resulting additional periods of notice are often three to six months.[53]

CONSTRUCTIVE DISMISSAL

If an employer changes the employment contract so that it is unacceptable to an employee, constructive dismissal can occur, even though the employee has not been formally terminated. Examples of constructive dismissal include demotion, reduction of pay and benefits, forced transfer, forced early retirement, and changes in job duties and responsibilities. An employee who believes he or she has been constructively dismissed can sue for wrongful dismissal. In many cases, financial settlements are reached without going to court.

Concept Quiz

Complete the following true–false quiz by circling the correct answer. Answers are at the end of the quiz. After marking your answers, remember to go back and check your understanding of any answers you missed.

True or False   1. One of the most important parts of performance evaluation starts before the interview begins.

True or False   2. Performance appraisals communicate and clarify performance expectations and results.

True or False   3. Specific objectives previously set with employees should be used as standards against which to measure progress.

True or False	4. Graphic rating scales use a list of critical incidents to provide examples to show the employee specific behaviours that are desirable and those that call for improvement.
True or False	5. Sometimes it is the standard that needs corrective attention, not the performance.
True or False	6. Many employees estimate their own performance level considerably more highly than managers do.
True or False	7. Feedback is an indirect form of recognition that can motivate people to higher levels of performance.
True or False	8. Negative feedback is most likely to be accepted when it comes from a distant source such as the human resource department and is in subjective form.
True or False	9. Feedback is most meaningful if a short interval separates the behaviour and the receipt of feedback about that behaviour.
True or False	10. Productive feedback is based on job-related performance, not the person.

Answers (1) True; (2) True; (3) True; (4) False; (5) True; (6) True; (7) True; (8) False; (9) True; (10) True

Behavioural Checklist

The following skills are important to effective performance evaluation. Use them when evaluating your performance evaluation skills and those of others.

Effective Performance Evaluation:

- Uses specific objectives previously set with employees as standards against which to measure progress.
- Puts the employee at ease and explains the purpose of the feedback interview.
- Encourages and supports while minimizing threats.
- When giving negative feedback, criticizes performance, not the person.
- Obtains employee participation and encourages self-evaluation.
- Uses specific examples to support ratings.
- Has the employee summarize the feedback to ensure understanding.
- Creates a future plan of development with the person receiving the feedback.

Modelling Exercise

Six common job performance dimensions of teaching post-secondary education classes are: knowledge of the subject, grading, organization and preparation, managing a comfortable learning environment, communicating ideas, and developing relevant and useful assignments. These dimensions are also included on the performance appraisal rating sheet at the end of this exercise.

INSTRUCTIONS A class leader is to be selected (either a volunteer or someone chosen by the instructor). The class leader will preside over a performance appraisal feedback session for the instructor.

The instructor will leave the room for 15 minutes. During this time the class members develop constructive feedback for the class leader to provide to the instructor on each performance dimension. The class leader should take notes from the class input to prepare his or her feedback. (No written documentation is required, however.)

After the 15-minute period is up, the class leader should invite the instructor back into the classroom and begin the feedback session. The class leader role-plays the performance feedback provider and the instructor plays him- or herself.

IMPORTANT NOTE: Your instructor understands that this session is only an exercise and is prepared to accept criticism (and, of course, any praise you may want to convey). Your instructor also recognizes that the class leader's feedback is actually a composite of many students' input. So be open and honest in your feedback and make the session valuable for the instructor's development.

TIME Not to exceed 15 minutes.

INSTRUCTOR PERFORMANCE EVALUATION RATING FORM

Evaluate your instructor for this course for each of the following performance dimensions by entering the appropriate rating. Provide explanatory feedback after your rating.

4 Strongly Agree	3 Agree	2 Disagree	1 Strongly Agree
_____ Demonstrates knowledge of the subject.			
_____ Grading is fair and impartial.			
_____ Creates a comfortable learning environment.			
_____ Organized and prepared for class.			
_____ Clearly explains topics and ideas.			
_____ Assignments are relevant and useful.			

Observer's Rating Sheet

On completion of the exercise, evaluate the performance appraisal feedback skills of the class member providing the feedback to the professor. Rate the feedback provider between 1 and 5 using the following scale. Write concrete examples in the space for comments below each criteria skill to use in explaining your feedback.

1 Unsatisfactory	2 Weak	3 Adequate	4 Good	5 Outstanding

_____ Used specific objectives previously set with employees as standards against which to measure progress.

_____ Put the employee at ease and explained the purpose of the feedback interview.

_____ Encouraged and supported while minimizing threats.

_____ When giving negative feedback, criticized performance, not the person.

_____ Obtained employee participation and encouraged self-evaluation.

_____ Used specific examples to support ratings.

_____ Had the professor summarize the feedback to ensure understanding.

_____ Created a future plan of development with the person receiving the feedback.

Group Exercises

Three different types of group exercise are presented here. First is a performance evaluation case for you to practise your analysis and action-planning skills. Second is an opportunity to practise, observe, and receive feedback in a performance appraisal role-play. Third is a peer review where you will both give and receive feedback on your own and your classmates' actual performance in this class.

Group Exercise 1: Case Analysis: Conducting a Performance Appraisal[54]

Plant manager Paul Dorn wondered why his boss, Leonard Hech, had sent for him. Paul thought Leonard had been tough on him lately; he was slightly uneasy at being asked to come to Leonard's office at a time when such meetings were unusual. "Close the door and sit down, Paul," invited Leonard. "I've been wanting to talk to you." After preliminary conversation, Leonard said that because Paul's latest project had been finished, he would receive the raise he had been promised on its completion.

Leonard went on to say that because it was time for Paul's performance evaluation, they might as well do that now. Leonard explained that the performance evaluation was based on four criteria: (1) the amount of high-quality merchandise manufactured and shipped on time; (2) the quality of relationships with plant employees and peers; (3) progress in maintaining employee safety and health; and (4) reaction to demands of top management. The first criterion had a relative importance of 40 per cent; the rest had a weight of 20 per cent each.

On the first item, Paul received an excellent rating. Shipments were at an all-time high, quality was good, and few shipments had arrived late. On the second item, Paul also was rated excellent. Leonard said plant employees and peers related well to Paul, labour relations were excellent, and no major grievances had arisen since Paul had become plant manager.

However, on attention to matters of employee safety and health, the evaluation was below average. His boss stated that no matter how much he bugged Paul about improving housekeeping in the plant, he never seemed to produce results. Leonard also rated Paul below average on meeting demands from top management. He explained that Paul always answered yes to any request and then disregarded it, going about his business as if nothing had happened.

Seemingly surprised at the comments, Paul agreed that perhaps Leonard was right and that he should do a better job on these matters. Smiling as he left, he thanked Leonard for the raise and the frank appraisal.

As weeks went by, Leonard noticed little change in Paul. He reviewed the situation with an associate. "It's frustrating. In this time of rapid growth, we must make constant changes in work methods. Paul agrees but can't seem to make people break their habits and adopt more efficient ones. I find myself riding him hard these days, but he just calmly takes it. He's well liked by everyone. But somehow, he's got to care about safety and housekeeping in the plant. And when higher management makes demands he can't meet, he's got to say, 'I can't do that and do all the other things you want, too.' Now he has dozens of unfinished jobs because he refuses to say no."

As he talked, Leonard remembered something Paul had told him in confidence once. "I take Valium for a physical condition I have. When I don't take it, I get symptoms similar to a heart attack—but I only take half as much as the doctor prescribed." Now, Leonard thought, I'm really in a spot. If the Valium is what is making him so lackadaisical, I can't endanger his health by asking him to quit taking it. And I certainly can't fire him.

Yet, as things stand, he really can't implement all the changes we need to fulfill our goals for the next two years.

QUESTIONS FOR DISCUSSION

1. Do you think a raise was justified in Paul's situation? Explain.
2. What could have been done differently in the performance appraisal session?
3. What can be done now to change the situation?

Group Exercise 2: Role-Play: A Difficult Performance Appraisal[55]

You have two responsibilities as a participant in a role-play. First, read *only* the background information on the exercise and *your own* role. Reading your counterpart's role will lessen the effectiveness of the exercise. Second, get into the character. Role-playing is acting. The role description establishes your character. Follow the guidelines it establishes. Do not change or omit the facts you are given. If you are an observer in an exercise, you should read everything pertaining to the role-play and review the Observer's Rating Sheet.

ACTORS Dana (director of human resources); Blair (employee relations manager).

DANA'S ROLE You are director of human resources for a manufacturing firm. You are well thought of in the firm and have excellent rapport with your boss, the vice-president of administration. Blair is your employee relations manager. You know that Blair is reasonably good at her job, but you also know that Blair believes herself to be "outstanding," which is not true. Blair is scheduled to have a meeting with you in five minutes, and you would like to establish clearer communication, as well as convince Blair to adopt a less grandiose self-image.

You believe that Blair is on the right track, but it will take her about two years to reach the stage at which she can be promoted. As to Blair's performance, you have received some good reports, as well as *three* letters of complaint. Blair prepared four research reports that you considered to be above average, but to keep her motivated and happy, you exaggerated and said they were "excellent." Maybe that was a mistake.

You are worried about the impact on other employees, whose performance is nearly as good as Blair's, if Blair is promoted. So you plan to set meaningful targets for Blair this year, evaluate her performance one or two years from now, and then give the promotion if it is deserved.

BLAIR'S ROLE You are the employee relations manager in a manufacturing firm. Dana is your boss and she is the director of human resources. You know that you are one of the best performers in your department, and may even be the best. However, you were not promoted last year, even though you expected to be, so you would like to be promoted this year.

You expect your boss to raise some obstacles to your promotion. Dana is bound to mention three letters of complaint against you, for instance. Dana seems to point out only your errors. Up front, you plan to remind Dana that you wrote four research reports that Dana herself said were *excellent*. If Dana tries to delay your promotion unnecessarily, you plan to confront her and, if necessary, take the issue to Dana's boss, the vice-president of administration. You think that in many instances you were rated better on performance than your colleagues in the department. You have decided that you will press your point of view firmly, but also rationally, in a professional manner.

TIME Not to exceed 15 minutes.

Observer's Rating Sheet

On completion of the exercise, evaluate the performance appraisal feedback skills of the class member playing Dana. Rate Dana's skills as a performance appraisal feedback provider between 1 and 5 using the following scale. Write concrete examples in the space for comments below each criteria skill to use in explaining your feedback.

1 Unsatisfactory	2 Weak	3 Adequate	4 Good	5 Outstanding

_____ Used specific objectives previously set with employees as standards against which to measure progress.

_____ Put the employee at ease and explained the purpose of the feedback interview.

_____ Encouraged and supported while minimizing threats.

_____ When giving negative feedback, criticized performance, not the person.

_____ Obtained employee participation and encouraged self-evaluation.

_____ Used specific examples to support ratings.

_____ Had the employee summarize the feedback to ensure understanding.

_____ Created a future plan of development with the person receiving the feedback.

Group Exercise 3: Peer Review of Class Members' Performance

PURPOSE To practise giving and receiving performance feedback.

INSTRUCTIONS

STEP 1 Form groups of five to seven students who have worked together in several class exercises. If permanent learning groups have already been formed, use them.

STEP 2 Put your name, followed by the words *Self-Appraisal*, on a piece of paper and draw a vertical line down the centre to form two columns. Write and underline the word *Strengths* at the top of the left column. Write and underline the words *Things to Work On* at the top of the right column. Then turn the paper over and do the same thing, except put the word *Others' Appraisal* after your name. These forms are illustrated in Exhibit 14-5, which you may want to tear out of the book and use for the exercise.

Exhibit 14-5 Class Performance Appraisal Feedback Form

Name: _____

Self-Appraisal

Strengths	Things to Work On

Exhibit 14-5 Class Performance Appraisal Feedback Form

Name: _____

Others' Appraisal

Strengths	Things to Work On

STEP 3 On the side of the paper titled *Self Appraisal*, do a self-appraisal of your class performance. In the left column of this side write a list of the strengths that you contribute to the class learning. Example strengths are things such as always prepared for class, ask relevant questions, encourage others to participate, and so on. In the right column of the same side, *Things to Work On*, write a list of things to work on to be a better contributor to the class.

STEP 4 When you are finished with your self-evaluation, turn your paper over. Be sure that your name followed by the word *other* is at the top and two columns are labelled *Strengths* and *Things to Work On*. Pass your blank form to the person on your left.

STEP 5 When you receive another student's *Others' Appraisal* form, fill in the strengths and things you think they could improve on in the appropriate columns. If others have previously written the same comments you were going to put down, just put a check mark after the comment. When you are finished writing your feedback, pass the form on to the next student to your left. Continue the process until you receive your own form.

Step 6 Compare your own evaluation of your strengths and things to work on to those listed by your classmates. Make notes of things you would like to clarify.

Step 7 One at a time, take about five minutes to ask others in your group to clarify and elaborate on the comments that you want to understand better. When receiving feedback, your goal is to listen to understand, not to rationalize or explain your behaviour. When providing feedback, follow the Behavioural Checklist of the skills for providing effective performance appraisal feedback.

Step 8 After all group members have clarified their performance appraisal feedback, the group should discuss the outstanding examples of skills exhibited by group members in providing effective performance appraisal feedback.

Time Plan about 10 minutes for self-appraisal, two to three minutes per student for writing feedback, approximately five to seven minutes per student for feedback clarification, and 10 minutes to examine examples of effective skills for providing effective performance appraisal feedback. So, if groups of five students participate, the time estimate would be 55 to 65 minutes. Experience suggests that you should be prepared for the longer times.

Application Questions

1. Examine the performance appraisal rating methods presented in this chapter. Which ones would work best in each of the following situations: college or university classroom; sports team; production line; research lab; sales team; middle management; top management?
2. By which of the performance appraisal rating methods would you prefer to be evaluated and why? Which method you would prefer if you were a manager and were required to evaluate employees and why? If there are differences between the methods, why do you think that the differences have developed?
3. What are the benefits of performance evaluation for the organization? For the individual?
4. Evaluate your own performance in all of your classes. How does your self-evaluation compare to how your teachers rate your performance? If a large variation exists, how do you account for this variation? Are the feedback methods effective? How could they be made more effective?
5. Which of the performance rating methods do you think is the fairest? Why?

Reinforcement Exercises

The following suggestions are activities you can do to reinforce your performance evaluation skills discussed in this chapter. You may want to adapt them to the Action Plan you will develop next, or try them independently.

1. Visit a local company and interview a manager or human resources staff member about how they conduct performance appraisals. Ask questions about their methods, the results that they obtain, and their confidence in the method. After the interview, critique the evaluation method that you researched.
2. Interview five students who have worked and ask them how they feel about performance evaluations. Ask them to describe the problems, fairness, or legal situations that might have occurred. Now, consider what the dangers would be if you only listened to one side of the story when it came to reviewing cases dealing with performance evaluation.
3. Find someone who is trying to accomplish a difficult goal within the next year. Help this person create a plan of development by applying the performance evaluation steps.

- Help the person set specific objectives against which progress can be measured and which are tangible, verifiable, and measurable.
- Help the employee draft a detailed step-by-step plan to achieve these objectives.
- Be sure this plan includes what has to be done and when.
- Determine how the person will use the previously set objectives as the standards to measure progress.
- Offer whatever assistance you can as a coach to help the person.

4. Design a performance appraisal to evaluate your own performance in one of your main lines of endeavour. Examples could be your success as a student, your performance on a job, or your contribution to your family.

Summary Checklist

Take a few minutes to reflect on your performance and look over others' ratings of your performance evaluation skills. Now assess yourself on each of the key learning behaviours. Make a check (√) next to those behaviours on which you need improvement.

_____ Using specific objectives previously set with employees as standards to measure progress against.

1. Make sure these objectives are tangible, verifiable, and measurable.
2. Use multiple sources to gather data for measurement: personal observation, statistical reports, oral reports, written reports, and computer-accessed databases.
3. Decide on appropriate measures for aspects such as individual task outcomes, behaviours, and traits.

_____ Putting the employee at ease and explaining the purpose of the feedback interview.

1. Explain what will transpire during the review and the resulting consequences.
2. Be supportive and understanding.

_____ Encouraging and supporting while minimizing threats.

1. Create a helpful and constructive climate.
2. Direct negative feedback toward work-related behaviour that the employee can do something about.

_____ When giving negative feedback, criticizing performance, not the person.

1. Be sure feedback is descriptive rather than judgmental.
2. Direct any criticism at specific job-related behaviours that negatively affect the employee's performance.

_____ Obtaining employee participation and encouraging self-evaluation.

1. Let employees do the majority of the talking.
2. Get the employee's perceptions of what you are saying, especially if you are addressing a problem.

_____ Using specific examples to support ratings through methods such as:

1. Written essays.
2. Critical incidents.
3. Graphic rating scales.
4. Behaviourally anchored rating scales.

5. Multiperson comparisons.
6. Group order ranking.
7. Individual ranking.
8. Paired comparison.
9. Combined methods.

_____ Having the employee summarize the feedback to ensure understanding.

1. Have the recipient rephrase the content of your feedback to see whether it fully captures the meaning you intended.
2. Encourage the employee to summarize the discussion that has taken place.

_____ Creating a future plan of development with the person receiving the feedback.

1. Help the employee draft a detailed, step-by-step plan to improve the situation.
2. Be sure this plan includes what has to be done, when, and how you will monitor the activities.
3. Offer whatever assistance you can to help the employee.

Action Plan

1. Which performance evaluation behaviour do I want to improve the most? (For examples, see Summary Checklist.)
2. Why? What will be my payoff?
3. What potential obstacles stand in my way?
4. What are the specific things I will do to improve? (For examples, see the Reinforcement Exercises.)
5. When will I do them?
6. How and when will I measure my success?

CHAPTER **15**
Developing Employees

Learning Objectives

After completing this chapter, you should be able to:

- Help employees through assistance and education.
- Develop others through delegation.
- Provide meaningful feedback for learning.
- Coach employees about performance problems at work.
- Counsel employees about personal problems and careers.
- Mentor employees for long-term development.

Self-Assessment Exercise

The Best Ways to Develop Employees

For each of the following actions, indicate whether you believe it is an effective developing behaviour by marking either True (T) or False (F).

_____	1. Tell employees the right way to do a job.
_____	2. Suspend judgment and evaluation.
_____	3. Act as a role model.
_____	4. Provide long-term career planning.
_____	5. Use a collaborative style.
_____	6. Apply active listening.
_____	7. Respect an employee's individuality.
_____	8. Focus on getting each employee's performance up to a minimum standard.
_____	9. Dismiss mistakes.
_____	10. Delegate responsibility for performance outcomes to the employee.
_____	11. If possible, assist rather than educate employees because assistance is much faster.

SCORING Check the following scoring key and add up the number of answers you had correct:

Answers   (1) False; (2) True; (3) True; (4) False; (5) True; (6) True; (7) True; (8) False; (9) False; (10) False; (11) False; (12) False; (13) True; (14) True; (15) True

Number of correct answers = _____

INTERPRETATION Scores of 12 or above indicate that you possess a valid working knowledge about developing employees. Scores of 8–11 indicate that you may be good at some aspects of helping but not at others. Scores of 7 or below indicate that you need to improve on most aspects of your helping behaviour.

Concepts

Whether you are a CEO or first-line supervisor, developing employees is an important part of any manager's job. CEOs need to develop managers at every level of the organization to be leaders in order to build a leadership succession plan and enhance organizational creativity and energy. They do this by creating positive emotional energy, instilling values that help the organization reach its goals, sharing their point of view about how to build and run the business, and developing vibrant stories that motivate others to reach for a better future.[1] For Deloitte & Touche, recently named to *Report on Business* magazine's 35 Best Companies to Work for in Canada, employee development is a corporate philosophy as well as a major company-wide initiative. "We've been nurturing an environment where talented men and women want to contribute their best because the firm supports them in doing so," states Colin Taylor, managing partner and chief executive of Deloitte & Touche.[2]

Developing employees is also important for two major reasons. First of all, more skilled and competent employees make a manager's job a lot easier because the manager can delegate more responsibilities without worrying so much about supervising every detail of the work. Second, by helping employees develop their skill competencies, build an exciting career plan, and resolve their personal problems, managers will motivate them to accomplish quality work. So developing employees is a win for the organization, the manager, and the employees.

This chapter is designed to help you develop employees by helping them resolve personal problems and enhance job competencies. It covers how you can help employees through assistance and education, develop them through delegation, provide meaningful feedback for learning, coach employees about performance problems at work, counsel them about personal problems and careers, and mentor employees for long-term development.

Determine the Best Approach for Developing Employees

ASSISTANCE OR EDUCATION[3]

Your concern as a developer of employees is to enable the receiver of your help to accomplish tasks independently at a high level of effectiveness when you are not there to assist. Although you could often assist and help the employee to do a better job by just doing it yourself or providing other people to help out, this response provides only a temporary solution. Assistance may be necessary in emergencies but in the long run the employee fails to learn how to handle similar situations independently and becomes more dependent on you, which takes more of your time.

Consequently, a better approach is education so that the employee can solve his or her own problems and perform effectively and independently in the future. Education may be frustrating for employees who want immediate relief, and it may cause some short-term resentment because you do not solve the problem for them, but in the long run, most employees will be grateful for the increased competence and self-esteem your coaching, training, or counselling has provided.

DETERMINE THE SOURCE OF THE PROBLEM

So what is the correct helping approach to take with employees who are not performing well? It depends upon what causes the problem. Unsatisfactory performance often has multiple causes, some of which lie within the control of the employee and some that do not. Here are some questions that managers can ask to determine what type of help would be most appropriate.[4]

1. Are employees unaware that their performance is unsatisfactory? If the answer is yes, the manager can provide feedback.
2. Does poor performance occur because employees are not really sure what is expected of them at work? If so, the manager can clarify the employee's role and provide clear expectations. (For more on this approach see the section on path-goal theory in Chapter 18, Leading Change).
3. Is employee performance hampered by obstacles that are beyond his or her control? If this is the case, the manager removes the obstacles.
4. Do employees not know how to do a task? If they do not, the manager provides coaching or training.
5. Is good performance followed by negative consequences? Managers should eliminate the negative consequences.
6. Is poor performance being rewarded by positive consequences? If so, eliminate the positive reinforcement. (For more information on how to eliminate enforcing poor performance, see the section on the folly of rewarding A while hoping for B in Chapter 9, Motivating Others.)

If all these steps have been taken to ensure good performance, and the employee is still not able or willing to perform well, it is time to try counselling to see if it is a personal problem. Although differences occur in coaching, counselling, and mentoring, common steps should be followed before, during, and after these helping sessions. These steps are summarized in Exhibit 15-1.

Exhibit 15-1 Guidelines for Conducting Effective Helping Sessions

Prior to the Helping Session:
- Acquire all the facts about the situation.
- Decide what type of coaching the situation requires.
- Consider how the employee might react and feel about the discussion.
- Think about the best way to present what you want to say to the employee.

During the Helping Session:
- Discuss the purpose of the session.
- Try to make the employee comfortable.

Exhibit 15-1 continued

- Establish a nondefensive climate characterized by open communication and trust.
- Praise the employee for positive aspects of performance.
- Mutually define the problem (performance or attitude).
- Mutually determine the causes. Do not interpret or psychoanalyze the employee's behaviour; instead, ask questions such as "What is causing the lack of motivation you describe?"
- Help the employee establish an action plan that includes specific goals and dates.
- Make sure the employee clearly understands what is expected of him or her.
- Summarize what has been agreed upon in the session.
- Affirm your confidence in the employee's ability to make needed changes based upon his or her strengths or past history.

After the Session:

- Follow up to see how the employee is progressing.
- Modify the action plan if necessary.

Note: For more detailed information on these guidelines, see D.C. Kinslaw, *Coaching for Commitment* (San Diego, CA: Pfeiffer & Company, 1993).

DEMONSTRATE POSITIVE REGARD

When you coach, counsel, and mentor employees you are engaging in a helping relationship. For a helping relationship to be successful it is important that the manager holds the employee in "unconditional positive regard." The manager accepts and exhibits warm regard for the employee as a person of unconditional self-worth and of value no matter what the condition, problem, or feelings. This kind of relationship provides a climate of warmth and safety because the employee feels liked and prized as a person. These feelings are a necessary condition for developing the trust that is crucial in a helping relationship.[5]

Positive regard for employees is also a motivational skill characteristic of high-performing managers. Assuming that employees mean well, rather than assuming the worst about them, creates a self-fulfilling prophecy when they try to live up to their boss's good opinion.[6]

Develop Others Through Delegation

Delegation occurs when a manager transfers to an employee authority for achieving goals and making decisions about how to do a job. Delegation empowers employees by increasing their involvement in their work through greater participation in decisions that control their work and by expanding responsibility for work outcomes.[7] Consequently, delegation helps develop employees by expanding their job capabilities and knowledge. Moreover, it helps them to develop their decision-making skills and prepares them for future promotion opportunities.

As a development tool, you should expect and accept some mistakes by your employees when you delegate. Mistakes are often good learning experiences, as long as their costs are not excessive. To ensure that the costs of mistakes do not exceed the value of the learning, you need to establish objectives, monitor progress, and provide effective feedback. These methods are described in Chapter 14, Evaluating Performance.

To become a more effective delegator, ask yourself the following questions:[8]

1. **Whom should I choose for this job?** Effective delegators choose a task that best suits the development needs of the particular employee. Be sure that the task doesn't exceed the ability of the employee. To avoid this problem, ask the employee how confident he or she is in his or her ability to complete the task. Also be sure the employee is motivated or sees "the pay-off" in completing the task.

2. **Have I clarified the assignment?** Provide clear information on what is being delegated, the results you expect, due dates, and any other performance expectations you hold.

   Unless the task requires adherence to specific techniques or methods, delegate only the end results. That is, get agreement on what is to be done and the end results expected, but let the employee decide on the means. By focusing on goals and allowing the employee the freedom to use his or her own judgment as to how those goals are to be achieved, you increase trust, improve that employee's motivation, and enhance accountability for the results.

3. **Does the employee know how far he or she can go without checking further with you?** You are delegating authority to act, but within certain parameters. You need to specify what those parameters or boundaries are so employees know the range of their discretion. Then, let go and trust others.

4. **Have I allowed the employee to participate?** If you allow employees to participate in determining what is delegated, how much authority is needed to get the job done, and the standards by which they will be judged, you increase employee motivation, satisfaction, and accountability for performance.

   Be alert, however, not to negotiate tasks and the amount of authority beyond what they need and beyond what they are capable of handling so that the delegation process is not undermined.

5. **Have I informed others?** Delegation should not take place in a vacuum. Inform others, both inside as well as outside the organization, who may be affected by the delegation. Essentially, you need to convey what has been delegated (the task and amount of authority) and to whom. If you fail to follow through on this step, the legitimacy of your employee's authority will probably be called into question. Failure to inform others makes conflicts likely and decreases the chances that the employee will be able to accomplish the delegated task efficiently.

6. **Have I established a reporting schedule to monitor progress?** Ideally, this should occur at the time of the initial assignment. After agreeing on a specific time for completion of the task, set progress dates when the employee will report back on how well he or she is doing and any major problems that have surfaced.

   A schedule to monitor the employee's progress increases the likelihood that important problems will be identified early and that the task will be completed on time and to the desired specifications.

   Be sure that the reporting schedule is not too constraining so that the employee will not be deprived of the opportunity to build self-confidence and motivation. A well-designed schedule permits the employee to make small mistakes, but quickly alerts you when big mistakes are imminent.

7. **Do I make myself available for consultation?** Beyond a progress schedule, be sure to be available and open to discussion. This can go a long way in clarifying expectations and avoiding misunderstandings.

8. **Do employees push decisions back on me?** When problems surface, insist on recommendations from the employee. Many managers fall into the trap of letting employees reverse the delegation process: the employee runs into a problem and then comes back to the manager for advice or a solution. Insist from the beginning that when employees want to discuss a problem with you, they come prepared with a recommendation and be prepared to help an employee develop his or her own solution.

9. **Did I review the entire job after it was finished for ways to improve the process next time?** Before moving on to your next challenge, review with the employee how the delegation process worked and didn't work. Use this feedback for the next project.

Provide Meaningful Feedback for Learning

Feedback is any communication to a person that provides information about some aspect of his or her behaviour and the impact of that behaviour.[9] Managers who are skilled at giving feedback can increase employee performance and provide positive personal development.[10]

Specifically, feedback can:

1. **Prompt** a person to develop goals, where none existed before.
2. **Inform** people how well they are progressing toward existing goals. If favourable, it acts as a positive reinforcer.
3. **Suggest** ways to improve performance.
4. **Induce** people to raise their goal sights after attaining a previous goal. It can be an indirect form of recognition that motivates people to higher levels of performance.[11]

Feedback involves observation, assessment, consequences, and development.[12] In other words, managers communicate to the employee what they observe, how they assess it, what impact it has, and how to improve or effectively address the observed behaviour and consequences. Development becomes an observation in the next communication loop. For example, a manager who observes sustained improvement and assesses it positively may consequently praise or promote that employee. Thus, feedback facilitates growth of employees because it provides information about how to improve performance and motivates development by informing them of the possible rewards.

This development assumes, of course, that feedback is effective. We have all been the recipients of ineffective feedback that just leaves us angry, confused, and frustrated. One example is vague feedback based on fuzzy impressions, such as "you really are not performing very well," which is generally hard to translate into the specific developmental goals that are so important to improvement. Some guidelines for providing effective feedback that promotes development are summarized in Exhibit 15-2. Other helpful hints can be found in Chapter 5, Interpersonal Communication, and Chapter 14, Evaluating Performance.

Coaching and Counselling

Coaching is similar but not synonymous with **counselling**. They both have the same objective—to improve the employee's performance—but coaching deals with ability issues while counselling deals with personal problems. When an employee needs help mastering skills and figuring out how to apply instructions, coaching is required. For example, when employees do not know how to run team meetings, they need to be taught

Exhibit 15-2 Characteristics of Effective Feedback

- Descriptive rather than evaluative.
- Specific and data-based rather than general.
- Directed toward controllable behaviours rather than personality traits or characteristics.
- Solicited rather than imposed.
- Close to the event under discussion rather than delayed for several months.
- Occurs when the receiver is most ready to accept it.
- Suggests rather than prescribes avenues for improvements.
- Is intended to help, not punish.

Source: Adapted from D.A. Kolb, I.M. Rubin, and J.S. Osland, *Organizational Behavior: An Experiential Approach* (Upper Saddle River, NJ: Prentice Hall, 1991) 448–50, who provide an extended discussion of each of these guidelines.

the specific steps in the process and given both practice and feedback. When an employee has an attitude, emotional, drinking, or family problem, the manager needs to engage in counselling behaviours.

Both coaching and counselling apply essentially the same problem-solving process of listening and understanding, identifying the problem, clarifying alternatives, deciding on an action plan, and implementing the action plan. Both also require the same behavioural skills of establishing a supportive climate, active listening, being nonjudgmental and understanding, joint problem solving, and educating the employee to solve his or her own problems rather than assisting by doing it yourself. The following sections explain these skills more thoroughly.

COACH EMPLOYEES ABOUT PERFORMANCE PROBLEMS AT WORK

Coaching is a day-to-day, hands-on process of helping employees recognize opportunities to improve their work performance. A coach analyzes the employee's performance; provides insight as to how that performance can be improved; and offers the leadership, motivation, and supportive climate to help the employee achieve that improvement. As a coach, you provide instruction, guidance, advice, and encouragement to help employees improve their job performance.

COACHING PREREQUISITES Coaching requires you to suspend judgment and evaluation. Managers, in the normal routine of carrying out their jobs, regularly express judgments about performance against previously established goals. As a coach, you focus on accepting employees the way they are and help them to make continual improvement toward the goal of developing their full potential.

Before discussing specific procedures and skills, it should be pointed out that not all coaching is done by managers. In most work groups, buddy systems develop where more experienced employees informally help new members develop necessary skills and offer them guidance when they have problems. Organizations sometimes formalize buddy systems into **mentoring** programs where senior employees are assigned junior proteges to whom they lend the benefit of their experience. Mentors perform as both coaches and counsellors as they guide their less experienced associates towards improved performance.

COACHING SKILLS AND BEHAVIOURS There are three general skills managers can apply to help their employees generate breakthroughs in performance.[13]

Ability to Analyze Ways to Improve an Employee's Performance and Capabilities A coach looks for opportunities for an employee to expand his or her capabilities and improve performance. To know what opportunities to provide you need to observe your employee's behaviour on a day-to-day basis. You can also *ask questions* of the employee: Why do you do a task this way? Can it be improved? What other approaches might be used? Then, *listen* to the employee. You need to understand the world from the employee's perspective. Finally, *show genuine interest* in the person as an individual, not merely as an employee. Respect his or her individuality. More important than any technical expertise you can provide about improving job performance is the insight you have into the employee's uniqueness.

Ability to Create a Supportive Climate It is the coach's responsibility to reduce barriers to development and facilitate a climate that encourages performance improvement. Through *active listening* and *empowering* employees to implement appropriate ideas they suggest, you can create a climate that contributes to a free and open exchange of ideas. You can also *offer help* by being available for assistance, guidance, or advice if asked.

By being *positive and upbeat*, you can encourage your employees. Do not use threats because they create a climate of fear and inhibition. Focus on mistakes as learning opportunities. Change implies risk and employees must not feel that mistakes will be punished. When failure occurs, ask "What did we learn that can help us in the future?"

Analyze the factors that you control and reduce all obstacles that you can to help the employee to improve his or her job performance. As a manager you must take personal responsibility for the outcome, but do not underplay employees' full responsibilities and contributions. Validate employees' efforts when they succeed and point to what was missing when they fail but never blame employees for poor results. Express to the employee the value of his or her contribution to the department's goals.

Ability to Influence Employees to Change Their Behaviour The ultimate test of coaching effectiveness is whether an employee's performance improves, but it is not a static concept. The concern is for ongoing growth and development. Consequently, you should help employees continually work toward improvement and encourage them by recognizing and rewarding even small improvements. Continual improvement, however, means no absolute upper limits to an employee's job performance.

By using a collaborative style with appropriate empowerment, employees will be more responsive to accepting change as they participate in identifying and choosing among improvement ideas. When confronted with a difficult job that shakes employees' confidence, it can help to break complex projects into a series of simpler tasks. This way the seemingly overwhelming project, which originally discouraged employees, becomes a number of achievable ones where employees are more likely to experience success. Achieving success on simpler tasks can encourage workers to take on more difficult ones.

As a manager you need to do more than tell and encourage. Model the qualities that you expect from your employees. If, for example, you want openness, dedication, commitment, and responsibility from your employees, you must demonstrate these qualities yourself. Your employees will look to you as a role model so make sure your deeds match your words.

Managers should also be aware of any company incentives for training and development. For example, Canada Post Corporation has an Individual Incentive Plan, which allows for a one time per year payment of 4.5 per cent of an employee's base salary. The criteria for the level of payment are based on a comparison of performance against goals that the employee set for that year. Other examples include Western Glove Works in Manitoba, which has established an education and training trust fund, and les Caisses populaires du Saquenay-Lac St-Jean, which pays employees for half the time they spend attending courses at a CEGEP (community college) or university.[14] A collaborative style, a supportive climate, identification of opportunities, modelling the qualities you wish to see in employees, and the provision of incentives can all help employees to improve performance.

The steps in coaching an employee who needs to develop new skills are summarized in Exhibit 15-3.

Exhibit 15-3 Behavioural Steps for Teaching New Skills

1. Explain the purpose and importance of what you are trying to teach.
2. Explain the process to be used.
3. Demonstrate how it is done.
4. Observe while the person practises the process.
5. Provide immediate and specific feedback (coach again or reinforce success).
6. Express confidence in the person's ability to be successful.
7. Agree on follow-up actions.

Source: W.C. Byham with J. Cox, *Zapp! The Lightning of Empowerment* (Pittsburg, PA: DDI Press, 1989) 129.

COUNSEL EMPLOYEES ABOUT PERSONAL PROBLEMS

Counselling is the discussion of an emotional problem with an employee in order to resolve the problem or, at a minimum, help the employee to cope with it better. Examples of problems that might require you to counsel an employee include divorce, serious illness, personal financial problems, difficulty in getting along with a co-worker, a drinking problem affecting work performance, or frustration over a lack of career progress in the company.

In counselling sessions, the purpose is to help employees gain insight into their feelings, behaviour, and alternatives. Counselling is appropriate for employees with attitude problems they themselves do not recognize. The focus in counselling is on problem recognition and solution.

When dealing with these emotional and personal problems, an important additional principle is to maintain confidentiality. To really open up and share the reasons for many personal problems, employees must feel that they can trust you and that you will not threaten their self-esteem or their reputation with co-workers. So, as soon as you determine that counselling is what is called for, emphasize that everything the employee says regarding personal matters will be treated in confidence.

Even though managers are not trained psychologists, there are several reasons for taking on a counselling role before referring the employee to a professional therapist. Sometimes an employee just needs a sounding board for the release of tension, which can become a prelude to clarifying the problem, identifying possible solutions, and taking corrective action. Emotions typically cloud rational thinking, and counselling can help employees clarify their thoughts into a more logical and coherent order.

Counselling can provide reassurance to employees that their problems have solutions and that they have the ability to improve. With more serious problems, counselling can identify employee problems requiring professional treatment. Severe depression, debilitating phobias, family and personality disorders, and substance abuse are examples of employee problems that require professional help. Psychological counselling is now included in employee assistance programs as part of most employee benefit health plans.

When successful, employee counselling can circumvent the need for disciplinary actions such as formal warnings, sanctions, or firing. In some instances it may be appropriate to give advice to an employee as to what you think he or she should do to correct a problem or improve performance. As mentioned earlier, however, employees grow by learning to solve their own problems, not from looking to others to solve their problems for them. Also, if the advice you give proves to be wrong, you are likely to be blamed.

Mentor For Long-Term Development

The role of a mentor is to help another person achieve his or her career goals. As a mentor, managers formally pair up with employees to help show them the ropes and provide emotional support and encouragement on an ongoing basis. It is similar to serving as the employee's permanent coach and counsellor. While some companies rely on informal mentoring, companies such as Deloitte & Touche[15] and Manulife Financial have formal mentoring programs where pair assignments are made.[16] Either way, helping others achieve success is an important attribute of successful managers. Mentors not only reduce the stress caused by uncertainty about how to do things and deal with challenging assignments, but they are a source of comfort when newer employees just need to let off steam or discuss career dilemmas.[17]

For new employees, mentoring sessions can help them gain a better understanding of the organization, its goals, and advancement criteria. Managers may also try to make employees more politically savvy and warn them of possible traps. In general, managers strive to help employees live up to their full potential and encourage them to be more proactive in managing their careers.

Concept Quiz

Complete the following true–false quiz by circling the correct answer. The answers are at the end of the quiz. After marking your answers, remember to go back and check your understanding of any answers you missed.

True or False   1. Coaching is the same as counselling.

True or False   2. You have to be judgmental with employees so they understand they need to improve.

True or False   3. Effective managers look for opportunities to teach employees how to improve their performance.

True or False   4. Effective managers think of mistakes as learning opportunities.

True or False   5. The test of helping effectiveness is whether an employee's performance improves.

True or False   6. Threats are a good development tool.

True or False   7. Sometimes it is more beneficial for the employee's development just to do the task yourself.

True or False   8. Once an employee has mastered a task satisfactorily your development job is done.

True or False   9. If you want your employees to behave in a certain way, model the behaviour yourself.

True or False   10. It's preferable to let employees develop their own ways to improve performance than to provide a solution yourself.

Answers   (1) False; (2) False; (3) True; (4) True; (5) True; (6) False; (7) False; (8) False; (9) True; (10) True

Behavioural Checklist

The following skills are important to developing employees. Use them when evaluating your own skills and those of others.

To Develop Employees:

- Ask questions to help discover sources of problems and how to best help employees improve.
- Actively listen to employees and show genuine interest.
- Demonstrate unconditional positive regard by suspending judgment and evaluation.
- Seek to educate rather than to assist.
- Delegate increased responsibilities and authority.
- Accept mistakes and use them as learning opportunities.
- Provide meaningful feedback for learning.
- Encourage continual improvement.
- Recognize and reward improvements no matter how small.
- Model qualities expected from employees.
- Help develop action plans for improvement.

Modelling Exercise

DIRECTIONS One volunteer assumes the role of the manager, Lorin Wilcox, and another assumes the role of the broker, T.J. Corsetti. Role-players read only their own role, and prepare for the role-play. Other class members read both roles and review the Observer's Rating Sheet. After the role-play discussion, observers will provide feedback to the person playing the manager, Lorin Wilcox, on his or her performance, using the Observer's Rating Sheet as a guide.

Building Problems in Edmonton

ACTORS Lorin Wilcox (manager); T.J. Corsetti (broker).

SITUATION Lorin Wilcox is the supervisor of the Edmonton office of a large mortgage brokering company that has 30 offices in Canada. Lorin supervises seven mortgage brokers, an assistant, and a secretary. The business entails helping home buyers find mortgages and acting as a link between lenders and borrowers in getting loans approved and processed.

T.J. Corsetti is one of the brokers. T.J. has been in the Edmonton office for two and a half years. Before that, he sold commercial real estate. Lorin Wilcox has been in the Edmonton job for 14 months, after having supervised a smaller office for the same company.

LORIN WILCOX'S ROLE You have not been pleased with T.J.'s job performance. So you decided to review his personnel file. T.J.'s first six-month review stated: "Enthusiastic. A bit disorganized but willing to learn. Seems to have good potential." After a year, T.J.'s previous supervisor had written, "T.J. seems to be losing interest. Seems frequently disorganized. Often rude to clients. Did not mention these problems to him previously. Hope T.J. will improve. Long-term potential now much more in question."

You have not spent much time with T.J. Your offices are far apart, but probably the real reason is that T.J. is not a person who is easy to talk to and you have little in common. When you took the Edmonton job, you decided that you would wait some time before attacking any problems to make sure you had a good grasp of the people and the situation.

T.J.'s problems, however, have become too visible to ignore. He is consistently missing quarterly sales projections. Based on mortgages processed, T.J. is your lowest performer. In addition, T.J.'s reports are constantly late. After reviewing last month's performance reports, you made an appointment yesterday to meet him today at 9:00 A.M. T.J. was not in his office when you arrived for that appointment, so you waited 15 minutes before giving up. Your secretary tells you that T.J. regularly comes in late for work in the morning and takes extra long coffee breaks.

Last week, Valerie Oletta, who has the office next to T.J.'s, complained to you that T.J.'s behaviour was demoralizing her and some of the other brokers.

You do not want to fire T.J. It would be difficult to find a replacement. Moreover, T.J. has many contacts with new-home builders, which bring in a number of borrowers to your office. In fact, maybe 60 per cent of the business generated by your entire office comes from builders who have personal ties to T.J. If T.J. were to leave your company and go to a competitor, he would probably be able to convince the builders to take their business somewhere else.

T.J. CORSETTI'S ROLE The mortgage brokering business has been pretty good for you. From your previous job in commercial real estate, you developed a lot of contacts with new-home builders, which bring in a number of borrowers to your office. In fact, maybe 60 per cent of the business generated by your entire office comes from builders who have personal ties with you.

Although your old builder buddies supply you with plenty of business, you realized early in your first year that the brokering business required some word-processing, mathematical, and computer skills that you never acquired 10 years ago when you graduated from high school. Most of the other brokers have either a diploma or degree in business administration and one even has an MBA. You have been embarrassed to ask for help because you are older than most of the other brokers. Consequently, it takes you quite a bit longer than other brokers to process the mortgages, which often makes your reports late because you have to type one key at a time.

To try and get up to speed, you have enrolled in an 8:00 A.M. extension course in typing and word-processing at Grant MacEwan College, which makes you about an hour late for work three days a week, but you think it certainly is going to be worth it in the long run. You are hoping that the evening course in business mathematics you signed up for will have an equal payoff. You are working on it three evenings a week and during your breaks at work.

These classes are a bit overwhelming at the moment, and you have fallen a little behind in your work. You overheard some of the other brokers discussing your lack of involvement with them a couple of weeks ago, but you are too busy to worry about that until you complete your courses. Then you will be right up with the best of them. Besides, you are still making a contribution in a way. It is your contacts with the builders that bring in a majority of the business for your office. In fact, you are also taking a broker course on weekends so you can take your contacts with you and start your own company next year.

The broker in the next office mentioned that your boss, Lorin Wilcox, was at your office for an appointment that Lorin had scheduled for 9:00 A.M. You went to your usual class and completely forgot about it. You decide to go up to Lorin's office to see what the appointment was about.

TIME Not to exceed 10 minutes.

Observer's Rating Sheet

On completion of the exercise, evaluate the development skills of Lorin Wilcox using the following scale. Write concrete examples in the space for comments to use in explaining your feedback.

1 Unsatisfactory	2 Weak	3 Adequate	4 Good	5 Outstanding

_____ Asked questions to help discover sources of problems and how best to help employees improve.

_____ Actively listened to employees and showed genuine interest.

_____ Demonstrated unconditional positive regard by suspending judgment and evaluation.

_____ Tried to educate rather than assist.

_____ Delegated increased responsibilities and authority.

_____ Accepted mistakes and used them as learning opportunities.

_____ Provided meaningful feedback for learning.

_____ Encouraged continual improvement.

_____ Recognized and rewarded all improvements no matter how small.

_____ Modelled qualities expected from employees.

_____ Helped develop action plans for improvement.

Group Exercises

Four group exercises follow. First is a short case presenting some dilemmas for developing employees in difficult situations. Second is an opportunity for you to receive feedback on your skills in actually coaching and counselling a classmate in a school-related performance problem. The third and fourth exercises are job-related role-plays dealing with coaching and counselling problems.

When conducting exercises three and four, follow the usual directions for role-plays: One volunteer assumes the role of the manager or supervisor and another assumes the role of the employee. Role-players read only their own role and prepare for the role-play. Other class members read both roles and review the Observer's Rating Sheet. After the role-play discussion, observers will provide feedback to the person playing the manager, on his or her performance, using the Observer's Rating Sheet as a guide.

Group Exercise 1: Writing Mike Off: Confessions of a Sales Manager[18]

During the managers' meeting when we were discussing difficult employees, I realized that I had completely written Mike off and had stopped any effective communication with him. Mike was a 53-year-old sales representative who had been with the company for more than 12 years. He was well liked by the central office staff but had not met his sales plan for five of the last six years. Furthermore, I was starting to hear complaints about him from some of our clients.

I first tried to put myself in Mike's shoes. What must it be like to be near the end of one's career and starting to go downhill? If I were Mike, how receptive would I be to criticism? I might then be able to understand one of his habitual behaviours that had been particularly annoying to me: his tendency to look only to external factors for his failures, to blame "bad luck," the market, competitors who used unfair tactics, and the like.

Still, before meeting with Mike, I did two things. I considered what would be a reasonable goal for him in six months—what exactly did I expect of him in terms of sales level, generating new business, and the like. Then I thought, "What is it in Mike's behaviour that would cause him trouble in making sales? Is it something in his style or is some knowledge lacking?"

I then sat down with Mike and began by acknowledging that our relationship had deteriorated, that I had been dissatisfied with him but had not confronted him before, and also that I probably had not helped him as much as I could have. Mike immediately blamed me for everything that had gone wrong. It was fortunate that I had thought this situation out before, because my first response was defensive, to attack back. What helped was that I had already thought about why Mike must be hurting—clearly his pain was greater than anything I was now feeling about his comments.

After Mike had vented his feelings, I repeated that I wanted to change our relationship so that I could be more helpful. In return, we needed to get agreement on some specific goals for Mike. Although I would help him, it would be his responsibility to meet certain objectives. He was to be accountable for them, and if he failed to meet or substantially reach them in six months, he would be placed on probation. We mutually negotiated these goals. When I felt he was setting them too low, I pointed out what other sales personnel would do. We ended up with my original list modified, but in a way both of us could live with.

I then asked Mike what he thought might cause him difficulty in going about reaching his goals. In what areas did he need more training, and were there ways he behaved that caused problems? (I also asked him to discuss what he thought was easy for him—what his especially strong areas were.) As he shared his self-perception, I also shared my perception. I tried to point to specific behaviours at specific times that illustrated the problem areas I saw. At one point, he got very defensive and offered external reasons why the problems I identified were not his fault. I used his response as an illustration of what I was pointing out in his behaviour.

In this discussion, we agreed to specific areas in which he could benefit from training. I sent him to a training program to work on his time-management problem. Also, we set up regular meetings (every two weeks) when we would review progress. I said that I was always available if he had a question, but that the initiative was up to him.

Mike did not meet the goals at the end of six months. I placed him on probation, with notice of termination in three months. I again met with him on a regular basis to offer assistance and coaching. Seven days before the end of his probation, Mike came in and said that the fit between him and the job was not right and quit.

As a result of this process, the office staff, who had very much liked Mike, had minimal reaction. Morale did not decrease, nor did any paranoia arise among the others. Mike found another job in an area both of us had discussed as being more in line with his skills. Perhaps most gratifying to me, he expressly thanked me for my concern. He is doing well in his new position and is much happier.

QUESTIONS FOR DISCUSSION

1. Is this manager acting as a coach or a counsellor? What did he do that made you answer the way you did?
2. Compare the sales manager's behaviours to those for developing employees on the Behavioural Checklist. How well did the manager do in helping Mike? What could he have done better?

Group Exercise 2: Helping with a Peer Problem

Divide the class into groups of three. Each trio will conduct three coaching/counselling sessions, allowing every student the opportunity to share a school-related performance problem to get help with, and to play the role of coach to help and counsel a peer.

If you are the person receiving help, think of a school-related problem you are currently experiencing or have had in the past. Briefly share the nature of the problem and its consequences with your coach. If you do not have a school-related problem you want to share, you can role-play someone else's problem from exercise three or four instead.

Now the coach takes over and conducts the most appropriate type of coaching or counselling session. At the conclusion of the session the observer will provide the coach with feedback based on the following Observer's Rating Sheet.

TIME   Not to exceed 20 minutes per helping session.

Observer's Rating Sheet

On completion of the exercise, evaluate the development skills of the person acting as the helper using the following scale. Write concrete examples in the space for comments following each behaviour to use in explaining your feedback.

1 Unsatisfactory	2 Weak	3 Adequate	4 Good	5 Outstanding

_____ Asked questions to help discover sources of problems and how best to help employees improve.

_____ Actively listened to employees and showed genuine interest.

_____ Demonstrated unconditional positive regard by suspending judgment and evaluation.

_____ Tried to educate rather than assist.

_____ Delegated increased responsibilities and authority.

_____ Accepted mistakes and used them as learning opportunities.

_____ Provided meaningful feedback for learning.

_____ Encouraged continual improvement.

_____ Recognized and rewarded all improvements no matter how small.

_____ Modelled qualities expected from employees.

_____ Helped develop action plans for improvement.

Group Exercise 3: Role-Play: Problems Everywhere[19]

ACTORS Lynn Bosco works in the blending department of a large pharmaceutical company; Ricky Thomas is Lynn's supervisor.

SITUATION Lynn works hard but recently she has been unable to concentrate well on the task at hand. At 45 years old, Lynn was divorced after a 15-year marriage. Six months later, Lynn married a 23-year-old aerobics instructor. In the last five years, Lynn has twice bid for a higher-paying job elsewhere in the company. In both cases Lynn was advised that she did not have the necessary educational qualifications for advancement into a skilled trade.

LYNN BOSCO'S ROLE Your mind is continually wandering to your debts. With easy credit, you have become a chronic borrower. This borrowing is not due to illness, rent payments, or any of the other common reasons people go into debt. You borrow for luxuries like the new Acura you just bought and the jet-ski boat you bought last year. You realize that your work is falling off somewhat but you are absolutely convinced you will get it straightened out soon.

RICKY THOMAS'S ROLE You have noticed that Lynn's work is beginning to deteriorate. The number of batches Lynn mixes per shift fell from 15 to 11 in the last six months, and on several occasions Lynn has scorched a batch. The last time you talked to Lynn about this slump, Lynn responded, "Everything is all right, I'm just a little untracked right now, I'll get it going again." Despite this assurance, however, Lynn's work has continued to be poor. You know about Lynn's bids for other jobs in the company and suspect the problems may be financial. Lynn has always been a good worker whom, up to this point, you've wanted to keep if possible. You feel that Lynn is not going to get over these problems without some help. You decide to call Lynn in and see if you can help.

TIME Not to exceed 15 minutes.

Group Exercise 4: Role-Play: Why Is the Camera Out of Focus?

ACTORS Fran Delano is a camera operator; Alex Maher is Fran's supervisor.

SITUATION Alex has supervised 11 camera operators at a major Canadian television network for more than five years. Fran has worked for Alex for more than four of those years and, in the last two years, Fran Delano has become the number-one-rated camera operator. Of the operators that the station employed, Fran was every producer's first choice. Fran had a choice of hours and shows. Fran was extremely competent, creative, and dependable. Fran's supervisor, Alex Maher, had even been a bit protective. As Alex said 18 months ago, "Everyone knows Fran's the best we've got. Everyone wants Fran for their shows. I've got to make sure we do not burn out our best camera operator."

ALEX MAHER'S ROLE You have become far less enthusiastic about Fran over the past four months. The problems began with Fran coming in late for assigned shifts. First it was just 10 or 15 minutes late. Then it got to be 30 minutes. Last week, Fran was over an hour late for shifts twice, and 15 to 20 minutes late each of the other three days. Yesterday, Fran called in sick just ten minutes before the show was to go "on the air." This morning, Fran came in 40 minutes late.

In addition to the lateness, you have noticed two other disturbing signs. Fran is not nearly as talkative and outgoing as usual. Also, several times last week, you are certain that you smelled alcohol on Fran's breath. Nick Randolph, another camera operator, told you two weeks ago that he was certain Fran had been drinking before coming to work, and again during the lunch break. Nick was particularly upset about the quality of Fran's work. Alex, of course, knew what he was talking about. Fran's mind seemed to be wandering during shows: she was missing directors' instructions, and slow in getting the camera into new positions.

You do not know much about Fran's personal life. You have heard Fran lives with or is married to a graphic artist but that is about all you know.

Up to this point, you have not said anything to Fran about this behaviour, but now something has to be done. After today's work shift, you called Fran into your office. As Fran walks in, you can't help noticing the smell of alcohol.

FRAN DELANO'S ROLE Becoming the number one-rated camera operator paid off in giving you your choice of hours and shows. The problem is you take every show you can possibly do. You feel that your place on the top rung is precarious because of the multitude of other talented camera operators jockeying to get some of your shows. It is lucrative for you right now and you feel that you had better get all you can while the getting is good. Actually, you do not have much choice if you are to maintain your house payments because your spouse has been unemployed as a graphic artist for the past two years and the prospects do not look good because hundreds of others are in the same situation. In fact, your spouse has quit looking recently, and is quite depressed.

This business is not easy and it requires all you have to handle it—the intense concentration when everything depends on you during the show, the relentless hours from the early morning news broadcasts to late night variety shows, and the constant worry that someone else will show their stuff if you miss a show for any reason. As if this pressure were not enough, you constantly worry about your spouse's deteriorating state of mind.

You are so exhausted when you get off work, often close to midnight, that you just go home and have a few drinks. That is what your spouse is doing anyway. You are usually happy when your spouse is already in bed because your relative success seems to cause hostile attacks or the silent treatment. You cannot decide which is worse, but your relationship is definitely floundering.

Lately you noticed that it takes a whole bottle of wine or more than a six pack of beer to calm you down enough to get to sleep. You have discovered that a shot of brandy in your morning coffee seems to help the dull headaches you wake up with. Also, a couple of glasses of wine at lunch can make the stress seem much less severe, and a short nip from the flask of Wild Turkey you keep in your coat pocket helps you relax between shows.

You know you are probably drinking a little too much, but it seems to be the only way you can avoid worrying about your problems enough to focus on your work or even get a little sleep. You are sure that as soon as your spouse finds a job and you can cut back a little, you will be just fine.

TIME Not to exceed 15 minutes.

Application Questions

1. Think of a particularly effective mentor or coach you had in high school, college or university, or any other situation (e.g., sports, debate, music, etc.). Describe why he or she was so effective. How do this helper's qualities match up with those in the Behavioural Checklist?

2. How have your parents served as helpers for your development? What did they do that was particularly helpful? What could they have done better?

3. How is coaching similar to counselling? How are the two different?
4. Which of the earlier skills in this book contribute to developing employees? How do they relate?
5. How can a manager tell whether he or she is being effective in developing others? When and how does a manager know the developing job is completed?
6. What are three things you should not do when developing others and why?
7. What are three things you should always do when developing others and why?

Reinforcement Exercises

1. Ask a coach of a local sports team (high school, college or university, club, or professional) for permission to observe him or her at work. Spend a few hours watching the coach do his or her job. How do this coach's behaviours match up with those in the Behavioural Checklist?
2. Watch several episodes of a television series. Determine incidences of people trying to develop others. Do they assist or educate, coach or counsel? How effectively do they use the skills described in this chapter?
3. Help someone develop. For example, help a less able student through a class-related problem; coach someone in developing an academic or athletic skill; counsel a friend who wants to improve a difficult relationship; or mentor a younger or less experienced sibling or friend.
4. Visit the counselling department at your college or university. Talk to a counselor about what procedures are used when helping students solve problems and which are most effective.

Summary Checklist

Review your performance and look over others' ratings of your development skills. Now assess yourself on each of the following key helping behaviours. Make a check (√) next to those behaviours on which you need improvement.

_____ Determining the best approach for developing employees.
   1. Use education whenever possible so that the employee can perform independently. Use assistance only in emergencies.
   2. Determine the source of the problem before trying to help the employee.
   3. Demonstrate unconditional positive regard.

_____ Empowering employees by delegating increased responsibilities and authority.
   1. Allow greater participation in decisions that control their work.
   2. Clarify expanded responsibilities for work outcomes.
   3. Specify the range of discretion.
   4. Inform others that delegation has occurred.
   5. Establish criteria to measure success.

_____ Providing meaningful feedback for learning.
   1. Communicate to the employee what behaviour you observe, how you assess it, what consequences it has, and how to effectively address the observed behaviour and consequences.
   2. Ensure that feedback is acceptable and effective by making it descriptive rather than evaluative, specific and data-based rather than general, directed toward controllable behaviours, and timely.

_____ Coaching employees about performance problems caused by ability or work skill issues.

1. Analyze ways to improve an employee's performance and capabilities by observing daily behaviour, asking questions, actively listening, and showing genuine interest in the person as an individual.

2. Create a supportive climate by reducing barriers to development, empowering employees to implement appropriate ideas, offering to help, being positive and upbeat, treating mistakes as learning opportunities, and validating employees' efforts.

3. Influence employees to change their behaviour by showing concern for ongoing development, rewarding improvements, using a collaborative problem-solving style, breaking complex tasks into simpler ones, and modelling desired behaviours.

_____ Counselling employees about personal problems.

1. Build trust by maintaining confidentiality.
2. Help clarify thoughts and feelings into a more logical and coherent order.
3. Provide reassurance that problems have solutions and can be solved.
4. Identify employee problems requiring professional treatment.

_____ Mentoring employees for long-term development.

1. Provide ongoing emotional support and encouragement.
2. Educate about the organization, its goals, and advancement criteria.
3. Coach to be more politically savvy and avoid possible traps.
4. Help employees live up to their full potential and encourage them to be more proactive in managing their careers.

_____ Helping to develop action plans for improvement.

1. Collaborate with participating employees to gain commitment.
2. Search for concrete and specific things to improve.
3. Establish a time schedule.
4. Determine criteria and how to get feedback to measure success.

Action Plan

1. Which helping behaviours do I most want to improve? (For examples, see Behavioural Checklist.)
2. Why? What will be my payoff?
3. What potential obstacles stand in my way?
4. What are the specific things I will do to improve? (For examples, see the Reinforcement Exercises and Summary Checklist.)
5. When will I do them?
6. How and when will I measure my success?

CHAPTER 16
Creating Teams

Learning Objectives
After completing this chapter, you should be able to:
- Identify the characteristics of effective teams.
- Design high-performing teams.
- Recognize the stages of team development.
- Adapt leadership style to different stages of team development.
- Identify obstacles to effective team performance.
- Facilitate team processes.
- Conduct effective meetings.

Self-Assessment Exercise
Do You Have a Team Mindset?
Circle the answer that most closely resembles your attitude.

	Strongly Disagree						Strongly Agree
1. Only those who depend on themselves get ahead in life.	7	6	5	4	3	2	1
2. To be superior a person must stand alone.	7	6	5	4	3	2	1
3. If you want something done right, you must do it yourself.	7	6	5	4	3	2	1
4. What happens to me is my own doing.	7	6	5	4	3	2	1
5. In the long run the only person you can count on is yourself.	7	6	5	4	3	2	1
6. Winning is everything.	7	6	5	4	3	2	1
7. I feel that winning is important in both work and games.	7	6	5	4	3	2	1
8. Success is the most important thing in life.	7	6	5	4	3	2	1
9. It annoys me when other people perform better than I do.	7	6	5	4	3	2	1

	Strongly Disagree						Strongly Agree
10. Doing your best is not enough; it is important to win.	7	6	5	4	3	2	1
11. I prefer to work with others in a group rather than working alone.	7	6	5	4	3	2	1
12. Given the choice, I would rather do a job where I can work alone rather than doing a job where I have to work with others in a group.	7	6	5	4	3	2	1
13. Working with a group is better than working alone.	7	6	5	4	3	2	1
14. People should be made aware that if they are going to be part of a group then they are sometimes going to have to do things they do not want to do.	7	6	5	4	3	2	1
15. People who belong to a group should realize that they are not always going to get what they personally want.	7	6	5	4	3	2	1
16. People in a group should realize that they sometimes are going to have to make sacrifices for the sake of the group as a whole.	7	6	5	4	3	2	1
17. People in a group should be willing to make sacrifices for the sake of the group's well-being.	7	6	5	4	3	2	1
18. A group is most productive when its members do what they want to do rather than what the group wants to do.	7	6	5	4	3	2	1
19. A group is most efficient when its members do what they think is best rather than doing what the group wants them to do.	7	6	5	4	3	2	1
20. A group is most productive when its members follow their own interests and concerns.	7	6	5	4	3	2	1

Source: Adapted from J.A. Wagner III, "Studies of Individualism-Collectivism: Effects on Cooperation in Groups," *Academy of Management Journal* (February 1995): 162.

SCORING AND INTERPRETATION Add your answers to calculate your score. Your total score will be between 20 and 140.

The higher your score, the higher your collectivist orientation, so high scores are more compatible with being a team player. For comparative purposes, 492 undergraduate students enrolled in an introductory management course at a large U.S. university scored an average of approximately 89. We might speculate that scores below 69 indicate a strong individualistic ethic, which would mean that you prefer to work alone. Scores above 109 indicate a strong team mentality and preference for collaborating with others.

Concepts

Successful managers are those who work with successful teams; however, working with others is not easy. Nevertheless, groups constitute the basic building blocks of any organization. For many tasks, teams can increase productivity by accomplishing more work in less time than the same number of individuals can working separately. Employees can also grow more quality conscious through group interaction as they learn about others' experiences, problems, and solutions as work-in-process flows through the organization.[1]

Groups can be defined as two or more people who meet regularly over a period of time, perceive themselves as a distinct entity distinguishable from others, share common values, and strive for common objectives.[2] Most of us are members of several different types of groups in organizations, ranging from the lunch bunch that meets to enjoy each other's company, to problem-solving task forces that are charged with developing plans for major organizational change.

All teams are groups, but they are more sophisticated forms. **Teams** are groups with complementary skills, who are committed to a common purpose, set of performance goals, and approach for which they hold themselves mutually accountable.[3] A team engages in collective work produced by coordinated joint efforts that result in more than the sum of the individual efforts, or **synergy**. Members are accountable for performance both as individuals and as a group.

The lunch bunch or people working independently in a radio assembly group would not be classified as a team, but their lack of team status is not a problem because they do not need coordinated joint efforts, complementary skills, and other ingredients necessary for group synergy. In other situations, such as a symphony orchestra or an emergency room hospital unit, complementary skills, coordinated joint efforts, shared and individual responsibility, and other team characteristics are necessary ingredients to produce the required synergistic output.

In Canada, teams play a central role in work redesign.[4] Without proper preparation, however, quality circles, self-directed work teams, and cross-functional teams may not live up to expectations.[5] A number of findings from studies of successful teams provide insights to the essential ingredients. In this chapter you will learn the skills to develop groups into high-energy teams and intervene when your team gets off track.

The Importance of Creating High-Performance Teams

Don Callahan and Brian Large huddled around a half-built Dodge Intrepid, trying to figure out why the warning light on the instrument panel was on even though the air conditioner was working fine. Both men were members of the LH cars' A platform at DaimlerChrysler's assembly plant at Brampton, Ontario. Don Callahan, an hourly assembly-line worker, and Brian Large, a product engineer, have worked together since the Intrepid prototype was first built. In a few hours, they managed to fix the electrical glitch and send their car down the line.

If DaimlerChrysler had developed the LH like most North American vehicles have been developed, Callahan wouldn't have contacted Large about the problem, because the two would never have met, and the early production cars would likely have reached customers' hands with the electrical system still on the fritz. However, the workers, designers, and engineers who collaborated in developing the first test batch of cars thrashed out the final stages of a vehicle development process that sought to blur the traditional lines between people in different functional work units.

The team approach paid off in a number of ways for DaimlerChrysler. The LH team, for example, shaved a full year off DaimlerChrysler's average vehicle development cycle, which historically averaged four and a half years, and team members did it with 40 per cent fewer engineers than a typical product program would use. At a price tag of just over $1 billion, the LH budget came in well under those of two other well-known team efforts, Ford's $3 billion Taurus/Sable and GM's $3.5 billion Saturn.[6]

At Waterloo-based NCR, which produces automatic teller machines and cheque processing machines, teams have also paid off. Teams of employees have influence over not only how they will get the job done but also what should be done. This has led to an improvement in the workplace climate, higher production worker satisfaction, and greater productivity as measured by increased on-time shipments, lower inventories, and reduced levels of scrap.[7]

What is it about teams that give them the potential to contribute these types of organizational benefits? Eight things that teams can provide are described in Exhibit 16-1. You should keep in mind, however, that these are only *potential* benefits that have a better chance of being realized if the skills in this chapter are applied. For each of these success stories of outstanding team performance, however, many times work groups do not work out at all.[8] What makes the difference between high-performing teams and group failures is the subject of this chapter. Let's start by taking a look at the characteristics of high-performing teams.

Exhibit 16-1 Eight Ways Your Organization Can Benefit From Teams

1. Team output usually exceeds individual output. Although a single person can make a big difference in an organization, he or she rarely has the knowledge, experience, or skill equal to a team. Research is clear that major gains on quality and productivity most often result from organizations with a team culture.

2. Complex problems can be solved more effectively. Complex problems usually require diverse, in-depth technical knowledge that can be found only among several subject-matter experts. Complexity mandates teams.

3. Creative ideas are usually stimulated in the presence of other individuals who have the same focus, passion, and excitement. Creative ideas, or leaps from conventional wisdom, are usually spawned in the tension of differences, which can most easily occur in teams.

4. Support arises among team members. Process improvement and product innovation are hard work and take a long time. It would be natural for one person's energy to drop during the long effort. The synergy and optimism that come from people working together productively can sustain team member enthusiasm and support even through difficult times.

5. Teams infuse knowledge. When many people work on an organizational problem, more organization members will see the need for change and a vision of what is better. Team members become "sensors" for how the rest of the organization will view the proposed change, as well as ambassadors for the proposed change.

6. Teams promote organizational learning in a work setting. The team setting naturally promotes both formal (training events and educational experiences) and informal learning because of the diverse knowledge and skills present in the group members, which then are ingested through problem identification and problem solving.

7. Teams promote individual self-disclosure and examination. Teams require flexibility in behaviour and outlook from individual team members. Egos must be checked at the door in favour of passionate commitment to a common goal.

8. Teams both appreciate and take advantage of diversity. Preconceived ideas about people and things will ultimately be challenged in teams. Emotions and ideas that do not support tolerance will be challenged in teams.

Source: S.F. Woodring, and D. Zigarmi, *The Team Leader's Idea-A-Day Guide* (Chicago, Dertnell, 1997) 5. Reprinted with permission. © by Dertnell, 360 Hiatt Drive, Palm Beach Gardens, FL 33418. All rights reserved. For more information on this or other products published by Dertnell, please call (800) 621-5463, ext 567.

Characteristics of High-Performing Teams

Studies of effective teams have found that they contain a small number of people with complementary skills who are equally committed to a common purpose, goals, and working approach for which they hold themselves mutually accountable.[9] Let's examine these characteristics in a little more depth.

SMALL SIZE

The best teams tend to be small. When they have more than about 10 members, it becomes difficult for them to get much done. They have trouble interacting constructively and agreeing on much. Large numbers of people usually cannot develop the common purpose, goals, approach, and mutual accountability of a real team, so in designing effective teams, keep them to 10 or less. If the natural working unit is larger, and you want a team effort, break the group into subteams. FedEx, for instance, has divided the 1,000 clerical workers at its headquarters into teams of 5 to 10 members each.

COMPLEMENTARY SKILLS

To perform effectively, a team requires three types of skills. First, it needs people with *technical expertise*. Second, it needs people with the *problem-solving and decision-making skills* to identify problems, generate alternatives, evaluate those alternatives, and make competent choices. Finally, teams need people with good *interpersonal skills*.

No team can achieve its performance potential without developing all three types of skills, but teams do not need to have all the complementary skills at the beginning. Where team members value personal growth and development, one or more members often take responsibility to learn the skills in which the group is deficient, as long as the skill potential exists. Additionally, personal compatibility among members is not critical to the team's success if the technical, decision-making, and interpersonal skills are in place.

COMMON PURPOSE

High-performing teams have a common vision and meaningful purpose that provide direction, momentum, and commitment for members. The development team at Apple Computer that designed the Macintosh, for example, was almost religiously committed to creating a user-friendly machine that would revolutionize the way people used computers. Production teams at NCR are united by the common purpose of working smarter, not harder, to gain greater efficiency. At New Brunswick Telephone Company, Ltd. (NB Tel), teams are motivated to adopt innovative workplace practices in order to survive in a highly uncertain and competitive industry environment.

Members of successful teams put a tremendous amount of time and effort into discussing, shaping, and agreeing upon a purpose that belongs to them collectively and individually. This common purpose, when accepted by the team, becomes the equivalent of what celestial navigation is to a ship captain: It provides direction and guidance under any and all conditions.

SPECIFIC GOALS

Successful teams translate their common purpose into specific, measurable, and realistic performance goals. Just as goals lead individuals to higher performance (see Chapter 11 for more on planning and goal setting), they also energize teams. Specific goals facilitate clear communication and help teams maintain their focus on getting results. Examples of specific team goals might be responding to all customers within 24 hours, cutting production-cycle time by 30 per cent over the next six months, or maintaining equipment at a level of zero downtime every month.

COMMON APPROACH

Goals are the ends a team strives to attain. Defining and agreeing upon a common approach ensures that the team is unified on the *means* for achieving those ends. Team members need to determine how to share the workload, set schedules, resolve conflicts, and make decisions. For example, at NB Tel, this approach has brought interdependent functions such as inside sales, installation, and cable repair in a particular area into a single team. The team members determine work scheduling, address budgeting issues, and determine their own training requirements.[10] Integrating individual skills to further the team's performance is the essence of shaping a common approach.

MUTUAL ACCOUNTABILITY

The final characteristic of high-performing teams is accountability at both the individual and group levels. Successful teams make members individually and jointly accountable for the team's purpose, goals, and approach. Members understand what they are individually responsible for and what they are jointly responsible for.

When teams focus only on group-level performance targets, and ignore individual contributions and responsibilities, team members often engage in **social loafing**.[11] They reduce their inputs because their individual contributions cannot be identified and become "free riders," coasting on the team's effort. The result is that the team's overall performance suffers. This issue reaffirms the importance of measuring individual contributions to the team as well as the team's overall performance.

Designing High-Performing Teams

The introduction of teams into the workplace can be more successful if a number of general business conditions exist. Greater success can be achieved when labour–management relations are cooperative, when innovative work practices are seen as a route to survival within a highly competitive industry environment, and when front-line managers are truly accepting and promote the idea of a team-based workplace.[12]

Lastly, it is easier to design high-performing teams when a new organization is being created than to impose them on an existing structure because appropriate applicants and technology can be selected for the new system. General Motors, for example, realized instant success when it started producing the Saturn automobile by establishing cross-functional teams with new members in an entirely new plant. The cross-functional teams were able to coordinate the entire project from the beginning, as opposed to GM's traditional method of having the design team pass its work on to the production team.

So what actions can be taken to get new teams off to a productive start? Exhibit 16-2 summarizes a set of questions that new teams need to address in the following order until all the answers are clearly understood and agreed upon by all team members.[13] Established teams also need to develop procedures to address the issues associated with these questions.

WHO ARE WE?

When team members share their strengths, weaknesses, work preferences, values, and beliefs with others, diversity can be dealt with before it causes unspoken conflicts. The end result is a set of common beliefs that creates a group identity, a feeling of "what we stand for." The "My Asset Base" exercise at the end of this chapter is a good way to answer this question in a structured manner. To start the team-building process, have each member

Exhibit 16-2 High Energy Team Development Model

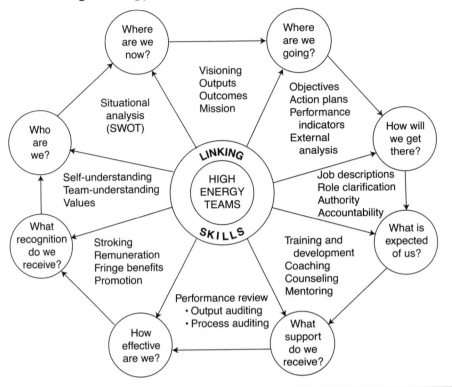

Source: C. Margerison and D. McCann, *The Team Development Manual* (Toowong, Queensland, Australia: Team Management Resources, 1990) 20.

answer the following questions and then share them with each other: What are my strengths that can be a resource for the team? What are my weaknesses where I may need some coaching or training? What are my work preferences where I will best fit team requirements? What are my values and beliefs?

After all have shared this personal information, the team should discuss the implications for working productively together. For example, what differences in basic values might cause conflicts? What are the common beliefs that allow for a shared identity regarding what the team "stands for"? What are the implications for working together as a team?

WHERE ARE WE NOW?

All teams have strengths and weaknesses, but most tend to concentrate on the things they do well and ignore those that they do not do well. Examining the team's strengths, weaknesses, opportunities, and threats (a team SWOT analysis as described in Chapter 11, Planning and Goal Setting) can be done by having the team address each of the following questions: What strengths should we reinforce, build on, and improve? What weaknesses can we improve on, and how can we do it? What opportunities do we have for improvement, learning new skills, and undertaking new tasks? What internal threats (e.g., role ambiguity or conflict) and external threats (e.g., budget decreases or increased competition) do we face?

WHERE ARE WE GOING?

Teams need to have a vision of the pot of gold at the end of the rainbow. They need a mission, purpose, and goals, as described in Chapter 11. They need to consider what the team will be like in one, two, or five years and develop a vision they are all excited about. They need an overriding reason for existing and concrete goals to strive for.

HOW WILL WE GET THERE?

Based on its mission and goals, the team needs to set specific team objectives and then integrate individual objectives. Objectives are the basis for action plans, which spell out who does what, when, and how, including external linkages with other departments and individuals who can facilitate goal attainment. Performance indicators need to be set up to measure how well the team is doing.

WHAT IS EXPECTED FROM US?

A team cannot perform if it does not know what is expected! Therefore, managers need to help team members understand their job description, roles on the team, responsibilities, and areas of authority and accountability. Teams will accomplish team objectives more effectively by better using the talents of all members appropriately. Roles and responsibilities should correspond with members' strengths and preferences. Questions to be considered when allocating roles and responsibilities include the following: Who is good at administering and maintaining systems? Who is good at initiating change? Who is good at whipping up enthusiasm? Who is comfortable managing details of implementation?[14] Two structured techniques that can facilitate clarifying role expectations are the role analysis technique and responsibility charting.

ROLE ANALYSIS TECHNIQUE   The **role analysis technique** is designed to clarify role expectations and obligations of team members through a structured process of mutually defining and delineating role requirements. Each individual analyzes the rationale, significance, and specific duties of his or her role with the inputs of other team members until all are satisfied that the role has been completely defined. Then each individual shares his or her expectations for other roles on the team, which are discussed until the entire team is in agreement. Finally, each member writes a **role profile** to summarize the activities in his or her role, the obligations of that role to each individual on the team, and the expected contributions of other roles to the member's role. This profile is shared and agreed upon by the entire team.[15]

RESPONSIBILITY CHARTING   This technique clarifies who is responsible for which decisions and actions. The first step is to construct a grid: The types of decisions and actions the team deals with go in a vertical column on the left side, and the team members who are involved in the decisions go across the top of the grid. Then each team member is assigned one of five behavioural expectations for each of the actions: responsibility to initiate action, approval or vetoing rights, support for implementation, right to be informed (but with no influence), and noninvolvement in the decision. This process is carried out with the entire team participating and reaching a consensus.

WHAT SUPPORT DO WE GET/NEED?

A review of each member's training and development needs (i.e., a personal SWOT analysis) can set the stage for individual training, counselling, and mentoring assignments that will strengthen both the individual and the team. The support given by key managers who ran interference for the LH team at DaimlerChrysler were crucial to its surviving intact throughout the initial three years. LH team "believers" helped protect the team from less enthusiastic factions in the company. Often, these executives signaled their support by simply staying out of the team's way. But even silent allies in high places were useful when company veterans began to feel threatened by a new team's deviations from the norm.[16]

HOW EFFECTIVE ARE WE?

Regular performance reviews of quantity and quality outputs should be set up to ensure achievement of team goals and provide members with standards. It is equally important to set up a regular review of the team process.

WHAT RECOGNITION DO WE GET?

As you read in Chapter 9, Motivating Others, managers get what they reward. The same is true for teams. Types of team recognition include stroking (psychological rewards such as saying "thank you"), praise when someone on the team makes a contribution, equitable remuneration and bonuses for outstanding achievements, fringe benefits including such team fringes as celebration lunches or parties, and promotions that include preparation for more responsibility. Team members will also be more motivated if their assigned roles and responsibilities match up with their strengths and preferences.

The Five Stages of Team Development

Several research-based theories suggest that most teams progress in sequence through the five stages of forming, storming, norming, performing, and adjourning.[17] Different groups, however, remain at various stages of development for different lengths of time, and some may stall at a given stage permanently. By being aware of a team's process, the manager can facilitate members' functioning at each stage and enhance the transition to the next stage of development.

Two variables can be observed to determine team development stage: productivity and morale.[18] The model in Exhibit 16-3 illustrates how productivity and morale vary during each stage of a team's development. **Productivity**, the team's ability to work together and achieve results, steadily increases from the initial team formation throughout the life of the team. **Morale**, the team's motivation, confidence, and cohesion, starts out high initially but then decreases as members realize that initial expectations are not being

Exhibit 16-3 Variations in Productivity and Morale During Team Development

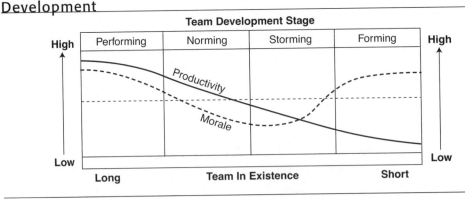

Source: Adapted from D. Carew, E. Parisi-Carew, and K. Blanchard, *Team Development and Situational Leadership II* (Escondido, CA: Blanchard Training and Development, Inc., 1998) 4.

met and conflicts develop. As differences are explored, expectations are aligned with reality and the team achieves positive results, raising morale again through the performance stage. If a manager can diagnose productivity and morale to determine a team's developmental stage, it will then be possible to make the necessary adjustments in leadership style to meet team needs at any specific stage, which will allow transition to the next stage.

To effectively diagnose the stage of a team's development, it is necessary to understand the characteristic behaviours at each stage. Then, to intervene to facilitate progression to the next stage of development, the manager needs to know the specific group needs at each stage and how to satisfy them. The following section will explain the characteristics and team needs at each stage of development. These are summarized in Exhibit 16-4.

Exhibit 16-4 Five Stages of Team Development

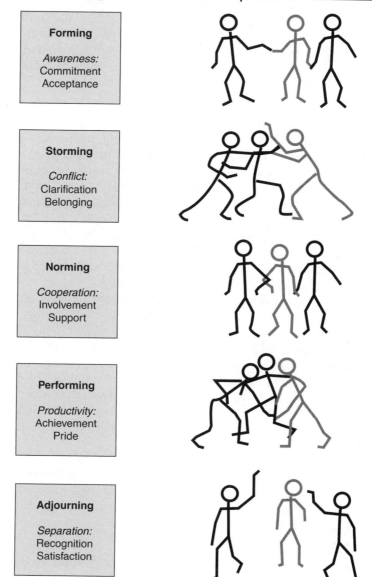

Forming

Awareness:
Commitment
Acceptance

Storming

Conflict:
Clarification
Belonging

Norming

Cooperation:
Involvement
Support

Performing

Productivity:
Achievement
Pride

Adjourning

Separation:
Recognition
Satisfaction

FORMING

In a newly formed group, many uncertainties exist about the group's purpose, structure, and leadership. Members are concerned about exploring friendship and task potentials. They do not have a strategy for addressing the group's task. They do not know yet what behaviours are acceptable as they try to determine how to satisfy needs for acceptance and personal goal satisfaction. As awareness increases, members begin to accept themselves as a group and commit to group goals.

Teams at the forming stage have a number of needs to satisfy before they can allay these concerns and move on to the next stage. A thorough and structured approach to satisfying these needs is for members to address the questions presented in the previous section for designing new teams. Answers to these questions will provide the information the team needs to know about its purpose, members' resources, ground rules for working together, roles, timelines, standards, decision-making authority, accountability, and available resources. Answering these questions to everyone's satisfaction will help the team move through not only the first, but all of the stages of development more efficiently.

The length of this stage depends on the clarity and difficulty of the task, as well as how easily the team members become comfortable working together. With fairly simple tasks, the forming stage may be a relatively short period of the team's life, say 5 to 10 per cent. With complex tasks, however, the team may spend 30 to 60 per cent of its existence at this stage.[19]

STORMING

After the team has spent some time forming, difficulties accomplishing the task and working together lead to frustration and conflict. Disagreement is inevitable as members attempt to decide on task procedures, role assignments, ways of relating, and power allocations. Then emerges a growing dissatisfaction with the team's dependence on the leader, who is blamed for a majority of the problems. Although productivity is increasing from stage one, it is still low. Communications begin to break down, which contributes to inability to problem solve and lowered trust. Negative reactions to each other develop, polarizing the team and leading to the formation of conflicting subgroups. Morale drops as team members deal with their concerns about power, control, and the discrepancy between their initial expectations and reality.

Before teams at the storming stage can move on, they need to resolve conflicts about power and task structure. They also need to work through the accompanying hostility and replace it with a sense of acceptance and belonging. Progress in these directions requires open and honest discussions of issues including emotional blocks, coalitions, and personality conflicts. Members need to simultaneously develop productive communication processes including active listening, the exchange of nonjudgmental feedback, and a problem-solving orientation. Team members also need to value differences, encourage and reassure each other, and recognize their accomplishments in order to: clarify the big picture; redefine their purpose, roles, goals, and structure; and regain commitment to essential values and norms.

The amount of time spent in this stage depends on the degree of conflict and emotions that develop. It also depends on the team's ability to resolve the issues. Occasionally groups with significant problems can become stuck in the storming stage, which leads to continued demoralization and little if any productivity.

NORMING

Cooperation is the theme of the norming stage. Resolving issues in the storming stage causes team members to value the differences among themselves and contributes to increased task accomplishment. Members agree on a structure that divides work tasks, provides leadership, and allocates other roles. This progress causes morale to rise and increases commitment to purpose, values, norms, roles, and goals. Trust and cohesion grow as communication becomes more open and task oriented. Members demonstrate a willingness to share responsibility and control as team members start thinking in terms of "we" rather than "I." On the down side, team members may avoid conflict for fear of losing the positive climate. This reluctance to deal with conflict can slow progress if remaining issues are not dealt with and less effective decisions are made.

Although productivity at this stage is moderately high and morale is improving, several needs still must be addressed before the team can move on to the performing stage. Among them are the further integration of roles, goals, norms, and structure with a focus on increasing productivity. The team members also need to continue skill development in areas such as sharing different perspectives and disagreeing in order to further develop problem-solving effectiveness and enhance their ability to learn from each experience. Finally, room still remains for continued building of trust and positive relationships through things such as the recognition and celebration of success.

This stage can be relatively short depending on the ease of resolving feelings of dissatisfaction and integrating new skills. If conflict avoidance is prolonged, the team could possibly return to the storming stage. On the other hand, if teams become too contented they can stall at this stage because they do not want to create conflict or challenge established ways of doing things.

PERFORMING

In this stage of development, group members are no longer conflicted about acceptance and how to relate to each other. Purpose, goals, and roles are clear. Now members work interdependently to solve problems and are committed to the group's mission. The primary focus is on performance, and productivity is at its peak. Morale is high, and members experience a sense of pride and excitement in being part of a high-performing team. Communication is open, and leadership is shared. Mutual respect and trust are the norms.

The major concerns include preventing loss of enthusiasm and sustaining momentum. The challenges are how to continue meeting the high standards of productivity through refinements and growth, and how to maintain morale through recognition and celebration of both team and individual accomplishments. For permanent work groups, this stage is hopefully the final and ongoing state of development. The performing stage is likely to continue with moderate fluctuations in feelings of satisfaction throughout the life of the team.

ADJOURNING

With ongoing teams this stage is not really relevant because it is never reached unless a drastic reorganization occurs. Termination, however, does occur in *ad hoc* teams or temporary task forces, and team members need to be prepared for its outcomes. Productivity may increase or decrease as the end approaches and team members strive for perfection or begin to disassociate with the team. Morale can also be impacted either positively, as team members pride themselves on their accomplishments, or negatively, as the end of the experience draws near and they feel sadness or loss. Feelings about disbanding range from sadness and depression at the loss of friendships to happiness and fulfillment due to what has been achieved. The leader can facilitate positive closure at this stage by recognizing and rewarding group performance. Ceremonial events bring closure to the desired emotional outcome, which is a sense of satisfaction and accomplishment.

Adapting Leadership Style to Facilitate Team Development[20]

Teams that are successful and productive in the performance stage do not just automatically start out that way. By understanding and diagnosing team needs at each stage of development, managers can provide appropriate leadership to move teams along the path from forming to performing.

Effective team leadership is the ability to diagnose the needs of the team and behave in ways that meet those needs. A manager can adapt leadership behaviours toward building productivity and morale as needed to achieve success in any given situation, which will allow transition to the next stage of team development.

A leader's productivity-related behaviours provide direction toward the team's task achievement. These behaviours are critical during the early stages of a team, but as time goes on, they are needed less. Morale-oriented behaviours, on the other hand, focus on how the team is working together and provide support. These behaviours are needed less in the forming stage of team development, but become critical during the storming and performing stages. The Leadership Style and Team Development model illustrated in Exhibit 16-5 provides a framework for identifying the leadership behaviours needed to build a high-performing team at each stage of team development.

Behaviours that *provide direction* focus on getting the job done. They include behaviours such as developing a compelling team purpose and values, clarifying team norms and ground rules, establishing roles, identifying goals and standards, agreeing on structure and strategies, and teaching team and task skills.

Behaviours that *provide support* focus on how the team is working together with the goals of developing harmony, involvement, and cohesion. These morale-related behaviours include involving others in decision making, encouraging participation, valuing differences, active listening, sharing leadership, acknowledging and praising, and building relationships.

Exhibit 16-5 illustrates how direction and support combine to form four leadership styles. These four styles—structuring, resolving, collaborating, and validating—vary in the amount of direction and support provided, which depends on the extent of leadership responsibility assumed by team members.

To determine appropriate leadership style, first diagnose the team's stage of development in relation to its goal, considering both productivity and morale. Then, locate the team's present stage of development in Exhibit 16-5 and follow a perpendicular line up to the curve. The point of intersection indicates the appropriate leadership style for the team. This model yields four matches of leadership style to stage of team development: structuring in the forming stage; resolving in the storming stage; collaborating in the norming stage; and validating in the performing stage. How to apply these different leadership styles will be explained next, then appropriate leader behaviours during the adjourning stage will be discussed.

STRUCTURING

When teams are initially formed, people usually are eager to be there and have high expectations. Therefore, morale is high at the start, but productivity is low due to lack of knowledge about the task and the resources each team member possesses. Direction is needed to provide the information and skills necessary to get the team started. Some need for support is present, but it is much less than the need for task-oriented behaviour. Structuring behaviours include: clarifying the team's relationship to organizational vision, purpose, and values; developing a clear and compelling team purpose; developing norms and ground rules to guide behaviour; orienting team members to one another; establishing and clarifying roles; setting goals, objectives, and standards; and developing structure and boundaries.

Exhibit 16-5 Leadership Style and Team Development

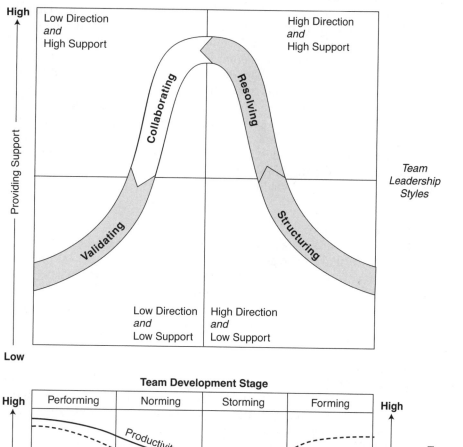

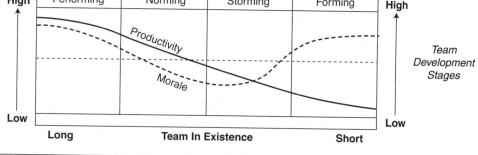

Source: Adapted from D. Carew, E. Parisi-Carew, and K. Blanchard, *Team Development and Situational Leadership II*, (Escondido, CA: Blanchard Training and Development, Inc., 1998) 5.

RESOLVING

At the storming stage of group development, anger, frustration, confusion, and discouragement can arise due to the discrepancy between initial expectations and reality. Appropriate leader behaviours are high direction and an increase in support to include more input on decision making and encouragement. Resolving behaviours include: redefining purpose, roles, goals, and standards; revisiting values and norms; encouraging active listening; providing big-picture perspective and rationale; encouraging and valuing different perspectives; encouraging feedback amid self-disclosure; recognizing and addressing difficult issues; and building supportive relationships.

COLLABORATING

The norming stage is characterized by increasing levels of morale and harmony and task competence as team members learn to work together. Goals and strategies are becoming clearer or have been redefined. Negative feelings are being resolved. Team members are more willing and able to assume leadership functions, but continued collaboration is needed to help team members develop confidence in their ability to work together. The team needs less direction in regard to the task and more support focused on building confidence, cohesion, and involvement. Collaborating behaviours include: facilitating involvement in problem solving and decision making; encouraging participation and open communication; acknowledging team accomplishments and individual contributions; encouraging interdependence and shared responsibility; integrating team purpose, norms, and structure into the team's operation; examining team functioning to reduce obstacles; and encouraging and valuing different perspectives.

VALIDATING

In the performing stage the team is providing its own direction and support. Both productivity and morale are high. At this point the manager can confidently share leadership and encourage full participation by all members. Validating behaviours include recognizing and celebrating team accomplishments, acknowledging individual contributions, continuing to evaluate and learn from experience, creating new challenges and higher standards, and encouraging continuous improvement.

TERMINATING

For adjourning teams with a distinct ending point, productivity can continue to increase, or it may go down because of a rush to complete the task. The approaching end of an important experience may also cause morale to increase or drop from its previous high levels. Accepting and acknowledging the feelings that are present during this stage may be helpful. A significant downturn in productivity and morale should be met with an increase in support, as well as some direction in order to maintain high performance.

Transforming Existing Work Groups Into High-Performing Teams

The newly created Saturn teams at GM had many benefits, including new members with common goals, agreed-upon work procedures, and shared responsibilities. Their creation is quite a contrast to DaimlerChrysler, which took people from functional work groups, with different backgrounds, who had previously competed for resources, and transformed them into cooperating LH teams. It took more than three years of team-building training in areas such as trust building and consensus decision making for the LH teams to overcome their history of buck passing, negative stereotypes, and competitiveness.[21]

Managers can learn valuable lessons about improving team performance by studying how coaches develop athletic teams. To win games, a sports team must coordinate the efforts of individual players. A sports team practises hours each week for that one hour of critical playing time where its performance counts. Members review films of past games, identify mistakes, set up goals, and plan strategies for the next game. Then the team practises until weaknesses are eliminated and it is skilled at implementing its new action plans.

Work teams also must coordinate the efforts of individual members to be effective. Most work teams, however, seldom take time out to review past actions to determine what worked and what did not. They do not spend time learning from past mistakes, nor do they consistently set goals, plan new strategies, practise new ways of behaving, or get coaching on new methods of communicating and working together. Work team members are usually intuitively aware of problems but just do not know what to do about them. So how can a manager assess problems and determine what is needed to improve team performance?

ASSESSING AND SOLVING OBSTACLES TO TEAM EFFECTIVENESS

A team-building program usually is initiated because someone (the leader, a higher-level manager, a team member, or consultant) recognizes that the group is having problems working productively as a team.[22] DaimlerChrysler managers became aware of serious difficulties on the new LH teams when they noticed symptoms such as overt hostilities between team members, chronic lateness and absenteeism at meetings, low quantity and quality of production, negative gossip and rumours, decisions not carried out because of misunderstandings, lack of willingness to take responsibility, and lack of interest in helping each other with problems. Remember that problem awareness is the first step in the problem-solving process described in Chapter 10, Innovation and Problem Solving. The rest of this section describes how to apply that process as it pertains to assessing and solving problems to team effectiveness.

PROBLEM AWARENESS: DETERMINING SYMPTOMS OF INEFFECTIVE TEAMS

The success of a team development program depends on the accurate identification of the group's specific needs and problems. It would make little sense, for example, to apply interventions aimed at increasing trust and openness of members of an executive staff if the primary problems it encountered centred on job ambiguity and role conflict. In becoming aware of and diagnosing ineffective team functioning, watch for the following key indicators.[23]

- **Failure to share issues and concerns** When team members are unwilling to get necessary information out in the open during group meetings, it usually means something is wrong in the functioning of the team. Signals that all is not well are closed-door meetings and hallway discussions to share issues and express concerns.

- **Overdependency on the leader** Even though the leader is an important initiator of team action, members should have enough confidence to move ahead when it is clear that action is needed, even if the leader is absent.

- **Unrealized decisions** Decisions made but not carried out indicate that people are working on matters of low concern or are not committed to the decisions that were made.

- **Hidden conflicts** To be effective, teams need to tolerate disagreements and work them through to mutually satisfactory solutions. Pretending that differences do not exist causes increased tension, which gets in the way of productivity and satisfaction.

- **Fighting without resolution** The continual presence of open infighting and attempts to put down, deject, or hurt others is a symptom of deep-rooted team problems.

- **Subgroups** When subgroups put themselves before the needs of the total unit, the common interests of the team are in jeopardy.

DATA GATHERING

Data need to be gathered about the team situation so that the correct diagnosis can be made. Why do negative factors exist, and what can be done about them? Data gathering can take a variety of forms.

One method for getting to the core of problems is to *interview* each team member privately, assuring confidentiality. Common and significant problems can later be shared with the team, but who mentioned them should not be disclosed. Usually, an outside expert who can gather and present the information in an unbiased manner can most effectively accomplish this interview process.

Interviews usually start with a set of common questions such as: What do you like best and least about the team? What obstacles keep you from being as productive as you could be? What are some of the strengths and weaknesses of the leader and of each member? What changes could make you and your team more effective? As the interview progresses, however, other significant factors can be investigated as they are revealed by the interviewees, in an attempt to understand and pinpoint all significant problems.

An alternative to face-to-face interviews is to distribute *written questionnaires* to team members and ask them to complete them (anonymously or not, depending on the office climate and content of the questionnaire). The team-building checklist in Exhibit 16-6 is one example of such a questionnaire.

DATA ANALYSIS

Content analysis of the interview or questionnaire data identifies common and significant problems, major themes, and suggested solutions. These results can then be summarized for presentation to team members.

If it is determined that some of the group's problems are caused by scarce resources, job ambiguity, role conflict, unrealistic workloads, and/or some other factors not directly related to how individuals function as a team, job redesign, allocation of additional resources, or better job–person matching may be called for. If outside difficulties are not the source of problems, then the manager needs to identify specific team problems.

PROBLEM IDENTIFICATION

After all the data are available, the team determines which issues are most important. Anything that will help clarify the issues already identified should be shared. Anything that keeps the group from being as effective as possible is fair game.

The next task is to set priorities and determine the group's agenda. It is vital that only those issues that the team can realistically do something about are included on the agenda so that the group can accomplish something positive and start to feel good about itself and its problem-solving abilities. Issues might be broken down into those that can be worked on immediately, those that are not possible for the group to influence and must be accepted, and those that should be delegated to someone else to act on. Following are critical obstacles that often prevent teams from being high performers.

- **Weak sense of direction** Teams perform poorly when members are not sure of their purpose, goals, and approach. Add weak leadership and you have the recipe for failure. Nothing will undermine enthusiasm for the team concept as quickly as the frustration of being an involuntary member of a team that has no focus.

- **Infighting** When team members are spending time bickering and undermining their colleagues, energy is being misdirected. Effective teams are not necessarily composed of people who all like each other; however, members must respect each other and be willing to put aside petty differences in order to facilitate goal achievement.

Exhibit 16-6 Team-Building Checklist

Identify to what extent you see evidence of the following problems in your work unit of either your present or a past job.

	Evidence		
	Low	**Some**	**High**
1. Loss of production or work unit output.	1	2 3 4	5
2. Grievances within the work unit.	1	2 3 4	5
3. Conflicts or hostility between unit members.	1	2 3 4	5
4. Confusion about assignments or unclear relationships between people.	1	2 3 4	5
5. Lack of clear goals, or low commitment of goals.	1	2 3 4	5
6. Apathy or general lack of interest or involvement of unit members.	1	2 3 4	5
7. Lack of innovation, risk taking, imagination, or initiative.	1	2 3 4	5
8. Ineffective staff meetings.	1	2 3 4	5
9. Problems in working with the boss.	1	2 3 4	5
10. Poor communications; people afraid to speak up, not listening to each other, or not talking together.	1	2 3 4	5
11. The lack of trust between boss and member or between members.	1	2 3 4	5
12. Decisions made that people do not understand or agree with.	1	2 3 4	5
13. People feel that good work is not recognized or rewarded.	1	2 3 4	5
14. People are not encouraged to work together for better team effort.	1	2 3 4	5

Scoring: Add up the score for the 14 items and interpret as follows:

14–28: Few indications of a need for team building.

29–42: Some evidence of a need, but no immediate pressure unless two or three items are high.

43–56: Seriously think about a team-building program.

57–70: Make team building a top priority.

Source: Excerpted from W. Dyer, R.H. Daines, and W.C. Giauque, *The Challenge of Management* (New York: Harcourt Brace & Company, 1990) 343.

- **Shirking of responsibilities** A team is in trouble if members exhibit lack of commitment to the team, manoeuvre to have others do part of their job, or blame colleagues or management for personal or team failures.

- **Lack of trust** When there is trust, team members believe in the integrity, character, and ability of each other. When trust is lacking, members are unable to depend on each other. Teams that lack trust tend to be short lived.

- **Critical skills gaps** When skill gaps occur, and the team doesn't fill these gaps, the team flounders. Members have trouble communicating with each other, destructive conflicts are not resolved, decisions are never made, or technical problems overwhelm the team.

- **Lack of external support** Teams exist within the larger organization. They rely on that larger organization for a variety of resources—money, people, equipment—and if those resources are not there, it is difficult for teams to reach their potential. For example, teams must live with the organization's employee selection process, formal rules and regulations, budgeting procedures, and compensation system. If these systems are inconsistent with the team's needs and goals, the team suffers.

MAKE ACTION PLANS TO SOLVE PROBLEMS

The task of finding solutions to problems can be assigned to subteams of concerned and qualified individuals, or the entire team can work through the prioritized agenda item by item to develop action plans. Action plans should include a statement of the problem, the recommended solution, people responsible for implementing action, and deadlines for results. Some of the things that can be done to overcome obstacles and help teams to reach their full potential are listed below.

- **Clarify goals** Members of high-performance teams have a clear understanding of their goals and believe that their goals embody a worthwhile or important result. The importance of these goals encourages individuals to sublimate personal concerns to these team goals. In effective teams, members are committed to the team's goals, know what they are expected to accomplish, and understand how they will work together to achieve these goals.

- **Encourage teams to go for small wins** The building of real teams takes time. New teams cannot be expected to hit home runs, right at the beginning, every time they come to bat. Team members should begin by trying to hit singles. Identifying and setting attainable goals can facilitate small wins. The eventual goal of cutting overall costs by 30 per cent, for instance, can be dissected into five or ten smaller and more easily attainable goals. As the smaller goals are attained, the team's success is reinforced. Cohesiveness is increased and morale improves. Confidence builds. Success breeds success.

- **Build mutual trust** Trust is fragile. It takes a long time to build and can be easily destroyed. Several things can be done to create a climate of mutual trust.[24] Keep team members informed by explaining upper-management decisions and policies and by providing accurate feedback. Create a climate of openness where employees are free to discuss problems without fear of retaliation. Be candid about your own problems and limitations. Make sure you are available and approachable when others need support. Be respectful and listen to team members' ideas. Develop a reputation for being fair, objective, and impartial in your treatment of team members. Show consistency in your actions, and avoid erratic and unpredictable behaviour. Finally, be dependable and honest. Make sure you follow through on all explicit and implied promises.

EVALUATE BOTH GROUP AND INDIVIDUAL PERFORMANCE

Team members should all share in the glory when their team succeeds, and they should share in the blame when it fails. So a large measure of each member's performance appraisal should be based on the overall team performance. But members need to know that they cannot ride on the backs of others. Therefore, each member's individual contribution should also be identified and made a part of his or her overall performance evaluation.

Four suggestions are provided for designing a system that supports and improves the performance of teams.[25]

1. **Tie the team's results to the organization's goals.** It is important to find measurements that apply to important goals that the team is supposed to accomplish.
2. **Begin with the team's customers and the work process the team follows to satisfy its needs.** The final product the customer receives can be appraised in terms of the customer's requirements. The transactions between teams can be appraised on

the basis of delivery and quality, and the process steps on the basis of waste and cycle time (the length of time it takes to complete the entire task).

3. **Measure both team and individual performance.** Define the roles of each team member in terms of accomplishments that support the team's work process. Then assess each member's contribution and the team's overall performance.

4. **Train the team to create its own measures.** Having the team define its objectives and those of each member ensures that every member understands his or her role on the team and helps the team develop into a more cohesive unit. This could be expanded to have teams evaluate themselves. Have teams ask themselves questions such as, "What are we doing that is working? What are we doing that is not working? How can we change that? As in an individual performance evaluation process, teams can start by creating an agreement or team contract about how to do things including standards against which to measure team results.

PROVIDE THE NECESSARY EXTERNAL SUPPORT

Managers are the link between the teams and upper management. It is their responsibility to make sure that teams have the necessary organizational resources to accomplish their goals. They should be prepared to make the case to key decision makers in the organization for tools, equipment, training, personnel, physical space, or other resources that the teams may require.

OFFER TEAM-BUILDING TRAINING

Teams, especially in their early stages of formation, will need training to build their skills. Typically, these skills would include problem solving, communication, negotiation, conflict resolution, and group processing. If you cannot personally provide this kind of skill training for your team members, look to specialists in your organization who can or secure the funds to bring in outside facilitators who specialize in this kind of training.

ROLE NEGOTIATION TECHNIQUE

When team ineffectiveness is based on problems of power and authority within the group, the role negotiation technique can be used to establish negotiations between team members. The process focuses on work behaviours, not personal feelings. Members write down what they want others to do more of, do less of, stop doing, and maintain unchanged. Then members agree to change certain behaviours if others will do the same, and a written contract is established.[26]

Conducting Effective Meetings

The most important team decisions are almost always reached in meetings.[27] As a manager of teams, you are the one in charge of them. You choose who will attend. You set and control the agenda. In fact, what you do or fail to do will largely influence the meeting's effectiveness. While no magic formulas guarantee success, managers can employ a number of skills and procedures to improve the quality of their meetings.

The suggestions that follow are divided into planning activities to carry out before the meeting, leadership activities to engage in during the meeting, and management activities to follow up on after the meeting. It is essential to be skilled at all phases of meeting management: the most thorough preparation will be wasted if you are careless during the meeting. Outstanding meeting leadership rarely overcomes poor planning, and if action plans are not implemented, then even the best decisions will not achieve expected results.

PREPARING FOR THE MEETING

Perhaps the most useful way to begin is simply to sit down with a blank sheet of paper and think through what you need to accomplish and what the meeting should be like. Write down all the issues that are likely to come up, what decisions need to be made, what you want to happen after the meeting, and what things have to happen before the meeting can take place. Now that you have reviewed the big picture, you can get down to planning the meeting. Your plan should include the following activities.

SET OBJECTIVES Most meetings are called either to exchange information or to solve team problems. Be explicit about your purposes because they have major implications for who should attend, which items belong on the agenda, when and where you hold the meeting, and what kinds of decision-making procedures you should use.

An information-exchange meeting can be an efficient mechanism if the information to be shared is complex or controversial, if it has major implications for the meeting participants, or if symbolic value comes through conveying the information personally. If none of these conditions is present, it may be more efficient, and just as effective, to write a memo, send an e-mail, or make a few telephone calls. Problem-solving meetings, however, provide an opportunity to combine the knowledge and skills of everyone on the team in an open-ended discussion, which usually produces more creative ideas than those the same people could produce working individually.

SELECT PARTICIPANTS Only invite people to the meeting who will either contribute to or be affected by its outcome. Select individuals who have knowledge or skills relevant to the problem, or who command organizational resources (time, budgets, other people, power, and influence) that you need access to. Do everything you can to keep the size of the group appropriate to your objectives. Although an information-exchange meeting can be almost any size, a problem-solving group should not exceed eight to 10 people if at all possible.[28]

PLAN THE AGENDA The agenda is the planning document that guides what you hope to accomplish at the meeting. The agenda should start by stating the meeting's purpose. It should also identify: who will be in attendance; what, if any, preparation is required of each participant; a detailed list of items to be covered; the specific time and location of the meeting; and a specific finishing time.

By defining the meeting's purpose, an agenda gives the participants a sense of direction and serves as a vehicle for premeeting discussions with participants. During the meeting, the agenda will be a valuable means of controlling the discussion and placing boundaries between relevant and irrelevant topics.

DISTRIBUTE THE AGENDA AND RELEVANT MATERIALS IN ADVANCE If you want to ensure that people will attend and be prepared for the meeting, get your agenda out well in advance. Providing adequate lead time will depend on the importance of the meeting and the amount of preparation necessary, but you should circulate the agenda and relevant background papers at least two or three days before the meeting. Keep your demands on their time reasonable, however. People are more likely to read and think about brief memos than long, comprehensive reports.

CONSULT WITH PARTICIPANTS BEFORE THE MEETING Few events are as frustrating as a meeting of people who are unprepared to discuss or decide the issues on the agenda. It is your responsibility to ensure that members are prepared by circulating relevant data and background materials far enough in advance that participants can prepare adequately. Encourage participants to do their homework. If all are prepared, the meeting can proceed much more quickly.

Another reason for contacting participants prior to the meeting is to collect all the relevant information you can, and to consider its implications. The more important and the more controversial the subject, the more contact you should have with other participants before the actual meeting. These contacts will help you anticipate issues and disagreements that may arise during the meeting.

SET A TIME AND PLACE   The timing and location of your meeting can have a subtle but significant impact on the quality of the discussion. When will the people you want at the meeting be available given scheduled work constraints? Given other activities, what time of day is best for your meeting? Be sure the time is sheltered to keep interruptions at a minimum. Also, gear your starting time to the meeting's desirable length. For example, if you want the meeting to last only an hour, a good time to schedule it is at 11 A.M.

Try not to plan meetings that last more than 90 minutes. Most people's endurance—or at least their creative capacity—will not last much longer than that. If the subject is so complex or lengthy that it will take longer, be sure to build in coffee and stretching breaks at least every 90 minutes.

Where you hold the meeting can have a marked influence on its tone and content. For example, consider the difference between calling three team members to your office versus meeting them for lunch in a restaurant. A "neutral" conference room creates a different climate than someone's office. Each setting implies a particular level of formality and signals what kind of discussion you expect to have. The appropriate setting depends on your purposes.

The discussion climate will also be affected by the arrangement of the furniture in the meeting room. In your office, you can choose to stay behind your desk and thereby be more authoritative, or to use a chair that puts you on a more equal basis with the other participants. In a conference room, you can choose to sit at the head of the table to symbolize your control, or in the centre to be "one of the team."

You should also be certain that you have arranged for any necessary mechanical equipment, such as an overhead or slide projector, an easel, or a blackboard. These vital aids can facilitate both information exchange and problem-solving discussions.

CONDUCTING THE MEETING

You called the meeting because you need something from the other participants, either information relevant to the problem or agreement and commitment to a decision. Your success in achieving those goals now depends not so much on what you know about the problem as on what you and the others can learn during the discussion. Thus, the primary concern as you begin the meeting should be with creating a healthy, problem-solving atmosphere in which participants openly confront their differences and work toward a joint solution. The following suggestions should help you achieve your goals.

BEGIN THE MEETING WITH THE AGENDA   The first thing you should do at the meeting is to get participants to review the agenda and the meeting objectives. Be careful not to simply impose the agenda on the team; others may have useful suggestions that will speed up the meeting or bring the problem into sharper focus. Some may disagree with some of your plans, but you will not learn about that disagreement unless you clearly signal that you consider the agenda open to revision. Do modifications need to be made? If so, make them. Clarify the issues that you plan to discuss. After this review, get participants to approve the final agenda. The more the others participate in defining the meeting, the more committed they will be to fulfilling that definition.

ESTABLISH SPECIFIC TIME PARAMETERS   Meetings should begin on time and have a specific time for completion.[29] This way no one has to waste their time waiting for latecomers and everyone can be sure that they will be able to attend later scheduled commitments. If you have set a specific ending time, and everyone knows you mean it, the tendency for the discussion to wander will be greatly reduced. It is your responsibility to specify these time parameters and to hold to them.

CONTROL THE DISCUSSION As the formal leader of the meeting, you have formal authority to influence the group's actions. You will normally want to exercise greater control when the topic generates strong, potentially disruptive feelings, when the group is moving toward a decision, or when time pressures are significant. A whole range of informal to formal control techniques is available for use if needed.

If you began the meeting with an explicit discussion of the agenda, you will find this focusing task easier to carry out. Often a simple reminder to the group, with a glance at the clock, is enough to get things back on track if the discussion wanders. Other times a pointed look, or even just a lifted eyebrow is all you need to indicate approval or disapproval of someone's behaviour.

If you need more formal control, you can permit participants to speak only when you call on them, or if you comment on or summarize each statement, direct confrontations between other individuals will be minimized. If you use a flip chart or blackboard to summarize ideas, you will also increase the level of formality and reduce the number of direct exchanges. In highly charged circumstances where destructive conflict is probable, you may even want to employ formal parliamentary procedures, such as requiring motions and limiting debate.

ENCOURAGE PROBLEM SOLVING As you read in Chapter 10, Innovation and Problem Solving, effective problem-solving meetings generally pass through several phases. Early in the discussion the team will be seeking to understand the nature of the problem. Understanding can be facilitated by encouraging factual, nonevaluative discussion that emphasizes describing symptoms and searching for all possible causes. As understanding is gained, the focus will shift to a search for solutions, which also is enhanced by nonevaluative suggestions. Only after all potential alternatives have been explored and the team moves toward a decision should the discussion become evaluative.

ENCOURAGE AND SUPPORT PARTICIPATION BY ALL MEMBERS Participants were not selected randomly. Each is there for a purpose. To maximize the effectiveness of problem-oriented meetings, each participant must be encouraged to contribute. Quiet or reserved personalities sometimes need to be drawn out so their ideas can be heard.

ENCOURAGE THE CLASH OF IDEAS, BUT DISCOURAGE THE CLASH OF PERSONALITIES You need to encourage different points of view, critical thinking, and constructive disagreement. Your goals should be to stimulate participants' creativity and to counter the group members' desire to reach an early consensus. An effective meeting is characterized by the critical assessment of ideas. If disagreements ever disintegrate into attacks on people, however, you should quickly intercede.

EXHIBIT EFFECTIVE LISTENING SKILLS Applying the listening skills you learned in Chapter 5, Interpersonal Communication, can contribute to encouraging participation and the expression of different ideas. Effective listening also reduces misunderstandings, improves the focus of discussion, and encourages the critical assessment of ideas. Even if other group members do not exhibit good listening skills, if you do, you can keep the discussion focused on the issues and facilitate critical thinking.

REACH A CONSENSUS Many teams fall into decision-making habits without thinking carefully about the consequences of those habits. The two major approaches to reaching a team decision are voting and reaching a consensus. Each strategy has its advantages and disadvantages.

Voting is often resorted to when the decision is important and the group seems deadlocked. The major benefit of taking a vote is that you are guaranteed a decision. However, voting requires public commitment to a position, and it creates a win–lose situation for the group members. Some individuals will be clearly identified as having favoured a minority position. Losers on one issue often try to balance their account on the next decision, or they may withdraw their commitment to the total group. Either way, you may have won the battle but lost the war.

Reaching a team consensus, where everyone agrees that the best solution under the circumstances has been reached, is generally a much more effective decision-making procedure. It is often more difficult, however, and is almost always more time-consuming. Working toward a genuine consensus means hearing all points of view, and usually results in a better decision—a condition that is especially important when the team members will be responsible for implementing the decision. Even when individuals do not fully agree with the team decision, they are more likely to support it (or less likely to sabotage it) when they believe their positions have had a complete hearing. As a caveat, never assume that silence means agreement; more often it signals some level of difference with the dominant theme of the discussion.

END THE MEETING BY CLARIFYING WHAT HAPPENS NEXT Close the meeting by summarizing the group's accomplishments, clarifying what actions need to follow the meeting, and allocating follow-up assignments.[30] If any decisions have been made, who will be responsible for communicating and implementing them? If the team will meet again, you can save a lot of time by scheduling your next meeting before people depart.

FOLLOW UP AFTER THE MEETING

Depending on the discussion topic and the decisions that have been made, either you or someone else should follow up after the meeting with a brief memo summarizing the discussion, the decisions, and the follow-up commitments that each participant has made. This kind of document serves not only as a record of the meeting, but also as a next-day reminder to the participants of what they decided and what they are committed to doing.

It can be a valuable learning experience for future meetings to spend the last five minutes debriefing the meeting process. Which processes contributed and which ones detracted from the meeting's success. How can they be improved for the next meeting? The best time to share your reactions to the meeting is right after it has ended.

Concept Quiz

Complete the following true–false quiz by circling the correct answer. Answers are at the end of the quiz. After marking your answers, remember to go back and check your understanding of any answers you missed.

True or False   1. All teams are groups, but not all groups are teams.

True or False   2. When teams are measured only on group-level performance, individual members often reduce their efforts.

True or False   3. The three types of complementary skills that a team needs to succeed are technical expertise, problem solving, and common purpose.

True or False   4. The five stages of team development proceed in the following order: forming, norming, storming, performing, and adjourning.

True or False   5. When a temporary team reaches the adjourning stage, a manager no longer needs to be concerned about members' feelings, morale, or productivity.

True or False   6. Task deadlines, team composition, and leader direction and support are all factors that can facilitate a team's progress through the five stages of development.

True or False	7. Failure to share issues and concerns, overdependency on the leader, and hidden conflicts are all signs that a team is ineffective.
True or False	8. Structuring is the most important team leadership style.
True or False	9. Effective meeting planning includes all of the following: setting objectives, selecting participants, planning the agenda, and consulting with participants in advance.
True or False	10. When the team is moving toward a decision, the leader should refrain from controlling the discussion.

Answers (1) True; (2) True; (3) False; (4) False; (5) False; (6) True; (7) True; (8) False; (9) True; (10) False

Behavioural Checklist

The following skills are important to effective team building. Use them when evaluating your own team-building skills and those of others.

The Effective Team Builder:

- Ensures that all members agree on a common team mission and goals.
- Establishes specific, measurable, and realistic goals for each member of the team.
- Develops agreement on a common approach for achieving goals.
- Makes sure that members are individually and jointly accountable for the team's performance.
- Facilitates the exploration of team process and structure issues before beginning on the task.
- Adapts leadership style to facilitate team development.
- Applies the rational problem-solving process to determine and overcome obstacles to team effectiveness.
- Prepares for team meetings by setting objectives and planning the agenda.
- Conducts team meetings by use of an agenda and encouraging productive participation.
- Follows up after team meetings to ensure that action commitments are being carried out.

Modelling Exercise

INSTRUCTIONS Seven volunteers form a circle in the front of the class. They will demonstrate team skills at completing an assigned task while the remainder of the class observes and rates the team's performance on the Observer's Rating Sheet. After the task has been completed, observers share their observations with the task team and each other. The last step is to draw conclusions about what helps and hinders team performance in tasks like the one observed and in general.

TEAM TASK Create a list of the 10 most important characteristics of high-performing teams. Then reach a consensus rank order of the importance of each characteristic.

TIME The total time for this exercise ranges from 45 to 55 minutes. Allow 30 minutes for the task team to complete the task. Allow 10 to 15 minutes for feedback to team members from the Observer's Rating Sheet. Allow 5 to 10 minutes for class generalizations and applications.

Observer's Rating Sheet

On completion of the exercise, evaluate the task group's team-building skills. Rate each skill set between 1 and 5 using the following scale. Write concrete examples in the space for comments below each criteria skill to use in explaining your feedback.

1 Unsatisfactory	2 Weak	3 Adequate	4 Good	5 Outstanding

_____ Agreed on a common team mission and goals.

_____ Established specific, measurable, and realistic goals for each member of the team.

_____ Developed agreement on a common approach for achieving goals.

_____ Made sure that members are individually and jointly accountable for the team's performance.

_____ Explored team process and structure issues before beginning on the task.

_____ Adapted leadership style to facilitate team development.

_____ Applied the rational problem-solving process.

_____ Set objectives and planned an agenda.

_____ Controlled the meeting by use of an agenda and encouraging productive participation.

_____ Followed up to ensure that action commitments are being carried out.

Group Exercises

Three different types of group exercises are presented here. First is a short case for you to practise your conceptual diagnostic skills to determine the best approach to team building. Second is an opportunity to experience a technique to inventory member assets at the forming stage of team development. Third is an exercise for established teams to build member recognition, appreciation, and cohesion in the norming and performing stages.

Group Exercise 1: Major Product Industries Case[31]

Through strategic acquisitions, Major Product Industries (MPI) had evolved from a mid-sized company into a unique multinational conglomerate with operations in a wide array of commercial products including aerospace and electronics. Additional acquisitions to strengthen the aerospace companies included Numero Company and Uno Incorporated. Both companies were placed under tremendous pressure from their new parent company to streamline operations and improve productivity, which they did to the tune of a 10 per cent improvement in productivity. Further improvement was mandated through the integration of functions and elimination of duplicate facilities.

The prescribed strategic plan for the newly merged Numero-Uno Company was to withdraw from mature industrial businesses and to concentrate on aerospace, electronics, and selected industrial products by developing new technologies and streamlining operations to improve productivity. These ambitious goals and sweeping changes put tremendous pressure on Numero-Uno's president and chief executive officer, who was overwhelmed by the challenge of picking up the pieces of the newly merged company, restructuring it, and developing a team from the chaos that could persevere and accomplish its assigned mission.

The Numero-Uno merger had created a multitude of significant structural and interpersonal changes that the financial officers who engineered the merger had not even contemplated. These issues included a considerable increase and redundancy in management layers, a new CEO with ambiguous power and goals, new operating procedures and responsibilities, and uncertain reward systems and career paths. These externally initiated changes led to a multitude of internal changes in organizational culture, interpersonal relationships, organizational structure, and career opportunities.

The staff members of each company were extremely competent in their areas of expertise, but they were now dependent on each other to make the new organization function effectively. The different styles of staff members, coupled with the anxiety and resentment spawned by the ambiguity of career paths and power bases, led to minimal communication, distrust of others' intentions, disorganization, and low productivity. The merger had transformed two effectively functioning companies into a group of disorganized and competing individuals whose disunity threatened to reverse previous progress and possibly destroy the new company and everyone in it.

This disunity was especially true of the corporate staff, which was made up of the president, vice-president, subsidiary company presidents, financial and legal division directors, and their immediate staffs. The need to streamline and increase productivity meant that not all of the current group, which represented officers of both the previous Numero and Uno companies, would remain at the end of the year because of considerable redundancies. The politics, lack of trust and openness, fear and hostility, and considerable differences in previous corporate cultures and decision styles created a group of territorial infighters. Clearly the Numero-Uno corporate staff was not a team.

QUESTIONS FOR DISCUSSION

1. Why wasn't the Numero-Uno corporate staff a team?
2. What team-building approach would you recommend for improving the Numero-Uno staff's effectiveness? Why? Explain the steps you would recommend.
3. Would you recommend the use of an outside consultant or inside facilitator? Why?

Group Exercise 2: My Asset Base[32]

PURPOSE To help team members get to know each other quickly and to build cohesiveness in the team.

INTRODUCTION Each of us has an asset base that supports our ability to accomplish the things we set out to do. We refer to our personal assets as talents, strengths, or abilities. When new teams form, one of the first items of concern is getting to know each other and what assets each member can contribute to the team.

DIRECTIONS The following steps will help you assess your own strengths and share them with others to provide an understanding of team member assets.

STEP 1 Individually fill out the following T chart. On the right-hand side of the T, list four or five of your accomplishments of which you are most proud. Your accomplishments would only include those things where you can take credit for achieving them. When you have completed the right-hand side of the chart, fill in the left-hand side by listing the talents, strengths, and abilities that have enabled you to accomplish the outcomes listed on the right-hand side. Try to be specific in describing what assets you have that have enabled you to do what you have done.

STEP 2 If you have already formed teams for class projects, meet with your assigned group. If not, form groups of four to six members. In a round-robin fashion, members share first their accomplishments, and then their talents, strengths, and abilities.

STEP 3 As a group, discuss the following questions.

1. How did your attitudes and feelings toward other members of the team change as you pursued this activity?
2. What does your reaction tell you about the process whereby we come to get to know and care about people?
3. What strengths does your team possess?
4. In what areas would you like to increase your team assets if you had a group research project to complete?

Group Exercise 3: Strength Acknowledgment[33]

PURPOSE To enhance team member awareness of individual strengths and barriers to group contributions in a constructive way that builds team cohesiveness and rapport.

MATERIALS Sheets of newsprint and markers for each participant.

DIRECTIONS

STEP 1. FOCUS ON STRENGTHS The class calls out what they view as team member strengths, which the instructor lists on the board. Examples are sensitivity, understanding, courage. Next, generate a list of barriers, factors that keep a person from using his or her strengths most effectively. (10 minutes)

MY ASSET BASE   Name: _____

Talents, Strengths, and Abilities	Achievements and Accomplishments

STEP 2. DIVIDE INTO GROUPS Meet in permanent small groups or form new groups of seven to 10 members who know each other fairly well. The remainder of this exercise is conducted within the small groups. (5 minutes)

STEP 3. SELF-ASSESSMENT OF STRENGTHS Each person is given a sheet of newsprint and a marker. On one side of the newsprint, the person's name is written. On the other, the person lists his or her strengths as a team member. When a person has finished listing his or her strengths, the newsprint is taped to the wall with only the name side showing. (15 minutes)

STEP 4. WRITING PERCEPTIONS OF OTHER MEMBERS' STRENGTHS When all participants have taped their newsprint sheets with names showing on the walls, everyone walks around the room writing the strengths they perceive about each member on that person's sheet. If someone else has previously written a strength you agree with, check it to indicate agreement. After you have written strengths on everyone's sheet, take a seat. (20 minutes)

STEP 5. SHARING AND RECEIVING FEEDBACK One at a time, team members share perceptions and receive feedback about their strengths. First, the focus person turns over his or her sheet, posts it on the wall, and reads to the group the list of self-perceived strengths. Next, the focus person turns the sheet over again and reads the strengths that others have listed. The focus person can ask for clarification of strengths that are not understood. (5 minutes per member)

STEP 6. RECEIVING AND CLARIFYING FEEDBACK ON BARRIERS The focus person asks the group to share what barriers they see as keeping him or her from using the strengths to the fullest. The focus person draws a line under his or her strengths and lists the barriers below the line as they are shared, asking for clarification as necessary. (5 minutes per member)

STEP 7. ACKNOWLEDGMENT OF STRENGTH FEEDBACK TO THE TEAM When all the strengths and barriers have been shared (additional ones can be added spontaneously anytime a team member thinks of one), the focus person shares with the team how he or she feels about the list. (2 minutes per member)

STEP 8. CONTINUE THE PROCESS FOR EACH MEMBER Each team member goes through the same process described in steps 5 through 7 above until all are finished. (10 minutes per member)

Application Questions

1. How would you build a high-energy team out of a group of students with differing talents, goals, and levels of motivation, who were randomly put together to complete a class project?
2. Have you ever been a member of a team that has social loafers going along for a free ride? How did this condition develop? What were the consequences? Was anything done to rectify the situation? If so, what? If not, what should have been done?
3. Contrast a team you have been on where members trusted each other versus another group where members did not trust each other. How did these conditions develop? What were the consequences in terms of interaction patterns and performance?
4. One way to avoid conflicts at meetings is to avoid having the meeting in the first place. But if you do need to have a meeting, how would you suggest managing potential conflicts?
5. How did the last formal meeting you participated in compare with the guidelines for effective meetings presented in this chapter? What were the main differences and consequences?

Reinforcement Exercises

1. Assess the skills of your friends and family. Who has the technical skills? Who has the problem-solving/decision-making abilities? Who has the interpersonal skills? If you can correctly identify them, you will be able to apply this to your team experiences.

2. Observe the interaction in a team you are on in a class or at work. Can you identify the team's strengths and weaknesses? If so, share them with the team and develop plans to make the team more effective.

3. Take a personal inventory of yourself as a team member. What are your strengths and weaknesses that would influence how you can most effectively contribute to a team?

4. Pay attention to what the leader does in meetings you attend, such as those of a club, sports team, or work group. Make mental notes of what principles of effective planning and conducting the leader put into effect and how they contributed to the effectiveness of the meeting. Then think about what the leader could have done better.

5. The next time you get the chance, volunteer to plan or help plan a meeting. Put your new skills to work!

Summary Checklist

Take a few minutes to reflect on your performance and look over others' ratings of your team-building skills. Now assess yourself on each of the key learning behaviours. Make a check (√) next to those behaviours on which you need improvement.

_____ Ensuring teams have the characteristics to make them effective.

1. Small size—no more than about ten members.
2. Complementary skills—technical, problem solving, interpersonal.
3. Common purpose—all agree on team mission and goals.
4. Specific goals—specific, measurable, and realistic.
5. Common approach—unified on the means for achieving goals.
6. Mutual accountability—individually and jointly accountable for the team's performance.

_____ Facilitating the exploration of issues necessary to design high-performing teams.

1. Who are we? (strengths, weaknesses, work preferences, values, and beliefs)
2. Where are we now? (the team's strengths, weaknesses, opportunities, and threats)
3. Where are we going? (mission, purpose, and goals)
4. How will we get there? (action plans, which spell out who does what, when, and how)
5. What is expected from us? (job description, roles, responsibilities, authority, and accountability)
6. What support do we get/need? (training, counselling, and mentoring)
7. How effective are we? (regular performance reviews of quantity and quality outputs)
8. What recognition do we get? (praise, remuneration, fringe benefits, and promotions)

_____ Recognizing and facilitating the stages of team development.

1. Forming—helping newly formed groups resolve uncertainties about purpose, structure, relationships, tasks, and leadership.
2. Storming—facilitating the resolution of conflicts about power and task structure.
3. Norming—integrating roles, goals, norms, and structure with a focus on increasing productivity. Continued building of trust and positive relationships.
4. Performing—preventing loss of enthusiasm and sustaining momentum.
5. Adjourning—preparing for termination of the team in temporary task forces.

_____ Adapting leadership style to different stages of team development.

1. Diagnose the needs of the team.
2. Use productivity-related behaviours to provide direction for task achievement.
3. Use morale-oriented behaviours to provide support and help the team work better together.
4. Structure style in the forming stage to provide needed direction.
5. Resolve style in the storming stage to provide both direction and support.
6. Collaborate style in the norming stage to provide continued support.
7. Validate style in the performing stage to reward and avoid interference with the team's demonstrated effectiveness.

_____ Assessing and solving problems to team effectiveness.

1. Become aware of problems by determining symptoms of ineffective teams.
2. Gather data through interviews or questionnaires.
3. Analyze data.
4. Identify problems.
5. Determine action plans to solve problems.
6. Follow up to ensure effective implementation of solutions.

_____ Preparing for team meetings by setting objectives, selecting participants, planning the agenda, setting a time and place, distributing the agenda in advance, and consulting with participants.

_____ Conducting team meetings.

1. Begin with a review of the agenda and the meeting objectives.
2. Establish specific time parameters.
3. Encourage participation by all members in problem solving by active listening and encouraging the clash of ideas, but not personalities.
4. Reach a consensus decision and debrief the meeting process.
5. End the meeting by clarifying what happens next.

_____ Following up after the meeting by distributing minutes that summarize the discussion, the decisions, and the action commitments that each participant has made.

Action Plan

1. Which team skills including conducting meetings do I most want to improve? (See the Summary Checklist.)
2. Why? What will be my payoff?
3. What potential obstacles stand in my way?
4. What are the specific things I will do to improve? (For examples, see the Reinforcement Exercises and Summary Checklist.)
5. When will I do them?
6. How and when will I measure my success?

Part V

Future-Building Competencies

Organizational environments are filled with change. The manager's job is increasingly one of juggling a dozen balls at once, in the dark, on the deck of a boat, during a typhoon! It requires turning an environment of chaotic change into an opportunity—the chance for well-managed organizations to gain a competitive advantage over rivals by being smarter, more flexible, quicker, more efficient, and better at responding to customer needs.

Future-building competencies involve creating a vision of what organizational members are working for and then directing and coordinating them so that they achieve their objectives. To be an effective leader, managers must have skills in promoting and leading change as well as diagnosing and modifying organizational culture.

Chapter 17, Diagnosing and Modifying Organizational Culture   Managers need to understand their own organization's culture as well as the cultures of other organizations with whom they interact. These cultures consist of the shared meanings, values, and accepted behaviours commonly agreed upon by members of the organizations. As such, cultures determine the attitudes of organization members toward how things are done and the ways members are supposed to behave. Managerial suggestions that are out of sync with the organizational culture face a formidable barrier. Fortunately, the manager's own behaviour is one of the primary factors that modifies the culture of an organization.

Chapter 18, Leading Change   Managers are catalysts and assume the responsibility for managing the change process. Managers need skills to create and articulate a realistic, credible, attractive vision of the future that grows out of and improves upon the present.[1] They need to design and execute planned change programs to improve interpersonal interactions within organizations, change work processes and methods, and redesign organization structures.[2] They also need to improve quality through seeking out and implementing continual changes to incrementally improve the organization.[3] Finally, because the world is undergoing dramatic change, managers must be willing to implement radical changes, which at times entail completely reinventing their organizations.[4]

Managers are on both the receiving end and the giving end of change. They have to adjust to change, and they also must be the catalyst for initiating change within their organizations. But they also realize that people often resist change. Accordingly, managers need to be in a position to appreciate the benefits of the change while simultaneously helping their employees deal with the uncertainty and anxiety that the changes may bring.

CHAPTER 17

Diagnosing and Modifying Organizational Culture

Learning Objectives

After completing this chapter, you should be able to:

- Identify an organization's culture.
- Assess how a person fits into a specific culture.
- Instill cultural values and norms in employees.
- Make appropriate changes to an organization's culture.

Self-Assessment Exercise

Respond as candidly as possible to the following statements designed to assess your understanding of organizational culture. Describe your level of agreement with each statement by circling the number in the appropriate column.

	Strongly Agree				Strongly Disagree
1. If a person can do well in one organization, he or she ought to do well in any organization.	1	2	3	4	5
2. An organization's culture is whatever the current CEO says it is.	1	2	3	4	5
3. Skills and experience are all that really matter; how a job candidate will "fit in" is not an important factor in hiring.	1	2	3	4	5

4.	Members of an organization explicitly tell people how to adhere to its culture.	1	2	3	4	5
5.	After appropriate study, astute managers can fairly quickly change a corporate culture.	1	2	3	4	5
6.	A common culture is important for unifying employees but does not necessarily affect the firm's financial health.	1	2	3	4	5
7.	Conscientious workers are not really influenced by an organization's culture.	1	2	3	4	5
8.	Strong organizational cultures are not necessarily associated with high organizational performance.	1	2	3	4	5
9.	Members of a subculture share the common values of the subculture but not those of the dominant organizational culture.	1	2	3	4	5
10.	A job candidate seeking to understand a prospective employer's culture can do so by just asking the interviewers.	1	2	3	4	5

SCORING AND INTERPRETATION Each of the preceding statements describes an important implication of organizational culture. The higher your score, the better you understand the organizational culture's ramifications. Add the numbers you have circled to obtain your total score.

40–50	You have excellent instincts about organizational cultures and how people respond to them.
30–39	You show average or better awareness of the principles of organizational culture.
20–29	You have some sense of how cultures affect workers, but you need to increase your knowledge.
0–19	You need to bolster your knowledge before trying to assess or modify a culture.

Concepts

- Delta Hotels, which now number 39 across Canada, believe the key to profitability is a healthy culture. This culture is built on the idea that highly satisfied employees provide excellent guest service. To achieve this, Delta has developed a supportive environment where employees feel valued, and high degrees of trust exist between managers and employee groups. Extensive training and regular feedback on performance is guaranteed. At a senior level, employee satisfaction scores are tied directly to bonuses. All of these efforts have paid off. Delta is a leading employer in the hospitality industry, and won a position on the 2001 *Report on Business* Top 35 Companies to Work For in Canada as well as the National Quality Institute's (NQI) Quality Award in 2000.[1]

- Northwood Technologies, an Ottawa wireless software developer, has created a culture where both quality of work and quality of life are important. Despite the demanding nature of their industry and the tight deadlines that come with it, Northwood provides as flexible a work environment as possible to its employees. One of the reasons why this culture developed was that, in the early years of the company, it couldn't offer above-market salaries to new recruits. This resulted in flextime, telecommuting or telework, and other work–life balance strategies being offered instead. Now more financially secure, the company realizes that it is the flexible culture that keeps the employees satisfied and loyal.[2]

- Legendary industrialist David Packard, who cofounded electronics giant Hewlett-Packard, once personally ordered an engineer to halt work on a new computer monitor. "When I come back next year I do not want to see that project in the lab," Packard said. The engineer, however, decided that if the model were in production, it wouldn't be in the lab, so he pushed ahead. The monitor turned out to be a huge success and created an entirely new market. Packard then rewarded the engineer with a "Medal of Defiance" for bucking his boss. As a result, young HP employees, knowing they won't be punished for aggressively pursuing ideas, still look for ways to get their products or prototypes completed before top managers have figured out whether they even want them.[3]

Each of those anecdotes suggests what that organization prizes. Those shared values are the cornerstone of an organization's culture, and they greatly influence behaviour at work. An organization's **culture** refers to the key characteristics that the organization values and that distinguish it from other organizations. Henry Mintzberg, a professor at McGill University, sees culture as the soul of an organization, holding it together and giving it life.[4] Managers need to be particularly aware of organizational culture because they are expected to be positive role models of the culture and to instill the same values and beliefs in their employees.

Most often the cultural imperatives are not written down or even discussed, but they are there, and all successful managers must learn what to do and what not to do in their organizations. In fact, the better the match between the manager's personal style and the organization's culture, the more successful he or she is likely to be.[5]

Why Organizational Culture Is So Important

When Pharmacia AB and Upjohn merged in 1995, many saw it as a perfect corporate marriage. Both firms were second-tier players fighting to survive in a world of global drug giants, and all the financial and marketing signals were positive for the merger. Pharmacia, based in Sweden, had a solid, if aging, product line but its distribution in the United States was weak. Upjohn, a U.S. firm, had some solid household name brands but suffered from stagnant sales. Thus, the merger was seen as a way to cut costs, improve global market penetration, and allow the new firm to better compete against Merck, Bristol-Myers Squibb, Pfizer, and other pharmaceutical giants.[6]

In the first few years after the merger, however, earnings plummeted, the stock fell sharply, many executives left, and company morale hit bottom. Why? Most experts point to the incompatibility between the two corporate cultures. For example:

- The hard-driving, mission-oriented American approach of Upjohn clashed with the consensus-oriented Swedish style of Pharmacia. Upjohn managers focused on ambitious cost-cutting and numerical accountability while Pharmacia managers emphasized keeping their employees informed and seeking feedback.

- The internationally experienced Pharmacia managers were surprised by the lack of global savvy and what they saw as the parochial attitudes of the Upjohn leaders. Upjohn's rules, for example, banned smoking and required all workers to take drug and alcohol tests. By contrast, at some Pharmacia sites, wine was poured freely in the company dining room and the boardrooms were well stocked with cigars.

- Pharmacia people, used to an open management system in which small teams were left largely on their own, were put off by Upjohn's tightly centralized management style. The Upjohn-based CEO required frequent reports, budgets, and staffing updates. Many of the Swedes viewed these reports as a waste of time and stopped taking them seriously.

Not surprisingly, such conflicts came to be reflected in the company's performance. Profits fell and top executives were replaced before stronger efforts were launched to blend the disparate styles. The case illustrates the importance of corporate cultures: Even though the two firms matched up well on traditional business criteria, they stumbled in blending their cultures.

It has been estimated that 83 per cent of mergers and acquisitions fail to produce benefit to shareholders.[7] Meshing corporate cultures to create a new culture can be a daunting task that requires frequent communication to let employees know how they fit in. To minimize expected losses in employee productivity, managers need to help people adapt, while at the same time, maintain focus on customers and markets.[8]

What Constitutes Organizational Culture?

Research suggests seven primary dimensions that, in aggregate, express the essence of an organization's culture.[9] Each characteristic exists on a continuum from low to high. In many organizations, especially those with strong cultures, one dimension often rises above the others and shapes the organization and the way its members work.

1. **Innovation and risk taking** The degree to which employees are encouraged to be innovative and take risks. For example, Diagnostic Chemicals Ltd. of Charlottetown, PEI, makers of blood analysis kits for hospitals, rewards independent action and offers the freedom to conduct research with little supervision. In an industry driven by innovation, the company subsidizes tuition as a means to encourage employees to upgrade their skills.[10]
2. **Attention to detail** The degree to which employees are expected to exhibit precision, analysis, and attention to detail. Such organizations make quality their driving theme. A well-known example is Motorola, whose "Six Sigma" program spearheaded a dramatic decrease in manufacturing defects.
3. **Outcome orientation** The degree to which management focuses on results rather than on the process used to produce those results. Delta Hotels, for instance, stresses customer service in which the employee is to do whatever is needed to make each guest's stay a positive one.
4. **People orientation** The degree to which management decisions take into account how people within the organization will be affected. Regina-based SaskTel, established in 1908, has never laid off an employee. Preferring to retrain workers, the company enjoys a high level of employee loyalty.[11] At Ottawa's MDS Nordion, a leading producer of medical isotopes for the diagnosis of cancer and heart disease, management has introduced many initiatives to assist employees achieve balance between their work and personal lives.[12]
5. **Team orientation** The degree to which work is organized around teams rather than individuals. An increasing number of smaller organizations and divisions of larger organizations are defining their culture around teams. A report issued by the Conference Board of Canada found that over 80 per cent of 109 survey respondents used teams.[13]
6. **Aggressiveness** The degree to which people are aggressive and competitive rather than easygoing. At General Electric, management sets demanding goals, as seen in the strategy to have either the number one or number two market share in each of GE's markets, or exit those markets.[14]

7. **Growth** The degree to which organizational activities emphasize growth rather than maintaining the status quo. Few firms better illustrate this than Samsung, South Korea's largest business with operations in electronics, chemicals, finance, and heavy machinery. It has ambitious plans to expand into many more industries, and it indoctrinates employees by, for example, displaying banners proclaiming the firm as "The Leader for the Twenty-First Century the World Will Notice."[15]

The more members accept the core values and the greater their commitment to them, the stronger the culture is.[16] Strong cultures have great influence on their members' behaviour. Seattle-based Nordstrom is an example of one of the strongest service cultures in retailing, and it conveys that culture succinctly. Exhibit 17-1 shows the 5-by-8-inch card that is given to employees.

Evidence indicates that strong cultures are associated with high organizational performance.[17] Why? A strong culture gives everyone a clear vision. Such a culture also increases employee commitment and loyalty as well as yielding a sustainable competitive advantage that competitors cannot easily replicate.[18] A strong culture in a large firm may have significant advantage. In Canada, large firms are more likely than smaller firms to perceive organizational culture as an important growth factor.[19]

Strong cultures have their downsides, however. For example, strong cultures that do not value adaptability may actually decrease performance in changing times. When the personal-computer revolution began, for instance, IBM's strong culture may have blinded its executives to the need to change its long-time emphasis on mainframes. A strong culture also may be a barrier to achieving workforce diversity and capitalizing on its benefits. Hiring new employees who are different in terms of race, gender, or ethnicity may fly in the face of the culture's pressure to conform.

On the other hand, employees in weak cultures are sure of neither what is expected of them nor how the organization will succeed. Real change may be even more difficult in weak cultures because members may feel impotent and unable to act decisively.[20]

Where Does Organizational Culture Come From?

An organization's culture often springs from what has worked for an organization before. Thus, the vision or mission of the founders of successful organizations is frequently reflected in the culture for decades, even centuries, to come.[21] The founders, not bound by previous approaches, projected an image of what the organization should be. Further,

Exhibit 17-1 The Essence of Nordstrom's Organizational Culture

Welcome to Nordstrom
We're glad to have you with our Company.
Our number one goal is to provide outstanding customer service.
Set both your personal and professional goals high.
We have great confidence in your ability to achieve them.
So our employee handbook is very simple.
We have only one rule...

Our only rule:

Use good judgment in all situations
Please feel free to ask your Department Manager, Store Manager, or Human Resource Manager any question at any time.

Source: Used with permission of Nordstrom.

because the new organization was small at first, the founders probably were able to stamp their vision on the members and the organization.

Founders create culture in three ways.[22] First, they hire and keep employees who think and feel the way they do. Second, founders indoctrinate and socialize these employees to their way of thinking. Third, the founder acts as a role model and his or her personality becomes central to the culture of the organization.

For example, the founder of McDonald's, Ray Kroc, died in 1984, but his philosophy of giving customers quality, service, cleanliness, and value continues to shape the fast-food chain. Frank Stronach, of Toronto-based Magna Corporation, is another founder whose company continues to reflect his values. Stronach's belief that employees should be entrepreneurial and work as if they owned the company led to the company allocating 10 per cent of pre-tax profit to profit-sharing programs for its employees.

Among the most effective means of transmitting the values, beliefs, and norms of culture are stories, rituals, material symbols, and language.

STORIES

Organizational "stories" typically anchor the present in the past and provide explanations and legitimacy for current practices.[23] At Nordstrom's, for example, one story goes like this: When the department store chain was in its infancy, a customer wanted to return a set of automobile tires. The flustered sales clerk was trying to handle the irregular request when Mr. Nordstrom walked by and overheard the conversation with the customer. The founder instructed the clerk to take back the tires and give the customer a full cash refund. After the satisfied customer left, the perplexed clerk said, "But, Mr. Nordstrom, we do not sell tires!" "I know," the boss replied, "but we do whatever we need to do to make the customer happy."[24] Thus, the story strongly conveys the company's policy toward customer satisfaction.

CEREMONIES AND RITUALS

Repetitive activities express and reinforce the key values of the organization. For example, awards dinners, company barbecues, retirement parties, and announcements of company success publicly recognize employees' contributions and strengthen commitment to company values. Similarly, you may have attended orientation sessions as a first-year student and, undoubtedly, look forward to your graduation ceremony.

MATERIAL SYMBOLS

These "perks" provided for employees convey what is important, the degree of egalitarianism desired by top management, and the kinds of behaviour that are expected. Such symbols might include size of offices, type of furnishings, "extras" such as country club memberships or use of the company gym, reserved parking spaces, or the existence of employee lounges or on-site dining rooms. At Husky Injection Moulding in Bolton, Ontario, founder and CEO Robert Schad has ensured that employees work in clean, environmentally friendly surroundings with access to child care and wellness and fitness programs. Space is open and allocated in a non-hierarchical way. Senior executives and technicians all park in the same lot, eat at the same cafeteria, and have open-concept offices.[25]

LANGUAGE

Many organizations and units within organizations use language to unite members of a culture. By learning the terminology or jargon, members show they accept the culture and are helping to preserve it. For example, Lucent Technologies Canada of Markham, Ontario uses the acronym GROWS to summarize the behaviours expected of employees. G is for global growth mind set; R is for results focus; O is for obsession with customers and competitors; W is for a workplace that is open, supportive, and diverse; and S is for speed to market. Lucent employees are evaluated by TOUCH. T is for teamwork; O is for obsession with customers; U is for uncompromising quality; C is for cost effectiveness; and H is for helping others to excel.[26]

The Role of Subcultures

Most large organizations have a dominant culture and numerous sets of subcultures.[27] These subcultures usually develop around departmental distinctions or around a geographical separation. The accounting department, for example, may have its own subculture. If so, those employees would share the core values of the dominant culture, plus additional values unique to the accounting department. Similarly, an office or unit of the organization that is physically separated from the main operation may take on different values.

How to Read an Organization's Culture

Being able to read an organization's culture is a valuable skill. Whether you are seeking to land a job, strike a business deal with a firm, or just understand the "rules" so you can perform well for your employer, accurately assessing the culture can be a big plus. It is not a simple task, though. Many organizations have given little thought to their culture and do not readily display it. Instead what they display are socially acceptable slogans or buzzwords ("Change is our only constant," "We empower our employees," or "People are our most important product") that mask the organization's true nature.

The way to get an accurate read is by observing a lot and by asking many members the same questions. For example, let's say you are a job applicant seeking to learn about the potential employer's culture. You might:

- **Observe the physical surroundings** Look at signs, pictures, styles of dress, length of hair, the degree of openness among offices, and how those offices are furnished and arranged.

- **Ask to sit in on a team meeting** Notice how the different ranks of employees are treated and to what degree they are encouraged to participate actively. How open is the communication?

- **Listen to the language** For example, do managers use military terms, such as "take no prisoners," and "divide and conquer"? Or do they speak about "intuition," "care," and "our family"?

- **Note to whom you are introduced and how they act** Do you meet just your prospective supervisor, or are you also invited to talk with potential colleagues, other managers, and senior executives? Are they formal or casual, serious or jovial?

- **Ask different people the same questions and compare their answers** You might ask: What is the background of the founders and of the senior managers? How does this company define success (e.g., annual profit, market share, favourable publicity, serving customers, growth)? For what are employees most rewarded (e.g., seniority, cost-cutting, innovation, performance)? Who is on the "fast track" and what put them there? Who is considered a deviant within the organization? Why? How has the organization responded to his or her unorthodoxy?

- **Get the views of outsiders** Talk with former employees, especially the job's previous incumbent. Also contact suppliers, customers, and maybe executive recruiters who have placed others in the organization.

Assessing the Individual-to-Organization Fit

The better the match between your personal values and behavioural style and the organization's culture, the better your chances of being satisfied at work and being perceived as doing well. Thus, a good individual-to-organization fit can be a critical factor in your career.[28] Though variations in culture are infinite, Exhibit 17-2 presents four symbolic descriptions that are helpful for understanding and classifying cultures.

An **academy** is a culture for steady climbers who prefer to master each new job they hold. Such firms like to recruit recent college and university graduates, train them, and then steer them through a myriad of specialized jobs within a particular function. Such firms as IBM, General Motors, and Procter & Gamble exemplify this traditional career path.

A **club** culture places a high value on fitting in and on loyalty and commitment. Age, experience, and seniority count for a lot at such employers, where supervisory personnel are groomed as generalists rather than specialists. United Parcel Service, government agencies, and the military are examples of clubs.

By contrast, risk takers and innovators fit best in entrepreneurial-oriented cultures known as **baseball teams**. Organizations with baseball team cultures seek talented workers of all ages and experiences and reward them for what they produce, not for their seniority or loyalty. Typically, employees are given great freedom, and those who excel are well paid. Thus, job-hopping is frequent. The kinds of organizations fitting this description include those in accounting, law, consulting, advertising, software, and bioresearch.

While baseball teams value innovation, organizations with **fortress** cultures are more concerned with survival. Many of these organizations were once academies, clubs, or baseball teams, but a turn of fortune caused them to change. Fortresses may offer little job security but can be an exciting workplace for those who are energized by the challenge of a turnaround. Large retailers may be among fortress organizations.

Each of these four cultural types tends to attract certain personalities. A good fit between the employee and the organization affects how far and how easily an employee may move up in the ranks. A risk taker, for example, will likely thrive at a baseball team but could fare poorly at an academy.

How compatible the attitudes of the individual are with the organization also may influence job offers, performance appraisals, and promotions. Not surprisingly, job satisfaction also will be higher when an employee matches up with the employer's culture.

Exhibit 17-2 Four Types of Organizational Culture

Type	Description
Academy	Employees stay within a narrow specialty and are promoted after they thoroughly master a new job.
Club	Employees are trained as generalists and promoted on the basis of seniority.
Baseball team	Employees are rewarded for what they produce. Risk taking and innovation are highly valued.
Fortress	Preoccupied with survival, these cultures reward employees who can reverse the organization's sagging fortunes.

Source: C. Hymowitz, "Which Culture Fits You?" *Wall Street Journal*, July 17, 1989, B1.

Sustaining an Organization's Culture

Once a culture is in place, the organization naturally tries to maintain and reinforce it. How? Much of that occurs as managers perform human resources duties such as identifying and hiring employees, giving performance evaluations, training and developing employees, and choosing candidates for promotion.[29] The following three managerial activities, however, play an especially important role in sustaining the culture.

1. **Selection practices** When hiring, the manager typically finds more than one candidate who meets the job's requirements. The final choice likely will take into account the important, but intangible, factor of how the candidates will "fit in." This consideration results in the hiring of candidates with values essentially consistent with those of the organization.[30] During the hiring process, the applicants also learn about the organization. Thus, they can self-select themselves out of the pool of candidates if they sense a mismatch. Selection, therefore, is a two-way street and tends to eliminate individuals who might be at odds with the organization's core values.

2. **Senior management's behaviour** The actions of senior executives have a major impact on an organization's culture.[31] By what they say and how they behave, these officials establish norms such as how much risk taking is desirable, how much freedom managers should grant employees, and what actions will pay off in terms of pay raises and promotions.

3. **Socialization** Organizations also help employees adapt to their cultures. The new worker, for instance, is taught what behaviours are rewarded and gradually assumes this new role, accepted by his or her peers and confident that he or she understands the "system." Though less explicitly, this socialization takes place throughout one's entire career in the organization.

At Starbucks, for example, each of the more than 20 000 employees goes through a set of formal classes during his or her first weeks on the job.[32] These classes include a history of the firm, coffee-making techniques, coffee-tasting classes, and even how to explain Starbucks' Italian drink names to baffled customers. The firm's socialization program turns out employees who are well-versed in the company's culture and understand management's obsession with "elevating the coffee experience," as one official puts it.

Changing an Organization's Culture

A culture commonly takes a long time to form, but once established, it's tough to change.[33] Reinforced by the selection process, top management behaviour, and socialization, the culture takes on a life of its own. At organizations where a given culture is judged to be no longer appropriate, management often finds there's little that can be done in the short run. Even in the most favourable conditions, changes in culture tend to be measured in years, not weeks or months.

CONDITIONS FACILITATING CULTURAL CHANGE

Still, as we have all experienced, change does happen. Cultural change is most likely to occur in organizations when most, or all, of the following conditions exist:

- **A dramatic crisis** A shock undermines the status quo and calls into question the relevance of the current culture; for instance, the loss of a major customer, a serious decline in market share, or a startling breakthrough by a competitor.

- **Turnover in leadership** An organization in crisis may turn to one or more new top leaders who seek to provide an alternative set of key values.

- **Young and small organization** The younger and smaller an organization, the easier it will be for top officials to instill new values, which is why multibillion-dollar corporations find the task especially difficult.
- **Weak culture** The more widely held a culture is and the higher the agreement among its members on the core values, the more difficult it will be to change. Thus, weak cultures are more amenable to a turnaround.

ACTIONS TO CHANGE CULTURE

All permanent changes are built on a foundation of trust, fairness, respect, and flexibility. If all of the above conditions or factors exist, how can change be encouraged? No single action is likely to succeed in changing a culture that is highly valued and entrenched. Thus, a comprehensive and coordinated strategy is needed.

DO A CULTURAL ANALYSIS The best place to begin is with a cultural analysis.[34] First, you would do a cultural audit to assess the current culture. Then compare the present culture with that which is desired, and finally, do a gap evaluation to identify what cultural elements require changing.

CREATE A SENSE OF URGENCY Management must make it clear to employees that the organization's survival is at risk if change does not occur. It is important, however, that the crisis be genuine and well explained to employees. If not, employee trust will be lost.

USE CHANGE AGENTS The appointment of a new top executive may dramatize that major changes are going to take place. The new chief may offer a new role model, a new vision, and new standards of behaviour. Ideally, the new executive will move promptly to introduce his or her new vision and to staff key management positions with similarly committed individuals.

CHANGE INTERNAL PROCESSES Changing culture is about changing the behaviour of people. New processes that demonstrate the new values must replace the old processes. For example, a firm may wish to replace a budgeting process that is perceived as secretive with one that is more open, transparent, and encourages employee input. To encourage employees, new reward structures must be created to support new behaviours.

CREATE SUPPORTING COMPONENTS This new leadership also will want to create new stories, symbols, rituals, and perhaps language to replace those that previously conveyed to employees the organization's dominant values. These new elements will need to be put in place rapidly so that the previous culture is not associated with the new leadership. Finally, management will need to change the selection and socialization processes and the appraisal and rewards system to support employees who share the new values.

Taking these steps does not guarantee that the change in culture will succeed. Asking employees to let go of values they understand and that have worked well in the past is, at best, a slow process. Managers will need to be on constant alert to prevent regression to the old, familiar practices.

Success stories of cultural change have several common denominators.[35] The turnarounds took from 4 to 10 years and were led by CEOs who were essentially outsiders, either brought in from outside the firms or from a division not in the corporate mainstream. In addition, all of the CEOs started their new jobs by trying to create an atmosphere of perceived crisis.

Concept Quiz

Complete the following true–false quiz by circling the correct answer. Answers are at the end of the quiz. After marking your answers, remember to go back and check your understanding of any answers you missed.

True or False   1. Usually, company stories about the founders have little validity and should be ignored.

True or False   2. Organizational culture is a system of shared meaning held by members, and distinguishes the organization from other organizations.

True or False   3. Employees learn their organization's culture through stories, rituals, material symbols, and language.

True or False   4. The words and deeds of senior executives rarely impact an organization's culture.

True or False   5. Two disadvantages of strong cultures are the pressure for conformity and resistance to change.

True or False   6. Leaders can affect an organizational culture, but they cannot unilaterally determine what that culture should be.

True or False   7. In many organizations, the nature of the culture is not something written down or even discussed.

True or False   8. The better the manager's personal style matches the organization's culture, the more successful the manager is likely to be.

True or False   9. A culture can be changed quickly if the conditions are right.

True or False   10. When subcultures develop, they usually develop around departmental lines or geographical separation.

Answers   (1) False; (2) True; (3) True; (4) False; (5) True; (6) True; (7) True; (8) True; (9) False; (10) True

Behavioural Checklist

The following behaviours are important for diagnosing and meshing with an organizational culture.

An Effective Manager of Organizational Culture:

- Identifies existing organizational culture.
- Assesses how people fit into specific cultures.
- Instills desirable values and norms in employees.
- Makes appropriate changes in organizational culture when needed.

Modelling Exercise
Diagnosing Organizational Culture

DIRECTIONS   The entire class should read the following situation. Then three students should be assigned to play the roles of Phyllis, Diane, and Pete. The rest of the class should observe and critique them.

Role-players should read and prepare for their roles but should not read the others' roles. After reading the situation, observers should read all three roles and study the sections on observations and the Observer's Rating Sheet.

Time 30 minutes.

Actors Phyllis, general manager of Booksco, a publishing firm; Diane, Booksco's managing editor; Pete, a job candidate.

Situation Phyllis is general manager of Booksco, where she has spent her entire 30-year career, rising from a stock clerk to general manager. The firm publishes books for pet owners and veterinarians. Diane is the managing editor, and has been with the company for 12 years. Diane has the major role in deciding which books Booksco should publish, then assigning writers and editors to produce them, and finally, overseeing production of the books. Diane answers to Phyllis, who is a businessperson, not an editor. But Phyllis, by authority of her position and her seniority, effectively has veto power over which book manuscripts are chosen. Pete is a writer who is considering joining Booksco.

During this exercise, Pete has a job interview with Diane, who will introduce him to Phyllis for a separate interview.

Phyllis' Role You have been here so long you sometimes think you *are* Booksco. In ways large and small, you've shaped this company to fit your values: hard-working, no-nonsense, profit-oriented, and tough but fair. As you like to say, "There are only two 'cant's' here: If you *can't* do the work, you *can't* stay." Such a hard-nosed philosophy has allowed Booksco to survive and prosper in a notoriously unstable publishing field. You would rather be respected than loved by your employees, which is probably what you are. If employees want state-of-the-art fringe benefits and/or a wimpy management that "empowers" them, they can go somewhere else. Here, what they get is hard work, decent pay, fair management, and a company that will be around when the others have gone belly up.

For example, Booksco does not give awards for writing; writers have their professional associations that can do that. Booksco does have annual awards, though, for those who come up with the best expense-cutting ideas. Those ideas and employees are what made this company strong and will keep it strong in the future.

Diane's Role In your dozen years here, you have learned a lot about publishing, and even more about how to get along with Phyllis. She's a good, if demanding, boss who consciously and unconsciously sets the tone for the company. You wish she were more open to new ideas and more sensitive about her employees. But you cannot deny that she oversees a commercially successful line of books. Employee turnover, though, is more than it should be, and the book line has become rather predictable. Phyllis's—and thus Booksco's—approach to publishing is that if something worked well in the past, it will work in the future. So why bother with change? Thus, she has rejected your idea for a line of children's books aimed at giving kids an appreciation of their pets and another suggestion for books about non-pet animals that serve the community, like seeing-eye dogs. Phyllis just wants basic pet books, geared to adults, that veterinarians and bookstores will sell and animal lovers will buy.

You think intuition is at the heart of publishing: sensing what people will read and then providing it. As a result, you think a publisher's got to take some chances, allow some mistakes in hopes of making a big score. But Phyllis likes things nailed down, distrusts intuition and spontaneity. "If it ain't broke, don't fix it" is one of Phyllis's favourite sayings. If you had a favourite, it would be: "You can be what you imagine."

You like Pete, whom you have come to know over the years from professional association meetings. He seems bright, creative, and easy to get along with. But you know that his previous job gave him a good deal of freedom in choosing what he wanted to write about. You wonder how he will fit into this organization, and you wonder what you will say if he asks you tough questions about what kind of place this is to work at.

PETE'S ROLE   Booksco has a reputation for being a good place to work. Not on the cutting edge perhaps, but stable: a place where someone can carve out a good career niche. You think it is time for a move to a stable company. Your previous employer, a rival of Booksco, satisfied you artistically. Management was so loose nobody knew what would happen next. Every day was an adventure, if not an accident. You were encouraged to write some things there of which you are especially proud. But because of poor management, the company was also flirting with financial disaster, and that made you nervous. Though you loved the creative, off-the-wall atmosphere and made many friends there, you are in your late thirties now and need a more solid place to roost. But you wonder: Is this the place? You hope to decide that during your next job interview with Diane, the firm's managing editor, and Phyllis, the GM.

INSTRUCTIONS   After Pete has talked to both Diane and Phyllis, he should tell the other class members what he concluded about the culture from the interviews, what else he observed, and what his feeling is about how he would fit in at Booksco.

Modelling Exercise Observations

During the dialogue, observers should watch Pete's interaction with Diane and with Phyllis. What questions does he ask of each? How do the two managers respond? What signals do they send? Be prepared to suggest additional questions for Pete and different ways for Diane and Phyllis to send out messages about the culture. What conclusions should Pete draw about Booksco's culture? Would it be a good place for him to work? What would be the pluses and the minuses for Pete?

Observer's Rating Sheet

Using the following scale, rate Pete's use of techniques discussed in this chapter for assessing and deciding whether he would fit into Booksco's culture. Also write comments that will help explain your feedback in the spaces between the criteria.

1 Unsatisfactory	2 Weak	3 Adequate	4 Good	5 Outstanding
				Rating

- Noted the physical surroundings.   _____

- Listened to the language.   _____

- Asked different people the same questions and compared answers.   _____

- Probed the meaning of stories and rituals.   _____

- Deduced how he will "fit in."   _____

Group Exercises

In the following four exercises you will be asked to show an understanding of organizational cultures. The first exercise involves maintaining a culture, the second concerns assessing the culture of your college or university, the third entails diagnosing the culture of a workplace, and the fourth concerns how you might go about changing a culture.

Group Exercise 1: Maintaining an Organizational Culture[34]

TIME 30 minutes.

INSTRUCTIONS Break into several groups of three to four persons each. Read the case study and discuss the questions within each group. The instructor will put each group's suggestions on the blackboard and encourage further discussion by the whole class.

THE BEAN QUEEN CASE The Bean Queen, the Bean Counters, and the Human Beans can all be found at Buckeye Beans and Herbs. Jill Smith is the Bean Queen. She's the self-proclaimed hippie artist-turned-entrepreneur who started the company in 1983 with an investment of just $1,000. From that small, inauspicious beginning, Buckeye Beans now has sales revenue approaching $8 million a year and employs 50 people (the aforementioned Human Beans).

Buckeye Beans has expanded its product lines. It began with just one product—Buckeye Bean Soup—but now includes a full line of "all-natural" soups as well as chili, bread mixes, and pasta. One innovation that Buckeye is especially fond of is special-occasion-shaped pasta: pasta molded into miniature Christmas trees, hearts, bunnies, dolphins, leaves, grapes, baseballs, and even golf balls. However, what is as unique as Buckeye's products is its organizational culture.

The firm's motto is: "We Make People Smile!" Jill Smith believes that cooking should be fun, not drudgery. Because of this philosophy, the first ingredient listed on all of Buckeye's product packages is a cup of good wine for the cook. Buckeye's strategy—crafted by Jill and her accountant–husband Jim (the Bean Counter)—is that its products go beyond a simple bag of beans and become entertainment.

Likewise, the Smiths believe running the company should be fun. Casual clothes are the rule, not the exception. On Fridays, employees are encouraged to dress in bean-related garb—wear hats made of beans, or shirts with bean buttons, or jewellery dotted with beans instead of gems. Each Friday, the most original bean couture is awarded—*you guessed it!*—a bag of beans.

Many of the employees are family and long-time friends, but they all share the belief that not only the products but the work environment should be built on a firm foundation of fun. Buckeye's employee and customer relationships run on the basis of trust, confidence, loyalty, and working together to get things done.

Jill and Jim have never given much thought to organizational culture. They have just made the company a projection of themselves, but they do perceive that it has a special flair.

They worry, though, that as it grows (and sales are climbing at more than 20 per cent each year) and more employees are added that this special flavour will be diluted and may be eventually lost. Imagine yourselves as consultants brought in to advise them about how to maintain and appropriately change Buckeye Beans' corporate culture.

QUESTIONS FOR DISCUSSION

1. How would you describe Buckeye's organizational culture? What are its dominant values? Its other values?
2. As Buckeye grows, what, specifically, can it do it perpetuate its culture?
3. How does it or could it use (a) stories, (b) rituals, (c) material symbols, and/or (d) language to transmit that culture? Give examples.
4. How difficult would it be to change this culture? Why?
5. What changes would you recommend?
6. What process would you recommend Jill use to make these changes?

Group Exercise 2: Assessing the Culture of Your College or University

TIME 45 minutes.

INSTRUCTIONS Break into teams of four or five. Assess your college or university's culture using the seven primary characteristics presented earlier in this chapter. As your team attempts to categorize your school, pay particular attention to the criteria various members use in order to draw their individual conclusions.

STEP 1. INDIVIDUAL RATINGS Rate your college or university in the following categories:

1. Innovation and risk taking: Low 1-2-3-4-5 High
Remarks:

2. Attention to detail: Low 1-2-3-4-5 High
Remarks:

3. Outcome orientation: Low 1-2-3-4-5 High
Remarks:

4. People orientation: Low 1-2-3-4-5 High
Remarks:

5. Team orientation: Low 1-2-3-4-5 High
Remarks:

6. Aggressiveness: Low 1-2-3-4-5 High
Remarks:

7. Growth: Low 1-2-3-4-5 High
Remarks:

STEP 2. TEAM DISCUSSION Team members share their ratings and reasons for each criterion and then reach a consensus.

STEP 3. CLASS COMPARISON Each team presents its findings to the class. Then the various teams' conclusions are compared and the class discusses the following questions:

- How much agreement was there?
- What explains the differences?
- Where were differences noted between individuals on a team? How did the group reconcile these differences?
- To what degree can the college or university's culture be traced to its founders?
- What rituals, stories, symbols, or language reflect the culture?
- If you were charged with changing this culture, how would you begin?

STEP 4. COMPARE AND CONTRAST The instructor asks students who have attended other colleges or universities to contrast the cultures of those schools with what the students perceive to be the culture at the present school.

Group Exercise 3: Deciding Whether You Mesh With the Culture

DIRECTIONS Split into three groups. Each group should read the situation and the dialogue, then try to answer the questions. Reconvene as a class and compare answers.

SITUATION Charlene, a middle-aged woman, is a candidate for a job as an investment counsellor at Goodman and Walters, a large multi-national brokerage firm. She previously worked for a small brokerage firm specializing in on-line trading. She began there as a clerk, then worked her way up to an account manager while going to school at night. But when the brokerage firm was merged with another, many of the best jobs were transferred to another city, and Charlene took a buyout and began looking for a new position. She is a single mother with two teenaged sons and does not want a job that involves a lot of travel or irregular hours. Thus, the position at a large brokerage has appeal.

But she wonders whether she can make the transition from the frenetic, but free-wheeling, atmosphere of the small brokerage to what she suspects is the almost glacial tempo of a large, button-down branch of a large company. Further, she wonders whether people will accept her. At her previous job, most of the business was done over the computer or the phone, so account managers were encouraged to dress casually, a style to which she has become accustomed. A lot of friendly, but spirited, banter went on among the account managers and even practical jokes (a dead fish was once hidden under a pile of papers on Charlene's notoriously untidy desk on the bet that she wouldn't find it for weeks!). She thinks Goodman and Walters will probably not be like that. As a broker, she was responsible for her results (each account manager's commission totals were published in the newsletter, adding to the firm's competitive atmosphere) but yet felt a part of the team. She is not sure Goodman and Walters will be like that, either. But she wants to be fair, and being rather adaptable, she thinks she could adjust to any culture as long as performance is valued.

Charlene has her first interview with William Wagner, the manager of the branch to which she would be assigned. They meet in his nicely furnished office. She notices that no one could ever hide a fish under the papers on his desk; it has no papers. All such material is neatly tucked into baskets, and his pens, stapler, and other stationery items are placed in seeming order on the desktop. Mr. Wagner is a distinguished-looking gentleman about her age. He seems quite proper yet gracious, speaking slowly and clearly with perhaps a hint of condescension.

Charlene and Mr. Wagner have the following conversation:

Mr. Wagner: Do you think you would enjoy working here? You haven't previously worked at a large brokerage, I see from your résumé.

Charlene: Well, I think I would, but I guess I need to know more about how you operate. How would you describe the work environment?

Mr. Wagner: In a word, "professional." Very professional. Our customers want a sense of stability in addition to good service. So we try to give them an experience that is both gracious and competent. How does that match with where you previously worked?

Charlene: Well, it was a different situation there. We worked mainly over the phones or on-line, so interacting personally with the customers was infrequent. It was probably more casual...but the bottom line was the same: We had to serve the customers and serve them well.

Mr. Wagner: Indeed. Our founder, whose picture hangs on the wall there, used to say, "Make every customer encounter a Moment of Magic, not a Moment of Misery." This company is built on that credo.

Charlene: What was he like?

Mr. Wagner: Well, in 1897 he rode a horse 27 kilometres through a howling storm to return a diamond stickpin that a customer had accidentally dropped in the office. That's how strongly he felt about winning the customers' respect and admiration.

Charlene: That's good to hear. How do you encourage "Moments of Magic"?

Mr. Wagner: In addition to our "How Was Your Service?" questionnaire available in the reception area, we include a similar form with each monthly statement mailed to our customers. So, we do a lot to encourage feedback. And we share those results with our staff, in private if the report is negative and in public, at our semi-annual Service Awards Ceremony, if a staff member gets repeated positive feedback. Employees who are exceptionally good and diligent about service can receive all manner of rewards, from tickets to major entertainment events to vacation holidays.

Charlene: And I would also be eligible for prizes?

Mr. Wagner: Of course. Usually our new employees are on probation for the first six months, during which time they are given monthly reviews by me or by their immediate supervisor and they are not considered fully trained and eligible until that probationary period is concluded. But in your case, because of your education and experience, we would waive that probation. You would be a full-fledged, permanent employee—a member of "Team One," as we call it—from your first day here.

Charlene: I like what I'm hearing. This sounds like, as you say, a "very professional" operation. But I must be honest and tell you that my previous employer, while highly successful, was very different. Competitive, but casual. We probably didn't do things by the book there, but we got things done. I'm used to a fast-paced, looser style of working than what I perceive to be the norm here. Do you think that will be a problem?

Mr. Wagner: Well, we do take our professionalism seriously. "Professional" is a word you hear around here a lot. What that means to me is that people take their jobs seriously and seek to project a certain decorum that customers expect from a major brokerage. We don't dress down on Fridays. We don't wear cutesy costumes on Valentine's Day or on Halloween. We don't post Dilbert cartoons in our workspaces. We're an investment firm, a *professional* investment firm.

Charlene nods, but says nothing.

Mr. Wagner: I like you and your credentials. I think you would fit in: you're articulate, well-dressed and, I gather, well-mannered. I'd like to offer you the job. But before you accept or reject it, I think you need to ask yourself: "Would I feel comfortable here?" In short, can you adapt? *We're* not going to change. If there is to be change, it will need to come from *you*. What do you think?

QUESTIONS FOR DISCUSSION

1. What good questions did Charlene ask? What other questions should she ask?
2. What did she learn about the firm's culture from William Wagner? Its stories? Its rituals? Its symbols?
3. Who else, if anyone, should she talk to inside the bank? Elsewhere?
4. How should she reply to Wagner's offer? Why?

Group Exercise 4: Changing a Culture

TIME 20 minutes.

INSTRUCTIONS Break into groups. Each group should study the following situation and answer the questions, then reconvene as a class and compare answers.

SITUATION You are an assistant store manager at Sports Choice, a sporting goods chain in Edmonton, when you are promoted to store manager in Regina. Your main task, as you understand it, is to shape up the store and the staff to go head-to-head with K-2 Sports, another sporting goods chain store, which also operates in Regina. However, you know of K-2's reputation for excellent service.

You do not know much about the new store yet, but you know the parent firm is sales conscious, sending managers like yourself weekly updates on how each store is performing. It also is fairly quick to replace managers whose sales lag. The most successful sales personnel—known as "QBs," or quota-busters—are annually feted at the headquarters in Vancouver.

Midway through your first week, you're wandering through the sportswear section when you see an item you might like to get your spouse for your anniversary. You examine it, decide to buy it, and look for a clerk. But the only clerk is at the other end of the floor helping a customer purchase a pair of skates.

You approach, and the lone clerk, not recognizing you, turns and says, "Look, I'm the only person up here, and I'm helping this customer right now. Why don't you come back another day when we have more help on the floor?" At that point, you realize just how big a job you face in reshaping this store.

QUESTIONS FOR DISCUSSION

1. How can the current culture be described?
2. What are its legends? Rituals? Symbols? Language?
3. What can you do to begin to change the culture?
4. Do you need to promote a "crisis"? Why or why not?
5. How much time should you give yourself?

Application Questions

Analyze the culture of an organization you know well by answering the following questions and then drawing conclusions. Ideally, this place is where you work, but a church or social group also will do.[35]

1. What is the background of the founders?
2. What explains the organization's growth and survival?
3. What does the organization stand for? What is its motto?
4. What values does the organization talk about?
5. What values does it act out?
6. What does it take for a person to do well in this organization? To stay out of trouble?
7. What kinds of mistakes are not forgiven?
8. How does the organization treat those who break the "rules"?
9. How are good employees/members rewarded?
10. How does the organization respond to crises?
11. What message does the physical setting convey?
12. How do things get done in this organization?
13. How does the group take in new members?
14. What kinds of stories are told about the organization?
15. Who are the heroes? Why?
16. How do the leaders exercise power?

Based on the answers to these questions, how would you describe the culture of this organization?

Reinforcement Exercises

1. Think of a favourite television show that portrays the members of an organization—perhaps a hospital emergency room, a law office, or a police force.
   a) How would you diagnose that organization's culture?
   b) Are leaders portrayed as those who exemplify that culture's values? Why? What do they do?
   c) Do some characters not "fit in"? Why? What do they do that puts them at cross-purposes with the culture? What happens to them?
2. Compare the cultures of the various classes you are taking this semester? How do they differ? How do they match, or clash, with your personal style?
3. What was the culture at your home when you were growing up? Identify its stories, rituals, symbols, and language.

Summary Checklist

Take a few minutes to reflect on your performance in the preceding exercises. Assess yourself as to how your analysis compared to other students (and if you were a presenter, how others rated your skill). Make a check (√) next to those behaviours on which you may need improvement.

_____ Identifying existing organizational cultures.

    1. Note the physical surroundings.

    2. Listen to the language.

    3. Ask different people the same questions and compare answers.

    4. Probe meaning of legends, rituals, and symbols.

_____ Deducing how people will "fit" into the culture.

    1. Choose candidates for hiring/promotion based in part on their organizational "fit."

    2. Determine whether they value what the organization values.

    3. See whether their personal style matches up with those who are getting ahead in the organization.

_____ Instilling desirable values and norms in employees.

    1. Speak and act in a way that models the appropriate behaviour.

    2. Continuously train employees.

_____ Making appropriate changes in culture when needed.

    1. Do a cultural audit of existing culture to see whether change is needed.

    2. Emphasize the urgency of the need for change.

    3. Put new leadership—with alternative values—in place.

    4. Create new stories, symbols, rituals, and perhaps language.

Action Plan

1. On what aspects of diagnosing and modifying organizational culture do I need to most improve? (For examples, see Summary Checklist.)
2. What benefits will I gain in my future workplace by improving my skills in this area?
3. How can I start improving in the organizations with which I am now associated?
4. When will I start?
5. How and when will I measure my success?

CHAPTER 18
Leading Change

Learning Objectives
After completing this chapter, you should be able to:
- Differentiate between management and leadership opportunities.
- Identify targets for change.
- Adapt leadership style to follower needs.
- Create and share compelling visions.
- Empower followers to achieve change goals.
- Facilitate the phases of planned change.
- Implement planned change.
- Recognize and overcome resistance to change.

Self-Assessment Exercise
Leadership Preferences[1]

For each statement, circle the number on the scale that best describes you.

	Strongly Agree				Strongly Disagree
1. I like to stand out from the crowd.	1	2	3	4	5
2. I feel proud and satisfied when I influence others to do things my way.	1	2	3	4	5
3. I enjoy doing things as part of a group rather than achieving results on my own.	1	2	3	4	5
4. I have a history of becoming an officer or captain in clubs and/or organized sports.	1	2	3	4	5
5. I try to be the one who is most influential in task groups at school or work.	1	2	3	4	5
6. In groups, I care most about good relationships.	1	2	3	4	5
7. In groups, I most want to achieve task goals.	1	2	3	4	5
8. In groups, I always show consideration for the feelings and needs of others.	1	2	3	4	5

	Strongly Agree				Strongly Disagree
9. In groups, I always structure activities and assignments to help get the job done.	1	2	3	4	5
10. In groups, I shift between being supportive of others' needs and pushing task accomplishment.	1	2	3	4	5

SCORING

Leadership Interest Score: Add the scale values you circled on items 1 through 5:_____

Leadership Style Score:

Task Emphasis Score: Add the scale values you circled on items 7 and 9: _____

Relationship Emphasis Score: Add the scale values you circled on items 6 and 8:_____

Difference between task and relationship scores:

Check the higher score: task _____ or relationship _____.

Adaptability Score: Your score on item 10: _____

INTERPRETATION

Leadership Interest. If your total score on items 1 through 5 is 20 or more, you likely have a strong interest in the role played by a leader. If your score is 10 or less, at this time in your life you are likely more interested in personal achievement. If you score in the middle range, your interests could go in either direction, depending on events.

Leadership Style. Your leadership style is suggested by your responses to items 6 through 10. Check the following totals to determine whether you prefer a task-oriented, relationship-oriented, or flexible leadership style.

Your *leadership style preference* is indicated by which is the highest of your task emphasis or relationship emphasis scores. The difference between these scores indicates how strong this preference is.

Your *style adaptability* is indicated by your Adaptability Score. A score of 4 or 5 on item 10 suggests you may adapt to circumstances as you see the need.

Concepts

Fortune magazine proclaimed Larry Bossidy "the most sought-after CEO in America."[2] Bossidy left the number two position at General Electric in 1991 to take the helm at ailing Allied-Signal, and has since been courted by IBM, Kodak, Westinghouse, and others. Brutally demanding and seldom satisfied, Bossidy sets challenging growth targets for his managers, helps them lay out strategies, provides resources, then grills them to make sure they follow through.

As a leader of other leaders and managers, Larry Bossidy promotes growth as a motivational force: "The biggest payoff from growth is with people." Expanding opportunities are necessary to attract and encourage talented people. Without growth, he believes firms resort to seeking productivity by laying off people. "Restructuring [with layoffs] is negative. You get a frightened workforce. Eventually you need to maintain or create jobs, not destroy them."

Bossidy is not a leader who stays in his executive suite to make only the big decisions. He immerses himself in the operating details of Allied-Signal's 20 businesses and guides unit managers in crafting business strategies. He claims, "A strategist divorced from operations is an incomplete person. You make far better judgments doing both."

Leaders such as Larry Bossidy are the people who create, grow, and transform organizations. They lead change processes and redirect people's energies towards transformation of products, technologies, and organizational practices to produce growth. On the other hand, they manage to preserve order and achieve productivity. They have to manage costs and timetables and coordinate tasks across departments so that quality and efficiency are achieved.

Bossidy is able to excel as a manager at driving down costs and developing innovative processes for getting work done more efficiently. He is also a visionary leader who provides a clear sense of direction for transforming ideas into commercial successes, and he energizes others by challenging them to help make possibilities come true. Larry Bossidy is both an accomplished manager and a superlative leader. This chapter is designed to help you develop the leadership skills essential to promote change effectively, but first, it is important to look at how leadership and management roles are integrated.

The Integration of Leadership and Management Roles

Leadership is different from management but not in the ways that many people think. Leadership is not mysterious or heroic and does not require special personality traits. It is not better than management or a replacement for it. Rather, leadership and management are different but complementary ways of acting.

Leadership is the set of skills and behaviours needed to create change—setting direction, communicating a vision of a brighter future, and transforming an organization. On the other hand, the management role requires skills and behaviours needed to keep an organization running smoothly and efficiently. Traditionally, leadership and management were seen as separate and distinct functions.

Today, the business landscape is quite different. Driven by the globalization of markets, changing consumer expectations, and advances in telecommunications and production technology, the pace of change has dramatically quickened. Organizations are faced with the task of operating in a world where change is the norm—very little is predictable or stable.

Because of these changes, management and leadership are no longer seen as separate and distinct functions but, rather, as integrated roles.[3] There are times when a manager/leader needs to innovate, adapt, and focus on change and other times when goals, planning, documentation, and stability become the centre of attention. It is not an issue of being *either* a leader *or* a manager but, rather, *both*. Organizations need to be both flexible, innovative, and adaptable *and* emphasize internal process controls. There is a need to create inspiring visions of the future and have planned objectives. More than ever, organizations need individuals who are adept at both roles. In other words, managers need to be good leaders and leaders need to be good managers.

THE MANAGER'S ROLE

A manager is a person granted **formal authority** to be in charge of an organization or one of its subunits. Managers exist at all levels of organizations, with titles symbolic of their scope of responsibilities, such as supervisors, managers, directors, administrators, or executives. Managers diagnose and influence systems and are responsible for controlling activities to keep the flow of work running smoothly. They keep activities and programs on track, maintain system predictability, and balance revenues against costs to achieve reasonable productivity and profitability. Authority is the right to make decisions and commit organizational resources based on one's position within the organizational hierarchy. Managers draw on their position authority to initiate problem solving, decision making, and action.

THE LEADER'S ROLE

Leadership is the process of providing direction, energizing others, and obtaining their voluntary commitment to the leader's vision.[4] A leader creates a vision and goals and influences others to share that vision and work toward the goals. Leaders are concerned with bringing about change and motivating others to support that vision of change. At an individual level, leaders coach, mentor, and motivate. At the group level, they build teams and resolve conflicts, and at the organizational level, they build culture. McGill University's Henry Mintzberg, in his observation of Bramwell Tovey, artistic director and conductor of the Winnipeg Symphony Orchestra, concluded that leadership is not about controlling situations or people from a corner office but, rather, behaving more like a foreperson who is intermeshed with operations on the shop floor.[5]

Informal leaders, who do not hold formal positions of authority, also stir up new ideas, champion new causes, and inspire co-workers to pursue strategic visions. This situation commonly occurs when a manager of one department influences peers in other departments to support a favoured program or a pilot project. In a similar situation, when several nonmanagerial people are put together on a "leaderless" task force or assigned to a self-managed team, one or two are likely to emerge as informal leaders. Consequently, leadership occurs at all organizational levels and is not dependent on formal authority.

All organizations need individuals who fulfill both manager and leadership roles. In contemporary organizations, one person fills the roles of both manager and leader. While a manager role involves controlling complexity, a leader's role involves initiating change.[6] Although the tasks are different, both roles involve deciding what needs to be done, creating networks of people and relationships that can accomplish an agenda, and then trying to ensure that those people actually do the job.[7] Exhibit 18-1 illustrates the basic distinction between how managers and leaders accomplish these tasks.

Exhibit 18-1 Task Distinctions Between Managers and Leaders

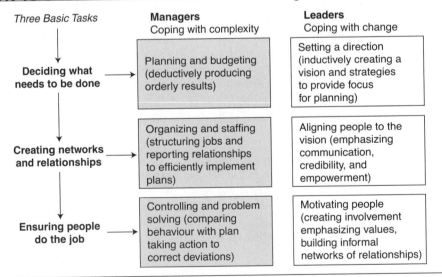

Three Basic Tasks	Managers Coping with complexity	Leaders Coping with change
Deciding what needs to be done	Planning and budgeting (deductively producing orderly results)	Setting a direction (inductively creating a vision and strategies to provide focus for planning)
Creating networks and relationships	Organizing and staffing (structuring jobs and reporting relationships to efficiently implement plans)	Aligning people to the vision (emphasizing communication, credibility, and empowerment)
Ensuring people do the job	Controlling and problem solving (comparing behaviour with plan taking action to correct deviations)	Motivating people (creating involvement emphasizing values, building informal networks of relationships)

Source: Summarized from J. Kotter, "What Leaders Really Do," *Harvard Business Review* 68 (May–June 1990): 103–11.

Leader Traits

Those who are successful in the leadership role do stand out from other people, but traits such as drive, honesty, and self-confidence by themselves are not sufficient to predict success. They are only preconditions or enablers from which leaders must initiate actions such as clarifying a vision, setting goals, and role modelling.[8]

Research has found that followers look for credibility in leaders.[9] **Credibility** refers to being honest, competent, forward looking, and inspiring. Another stream of research concludes that six traits distinguish leaders from non-leaders: drive, leadership motivation, honesty and integrity, self-confidence, cognitive ability, and knowledge of the business.[10] Exhibit 18-2 summarizes these qualities. When followers look to leaders for direction and inspiration, they expect to find these types of characteristics.

Other research points to "adaptive capacity" as being critical to success. This means the combination of perseverance, mental toughness, and an ability to grasp the big picture. These characteristics allow an individual to draw wisdom from trying circumstances and emerge stronger and more committed than before.[11]

The findings from more than 50 years of research, however, conclude that although some traits increase the likelihood of success as a leader, none of the traits guarantees success.[12]

Leader Behaviours

Ultimately people evaluate leaders on the basis of their behaviour and decide whether they want to follow their lead voluntarily. Years of research on leader behaviour have essentially differentiated between behaviours that focus on task production and behaviours that focus on building positive employee relationships.[13] **Task-oriented behaviour** focuses on careful supervision of group members to obtain consistent work methods and

---

Exhibit 18-2 Leader Traits

As you read the following descriptions of these six traits, try to create an image of a leader at work. Does this describe you?

- Drive—has the need for achievement through challenging assignments, the desire to get ahead, high energy to work long hours with enthusiasm, tenacity to overcome obstacles, and initiative to make choices and take action that leads to change.

- Leadership motivation—exemplifies a strong desire to lead, the willingness to accept responsibility, the desire to influence others, and a strong socialized desire for power (which means the desire to exercise power for the good of the organization).

- Honesty and integrity—demonstrates truthfulness or nondeceitfulness (honesty) and consistency between word and deed, is predictable, follows ethical principles, is discreet, and makes competent decisions (integrity).

- Self-confidence—gains the trust of others by being sure of own actions (and not being defensive about making mistakes), being assertive and decisive, maintaining emotional stability (not losing one's cool), and remaining calm and confident in times of crisis.

- Cognitive ability—has a keen mind and thinks strategically, reasons analytically, and exercises good judgment in decisions and actions; has the ability to reason deductively and inductively.

- Knowledge of the business—beyond formal education, develops technical expertise to understand the concerns of followers, comprehends the economics of the industry, and knows the organization's culture and behaviour.

Source: S.A. Kirkpatrick and E.A. Locke, "Leadership: Do Traits Matter?" *Academy of Management Executive* 5 (May 1991): 48–60. © Irwin Co. Reprinted by permission of the McGraw-Hill Companies.

accomplishment of the job. It centres on initiating structure and processes intended to establish "well-defined patterns of organization, channels of communication, and methods of procedure" between leader and group. **Employee-oriented behaviour** aims at satisfying the social and emotional needs of group members. It focuses on showing consideration to develop "friendship, mutual trust, respect, and warmth in the relationship between leader and staff members."[14] Research also indicates that followers look to leaders who display employee-oriented behaviours such as developing the workplace community, enhancing the significance of work, and offering excitement.[15]

Neither task-oriented nor employee-oriented behaviour, however, ensures maximum performance effectiveness and work-group satisfaction.[16] Although leaders high in *both* task orientation and employee orientation tended to have better follower performance and satisfaction, enough negative side effects (absenteeism and grievances) were present that the positive outcomes were not unconditional. Research trying to predict group performance solely on the basis of consistent leader behaviour turned out to be a futile endeavour.

A related line of research concentrated on studying leader behaviour in decision making and its impact on productivity and satisfaction. Four principal leader decision styles were identified. The first is autocratic, characterized by unilaterally taking charge and giving assignments to others. The democratic style is easygoing, using suggestions and encouragement to reach a group consensus. With the laissez-faire style the leader is passive and noncommittal, which allows others to make their own decisions independently. The fourth decision style is participative. It emphasizes consulting with those who are involved to gather data and opinions before making a decision.[17] Exhibit 18-3 shows how these four descriptors of a leader's decision style can be distinguished when superimposed on the two broad behavioural dimensions of initiating structure (task orientation) and showing consideration (relationship orientation).[18]

The appropriate use of these different leader behaviours depends on the situation, such as the task complexity, the leader's formal power, and the time frame available, as well as such follower characteristics as competency, motivation, goals, and attitude toward the leader. Two approaches to leadership that address these issues are the situational leadership model and path-goal theory.

THE SITUATIONAL LEADERSHIP MODEL

In Paul Hersey and Kenneth Blanchard's situational leadership model, combinations of task and relationship behaviours are prescribed based on the job maturity of followers.

Exhibit 18-3 Leader Behaviours and Decision Styles

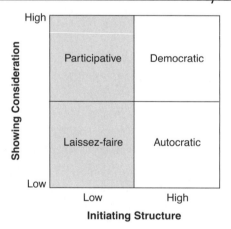

Task behaviours include things such as organizing and defining roles, explaining what activities need to be done, establishing organization structure, channels of communication, and methods of getting jobs accomplished. **Relationship behaviours** include maintaining personal relationships with followers by opening channels of communication, providing recognition and praise, being empathetic, and facilitating behaviours.[19]

Followers' maturity, or job readiness, consists of the degree of "the capacity to set high but attainable goals, willingness and ability to take responsibility, and education and/or experience of an individual or a group."[20] Maturity ranges along a continuum according to the degree to which followers are willing and able to complete tasks on their own. This ability, of course, varies with the task. For example, a salesperson may be particularly responsible in securing new sales but very casual about completing the paperwork necessary to close on a sale. As a result, it is appropriate for the manager to leave him or her alone in terms of closing on sales, but to supervise closely in terms of paperwork until he or she can start to do well in that area too.[21]

The pattern of effective leader behaviours in relation to follower maturity is presented in Exhibit 18-4. To determine the appropriate leadership style, select one of the four boxes indicating your estimate of a follower's readiness. Draw a line straight upward

Exhibit 18-4 The Situational Leadership Model

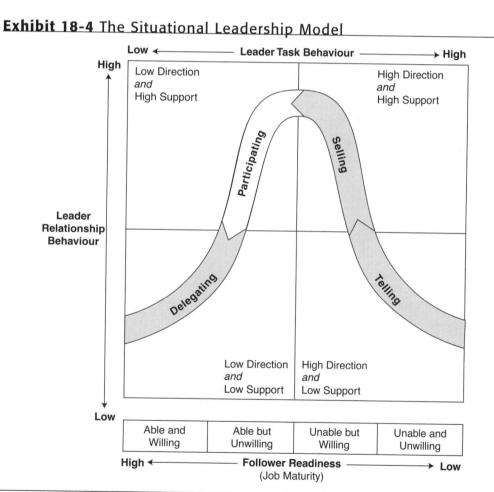

Source: Based on P. Hersey and K.H. Blanchard, *Management of Organizational Behavior,* 6th ed. (Upper Saddle River, NJ: Prentice Hall, 1993) 186. Adapted by permission. Situational Leadership® is a registered trademark of the Center for Learning, Escondido, CA.

and where it intersects the normal curve indicates the appropriate leader behaviour. Ideally, as a follower's job maturity changes, the leader's behaviour toward that person should change also. Leadership behaviours should be adjusted over time to develop employee competencies as well as to guide and influence current performance.

Consider a leader who has two employees low in job maturity—for example, inexperienced supermarket cashiers both of whom are in their first full-time job. The assistant store manager begins their socialization by emphasizing responsibilities and training them in how tasks should be performed (high concentration on task, or "telling"). As the cashiers begin to demonstrate that they can handle basic jobs, the leader shifts to also providing reassurance and praise and making each worker feel valued (high relationship, or "selling" behaviours).

Over time, the leader's task guidance diminishes, as performance becomes self-sustaining. Once the cashiers reach a high level of competence, the leader grants greater autonomy (for example, to cash cheques without approval by the manager). Interaction then occurs on an "as-needed," or "participating" basis. In professional occupations, such a pattern often occurs between a mentor and protege as the younger person gains professional skill, stature, and reputation, ultimately becoming independent of the mentor.[22]

PATH-GOAL THEORY

The major emphasis of **path-goal theory** is how to increase employees' motivation to attain organizational goals. As illustrated in Exhibit 18-5, a leader can increase follower motivation by clarifying employees' pathways to obtaining organizational goals and by

Exhibit 18-5 Path-Goal Theory

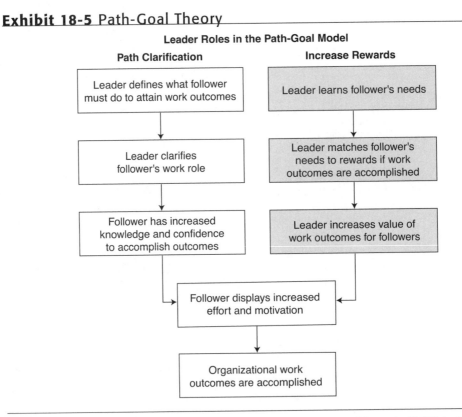

Source: Based on B.M. Bass, "Leadership: Good, Better, Best," *Organizational Dynamics* 13 (Winter 1985): 26–40.

providing meaningful personal rewards.[23] When clarifying paths to goals, leaders help employees identify and learn the behaviours that will enable them to accomplish tasks successfully. Second, leaders consult with employees to determine which rewards are important to them. Then the leader's job is to increase personal payoffs to employees for goal attainment and to make the paths to these payoffs clear and easy to travel.

Like situational leadership, the path-goal approach indicates that leaders engage in task behaviours and supportive or relationship behaviours that combine into four leadership styles.[24] *Directive leadership* (highly task oriented) lets followers know what is expected of them, provides guidance as to what is to be done and how, clarifies performance standards and time schedules, and calls attention to work procedures and policies. *Achievement-oriented leadership* (highly task and relationship oriented) establishes challenging goals, seeks performance improvement, and displays confidence that people will exert high levels of effort. *Participative leadership* (moderately task and highly relationship oriented) involves consulting with and soliciting the ideas of others in decision making and action taking. *Supportive leadership* (highly relationship oriented) shows concern for the needs and goals of others and strives to make the work situation pleasant and equitable.

The path-goal approach suggests two important factors that determine which leadership style will be most effective for motivating employees in different situations. The first one, like situational leadership, concerns the personal readiness level of employees: ability, skills, needs, and motivations. The second factor concerns three environmental conditions: task structure, formal authority, and work group characteristics. The degree of task structure is the extent to which tasks are well defined and have clear job descriptions. The nature of the formal authority system refers to the degree of legitimate power the leader has and the extent of policies and rules that exist. Work group characteristics concern the quality of interpersonal relationships among group members.

Researchers have found the most useful application of path-goal leadership occurs when the follower's task is perceived to be ambiguous, ill-defined, and lacking in routine or standardization, such as jobs in product development or marketing research.[25] A task-focused leader helps followers clarify ambiguous roles. Under conditions of low task structure (complex and/or ambiguous jobs), task-focused leaders have higher follower job satisfaction and goal attainment, but in highly structured tasks, such as purchasing or accounts payable jobs, group members view task-oriented leader behaviour as an attempt to exert added, unnecessary structure and control over their lives—too much management. In situations where substantive conflict exists, task-oriented leader behaviour is more appropriate. In well-defined and routine situations with strong lines of formal authority, supportive relationship behaviour from the leader is more appropriate. Similarly, supportive behaviour is likely to be well received by employees who have ability and considerable experience. The relationship-building behaviour aims to increase morale and cooperation by building on a base of rewards.

If the leader's path-goal behaviour is effective, it will produce greater employee effort by clarifying how employees can receive rewards, or changing rewards to fit their needs. The payoff to leaders is that those who are being influenced are likely to accept the leader, expect that personal effort leads to better performance, expect that effective performance leads to relevant rewards, and be satisfied with their work and work situation.[26]

Identifying Targets for Change

Exhibit 18-6 illustrates six primary organizational factors that a leader can target for change. Changes in strategy, structure, management, and culture are generally initiated by senior management and are implemented from the top down. On the other hand, technology changes are usually initiated at the operating levels of the organization and channeled

Exhibit 18-6 Organizational Change Targets

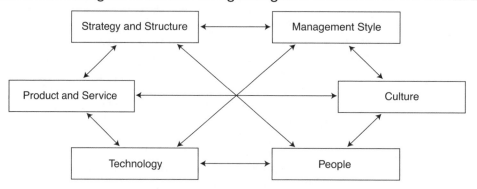

upward for approval. Managers are always searching for, and supportive of, these bottom-up ideas because they know that employees at operating levels have the most expertise to propose meaningful changes in the jobs they perform.

STRATEGY AND STRUCTURE

Strategy and structure changes originate with top management. Chapter 11, Planning and Goal Setting, described how management creates new visions, missions, and strategic plans for an organization, which include, at the operating level, changes in policies, reward systems, coordination, and control systems. Examples of changes in the organization's structure would be things such as adding a new department or changing from a functional structure to a product division structure.

PRODUCT AND SERVICE

Product and service changes pertain to organization outputs to meet customer needs. New products are normally designed to increase market share or to develop new markets, customers, or clients. Although ideas for new products or services often originate at operating levels, they also flow horizontally across departments because they generally require expertise from several different departments simultaneously. For example, people in research might inform marketing of new developments to learn whether they will be useful to customers, or marketing people could pass customer complaints to research to use in the design of new products.

TECHNOLOGY

Changes in technology are designed to make production more efficient or to produce greater volume. They include such things as upgrading a data processing system or installing a robotic manufacturing operation. They might also be changes in work methods, equipment, and work flow.

PEOPLE

People are let go during downsizing and hired during expansions. People changes also consist of upgrading knowledge and skill bases of existing employees. At times a leader attempts to change an employee's attitude or behaviour. When this type of transformation is attempted on the organizational level for all employees, the focus shifts to changing the entire culture.

CULTURE

Cultural changes transform the values, attitudes, expectations, beliefs, and behaviours of all employees in the organization. An example is implementing a program to encourage valuing quality and service. Chapter 17, Diagnosing and Modifying Organizational Culture, provides more information on changing organizational culture.

MANAGEMENT

Changes in management style refer to the degree of task and relationship behaviours that managers exhibit with employees in different situations, as well as the degree of participation they allow in decision making and problem solving. For example, a manager might encourage bottom-up participation in problem solving from employees to replace a former top-down approach.

INTERDEPENDENCY OF CHANGE TARGETS

The arrows connecting the types of change targets in Exhibit 18-6 indicate that a change in one target may affect others as well. For example, a new strategic plan may lead to new products, which in turn creates stretch goals for people and requires changes in technology.

Managing the Planned Change Process

Planned change is the result of consciously preparing for and taking actions to reach a desired goal or organizational state. It involves proactively making things different rather than reacting to changes imposed from outside the organization. Major change does not happen easily and requires a significant amount of time. Changes in people and culture may also be necessary to overcome resistance to change.

In a very general sense, there are three phases of planned change. The three phases, as illustrated in Exhibit 18-7, are unfreezing, changing, and refreezing.[27]

Phases of Planned Change

UNFREEZING

This involves helping people to see that a change is needed because the existing situation is not adequate. Existing attitudes and behaviours need to be altered during this phase

Exhibit 18-7 Three Phases of Planned Change in Organizations

Current State	Transitional State	New State
• Existing roles and structures • Comfortable, familiar, and secure • Controllable, certain, and proven • Creating a felt need for change • Minimizing resistance to change	• Letting go of old work • Taking on new work • Changing tasks, routines, demands, and relationships • Coping with the loss • Changing people; individuals and groups; tasks; structure; technology	• New roles and structures • New work and routines • Unfamiliar and risky • Reinforcing outcomes • Evaluating results • Making constructive modification
Unfreezing	**Changing**	**Refreezing**

Source: Adapted from K. Lewin, *Field Theory in Social Science* (New York: Harper & Row, 1951).

so that resistance to change is minimized. The manager may do this by explaining how the change can help increase productivity, but it will also probably be necessary to convince participants that their work satisfaction will not be lowered or that the cost will be worth some other gain they care about. The manager's goal is to help the participants see the need for change and to increase their willingness to make the change a success.

CHANGING

The second phase involves actually making the change. It requires participants to let go of old ways of doing things and to develop new ones. This phase is difficult because of the anxiety involved in letting go of the comfortable and familiar to learn new ways of behaving, doing different tasks with new people and, perhaps, with more complex technology. In more complex changes, several targets of change may need to be changed simultaneously.

REFREEZING

The third phase, refreezing, reinforces the changes made so that the new ways of behaving become stabilized. If people perceive the change to be working in their favour, positive results will serve as reinforcement. If they perceive the change as not working in their favour, it may be necessary for the manager to use external reinforcers, which can be positive or negative.[28] For example, the manager might encourage the employees to keep working at the change by predicting that desired positive results will come, or a small reward, such as a lunch or an afternoon off, might be awarded when the change has been completed successfully. The goal of this phase of the change process is to cause the desired attitudes and behaviours to become a natural, self-reinforcing pattern.

The change process goes through stages, each of which is important. Exhibit 18-8 presents an eight-stage sequence of skills that managers need to apply to successfully bring about planned change.[29] Stages in the change process generally overlap, but skipping stages or making critical mistakes at any stage can cause the change process to fail.

Exhibit 18-8 Eight-Stage Sequence of Skills for Planned Change

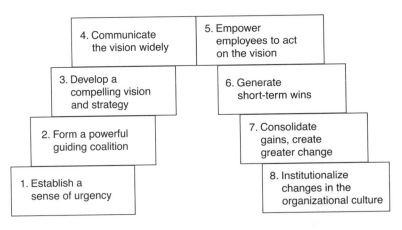

ESTABLISH A SENSE OF URGENCY

At stage 1, leaders unfreeze people by establishing a sense of urgency that change is really needed. Sometimes the need for change is obvious, as when results are not in line with expectations, when things clearly are not working well, or dissatisfaction is apparent. As the "pain" in such situations increases, so does the incentive to change. For example, dramatically declining profits provide a sense of urgency for all **stakeholders**. In many cases, however, no current crisis is obvious but leaders have identified potential problems by scanning the external environment, looking at such things as competitive conditions, market position, and social, technological, and demographic trends. In these cases, leaders need to find ways to communicate the information broadly and dramatically to make others aware of the need for change.

FORM A POWERFUL GUIDING COALITION

Stage 2 involves establishing a team of opinion leaders with enough power to guide the change process. The critical variable at this point is the development of a shared commitment to the need and direction of organizational change. Mechanisms such as off-site retreats can get people together and help them develop a shared assessment of problems and how to approach them. It is also important to include all levels of management in this coalition to ensure support from top leaders and enthusiastic implementation from middle and front-line managers.

DEVELOP A COMPELLING VISION AND STRATEGY

As discussed in Chapter 11, Planning and Goal Setting, senior management is responsible for formulating and articulating a compelling vision that people will aspire to and that will guide the change effort. A picture of the future needs to be created that is easy to communicate and is attractive to all stakeholders. To achieve that vision, management must continually develop, examine, and adjust strategies.[30]

In general, planned change goals prepare an organization to cope with external changes and enhance its employees' competencies. The first thing that leaders need to do is determine what specific factors need to be changed to achieve the desired situation. In doing so, it is important to determine immediate and longer-term objectives and the means by which these objectives will be accomplished. When planning a change, all stakeholders, such as employees, managers, investors, suppliers, customers, and even regulators who might be affected by the change, should be considered. Why? Let us say, for example, that management decides to increase employees' pay to encourage motivation. Choosing this particular action, however, might irritate investors who may view the increase as an unnecessary expense that cuts into earnings.

The best way to change a given situation will depend on critical factors in the situation that make one strategy more appropriate than another. Factors to consider include: the timing of changes; how important the changes are; anticipated resistance; the relative power of stakeholder groups; and the abilities, knowledge, and resources required.[31] The key point is that managers should assess the situation considering all critical factors and then select the most appropriate strategy for intervention. For example, if the change is important, resistance is anticipated, and the changes widespread, a participative approach is most suitable.

COMMUNICATE THE VISION WIDELY

Leaders need to use every means possible to communicate the vision and strategy to all stakeholders. Transformation is impossible unless a majority of people in the organization are involved and willing to help. This process should start with the managers in the change coalition themselves, who should set an example by modeling the new behaviours needed from employees. Leader/managers also need to continuously remind people of the importance and the meaning of the work they do.[32]

EMPOWER EMPLOYEES TO ACT ON THE VISION

At this stage, people are empowered with knowledge, resources, and discretion to make things happen. Leaders should encourage and reward risk taking and nontraditional ideas and actions. Also, they need to revise systems, structures, or procedures that hinder or undermine the change effort. For example, with the survival of the company at stake, labour and management at Rolls-Royce Motor Company revised hundreds of precise job descriptions that were undermining the change into a new contract specifying that all employees will do anything within their capabilities to support the company.[33]

GENERATE SHORT-TERM RESULTS

Introducing and implementing change seldom leads immediately to the desired results because people often require time to learn how to behave differently.[34] Individual performance usually declines during the learning period, inducing fear and anxiety among participants. Initial enthusiasm can fade as changes encounter operating problems. During this period, many participants may experience a strong desire to return to more familiar and proven behaviours. This doubt and fear may be reinforced if individuals share their concerns and complaints with one another.

As a leader/manager, it is your responsibility to determine whether the change is progressing as planned and accomplishing desired results.[35] Information needs to be gathered through feedback mechanisms such as surveys, discussions, or interviews, and then compared to desired outcomes.

Organizations often fail to recognize that the most significant change issues are the people issues. Unfortunately, they are often given little attention. Managers can help people get through the transition period by anticipating sub-par performance and attitudinal problems and by being ready with answers and constructive solutions. Organizations and their leader/managers need to provide specific answers to the questions: What is changing? What will actually be different because of the change? Who's going to lose what?[36] Increased support, education, encouragement, and resources also help employees adapt. For example, it helps to develop support groups, set up special meetings and off-site retreats, and provide the means for steady reinforcement (e.g., praise, bonuses, award dinners, etc.) of those changing. As people learn how to perform under the changed conditions, and as they begin to perceive positive results, they begin to internalize their newly learned behaviours. When the new behaviours are in place, the external supports given by the manager can be reduced.

Short-term accomplishments need to be recognized and celebrated by employees. Consequently, leaders should plan for performance improvements that are visible, enable them to happen, and celebrate employees who were involved in the improvements. These successes can boost the credibility of the change process and renew the commitment and enthusiasm of employees.[37]

BUILD MOMENTUM: CONSOLIDATE GAINS AND CREATE GREATER CHANGE

This stage builds on the credibility achieved by short-term results to consolidate improvements, tackle bigger problems, and create greater change. At this point, leaders change systems, structures, and policies that do not fit the vision but have not yet been confronted.[38] They hire, promote, and develop employees who can implement the vision and create new change projects. A common mistake is to over-emphasize structure and systems at the expense of communication and the development of formal and informal networks. When Rolls-Royce was at this stage, for example, leaders overcame this problem by setting up "change teams" made up of members who were horizontally cross-trained to perform one another's jobs, and vertically integrated from executives to shop floor workers, and charged them to communicate and develop new ideas together.[39]

EMBED NEW BEHAVIOURS INTO THE ORGANIZATIONAL CULTURE

At this refreezing stage new values and beliefs are instilled in the culture so that employees view the changes not as something new but as a normal and integral part of how the organization operates. Old habits, values, traditions, and mindsets are permanently replaced by emphasizing and rewarding new behaviours. Because of the volume, complexity, and rate of change in today's workplaces, leaders need to encourage a learning culture—the capacity to learn and adapt all of the time.[40]

Recognizing Resistance to Change

It is not difficult to recognize resistance to change when it is explicitly manifested through such actions as strikes, slowdowns, and complaints. It is more difficult to detect and cope with implicit resistance, such as decreased motivation or loyalty, errors, and absenteeism. Resistance to change is sometimes beneficial because it promotes functional conflict and debates, which can promote more thorough analyses of alternatives and their consequences. On the other hand, excessive or irrational resistance can hinder progress and even survival. Why is change often resisted even when its benefits clearly outweigh its costs? Several overlapping reasons address why people and organizations resist change.

WHY INDIVIDUALS RESIST CHANGE[41]

Chapters in this book that cover such topics as communication, diversity, ethics, and motivation provide a number of clues about why people are inclined to resist change. The following paragraphs describe five of the main reasons individuals resist change.

SELF-INTEREST People often perceive the same things differently. When changes are initiated, individuals tend to focus on how they will be personally affected rather than seeing the big picture for the entire organization. For example, assume a manager introduces a new software system in accounting. Anique, who loves computers and is highly skilled in their use, may eagerly embrace the change as an opportunity to demonstrate her abilities. Chris, another employee who is very familiar with the old system, may object because he senses a loss of personal control. At other times, individuals may perceive that change is incompatible with personal beliefs and values.

LACK OF INFORMATION People will resist change if they lack knowledge as to what is expected or why the change is important. Many people take the attitude that "if it's not broken, don't fix it." If the reasons for change are not clearly presented, employees tend to fill in the missing pieces with speculation, which often assumes the worst in terms of initiator intentions and personal impact. In addition, if people do not have enough information about how to change, they may fear making mistakes, so they will not try. Change may also be resisted where leaders and those affected by the change have radically different assessments of the situation or the effectiveness of the proposed change.

FEAR OF THE UNKNOWN Individuals resist change when they are uncertain about how it will affect their well-being. They ask themselves, for example, "How will downsizing or new automation affect my job security?"[42] Other fears include uncertainties about not knowing how to change or of not being able to perform as well as before the change; losing position, income, status, or power; the possibility that work will be less convenient or more difficult; and the potential of losing desirable social interactions.

HABIT People prefer familiar actions and events, even if they are not optimal. Have you ever tried to break a bad **habit** like smoking, drinking too much coffee, or not exercising? Breaking a habit is difficult because it takes hard work and involves giving up perceived benefits from the habit, even if the new behaviour has more desirable consequences.

LACK OF TRUST Without trust in the manager's intentions, people resist change. Similarly, if a change seems arbitrary or unreasonable, or its timing and manner of implementation lack concern for the people, resentment and anger are often directed toward those initiating the change. A 1999 study by the Canadian Federation of Independent Business found that 70 per cent of employees in major corporations don't trust their boss.[43]

COMMON REASONS ORGANIZATIONS RESIST CHANGE

Organizations resist change for many of the same reasons individuals do. In addition, many organizational practices minimize risk taking; if a process is working satisfactorily an organization quite often will not move to change it until forced to.[44] Many forces inside an organization also create resistance to changes initiated by environmental conditions.[45] Some of the main reasons are summarized here.

POWER MAINTENANCE Changes in decision-making authority and control of resource allocations threaten the balance of power in organizations. Units benefiting from the change will endorse it, but those losing power will resist it, which can often slow or prevent the change process. Managers, for example, often resist the establishment of self-managed work teams, and manufacturing departments often resist letting purchasing departments control input quality. Functional units usually think of themselves first when evaluating potential changes. They support those that enhance their own welfare, but resist the ones that reduce it or seem inequitable.

STRUCTURAL STABILITY Organizational structures, rules, and socialization are designed to develop consistent, predictable behaviours. Such behaviours resist change. Furthermore, an organization is a system of interrelated structures or subsystems. A change in any one area will have effects on others, which may not be acceptable.

ORGANIZATIONAL CULTURE Organizational culture establishes values, norms, and expectations to promote predictable ways of thinking and behaving. Organizational members will resist changes that force them to abandon established and approved ways of doing things.

TEAM NORMS Teams develop their own norms to promote desirable behaviours. Most members conform to these norms, especially in cohesive teams. Consequently, any change that disrupts group norms, tasks, or role relationships will probably be resisted. Teams also act to ensure their own interests, often at the expense of the larger organization, which means that teams will often resist changes that do not directly benefit them individually.

Managers sometimes mistakenly assume that employees will perceive the desired changes in the same way they do; thus, they have difficulty understanding the resistance. As we have just discussed, a number of reasons indicate that people will perceive the desired change differently. A key task is to determine and understand the reasons behind people's resistance when it occurs. Then the challenge is to find ways to reduce or overcome that resistance.

Overcoming Resistance to Change

It is only when employees truly understand the need for change, the direction that has been set, and are actively engaged in the process that change can happen. The real emphasis has to be on changing the behaviours of employees and changing the reward systems to reinforce the desired employee behaviours. Moreover, senior management must be visible throughout the organization and its commitment continuous.[46]

Research has identified six general strategies for overcoming resistance to change.[47] It is the manager's job to match the demands of a change situation with the best approach to overcoming resistance with minimum disruption. Sometimes you can apply several of the following strategies simultaneously.

NEGOTIATION AND AGREEMENT

This tactic is often necessary when dealing with powerful resisters, such as unions. Bargain to offer incentives in return for agreement to change. Sometimes specific things can be exchanged in return for help in bringing about a change, such as the introduction of new technology in exchange for increased job security provisions. Other times, general perks can be widely distributed to help make the change easier to undertake.

MANIPULATION AND CO-OPTATION

Manipulation is framing and selectively using information and implied incentives to maximize likelihood of acceptance. An example would be if management tells employees that accepting pay cuts is necessary to avoid a plant shutdown, when it is possible that plant closure would not really have to occur. **Co-optation** is influencing resistant parties to endorse the change effort by providing them with benefits they desire and opportunities to fill desired roles in the process. The use of either or both of these tactics is likely to lead to a loss of employee trust and to charges of dealing in "bad faith."

EXPLICIT AND IMPLICIT COERCION

Some managers use the authority of their position to threaten negative incentives, thereby forcing acceptance of the proposed change. For example, if employees do not accept proposed changes, management may threaten to close the company, decrease salaries, or lay people off. Although this approach may appear to speed change, it is risky, shortsighted, and can create long-lasting animosity toward management.

EDUCATION AND COMMUNICATION

Even if the consequences of a change are generally perceived as positive, extensive communication will help reduce anxiety and ensure that people understand what is happening, what will be expected of them, and how they will be supported in adapting to change.[48] The objective is to help people learn beforehand the reasons for the change, how it will take form, and what the likely consequences will be. Communication is only effective, however, when there is a trusting relationship between the parties, which can take considerable time and effort to develop.

PARTICIPATION AND INVOLVEMENT

Participation increases understanding, enhances feelings of control, reduces uncertainty, and promotes a feeling of ownership when change directly affects people. Encourage those involved to help design and implement the changes in order to draw out their ideas and to foster commitment. It is difficult for people to resist changes that they themselves have helped bring about. However, participation processes can be very time consuming and may not lead to results unless well facilitated.

FACILITATION AND SUPPORT

By accepting people's anxiety as legitimate and helping them cope with change, managers have a better chance of gaining respect and the commitment to make it work. Provide encouragement and support, training, counselling, and resources to help those affected by the change adapt to new requirements.

Concept Quiz

Complete the following true–false quiz by circling the correct answer. The answers are at the end of the quiz. After marking your answers, remember to go back and check your understanding of any answers you missed.

True or False   1. Planned change involves proactively making things different rather than reacting to changes imposed from outside the organization.

True or False   2. Path-goal leadership is most effective when applied in highly structured and routine job situations.

True or False   3. Management and leadership are integrated roles that require different skills.

True or False   4. Informal leaders draw on their position authority to initiate problem solving, decision making, and action.

True or False   5. Leaders bring about change because they can create a vision and, most importantly, motivate and empower followers to work toward that vision and change.

True or False   6. Product and service changes are most often introduced by top management with the top-down approach.

True or False   7. The three phases of planned change are unfreezing, change, and refreezing.

True or False   8. The need for organizational change is usually obvious, so if everything is going well management need not worry about it.

True or False   9. Leader/managers should adjust their leadership style to be relevant to the circumstances and follower needs.

True or False   10. Leader/managers can drastically improve employees' transition through change by anticipating that they will have problems.

Answers (1) True; (2) False; (3) True; (4) False; (5) True; (6) False; (7) True; (8) False; (9) True; (10) True

Behavioural Checklist

The following skills are important to leading change. Use them when evaluating your own leadership skills and those of others.

Effective Leaders of Change:

- Focus more on being effective (doing the right things) to accomplish the organization's mission rather than being efficient (doing things right).
- Motivate others to support their vision of change.
- Appropriately adjust leadership style—degrees of task and relationship behaviours—to relevant environmental contingencies (e.g., followers, task structure, formal authority, work group cohesiveness, etc.).
- Identify appropriate targets for change.
- Manage all phases of the planned change from unfreezing through refreezing.
- Determine reasons for resistance to change and intervene to overcome them.
- Create a sense of urgency.
- Form a guiding coalition.
- Generate short-term wins.

Modelling Exercise

What Does the Leader Do Now?

PURPOSE What would you do as a leader as you encounter changing situations? This role-play gives several members of the class the opportunity to test their approach.

TIME 20 minutes.

DIRECTIONS Two people volunteer to be leaders; one to be the leader for situation A, the other for B. Next, everyone reads the background in situation A. Then, leader A conducts a meeting for 7 to 8 minutes to review the issues generated by the grand opening of your computer store. After concluding A, leader B will conduct a group discussion for 7 to 8 minutes pertaining to situation B issues.

SITUATION A You are the newly appointed manager of a new computer store, the 21st in a fast-growing regional chain. The grand opening just concluded, which turned in a better-than-expected sales performance, but it was a week scarred by confusion and numerous problems serving customers. With two exceptions, the full-time sales service staff you hired have no previous computer sales experience. You personally did all the hiring two to three weeks before the store opened, looking for people experienced in working with computers. The glitches during the last week were a combination of the staff not knowing the technical specifications of inventory items they had not personally used and at times resorting to faking their recommendations to customers—or acting with indifference toward customers. You decide to meet with your entire staff before the store opens on Monday morning to share with them the sales success of opening week, and to begin correcting the types of customer-related problems that caused you to be less than pleased with their overall performance during the opening.

SITUATION B Your store is now into its second quarter of operation. You have hired four more staff. With a couple of exceptions, the staff has settled into their roles quite nicely. People have learned the technical side of the business and have generally become versatile across several brands of equipment. They demonstrate a basic knowledge of most software products. Paul, however, continues to generate two to four customer complaints per week, usually about his impatient, condescending attitude in working with customers who lack technical expertise. Samantha has proven to be a capable technician, especially in configuring hardware and installing software, but she is often hesitant to make specific recommendations when serving customers. You have decided to hold your first staff meeting of the quarter to review progress to date and engage your people in a quest for continuous improvement.

DEBRIEFING Select a third volunteer to conduct a class discussion of the following questions:

1. What did leader A do that seemed effective? What was not so effective?
2. Which leadership theories seem to have relevance for the way leader A handled the group? What is your assessment of the job maturity of group members in situation A? Did the leader's behaviour seem to take this factor into account? How?
3. What did leader B do that was effective? What was not so effective?
4. Again, what leadership theories appear to have relevance for leader B's handling of the situation? To what degree has employee job maturity changed in situation B? Did the leader seem to take this change into account? How?

Observer's Rating Sheet

After completing the two role-plays and the debriefing, rate the leadership skills of each of the leader volunteers between 1 and 5 using the following scale. First rate and provide feedback for the volunteer in situation A. Then do the same for the leader volunteer in situation B. Finally, complete the process for the third volunteer who led the debriefing. Write concrete examples to use in explaining your feedback in the spaces following each behaviour.

1 Unsatisfactory	2 Weak	3 Adequate	4 Good	5 Outstanding

_____ Is effective: does the right things to accomplish the organization's mission.

_____ Motivates others to support the vision of change.

_____ Adjusts leadership style to relevant circumstances and follower needs.

_____ Identifies appropriate targets for change.

_____ Manages all phases of the planned change from unfreezing through refreezing.

_____ Determines reasons for resistance to change and intervenes to overcome them.

_____ Creates a sense of urgency.

_____ Forms a guiding coalition.

_____ Generates short-term wins.

Group Exercises

Two different types of group exercises are presented here. First is a role-play to utilize your change skills. Second is the Card Tower exercise to practise your leadership skills in a competitive task situation.

Group Exercise 1: Role-Play: Dividing Up Leadership

PURPOSE This role-playing exercise initially involves all class members and gives everyone an opportunity to exert leadership influence in one of six groups. Through the two-phase dynamics of the exercise, students form impressions about their own leadership tendencies and learn through social observation what leadership behaviours do and do not work in the present situation. The first phase focuses on emergent leadership within self-selected groups; in the second phase, representatives from each group vie to influence others as to the merits of their group's recommendation and their share of a $500,000 budget.

TIME 45 minutes.

MATERIALS NEEDED Six group background notes are provided by the instructor from the Instructor's Guide. Each note represents one of the six major activity centres for the Multi-Phase Products Company: research, manufacturing, marketing, administration, scientific instruments division, and medical instruments division.

PREGROUP PREPARATION: A BACKGROUND NOTE ON MULTI-PHASE PRODUCTS CO.

Everyone should read the following background material before beginning phase 1:

Multi-Phase Products, Inc., is a midsize firm in the medical and scientific instruments industries that has begun to experience difficulties. The firm is organized along functional lines, and it has two business divisions that produce and sell products. Now 12 years old, the firm currently employs about 700 people. Last year it generated revenues of $120 million with profits before taxes of $3 million. Now, three months into the fiscal year, managers are troubled by declining profit margins. Three years ago, net profit margins before taxes peaked at 10 per cent of gross revenues. This quarter a loss is projected. Gross margins have also declined (from 55 per cent three years ago to 40 per cent this quarter). In part, this decline is because of higher costs involved in introducing a new technology within the Medical Instruments Division. Price points have also eroded in the maturing Scientific Instruments Division, which is facing intensified competition in both domestic and foreign markets. In several specific product market areas, customers have the perception that the quality of Multi-Phase products has slipped relative to that of competitors.

PROCEDURE FOR PHASE 1: GROUP SELECTION AND RECOMMENDATIONS

After everyone has read the background note, progress through the following three steps:

1. The instructor asks for six volunteers whose jobs are simply to act as resource persons and pass along information to group members once groups form. Each volunteer is handed one of the six group background information notes and a sign indicating the group's organizational unit. The six then stand around the perimeter of the room (at the four corners and midpoints of the two longest sides) and hold up their organizational unit sign.

2. All others in the class then stand and move to one of the six locations. Use any criteria you wish in selecting a group, such as its function, the people who seem to be attracted to it, or the number of people in the group. Groups need not be equal in numbers, but the largest must have no more than twice as many members as the smallest.
3. Now the work begins. The resource volunteer shares verbally (by paraphrasing, not reading) information contained in the group note with his or her group. Members discuss ideas for improving the firm, restoring quality, and selecting an approach that seems reasonable. They also decide what share of a $500,000 quality improvement budget they believe their recommendation merits. They then select one member to represent their interests as a leader at the task force meeting. (10 minutes)

PROCEDURE FOR PHASE 2: TASK FORCE BUDGET MEETING

The six task force leaders now assemble in front of the room (seated, if movable chairs are available). Each presents his or her group's recommendations and discusses them with the other five. This group is leaderless in the sense that no one is appointed to officiate as chairperson.

The six-person group will then decide on the merits of the six proposals by allocating the $500,000 quality improvement pool of funds the CEO has budgeted for this purpose. The allocation that is finally accepted by the task force group should be proportionate to the perceived value of the six proposals for improving Multi-Phase Products. (15 minutes)

DEBRIEFING The instructor guides a discussion of questions such as:

1. Why did you choose to volunteer (or not to volunteer) as a resource person? To what extent did resource persons become group leaders at the multigroup negotiations?
2. What behaviours were influential in deciding on the group's recommendations? Were the influential persons examples of leaders showing relationship behaviour or task behaviour or both? Did some people actively seize the opportunity to influence the group? For people who were influential, what were you seeking to accomplish by both the content and manner of expressing your ideas?
3. Why were some of the leaders apparently more able to convey a vision of their plan in the budget negotiations? Did the most visionary exert greater influence on the task force? What was the basis for leadership at the phase 1 group level? To what extent was the outcome of the budget allocation process in phase 2 a reasonable reflection of the pathfinding leadership qualities of the group leaders?

Group Exercise 2: Do Not Topple the Tower[49]

PURPOSE This action exercise helps to examine leader–member relationships that affect team performance on a tangible production project. In teams of three or four people, the objective is to see how many folded index cards can be stacked two cards per tier, with each tier at a ninety-degree angle to the tier below, to form a multi-tiered tower of up to twenty cards. You say it sounds easy? Wait until you are a worker and try to do it blindfolded!

Primary attention is on the thoughts and interaction behaviours of the leader. During each production debriefing, other situational factors are examined: skill differences among workers; worker needs, expectations, and perceptions; physical factors; and so on.

TIME 35 to 65 minutes.

MATERIALS NEEDED

1. Large index cards (5″ × 7″ recommended), 20 per team.
2. Strips of cloth suitable for blindfolds, two per team.

PROCEDURES

1. Assign participants to teams of three or four persons. If the available time is limited to about 45 minutes, three-person teams allow sufficient time for each member to serve in a leadership role during one five-minute building period. If time is not so limited, four-person teams provide more comparison data.
2. The production exercise will be repeated (in five-minute intervals, timed by the instructor) as many times as there are persons per team. Roles are to be rotated following each action cycle. The roles are:
   • Leader or supervisor (one person)
   • Employees, builders (two people)
   • Process observer (one person, but only if using four-person teams)
3. Once teams are assembled, each team receives its 20 index cards and two blindfolds. Fold cards lengthwise in the middle to form "tents." If 5″ × 7″ cards are used, each tent will be 2 1/2″ × 7″, flared about an inch at the bottom.
4. After teams and materials are assembled, develop whatever procedures you believe will be necessary to ensure good performance, as long as they are consistent with the instructions. During the planning and preparation time, it will be the leader's responsibility to establish a team output goal (expressed as number of cards stacked without toppling the tower). Blindfold the two initial builders, and designate them as worker A and worker B. If you have time, practise until the instructor is ready to start all teams on the first five-minute production period.

PRODUCTION INSTRUCTIONS

1. Using the nondominant hand for stacking cards, blindfolded worker A will place the first card tent in the middle of a desk or table. Blindfolded worker B places the second card, parallel to the first, as close or far apart as directed by the leader. These cards form the base tier. Worker A then places the third card at right angles to the base; worker B places the fourth card parallel to the third. Work continues in this manner, with workers alternating the stacking of each card, with two parallel cards per tier.
2. Because workers are blindfolded, the leader/supervisor must guide the work verbally through instructions to the work team. The supervisor cannot touch either the workers or the cards at any time during the five-minute timed production period.
3. The round is terminated for a work team when (a) the goal is achieved, i.e., the tower is 10 tiers high; (b) a card that was previously stacked on the tower is knocked off; (c) the entire tower topples; (d) the instructor calls time at the end of five minutes. If a worker is placing a card that slips off without knocking off another card, the leader may direct the worker to retrieve the card and resume building.
4. After each round, the instructor records on the board each team's goal and actual results. This record can be made in matrix form with numbers inserted as each round is completed.
5. At the end of each round, each team privately debriefs the factors that contributed to productivity or problems, satisfaction, and developmental learning. The observer (if one is used) should lead this discussion using notes of observed behaviours. Questions can be asked of workers and leader about their experience: Did they feel anxiety, tension, or frustration? What were their thoughts, motives, and suggestions for improving performance? Following a few minutes for team debriefing and planning, the instructor may debrief the class with one or more focusing questions. If time is

scarce, the debriefing can be held until after the final round. The objective of the debriefing phase is to move beyond having fun and help focus learning from this direct experience.

Application Questions

1. Describe the best leader you have known. What were his or her particular leadership qualities and strengths or weaknesses? How did this leader acquire his or her capability?
2. What do you consider your own strengths and weaknesses for leadership? What activities should you undertake to improve your leadership capability in areas where you are weak?
3. If the need for change is not obvious, what are some ways that leaders can recognize trends that signal to them that change is necessary for the organization's success in the long run?
4. Why do you think so few people succeed at both management and leadership?
5. Why do employees resist change? What are some ways leaders can overcome this resistance?

Reinforcement Exercises

1. Interview several managers about how they make decisions. Compare the answers you receive to the steps in the problem-solving model. Also, check the degree of participation that these managers used against those recommended by the participation decision tree.
2. Think of a situation when you were involved in change, whether in a club, school, or at work. Can you identify the leaders who made it happen? Outline specifically how they contributed to or held back the change.
3. Identify an area in your work, school, or club situation where you see a need for change. Then formulate a strategy and vision of how you would motivate those involved to accept the change and how you would implement the results of the change. What resistance do you anticipate? How do you plan to overcome this resistance?

Summary Checklist

Take a few minutes to reflect on your performance and look over others' ratings of your leadership skills. Now assess yourself on each of the key learning behaviours. Make a check (√) next to those behaviours on which you need improvement when leading change.

_____ Focusing more on being effective, or doing the right things to accomplish the organization's mission, than on being efficient, or doing things right.

1. Excite people about visions of opportunities and empower them to innovate and excel.
2. Use resources and meet project deadlines to achieve stated organizational objectives.

_____ Motivating others to support the vision of change.

1. Find a vision for change that is significantly better than the current situation, which provides a dream to launch people into action.
2. Inspire followers to strive for the good of the group.
3. Motivate by providing opportunities for growth and development.
4. Develop followers into leaders.

_____ Adjusting leadership style to relevant circumstances.

1. Demonstrate task-oriented behaviour consisting of careful supervision of group members to obtain consistent work methods and accomplishment of the job.

2. Demonstrate relationship-oriented behaviour for satisfying the social and emotional needs of group members and developing friendships, mutual trust, respect, and warmth in the relationship between the leader and followers.

3. Adapt to relevant environmental contingencies such as differences in followers, task structure, formal authority, and work group cohesiveness.

_____ Identifying targets for change.

1. Strategy and structure.

2. Product and service.

3. Technology.

4. People.

5. Culture.

6. Management.

_____ Managing all phases of the planned change.

1. Recognize the need for change.

2. Diagnose and determine the best interventions.

3. Manage the transition: unfreezing, changing, and refreezing.

_____ Employing skills for leading change.

1. Create a sense of urgency.

2. Form a guiding coalition.

3. Develop a compelling vision and strategy.

4. Communicate the vision widely.

5. Empower employees to act on the vision.

6. Generate short-term wins.

7. Consolidate gains and create greater change.

8. Institutionalize changes in the organizational culture.

_____ Recognizing resistance to change.

1. Address individual reasons: selective perception, lack of information, fear of the unknown, habit, resentment toward the initiator.

2. Assess organizational reasons: power maintenance, structural stability, organizational culture, team norm.

_____ Overcoming resistance to change.

1. Education and communication.

2. Participation and involvement.

3. Facilitation and support.

4. Negotiation and agreement.

5. Manipulation and co-optation.

6. Explicit and implicit coercion.

Action Plan

1. Which leadership behaviour do I most want to improve? (For examples, see Summary Checklist.)
2. Why? What will be my payoff?
3. What potential obstacles stand in my way?
4. What are the specific things I will do to improve? (For examples, see the Reinforcement Exercises.)
5. When will I do them?
6. How and when will I measure my success?

Appendix A

Oral Presentation Skills[1]

Many adults fear speaking in public. Nevertheless, studies conducted by the Conference Board of Canada identify all communications, including oral presentations, as critical employability skills.[2] These skills are especially important for those who supervise the work of others. This appendix will provide ideas on three skills necessary for making effective oral presentations: managing anxiety, planning and preparing, and delivery of the presentation.

Managing Anxiety

Stage fright is a normal reaction. Almost every speaker, actor, musician, or performer experiences some degree of stage fright. Although anxiety never goes away entirely, you can learn to manage your fear so that it can actually help you perform better.[3] Exhibit A-1 provides 10 tips for overcoming stage fright.

Planning and Preparing

Once you have your stage fright under control, the success of your public speaking is determined primarily by the time you spend preparing before you step in front of your audience. You want to avoid presentations that are too long, too detailed, confusing, vague, boring, or off-track. The following steps will help you prepare an effective presentation.

Identify the Purpose

The first and most critical step in preparation is understanding the "what" and the "why" of your presentation. Your *purpose* is the broad general outcome you want the presentation to achieve. Ask yourself three questions to clarify the objective of your presentation:

- *Why* am I giving this presentation: to persuade, to explain, to instruct, to report on something?
- *What* do I want the audience to know or do at the end of the presentation?
- *How* do I want the audience to feel?

Analyze Your Audience

After you are clear on what you want to accomplish, mold your presentation to fit the specific characteristics of the audience. You can acquire information about your audience by:

- Asking the presentation host about the audience.
- Talking to people who will be in the audience.
- Talking to other speakers who have spoken to the same group.

Exhibit A-1 Tips for Overcoming Stage Fright

- **Know your material well** Being the expert gives you confidence because you know more than the audience does.
- **Practise** your presentation and, if possible, videotape yourself so that you know how you look to others.
- Get **audience participation** It shifts attention from you to the audience and generates more of an easy-going conversational atmosphere.
- **Use names and eye contact** to establish rapport. It is easier to talk to friends than strangers.
- **Check the facilities and audiovisual equipment in advance** Checking beforehand eliminates worry about whether the equipment works, and you avoid having to figure things out in front of the audience if it does not work.
- **Research your audience** Being familiar with your audience gives you confidence because you know their needs. You might even discover that you have friends in the audience who will support you.
- **Relax** Take time out right before your presentation to relax. Different things will relax different people. Some concentrate on breathing deeply. Others visualize themselves successfully presenting. Some do progressive muscle relaxation (i.e., focus on relaxing specific muscle groups one at a time: neck, shoulders, arms, legs).
- **Dress comfortably and appropriately** to avoid anxiety about your image.
- **Use your own style** You do not need the stress of trying to imitate someone else.
- **Use audiovisual aids** They can reduce anxiety by providing prompts and taking the visual impact off you personally for a while.

Source: D.A. Level and W.P. Galle, Jr., *Managerial Communications* (San Diego, CA: Business Publications, Inc., 1988) 44.

Organize the Presentation

Once you know your audience and are clear about your purpose and objectives, you are ready to start organizing your presentation. The first step is to find your focus or the "big idea" of your material. The second is to develop an outline so that you can visualize the flow of your presentation.

PRIMARY FOCUS

What is the one thing you want your audience to walk away with? Say, for example, that you are going to explain a new marketing plan to your company's board of directors. It probably has several sections that are supported by reams of documented research and facts, but you only have 20 to 30 minutes to summarize the plan in a way that will gain the board's approval. What is it about the plan that will capture their imagination? A new theme? A new program? A high payoff possibility?

How well you translate your message into benefits for the audience determines its effectiveness. You need to structure your presentation so that it supports your one big idea. Of course, your message will contain more than one idea but they should all reinforce the primary purpose.

DEVELOP AN OUTLINE

One way to make sure you are clear on your focus is to develop a basic outline for your presentation. Begin by listing no more than five independent ideas that the audience must understand for the objectives to be accomplished. Be sure that the sequence of these ideas is logical and will flow smoothly. Then outline your plan for presenting the detail and persuasive material needed to allow your audience to understand those points. For the most effective delivery, break your presentation down into its three main parts: the introduction, body, and conclusion.

THE INTRODUCTION It is important to write out your introduction completely, word-for-word. This part of your presentation is too important to leave to chance, hoping you have the right words when you get there. It also acts as a security blanket. If you can get through those first few minutes, the butterflies will settle down and the rest of the presentation will flow more easily. The introduction should take 5 to 15 per cent of the allowed speaking time, and it should prepare the audience for the main points of the presentation.[4]

- **Start the introduction with a bang** At this point you need to get the audience's attention and convince them to listen to you. Grab the audience with something vitally interesting to them. Give them an interesting story or example that ties into your focus. Or you might use a strong, meaningful quotation, a startling statistic, or appropriate humour that makes a relevant point.

- **Increase your credibility** Relate something about your background and experience that makes you an expert on the topic you are speaking about. This point, of course, is one of the purposes of having someone share your credentials when they introduce you before the talk. But, referring to a time when you successfully applied your expertise provides a relevant example and further amplifies your credibility.

- **Present your agenda** Keep in mind the familiar slogan: "Tell them what you are going to tell them, tell them, and then tell them what you just told them."

- **Share what you expect of the audience** At the beginning of your presentation, tell listeners about the question-and-answer session at the end, or the ensuing reception, or the cards you want them to fill out before they leave.

- **Use icebreakers if appropriate** In some presentations it is helpful to do an opening icebreaker to set an emotional climate for the presentation. The most common icebreaker is having people introduce themselves and explain their reason for attending the presentation. Make sure your icebreakers are short, appropriate, and participative.[5] They should last no longer than 5 to 10 minutes, have something to do with the topic, and be something that each person can, and wants to, get involved with.

THE MAIN MESSAGE Once you have obtained the audience's attention, you need to deliver what you promised in the shortest, most interesting way possible. Be sure to support your points with evidence using examples, the conclusions of others, or statistics. Keep two things in mind as you structure your message: the attention cycle of your audience and pace of your presentation.[6]

Material at the beginning and end of a presentation will be remembered more than the material in the middle.[7] Our attention span only lasts for a short time and then it tapers off. When we sense the end of a message, we pull our attention back in time to catch the last material. Fluctuation of the attention cycle is one of the main reasons we put such emphasis on the introduction and conclusion.

You can also change the pace every 10 to 15 minutes to break up your talk and keep attention riveted. You can create this change by including appropriate humour, stories, exercises requiring people to move their bodies (even if it is just raising their hands), or calls for a verbal response.

Other things you do can help retention. First, use repetition. Your main ideas need to be communicated several times to make sure they get through accurately and are remembered. Second, use stories and analogies to associate and connect your ideas to something the listeners already understand. Third, change the intensity in the pitch, tone, and loudness of your voice to focus audience attention. Fourth, use audience involvement. Use visual aids, questions, hand gestures, and sound effects, anything that gets the audience involved with the message.

THE CONCLUSION Your conclusion should repeat your main ideas to reinforce your objectives and expectations for the audience. It should be strong, succinct, and persuasive. Many speakers consider this section almost as important as the introduction and they write it out word-for-word.

Practise and Visualize Success[8]

You know your audience. You know your material. You have written a dynamite presentation. The last step is to practise delivering it. The following guidelines may assist you in the process.

REHEARSE

Rehearse aloud at least four or five times in order to check your timing (you read out loud more slowly than you read in your mind), and to make sure your presentation flows and sounds the way you want it to. You should feel comfortable explaining all of your ideas. Do not try to memorize your presentation. You may end up sounding stale, as if you are reciting or reading.

Rehearse in the actual location of the presentation, if possible. It is better to work out the technicalities of visual aids, sound equipment, outlets, and positioning during a rehearsal, rather than be surprised on the day of your presentation.

You can get used to public speaking through rehearsing with family or friends. Ask them to explain what they heard. This feedback will give you a chance to make sure your message is clear. Ask them whether your visual aids are effective and whether they make your message more understandable. Ask them what you can do better.

VISUALIZE

Once you have rehearsed your presentation and feel comfortable with the material, visualize yourself presenting it successfully. Olympic athletes use visualization to reach their peak performance. Studies have shown that visualized practice has a similar effect to actual practice. Visualizing a successful conclusion to any activity gives you a chance to experience success and become more confident in your delivery.

Delivery of the Presentation

Planning and rehearsing are necessary, but not sufficient to ensure a successful presentation. No matter how well organized, logical, and supported with visual aids, if a presentation is poorly delivered it is doomed to failure. Following are some guidelines for using delivery to enhance your presentation.[9]

Be Enthusiastic

Students usually forgive a presenter's lack of platform skills if he or she appears devoted to the subject and is trying to share that appreciation with them. An audience can become oblivious to similar speaker deficiencies if his or her gestures, vocal intonations, and attitude convey enthusiasm for the message. Your interest in your topic tends to be contagious. An enthusiastic introduction will perk audience interest to learn why you are so enthusiastic. Speak as if you are in a lively conversation with friends, but avoid shouting or preaching.

Maintain Eye Contact

Eye contact enhances audience involvement. It makes the audience feel that they are being spoken to personally and that you are sincere. It is most effective to rotate looking at audience members one at a time on a random basis.

Use Space and Movement for Maximum Impact

The arrangement and use of physical space can enhance or detract from your presentation. It is better not to hide behind a podium. Eliminate distracting items from the area such as unnecessary equipment, furniture, papers, writings on the board, and irrelevant signs. You want to keep the audience's attention on you.

Body movement keeps the audience's attention. It can emphasize key points, build rapport, and signal transitions. Variety is the key, so keep alternating standing, moving, sitting, speaking, listening, and gesturing. Move closer to the audience to build rapport with particular members and make points. Back off when you are awaiting responses or addressing the entire group.

Use Appropriate Gestures

You should obviously avoid alienating or distracting gestures such as jingling keys, twisting hair, or adjusting notes. Appropriate gestures appear to be spontaneous and accentuate your verbal message. Small audiences can pick up minor variances in facial expression and hand movements, but with large audiences, your gestures need to be more accentuated and dramatic.

Never Apologize

Do not apologize for the way you look or sound, do not apologize for not being the best speaker in the world, do not apologize because your slides are upside down...do not apologize for anything! The minute you apologize, your ability to influence your audience is decreased. Start your presentation with impact. Make your audience think they are going to be informed, entertained, or enlightened. Do not let them think they are getting anything except your best.

Concept Quiz

Complete the following true–false quiz by circling the correct answer. Answers are at the end of the quiz. After marking your answers, remember to go back and check your understanding of any answers you missed.

True or False	1. The three main sections of an oral presentation are the primary focus, the introduction, and the conclusion.
True or False	2. Because you are the expert, it is not a good idea to involve the audience in your presentation.
True or False	3. You should never apologize during oral presentations.
True or False	4. You can minimize anxiety by dressing comfortably and appropriately.
True or False	5. An information technology manager should avoid using computer jargon when addressing the general public.
True or False	6. You should never use gestures because they are confusing.

True or False	7. Being enthusiastic about your topic can discredit your presentation.
True or False	8. Develop your own style rather than imitating the presentation style of others.
True or False	9. You should not check on the technological capabilities of the location where you are speaking because they are your host's responsibility.
True or False	10. Preparing by practising out loud can be detrimental and throw you off during the actual presentation.

Answers (1) False; (2) False; (3) True; (4) True; (5) True; (6) False; (7) False; (8) True; (9) False; (10) False

Behavioural Checklist

The following skills are important to effective formal oral and written communication. Use them when evaluating your communication skills and those of others.

The Effective Oral Presenter:

- Includes content appropriate for the audience.
- Determines the presentation's purpose and behavioural objectives.
- Productively manages anxiety.
- Includes an introduction, body, and conclusion.
- Speaks clearly and enthusiastically.
- Effectively uses visual aids.
- Utilizes space for maximum impact.
- Maintains eye contact and uses appropriate gestures.

Group Exercise
Oral Presentations

Many students steer clear of classes and situations requiring oral presentations. The problem is that most management jobs require them. By choosing to avoid earlier discomfort in the classroom where they are expected to make oral presentation gaffes and where others can help them improve, these individuals miss opportunities that might help them avoid making common mistakes in front of co-workers, clients, or bosses where career goals could be jeopardized.

Nothing substitutes for experience in honing your oral presentation skills. Consequently, this group exercise consists of everyone making and evaluating oral presentations in order to gain confidence and feedback to become better presenters.

DIRECTIONS Each class member is to prepare and deliver a three- to five-minute oral presentation to other class members. Use the following Observer's Rating Sheet as a guide for preparing and delivering your presentation. The topic can be anything relevant to this class. Some suggestions are:

- Ideas about how to make grading more fair in this class.
- Strategies for reducing stage fright.
- Your most embarrassing moment.
- A sales presentation on some service or product you can provide.

- Why the CEO should serve as an ethical example for others.
- The most interesting person you ever met.
- The advantages of your chosen career.
- A funny story.

TIME Take 10 to 15 minutes for the class members to prepare their presentations. Each presenter will be timed by the next presenter. The timer will signal after four minutes to help the presenter conclude on time. The class may need to be divided into subgroups in order to finish within schedule time constraints.

Observer's Rating Sheet

On completion of each presentation, observers rate the presenter's application of oral presentation skills. Use the following rating scale. Write concrete examples in the space for comments below each criterion to use when explaining your feedback.

Name of Presenter: _____ **Rating** _____

1 Unsatisfactory	2 Weak	3 Adequate	4 Good	5 Outstanding

■ Content appropriate for the audience.   _____

■ Determined the purpose and behavioural objectives.   _____

■ Productively managed anxiety.   _____

■ Included an introduction, body, and conclusion.   _____

■ Spoke clearly and enthusiastically.   _____

■ Effectively used visual aids.   _____

■ Utilized space for maximum impact.   _____

■ Used appropriate eye contact and gestures.   _____

Application Questions

1. Think of a speaker who really connected with the audience. What did the speaker do to establish and maintain the connection, e.g., tell an appropriate joke, use vivid examples, maintain eye contact, and so on?
2. Think of a situation in which you saw a speaker do a poor job presenting. What did he or she do that contributed to this failure?
3. What are some of the best visual aids you have seen? What are some of the worst? What makes the difference?
4. Have you ever been nervous before making a presentation? If so, how did you get through it? What could you do to be more relaxed? If not, what do you do to retain your cool?

Reinforcement Exercises

The following suggestions are activities you can do to reinforce the oral skills in this appendix. You may want to adapt them to an Action Plan, or try them independently.

1. Attend a local meeting of Toastmasters. Watch how others make oral presentations and learn from the feedback that is given to the presenters. Try participating yourself if you have the time and inclination.
2. Take a course that requires public speaking and presentations. As with anything else, you will become more comfortable the more you practise.
3. Volunteer to speak in front of a group, no matter how large or small. Ask family and friends for feedback on your presentation.
4. Join a campus club or organization. It will give you an opportunity to get involved and make new friends, and give your input on the club's activities. You will learn to be more used to speaking in front of others, without the need for a structured presentation.

Appendix B

Written Presentation Skills[1]

As soon as you move one step up from the bottom, your effectiveness depends on your ability to reach others through the spoken or written word.
—Peter Drucker

You may be bright, ambitious, and hardworking but having poor writing skills can stall a career. Writing abilities are as visible as a person's wardrobe, yet the impressions you leave through your written work last even longer. Memos, reports, and letters are read, often reread, and can be kept forever. By developing your writing skills, you will be better equipped to persuade, direct, and influence the course of your day-to-day work and the direction of your career.

Poor writing smothers even the most important messages. The reader may spend more time interpreting the message than acting on it. Writing well takes practice, effort, and a bit of talent. In the end you want your writing to be organized and coherent, not open to multiple interpretations. You want your reader to understand your message, not point at it and exclaim, "What does *this* mean?"

The ingredients of effective writing are content, style, technique, and format. The first section of this appendix will help you understand how to powerfully focus your content and to use each of the most common business formats (memos, letters, and reports) effectively. The second section will give you guidelines on style and techniques to avoid some of the most common writing mistakes.

Content

Grasp the subject, the words will follow.
—Cato the Elder

Good business writing is more about clear thinking than it is about writing style. Writing can only be as good as the thinking that precedes it. You must know what you want to say, what your objective is in saying it, and why it is important for your audience to read it.

Getting Organized

Organizing a writing project is similar to organizing a presentation. The good writer is just as aware of the intended audience as a good public speaker is. The good writer also spends time developing an outline of the content. One useful technique for organizing your thoughts is *mindmapping*, which was described in Chapter 10, Innovation and Problem Solving. This technique allows a writer to pull ideas together quickly as information flows from mind to paper.

Focus On Your Purpose

After you have organized the subject of your memo, report, or letter, you should have a clear idea of your main focus. *Focus* in your business report or memo refers to your objective. It is the "why" of why you are bothering to write at all. A lot of business writing has its purpose buried. It has no focus: no goal, no call for action, no desired end result. If you do not provide the focus, your readers may be confused about why they are reading your document. You should have answered this question for yourself before using your word processing software. Ask yourself:

- Who is my audience?
- What do I want them to do?
- What reasons will they have for not wanting to do what I want them to do?
- What might stop the reader from doing what I suggest?
- Will someone other than the reader make the decision?
- What are the politics involved?

You are not ready to start writing until you can complete this sentence: I want (WHOM) to do (WHAT) because (REASON). If you can fill in that sentence, you are ready to proceed with the writing.

Analyze Your Audience

Knowing your audience will help you to organize your material so that it has the best chance of being read and understood. Put yourself in your reader's shoes, listen, and you will be better received. Do not be condescending. Phrases such as, "As you can clearly see" and "I am sure you will agree" only serve to turn your audience off.

Choosing the Appropriate Format

The format of what you are writing should fit its function. If you receive a memo and your response is a short note or decision, you may want just to jot your response on the memo and send it back. If you are responsible for presenting an analysis of a new market, however, you will need a formal report complete with charts, graphs, and documentation.

Making the format fit the function of your writing seems simple, but all too often a brief request triggers a three-page memo. Review the following hierarchy of communication formats so that you are sure your situation fits the requirements.

- **Verbal** informal conversations where no documentation is required.
- **Handwritten** informal communication requiring a minimum of documentation.
- **Memos** broad communication (to more than three people) where formal documentation is required.
- **Reports** broad communication involving complex issues that require supporting documentation, and decisions that need to be documented.
- **Business letters** written communication generally to people outside your organization, serves several different functions and provides documentation.

MEMOS: USE AND ABUSE

Memos are most often boring, confusing, unnecessary, or all of the above. The first thing you should ask yourself is whether you really need to write it at all. Can you phone the people involved and *talk* to them? Talking to people has wonderful advantages over writing: you get immediate feedback; you strengthen your social contacts; and you save trees.

Eliminating written communication probably is not practical or even desirable for most organizations. Whenever possible, however, talk to people and save your written communications for complex issues requiring extensive explanation or documentation.

When you do decide to write a memo, it should facilitate, simplify, and accelerate internal communication. When used effectively, memos provide a simple method to communicate an identical message to several people. In effect, memos are kind of a meeting on paper. Use them to give instructions, to ask for information or action, to announce or clarify a new policy or procedure, to announce changes or personnel transfers, or as "covers" for lengthier material such as reports.

Memos are an appropriate method of giving instructions to a number of people. Putting directions in writing, when done clearly, prevents misunderstandings about what is to be done, whose responsibility it is, and the date it is due.

Memos should be short (one page for most). Use every possible trick for quick communication including: headlines, short paragraphs, bullets, bolding of important points, and a modified outline format. A common heading for memos is illustrated in Exhibit B-1.

REPORTS: MORE THAN LONG MEMOS

Many people get anxious at the thought of writing a business report. Reports are generally long and deal with complex, often controversial, subjects. They require a great deal of research and critical thought. Perhaps even more anxiety-producing is the realization

Exhibit B-1 Example Memo Format

```
DATE: _____

TO: _____

FROM: _____

SUBJECT: _____

ACTION REQUIRED: _____
```

TO should include all intended recipients of the memo. The form of address depends on the culture of your organization. Some companies use Mr./Mrs./Ms. and titles; others use only first names. *FROM* includes your name.

The *SUBJECT* of your memo should be specific. Clarify it, including only the relevant information: who, what, when, where, how, and why. This line should instantly give the reader enough information to know how to deal with it. A memo with the subject *New Marketing Plan Review Meeting* will receive a much different response than one with the subject *Salary Freeze Policy*.

The *ACTION REQUIRED* line makes it clear to the reader that the writer expects an action. It also helps the writer consider the purpose of the memo. If you are writing too many *Info Only* memos, it is time to rethink your communication strategy. If you refer to an earlier memo, include it, preventing inconvenience for the receiver.

Keep your message brief, informal, and simple. Keep the specific readers' needs and circumstances in mind. Clarify the purpose and be specific about the actions the reader should take and when. Avoid words with double meanings, hidden agendas, jokes, or jargon. Artificial embellishments, fancy words, and wasteful sentences have no place in the office memo. Short and informal, a memo should never be written so hastily that it is ambiguous. Write it well and avoid misunderstandings, hurt feelings, and time spent correcting errors.

that business reports generally influence major company decisions. The people who determine your future in the organization will read it, and a well-written report can enhance your opportunity for advancement. Conversely, a poorly thought-out and written report leaves a black mark that may be difficult to overcome.

The business report is a highly organized, fact-oriented document. You should use headings, subheadings, bulleted points, and details to support any conclusions. Use a variety of graphs and charts to help the reader understand the data you are presenting.

BEFORE YOU START WRITING Know the purpose of your report before you begin writing. Is it for information only? Will it recommend a specific solution?

As with every other form of communication, you should also know your intended audience. Make sure you do not insult their intelligence by presenting in detail information they already know, or confuse them with terms they may not be familiar with. Here are some excellent questions to ask yourself before you proceed with your report.

- What is the familiarity of the reader with the problem?
- What expertise does the reader have in this area?
- What conclusions are of importance to the reader?
- What are the preconceived notions of the reader?
- Why was the report requested?
- What does the reader need to know to make a decision?

STRATEGIES FOR PRESENTING INFORMATION IN A REPORT You should also be thoroughly familiar with the ramifications of your suggestion and any drawbacks to it. Few solutions are perfect, so make sure you understand the limitations of yours. The purpose of the report, the proposed solution, and the intended audience will all affect the strategy you choose for your report. You should understand your strategy before you begin to write. Here are three typical strategies:

1. **Most important to least important** This strategy works well when the decision or action is logical and not highly political, and the readers are objective.
2. **Least controversial to most controversial** Builds support gradually and is best used when the decision is expensive, controversial, politically sensitive, or when the readers are emotionally attached to a different solution than the one proposed.
3. **Negative to positive** Works well when readers are familiar with the problems involved with the situation and the proposed solution. It establishes a common ground and puts the positive argument last in a place of strength.

Business reports are fact-oriented and should not include opinion. If you want to add your personal opinions, they can be included in the cover letter. Opinions in the body of your report will make it seem less factual and objective.

ORGANIZATION OF BUSINESS REPORTS Informal business reports have a fairly standard organization. This organization is outlined here.

- **Introduction** The introduction is similar to the opening of a presentation. It is where you grab the reader, introduce the key issues, and give the reader a sense of who, what, where, when, why, and how. It should give the reader the background of the problem, state the problem clearly and indicate why its solution is important to the reader, and define the scope and limitations of the proposed solution.
- **Table of contents** This table makes it easy for the reader to find key information. In a 10-page report, it is not critical, but in a 100-page report, a great deal of time can be wasted looking for information. Reports are often reviewed in meetings, and trying to find a key point can be frustrating.

- **Main body** The body is where the writer presents the findings from the research, analyzes the data, evaluates the possible solutions, and develops a rationale for selecting the proposed solution. This section is often broken down into the following subsections:
  - **Background material and facts** The two functions of this section are to give readers essential background material they may lack, and to clarify the report writer's understanding of the situation, which may well differ from the perceptions of others.
  - **Statement of problem** This section explicitly defines the problem (as opposed to the symptoms) to be solved.
  - **Analysis** This section contains the logical thought processes used to develop the solution; it is designed to persuade the reader regarding the advantages of the solution and thoroughness of the writer's analysis. This section could be further divided into such topics as alternatives considered, objectives for solution, evaluation of alternatives, alternatives rejected, or assumptions.
  - **Solutions and implementation** This final section details solutions to the problem.
- **Conclusions and recommendations** The entire report leads up to this point. No new information is presented but the key ideas are recapped and summarized in a way that reinforces the validity of the recommendation.
- **Appendices** Data that are lengthy or complex should be in this section. The body of the text can reference data in a particular appendix without bogging the reader down with the entire set of data. It is not unusual to have the body of a report be a few pages of text backed up by hundreds of pages of detailed data.

BUSINESS LETTERS: YOUR MESSENGERS TO THE OUTSIDE WORLD

Business letters are your written contact with people outside the organization. Unlike telephone conversations, letters document your communication, providing a long-lasting record that can be referred to whenever necessary. Writing a business letter is done for many different reasons. Each purpose dictates a slightly different style and tone. Some common reasons are

- To request specific information or action from someone outside the company.
- To provide information to someone who requests it.
- For ceremonial purposes (congratulations, thank-you's, commendations).
- To exchange ideas, handle arguments, present a point of view, or explain why an action was taken or why a requested action was rejected.
- To sell goods or services or to provide information about the company.

You are representing your company when you write a business letter. Get to the point quickly. Be clear, courteous, and concise.

Your first paragraph is where you hook your reader's attention and get the reader involved with your purpose. It is not the time for mumbling, stuttering, or vagueness. It is where you persuade the reader to consider your ideas. Give a clear idea of the benefits your proposal brings to the reader or why you need the information the reader has.

Write so that the reader enjoys reading it. Write the entire letter from the reader's point of view. Answer questions and objections the reader might have. Be positive. Be nice. Be natural.

Conclude by urging the reader to act on your solution. You should get your message across in one or two pages. If not, add an appendix of materials. Read your letter out loud to see whether it sounds natural and pleasant, and clearly addresses your purpose.

Good business writing is a combination of clear thinking, good organization, and effective presentation. The previous sections have given suggestions to help you think through your writing project and organize it effectively. They have also given you a guide to using the three most common formats in business writing: memos, reports, and business letters. The next few sections will help you improve your style and avoid some of the most common pitfalls in writing.

Style

Colors fade, temples crumble, empires fall, but wise words endure.

> —Edward Thorndike

What exactly is style? Hemingway had style. Stephen King has style. Does that mean you have to be a professional writer to have style? No. In fiction, *style* is used to describe a distinctive voice in writing—a certain grace with words that sets the truly great writer apart from the rest. In business writing, we are talking about something much more basic. In business writing, we are looking for clarity, conciseness, and readability more than eloquence.

Think about the memos that you absolutely dread reading. Those with sentences so long you get lost along the way? Those that strangle you with confusing phrases, technical terms, acronyms, and words that only a dictionary could love? Those that ramble for pages without a break or even a sense of where they are going?

You have probably seen them all...and maybe worse. These are the memos, letters, and reports that you want to pass along to someone else to read, no matter how important the information inside may seem to be. The overwhelming temptation is to set it aside in the "To Read" file, or, better yet, the circular file. Style is what makes the difference.

The Big Three: Clear, Concise, Readable

By now you are well aware of the importance of clarity in your thinking before you begin writing. To write clearly demands a high level of preparation. If you lack confidence when you write, it shows up in the use of passive voice, jargon, indirect expressions, and lengthy, unfocused writing. To be clear, you need to say what you want to say directly rather than tiptoeing gently around the topic. Most readers are not likely to tiptoe with you, which makes you, the writer, seem to be hiding something.

To write concisely, you should use short words, sentences, and paragraphs, to grab the attention of the reader. Finally, to make your business document readable, you should consider the words you use, the voice you choose, and your level of formality.

DO NOT MUDDY THE WATER

Once you are confident about what you want to say and have it well organized and structured, three actions will help you to improve the clarity of your writing: use active voice, avoid jargon, avoid indirectness.

Use Active Voice Active voice is open and up-front. Business writing is about action. It requests action, suggests action, encourages action. If you want people to act, use active rather than passive voice. Example:

> *Passive:* It is suggested that you have a meeting called at your earliest convenience.
> *Active:* Please call a meeting ASAP.

We get into passive voice primarily in two ways: delaying the subject and using a *be* verb or past participle of an active verb. Here are two examples. The subject of the sentence is in italics and the verb is underlined:

Passive: There <u>seems</u> to be a need to review our health plan.
Active: We <u>will review</u> our health plan Friday.

Note that the first sentence is so passive, the subject fails to even make an appearance.

Passive: A new phone system <u>was chosen</u> by the committee.
Active: The committee <u>chose</u> a new phone system.

Notice that it is the same basic verb—chose—but the passive voice uses the past participle form. The active sentence is clean, clear, and simple. Active voice is much closer to the way we talk. As a writer you are talking with your reader through the written word. If you were talking to a co-worker, you would say "I suggest" and not "it is suggested." The active voice not only adds vitality to your writing, but it is more direct, forceful, and personal.

Active voice depends on action verbs. Decide. Talk. Meet. Sell. Start. Buy. Merge. Choose. Hire. Fire. Plan. Negotiate. Make. Build. Ask. These action words of business are more meaningful when not surrounded by muddy, indirect phrases.

Passive voice is a shield to hide behind. It is flat and dull, and you should only resort to it when you want to soften bad news, you want to avoid responsibility for some occurrence or remain detached, or you do not know who the main "actor" is in a sentence.

AVOID JARGON Every profession has its terminology, acronyms, and jargon. When everyone understands the terms, it provides a quick and efficient shorthand. When everyone does not understand the terms, it creates miscommunication and misunderstandings. It is almost impossible to avoid jargon and acronyms, and when you are writing for people within your organization, you are probably safe. If you have any doubt that your readers will understand a term or acronym, define the term the first time it is used, or find a different way of expressing your idea. Example:

Jargon: The LOE required to respond to the RFP is too high.
Translation: The level of effort required to respond to the request for proposal is too high.
Plain English: We cannot afford to bid on this project.

BE DIRECT Say what you mean. If you try to hide behind indirect expressions, people will either not understand what you are saying or they will figure it out anyway and just think you are a poor writer. Examples:

Indirect: It is suggested that you have a meeting called at your earliest convenience regarding the possibility of determining the feasibility of implementing a new marketing plan.
sirect: Please call a meeting ASAP to discuss a new marketing plan.

People generally go into indirect mode when they are hedging. Common hedging words are *seems, appears, might possibly be,* and *could be.* These words and phrases indicate a lack of confidence and a fuzziness of thinking. They do not inspire confidence and action in your reader.

Writing is an act of communication. We are trying to pass a message from one mind to another. It is our job as writers to make the message as clear as possible to the reader. The more active, jargon-free, and direct our writing is, the more the reader will understand what our message is.

SHORT IS BEST

The second goal of business writing is conciseness. We are not writing a novel; we are transmitting information or requesting action from people who have little time or inclination to read what we are writing. If we are asking someone to take action and we can clearly convey that request in one paragraph, great! Business writing is not a term paper with a fixed page requirement. We want to state our business in the clearest and shortest way possible. Cut out all the fluff and improve your chances of having your memos and reports read and acted on.

SHORT WORDS Start with short words. Big words are no substitute for clear thinking and often they are not as powerful as short, punchy, crisp, lean, exact, sharp, tight, and to-the-point small words. Here are a few examples of big words that have smaller alternatives. You may want to use the big word but consider the little one:

Viable = workable, useful
Interface with = meet with, work with
Optimize = make the most of
Sufficient = enough
Utilize = Use

SHORT PHRASES Just as we often opt for a long word when a short one would do, we have developed a lot of wordy phrases that need to be trimmed back. Here are some examples:

With reference to = about, regarding
On the grounds that = because
In accordance with = by, following
To tell the truth = (avoid this one, it sounds like a lie is coming)
To the best of my ability = (eliminate)
Hold a discussion = discuss
Take action = act
At this point in time = now

SHORT SENTENCES Short sentences are active. They have punch. Although not all sentences can be short, watch out for these three tiny words: and, but, or. They often lead into long sentences full of dependent clauses and twists and turns that may lose the reader. The most interesting writing uses a variety of sentence lengths with the short sentence being used as the power punch. Look at a recent memo or report and count the words in three or four sentences. A common guideline is 17 words. It is okay to go over that limit occasionally, but if all your sentences are more than 17 words, your readers are going to go brain dead. (This last sentence contained 26 words. It could have been two sentences: It is okay to go over that limit occasionally. However, if all your sentences are more than 17 words, your readers are going to go brain dead.)

SHORT PARAGRAPHS Two reasons support the use of short paragraphs: one idea and white space. Powerful paragraphs transmit one idea. Each sentence in the paragraph develops the idea. When that idea is complete, go to the next idea in the next paragraph.

Take a lesson from the advertising folks. White space sells. The space between paragraphs gives the reader time to process information and makes it easier to transition to the next idea. Short paragraphs broken by white space please the eye more than an unbroken mass of words on a page.

SHORT WRITING If you can say it in one page, do not take two. Brief is better. Short has more chance of being read. However, short is not easier. It is much harder to write a one-page memo than to ramble on for two. It requires clear thinking and clear writing. But, it is worth the effort.

Business is about productivity and efficiency. Business writing that is clear and concise promotes those ideals. Business writing is almost never about entertaining the reader. Reading memos is not a leisure activity. Respect your reader's time by saying what you need to say as clearly and concisely as possible.

MAKE IT READABLE

Once your message is clear and concise, make your memo readable and etch it to your reader's mind with a powerful format. Make it as easy to read as possible. When considering format, always keep these business principles in mind:

First and foremost: *No one wants to read it!*
Second and important: *Almost no one will read all of it!*
Third and critical: *Almost everyone will misunderstand some part of it!*

No one exclaims, "Oh wow! A new report for me to read!"—except with sarcasm. In the business world, a written message is usually a call to do something, to make decisions, to add to an already overcrowded schedule. Too often we blow it from the first line. *Per your request, please find enclosed the report on the possible involvement of management in a...Yawn. Z-Z-Z-Z.*

You are competing for the time of busy people. Unless you are the chair of the board or president, you probably have about 30 seconds to grab the interest of your reader. Just as we buy magazines based on the front-page headline or picture, we are more likely to read a memo that captures our attention. Otherwise, the magazine stays on the stand and the memo ends up in the "To Read" cemetery.

Borrowing from the journalism and advertising trade, energize your writing with the main tools for improving readability: headlines, subheads, visuals, highlighting and bullets, the use of white space, and dynamic delivery. Grab the reader's attention.

HEADLINES ARE GOLDEN   They must never be boring. Do not waste a headline with *Summary of Benefits* when you could have stated: *Three Million in Savings*. When writing a report, proceed in this order: start with the headlines, then plan the graphics and subheads and, perfecting those, add the main body. This way is best to maintain focus and flow in your writing.

VISUALS SELL YOUR MESSAGE   Pictures, graphs, or illustrations will help you get an idea across quickly or emphasize a particular point. Keep these suggestions in mind when incorporating graphics:

- Graphs and charts have more impact than tables.
- Each graph, chart, or picture should make only one point. Better to have several graphs, each making one point, than one confusing graph with little impact.
- Add colour if at all possible.
- Keep the graph or picture as close to the related text as possible.

HIGHLIGHTING   Use bolding and italics to highlight key ideas and introduce new topics, and bullets to emphasize list items. For example:

- **Bolding and *Italics*** key ideas and new topics
- **Bullets** emphasize list items

Even though they can be extremely useful at the appropriate times, you should use these tools sparingly. When you are speaking in public, you can use your voice to emphasize certain ideas. When you are writing, you are using these highlighting mechanisms in the same way you would use your voice. Just as you would not try to emphasize every word to your audience, you do not emphasize every word on the page. For example, the exclamation point should be used infrequently in business writing! *Also*, if you *try* to **emphasize** *too* many words, **it** becomes *visually* **chaotic** and *makes* the **reader** want to **quit** *reading*. Did the previous sentence make the point?

WHITE SPACE   Again, white space makes a page more readable. Use it to produce a page that is clean and attractive. Use wide margins and a break between paragraphs. It is much easier to read narrow columns than wide lines. Wide margins also make it easy for the reader to make notes while reading. It makes the page look clean and professional.

ADDITIONAL READABILITY TIPS   These housekeeping tips help to make your memos and reports more readable.

- **Limit upper case**   Although upper case may be used OCCASIONALLY for emphasis, long blocks of text in upper case are difficult to read. It is almost always better to use bolding and italics for emphasis and save uppercase for titles and headings.
- **Numbers**   Numbers should be written in a way that makes them easier to read. $4 million is easier to read than $4 000 000.
- **Page numbers**   For reports of more than three pages, page numbers are mandatory. Trying to discuss unnumbered pages has ruined many meetings.
- **Hyphens**   Before we had word processing, we seldom thought about breaking a word at the end of a line. The only purpose for hyphenation is to even out spacing. Hyphens do not improve readability. Avoid them if you can and if you cannot, review them carefully to make sure they do not break the flow of words.
- **Right justification**   This technique is popular because magazines and newspapers use it. It makes the page look "professional." However, they use it because it packs more words into a smaller space and saves paper. The uneven spaces created by right justification make reading more difficult and should be avoided when possible.

If you use these guidelines to help you write clearly and concisely in a readable format, your writing will become far more powerful and effective. And, as your memos and reports become more powerful, you will begin to have more of an impact on your organization. The following paragraphs will give you a few more tips to help your writing style.

AVOID SEXISM

A recent study of 500 college students (50 per cent male and 50 per cent female) showed that when they read a story using he, him, or his where the subject could be male or female, 65 per cent of the study group assumed the subject was male. Recently, people have been sensitized to sexism in writing; therefore, you should avoid sexism whenever possible. However, using awkward constructions such as he/she or (s)he can break the flow of your writing and lessen readability.

Here are some ways to avoid sexism without sacrificing readability:

- Specify the person you are discussing.
- Use plurals. For example:

  A manager should listen to his staff.
  Managers should listen to their staff.

- Alternate he and she.

  A manager should listen to her staff.

- Substitute less offensive words: person for man; synthetic for man-made; representative for spokesman; worker for workman; labour hours for man-hours.

HUMOUR

Humour can be effective in informal writing. However, unless you are positive that the humour will not give offence, it is better not to use it. If you are a boss writing to your staff, humour directed at yourself can establish a warm, human tone. If you are a staff member, humour directed at yourself might be perceived as a lack of self-confidence or weakness.

Even if you are extremely good at humour, you should limit it in your business writing. People will come to expect it and your serious communications will be more difficult.

PUNCTUATION

Punctuation is another way we approximate in writing what we can do with our voice in speaking. Punctuation creates pauses, clarifies meaning, and adds rhythm to our writing. Reading is like listening: the more fluent and lyrical the words, the more willing the reader is to read on. Writers use punctuation to control the timing and pace of their work.

- The period stops the sentence. The semicolon creates a pause between two ideas. And, the comma is a brief rest before going on.
- Dashes separate an important aspect of a larger idea—such as our discussion of punctuation—and draw attention to it.
- The colon is a pause longer than a semi-colon but not as long as a period. Colons are most commonly used for two purposes: to introduce a list, or to serve as a link between an introductory statement and an important point.
- Parentheses tell the reader that the enclosed information is useful but not vital.

Two punctuation marks affect the tone of a paper: the question mark and quotation marks. Questions are unassuming and can add a warm, easygoing tone to your writing. Questions also facilitate transitions. For example, after explaining a change in procedure you might interject, "How are we going to do it?" Then you could explain the implementation procedure. Quotation marks not only enclose direct quotes, but also set off and denote words or phrases used in a special sense.

EDITING

You have not finished your report until you have edited it thoroughly for typos, misspellings, and errors in numbers or dates. Whether you write one memo a month or 40, you should have a minimum of three reference books: a good dictionary, a thesaurus, and a style guide. Keep these by your desk and do not hesitate to refer to them. The time you take now to double-check a spelling or find the right word will make all the difference later.

COMMON ERRORS

We make many word errors—words with the wrong meaning, imprecise words, redundant words, out-of-date words. Know your words and, when in doubt, check a dictionary. Certain words are confused with others over and over again, which in turn confuses the reader. Here are a few of the culprits:

- *It's* vs. *Its: It's* is a contraction of "it is." *Its* is the possessive form of "it."
- *Imply* vs. *Infer: Imply* means to suggest indirectly. *Infer* means to draw meaning out of something.

He implied that he wanted to go.
I inferred from his actions that he wanted to go.

I.e. vs. *e.g.*: *I.e. (id est)* means "that is." *E.g. (exampli gratia)* means "for example."

Appraise vs. *Apprise*: *Appraise* means to measure, to assess the value or nature of something. *Apprise* means to inform in detail.

Style Strategies

Once you thoroughly understand style, you can select the style that fits your reader and the type of writing situation you face. These situations generally fall into the following four categories:

1. **Positive situations** Where you are saying yes or relating good news.
   Style: Personal, at times Colourful
2. **Situations where you are asking something of the reader** Where you are giving instructions or persuading someone to do as requested.
   Style: Active, at times Personal and Colourful
3. **Information-conveying situations** Where you are passing along factual, detailed information.
   Style: Impersonal
4. **Negative situations** Where you are delivering information that the reader would prefer not to know.
   Style: Passive, Impersonal

Here is a list of the highlights of each style:

ACTIVE STYLE

- Helps you be forceful, confident, and sure as in action requests or when you are saying no firmly but politely to an employee.
- Depends on active verbs.
- Uses short sentences.
- Makes direct statements that start with the subject.
- Speaks in first person—*I want, We need*.

PASSIVE STYLE

- Is useful when you are in a negative situation or are in a lower position than the reader.
- Avoids the imperative—never give an order.
- Puts the subject at the end of the sentence or buries it completely.
- Attributes responsibility for negative statements to nameless, faceless, impersonal "others."
- Uses long sentences or dense paragraphs to slow down the reader's attention to sensitive or negative information.

PERSONAL STYLE

- Is useful when you are relating good news or a persuasive action-request.
- Refers to people by name (first name, when appropriate) instead of by title.
- Uses personal pronouns (especially "you" and "I" when you have positive things to say).

- Incorporates short, informal, and conversational sentences, with contractions if necessary.
- Asks the reader direct questions.
- Includes personal notes and references.

IMPERSONAL STYLE

- Is useful in negative and information-conveying situations, and especially in technical and scientific writing.
- Refers to people by title or job description if necessary, not by name (particularly first name).
- Avoids using personal pronouns, although a faceless "we" may be appropriate.
- Uses passive verbs.
- Uses longer sentences including complex sentences and long paragraphs.

COLOURFUL STYLE

- Is useful for highly persuasive writing such as sales letters or for good-news situations.
- Includes more descriptive adjectives and adverbs.
- Incorporates metaphor and simile when appropriate.
- Allows unusual words or slang.

Memos, reports, and business letters are a critical part of an organization's communication environment. As you develop your ability to write in a clear, concise, forceful style, you will improve your personal effectiveness and the productivity of your organization. "Style," as it applies to business writing, is not as mysterious as it sounds. It is more a matter of common sense: understanding the needs of your reader, as well as your own objectives, and then presenting your message clearly and concisely in a readable format.

Concept Quiz

Complete the following true–false quiz by circling the correct answer. Answers are at the end of the quiz. After marking your answers, remember to go back and check your understanding of any answers you missed.

True or False   1. If you are bright, ambitious, or successful, poor business writing will not have a negative effect on your career.

True or False   2. The first steps in writing are to organize your thoughts and analyze your audience.

True or False   3. You are ready to write when you can complete this sentence: I want (WHOM) to do (WHAT) because (REASON).

True or False   4. Tables have more of an impact than charts and graphs.

True or False   5. In a business report, it is acceptable and appropriate to place lengthy data in appendices.

True or False   6. Three ways to improve clarity of style are by using the active voice, avoiding jargon, and being direct.

True or False   7. Business writing is often about complex issues, so long words or sentences are necessary.

True or False   8. To improve readability, one should use all capital letters and right justification.

True or False   9. Highlighting, bullets, and headlines are unprofessional and have no place in business writing.

True or False   10. In positive situations, your style should be personal and perhaps colourful, and use active voice.

Answers (1) False; (2) True; (3) True; (4) False; (5) True; (6) True; (7) False; (8) False; (9) False; (10) True

Behavioural Checklist

The following skills are important to effective business writing. Use them when evaluating your writing skills and those of others.

The Effective Business Writer:

- Organizes thoughts before writing, so that the document flows naturally.
- Considers the audience when writing.
- Uses graphs, charts, headlines, and bullets to enhance memos and reports.
- Indicates the need for action, if there is one.
- Uses short words, sentences, and paragraphs.
- Avoids sexism, inappropriate humour, jargon, and indirectness.
- Knows what style strategy is appropriate for each type of business situation.
- Lives by the Big Three—clear, concise, and readable.

Group Exercise

Written Presentations

Many students agonize over writing papers for class. However, once you enter the business world, effective business writing is expected in virtually every type of position. Just like public speaking, good business writing requires practice. Although the prospect of writing papers may seem daunting, students are getting valuable practice toward successful careers. Consequently, the group exercise for this module consists of students preparing two different types of business documents in order to practise and receive feedback on their writing.

DIRECTIONS The students should form groups of three or four. Each member will prepare a memo and an outline for a business report based on a business scenario of mutual interest.

STEP 1 Group members should describe interesting business situations they have been involved in or have heard about. Then they agree on one to write about. Examples of situations might be:

- New Marketing Plan
  - The memo might announce the introduction of the marketing plan.
  - The outline might reflect how a report on the new marketing plan should be structured.
- CEO announces hiring freeze based on low profits
  - The memo should announce the news to the employees.
  - The outline should reflect the business report stating the findings and making the recommendations for a hiring freeze.

STEP 2   Students individually write their own memo and report outline.

STEP 3   Students read and critique the others' work based on the effective business writer Behavioural Checklist.

STEP 4   Students discuss what they have learned from their experience and make recommendations based on the exercise.

TIME   Each group will have 10 minutes to brainstorm a scenario to work on. Next, students will have 10 minutes to write their own memo, and another 15 minutes to write the outline. After every member has finished, the other group members will have 20 minutes to look over and critique the others' work. Finally, in the time remaining, students will discuss what they learned from their experience and make recommendations based on the exercise.

Application Questions

1. Evaluate your professor's writing. Do the course outline and project assignments follow the guidelines outlined in this section?
2. Think of a paper or a memo that you had to read that was exceptionally well written. What tactics did the writer use to capture your attention?

    Conversely, think of a paper or memo that you considered poorly written and boring. What mistakes do you remember that the writer made?

    Based on what you have just learned, how could he or she have avoided those errors?
3. Do you feel that you have a noticed a distinct writing "style" in your writing or the writings of your classmates? What distinguishes different styles in your mind?
4. Name some instances when you or others have used humour in business writing. What was the effect on you? What was the ultimate outcome of using humour?

Reinforcement Exercises

The following suggestions are activities you can do to reinforce the skills in this chapter. You may want to adapt them to an Action Plan or try them independently.

1. Practise your writing. Pretend that each paper, no matter how small, will be viewed by the CEO of your company, and put the appropriate effort into it.
2. Take a course on business writing. It can enhance the basic lessons taught in this section, and you can keep reinforcing these guidelines so they become a routine in your writing.
3. Visit your school's writing centre, and ask someone there to review your written work. Ask for feedback and suggestions.
4. Play around with your style and effective writing. When sending e-mail to friends or writing letters, structure them as you would a business document. Again, this practice will help embed the lessons in your writing.
5. Volunteer to contribute to a newsletter of an organization that interests you.
6. When reading business documents written by others, try to identify all the errors and broken rules of effective business writing. Once you see it from the other side, you will be less likely to make the same mistakes yourself.

Glossary

ABC system a prioritizing approach developed by time management expert Alan Lakein in which tasks are given a value of A, B, or C, depending upon their urgency and importance.

Academy a type of organizational culture in which employees stay within a narrow specialty and are promoted after they thoroughly master a job.

Accommodation a conflict resolution approach of placing another's needs and concerns first in order to maintain a harmonious relationship.

Achievement motive the desire to perform tasks that will provide a sense of accomplishment.

Achievement-oriented leadership a highly task- and relationship-oriented leadership style that establishes challenging goals, seeks performance improvement, and displays confidence that people will exert high levels of effort.

Active listening the process of listening in which the listener refrains from evaluating other people's words, tries to see things from their point of view, and demonstrates a sincere effort to understand.

Adjourning the last of the five stages of team development in which the group goals have been met and the team is disbanded.

Affiliation motive the desire to perform tasks that provide satisfaction through quality social and interpersonal relationships.

Attending the ability of an active listener to send verbal, vocal, and visual messages to the speaker to indicate the listener's full attention.

Authority the right to give orders and expect the orders to be obeyed; the right to make decisions and commit organizational resources.

Avoidance a conflict resolution approach of withdrawing from or postponing the conflict.

Bargaining a process in which two or more parties exchange goods or services and attempt to agree upon the exchange rate for them; also known as negotiating.

Baseball team a type of organizational culture in which employees are rewarded for what they produce, and where risk taking and innovation are highly valued.

Behaviour modification a technique of changing behaviour through the use of contingent rewards or punishments.

Behaviours a set of criteria used in appraising performance in which individual actions are the basis of measurement.

Benchmark a specific level of performance against which actual results are measured and compared.

Bias occurs when managers develop feelings—positive, negative, or neutral—about employees based on work-related interactions that have little to do with worker performance.

Brainstorming a highly participative group decision-making process in which group members generate as many ideas as possible without criticism or evaluation of the ideas in order to accumulate a large number of solution alternatives that can be evaluated later for feasibility.

Cause-and-effect diagram a construction that represents the relationship between some effect and all possible causes influencing it; also known as a fishbone chart.

Central tendency the grouping of employee evaluation ratings at average or just above average on the performance scale even though employees do not perform the same all the time on specific tasks.

Certainty a situation in which the exact results of implementing a problem solution are known in advance.

Changing a phase of planned change that involves moving or actually altering the way things are done.

Club a type of organizational culture in which employees are trained as generalists and promoted on the basis of seniority.

Coaching a problem-solving process that helps an employee in mastering skills and figuring out how to apply instructions.

Collaboration a conflict resolution approach in which all parties to the conflict seek to satisfy their interest through a solution that is advantageous to all parties.

Communication the process that occurs when one person sends a message to another with the intent of evoking a response.

Competitive strategy plans that provide a distinct advantage by capitalizing on the strengths of the organization and the industry it is in.

Compromise a conflict resolution approach that requires each party to give up something of value.

Conflict a disagreement between two or more parties who perceive that they have incompatible concerns.

Continuous reinforcement to reward a desired behaviour continuously each and every time it occurs.

Co-optation influencing resistant parties to endorse the change effort by providing them with benefits they desire.

Cost leadership a competitive strategy in which the organization strives to be the low-cost producer in the industry.

Counselling a problem-solving process that helps employees deal with personal issues and attitudes.

Credibility others' perceptions of the degree to which an individual is honest, competent, forward looking, and inspiring.

Criteria specific, measurable, attainable, complementary, and ethical statements of objectives that need to be met for a problem to be solved.

Culture the key characteristics that the organization values and that distinguish it from other organizations.

Decision making the process of selecting the best solution from among feasible alternatives.

Decode the process of perceiving a communication and interpreting its meaning.

Delegation the transfer from a manager to an employee of authority for achieving goals and making decisions about how to do a job.

Delphi technique an independent group decision-making process in which participants at their own individual locations write and then pool a variety of ideas that they may comment on and eventually vote to give a specific solution priority.

Differentiation a competitive strategy in which the organization seeks to be unique in its industry in ways that are widely valued by buyers.

Directive leadership a highly task-oriented leadership style that lets followers know what is expected of them, provides guidance as to what is to be done and how, clarifies performance standards and schedules, and calls attention to work procedures and policies.

Distinctive competence unique skills or resources that give an organization a competitive edge.

Distributive bargaining a negotiation process that operates under a zero-sum condition; that is, any party's gain comes at the expense of the other party.

Diversity the individual variations in the values, needs, interests, and expectations of a group of people.

Employee-oriented behaviour a pattern of organizational actions that aim to satisfy social and emotional needs of group members.

Empowerment the process of encouraging and providing tools to another to complete a task.

Encode the process of putting a message in a format that the receiver will understand.

Environmental scanning the process in which managers look outside their organization to ensure that their goals align well with current and future environments.

Equity theory a theory suggesting that motivation is moderated by the perceived fairness or discrepancy between personal contributions and rewards relative to others.

Ethical guideposts company policies on ethics that describe what the organization perceives as ethical behaviour and what it expects its stakeholders, specifically its workers, to do.

Ethics the rules or principles that define right and wrong conduct.

Evaluation the process of monitoring activities to ensure that they are accomplishing planned goals and of correcting any significant deviations.

Evaluation process a system in which: (1) actual performance is measured; (2) actual performance is compared against a standard; and (3) managerial actions are taken to correct any deviations or inadequate standards.

Experiential learning model a theory stating that the development of behavioural skills comes from observation and practice.

Extinction a process of not rewarding or acknowledging undesired behaviour so that it will cease to occur.

Extrinsic rewards rewards that are externally bestowed, such as praise, monetary compensation, or promotion.

Extrovert a person characterized by an interest in the outer world, a responsiveness to external events, a desire to influence and be influenced by events, and a strong association with image.

Feedback a primary tool for determining how clearly a message was understood and what effect it had on the receiver.

Filtering selectively omitting certain information from messages that are sent.

Flextime a work schedule that allows workers some discretion over when they arrive at and leave work; short for "flexible hours."

Focus a competitive strategy in which an organization seeks uniqueness in a narrow market segment, or niche.

Focusing on activities occurs when a manager rates employees on how busy they appear versus how well they perform in achieving results.

Forcing a conflict resolution approach that attempts to satisfy personal needs at the expense of the other party; used when quick resolutions on important issues are needed or where unpopular actions must be taken.

Formal authority individuals who hold positions of leadership through office or title.

Forming the first of five stages of team development in which a group of people come together to answer questions as to a team's purpose, its resources, its ground rules, roles, timelines, and accountability, and its authority.

Fortress a type of organizational culture in which employees who can reverse the organization's sagging fortunes are rewarded.

Gantt chart a graphic planning and control method that breaks a project down into separate tasks and estimates the time needed for their completion.

Goal the specific desired outcome of individual, group, or organizational action.

Group two or more people who meet regularly over a period of time, who perceive themselves as a distinct entity, who share common values, and who strive for common objectives.

Group order ranking an evaluation of an individual's performance by comparing it against all employees' performances and then placing it in a particular hierarchical classification.

Groupthink a phenomenon that occurs when group members' desire to agree is so great that it tends to override the concern for realistic appraisal of alternative courses of action.

Habit a familiar action or event that is continued because it is familiar even when it may not be optimal.

Halo effect occurs when a manager's positive feelings about an employee influence the performance ratings for that employee more positively in all areas because of outstanding performance in a single area.

Horns effect occurs when a manager's negative feelings about an employee influence the performance ratings for that employee more negatively in all areas because of unfavourable performance in a single area.

Human resources management (HRM) the title or department under which much of an organization's staffing activities are grouped.

Impression management an individual's process of shaping the image projected during interactions with others in order to favourably influence how others see and evaluate that individual.

Individual ranking an approach to evaluating an employee's performance by placing that employee in a rank-order from best to worst.

Individual task outcomes a set of criteria used in appraising performance in which ends rather than means are the basis for measurement.

Informal leaders individuals who inspire new ideas or champion causes without the benefit of formal authority.

Integrative bargaining a negotiation process that operates under the assumption that at least one settlement exists that can create a win-win solution.

Intermediate goals the steps that are required in order to accomplish long-term goals.

Intermittent reinforcement the reward for a desired behaviour on a random basis that is frequent enough to encourage the person to continue performing the desired behaviour.

Intrinsic rewards an individual's personal feelings about how well a task was performed or simply the satisfaction of completing the task.

Introvert a person who is introspective and preoccupied with personal thoughts and reflections.

Job burnout a feeling of exhaustion that develops when an individual simultaneously experiences too much pressure and too few sources of satisfaction.

Job characteristics model (JCM) the description of a job according to its skill variety, task identity, task significance, autonomy, and feedback.

Job description a listing of activities to be performed by an employee, how they are done, and why they are done.

Job design the way tasks are combined to form complete jobs.

Job enlargement an approach that attempts to overcome the drawbacks of specialization by horizontally expanding a job and increasing job scope, or the number of different tasks required within the job.

Job enrichment an approach that attempts to design more meaning and challenge into jobs by adding planning and evaluation responsibilities, thereby increasing job depth and employees' control over their own work.

Job sharing a work arrangement that allows two or more people to split a traditional 40-hour-a-week job.

Job specification a listing of the minimal acceptable qualifications that an employee must have to perform the job successfully.

Known risk the probability that a given alternative will produce specific outcomes as predicted.

Leniency the grouping of employee evaluation ratings at the positive end of the performance scale in which employees are rated higher than actual performance warrants.

Long-term goals achievements a person wishes to bring about in the areas of career, family, religion, recreation, and relationships during the person's life.

Management by objectives (MBO) a management system in which employees and supervisors apply goal-setting skills in jointly determining specific performance objectives, which are then periodically reviewed and rewarded according to progress toward those goals.

Management skills the abilities or behaviours that are crucial to success in a managerial position, including planning, organizing, leading, controlling, and evaluating.

Managers organizational members who oversee the activities of other people with the purpose of accomplishing organizational goals.

Manipulation framing and selectively using information and implied incentives to maximize the likelihood of acceptance.

Maslow's hierarchy of needs Maslow's proposal that all individuals have a five-level hierarchy of needs that they attempt to satisfy, beginning with physical well-being, and progressing successively through safety, belonging, esteem, and self-actualization.

Mentoring guiding a less experienced associate toward improved performance.

Merit pay compensation that is tied to output over which the employee has control.

Mission statement an articulation that defines an organization's purpose and answers the questions: Why do we exist? What do we do? What business are we in?

Morale the team's motivation, confidence, and cohesion.

Motivation the conscious decision to direct effort in an activity to achieve a goal that will satisfy a predominate need.

Negotiation a process in which two or more parties exchange goods or services and attempt to agree upon the exchange rate for them; also known as bargaining.

Niche a unique set of opportunities that provide an organization with a competitive advantage.

Noise anything that interferes, at any stage, with the communication process.

Nominal group technique a highly structured group decision-making process in which participants write ideas independently; the ideas are then evaluated and ranked, with the alternative with the highest ranking being the solution of choice.

Norming the third of five stages of team development in which members agree on a structure, experience increased morale and commitment, and communicate more openly as they work toward the team's goals.

Objectives the desired outcomes for individuals, groups, or entire organizations.

Operational plans plans, usually short-term in nature, that specify the details of how the overall objectives in the strategic plan are to be achieved.

Opportunities situations that an organization can take advantage of in working to meet its goals.

Overload the experience of a person who is expected to accomplish more than ability or time permits.

Paired comparison an approach to evaluating an individual's performance by comparing that person with every other employee and rating the employee as either superior or weaker in comparison.

Participative leadership a moderately task-oriented and highly relationship-oriented leadership style that involves consulting with and soliciting the ideas of others in decision making and action taking.

Path-goal theory an approach to leadership in which leaders motivate through clarification of employees' pathways to meet organizational goals and through providing meaningful rewards.

Perceiving becoming aware of ideas, facts, and occurrences.

Performance appraisal a managerial assessment of a worker's actions and productivity and the worker's effectiveness in meeting specific goals of the organization.

Performing the fourth of five stages of team development in which team members work to solve problems and are committed to the group's mission.

Piecework system a reward system based on payment for the amount produced consistent with specified quality standards.

Planning the management function that encompasses defining an organization's goals, establishing an overall strategy for achieving those goals, and developing a comprehensive hierarchy of plans to integrate and coordinate activities.

Positive reinforcement occurs when a reward is given after a desired behaviour.

Power the capacity or potential to influence the behaviour of others.

Power motive the desire to perform tasks that will provide satisfaction from being in charge and controlling and influencing others.

Problem solving the process of eliminating the discrepancy between actual and desired outcomes.

Productivity a team's ability to work together and achieve results.

Punishments an organization's negative response to employees' undesirable behaviour, which employees generally try to avoid.

Recency emphasis performance evaluations that are based on the most recent work performance rather than the performance of the entire evaluation period.

Referent power the influence of a person's image over others' behaviour or values.

Reflecting summarizing and giving feedback to the speaker about the content and feeling of the speaker's message.

Reframing changing personal perception from being helpless to being in control of altering the situation to cope with life stressors.

Refreezing a phase of planned change in which changes that have been made are reinforced, causing desired attitudes and behaviours to become a natural, self-reinforcing pattern.

Relationship behaviours aspects of the situational leadership model that include maintaining personal relationships through opening channels of communication, providing socio-emotional support, and facilitating productive behaviours.

Reliability the extent to which a selection device measures the same thing consistently.

Rewards organizational behaviour or recognition that employees value and that may motivate performance.

Role ambiguity occurs when a worker is expected to work without a clear understanding of job definition, performance expectations, or consequences of behaviour.

Role analysis technique a definition of a group member's role based on the individual's analysis of the rationale, significance, and specific duties of the role.

Role conflict a situation that occurs when an individual's duties or responsibilities conflict with one another.

Role profile a summary of a group member's activities and obligations to the group.

Rushing occurs when a manager hurries through the appraisal process because of insufficient time or a heavy workload.

Satisficing choosing the first satisfactory alternative that meets minimal requirements.

Semantics the meanings and uses of words.

Sensing the ability to recognize the silent messages that the speaker is sending.

Short-term goals the steps that are compatible and contribute to the next longer-term goal.

Small-wins strategy a method of breaking a large, perhaps overwhelming, situation into smaller parts that are more likely to be attained and provide visible success on the way to accomplishing the larger task.

Smoothing a means of providing conflicting groups with some incentive to repress their conflict and avoid its open expression.

Social information processing model (SIP) the description of a job based on the attitudes and behaviours of employees in response to social feedback provided by others.

Social loafing a reduction in a group member's input to the group based on the reasoning that individual contributions, or lack thereof, cannot be identified.

Stakeholders an organization's employees, managers, stockholders, suppliers, customers, and regulators.

Standard-hour plan a pay-for-performance system in which the normal time required to complete the task is associated with a standard rate of pay.

Storming the second of five stages of team development in which the team needs to resolve conflicts about power and task structure.

Strategic plans overall objectives determined by top-level managers, which set out the long-term focus and direction of the entire organization.

Strengths an organization's available internal resources or things that an organization does well.

Stress the body's psychological, emotional, and physiological response to any demand perceived as threatening to a person's well-being.

Superordinate goal an overriding goal that requires the cooperative effort of conflicting groups.

Supportive leadership a highly relationship-oriented leadership style that shows concern for the needs and goals of others and strives to make the work situation pleasant and equitable.

SWOT analysis an examination of the fit between an organization's strengths and weaknesses, and the environmental opportunities and threats.

Synergy coordinated joint efforts that result in more than the sum of the individual efforts.

Task behaviours aspects of the situational leadership model that include organizing and defining roles, explaining activities, and establishing structure, channels of communication, and methods of getting jobs done.

Team a group of people with complementary skills, who are committed to a common purpose, a set of performance goals, and an approach for which they hold themselves mutually accountable.

Technical skills the ability to apply specialized knowledge or expertise.

Telecommuting a work arrangement in which employees do their tasks at home or on the road using a computer linked to the office.

Threats environmental situations that may endanger an organization's ability to meet its goals.

Training in management skills (TIMS) a 10-step training program for acquiring managerial skills, based on the experiential learning model.

Traits a set of criteria used in appraising performance in which individual characteristics are the basis of measurement.

Transmit the process of sending a message to a receiver, whether in oral, nonverbal, written, or electronic format.

Turbulence the irregularity of a rapidly changing environment in which decision makers are not clear about relevant variables, available solution options, or potential consequences of decisions.

Uncertainty a situation in which decision-makers are unable to assign any probabilities to the consequences associated with an alternative.

Underutilization occurs when an organization requires less of a person's time or abilities than the person is able to and wants to give or perform.

Unfreezing a phase of planned change in which leaders help people to see that change is needed and motivate employees to make those needed changes.

Validity the characteristic of a selection device that demonstrates a proven relationship between the device and some relevant criterion.

Value judgments an evaluation based on a message hearer's own experience or culture.

Values enduring personal beliefs about what is worthwhile.

Weaknesses activities that an organization does not do well or resources it needs but does not possess.

Notes

Preface

1. A. Bandura, *Social Learning Theory* (Upper Saddle River, NJ: Prentice Hall, 1977).

Chapter 1

1. S.P. Robbins, *Managing Today!* (Upper Saddle River, NJ: Prentice Hall, 1997) 32–33.
2. H. Mintzberg, "The Manager's Job: Folklore and Fact," *Harvard Business Review*, March–April, 1990.
3. H. Mintzberg, *The Nature of Managerial Work*, Addison-Wesley Educational Publishers Inc., 1973.
4. R.D. Fowler, "Psychologists as Managers," *Monitor on Psychology* (March 1999): 3.
5. D. Stafford, "For Managers, People Skills Are Paramount," *San Diego Union-Tribune*, October 5, 1998, E-3.
6. G.W. Dauphinalis and C. Price, "The CEO as Psychologist," *Management Review* (September 1998): 3–9.
7. J.A. Waters, "Managerial Skill Development," *Academy of Management Review* 5, no. 3 (1980): 449–453; American Assembly of Collegiate Schools of Business, "The Cultivation of Tomorrow's Leaders: Industry's Fundamental Challenge to Management Education," *Newsline* 23, no. 3 (Spring 1993): 1–3.
8. K.L. Fowler and D.M. Scott, "Experiential Learning in the Capstone Strategic Management Course: Collaborative Problem Solving, the Student Live Case, and Modeling," *Journal of Business and Management* (Spring 1996): 103–20.
9. M.J. Burke and R.R. Day, "A Cumulative Study of the Effectiveness of Management Training," *Journal of Applied Psychology* (May 1986): 232–45; L. Cummings, "Reflections on Management Education and Development: Drift or Thrust Into the 21st Century?" *Academy of Management Review* 15, no. 4 (October 1990): 694–6.
10. Ibid.
11. S.B. Parry, "Just What is a Competency? (And why should you care?)," *Training* 35,6 (1998), pp. 58–64 and McMaster University, *Final Report of the Core Competencies Task Team: Staff Survey Implementation Project*, June, 2001.
12. The following is a sample of studies that have identified the key competencies of managers: American Management Association, *Managerial Skills and Competence*, March–April 2000; Anderson Consulting Company, *Skills Needed for the E-Business Environment*, 2000; D. Goleman, *Emotional Intelligence*, New York: Bantam, 1995; D. Goleman, *Working with Emotional Intelligence*, New York: Bantam, 1998; R. Camp, M. Vielhaber, and J.L. Simonetti, *Strategic Interviewing: How to Hire Good People*, San Francisco: Jossey-Bass, 2001; E. Van Velsor and L.J. Brittain, "Why Executives Derail: Perspectives across Time and Cultures," *Academy of Management Executive*, 9, 62–72.
13. D.W. Johnson, and F.P. Johnson, *Joining Together: Group Theory and Group Skills* (Upper Saddle River, NJ: Prentice Hall, 1975) 8–10.
14. The experiential learning model is consistent with social-learning theory presented by A. Bandura, *Social Learning Theory* (Upper Saddle River, NJ: Prentice Hall, 1977).
15. D.A. Kolb, I.M. Rubin, and J.M. McIntyre, *Organizational Psychology: Readings on Human Behavior in Organizations*, 4th ed. (Upper Saddle River, NJ: Prentice-Hall, 1984) 29–31.
16. H.B. Clark, R. Wood, T. Kuchnel, S. Flanagan, M. Mosk, and J.T. Northrup, "Preliminary

Validation and Training of Supervisory Interactional Skills," *Journal of Organizational Behavior Management* (Spring–Summer 1985): 95–115.

17. S.R. Robbins, and P.L. Hunsaker, *Training in Interpersonal Skills*, 3rd ed. (Upper Saddle River, NJ: Pearson Education Inc., 2003).

18. C.R. Rogers, *On Becoming a Person* (Boston: Houghton Mifflin, 1961) 12.

19. G.A. Miller, "The Magical Number Seven, Plus or Minus Two: Some Limits on Our Capacity for Processing Information," *Psychological Review* (March 1956): 81–97.

20. This section is adapted from M.R. McKnight, "The Nature of People Skills," *Journal of Management Education* 10, no. 2 (May 1995): 193–8.

21. S.R. Covey, *The 7 Habits of Highly Effective People* (New York: Simon & Schuster, 1989) 204–34.

22. The idea for this exercise came from B. Goza, "Graffiti Needs Assessment: Involving Students in the First Class Session," *Journal of Management Education* 17, no. 1 (February 1993): 99–106.

Part 2 Self-Management Competencies

1. L. Smith, "Burned-Out Bosses," *Fortune*, July 25, 1994, 44.

2. R.C. Barnett and R.T. Brennan, "The Relationship Between Job Experiences and Psychological Distress: A Structural Equation Approach," *Journal of Organizational Behavior* (May 1995): 250–76; Hammonds, *The New World of Work*; B. Baumohl, E.W. Desmond, W. McWhirter, R. Woodbury, and S. Ratan, "We're #1 and It Hurts," *Time*, October 24, 1994, 48–56; and J. Connelly, "Have We Become Mad Dogs in the Office?" *Fortune*, November 28, 1994, 197–9.

3. K. Weick, "The Collapse of Sensemaking in Organizations," *Administrative Science Quarterly* 38 (1993): 628–52.

4. T.D. Wall, P.R. Jackson, S. Mullarkey, and S.K. Parker, "The Demands-Control Model of Job Strain: A More Specific Test," *Journal of Occupational and Organizational Psychology* (June 1996): 153–66.

Chapter 2

1. T. Gabriel, "Away at Management Camp and Feeling Alone," *New York Times*, April 28, 1996, 10.

2. Ibid.

3. P.F. Drucker, "Managing Oneself," *Harvard Business Review* (March–April 1999): 65.

4. B. Van Buskirk and J. Seltzer, *LaSalle University's Model of Teaching Management Skills*, Paper presented at the Symposium for Management Education and Development, Academy of Management 1995 Meeting, 11.

5. R.L. Hughes, R.C. Ginnett, and G.J. Curphy, *Leadership: Enhancing the Lessons of Experience*, 3d ed. (Burr Ridge, IL: Irwin McGraw-Hill, 1999) 487.

6. P.F. Drucker, "Managing Oneself," *Harvard Business Review* (March–April 1999): 66.

7. Ibid., 66–7.

8. Ideas about how to keep and apply a journal for optimal results can be found in M. Csikszentmihalyi, *Flow: The Psychology of Optimal Experience* (New York: Harper & Row, 1990).

9. H. McIntosh, "Solitude Provides an Emotional Tune-up," *Monitor on Psychology* 27, no. 3 (March 1996): 9–10.

10. K. Blanchard, *A Call to Solitude*, Handout for the Master of Science in Executive Leadership seminar, University of San Diego, San Diego, California, November 10, 1999.

11. It should be noted that these assessment instruments have all been validated in North

American cultures and that the implications drawn are predominately oriented for North American business organizations. Different implications may be drawn for managers in other countries.

12. The idea for this assessment came from J.B. Miner and N.R. Smith, "Decline and Stabilization of Managerial Motivation over a 20-Year Period," *Journal of Applied Psychology* (June 1982): 298.

13. Adapted from H. Weisinger, *Emotional Intelligence at Work* (San Francisco: Jossey-Bass, 1998): 214–5.

14. This discussion is based on B. Murray, "Does Emotional Intelligence Matter in the Workplace?" *Monitor on Psychology* (July 1998): 21; A. Fisher, "Success Secret: A High Emotional IQ," *Fortune*, October 26, 1998, 293–8; D. Goleman, *Working with Emotional Intelligence* (New York: Bantam Books, 1998); R. Daft, *Leadership: Theory and Practice* (Fort Worth, The Dryden Press, 1999) 346–7.

15. H. Weisinger, *Emotional Intelligence at Work* (San Francisco: Jossey-Bass, 1998) 214–5.

16. N. Gibbs, "The EQ Factor," *Time*, October 2, 1995, 65.

17. D. Ancona, T. Kochan, M. Scully, J. Van Maanen, and D.E. Westney, *Managing for the Future: Organizational Behavior and Process*, 2d ed. (Cincinnati: South-Western College Publishing, 1999) C5–C15.

18. Adapted from D. Maric, *Organizational Behavior: Experiences and Cases*, 3d ed. (New York: West Publishing Company (1992) 376–79). Copyright 1985 by Dorothy Marcic. All rights reserved.

19. I.B. Myers, *The Myers-Briggs Type Indicator Manual* (Princeton, NJ: Education Testing Service, 1962).

20. C.J. Jung, *Psychological Types* (Princeton, NJ: Princeton University Press, 1971).

21. Myers, 1962.

22. Myers, 1962.

23. Jung, 1971.

24. Myers, 1962.

25. Myers, 1962.

26. Myers, 1962, 50.

27. Myers, 1962.

28. Jung, 1971.

29. Myers, 1962, 80.

30. Myers, 1962.

31. H. Mann, M. Siegler, and H. Osmond, "The Many Worlds of Time," *Journal of Analytical Psychology* 13, no. 1 (1968): 33–56.

32. D. Hellriegel and J.W. Slocum, Jr., "Managerial Problem-Solving Styles," *Business Horizons*, December 1975, 29–37.

33. R. Kilmann, "Stories Managers Tell: A New Tool for Organizational Problem Solving," *Management Review* (July 1975): 18–28.

34. Hellriegel and Slocum, 1975.

35. R. Kilmann, "Stories Managers Tell: A New Tool for Organizational Problem Solving," *Management Review* (July 1975): 18–28.

36. Hellriegel and Slocum, 1975.

37. Adapted from S.P. Robbins and P.L. Hunsaker, *Training in Interpersonal Skills*, 2d ed. (Upper Saddle River, NJ: Prentice Hall, 1996) 12–14.

38. D. McGregor, *The Human Side of Enterprise* (New York: McGraw-Hill, 1960).

39. J. Powell, *Why Am I Afraid to Tell You Who I Am?* (Chicago: Argus Communications, 1969); W.J.A. Marshall, "The Importance of Being Earnest: A Primer for Leaders," *Management Quarterly* 27, no. 2 (Summer 1986): 7–12; J. Luft, *Group Processes*, 3d ed. (Palo Alto, CA: Mayfield Publishing Company, 1984) 11–20.

40. R.L. Weaver II, *Understanding Interpersonal Communications* (New York: Harper Collins College Publishers, 1993).

41. S. Ashford, "Feedback-Seeking in Individual Adaptation: A Resource Perspective," *Academy of Management Journal* (September 1986): 465–87; P.L. McLeod, J.K. Liker, and S.A. Lobel, "Process Feedback in Task Groups: An Application of Goal Setting," *Journal of Applied Behavioral Science* 28, no. 1 (March 1992): 15–41.

42. G.B. Northcraft and S.J. Ashford, "The Preservation of Self in Everyday Life: The Effects of Performance Expectations and Feedback Context on Feedback Inquiry," *Organizational Behavior and Human Decision Processes* 47, no. 1 (October 1990): 42–64.

43. For a comprehensive discussion of the Johari Window, see J. Luft, *Group Processes*, 3d ed. (Palo Alto, CA: Mayfield Publishing Company, 1984): 11–20; J. Hall, "Communication Revisited," *California Management Review* 15, no. 3 (Spring 1973).

44. R.L. Weaver II, *Understanding Interpersonal Communications* (New York: Harper Collins College Publishers, 1993).

45. L.W. Mealiea and G.P. Latham, *Skills for Managerial Success* (Chicago: Irwin, 1996) 50.

46. C. Cherniss and D. Goleman, *Bringing Emotional Intelligence to the Workplace*, Technical Report Issued by the Consortium for Research on Emotional Intelligence in Organizons (Piscataway, NJ: Rutgers University, 1998) 4.

47. Ibid.

48. P.F. Drucker, "Managing Oneself," *Harvard Business Review* (March–April 1999): 70–71.

49. J.H. Greenhaus, *Career Management* (Chicago: The Dryden Press, 1987).

50. J.G. Clawson, J.P. Kotter, V.A. Faux, and C.C. McArthur, *Self-Assessment and Career Development* (Upper Saddle River, NJ: Prentice-Hall, 1985).

51. O.C. Brenner, "The Impact of Career Exploration on the Career Decision-Making Process," *Journal of College Student Personnel* 24 (1983): 495–502; Greenhaus, 1987.

52. J.H. Greenhaus, *Career Management* (Chicago: The Dryden Press, 1987) 18.

53. B. Filipczak, "You're On Your Own: Training, Employability, and the New Employment Contract," *Training* (January 1995): 29–36.

54. See Chapter 11 for skills on planning, goal setting, and strategy development.

55. See Chapter 14 for a review of the skills necessary for effectively evaluating performance.

56. K. Labich, "Taking Control of Your Career," *Fortune* 124, part 2 (November 18, 1991): 87; J.E.A. Russell, "Career Development Interventions in Organizations," *Journal of Occupational Behavior* 38 (1991): 237–87.

57. M. Calabresi, J. Van Tasel, M. Riley, and J.R. Szczesny, "Jobs in an Age of Insecurity," *Time*, November 22, 1993, 38.

58. J.G. Clawson, J.P. Kotter, V.A. Faux, and C.C. McArthur, *Self-Assessment and Career Development* (Upper Saddle River, NJ: Prentice-Hall, 1985).

59. These ideas are based on D.T. Hall and Associates, eds., *The Career Is Dead—Long Live the Career* (San Francisco: Jossey Bass, 1996); M. Cianni and D. Wnuck, "Individual Growth and Team Enhancement: Moving Toward a New Model of Career Development," *Academy of Management Executive* (February 1997): 105–15; D.T. Hall, "Protean Careers of the 21st Century," *Academy of Management Executive* (November 1996): 8–16.

60. S.P. Robbins, *Managing Today!* 2d ed. (Upper Saddle River, NJ: Prentice Hall, 2000): 295–6.

Chapter 3

1. Adapted from numerous sources, including A.J. DuBrin, *Human Relations: Interpersonal, Job-Oriented Skills*, 6th ed. (Upper Saddle River, NJ: Prentice Hall, 1997) 249–50; S.P. Robbins and D.A. De Cenzo, *Supervision Today!* 2d ed. (Upper Saddle River, NJ: Prentice Hall, 1998) 65.

2. Adapted from G. Dessler, *Management: Leading People and Organizations in the 21st Century* (Upper Saddle River, NJ: Prentice Hall, 1998) 78.

3. Adapted from T. Kelly, "Ethics Officers Guide Workers to Right Choices," *New York Times* News Service Report in *San Diego Union-Tribune*, March 3, 1998, C2.

4. K. Ireland, "The Ethics Game," *Personnel Journal* no. 5 (1979): 171–81.

5. K. Davis and W.C. Frederick, *Business and Society: Management, Public Policy, Ethics*, 5th ed. (New York: McGraw-Hill, 1984) 76.

6. K. Durham, "Right and Wrong: What's Ethical in Business? It Depends on When You Ask," *Wall Street Journal*, January 11, 1999, R48.

7. D. Simpson, "Understanding Employee Loyalty and Commitment: Ethics Matter," *Management Ethics*, Canadian Centre for Ethics & Corporate Policy, December 2000.

8. Ibid.

9. Adapted from G. Stock, *The Book of Questions: Business, Politics and Ethics* (New York: Workman Publishing, 1991) 88.

10. B. Domaine, "Exporting Jobs and Ethics," *Fortune* (October 5, 1992): 10.

11. E. Jansen and M.A. Von Glinow, "Ethical Ambivalence and Organizational Rewards Systems," *Academy of Management Review*, no. 10 (1985): 814–22.

12. D.M. Wolfe, "Is There Integrity in the Bottom Line? Managing Obstacles to Executive Integrity," in S. Srirastava, ed., *Executive Integrity: The Search for High Values in Organizational Life* (San Francisco: Jossey-Bass, 1988) 140–71.

13. N.J. Adler, *International Dimensions of Organizational Behavior*, 3d ed. (Cincinnati: South-Western College Publishing, 1997) 174.

14. Kelly, *New York Times* News Service Report in *San Diego Union-Tribune*, March 3, 1998, C2.

15. L.K. Trevino and S.A. Youngblood, "Bad Apples in Bad Barrels: A Causal Analysis of Ethical Decision-Making Behavior," *Journal of Applied Psychology* (August 1990) 378–85.

16. Cited in C. Fredman, "Nationwide Examination of Corporate Consciences," *Working Woman* (December 1991): 39.

17. F.R. David, *An Empirical Study of Codes of Business Ethics: A Strategic Perspective*, Paper presented at the 48th Annual Academy of Management Conference; Anaheim, CA (August 1988).

18. Nortel's Code of Business Conduct is available at http://www.nortel.com/corporate/community/ethics/.

19. R. Sweeney and H. Siers, "Survey: Ethics in Corporate America," *Management Accounting* (June 1990): 34–40.

20. B.Z. Posner and W.H. Schmidt, "Values and the American Manager: An Update," *California Management Review* (Spring 1984): 202–16; R.B. Morgan, "Self- and Co-Workers Perceptions of Ethics and Their Relationships to Leadership and Salary," *Academy of Management Journal* (February 1993): 200–14.

21. P.F. Miller and W.T. Coady, "Teaching Work Ethics," *Education Digest* (February 1990): 54–5; Robbins and Coulter, 170.

22. Kelley, *New York Times* News Service Report in *San Diego Union-Tribune*, March 2, 1998, C2.

23. S.P. Robbins and M. Coulter, *Management*, 6th ed. (Upper Saddle River, NJ: Prentice-Hall, 1999) p.171.

24. Kelley, *New York Times* News Service Report in *San Diego Union-Tribune*, March 2, 1998, C2.

25. Adapted from L.K. Trevino and K.A. Nelson, *Managing Business Ethics: Straight Talk About How to Do It Right* (New York: John Wiley, 1995) 71–5.

26. Adapted from J.R. Boatright, *Ethics and the Conduct of Business* (Upper Saddle River, NJ: Prentice Hall, 1993) 1.

27. Adapted from G. Sammet Jr., *Gray Matters: The Ethics Game* (Orlando: Martin Marietta Corporation, 1992).

Chapter 4

1. S. Eng, "Time Out," *The San Diego Union-Tribune,* September 14, 1998, C1–C2.
2. L. Duxbury and C. Higgins. *2001 National Work-Life Conflict Study.* Health Canada. July 2002.
3. C.W. Cook, P.L. Hunsaker, and R.E. Coffey, *Management and Organizational Behavior,* 2d ed. (Burr Ridge, IL: Irwin, 1997) 498.
4. Selye, Hans. *The Stress of Life.* New York: McGraw-Hill Book Company, 1956.
5. Health Canada. *The Business Case for Active Living at Work: Helping Employees Get Off Their Bottoms Improves Health and the Bottom Line.* 2000.
6. J. Bales, "Work Stress Grows, but Services Decline," *Monitor on Psychology* 22, no. 11 (November 1991): 32.
7. M. Shain. *Best Advice on Stress Risk Management in the Workplace.* Health Canada. 2000.
8. L. Duxbury and C. Higgins. *2001 National Work–Life Conflict Study.* Health Canada. July 2002.
9 Felix, Sonya. "Taking the Sting Out of Stress," *Benefits Canada Magazine,* November 1998.
10. The basis of this discussion is R.L. Kahn and P. Byosiere, "Stress in Organizations," in M.D. Dunnette, and L.M. Hough, *Handbook of Industrial and Organizational Psychology,* 2d ed., vol. 3 (Palo Alto, CA: Consulting Psychologists Press, 1992): 573–80.
11. B. Fletcher, "The Epidemiology of Occupational Stress," in C.L. Cooper and R. Payne, *Causes, Coping and Consequences of Stress at Work* (New York: John Wiley & Sons, 1988) 3–52.
12. J.W. Jones, "A Cost Evaluation for Stress Management," *EAP Digest* 1 (1984): 34–39.
13. D. Schwimer, "Managing Stress to Boost Productivity," *Employee Relations Today* (Spring 1991): 23–27.
14. K. Matthews, E. Cottington, E. Talbott, L. Kuller, and J. Siegel, "Stressful Work Conditions and Diastolic Blood Pressure Among Blue-Collar Factory Workers," *American Journal of Epidemiology* (1987): 280–291.
15. B. Fletcher, "The epidemiology of occupational stress," in C.L. Cooper and R. Payne, *Causes, Coping and Consequences of Stress at Work* (New York: John Wiley & Sons, 1988) 3–52.
16. *Employee Burnout: America's Newest Epidemic,* (Milwaukee: Northwestern Life Insurance Company, 1991).
17. R.R. Golembiewski and R.F. Munzenrider, *Phases of Burnout: Developments in Concepts and Application* (New York: Praeger, 1988) 6–10.
18. D.P. Rogers, "Helping Employees Cope with Burnout," *Business* (October–December 1984): 3–7.
19. S.E. Jackson, R.L. Schwab, and R.S. Schuler, "Toward an Understanding of the Burnout Phenomenon," *Journal of Applied Psychology* 71 (1986): 630–40.
20. D. Schwimer, "Managing Stress to Boost Productivity," *Employee Relations Today* (Spring 1991): 23–7.
21. M. Jamal, "Relationship of Job Stress to Job Performance: A Study of Managers and Blue-Collar Workers," *Human Relations* (May 1985): 409–24.
22. Felix, Sonya. "Taking the Sting Out of Stress," *Benefits Canada Magazine,* November 1998.
23. D. Schwimer, "Managing Stress to Boost Productivity," *Employee Relations Today* (Spring 1991): 23–7.
24. B. Fletcher, "The epidemiology of occupational stress," in C.L. Cooper and R. Payne, *Causes, Coping and Consequences of Stress at Work* (New York: John Wiley & Sons, 1988) 3–52.
25. For a review of recent organization stressors see R.S. DeFrank and J.M. Ivancevich, "Stress on the job: An executive update," *Academy of Management Executive* (August 1998): 55–66.
26. Ibid., 56–7.
27. T.D. Schellhardt, "The Pressure's On," *Wall Street Journal,* February 26, 1996, B4.
28. R. Zemke, "Workplace Stress Revisited," *Training* (November 1991): 36.
29. *Employee Burnout: America's Newest Epidemic* (Milwaukee: Northwestern Life Insurance Company, 1991) 8.

30. R. Hogan, and J. Morrison, *Work and Well-Being: An Agenda for the '90s*, Paper presented at the American Psychological Association and National Institute for Occupational Safety and Health Conference, Washington, DC, November 1990.

31. A.L. Delbecq and F. Friedlander, "Strategies for Personal and Family Renewal: How a High-Survivor Group of Executives Cope with Stress and Avoid Burnout," *Journal of Management Inquiry* (September 1995): 262–9.

32. T.H. Holmes and R.H. Rahe, "The Social Readjustment Rating Scale," *Journal of Psychosomatic Research* 11 (1967), 213–8.

33. M. Friedman and R. Rosenman, *Type A Behavior and Your Heart* (New York: Knopf, 1974).

34. R.B. Williams, Jr., "Type A Behavior and Coronary Heart Disease: Something Old, Something New," *Behavior Medicine Update* 6 (1984): 29–33.

35. A. Lakein, *How to Get Control of Your Time and Your Life* (New York: Peter H. Wyden, 1973).

36. S.R. Covey, *The 7 Habits of Highly Effective People* (New York: Simon & Schuster, 1990) 95–144.

37. R. Garters, *Time to Manage Time* (Christchurch, New Zealand: New Zealand Institute of Management, 1990) 47–55.

38. M.T. Matteson, and J.M. Ivancevich, *Controlling Work Stress* (San Francisco: Jossey-Bass, 1987) 88–91.

39. D.A. Girdano, G.S. Everly, Jr., and D.E. Dussek, *Controlling Stress and Tension: A Holistic Approach, 3d ed.* (Upper Saddle River, NJ: Prentice Hall, 1990) 114–5.

40. N. Branden, *Self-Esteem at Work* (San Francisco, Jossey-Bass, 1998) 33–6.

41. L.R. Murphy, "A Review of Organizational Stress Management Research," *Journal of Organizational Behavior Management* (Fall–Winter 1986): 215–27.

42. S.J. Motowidlo, J.S. Packard, and M.R. Manning, "Occupational Stress: Its Causes and Consequences for Job Performance," *Journal of Applied Psychology* (November 1987): 619–20.

43. R.C. Cummings, "Job Stress and the Buffering Effect of Supervisory Support," *Group & Organization Studies* (March 1990): 92–104; J.J. House, *Work Stress and Social Support* (Reading, MA: Addison-Wesley, 1981).

44. J.G. Anderson, "Stress and Burnout Among Nurses: A Social Network Approach," *Journal of Social Behavior and Personality* 6, no. 7 (1991): 251–72.

45. K. Mobily, "Using Physical Activity and Recreation to Cope with Stress and Anxiety: A Review," *American Corrective Therapy Journal* (May–June 1982): 62–8.

46. H. Benson, *The Relaxation Response* (New York: William Morrow, 1975).

47. J.C. Smith, *Cognitive-Behavioral Relaxation Training* (New York: Springer Publishing Company, 1990).

48. K.E. Hart, "Managing Stress in Occupational Settings: A Selective Review of Current Research and Theory," in C.L. Cooper, *Stress Management Interventions at Work* (Rochester, England: MCB University Press Limited, 1987) 11–7.

49. Shain, Martin. *Best Advice on Stress Risk Management in the Workplace*. Health Canada. 2000.

50. A.L. Delbecq, and F. Friedlander, "Strategies for Personal and Family Renewal: How a High-Survivor Group of Executives Cope with Stress and Avoid Burnout," *Journal of Management Inquiry* (September 1995): 266.

51. R.S. Schuler and S.E. Jackson, "Managing Stress through PHRM Practices: An Uncertainty Interpretation," in K. Rowland and G. Ferris, eds, *Research in Personnel and Human Resources Management,* vol. 4 (Greenwich, CT: JAI Press, 1986): 183–224.

52. "Workplace Flexibility Is Seen as Key to Business Success," *Wall Street Journal,* November 23, 1993, A1.

53. Health Canada, *National Wellness Survey Report 2000,* 2001.

54. C.E. Beadle, "And Let's Save 'Wellness.' It Works," *New York Times,* July 24, 1994, F9.

55. Health Canada. *Business Case for Active Living at Work*, 2001.

56. Adapted from Cook, et. al., (1997) 526.

Chapter 5

1. Adapted from S.P. Robbins and D.A. De Cenzo, *Supervision Today*, 2d ed. (Upper Saddle River, NJ: Prentice Hall, 1998) 388–9.

2. B.L. Reece and R. Brandt, *Effective Human Relations in Business*, 5th ed. (Boston: Houghton Mifflin, 1993) 97.

3. Ibid., 27.

4. D.K. Berlo, *The Process of Communication* (New York: Holt, Rinehart & Winston, 1960) 30–2.

5. E. Weiner, "Right Word Is Crucial in Air Control," *New York Times*, February 29, 1990, B-5.

6. J. Ritter, "Poor Fluency in English Means Mixed Signals," *USA Today*, January 18, 1996, 1A.

7. L.L. Tobias, "Twenty-Three Ways to Improve Communication," *Training and Development Journal* (1989): 75–7.

8. E. Lewis and B.K. Spiker, "Tell Me What You Want Me to Do," *Manufacturing Systems* (December 1991): 46–9.

9. R. McGarvey, "Now Hear This," *Entrepreneur* (June 1996): 87–9.

10. T. Alessandra and P. Hunsaker, *Communicating at Work* (New York: Simon & Schuster, 1993) 54–68.

11. A. Mehrabian, *Nonverbal Communication* (Chicago: Aldine/Atherton, 1972) 25–30.

12. T. Alessandra and P. Hunsaker, *Communicating at Work* (New York: Simon & Schuster, 1993) 111–9.

13. P. Ekman, "Facial Expression and Emotion," *American Psychologist* (April 1993): 384–92.

14. D. Blum, "Face It," *Psychology Today* (September–October 1998): 32–9, 66–70.

15. F. Williams, *The New Communications* (Belmont, CA: Wadsworth, 1989) 45.

16. J.W. Gibson and R.M. Hodgetts, *Organizational Communication: A Managerial Perspective* (Orlando, FL: Academic Press, 1986) 95.

17. "What's A-O-K in the U.S.A. Is Lewd and Worthless Beyond," *New York Times*, August 18, 1996, E7.

18. M. Henricks, "More Than Words," *Entrepreneur* (August 1995): 54–7.

19. See O.P. Kharbanda and E.A. Stallworthy, "Verbal and Non-Verbal Communication," *Journal of Managerial Psychology* 6, no. 4 (1991): 10–3, 49–52, for an expansion of these ideas.

20. For elaboration see R.T. Barker and C.G. Pearce, "The Importance of Proxemics at Work," *Supervisory Management* 35 (1990): 10–1.

21. T. Carney, "The Four-Communication-Styles Approach," *The 1980 Handbook for Group Facilitators* (San Diego: University Associates, 1980) 127–32.

22. P. Harris and R. Moran, *Managing Cultural Differences*, 3d ed. (Houston: Gulf Publishing, 1991) 13.

23. D. Tannen, *You Just Don't Understand: Women and Men in Conversation* (New York: Ballantine Books, 1991) 24–5.

24. J. Bard and P. Bradley, "Styles of Management and Communication: A Comparative Study of Men and Women," *Communication Monographs* 46 (1979): 101–11.

25. J. Hunsaker and P. Hunsaker, *Strategies and Skills for Managerial Women* (Cincinnati: South-Western Publishing, 1991) 252–3.

26. B. Eakins and R. Eakins, *Sex Differences in Human Communication* (Boston: Houghton Mifflin Company, 1978) 117–9.

27. J. Hunsaker and P. Hunsaker, *Strategies and Skills for Managerial Women*, 139.
28. N.J. Adler, *International Dimensions of Organizational Behavior*, 2d ed. (Boston: Kent Publishing, 1991) 83–4.
29. N. McDonald and G. Hasselfield, *Communicating Across Cultures: A Practical Handbook to Cross Cultural Communication Skills* (Winnipeg, Manitoba, Cross Cultural Communications International, Inc.) 20-22.
30. Case based on J. Cushman, "Avianca Flight 52: The Delays That Ended in Disaster," *New York Times*, February 5, 1990, B-1; and E. Weiner, "Right Word Is Crucial in Air Control," *New York Times*, February 29, 1990, B-5.

Chapter 6

1. R.L. Daft, *Leadership: Theory and Practice* (Fort Worth: Dryden Press, 1999) 302.
2. F. Milliken and L.I. Martins, "Searching for Common Threads: Understanding the Multiple Effects of Diversity in Organizational Groups," *Academy of Management Review* 21, no. 2 (1996): 402–33.
3. Daft, 1999, p. 318.
4. L.E. Wynter, "Minorities Play the Hero in More TV Ads as Clients Discover Multicultural Sells," *Wall Street Journal*, November 24, 1993, B6.
5. C. Hall, "Hoechst Celanese Diversifying Its Ranks," *Dallas Morning News*, September 27, 1992, 1H, 7H.
6. The text under this heading is extracted from: G. Dessler, N.D. Cole, and V.L. Sutherland, *Human Resources Management in Canada*, 8th Canadian ed. (Toronto: Prentice Hall, Inc., 2002) p. 75. Reprinted with permission by Pearson Education Canada Inc.
7. S. Jackson and Associates, *Diversity in the Workplace: Human Resource Initiatives* (New York: Guildford Press, 1992).
8. S. Rynes and B. Rosen, "A Field Survey of Factors Affecting the Adoption and Perceived Success of Diversity Training," *Personnel Psychology* (Summer 1995): 247–70.
9. N. Spinks, *The Manager's Work-Family Toolkit*, The Vanier Institute of the Family Ottawa, 1998.
10. I. Harpaz, "The Importance of Work Goals: An International Perspective," *Journal of International Business Studies* (First Quarter 1990): 75–93.
11. G. Hofstede, "Motivation, Leadership and Organizations: Do American Theories Apply Abroad?" *Organizational Dynamics* (Summer 1980): 55.
12. T. McDermott, "TQM: The Total Quality Maquiladora," *Business Mexico* 4, no. 11 (1994): 42–5.
13. N. Adler, *International Dimensions of Organizational Behavior*, 3d ed. (Boston: PWS—Kent, 1997); and T. Cox and S. Blake, "Managing Cultural Diversity: Implications for Organizational Competitiveness," *Academy of Management Executive* 5 (August 1991): 45–66.
14. Adapted from D. Bowen, et al. *Experiences in Management and Organizational Behavior*, 4th ed. (New York: Wiley, 1996) 329.
15. Adapted from A.J. Kinicki, *Valuing Diversity* (Chandler, AZ: Angelo Kinicki, 1994) 1–5.
16. Adapted from Greenberg, 99.

Chapter 7

1. D.W. Johnson, *Reaching Out: Interpersonal Effectiveness and Self-Actualization* (Boston: Allyn and Bacon, 1993) 205-7.
2. D. Tjosvold and D.W. Johnson, *Productive Conflict Management: Perspectives for Organizations* (New York: Irvington Publishers, 1983) 10.

3. M.A. Rahim, *Managing Conflict in Organizations,* 2d ed. (Westport, CT: Praeger, 1992).

4. S.P. Robbins, "'Conflict Management' and 'Conflict Resolution' Are Not Synonymous Terms," *California Management Review* (Winter 1978): 67–75; D. Tjosvold, *Working Together to Get Things Done* (Lexington, MA: D.C. Heath, 1986) 111–2.

5. S.P. Robbins, *Managing Organizational Conflict: A Nontraditional Approach* (Upper Saddle River, NJ: Prentice Hall, 1974) 31–55; and Yuan-Duen Lee "Managing Workplace Conflict," *Management Review* (July 1993): 57.

6. C.O. Kursh, "The Benefits of Poor Communication," *Psychological Review* (Summer–Fall 1971): 189–208.

7. L. Greenhalgh, "Managing Conflict," *Sloan Management Review* (Summer 1986): 45–51.

8. R.H. Kilmann and K.W. Thomas, "Developing a Forced-Choice Measure of Conflict Handling Behavior: The MODE Instrument," *Educational and Psychological Measurement* (Summer 1997): 309–25.

9. K.W. Thomas, "Conflict and Conflict Management," in M. Dunnette, ed., *Handbook of Industrial and Organizational Psychology* (Chicago: Rand McNally, 1976) 889–935.

10. N.J. Adler, *International Dimensions of Organizational Behavior,* 3d ed. (Cincinnati: South-Western College Publishing, 1997) 189–90.

11. See for example, S.D. Weiss, "International Negotiations: Bricks, Mortar, and Prospects," in B.J. Punnett and O.J. Shenkar, eds., *Handbook for International Management Research* (Cambridge, MA: Blackwell, 1996) 209–65.

12. N.J. Adler, *International Dimensions of Organizational Behavior,* 3d ed. (Cincinnati: South-Western College Publishing, 1997) 194–5.

13. S.P. Robbins, *Managing Organizational Conflict: A Nontraditional Approach* (Upper Saddle River, NJ: Prentice Hall, 1974) 31–55.

14. D. Cyr, "How To Argue," *Attache* (US Airways, January 1998) 49–51.

15. S.R. Covey, *The 7 Habits of Highly Effective People* (New York: Simon & Schuster, 1990) 207–14.

16. J.A. Wall, Jr., *Negotiation: Theory and Practice* (Glenview, IL: Scott, Foresman, 1985).

17. D.J. McConville, "The Artful Negotiator," *Industry Week* (August 15, 1994): 40.

18. R. Fisher and W. Ury, *Getting to Yes: Negotiating Agreement Without Giving In* (New York: Penguin Books, 1986) 84–98.

19. See, for instance, D. Tjosvold and D.W. Johnson, *Productive Conflict Management Perspectives for Organizations* (New York: Irvington, 1983).

20. S.P. Robbins, *Managing Organizational Conflict: A Nontraditional Approach* (Upper Saddle River, NJ: Prentice Hall, 1974) 31–55.

21. D.G. Ancona, "Outward Bound: Strategies for Team Survival in an Organization," *Academy of Management Journal* (June 1990): 334–56.

22. R.A. Cosier and C.R. Schwenk, "Agreement and Thinking Alike: Ingredients for Poor Decisions," *Academy of Management Executive* (February 1990): 69–74.

23. W.L. Ury, J.M. Brett, and S. Goldberg, *Getting Disputes Resolved: Designing Systems to Cut the Costs of Conflict* (San Francisco: Jossey-Bass, 1988).

24. D.H. Schein, *Organizational Psychology,* 3d ed. (Upper Saddle River, NJ: Prentice Hall, 1980) 177–8.

25. M. Afzalur Rahim, ed., *Managing Conflict: An Interdisciplinary Approach* (New York: Praeger Publishers, 1989); R. Likert and J. Likert, *New Ways of Managing Conflict* (New York: McGraw-Hill, 1976).

26. "A Smarter Way to Manufacture," *Business Week,* April 30, 1990, 110–7.

27. R.J. Lewicki, J.A. Litterer, J.W. Minton, and D.M. Saunders, *Negotiation,* 2d ed. (Burr Ridge, IL: Irwin, 1994) 45–128.

28. J.W. Galbraith, *Designing Complex Organizations* (Reading, MA: Addison-Wesley, 1973) 15.

29. C.W. Cook, R.E. Coffey, and P.L. Hunsaker, *Management and Organizational Behavior* (Chicago: Irwin, 1997) 376–7.

30. R. Charan, "How Networks Reshape Organizations for Results," *Harvard Business Review* (September–October 1991), 179; and "Theory P Stresses How Departments Interact" *Wall Street Journal,* December 13, 1991, B1.

31. Adapted from A. Zoll, *Explorations in Managing* © 1974, Addison-Wesley Publishing Company, Inc. Based on a format suggested by Allen A. Zoll, III. Reprinted with permission.

32. Adapted from a role-play developed by Prof. Leonard Greenhaigh, Dartmouth College, as presented by R.J. Lewicki, J.A. Litterer, D.M. Saunders, and J.W. Minton, *Negotiation: Readings, Exercises, and Cases,* 2d ed. (Homewood, IL: Richard D. Irwin, 1993) 573–5. Used with permission.

33. Adapted from S.B. Simon, H. Kirschenbaum, and L. Howe, *Values Clarification, The Handbook,* rev. ed. (Sunderland, MA: Values Press, 1991).

Chapter 8

1. This instrument appeared in E. Raudsepp and J.C. Yeager, "Power in the Pecking Order: Do You Act Like a Top Chicken?" *Inc.* 3, no. 3 (March 1981): 42–6.

2. See, for instance, H. Mintzberg, *Power In and Around Organizations* (Upper Saddle River, NJ: Prentice Hall, 1983); K. Pfeffer, *Managing with Power* (Boston: Harvard Business School Press, 1992); and R.I. Dilenschneider, *On Power* (New York: Harper Business, 1994).

3. R.E. Emerson, "Power-Dependence Relations," *American Sociological Review* 27 (1962): 31–41.

4. D. Tjosvold, I. Andrews, and J.T. Struthers, "Power and Interdependence in Work Groups," *Group and Organizational Studies*, Vol. 16 No. 3, 1991, pp. 285-99.

5. Based on J.R.P. French, Jr. and B. Raven, "The Bases of Social Power," in D. Cartwright, ed., *Studies in Social Power* (Ann Arbor: University of Michigan, Institute for Social Research, 1959), 150–67; G.E. Littlepage, J.L. Van Hein, K.M. Cohen, and L.L. Janiec, "Evaluation and Comparison of Three Instruments Designed to Measure Organizational Power and Influence Tactics," *Journal of Applied Social Psychology* (January 1993): 107–25.

6. N.W. Biggart, "The Power of Obedience," *Administrative Science Quarterly* 29 (1984): 540–9.

7. S.H. Ng, *The Social Psychology of Power* (London: Academic Press, 1980) Chapter 3.

8. A. Schweitzer, *The Age of Charisma* (Chicago: Nelson-Hall, 1984).

9. R.E. Quinn, S.R. Faerman, M.P. Thompson, and M.R. McGrath, *Becoming a Master Manager: A Competency Framework,* 2nd ed, (New York: John Wiley & Sons, Inc., 1996, p. 297.

10. B.R. Schlenker and M.F. Weigold, "Interpersonal Processes Involving Impression Regulation and Management," in M.R. Rosenzweig and L.W. Porter, eds., *Annual Review of Psychology* 43 (Palo Alto, CA: Annual Reviews Inc., 1992), 133–68.

11. M.R. Leery and R.M. Kowalski, "Impression Management: A Literature Review and Two-Component Model," *Psychological Bulletin* 107 (1990): 34–47.

12. D. McLellan, "That's a Lie," *Los Angeles Times*, February 9, 1993, E3.

13. This section is adapted from D. Kipnis, S.M. Schmidt, C. Swaffin-Smith, and I. Wilkinson, "Patterns of Managerial Influence: Shotgun Managers, Tacticians, and Bystanders," *Organizational Dynamics* (Winter 1984): 58–67; B. Keys and T. Case, "How to Become an Influential Manager," *Academy of Management Executive* (November 1990): 38–51; G. Yukl, H. Kim, and C.M. Falbe, "Antecedents of Influence Outcomes," *Journal of Applied Psychology* (June 1996): 309–17.

14. M. Knapp and M. Comadena, "Telling It Like It Isn't: A Review of Theory and Research on Deceptive Communication," *Human Communication Research* 5 (1979): 270–85.

15. D.J. Lawless, *Effective Management* (Upper Saddle River, NJ: Prentice Hall, 1972) 243.

16. P.A. Wilson, "The Effects of Politics and Power on the Organizational Commitment of Federal Executives," *Journal of Management* (Spring 1995): 101–18.

17. Adapted from N.R.F. Maier, *Problem Solving and Creativity in Individuals and Groups* (Belmont, CA: Brooks/Cole Publishing Company, 1970) 298–302.

18. Based on L. Berman, "The Gospel According to Mary," *Working Woman* (August 1995): 47–9, 68–72; and P.W. Bernstein, "Things the B-School Never Taught," *Fortune*, November 3, 1980, 53–6.

Chapter 9

1. Adapted from D.A. Whetten and K.S. Cameron, *Developing Management Skills*, 4th ed. (Reading, MA: Addison-Wesley, 1998) 293.

2. C.W. Cook, P.L. Hunsaker, and R.E. Coffey, *Management and Organizational Behavior*, 2d ed. (Homewood, IL: Irwin, 1997) 185.

3. *Manpower Argus* no. 375 (December 1999), 11.

4. Ibid.

5. See for example, K.A. Kovach, "What Motivates Employees? Workers and Supervisors Give Different Answers," *Business Horizons* (September–October 1987): 60–6.

6. D.A. Whetten and K.S. Cameron, 4th ed.

7. For elaboration, see V. Vroom, *Work and Motivation* (New York: Wiley, 1964); R.M. Steers, L.W. Porter, and G.A. Begley, *Motivation and Leadership at Work* (New York: McGraw-Hill, 1996).

8. A. Maslow, *Motivation and Personality* (New York: Harper & Row, 1954).

9. D.C. McClelland, *The Achieving Society* (New York: Van Nostrand Reinhold, 1961).

10. D.C. McClelland, "Achievement Motivation Can Be Developed," *Harvard Business Review* 43 (November– December 1965), 6–8.

11. D.C. McClelland and D.H. Burnham, "Power Is the Great Motivator"; D.C. McClelland, *Power: The Inner Experience* (New York: Irvington, 1975).

12. C.M. Kelly, "The Interrelationship of Ethics and Power in Today's Organizations," *Organizational Dynamics* 5 (Summer 1987).

13. Ibid.

14. D.C. McClelland and D.H. Burnham, "Power Is the Great Motivator," *Harvard Business Review* 73 (January– February 1995): 126–39.

15. P.C. Earley and R. Kanfer, "The Influence of Component Participation and Role Models on Goal Acceptance, Goal Satisfaction and Performance," *Organizational Behavior and Human Decision Processes* 36 (1985): 378–90.

16. M. Erez, P.C. Earley, and C.L. Hulin, "The Impact of Participation on Goal Acceptance and Performance: A Two-Step Model," *Academy of Management Journal* 28 (February 1985): 50–66.

17. G.P. Latham and H.A. Marshal, "The Effects of Self-Set, Participatively Set and Assigned Goals on the Performance of Government Employees," *Personnel Psychology* 35 (1982): 399–404.

18. G. Dangot-Simpkin, "Getting Your Staff to Do What You Want," *Supervisory Management* 36 (January 1991): 4–5.

19. J.P. Wanous, T.L. Keon, and J.C. Latack, "Expectancy Theory and Occupational/Organizational Choices: A Review and Test," *Organizational Behavior and Human Performance* (August 1983): 66–86.

20. L.W. Porter and E.E. Lawler III, *Managerial Attitudes and Performance* (Homewood, IL: Irwin, 1968); and E.E. Lawler III, *Motivation in Work Organizations* (Monterey, CA: Brooks/Cole, 1973).

21. J.M. George, "Extrinsic and Intrinsic Origins of Perceived Social Loafing in Organizations," *Academy of Management Journal* 35 (March 1992): 191–202.

22. R.M. Steers and L.W. Porter, *Motivation and Work Behavior*, 4th ed. (New York: McGraw-Hill, 1987).

23. R.T. Mowday, "Equity Theory Predictions of Behavior in Organizations," in R.M. Steers and L.W. Porter, eds., *Motivation and Work Behavior*, 4th ed. (New York: McGraw-Hill, 1987) 91–113.

24. Ibid.

25. J. Brockner et al., "Layoffs, Equity Theory, and Work Performance: Further Evidence of the Impact of Survivor Guilt," *Academy of Management Journal* 29 (June 1986): 373–84.

26. P.K. Tyagi, "Inequities in Organizations, Salesperson Motivation and Job Satisfaction," *International Journal of Research in Marketing* 7 (December 1990): 135–48.

27. J.A. Bradt, "Pay for Impact," *Personnel Journal* 70 (May 1991): 76–9.

28. T.L. Quick, "Simple Is Hard, Complex Is Easy, Simplistic Is Impossible," *Training and Development Journal* 44 (May 1990): 94–9.

29. J.T. Knippen and T.B. Green, "Boost Performance Through Appraisals," *Business Credit* 92 (November–December 1990): 27.

30. M.F. Villere and S.J. Hartman, "The Key to Motivation Is in the Process: An Examination of Practical Implications of Expectancy Theory," *Leadership and Organization Development Journal* 11, no. 4 (1990): 1–3.

31. "More Benefits Bend with Workers' Needs," *Wall Street Journal*, January 9, 1990, B1.

32. S. Kerr, "On the Folly of Rewarding A, While Hoping for B," in B.M. Staw, ed., *Psychological Dimensions of Organizational Behavior* (New York: Macmillan, 1991) 65–75. Originally in *Academy of Management Journal* 18 (1975): 769–83.

33. W.C. Hamner, "Reinforcement Theory in Management and Organizational Settings," in H. Tosi and W.C. Hamner, *Organizational Behavior and Management: A Contingency Approach* (Chicago: Saint Claire, 1974), 86–112.

34. W.C. Hamner, "How to Ruin Motivation with Pay," *Compensation Review* 21 (1975): 88–9.

35. "When Are Employees Not Employees? When They're Associates, Stakeholders...," *Wall Street Journal*, November 9, 1988, B1.

36. S. Walton with J. Huey, *Sam Walton: Made in America* (New York: Doubleday, 1992) 132–3.

37. T.M. Welbourne and L.R. Gomez-Mejia, "Gainsharing: A Critical Review and a Future Research Agenda," *Journal of Management* 21 (September 1995): 5591.

38. S. Payette, Performance-Based Pay", *Workplace Gazette*, Vol. 4, No. 3, 2001.

39. J.A. Conger and R.N. Kanungo, "The Empowerment Process: Integrating Theory and Practice," *Academy of Management Review* 13 (July 1988): 471–82.

40. A.R. Cohen and D.L. Bradford, *Managing for Excellence: The Guide to High Performance in Contemporary Organizations* (New York: John Wiley & Sons, 1984).

41. L.A. Kappelman and V.R. Prybutok, "A Small Amount of Empowerment Pays Off Big in a Regional Bank," *National Productivity Review* 14 (September 1995): 39–42.

42. K.W. Thomas and B.A. Velthouse, "Cognitive Elements of Empowerment: An 'Interpretative' Model of Intrinsic Task Motivation," *Academy of Management Review* 15 (October 1990): 673.

43. R. Chamberland, "BPCO Participatory Management Approach," *Human Resources Canada, Collective Bargaining Review*, (June 1997) pp. 93–98.

44. R. Chamberland, "Employee Empowerment at Kruger Bromptonville," *Human Resources Development Canada, Collective Bargaining Review*, (May 1997) pp. 73–79.

45. J.R. Hackman, G. Oldham, R. Janson, and K. Purdy, "A New Strategy for Job Enrichment," *California Management Review* 16 (Fall 1975): 57–71.

46. The Conference Board of Canada, *Workplace Literacy Best Practices Reader*, 1998, p. 5.

47. Ibid., p. 19.

48. T.L. Prior, "If I Were President," *Inc*. (April 1995): 56–61.

49. Adapted from Whetten & Cameron, 1998, pp. 312–4.

50. A.J. DuBrin, *Applying Psychology: Individual & Organizational Effectiveness*, 5th ed. (Upper Saddle River, NJ: Prentice Hall, 2000) 136.

Chapter 10

1. S. Bernhut, "Leading the Revolution: Gary Hamel In Conversation," *Ivey Business Journal* July/August 2001, p. 40.
2. Canadian Labour and Business Centre, *Dofasco's Inc.'s Healthy Lifestyle Activities*, Ottawa, March 2002.
3. Dofasco News Release, *Dofasco Listed on Dow Jones Sustainability World Index*, October 5, 2001.
4. Industry Canada, *Sector Competitiveness Framework Series: Primary Steel*, 2002 and Canadian Labour and Business Centre, *Dofasco's Inc.'s Healthy Lifestyle Activities*, Ottawa, March 2002.
5. Address by John Mayberry, Materials and Manufacturing Ontario (MMO) Partnerships 2002 Conference, Toronto, June 2002.
6. B.M. Bass, *Organizational Decision Making* (Homewood, IL: Richard D. Irwin, 1983).
7. S. Bernhut, Ibid., p.39.
8. Canada's innovation challenges and strategy is outlined in *Achieving Excellence: Investing in People, Knowledge and Opportunity*, Government of Canada, 2001 and *Knowledge Matters: Skills and Learning for Canadians*, Government of Canada, 2001.
9. D. Campbell, "Some Characteristics of Creative Managers," *Center for Creative Leadership Newsletter*, No. 1 (February 1978): 6–7.
10. S. Bernhut, Ibid., p.41.
11. *Harvard Business Review*, Vol. 80 No. 6, August 2002, is entirely devoted to the managerial techniques and business processes of corporate innovation.
12. Descriptions of Dofasco's innovative direction can be found at www.dofasco.com.
13. A. Stewart, "3M Fights Back," *Fortune*, February 5, 1996, 94–9.
14. C. Henderson, "Finding, Examining Lead Users Push 3M to Leading Edge of Innovation," *The CEO Refresher*, 2000.
15. The Conference Board of Canada, "The Road to Global Best: Leadership, Innovation and Corporate Culture," *Innovation Challenge Paper #1*, May 2002, p. 1.
16. D.A. Whetten and K.S. Cameron, *Developing Management Skills* 5 ed. (Upper Saddle River, N. J. Pearson Education, 2002) p.191. For other discussions of facilitating innovation, see S.K. Markham and L. Aiman-Smith, "Product Champions: Truths, Myths and Management," *Research Technology Management* 44 (3), 44–50, 2001; J. Howell and C. Higgins, "Champions of Change: Identifying, Understanding and Supporting Champions of Technological Innovations," *Organizational Dynamics* 19 (1), 40–55, 1990; and Y.T. Chen and A.H. Van de Ven, "Learning the Innovation Journey: Order out of Chaos?," *Organization Science* 7 (6), 593–614, 1996.
17. The Conference Board of Canada, ibid., p. 3.
18. The Conference Board of Canada, ibid., p. 5.
19. W.F. Pounds, "The Process of Problem Finding," *Industrial Management Review II* (Fall 1969): 1–19.
20. Ibid.
21. M. Brassard, *The Memory Jogger: A Pocket Guide of Tools for Continuous Improvement* (Methuen, MA: GOAL/QPC, 1988) 24-9.
22. M. Michalko, *Thinkertoys (A Handbook of Business Creativity)*, Ten Speed Press, 1991, Chapter 9.
23. See T. Buzan, *The Mind Map Book: How to use Radiant Thinking to Maximize Your Brain's Untapped Potential* (Plume, 1996) and J. Wycoff, *Mindmapping: Your Personal Guide to Exploring Creativity and Problem-Solving* (Berkley Publishing Group, 1991).
24. A.F. Osborn, *Applied Imagination* (New York: Scribner, 1957).
25. A.H. Van de Ven and A. Delbecq, "The Effectiveness of Nominal, Delphi, and Interacting Group Decision-Making Processes," *Academy of Management Journal* 17 (1974): 605–21.

26. N.C. Dalkey and O. Helmer, "An Experimental Application of the Delphi Method to the Use of Experts," *Management Science* 9 (1963): 458–67.

27. S.M. Natale, C.F. O'Donnell, and W.R.C. Osborne Jr., "Decision Making: Managerial Perspectives," *Thought* 63, no. 248 (1990): 32–51.

28. H.A. Simon, *Administrative Behavior*, 2d ed. (New York: Free Press, 1957).

29. J.L. Cotton, D.A. Vollrath, and K.L. Froggatt, "Employee Participation: Diverse Forms and Different Outcomes," *Academy of Management Review* (January 1988): 8–22.

30. V.H. Vroom and A.J. Jago, *The New Leadership: Managing Participation in Organizations* (Upper Saddle River, NJ: Prentice Hall, 1988).

31. Ibid.

32. Ibid.

33. M.E. Shaw, *Group Dynamics*, 3d ed. (New York: McGraw-Hill, 1981) 78.

34. R.G. Fulmer, C.P. Koelling, A.R. Doss, and H.A. Kurstedt Jr., "The Effects of Information Availability on the Group Consensus Process," *Computers & Industrial Engineering* 19, Nos. 1–4 (1990): 510–3.

35. N.R.F. Maier, "Assets and Liabilities in Group Problem Solving," *Psychological Review* 74 (July 1967): 239–49.

36. I. Janis, *Victims of Groupthink* (Boston:Houghton Mifflin, 1972); and "Groupthink," *Psychology* (November 1971): 43-6.

37. I. Janis, *Groupthink: Psychological Studies of Policy Decisions and Fiascoes*, 2d ed. (Boston: Houghton Mifflin, 1982).

38. J.E. Driskell and E. Salas, "Group Decision Making Under Stress," *Journal of Applied Psychology* (June 1991): 473–8.

39. A.E. Schwartz and J. Levin, "Better Group Decision Making," *Supervisory Management* (June 1990): 319–42.

40. Janis, "Groupthink," 43–5.

41. Adapted from D.A. Whetton and K.S. Cameron, *Developing Management Skills*, 2d ed. (New York: Harper Collins, 1991) 438–9.

42. The case was prepared based on material appearing in B. Murray, "Are Professors Turning a Blind Eye To Cheating?" *Monitor on Psychology* (January 1996): 1, 42; D. McBurney, "Cheating: Preventing and Dealing With Academic Dishonesty," *APS Observer* (January 1996): 32–5.

43. The three cases cited in this exercise are from V.H. Vroom and A.G. Jago, "Decision Making as a Social Process," *Decision Sciences* 5, no. 4 (October 1974): 734–69.

44. Adapted from D. Johnson and F. Johnson, *Joining Together*, 5th ed. (Boston: Allyn and Bacon, 1994) 261–6.

Chapter 11

1. Copyright 1994 by National Research Bureau, P.O. Box 1, Burlington, IA 52601–0001. Reprinted by permission.

2. Adapted from R.E. Quinn, S.R. Faerman, M.P. Thompson, and M.R. McGrath, *Becoming a Master Manager* (New York: Wiley, 1990) 33–4.

3. Cited in Rubbermaid's *Philosophy, Management Principles, Mission, and Objectives*, April 1993.

4. N. Venkatraman and J.E. Prescott, "Environment-Strategy Coalignment: An Empirical Test of Its Performance Implications," *Strategic Management Journal* (January 1990): 1–23.

5. A.A. Thompson and A.J. Strickland, III, *Crafting and Implementing Strategy* (Burr Ridge, IL: Richard D. Irwin, 1995) 85.

6. A.A. Thompson and A.J. Strickland, III, *Strategic Management: Concepts and Cases*, 9th ed. (Burr Ridge, IL: Irwin, 1996) 78–89.

7. Ibid., 90–104.

8. J. Lardner, "Hollywood vs. High-Tech," *Business 2.0*, May 2002.

9. H.G. DeYong, "Thieves Among Us," *Industry Week* (June 17, 1996): 12–6.

10. S.E. Jackson and J.E. Dutton, "Discerning Threats and Opportunities," *Administrative Science Quarterly* (September 1988): 370–87.

11. J.C. Collins and J.I. Porras, "Building a Visionary Company," *California Management Review* 37 (Winter 1995): 80–100.

12. Wal-Mart, 1995 Annual Report.

13. M.E. Porter, *Competitive Advantage: Creating and Sustaining Superior Performance* (New York, Free Press, 1985).

14. H. Mintzberg, "Five P's for Strategy," *California Management Review*, 1987 30(1): 11–24.

15. Canadian Tire: website: http://www2.canadiantire.ca/CTCwebsite/about/way.html.

16. M. E. Porter, "What is Strategy?" *Harvard Business Review*, 74, 6: 61–78.

17. R. Kaplan and D. Norton, "Using the Balanced Scorecard as a Strategic Management System," *Harvard Business Review* (January–February 1996); 75–85.

18. BC Hydro, *2002 Triple Bottom Line Report*, 2002.

19. C.C. Miller and L.B. Cardinal, "Strategic Planning and Firm Performance: A Synthesis of More Than Two Decades of Research," *Academy of Management Journal* (March 1994): 16–61.

20. G.L. Morrisey, *Management by Objectives and Results for Business and Industry*, 2d ed. (Reading, MA: Addison-Wesley, 1977).

21. E.A. Locke, "Motivation Through Goal Setting," in R.T. Golembiewski, ed., *Handbook of Organizational Behavior* (New York: M. Dekker, 1999) 4.

22. P.F. Drucker, "Managing Oneself," *Harvard Business Review* (March–April, 1999): 71.

23. J. Quinn, P. Anderson, and S. Finkelstein, "Managing Professional Intellect: Making the Most of the Best," *Harvard Business Review* (March–April 1996): 71–80.

24. E.A. Locke, "Motivation Through Goal Setting," in R.T. Golembiewski, ed., *Handbook of Organizational Behavior* (New York: M. Dekker, 1999) 14–15; G.P. Latham and G.A. Yukl, "A Review of Research on the Application of Goal Setting in Organizations," *Academy of Management Journal* (December 1975): 824–45.

25. G.P. Latham and E.A. Locke, "Goal Setting—A Motivational Technique That Works," *Organizational Dynamics* (Autumn 1979): 68–80.

26. E.A. Locke, "Motivation Through Goal Setting," in R.T. Golembiewski, ed., *Handbook of Organizational Behavior* (New York: M. Dekker, 1999); G.P. Latham and L.M. Saari, "The Effects of Holding Goal Difficulty Constant on Assigned and Participatively Set Goals," *Academy of Management Journal* (March 1979): 163–8.

27. G.P. Latham, T.R. Mitchell, and D.L. Dossett, "Importance of Participative Goal Setting and Anticipated Rewards on Goal Difficulty and Job Performance," *Journal of Applied Psychology* (April 1978): 163–71.

28. E.A. Locke, and D.M. Schweiger, "Participation in Decision Making: One More Look," in B. M. Staw, ed., *Research in Organizational Behavior*, vol. 1 (Greenwich, CT: JAI Press, 1979) 265–339.

29. P.C. Early, G.C. Northcraft, and T.R. Litucy, "The Impact of Process and Outcome Feedback on the Relation of Goal Setting to Task Performance," *Academy of Management Journal* 33 (1990): 87–105.

30. J.M. Ivancevich and J.T. McMahon, "The Effects of Goal Setting, External Feedback, and Self-Generated Feedback on Outcome Variables: A Field Experiment," *Academy of Management Journal* (June 1982): 359–72.

31. Maple Leaf Foods Inc., 2001 Annual Report.

32. Government of Canada, Department of Canadian Heritage, Multicultural Program.

33. E. Locke and G. Latham, *A Theory of Goal Setting and Task Performance* (Upper Saddle River, NJ: Prentice Hall, 1990).

34. E.A. Locke, "Motivation Through Goal Setting," in R.T. Golembiewski, ed., *Handbook of Organizational Behavior* (New York: M. Dekker, 1999) 11–2.

35. Ibid., 14.

36. Ibid., 12–3.

37. R. Kaplan and D. Norton, "Using the Balanced Scorecard as a Strategic Management System."

38. G.P. Latham, and E.A. Locke, "Goal Setting—A Motivational Technique That Works," *Organizational Dynamics* (Autumn 1979): 68–80; E.A. Locke, "Motivation Through Goal Setting," in R.T. Golembiewski, ed., *Handbook of Organizational Behavior* (New York: M. Dekker, 1999) 6–7.

39. P.F. Drucker, "Managing Oneself," *Harvard Business Review* (March–April 1999): 71.

40. The Conference Board of Canada, "Business Basics for the Workplace: A Practical Approach to Workplace Learning," *Workplace Gazette*, Vol. 2, No. 1, 1999.

41. "Female Managers Discover Secret Weapon at Carleton," *Ottawa Citizen*, June 8, 2002.

42. P.F. Drucker, *The Practice of Management* (New York: Harper & Row, 1954).

43. M.A. Verespej, "Future Vision," *IW*, February 17, 1997, 50–5.

Chapter 12

1. S. Caudron, "The De-Jobbing of America," *Industry Week*, September 5, 1994, 31–6.

2. K.H. Hammonds, K. Kelly, and K. Thurston, "Rethinking Work," *Business Week*, October 12, 1994, 75–87.

3. C. Powell, "When Workers Wear Walkmans on the Job," *Wall Street Journal*, July 11, 1994, B1, B8; J. Stuller, "Games Workers Play," *Across the Board* (July–August 1997): 16–22; C. Harmon, "Goofing Off at Work: First You Log On," *International Herald Tribune*, September 23, 1997, 1, 10.

4. S. Melamed, I. Ben-Avi, J. Luz, and M.S. Green, "Objective and Subjective Work Monitoring: Effect on Job Satisfaction, Psychological Distress, and Absenteeism in Blue-Collar Workers," *Journal of Applied Psychology* (February 1995): 29–42.

5. M.A. Campion, and C.L. McClelland, "Follow-up and Extension of the Interdisciplinary Costs and Benefits of Enlarged Jobs," *Journal of Applied Psychology* (June 1993): 339–51.

6. Description based on L. Jaroff, "Age of the Road Warrior," *Time* (Spring 1995) 38–40.

7. J.R. Hackman and G.R. Oldham, "Motivation Through the Design of Work: Test of a Theory," *Organizational Behavior and Human Performance* (August 1976): 250–79; J.R. Hackman and G.R. Oldham, "Development of the Job Diagnostic Survey," *Journal of Applied Psychology* (April 1975): 159–70.

8. J.R. Hackman, "Work Design," in J.R. Hackman and J.L. Suttle, eds., *Improving Life at Work*, (Glenview, IL: Scott Foresman, 1977) 129.

9. M. Campion and G. Sanborn, "Job Design," in G. Salvendy, ed., *Handbook of Industrial Engineering* (New York: Wiley, 1991).

10. J.R. Hackman, G. Oldham, R. Janson, and K. Purdy, "A New Strategy for Job Enrichment," *California Management Review* 16 (Fall 1975): 57–71.

11. G. Oldham and A. Cummings, "Employee Creativity: Personal and Contextual Factors at Work," *Academy of Management Journal* 39 (1996): 607–34.

12. A. Haasen, "Opel Eisenach GMBH—Creating a High-Productivity Workplace," *Organizational Dynamics* (Spring 1996): 80–5.

13. R. Cumberland, "High-Performance Work Practices at Abitibi-Price," *Collective Bargaining Review*, Human Resources Development Canada (March 1997) 115–119.

14. P.F. Drucker, "Managing Oneself," *Harvard Business Review* (March–April 1999): 67.

15. G.R. Salancik and J. Pfeffer, "A Social Information Processing Approach to Job Attitudes and Task Design," *Administrative Science Quarterly* (June 1978): 224–53.

16. Hackman, "Work Design," 129.

17. Ibid., 136–40.

18. R.W. Griffin and G.C. McMahan, "Motivation Through Job Design," in J. Greenberg, ed., *Organizational Behavior: The State of the Science* (Hillsdale, NJ: Lawrence Erlbaum Associates, 1994) 36–8.

19. J.R. Hackman, "The Design of Work Teams," in J.W. Lorsch, ed., *Handbook of Organizational Behavior* (Upper Saddle River, NJ: Prentice Hall, 1987): 324–7.

20. K. Johnson, D. Lero and J. Rooney. *Work–Life Compendium 2001: 150 Canadian Statistics on Work, Family & Well-Being*. Centre for Families, Work and Well-Being, University of Guelph and Human Resources Development Canada, 2001.

21. D.R. Dalton and D.J. Mesch, "The Impact of Flexible Scheduling on Employee Attendance and Turnover," *Administrative Science Quarterly* (June 1990): 370–87; and K.S. Kush and L.K. Stroh, "Flextime: Myth or Reality?" *Business Horizons* (September–October, 1994): 53.

22. S. Biouele, I. Savary, and S. St-Onge, "Merck Frosst Canada & Co.: Practices to Promote a Better Work–Family Balance," *Workplace Gazette* (Vol. 3, No. 2, 2000): 80–81; Royal Bank Financial Group, *Flexible Work Arrangements*, April 1998.

23. K. Johnson, D. Lero, and J. Rooney. *Work–Life Compendium 2001: 150 Canadian Statistics on Work, Family & Well-Being*.

24. Kush and Stroh, "Flextime."

25. Statistics Canada, *Survey of Work Arrangements*, 1995.

26. Canadian Labour Market and Productivity Centre, *Case Studies of Alternative Working Arrangements and Changes in Working Time*, April 1997.

27. S. Shellenbarger, "Two People, One Job: It Can Really Work," *Wall Street Journal*, December 7, 1994, B1.

28. L. Calderwood-Parsons, "Family-Friendly Policies at CIBC," *Collective Bargaining Review* (October 1997): 73–80.

29. "Face-to-Face Communications: Press the Flesh, Not the Keyboard," *The Economist* (Volume 364, Number 8287 August 2002): 50–51.

30. K. Johnson, D. Lero, and J. Rooney, *Work–Life Compendium 2001: 150 Canadian Statistics on Work, Family & Well-Being*.

31. Adapted from D.D. Bowen, R.J. Lenicki, et al., *Experiences in Management and Organizational Behavior*, 4th ed. (New York: Wiley, 1997) 51–3.

32. Adapted from D.L. Nelson and J.C. Quick, *Organizational Behavior: Foundations, Realities, and Challenges* (Minneapolis/St. Paul:West Publishing, 1997) 431.

33. Adapted from "Group Dynamics and Intergroup Relations" by A. Bavelas and G. Strauss (under the title "The Hovey and Beard Case") in W.F. Whyte, ed., *Money and Motivation* (New York: Harper & Row, 1955).

34. This checklist is extracted from: "Work–Life Balance in Canadian Workplaces": http://labour-travail.hrdc-drhc.gc.ca/worklife/welcome-en.cfm, Checklist for Employers, Human Resources Development Canada. Reproduced with the permission of the Minister of Public Works and Government Services Canada, 2003.

35. J.R. Hackman and G.R. Oldham, "The Job Diagnostic Survey: An Instrument for the Diagnosis of Jobs and the Evaluation of Job Redesign Projects," *Technical Report No. 4* (New Haven, CT: Department of Administrative Sciences, Yale University, 1974) 2–3 of the Short Form.

Chapter 13

1. A. Fisher, "The World's Most Admired Companies," *Fortune*, October 27, 1997, 220–40.

2. Various studies have concluded that an organization's human resources can be a significant source of competitive advantage. See P.M. Wright and G.C. McMahan, "Theoretical Perspectives for Strategic Human Resources Management," *Journal of Management* 18, no.

1 (1992): 295–320; A.A. Lado and M.C. Wilson, "Human Resource Systems and Sustained Competitive Advantage," *Academy of Management Review* (October 1994): 699–727; and J. Pfeffer, *Competitive Advantage Through People* (Boston: Harvard Business School Press, 1994).

3. "In Quest of the Ideal Employee," *Nation's Business* (November 1986): 38; E. Dickerson, "The Hiring Decision: Assessing Fit into the Workplace," *Management Review* (January 1987): 24; D.S. Campbell, "Hiring Smart," *Knight Ridder News Service* report in the *San Diego Union-Tribune*, July 19, 1999, C1.

4. http://www.globetechnology.com/robmag/robmag_04.html

5. "Fitting in Determines Job Success," *Training and Development Journal* (August 1986): 11.

6. E.H. Burack and N.J. Mathys, *Human Resource Planning: A Pragmatic Approach to Manpower Staffing and Development* (Lake Forest, IL: Brace-Park Press, 1980).

7. J.C. Ullman, "Employee Referrals: Prime Tool for Recruiting Workers," *Personnel* (May–June, 1996): 30–5; J.P. Kirnan, J.A. Farley, and K.F. Geisinger, "The Relationship Between Recruiting Source, Applicant Quality, and Hire Performance," *Personnel Psychology* (Summer 1989): 293–308; C.R. Williams, C.E. Labig Jr., and T.H. Stone, "Recruiting Sources and Posthire Outcomes for Job Applicants and New Hires," *Journal of Applied Psychology* (April 1993): 163–72.

8. L.M. Litvan, "Casting a Wider Net," *Nation's Business* (December 1994): 49–51.

9. Canadian Human Rights Commission, 2002.

10. R. Resnick, "Leasing Workers," *Nation's Business* (November 1992): 20–8; T.G. Block, "Brains for Rent," *Forbes*, July 31, 1995, 99–100; J. Alex, "The Temp Biz Boom: Why It's Good," *Fortune*, October 17, 1995, 53–6.

11. For example, see M. Klimas, "How to Recruit a Smart Team," *Nation's Business* (May 1995): 26.

12. J.J. Asher, "The Biographical Item: Can It Be Improved?" *Personnel Psychology* (Summer 1972): 266.

13. According to Carl King, president of Team Building Systems of Houston, TX, as cited in E.E. Spragins, "Screening New Hires," *INC.* (August 1992): 82; Randall Scott Echlin, "How to Avoid Traps When Hiring or Applying", *Globe & Mail* (December 7, 1998): B15

14. Survey conducted by the Conseil Quebecois du Commerce de Detail (CQCD) in cooperation with Samson, Belair, Deloitte & Touche, 2001.

15. J. Aberth, "Pre-Employment Testing Is Losing Favor," *Personnel Journal* (September 1986): 96–104; C. Lee, "Testing Makes a Comeback," *Training* (December 1988): 49–59.

16. E.E. Ghiselli, "The Validity of Aptitude Tests in Personnel Selection," *Personnel Psychology* (Winter 1973): 475; G. Grimsley and H.F. Jarrett, "The Relation of Managerial Achievement to Test Measures Obtained in the Employment Situation," *Personnel Psychology* (Spring 1973): 31–48; A.K. Korman, "The Prediction of Managerial Performance: A Review," *Personnel Psychology* (Summer 1986): 295–322.

17. I.T. Robertson and R.S. Kanola, "Work Sample Test: Validity, Adverse Impact, and Applicant Reaction," *Journal of Occupational Psychology* 55, no. 3 (1987): 171–83.

18. G.C. Thornton, *Assessment Centers in Human Resources Management* (Reading, MA: Addison-Wesley, 1992) and Stephen Jackson, "Hire Top Performing Managers with Performance-Based Micro-Assessments", *Canadian HR Reporter*, Article 372.

19. *Human Resource Management: Ideas and Trends* (Commerce Clearing House, May 17, 1992) 85.

20. "Understanding the Liability of Negligent Hiring," *Security Management Supplement* (July 1990): 7A.

21. "If You Can't Say Something Nice," *Wall Street Journal*, March 4, 1988, 25.

22. Canadian Human Rights Commission, *Policy on Alcohol and Drug Testing* (July 2002).

23. R.L. Dipboye, *Selection Interviews: Process Perspectives* (Cincinnati: South-Western, 1992) Chapter 2.

24. A.I. Huffcutt and W. Arthur Jr., "Hunter and Hunter (1984) Revisited: Interview Validity for Entry-Level Jobs," *Journal of Applied Psychology* (April 1994): 184–90; M.A. McDaniel, D.L. Whetzel, F.L. Schmidt, and S.D. Maurer, "The Validity of Employment Interviews: A Comprehensive Review and Meta-Analysis," *Journal of Applied Psychology* (August 1994): 599–616; and J.M. Conway, R.A. Jako, and D.F. Goodman, "A Meta-Analysis of Interrater and Internal Consistency Reliability of Selection Interviews," *Journal of Applied Psychology* (October 1995): 565–79.

25. See, for example, Dipboye, *Selection Interviews*, 42–4; R.D. Arveny and J.E. Campion, "The Employment Interview: A Summary and Review of Recent Research," *Personnel Psychology* (Summer 1982): 281–322; M.D. Hakel, "Employment Interview" in K.M. Rowland and G.R. Ferris, eds., *Personnel Management: New Perspectives* (Boston: Allyn and Bacon, 1982): 192–255; E.C. Webster, *The Employment Interview: A Social Judgment Process* (Schomberg, Ont.: S.I.P. Publications, 1982); and M.M. Harris, "Reconsidering the Employment Interview: A Review of Recent Literature and Suggestions for Future Research, *Personnel Psychology* (Winter 1989): 691–726.

26. W.F. Cascio, *Applied Psychology in Personnel Management* (Upper Saddle River, NJ: Prentice Hall, 1991) 271.

27. T.J. Hanson and J.C. Balesteri-Spero, "An Alternative to Interviews," *Personnel Journal* (June 1985): 114.

28. Based on Lussier, 296–7.

29. Adapted from various sources, including S.P. Robbins and D.A. DeCenzo, *Supervision Today* (Upper Saddle River, NJ: Prentice Hall, 1998) 249; Campbell, "Hiring Smart," *Knight Ridder News Service* report; W.C. Donaghy, *The Interview: Skills and Applications* (Glenview, IL: Scott, Foresman, 1984) 245–80; J.M. Jenkins and B.L. Zevnik, "ABCs of Job Interviewing," *Harvard Business Review* (July–August 1989): 38–42.

30. Adapted from S.C. Certo, *Supervision: Quality, Diversity, and Technology* (Chicago: Irwin, 1997) 500–1.

31. Adapted from Lussier, 307–9.

32. Adapted from S. Robbins, *Managing Today* (Upper Saddle River, NJ: Prentice Hall) 289.

33. Adapted from Lussier, 311.

Chapter 14

1. D. Hirshberg, "Quotes taken from employee evaluations," *PACE (Policy Analysis for California Education)*, School of Education University of California, Berkeley, CA 94720-1670, November 5, 1999.

2. M.A. Huselid, S.E. Jackson, and R.S. Schuler, "Technical and Strategic Human Resource Management Effectiveness as Determinants of Firm Performance," *Academy of Management Journal* (February 1997): 171–88.

3. J.A. Segal, "86 your Appraisal Process?," *HR Magazine* (October 2000): 199.

4. W.R. Boswell and J.W. Boudreau, "Employee Satisfaction with Performance Appraisals and Appraisers: The Role of Perceived Appraisal Use," *Human Resource Development Quarterly* (Fall 2000): 283 and Chris Argyris, "Good Communication That Blocks Learning," *Harvard Business Review*, Vol. 72 No. 4.

5. C.O. Longenecker and L.S. Fink, "Creating Effective Performance Appraisals," *Industrial Management* (September/October 1999): 18–23.

6. Ibid.

7. Ibid.

8. G.C. Reed, "Employers' New Burden of Proof in Discrimination Cases," *Employment Relations Today* (Summer 1989): 112.

9. A.H. Locher and K.S. Teel, "Appraisal Trends," *Personnel Journal* (September 1988): 139–45.

10. Adapted from S.P. Robbins, *Managing Today!* 2d ed. (Upper Saddle River, NJ: Prentice Hall, 2000) 289–91.

11. S.E. Catt and D.S. Miller, *Supervision: Working with People* 2d ed. (Homewood, IL: Richard D. Irwin, 1991) 373–4.

12. J.A. Segal, "Evaluating the Evaluators," *HR Magazine*, October 1995.

13. A. Tsui and B. Barry, "Interpersonal Affect and Rating Errors," *Academy of Management Journal* (September 1986): 595.

14. W.K. Blazer and L.M. Sulsky, "Halo and Performance Appraisal Research: A Critical Examination," *Journal of Applied Psychology* (December 1992): 976–85.

15. Ibid.

16. Ibid.

17. K. Phillips, Red Flags in Performance Appraisal," *Training and Development Journal* (March 1987): 80–5.

18. C. Lee, "Performance Appraisal: Can We 'Manage' Away the Curse?" *Training* (May 1996): 44–59.

19. H.H. Meyer, "A Solution to the Performance Appraisal Feedback Enigma," *The Executive* (February 1991): 68–76.

20. B.R. Nathan, A.M. Mohrman Jr., and J. Milliman, "Interpersonal Relations as a Context for the Effects of Appraisal Interviews on Performance and Satisfaction: A Longitudinal Study," *Academy of Management Journal* (June 1991): 352–69.

21. J.L. Komaki, R.L. Collins, and P. Penn, "The Role of Performance Antecedents and Consequences in Work Motivation," *Journal of Applied Psychology* (June 1982): 334–40; E.A. Locke, and G.P. Latham, *Goal-Setting: A Motivational Technique That Works!* (Upper Saddle River, NJ: Prentice Hall, 1984).

22. C.W. Cook, R.E. Coffey, and P.L. Hunsaker, *Management and Organizational Behavior*, 2d ed. (Burr Ridge, IL: Austin Press/Irwin, 1997) 271–3.

23. D. Ilgen, C.D. Fisher, and M.S. Taylor, "Consequences of Individual Feedback on Behavior in Organizations," *Journal of Applied Psychology* (August 1979): 349–71.

24. F. Bartolome, "Teaching About Whether to Give Negative Feedback," *The Organizational Behavior Teaching Review*, XI, no. 2 (1986–1987): 95–104.

25. K. Halperin, C.R. Snyder, R.J. Shenkel, and B.K. Houston, "Effect of Source Status and Message Favorability on Acceptance of Personality Feedback," *Journal of Applied Psychology* (February 1976): 85–8.

26. M.J. Kavanagh, "Evaluating Performance," in K.M. Rowland and G.R. Ferris, eds., *Personnel Management* (Boston: Allyn & Bacon, 1982) 187–226.

27. N.R.F. Maier, *The Appraisal Interview: Three Basic Approaches* (La Jolla, CA: University Associates, 1976).

28. M. Beer, "Performance Appraisal," in J.W. Lorsch, ed., *Handbook of Organizational Behavior* (Upper Saddle River, NJ: Prentice Hall, 1987) 286–300.

29. D.L. Kirkpatrick, "Performance Appraisal: Your Questions Answered," *Training and Development Journal* (May 1986): 68–71.

30. Beer, 1987.

31. C.R. Mill, "Feedback: The Art of Giving and Receiving Help," in L. Porter and C.R. Mill, eds., *The Reading Book for Human Relations Training* (Bethel, ME: NTL Institute for Applied Behavioral Science, 1976) 18–9.

32. K.S. Verderber and R.F. Verderber, *Inter-Act: Using Interpersonal Communication Skills*, 4th ed. (Belmont, CA: Wadsworth, 1986).

33. L.E. Bourne, Jr. and C.V. Bunderson, "Effects of Delay of Information Feedback and Length of Post-Feedback Interval on Concept Identification," *Journal of Experimental Psychology* (January 1963): 1–5.

34. P.W. Dorfman, W.G. Stephan, and J. Loveland, "Performance Appraisal Behaviors: Supervisor Perceptions and Subordinate Reactions," *Personnel Psychology* (Autumn 1986): 579–97.

35. H.K. Baker and P.L. Morgan, "Two Goals in Every Performance Appraisal," *Personnel Journal* (September 1984): 74–8.
36. Verderber and Verderber, 1986.
37. Ibid.
38. T. Alessandra and P. Hunsaker, *Communicating at Work* (New York: Simon & Schuster, 1993) 86–90.
39. C. Fletcher, "The Effects of Performance Review in Appraisal: Evidence and Implications," *Journal of Management Development* 5, no. 3, (1986): 3–12.
40. Cook, Hunsaker, and Coffee, 1997, 271–3.
41. Beer, 1987.
42. Fletcher, 1986.
43. L.L. Cummings, *Appraisal Purpose and the Nature, Amount, and Frequency of Feedback*, Paper presented at the American Psychological Association meeting, Washington, DC, September 1976.
44. C.R. Mill, "Feedback: The Art of Giving and Receiving Help," in L. Porter and C.R. Mill, eds., *The Reading Book for Human Relations Training* (Bethel: NTL Institute for Applied Behavioral Science, 1976) 18–9.
45. R. Brett and A.J. Fredian, "Performance Appraisal: The System Is Not the Solution," *Personnel Administrator* (December 1981): 62.
46. Beer, 1987.
47. Dorfman, Stephan, and Loveland, 1986.
48. Adapted from: G. Dessler, N.D. Cole, and V.L. Sutherland, *Human Resources Management in Canada*, 8th Canadian ed. (Toronto: Prentice Hall, Inc., 2002): 543–46.
49. S. Ray and D. Holmes, "How to Discipline Without Exposure to Lawsuits," *Canadian HR Reporter* (September 6, 1999): 31.
50. Adapted from: G. Dessler, N.D. Cole, and V.L. Sutherland, *Human Resources Management in Canada*, 8th Canadian ed. (Toronto: Prentice Hall, Inc., 2002): 546–48.
51. E.E. Mole, *Wrongful Dismissal Practice Manual* (Toronto: Butterworths Canada Ltd., 1993) Chapter 7.
52. K. Blair, "Sports Editor Scores 28-Month Severance," *Canadian HR Reporter* (April 7, 1997): 5.
53. M.J. MacKillop, *The Perils of Dismissal: The Impact of the Wallace Decision on Reasonable Notice*, paper presented at the Human Resources Professionals Association of Ontario Law Conference, October 1999, Toronto.
54. R.W. Rue and L.L. Byars, *Management: Skills and Applications*, 9th ed. (Burr Ridge, IL: Irwin McGraw-Hill, 2000) 418–9.
55. Based on S. Umapathy, "Teaching Behavioral Aspects of Performance Evaluation: An Experiential Approach," *The Accounting Review* (January 1985): 107–8.

Chapter 15

1. N.M. Tichy, *The Leadership Engine* (New York: HarperCollins Publishers, 1997)
2. *Report on Business* magazine, *Globe and Mail*, January 2001.
3. More on the distinction between assisting and educating can be found in D.A. Kolb, I.M. Rubin, and J.S. Osland, *Organizational Behavior: An Experiential Approach* (Upper Saddle River, NJ: Prentice Hall, 1991) 277.
4. F. Fournies, *Coaching for Improved Work Performance* (New York: Van Nostrand Reinhold, 1978).
5. C. Rogers, *On Becoming a Person* (Boston: Houghton Mifflin, 1961) 34.
6. C.R. Leana, "Predictors and Consequences of Delegation," *Academy of Management Journal* (December 1986): 754–74.
7. S.P. Robbins and D.A. DeCenzo, *Supervision*, 2d ed. (Upper Saddle River, NJ: Prentice Hall, 1998) 212.

8. L.L. Steinmetz, *The Art and Skill of Delegation* (Reading, MA: Addison-Wesley, 1976) 248.

9. C.R. Mill, "Feedback: The Art of Giving and Receiving Help," L. Porter and C.R. Mill, eds., *The Reading Book for Human Relations Training* (Bethel, ME: NTL Institute for Applied Behavioral Science, 1976) 18–9.

10. J.C. Kunich and R.I. Lester, "Leadership and the Art of Feedback: Feeding the Hands That Back Us," *The Journal of Leadership Studies* 3 (1996): 3–22.

11. C.W. Cook, P.L. Hunsaker, and R.E. Coffey, *Management and Organizational Behavior*, 2d ed. (Burr Ridge, IL: Irwin, 1997) 271–3.

12. M. Mavis, "Painless Performance Evaluations," *Training and Development* (October 1994): 40–4.

13. C.D. Orth, H.E. Wilkinson, and R.C. Benfari, "The Manager's Role as Coach and Mentor," *Organizational Dynamics* (Spring 1987): 67.

14. C. Laporte, "Innovative Workplace Practices," *Workplace Gazette*, Vol. 2 No. 1, 1999.

15. Deloitte & Touche, January 2001.

16. Manulife Financial, and Company-Wide Rotational Program.

17. K.E. Kram and D.T. Hall, "Mentoring as an Antidote to Stress During Corporate Trauma," *Human Resource Management* (Winter 1989): 493–511.

18. Excerpted from D. Bradford and A.R. Cohen, *Managing for Excellence* (New York: John Wiley, 1984) 157–8.

19. Adapted from W.C. Donaghy, *The Interview: Skills and Applications* (Glenview, IL: Scott, Foresman, 1984) 299–300.

Chapter 16

1. M. Gates, "The Quality Challenge: Can Managers and Workers See Eye to Eye?" *Incentive* 163, no. 8 (August 1989): 20–2.

2. M.E. Shaw, *Group Dynamics: The Psychology of Small Group Behavior*, 3d ed. (New York: McGraw-Hill, 1981) 11–2.

3. J.R. Katzenback and D.K. Smith, *The Wisdom of Teams: Creating the High-Performance Organization* (Boston: Harvard Business School Press, 1993) 45.

4. E.T. Jackson and G. DiGiacomo, "Lessons from Nine Case Studies," *Collective Bargaining Review*, Human Resources Development Canada (October 1997): 81–88.

5. R.D. Smither, "The Return of the Authoritarian Manager," *Training* (November 1991): 40.

6. A. Harmon, "TEAMWORK: Chrysler Builds a Concept as Well as a Car," *Los Angeles Times* (April 26, 1992): D1–D3.

7 E.T. Jackson and G. DiGiacomo, "Self-Directed Work Teams at NCR," *Collective Bargaining Review*, Human Resources Development Canada (February 1997): 61–66.

8. J.R. Katzenback and D.K. Smith, *The Wisdom of Teams: Creating the High-Performance Organization* (Boston: Harvard Business School Press, 1993); and P.F. Drucker, "There's More Than One Kind of Team," *Wall Street Journal* (February 11, 1992): A16.

9. J.R. Katzenback and D.K. Smith, *The Wisdom of Teams: Creating the High-Performance Organization* (Boston: Harvard Business School Press, 1993) 43–64.

10. E.T. Jackson and G. DiGiacomo, "High Involvement Work Reorganization at NB Tel," *Collective Bargaining Review*, Human Resources Development Canada (January 1997): 91–99.

11. J.A. Sheppard, "Productivity Loss in Performance Groups: A Motivation Analysis," *Psychological Bulletin* (January 1993): 67–81.

12. E.T. Jackson and G. DiGiacomo, "Lessons from Nine Case Studies," *Collective Bargaining Review*, Human Resources Development Canada (October 1997): 81–88.

13. C. Margerison and D. McCann, *Team Management Systems: The Team Development Manual* (Toowong, Queensland, Australia: Team Management Resources, 1990) 19–36.

14. T.G. Cummings and C.G. Worley, *Organizational Development and Change*, 5th ed. (St. Paul, MN: West, 1993) 226–8.

15. W.L. French and C.H. Bell, Jr., *Organization Development: Behavioral Science Interventions for Organization Improvement* (Upper Saddle River, NJ: Prentice Hall, 1990) 133–4.

16. A. Harmon, D1.

17. B.W. Tuckman and M.A.C. Jensen, "Stages of Small Group Development Revisited," *Group and Organizational Studies* 2 (1977): 419–27; M.F. Maples, "Group Development: Extending Tuckman's Theory," *Journal for Specialists in Group Work* (Fall 1988): 17–23; and C. Kormanski and A. Mozenter, "A New Model of Team Building: A Technology for Today and Tomorrow," in J.W. Pfeiffer and J.E. Jones, eds., *The 1987 Annual: Developing Human Resources* (San Diego: University Associates, 1987) 255–68.

18. D. Carew, E. Parisi-Carew, and K. Blanchard, *Team Development and Situational Leadership II* (Escondido, CA: Blanchard Training and Development, Inc., 1998) 4.

19. Information about length of duration of each stage of team development is based on R.B. Lacoursiere, *The Life Cycle of Groups: Group Development Stage Theory* (New York: Human Service Press, 1980).

20. This section is adapted from D. Carew, E. Parisi-Carew, and K. Blanchard, *Team Development and Situational Leadership II* (Escondido, CA: Blanchard Training and Development, Inc., 1998).

21. A. Harmon, D1.

22. W.G. Dyer, *Team Building: Issues and Alternatives*, 2d ed. (Menlo Park, CA: Addison-Wesley, 1987) 97–108.

23. W.G. Dyer, R.H. Daines, and W.C. Giauque, *The Challenge of Management* (New York: Harcourt Brace Jovanovich, 1990) 343.

24. F. Bartolome, "Teaching About Whether to Give Negative Feedback," *The Organizational Behavior Teaching Review* XI, no. 2 (1986–1987): 95–104.

25. J. Zigon, "Making Performance Appraisal Work for Teams," *Training* (June 1994): 58–63.

26. R. Harrison, "When Power Conflicts Trigger Team Spirit," *European Business* (Spring 1972): 27–65.

27. E.A. Michaels, "Business Meetings," *Small Business Reports* (February 1989): 82–8.

28. A.S. Grove, "How (and Why) to Run a Meeting," *Fortune*, July 11, 1983, 132–9.

29. D. Stoffman, "Waking Up to Great Meetings," *Canadian Business* (November 1986): 75–9.

30. Ibid.

31. Adapted from M.J. Driver, K.R. Rousseau, and P.L. Hunsaker, *The Dynamic Decision Maker* (San Francisco: Jossey-Bass Publishers, 1990) 215–6.

32. Adapted from D.D. Bowen, R.J. Lewicki, D.T. Hall, and F.S. Hall, eds., *Experiences in Management and Organizational Behavior*, 4th ed. (New York: John Wiley & Sons, 1982) 14–6.

33. Adapted from H.A. Otto, *Group Methods to Actualize Human Potential: A Handbook* (Beverly Hills, CA: The Holistic Press, 1970) 50–9.

Part 5 Future-Building Competencies

1. N.H. Snyder and M. Graves, "Leadership and Vision," *Business Horizons* (January–February 1994): 1.

2. See, for example, K. Lewin, *Field Theory in Social Science* (New York: Harper & Row, 1951); N. Margulies and J. Wallace, *Organizational Change: Techniques and Applications* (Glenview, IL: Scott Foresman, 1973); and W.L. French and C.H. Bell, Jr., *Organization Development*, 4th ed. (Upper Saddle River, NJ: Prentice Hall, 1990).

3. See, for example, M. Walton, *The Deming Management Method* (New York: Putnam/Perigee, 1986).

4. M. Hammer and J. Champy, *Reengineering the Corporation: A Manifesto for Business Revolution* (New York: Harper Business, 1993).

Chapter 17

1. Human Resources Development Canada, *Work-Life Balance in Canadian Workplaces*, 2002.
2. Ibid.
3. N.K. Austin, "Managing by Parable," *Working Woman* (September 1995): 14–6.
4. H. Mintzberg, "Organization Man: Henry Mintzberg Has Some Common Sense Observations About the Ways We Run Companies," *Financial Post* (November 22, 1997): 14–16.
5. A. Ede, "Leadership and Decision Making: Management Styles and Culture," *Journal of Managerial Psychology* (July 1992): 28–31.
6. Based on J. Flynn and K. Naughton, "A Drug Giant's Allergic Reaction," *Business Week* (February 3, 1997): 122–5; and R. Frank and T.M. Burton, "Cross-Border Merger Results in Headaches for a Drug Company," *Wall Street Journal* (February 4, 1997): A1.
7. G. Gitelson, J. Bing, and L. Laroche, "Culture Shock," *CMA Management* (March 2001): 41–44.
8. Ibid.
9. C.A. Reilly III, J. Chatman, and D.F. Caldwell, "People and Organizational Culture: A Profile Comparison Approach to Assessing Person-Organization Fit," *Academy of Management Journal* (September 1991): 487–516; and J.A. Chatman and K.A. Jehn, "Assessing the Relationship Between Industry Characteristics and Organizational Culture: How Different Can You Be?" *Academy of Management Journal* (June 1994): 522–53.
10. D. Jenish and B. Woodward, "Canada's Top 10 Employers," *Maclean's* (November 5, 2001): 46–56.
11. Ibid.
12. P. Chisholm, "Redesigning Work" *Maclean's* (March 5, 2000): 34–41.
13. P. Booth, *Challenge and Change: Embracing the Team Concept*, Report 123-94, Conference Board of Canada, 1994.
14. J. Castro, T. McCarroll, J. Moody, and W. McWhirter, "Jack in the Box," *Time* (October 3, 1994): 56–8.
15. S. Glain, "Korea's Samsung Plans Very Rapid Expansion into Autos, Other Lines," *Wall Street Journal* (March 3, 1995): A1.
16. Y. Wiener, "Forms of Value Systems: A Focus on Organizational Effectiveness and Cultural Change and Maintenance," *Academy of Management Review* (October 1988): 536.
17. See, for example, D.R. Denison, *Corporate Culture and Organizational Effectiveness* (New York: Wiley, 1990); G.G. Gordon and N. DiTomaso, "Predicting Corporate Performance from Organizational Culture," *Journal of Management Studies* (November 1992): 784–98; and D.R. Denison and A.K. Misha, "Toward a Theory of Organizational Culture and Effectiveness," *Organization Science* (March–April 1995): 204–23.
18. J.P. Kotter and J.L. Heskett, *Corporate Culture and Performance* (New York: Free Press, 1992) 16; and J. Pfeffer, "Will the Organization of the Future Make the Mistakes of the Past?" in F. Hesselbein, M. Goldsmith, and R. Beckhard, eds., *The Organization of the Future* (San Francisco: Jossey-Bass, 1997) 48.
19. G. McDougall and D. Swimmer, "Business Strategies of SMEs and Large Firms in Canada," *Industry Canada* (October 1997).
20. H.M. Rice and J.M. Beyer, "Studying Cultures through Rites and Ceremonies," *Academy of Management Review* 9 (October 1984): 666.
21. E.H. Schein, "The Role of the Founder in Creating Organizational Culture," *Organizational Dynamics* (Summer 1983): 13–28.
22. E.H. Schein, "Leadership and Organizational Culture," in F. Hesselbein, M. Goldsmith, and R. Beckhard, eds., *The Leader of the Future* (San Francisco: Jossey-Bass, 1996) 61–2.
23. A.M. Pettigrew, "On Studying Organizational Cultures," *Administrative Science Quarterly* (December 1979): 576.

24. S. Robbins, *Managing Today* (Upper Saddle River, NJ: Prentice Hall, 1999) 347.

25. Human Resources Development Canada, *Organizational Profiles: Husky Injection Moulding Systems*, 2002.

26. C. Stephenson, "Corporate Values Drive Global Success at Lucent Technologies," *Canadian Speeches* (November/December 1999): 23–27.

27. S.A. Sackmann, "Culture and Subcultures: An Analysis of Organizational Knowledge," *Administrative Science Quarterly* (March 1992): 140–61.

28. S.P. Robbins and D. DeCenzo, *Supervision Today!* 2d ed. (Upper Saddle River, NJ: Prentice Hall, 1998) 584.

29. J.R. Harrison and G.R. Carroll, "Keeping the Faith: A Model of Cultural Transmission in Formal Organizations," *Administrative Science Quarterly* (December 1991): 552–82.

30. B. Schneider, "The People Make the Place," *Personnel Psychology* (Autumn 1987): 437–53.

31. D.C. Hambrick and P.A. Mason, "Upper Echelons: The Organization as a Reflection of Its Managers," *Academy of Management Review* (April 1984): 193–206; and B.P. Niehoff, C.A. Enz, and R.A. Grover, "The Impact of Top Management Actions on Employee Attitudes and Perceptions," *Group & Organization Studies* (September 1990): 337–52.

32. Based on J. Reese, "Starbucks: Inside the Coffee Cult," *Fortune* (December 9, 1996): 190–200.

33. T.H. Fitzgerald, "Can Change in Organizational Culture Really Be Managed?" *Organizational Dynamics* (Autumn 1988): 5–15; and B. Doumaine, "Creating a New Company Culture," *Fortune* (January 15, 1990): 127–31.

34. M. Albert, "Assessing Cultural Change Needs," *Training and Development Journal* (May 1985): 94–8.

35. Kotter and Heskett, 94–106.

34. Based on Small Business 2000, Show 203.

35. Adapted from D. Kolb , J. Osland, and I. Rubin, *Organizational Behavior: An Experiential Approach*, 6th ed. (Upper Saddle River, NJ: Prentice Hall, 1995) 369–71.

Chapter 18

1. Adapted from C.W. Cook, P.L. Hunsaker, and R.E. Coffey, *Management and Organizational Behavior*, 2d ed. (Homewood, IL: Irwin, 1997) 465.

2. S. Tully, "So, Mr. Bossidy, We Know You Can Cut. Now Show Us How to Grow," *Fortune* (August 21, 1995): 70–80.

3. For discussions of the integration of leadership and management roles, see: R.E. Quinn, S.R. Faerman, M.P. Thompson, and M.R. McGrath, *Becoming A Master Manager: A Competency Framework* 2nd ed. (New York: John Wiley & Sons, Inc., 1996) and D.A. Whetten and K.S. Cameron, *Developing Management Skills* 5th ed. (Upper Saddle River, N. J.: Pearson Education, Inc., 2002): 15–17.

4. W. Bennis and B. Nanus, *Leaders: The Strategies for Taking Charge* (New York: Harper & Row, 1985) 20.

5. H. Mintzberg, "Covert Leadership: Notes on Managing Professionals," *Harvard Business Review* (November–December 1998).

6. J.P. Kotter, "What Leaders Really Do," *Harvard Business Review* 68 (May–June 1990): 103–11. For a more expansive distinction, see Kotter, *A Force for Change: How Leadership Differs from Management* (New York: Free Press, 1990).

7. Kotter, "What Leaders Really Do," p. 104.

8. S.A. Kirkpatrick and E.A. Locke, "Leadership: Do Traits Matter?" *Academy of Management Executive* 5 (May 1991): 48–60.

9. W.H. Schmidt and B.Z. Posner, *Managerial Values and Expectations: The Silent Power of Personal and Organizational Life* (New York: American Management Association, 1982).

10. Kirkpatrick and Locke, "Leadership: Do Traits Matter?" 48–60.
11. W.G. Bennis and R.J. Thomas, "Crucibles of Leadership," *Harvard Business Review* Vol. 80, No. 9, 2002.
12. G. Yukl and D.D. Van Fleet, "Theory and Research on Leadership in Organizations," in M.D. Dunnette and L.M. Hough (eds.), *Handbook of Industrial and Organizational Psychology* 2nd ed., vol. 3 (Palo Alto, CA: Consulting Psychologists Press, 1992) 150.
13. For comprehensive reviews of this early research see R. Likert, *New Patterns of Management* (New York: McGraw-Hill, 1961) 36; and R.M. Stodgill and A.E. Coons, *Leader Behavior: Its Description and Measurement* (Columbus, OH: Ohio State University, Bureau of Business Research, 1957) 75.
14. A.W. Halpin, *The Leadership Behavior of School Superintendents* (Chicago: Midwest Administration Center, The University of Chicago, 1959) 4.
15. R. Goffee and G. Jones, "Followership: It's Personal, Too," *Harvard Business Review*, Vol. 79, No. 11, 2001.
16. A.K. Korman, "Consideration, Initiating Structure, and Organizational Criteria—A Review," *Personnel Psychology* (Winter 1966): 349–61.
17. L. Berkowitz, "Group Standards, Cohesiveness, and Productivity," *Human Relations* 7 (1954): 509–14; and S.E. Seashore, *Group Cohesiveness in the Industrial Work Group* (Ann Arbor: University of Michigan Survey Research Center, 1954).
18. K. Lewin and R. Lippitt, "An Experimental Approach to the Study of Autocracy and Democracy: A Preliminary Note," *Sociometry* 1 (1938): 292–300.
19. P. Hersey and K.H. Blanchard, *Management of Organizational Behavior: Utilizing Human Resources*, 7th ed. (Upper Saddle River, NJ: Prentice Hall, 1996) Chapter 8.
20. Ibid., 161.
21. Ibid.
22. K.E. Kram, *Mentoring at Work* (Glenview, IL: Scott, Foresman, 1984).
23. R.J. House and T.R. Mitchell, "Path-Goal Theory of Leadership," *Journal of Contemporary Business* 3 (Autumn 1974): 81–97.
24. House and Mitchell, pp. 81–97.
25. C. Schriesheim and M.A. Von Glinow, "The Path-Goal Theory of Leadership: A Theoretical and Empirical Analysis," *Academy of Management Journal* 20 (September 1977): 398–405.
26. P. Strebel, "Choosing the Right Change Path," *California Management Review* 36 (Winter 1994): 29–51.
27. K. Lewin, *Field Theory in Social Science* (New York: Harper & Row, 1951).
28. T.G. Cummings and C.G. Worley, *Organization Development and Change*, 5th ed. (St. Paul, MN: West Publishing Company, 1993) 63.
29. J.P. Kotter, "Leading Change: Why Transformation Efforts Fail," *Harvard Business Review* (March–April 1995): 59–67.
30. S. Bernhut, "Managing the Dream: Warren Bennis on Leadership," *Ivey Business Journal* (May/June 2001): 41.
31. Kotter and Schlesinger.
32. Bernhut, 39.
33. C. Matthews, "How We Changed Gear to Ride the Winds of Change," *Professional Manager* (January 1995): 6–8.
34. J.M. Groves, "Leaders of Corporate Change," *Fortune* (December 14, 1992): 104–14.
35. Cummings and Worley, 155.
36. For a discussion of a conceptual model of transition and how managers can assist others through transitions, see W. Bridges, *Managing Transitions: Making the Most of Change* (New York: Addison-Wesley Publishing Company, 1991).
37. J.P. Kotter, "Leading Change: Why Transformation Efforts Fail," *Harvard Business Review* (March–April 1995): 59–67.

38. For a discussion of how to sustain change, see: P. Senge, A. Kleiner, C. Roberts, R. Ross, G. Roth, and B. Smith, *The Dance of Change: The Challenges to Sustaining Momentum in Learning Organizations* (New York: Doubleday, 1999).

39. Matthews, 1995.

40. D. Shepherdson, "Meeting the Challenge: Managing Change in the Nineties," Canadian Centre for Management Development, The Conference Board of Canada, *Management Practices* No. 9, April 1995.

41. R. Likert, *The Human Organization* (New York: McGraw-Hill, 1967).

42. C. Argyris, *Personality and Organization* (New York: Harper and Row, 1957).

43. Canadian Federation of Independent Business, *Study of Workplace Satisfaction in Private, Public Sectors*, Toronto, 1999.

44. R.H. Hall, *Organizations: Structures, Processes, and Outcomes*, 4th ed. (Upper Saddle River, NJ: Prentice Hall, 1987) 29.

45. R.M. Kanter, *When Giants Learn to Dance: Mastering the Challenges of Strategy* (New York: Simon and Schuster, 1989).

46. Bernhut, 40.

47. J.P. Kotter and L.A. Schlesinger, "Choosing Strategies for Change," *Harvard Business Review* 57 (March–April 1979): 106–14.

48. J.B. Keffeler, "Managing Changing Organizations: Don't Stop Communicating," *Vital Speeches* (November 15, 1991): 92–6.

49. Adapted from C.W. Cook, "Debriefing with Serialized Theory Development for Task-Team Development," *Exploring Experiential Learning: Simulations and Experiential Exercises* (Tempe, AZ: Bureau of Business and Economic Research, Arizona State University, 1978) 7–8.

Appendix A

1. The conceptual outline for this appendix is adapted from J.S. Hunsaker and P.L. Hunsaker, "Effective Presentation Skills," *Industrial Management* (March 1985): 13–7.

2. Conference Board of Canada, *Employability Skills Toolkit*, September 2001.

3. D.A. Level, Jr. and W.P. Galle, Jr. *Managerial Communications* (San Diego, CA: Business Publications, Inc., 1988) 34.

4. T. Alessandra and P. Hunsaker, *Communicating at Work* (New York: Simon & Shuster, 1993) 177.

5. Alessandra and Hunsaker, 178.

6. Alessandra and Hunsaker, 179.

7. Alessandra and Hunsaker, 179.

8. Alessandra and Hunsaker, 181–2.

9. D.A. Peoples, *Presentations Plus* (New York: QED/John Wiley and Sons, 1992).

Appendix B

1. The material in this appendix is adapted from T. Alessandra and P. Hunsaker, *Communicating at Work* (New York: Simon & Schuster, 1993) Chapters 16 and 17.

Index

management competencies, 4–5
management skills
    described, 3–4
    effective skill performance guide-
        lines, 7–8
    importance of, 4
    key competencies, 4–5
    learning, 5–7
    types of, 4
managerial effectiveness,
    maximization of, 175–176
managers
    authority of, 3
    of creativity, 221–222
    described, 2
    diversity, importance of, 124
    and employees' career development,
        36
    group decision making, role in, 237
    institutional-power, 197
    objectives, 3
    personal-power, 196–197
    role of, 2–3, 427–428
    task distinctions between
        managers and leaders, *428*
The Manager's Work-Family Toolkit
    (Vanier Institute of the Family),
    125–126
manipulation, 441
Manulife Financial, 358
Marshall Industries, 153
Maslow, Abraham, 194
Mayberry, John, 2
McClelland, David, 196
McDonald's Restaurants, 409
MDS Nordion, 407
meetings. *See* effective meetings
memos, 462–463, *463*
mental blocks, common causes of, 226
mentoring, 356, 358–359
Merck Frosst Canada & Co., 283
merit pay, 204
Microsoft Corporation, 254
Microsoft Network, 254
mindmapping, 226–227, *227*
Minnesota Mining & Manufacturing
    Company (3M), 222
minority workers. *See* diversity
Mintzberg, Henry, 3, 255, 406, 428
mirroring phenomenon, 7
mission statement, 252
morale, 378, *378*
motivation
    basic needs, 194–196
    content theories of. *See* needs-based
        theories of motivation
    defined, 192–193
    effort, expectancies about, 198
    equity, perceptions of, 199–200
    expectancy theory, 198–199, 204
    factors, 193–197
    and goals, 198
    individual, and diversity
        management, 126
    learned needs, 196–197

needs-based theories of. *See* needs-
    based theories of motivation
to perform well, 193–197
performance, expectancies about,
    198
process theories of, 197–200
and reward systems, 193
rewards, expectancies about, 199
rewards, nature of, 199
self-assessment exercise, 191–192
to stay on the job, 193
motivation methods
    behaviour modification, 202–203
    continuous reinforcement, 203
    effort-performance-reward
        expectancies, strengthening, 201
    employee empowerment, 205–206
    equitable administration of
        rewards, 203–204
    extinction, 202
    goals, commitment to, 200–201
    intermittent reinforcement, 203
    job redesign, 206
    opportunities to learn, 206
    performance-based compensation,
        204–205
    performance feedback, 201
    performance-reward linkages, clarifi-
        cation of, 201
    positive reinforcement, 202
    punishment, 202
    reinforcement of right
        behaviour, 202–203
    rewards, timeliness of, 203
    salient rewards, 201–202
Motorola, 407
multiculturalism. *See* diversity
multiperson comparisons, 327
multiple channels, 104
Myers-Briggs Type Indicator, 24

N

national culture. *See* culture
National Quality Institute, 405
national styles of persuasion, 144t
National Wellness Survey, 81
natural work units, 281
NB Tel Company, Ltd., 374
NCR Corp., 153, 372–373, 374
needs-based theories of motivation
    basic needs, 194–196
    hierarchy of needs, 194–196, 195
    learned needs, 196–197
negative feedback, 332
negotiation
    bargaining strategies, 147–149
    bargaining zone, staking out, *148*
    defined, 147
    distributive bargaining, 147t, *148*
    guidelines for effective negotiation,
        149–150
    integrative bargaining, 147t,
        148–149
    intergroup conflict management, 153
    and resistance to change, 441

networking, 173–174
niche, 254
noise, 102
nominal group technique, 228
nonroutine problems, 223–224
nonverbal communication, 106, 107t
Nordstrom, 408, 409
norming stage, 380–381
Nortel Networks, 48
Northwood Technologies, 405–406

O

objectives
    see also goals
    clarification of, 223
    of conflict management, 145
    focus on, and evaluation process, 324
    general, 258
    of managers, 3
    meetings, 390
    operational, 254
    prioritization of, 76
Opel, 280
open communication, 80
open-ended questions, 309
operational objectives, 254
operational plans, 251
oral presentation skills
    audience, analysis of, 452
    delivery of presentation, 455–456
    enthusiasm, 455–456
    eye contact, 456
    focus, 453
    gestures, 456
    movement, use of, 456
    never apologize, 456
    organization, 453–455
    outline, 453–455
    physical space, use of, 456
    planning and preparation, 452–453
    purpose, 452
    rehearsal, 455
    stage fright, 452, 453t
    visualization, 455
organizational coping strategies
    employee assistance programs, 81
    employee participation in
        decision making, 80
    job design, 81
    open communication, 80
    person-job fit, 81
    training, 81
    wellness initiatives, 81
organizational culture
    academy, 411
    aggressiveness, 407
    baseball teams, 411
    ceremonies and rituals, 409
    and change resistance, 440
    change target, 433
    changing, 412–413
    club culture, 411
    defined, 406
    detail, attention to, 407
    dimensions of, 407–408